SALEM HEALTH

ADDICTIONS, SUBSTANCE ABUSE & ALCOHOLISM

SALEM HEALTH

ADDICTIONS, SUBSTANCE ABUSE & ALCOHOLISM

Second Edition

Volume 1

Editor
Paul Moglia, Ph.D.

SALEM PRESS
A Division of EBSCO Information Services, Inc.
Ipswich, Massachusetts

GREY HOUSE PUBLISHING

Note to Readers

The material presented in *Salem Health: Addictions, Substance Abuse & Alcoholism* is intended for broad informational and educational purposes. Readers who suspect that they or someone they know has any disorder, disease, or condition described in this set should contact a physician without delay. This set should not be used as a substitute for professional medical diagnosis. Readers who are undergoing or about to undergo any treatment or procedure described in this set should refer to their physicians and other health care providers for guidance concerning preparation and possible effects. This set is not to be considered definitive on the covered topics, and readers should remember that the field of health care is characterized by a diversity of medical opinions and constant expansion in knowledge and understanding.

Library of Congress Cataloging-in-Publication Data

Names: Moglia, Paul, editor.
Title: Addictions, substance abuse & alcoholism / editor, Paul Moglia, Ph.D.
Other Titles: Addictions, substance abuse and alcoholism
Description: Second edition. | Ipswich, Massachusetts : Salem Press, a division of EBSCO Information
    Services, Inc. ; Amenia, NY : Grey House Publishing, [2018] | Series: Salem health | Originally
    published as: Addictions and substance abuse. ©2013. | Includes bibliographical references and index.
Identifiers: ISBN 9781682179444 (set) | ISBN 9781682179451 (v. 1) | ISBN 9781682179468 (v. 2)
Subjects: LCSH: Substance abuse–Treatment–United States. | Drug abuse–Treatment–United States. |
    Alcoholism–Treatment–United States.
Classification: LCC RC564 .A356 2018 | DDC 362.29–dc23

FIRST PRINTING
PRINTED IN THE UNITED STATES OF AMERICA

Contents

Publisher's Note

This second edition of *Salem Health: Addictions, Substance Abuse & Alcoholism* presents essays on a variety of topics concerning substance abuse and behavioral addictions and their related issues. The U.S. Centers for Disease Control and Prevention (CDC) report that more Americans die from the effects of drug abuse than from traffic accidents, and attributes the death of nearly 100,000 Americans annually to the excessive consumption of alcohol. These startling statistics, coupled with the staggering rise in deaths from prescription drug misuse in the twenty-first century, have thrown the spotlight on how the allied health community and society at large approach, track, and treat alcohol and drug dependency and other addictive behaviors.

As addictions and their related disorders continue to escalate, so has society's understanding and treatment of them, from increased and more thorough comprehension of maladaptive behavior to a clearer picture of the physiological effects of substance abuse, both in the short and long term. Also important is being aware of the role that substance abuse and misuse and addiction play in society, whether through glorification or stigmatization in the media, or experienced firsthand in a home or social setting by a parent or child, and the agencies and preventative strategies in place to curb abuse and its effects. *Salem Health: Addictions, Substance Abuse & Alcoholism* surveys the decades of progress in understanding and treating addictive behaviors and substance abuse, analyzing trends and treatment, offering historical and technical background, and providing socioeconomic, psychological, and physiological understanding of the influence and impact of addiction and substance abuse.

SCOPE AND COVERAGE

This two-volume work includes 329 essays covering all aspects of addiction and substance abuse, including diseases or conditions, substances of abuse, treatment and addiction overviews, organizations and foundations dedicated to treatment and prevention, physiological and psychological issues and behaviors, trends and statistics, and social contexts and concerns related to substance abuse and treatment such as advertising and media influence, aging, ethnicity, and children and substance abuse. The essays, written for non-specialists by medical professionals, professors in science and medicine, and medical writers, will appeal to students studying science, premed, psychology, addictive behaviors, drug abuse epidemiology and public health issues, as well as to librarians and their patrons, and of course to individuals, family and friends directly affected by addiction.

Salem Health: Addictions, Substance Abuse & Alcoholism examines the various concepts and models of both the addiction and its associated behaviors and impulses and the therapeutic and treatment practices that enable an individual to regain the traction of an addiction and abuse-free life. Comprehensive essays on drug and alcohol abuse constitute the core coverage, while a significant number of essays survey behavioral addictions and disorders, as well as the sociocultural and economic impact of addiction. Essays, where applicable, provide overviews of prevention, diagnosis, and treatment, and outline causes, risk factors, and symptoms. The work's scope also embraces ethical questions raised by the convergence of alternative therapy and addiction and the legalized use of substances of abuse in the allied health field. Also prominent is the discussion of the preventative and educational work of the government and other agencies in addressing addictions and substance abuse.

ORGANIZATION AND FORMAT

Essays are alphabetized, vary in length from one to five pages, and include the following ready-reference top matter:

- **Category** lists the focus of the essay, including Diagnosis and Prevention; Health Issues and Physiology; Psychological Issues and Behaviors; Social Issues; Substance Abuse/Misuse; Substances; and Treatment.
- **Also Known As** provides alternative names used, where applicable.
- **Definition** introduces, defines, and describes the essay topic.
- Essays can include the following sections: **Overview**, **Introduction**, **Causes**, **Risk Factors**, **Symptoms**, **Screening and Diagnosis**, **Treatment and Therapy**, and **Prevention**.

Substances of abuse essays include Status and Classification, Source, Transmission Route, History of Use, and Effects and Potential Risks.

Essays covering **organizations**, **programs**, and **treatment centers** include Background, Dates established or founded, and Mission and Goals.

Essays that discuss **diagnosis**, **physiology**, **prevention**, **psychological issues**, **social issues**, and **treatment** include unique subsections, chosen by the author, that divide the main text and guide readers through the essay.

All entries end with the author's byline, and list of sources for further reading. Many essays feature sidebars, graphs and photographs to enhance the information offered.

SPECIAL FEATURES

The articles in the *Salem Health: Addictions, Substance Abuse & Alcoholism* are arranged alphabetically by title. Both volumes offer a Complete List of Contents for easy identification of desired topics.

Appendixes include a geographical listing of treatment centers and programs, a cross-referenced list of substances of abuse, a glossary of definitions of commonly used terms and concepts related to addiction and substance abuse; pharmaceutical treatments, categorized by brand name; a bibliography which offers citations for both classic and recently published sources for additional research; and a time line which details major developments in addictions and substance abuse.

Indexes include a category index and a comprehensive subject index.

ACKNOWLEDGMENTS

The editor wishes to thank the many medical practitioners and other scholars who contributed to this new edition; their names and academic affiliations and other credentials appear in the list of contributors that follows.

This second edition of *Salem Health: Addictions, Substance Abuse & Alcoholism* is a valuable addition to the Salem Health series, which includes both print and electronic versions of *Salem Health: Adolescent Health & Wellness* (2015); *Salem Health: Nutrition* (2016); *Salem Health: Cancer* (second edition, 2016); *Salem Health: Psychology & Behavioral Health* (second edition, 2015); *Salem Health: Genetics & Inherited Conditions* (second edition, 2017), *Salem Health: Complementary & Alternative Medicine* (2012), and the core set *Magill's Medical Guide* (eighth edition, 2018).

More news on the Salem Health front include a second edition of *Salem Health: Infectious Diseases & Conditions* and the first edition of a brand new title, *Salem Health: Women's Health,* both due out in Spring 2019.

Editor's Introduction

The timing for publishing this, the second edition of *Salem Health: Addictions, Substance Abuse & Alcoholism,* could not be more opportune or fortuitous. Of the 300 million souls living in the United States, more than 30 million, one in ten, struggle with misuse of substances including alcohol. Add to this number, the ten million who struggle with one or more behavioral addictions. As large as these numbers are, the impact on the nation is far greater. Though each individual is unique, the average person with addiction is closely involved with five others who have no addiction. Addictions of all types, including alcohol misuse, touch the lives of almost everyone living in the United States. It would be hard to find a person who is either, not an addicted person, or not emotionally and psychologically close to someone who is. In spite of a decades-long war on drugs, omnipresent psychoeducation programs for children and adolescents in schools, advances in drug enforcement, prescription medication scrutiny, the expansion of professional organizations targeting addiction like the American Academy of Addiction Medicine and the American Psychological Association's Division on Addictions, the de-criminalization of some substances, the increasing substitution of treatment in lieu of incarceration, the expansion of treatment centers, the inclusion of substance misuse as treatment covered by third-party payers, published best practices and protocols for acute and long-term treatment, and the pandemic availability of emergency, life-saving administration of naloxone and suboxone, for most segments of our population, the occurrence of substance use disorders and occurrence of behavioral addiction are on the rise.

I used the word "struggle" in describing the psycho-social-spiritual state of addicted persons. Many have not found the road back to normalcy, to their pre-drug misuse selves or to their pre-obsessive compulsive behaviorally-addicted selves. Some have not begun the journey. Some began, faltered, and stopped. Some remain on the road, fall, relapse, but then get up and renew their painful pilgrimage.

The goal of this edition is to provide user-friendly scholarship to those likely to pick up this book or access its online content. The first group this work is written for are students assigned to research on, write about, and report to others on one of the hundreds of topics here. You will find the information readily intelligible, accurate, and up-to-date, with suggestions on where to learn more.

The second group is friend or family to someone who is behaviorally or chemically addicted whose primary motivator is to fulfill the needs of addiction, specifically their addiction. For you, one primary motivator in your life is to help where you can, when you can, and how you can without developing an unhealthy enmeshed, co-dependent, or apathetic response. The disease model of addiction, though we cover much more than it, understands that addiction, whatever kind, can define the life of the addicted. It also understands that addiction, of whatever kind, profoundly affects those who care. As a number of our articles discuss, individual addiction is a dangerous, misleading myth. All individual addiction is family addiction.

The third audience for this work is the addicted, those with substance misuse or behavioral addiction, or both. There is nothing about having either that precludes or protects from having both. For you we provide a scientifically-based presentation of the addiction's history, its causes, signs and symptoms of its presence, and its treatment. Every clinically oriented article describes what treatment looks like and where to learn more and, ultimately, do more. While this work is not treatment, nor even assessment, and should not be used this way, all articles provide sources that can lead to clearer conceptualization. Many, perhaps most, also provide information leading to treatment itself.

Tapping into a remarkable array of educational backgrounds, professional practices, and clinical experiences of our authors, we provide solid but succinct information about addiction. Our contributors discuss the latest developments, from those broadly affecting our society as in legal developments in the decriminalization of marijuana and the insidious invasion of opioids, to those of family and individual concerns, as in parenting and substance misuse or second-hand smoke. Hardly the last word on any of the hundreds of topics we have, we thank you for the privilege of providing, perhaps, the first word on your or a loved one's road to recovery and resiliency,

Paul Moglia, PhD

Contributors

Christopher M. Aanstoos, PhD
University of West Georgia

Richard Adler, PhD
University of
    Michigan—Dearborn

Wendell Anderson, BA
American Medical Writers
    Association

Tammi Arford, MA
Northeastern University

Bryan C. Auday, PhD
Professor, Department of
    Psychology
Director, Neuroscience Program,
    Gordon College

Allison C. Bennett, PharmD
Duke University Hospital

R. L. Bernstein, PhD
New Mexico State University

Lillian J. Breckenridge
Oral Roberts University

Michael A. Buratovich PhD
Spring Arbor University

Byron D. Cannon, PhD
University of Utah

Shiliang (Alice) Cao MD-ScM
    Candidate 2019
Brown University Warren Alpert
    Medical School

Richard Capriccioso, MD

Christine M. Carroll, RN, BSN,
    MBA
American Medical Writers
    Association

Jack Carter, PhD
University of New Orleans

Robert S. Cavera, Psy.D
Merrick, NY

Paul J. Chara, PhD
Professor of Psychology
University of Northwestern
    – St. Paul

Ruth M. Colwill, PhD
Brown University

Jackie Dial, PhD
Medical Writer & Illustrator

Ronna F. Dillon, PhD
Southern Illinois University

Sally Driscoll, MLS
State College, Pennsylvania

Patricia Stanfill Edens, MBA,
    PhD, RN, LFACHE
Nashville, TN

Karen Nagel Edwards, PhD
Midwestern University

Denis Folan, DO

Anthony J. Fonseca, PhD
Nicholls State University

Rebecca J. Frey, PhD
Yale University

Christine Gamble, MD, MPH

Jennifer L. Gibson, PharmD
Excalibur Scientific, LLC

Lenela Glass-Godwin, MS
Texas A&M University/Auburn
    University

Meika Harris, BSN, RN, CWCN

P. Graham Hatcher, PhD
University of Alabama

Brandy Henry, PhD Candidate,
    MA, MSW, LICSW
NIAAA Predoctoral Fellow
Institute for Behavioral Health
Brandeis University Heller
    School for Social Policy &
    Management

Julie Henry, RN, MPA
Myrtle Beach, South Carolina

David Hernandez
Brown University '16 - Biology
    ScB
MD Candidate 2020 - Warren
    Alpert Medical School of
    Brown University

Michelle Holliday-Stocking, PhD
Adjunct Assistant Professor
Natural and Applied Sciences
    Department
Bentley University

Christine G. Holzmueller, BLA
Glen Rock, Pennsylvania

Glenn Hutchinson, PhD
Decatur, Georgia

April D. Ingram, BS
Kelowna, British Columbia

Pamela Jones, MA
Emerson College/Tufts
    University School of Medicine

Stefanie M. Keen, PhD
University of South Carolina,
    Upstate

xi

Contributors

Mary C. Ware, PhD
SUNY, College at Cortland

Robert J. Wellman, PhD
Fitchburg State University

Lindsey L. Wilner, Psy.D.
Wisconsin & New York

Barbara Woldin, BS
American Medical Writers
Association

Robin L. Wulffson, MD
FACOG Faculty, American
College of Obstetrics and
Gynecology

Complete List of Contents

Volume 1

Volume 2

A

Abstinence-based treatment

CATEGORY: Treatment

ALSO KNOWN AS: Minnesota model of addiction treatment

DEFINITION: Abstinence-based treatment of drug and alcohol addiction is based on addiction as a disease. According to this treatment model, no cure exists for the disease of addiction. Through counseling and continued support, the addicted person can recover as long as he or she maintains lifelong abstinence from drugs and alcohol.

HISTORY

Abstinence-based treatment was first developed at Willmar State Hospital and Hazelden Treatment Center in Minnesota in 1949. The treatment was targeted at "hopeless" alcoholics and was based on the principles of Alcoholics Anonymous (AA). Borrowing from the twelve-step meetings of AA, developed in the 1930s, these alcoholic treatment centers added residential treatment that included lectures, open discussions, small group therapy, and peer interaction.

First known as the Willmar or Hazelden model, and then the Minnesota model in the 1970s, abstinence-based treatment centers became the predominant model for treating both alcohol and drug misuse in the 1980s. Private treatment in twenty-eight-day residential treatment centers dominated the treatment landscape but was affected by cost-cutting managed-care by the 1990s.

Most abstinence-based treatment now occurs in outpatient settings. Treatment focuses on individualized treatment plans, family involvement, and frequent use of group meetings such as AA, Narcotics Anonymous, and Al Anon. Studies show that more than 90 percent of drug and alcohol treatment programs in the United States are abstinence-based, and most use the twelve-step program of AA as a core principle.

BASIC PRINCIPLES

The first treatment principle is that all addiction, no matter the substance, is caused by lifelong physiological, social, and psychological disease processes. No cure exists for the disease of addiction, but recovery is possible through peer support and positive change. This principle removes the guilt that is associated with addiction and focuses on the disease instead of the addicted person. The addicted person begins by admitting that the disscease makes him or her powerless over drugs and alcohol.

Recovery involves taking responsibility for the disease and making necessary changes in thinking and behavior. This type cognitive behavioral therapy may include individual and group therapy. Personal change may include recognizing denial and other self-defeating behaviors and replacing these negative thoughts with gratitude, honesty, forgiveness, and humility. For many addicts and alcoholics, key components of successful abstinence include a spiritual awakening, faith in a higher power, and faith in the power of being part of a recovery community. A final principle is that without continued abstinence, addiction is a progressive and ultimately fatal disease.

BASIC COMPONENTS

Diagnosis should begin with a comprehensive evaluation that recognizes that addiction is a social, biological, and psychological disease. The initial phase of treatment may require medically supervised detoxification. Comorbid diseases related to alcohol or drug misuse and dual diagnosis such as bipolar disorder, attention deficit/hyperactivity disorder, or depression should also be recognized and treated.

Treatment for primary addiction may include the use of control-craving drugs, individual cognitive behavioral therapy, group therapy, family therapy, and relapse prevention therapy. Abstinence-based treatment may be adapted to a long period of residential treatment or may occur through outpatient care.

Because this treatment considers addiction a lifelong disease, addicts are encouraged to attend after-care programs and twelve-step meetings, where they can benefit from the reinforcement of core principles and the support of other recovering people.

SUCCESS AND CRITICISM

Abstinence-based treatment is often criticized for having a low success rate, but because relapse is accepted as part of the natural course of the disease of addiction, it is difficult to give much credence to studies that look at one-year or even five-year success rates. Many addicted people fail initial treatment, have several relapses, and then continue with many years of sustained abstinence. According to the National Institute on Drug Abuse, relapse rates for addictions are similar to those for other chronic diseases, such as diabetes, hypertension, and asthma.

The abstinence-based treatment model also is criticized for being one-size-fits-all; for not allowing other treatment options, such as the harm-reduction model; for not being adaptable to persons who cannot accept the spiritual concept of a higher power; and for encouraging unattainable goals. These criticisms and alternatives are under discussion and study.

Still, most experts agree that abstinence should be the first and primary goal of addiction treatment. In the United States, therefore, abstinence-based treatment remains the treatment of choice for drug and alcohol addiction.

Christopher Iliades MD

FOR FURTHER INFORMATION

Cherkis, Jason. "Dying to Be Free: There's a Treatment for Heroin Addiction That Actually Works. Why Aren't We Using It?" *Huffington Post.* TheHuffingtonPost.com, 28 Jan. 2015. Web. 26 Oct. 2015.

Galanter, Marc, Herbert D. Kleber, and Kathleen T. Brady. *The American Psychiatric Publishing Textbook of Substance Abuse Treatment.* 5th ed. Washington, DC: Amer. Psychiatric Assn., 2015. Print.

Mignon, Sylvia I. *Substance Abuse Treatment: Options, Challenges, and Effectiveness.* New York: Springer, 2015. Print.

Ries, Richard, and Shannon C. Miller. *Principles of Addiction Medicine.* Philadelphia: Lippincott, 2009. Print.

Scott, Christy K., et al. "Surviving Drug Addiction: The Effect of Treatment and Abstinence on Mortality." *American Journal of Public Health* 101.4 (2010): 737–44. Print. Print.

Spicer, Jerry. *The Minnesota Model: The Evolution of the Multidisciplinary Approach to Recovery.* Center City: Hazelden, 1993. Print

Derived from: "Abstinence-based treatment." *Addictions & Substance Abuse.* Salem Press. 2012.

See also: Alcoholics Anonymous: The Twelve Steps; Hazelden Foundation; Minnesota model; Relapse

Addiction

CATEGORY: Health issues and physiology

DEFINITION: Addiction is a chronic brain disease and is identified as substance use disorder by the American Psychiatric Association in their most recent publication of the *Diagnostic and Statistical Manual of Mental Disorders* (2013), the *DSM-5*, which is compiled to describe and diagnose all currently identified mental health problems that may receive a formal medical diagnosis in the United States.

THE COSTS OF ADDICTION

According to the National Institute on Drug Abuse in April 2017, the societal cost of drug and alcohol addiction, in terms of lost productivity, crime, and health-care associated costs, is more than $740 billion per year. Perhaps an even greater cost, but one that is far more difficult to calculate, is the harm of addiction to those addicted and the "collateral damage" that often occurs to the loved ones of the addicted individual.

Most people can think of someone in their lives—a friend, partner, parent, or child—who is affected by addiction. Addiction is far too common, and its effects can be devastating. Researchers are making considerable progress in understanding the illness, and with greater understanding should come better treatment and more reason for hope.

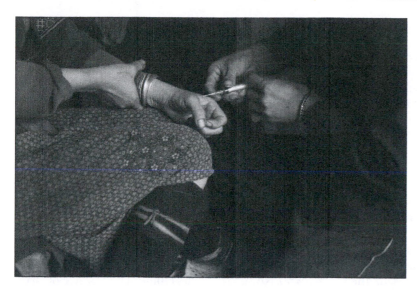

A drug addict injects a fellow user. (via Wikimedia Commons)

DIAGNOSTIC CATEGORIES RELATED TO ADDICTION

Substance use disorder involves a set of maladaptive set of behaviors associated with the taking of substances, including drugs and alcohol, that lead to significant impairment or distress. Maladaptive behaviors include the failure to fulfill one's responsibilities at work, school, or home; engaging in risky or dangerous situations while using substances (such as driving while intoxicated or operating machinery while under the influence of drugs); or continuing to use substances despite recurrent negative consequences (such as losing one's job or arguments or physical altercations with others).

Tolerance of a substance is also an diagnostic criteria of addiction and substance use disorder. Tolerance is the need for increased amounts of a substance to achieve the desired effect or to reach intoxication. Tolerance is also marked by noticeably diminished effects despite continued use of the same amount of the substance. Other criteria include withdrawal (unpleasant symptoms associated with drug removal). Additional criteria for substance dependence include the tendency to escalate drug use; taking the drug more frequently, in greater doses, or for longer periods of time; loss of control over drug use; and an inability to limit one's use.

The term "addiction" has been expanded in the DSM-5 to include excessive, compulsive, or destructive habits that have nothing to do with drugs or alcohol, such as gambling disorder. Although several societal addictions have not been formally recognized in the DSM-5, two terms, *workaholics* and *shopaholics* are commonly used by individuals to reflect society's belief that a person can be addicted to working or to shopping. The concept of addiction also is commonly applied to cigarette smoking, Internet use, overeating, and sexual behavior, though not formally recognized in the DSM-5.

GENERAL FEATURES OF ADDICTION

Addictions occur with behavioral rewards. Behavioral rewards include experiences that a person wants, experiences for which a person is willing to behave in a particular way. In short, the objects of addictions always feel good, at least in the beginning. While certain potentially addicting drugs and behaviors may indeed be harmful in all circumstances, this is not true across the board. There is nothing inherently unhealthy in things that feel good, or in the tendency to engage in certain behaviors to obtain those things. These behaviors have evolved, and they are tendencies that have served well for human survival.

The problem with addiction is that the effect of the behavioral reward changes in particular ways. With time and repeated exposure, a person's reaction to the behavioral reward changes in three observable ways. First, the person may develop a tolerance and then experience withdrawal. More and more of the behavioral reward will be needed to get the same amount of pleasure (tolerance), and the behavior may need to continue to keep feeling pleasure (withdrawal).

The presence of tolerance and withdrawal has been used as the primary indicator of addiction in years past. However, a person can vary in the extent to which he or she experiences tolerance and, especially, withdrawal, in his or her addiction, even with drugs such as alcohol, which produce symptoms of physical dependence.

In addition, other changes in a person's reaction to behavioral rewards also typically accompany the development of addictions. For example, the value of the addictive behavior, relative to other possible behaviors, changes. The person's behavioral repertoire shifts from one in which variable behaviors and responses occur to a far narrower focus, in which behaviors associated with the addiction come to predominate. Finally, the person seems to lose control of the addiction. Once he or she gets started with the behavior in question, they "overdo it" in ways that they did not intend and that they frequently regret. Efforts to permanently curtail or eliminate the addiction are extraordinarily difficult. Relapse, or returning to the behavior after successfully staying away from it for a time, is a common problem.

MODELS OF ADDICTION

Many different models, from widely diverse theoretical orientations within the field of psychology and medicine, have been proposed to account for addiction. Advances in brain imaging, however, have allowed scientists and researcher to see inside the brain of addicted individuals and study the areas of the brain that are affected by drugs and alcohol. Research has found that addiction is a brain disease because alcohol and drugs change the structure and function of the brain itself. Although many outside the scientific and research communities still consider addiction to be learned behavior, research is proving otherwise.

Other experts have sought to explain addiction in terms of personality variables, emphasizing the role of inner conflict or inadequate psychological coping mechanisms. Finally, numerous biological models search for the root of addictive behaviors in genetics and neurochemistry. It seems likely that a complete understanding of addiction may ultimately require a synthesis of several, if not all, of these approaches.

Linda R. Tennison PhD

FOR FURTHER INFORMATION

DiClemente, Carlo C. *Addiction and Change: How Addictions Develop and Addicted People Recover.* New York: Guilford, 2006. Print.

Granfield, Robert, and Craig Reinarman, eds. *Expanding Addiction: Critical Essays.* New York: Routledge, 2015. Print.

Hart, Carl L., and Charles Ksir. *Drugs, Society, and Human Behavior.* 16th ed. New York: McGraw-Hill, 2014. Print.

Julien, Robert M., Claire D. Advokat, and Joseph E. Comaty. *A Primer of Drug Action.* 13th ed. New York: Worth, 2014. Print.

Koob, George F., Michael A. Arends, and Michel le Moal. *Drugs, Addiction, and the Brain.* Boston: Academic, 2014. Print.

Miller, Peter M. *Biological Research on Addiction.* Amsterdam: Elsevier, 2013. Print.

Nutt, David J., and Liam J. Nestor. *Addiction.* Oxford: Oxford UP, 2013. Print.

Rosenberg, Kenneth Paul, and Laura Curtiss Feder. *Behavioral Addictions: Criteria, Evidence, and Treatment.* Boston: Academic, 2014. Print.

Rosner, Richard. *Clinical Handbook of Adolescent Addiction.* Chichester: Wiley-Blackwell, 2013. Print.

Sheff, David, *Clean: Overcoming Addiction and Ending America's Greatest Tragedy.* Boston: Houghton Mifflin Harcourt, 2013. Print.

"Trends & Statistics." *NIH National Institute on Drug Abuse,* National Institutes of Health, Apr. 2017, www.drugabuse.gov/related-topics/trends-statistics. Accessed 9 Oct. 2017.

Volkow, Nora. "Teacher's Guide: The Essence of Drug Addiction." *The Brain: Understanding Neurobiology Through the Study of Addiction.* Natl Inst of Health, 2010. Web. 8 Sept. 2014.

See also: Models of addiction; Psychological dependence; Risk factors for addiction; Science of addiction; Substance misuse

---

Addiction medications

CATEGORY: Treatment

DEFINITION: Addiction medications are drugs used to treat substance use disorders. The drugs are best used when combined with psychosocial treatment.

INTRODUCTION

Addiction is a brain disease. Once a person becomes addicted, changes typically occur in the body and the brain that make these systems function differently than before the development of the addiction. The functional (and perhaps structural) changes to the brain that occur with addiction can sometimes be treated with medications that allow the brain to function normally in the absence of the drug.

Medications are available for the treatment of opiate, alcohol, and cocaine use disorders and for nicotine use. Each of these medications will be considered individually here. No medication exists for the treatment of methamphetamine addiction, but about one-half dozen are being studied.

Many of the medications used in the treatment of addiction are used "off-label." In other words, the medications are used for addiction even though they have been approved by US Food and Drug Administration (FDA) to treat other disorders, such as depression, muscle spasms, insomnia, and nausea. Only those medications currently legal to use in the United States (including those used off-label) are presented here. When available, both the clinical name and the more commonly used name will be included. The common name will appear in parentheses.

Many of the medications discussed fall under one of three categories: antagonist, full agonist, or partial agonist. An antagonist is a substance that binds to receptor cells so tightly that it will block any other substance from binding to that cell. Antagonists also bind to the cell without stimulating the cell or otherwise causing a response. Examples of antagonists include naltrexone and ondansetron.

A full agonist is similar to an antagonist in that it completely binds to a receptor cell. Unlike antagonists, however, full agonists will activate that receptor site. Examples of full agonists include morphine and topiramate (a gamma-aminobutyric acid, or GABA, agonist).

Partial agonists, like agonists, bind to receptor cells and activate them, but they cannot bind fully, so the receptor is only partially activated. Examples of partial agonists include varenicline and buprenorphine.

Medications are wonderful tools in the treatment of both physical and mental illnesses and disorders. It should be noted, however, that patients receiving medication also should receive psychosocial treatment.

MEDICATIONS FOR ALCOHOL ADDICTION

Alcohol is a central nervous system depressant. It works by interfering with communication between nerve cells and by interacting with the receptors on some cells. Alcohol suppresses excitatory nerve pathway activity (for example, glutamine) and increases inhibitory nerve pathway activity (for example, GABA). Thus, alcohol lowers inhibitions, which is why it is often found to be a significant factor in violent and sexually motivated crimes. Medications used (or under study) to treat alcohol use disorders include baclofen, campral (Acamprosate), disulfiram (Antabuse), naltrexone (ReVia or Vivitrol), ondansetron (Zofran), and topiramate (Topamax).

Baclofen. Baclofen treats muscle tightness and cramping or spasms that are often associated with spinal cord injury, spinal cord disease, or multiple sclerosis. The drug is a derivative of GABA and works with alcohol dependence by decreasing withdrawal symptoms and cravings. These effects are achieved by inhibiting the activation of the receptors in the brain that become stimulated during withdrawal.

Campral. The FDA approved campral for the treatment of alcohol use disorder in 2004. Before this time, campral was used widely across Europe in the treatment of alcohol use disorders. Campral works by stimulating GABA receptors and thereby reducing the negative symptoms a person may experience when attempting to abstain from alcohol.

Disulfiram. Disulfiram has been used to treat alcohol use disorders since the 1950s. Originally thought to work well as a treatment for parasites, experts began to notice that persons who took the medication and who also drank alcohol became ill. The medication disrupts the metabolism of alcohol, resulting in a hangover type of physical illness. The physical effects caused by disulfiram in persons also ingesting alcohol include headache, flushing nausea, dizziness, and vomiting.

Naltrexone. Naltrexone is an antagonist; it binds to the mu (μ) opioid receptors in the brain, but it does not stimulate them. This is important because naltrexone is used to treat addictions but does so without causing euphoria, like some addiction medications. Naltrexone is available in two different administrations: oral and injection.

The oral version of naltrexone, ReVia, was approved for the treatment of alcohol use disorders in 1995. However, because it must be taken daily, its effectiveness varies for those who are not medication compliant or not committed to treatment. In addition, side effects may be substantial because the medication levels vary throughout the day. The injection form of naltrexone, Vivitrol, was approved in 2006. Vivitrol is a long acting, once-a-month, injection that works the same way as ReVia, but it has fewer side effects and better medication compliance.

Ondansetron. Ondansetron is an antiemetic that reduces the nausea and vomiting that often accompany chemotherapy treatment. Ondansetron is a serotonin receptor antagonist and works by reducing the activity of the vagus nerve, thereby blocking the sensation of the need to vomit. This medication also has been studied as a treatment for other disorders, including alcohol use disorder, and although it is not approved for this, it can be prescribed off-label.

Topiramate. Topiramate treats epilepsy; however, research also indicates that it may be useful as a treatment for alcohol, cocaine, and nicotine dependence. Topiramate is a glutamate antagonist and a GABA agonist. It works by blocking the glutamate receptors and by increasing the effects of GABA, which help to calm over-excited nerve cells. Topiramate has been shown useful in the treatment of alcohol dependence. Topiramate has a number of side effects, including weight loss, impaired memory and concentration, numbness and tingling of extremities (although this side effect is transient), and the development of kidney stones.

MEDICATIONS FOR COCAINE ADDICTION

Cocaine is a stimulant of the central nervous system derived from the coca plant (not to be confused with the cocoa plant, which is used for chocolate). Cocaine is a serotonin-norepinephrine-dopamine reuptake inhibitor, which means that cocaine can increase alertness, euphoria, energy, motor activity, and feelings of competence. However, it also can result in anxiety, paranoia, restlessness, delusions, hallucinations, and tachycardia. Medications used (or under study) to treat cocaine use disorders include baclofen, disulfiram, gabapentin (Gabitrol), and modafinil (Provigil), and the dietary supplement N-acetylcysteine (NAC).

Baclofen. Baclofen, which is used to treat muscle spasticity (found in persons with multiple sclerosis), also has been studied as a potential treatment for cocaine addiction. Baclofen is said to work by decreasing the effects of dopamine in the brain and, thereby, reducing cocaine-induced euphoria.

Disulfiram. Disulfiram, which is used to treat alcohol use disorders, also has been studied as a treatment for cocaine disorders. In one study conducted at Yale University, disulfiram was found to work well in decreasing cocaine use. Similar to its effect with alcohol users, the study showed that is caused cocaine users to become physically ill. This research has since been replicated.

Gabapentin. Gabapentin is an anticonvulsant medication used to treat seizure disorders, depression, and pain. The medication also has been studied as a treatment for cocaine use disorders. The medication works

by making cravings less intense and by lessening the severity of any relapse to cocaine use. Because of these positive effects, however, some doctors are hesitant to prescribe gabapentin for cocaine use disorders; it is believed that the medication will reinforce cocaine use rather than discourage it.

Modafinil. Modafinil is FDA approved for the treatment of narcolepsy and other sleep disorders. It also has been studied in the treatment of cocaine use disorders. However, findings have proven inconclusive.

N-acetylcysteine. N-acetylcysteine is an over-the-counter herbal supplement with purported antioxidant effects. It has been used to treat everything from carbon monoxide poisoning to acetaminophen overdose. Its effectiveness in treating cocaine use disorders has not been determined.

MEDICATIONS FOR METHAMPHETAMINE ADDICTION

Methamphetamine is a synthetic drug. Although chemically similar to amphetamine, its effects are much longer lasting. Methamphetamine is a central nervous system stimulant with euphoric effects similar to those found with cocaine. Methamphetamine works by increasing the release of dopamine in the brain. No approved medications are on the market to treat methamphetamine addiction, and no medication is used off-label to treat methamphetamine addiction. However, a few drugs are under study, including paroxetine (Paxil), ondansetron, and gabapentin.

Paroxetine. Paroxetine is indicated for the treatment of mood disorders (depression and anxiety) and obsessive-compulsive disorder and panic disorder. It also is under study for the treatment of methamphetamine misuse.

Ondansetron. Ondansetron, used to treat alcohol use disorders, is FDA approved as an antinausea drug that may work to block specific binding sites for the neurotransmitter serotonin. Some preliminary studies have indicated that ondansetron may block the effects of methamphetamine.

Gabapentin. Gabapentin, in addition to being a potential medication for the treatment of cocaine use disorders, also may be a viable option for the treatment of methamphetamine use disorders.

MEDICATIONS FOR NICOTINE ADDICTION

Nicotine is a stimulant found in tobacco and tobacco products. The American Heart Association reports that nicotine dependence is one of the most difficult addictions to break. Some medications, including bupropion (Wellbutrin) and varenicline (Chantix), and other products, such as nicotine replacements, are available to assist persons addicted to nicotine. The use of bupropion and varenicline in nicotine addiction treatment, however, has been linked to serious side effects, including depression and suicidal ideation. Nicotine replacement products (such as patches and gum) provide the user with nicotine, but they do not have the harmful carcinogens that accompany many of the delivery systems (such as smoking or tobacco chewing).

Bupropion. Bupropion is a well-known antidepressant that has been used in the treatment of nicotine dependence. The drug works by reducing the urge to smoke.

Varenicline. Varenicline is a nicotine receptor partial agonist. It works by decreasing the cravings for nicotine and by decreasing the pleasurable effects of nicotine consumption.

MEDICATIONS FOR OPIATE ADDICTION

Opiates are narcotic analgesics (painkillers) that are derived from the poppy plant and from several artificial means. Opiates work by binding to specific receptors in the brain. Because the human body creates its own form of opiate, the brain has specific receptors created just for this substance. The receptors where opiates bind typically control movement, digestion, mood, the experience of pain, and, most problematic, body temperature and respiration.

Opiate use disorders vary and can include addiction to heroin and painkillers (such as vicodin and oxycodone). Medications used to treat opiate use disorders include buprenorphine, methadone, and naltrexone.

The FDA approved buprenorphine in 2002 as a treatment for opiate use disorders. The drug works by binding to the same receptors as opiates, but because it is a partial agonist it does not completely fill the receptor; therefore, little euphoria is achieved when taken as prescribed. A doctor prescribes buprenorphine, and induction (introduction of buprenorphine into the system) can be done in a doctor's office rather than at a substance misuse treatment facility. The effects of buprenorphine can last up to three days, so unlike the common drug methadone, daily doses are not required.

There are two different formulations of buprenorphine: Subutex and Suboxone. Subutex contains only buprenorphine and is the formulation used during the first few days of induction. Suboxone includes both buprenorphine and naloxone. Naloxone is a powerful substance that blocks the effects of opiates and is often used to treat opiate overdose. When combined with buprenorphine, it greatly reduces the misuse potential of this medication.

Methadone. Methadone, perhaps the best-known medication to treat opiate use disorders, is a synthetic opiate and a narcotic pain reliever similar to morphine. It has been used in the treatment of opiate addiction since the 1960s. Methadone is a full mu (μ) opioid agonist and works by binding to this receptor and by preventing other opiates from binding to that same receptor. However, methadone, if given in the incorrect dosage or through certain routes, can result in euphoria similar to that of illicit opiates.

Withdrawal from methadone can take several weeks to several months and has been described as more difficult to withdraw from than other opiates. Methadone is taken orally and is typically taken daily.

Naltrexone. Naltrexone, in addition to treating alcohol use disorders, also has been shown to be effective in the treatment of opiate use disorders. When used for opiate use disorders, naltrexone works as it does for alcohol: It binds tightly to the mu (μ) opioid receptors and prevents any other drug from binding to those same receptors. The binding action reduces cravings for the substance and also prevents the high that is normally experienced from opiate use. Because naltrexone is an antagonist, it is powerful enough to push the opiates out of the receptors to bind to them. This is important because naltrexone will place a patient into precipitated withdrawal from opiates if the patient has not abstained from opiates before receiving naltrexone.

There are two ways to administer naltrexone: orally (ReVia) and through an intramuscular injection (Vivitrol). Both forms are FDA approved for the treatment of opiate use disorders.

Desirée A. Crèvecoeur-MacPhail PhD

FOR FURTHER INFORMATION

Anderson, David. "Narrative of Discovery: In Search of a Medication to Treat Methamphetamine Addiction." *NIDA Notes.* Natl. Inst. on Drug Abuse, 14 Jan. 2015. Web. 26 Oct. 2015.

Anglin, M., et al. "Longitudinal Effects of LAAM and Methadone Maintenance on Heroin Addict Behavior." *Journal of Behavioral Health Services and Research* 36.2 (2009): 267–82. Print.

Diehl, A., et al. "Why Is Disulfiram Superior to Acamprosate in the Routine Clinical Setting? A Retrospective Long-Term Study in 353 Alcohol-Dependent Patients." *Alcohol and Alcoholism* 45.3 (2010): 271–77. Print.

Dranitsaris, G., P. Selby, and J. C. Negrete. "Meta-Analyses of Placebo-Controlled Trials of Acamprosate for the Treatment of Alcohol Dependence: Impact of the Combined Pharmacotherapies and Behavior Interventions Study." *Journal of Addiction Medicine* 3.2 (2009): 74–82. Print.

Johnson, B. A., et al. "Improvement of Physical Health and Quality of Life of Alcohol-Dependent Individuals with Topiramate Treatment." *Archives of Internal Medicine* 168.11 (2008): 1188–99. Print.

Kahan, M., et al. "Buprenorphine: New Treatment of Opioid Addiction in Primary Care." *Canadian Family Physician* 53.3 (2011): 281–89. Print.

Koob, George F., Michael A. Arends, and Michel le Moal. "Medications for the Treatment of Addiction—A Neurobiological Perspective." *Drugs, Addiction, and the Brain.* Boston: Academic, 2014. 310–34. Print.

Mattick, R. P., et al. "Methadone Maintenance Therapy versus No Opioid Replacement Therapy for Opioid Dependence." *Cochrane Database of Systematic Reviews* 3 (2009): CD002209. Print.

Szabo, Liz. "Advocates Push to Expand Use of Medications to Treat Addiction." *USA Today.* Gannett, 8 July 2015. Web. 26 Oct. 2015.

See also: Baclofen; Bupropion; Methadone; Naltrexone

Addictive personality

CATEGORY: Psychological issues and behaviors

DEFINITION: Addiction is a chronic, relapsing medical condition. Researchers have been unable to provide evidence of the addictive personality type. It was thought that there is a character flaw that leads inevitably to addiction. Another theory is that people develop addictions because they are risk-takers or impulsive, and are out of control of their lives. Recent research into addiction and personality focuses on the behaviors seen more frequently in persons with addictions. There is evidence that addiction can develop in a person with any type of personality. Addictions do not just include alcohol and opioid drugs. There can be addictions related to such things as: computer gaming, cell phones, eating, smoking, sex, exercise, gambling, and shopping.

PREVALENCE

Researchers studying addictions have found that roughly 47% of people in the U.S. may be addicted within a 12 month period.

CAUSES

About 50% of people have a genetic predisposition for developing addictions. The genes are inherited from a family member. Persons with one of these genes often have family members with addictions. Most of the genes causing the predisposition for addiction have been identified with research using rodents.

Recent research suggests that it is common that people become addicted due to stressful life events and difficulty coping with them. Originally, addiction was thought to be a disease of adolescents. Now it has been diagnosed in people of all ages and stages of their lives. An example is seen in midlife persons who suddenly lose their jobs, and are unable to find another comparable job. Other possible life events are: death of a child or other family members; divorce; the onset of a chronic, life-threatening disease; and financial problems. One researcher feels that loneliness and lack of human contact is actually the cause of addictions. If addiction is caused by stressful life events, it is more common in a person unable to self-regulate their feelings.

RISK FACTORS

There are a number of factors that are thought to increase a person's risk for developing an addiction. One risk factor is the presence of other mental health problems, such as anxiety, depression, schizophrenia and Post Traumatic Stress Disorder (PTSD). Others at risk for addiction are persons who have an anti-social personality, apathy, or loneliness. Another researcher thinks that people who struggle with addiction may be risk-takers and adventurous. More unusual problems that may lead to addiction are low levels of dopamine, desire for self-harm, and difficulty regulating one's behaviors or thoughts.

ASSESSMENT

Some behaviors are more common in persons with an addiction. These behaviors are thought to be related to the disease of addiction. They are impulsive behavior, negative feelings about values that society values, trouble dealing with stress, denial of the seriousness of an addiction, the need for instant gratification, erratic moods, and unwilling to ask others for help with their problems. These behaviors are often one of the signs that a person has developed an addiction.

DIAGNOSIS

The compulsions and lack of control that characterize addiction are signs that the brain's neurophysiology is changing. Neuro-imaging techniques are able to identify the parts of the brain that have been affected. There are two tests that can diagnose an addiction. They are functional magnetic resonance imaging (fMRI) and positron emission tomography (PET) scan. Both of these tests assess the activity of specific areas of brain tissue and brain anatomy. The fMRI maps blood flow and oxygenation of the brain. This increase in blood flow represents an increase in the brain metabolism. These areas are the areas of brain pathology. The PET scan measures areas of increased metabolism by analyzing the locations of increased glucose. The glucose is marked by an irradiated tracer. The results of both tests highlight the areas of the brain that are active with addiction.

With addiction, the prefrontal cerebral cortex uses glutamine to interact with dopamine. This combination initiates cravings and visualizations. The next area of the brain is the orbitofrontal cortex where other pleasurable hormones are released. They start to affect decision making and regulation of emotional behavior. The prefrontal cortical regions govern the reward-related behavior that is impaired in addicted persons. The orbitofrontal cortex can stop the progression on the pathway if it feels that too much drug has been used. The orbitofrontal cortex can initiate a decision to reject immediate gratification in favor of greater delayed rewards.

Involvement of the neurotransmitter dopamine is further evidence of neural participation in addictive processes. Dopamine is believed to act on mechanisms of expectation and reward. Most addictive drugs increase dopamine levels and dopaminergic transmission. Appetizing food and addictive drugs have a comparable effect in raising levels of dopamine. The other areas of the brain that are affected by addiction include: the nucleus accumbens (NAC), the ventral palladium, the habenula, the insula, the anterior cingulate, and the amygdala. The parts of the brain involved with the production of dopamine, are the source of the "high" that causes craving for a drug. The NAC is a source of dopamine which rewards pleasant behavior in the non-addicted person, and rewards the addicted person with high levels of dopamine.. The NAC also helps a person to decide whether they wish to get involved with drug taking. The ventral palladium is another area of the brain that is involved with the reward for the addicted person. The habenula seems to initiate negative feelings, and to stimulate the insula.

The insula gives a person another chance to decide whether they wish to take an addicting drug, and it processes a person's feelings, like disgust, hunger or thirst. The anterior cingulate works with the insula to help a person to reconsider their decisions as they make them. The insula is involved in the person's judgments and conflicting feelings to assist in making a decision related to drug-taking. The anterior cingulate analyzes their plans and whether they are good or bad. The insula attempts to change the plans until they are right for the person. The amygdala helps a person to identify their feelings about their drug taking plan. If the plan is not a good one it may cause feelings of fear.

TREATMENTS

There are several ways of treating addiction problems. They are counseling, and medications. For the treatment to be successful, the person must be motivated to make the change. Recovery involves counseling, or meetings like Alcoholic Anonymous (AA) or the 12 step programs. A counselor teaches Cognitive Behavioral Therapy (CBT), which is a way to deal with the tough occurrences in life, and to self-sooth. AA has group meetings where each person shares their story. A member who has been successful in giving up their addiction becomes an advisor to a new member. The new member can telephone the advisor whenever they feel like going back to their addiction. The 12 step programs are group meetings.

The drugs used to treat alcoholism are Antabuse, Campral, and Naltrexone. The person has to agree to take Antabuse because it causes uncomfortable symptoms if you drink alcohol. The symptoms are nausea, flushing and irregular heartbeat. Both Campral and Naltrexone decrease the symptoms of withdrawal from alcohol. For drug addiction, the drugs include Naloxone (Narcan), methadone, suboxone (buprenorphine), and Naltrexone. Naloxone is used in an overdose to reverse the symptoms of the drugs. Naloxone is life-saving if administered soon after the overdose. Naltrexone, methadone, and suboxone reduce the symptoms of withdrawal from drugs. Methadone must be obtained from a methadone clinic, and the person is given a few pills.

FUTURE/OUTCOMES
There are no easy solutions for addictions, especially addiction of alcohol and drugs. It would be easier if drugs and alcohol were less available. Cocaine, Heroin, amphetamines, and Fentanyl are readily available on the street. Alcohol is even more available than drugs, and drinking alcohol is socially acceptable. We have limited numbers of psychiatrists and drug treatment programs. There is a federal parity law that requires the same payments to psychiatrists and drug treatment centers, as medical care. Despite the parity law, most health insurance does not pay for addiction treatment at a treatment center. The only hope is to more aggressively educate both children and adults about the dangers of drug and alcohol addiction.

Judith Weinblatt, MS, MA;
Updated by Christine M. Carroll, MBA

FOR FURTHER INFORMATION
Griffiths, Marc D., Ph.D. (11 May 2015) "The Myth of the Addictive Personality." Retrieved July 12, 2018 from www.PsychologyToday.com/us/blog/in excess/201605/The-Myth-of-the-Addictive-Personality/ This author wrote about the role that addictions have in human life.

Smith, Fran. "The Addicted Brain." *National Geographic*, September 2017. This article is about the basics of addiction, including the effect on newborns. There is also information about the experimental use of magnets to restore normal brain functions.

Szalavitz, Maia. *The Unbroken Brain: A Revolutionary New Way of Understanding Addiction:* St. Martin's Press, April 5, 2016. Szalavitz writes about her own addiction as a child, and how she believes that addiction is a learning disorder.

Szalavitz, Maia. (5 April, 2016) "The Addictive Personality Isn't What You Think It Is." Retrieved July 12, 2018, from https://ScientificAmerican.com/article/The-Addictive-Personality-isn't-what-You-think-it-is/ The author writes about her own experience with addiction and her feeling that tolerance, prevention and treatment should be used for addicts.

See also: Addiction; Behavioral addictions: Overview; Impulse control disorders; Risk factors for addiction; Science of addiction

---

Adolescents and alcohol misuse

CATEGORY: Social issues

DEFINITION: Alcohol misuse is a pattern of heavy drinking that significantly compromises a person's physical health and social functioning. According to the US National Institute on Alcohol Abuse and Alcoholism (NIAAA), an estimated 855,000 American adolescents aged twelve to seventeen years qualified for a diagnosis of alcohol use disorder (AUD) in 2012, accounting for 3.6 percent of American teenaged girls and 3.2 percent of American teenaged boys. Despite intensive government efforts to curb the problem, the prevalence of underage alcohol misuse has remained constant since about 1990.

SCOPE OF THE PROBLEM
Alcohol use and misuse among young people in the United States is pervasive and destructive. In the United States, adolescents misuse alcohol more than any illicit drug, and it causes the most harm. Despite a nationwide minimum legal drinking age of twenty-one years, the Substance Abuse and Mental Health Services Administration (SAMHSA) reports that 61 percent of high school students have consumed alcohol by the end of high school, 23 percent have consumed alcohol by 8th grade, 46 percent of 12th

graders have been drunk at least once in their life, and 9 percent of 8th graders have been drunk at least once in their life. The National Institute on Alcohol Abuse and Alcoholism (NIAAA) reports that, on average, young people have about five drinks in a night, which many health experts believe qualifies as binge drinking. More specifically, the NIAAA also defines binge drinking as consuming enough alcohol within about two hours to bring blood alcohol levels (BAC) to 0.08 grams of hemoglobin per deciliter (g/dL). According to the NIAAA, approximately five thousand youths under the age of twenty-one die each year in the United States due to alcohol-related car crashes, homicides, suicides, alcohol poisoning, and other injuries. Nearly two thousand college-aged students aged eighteen to twenty-four die from alcohol-related injuries each year. According to the 2013 Youth Risk Behavior Surveillance System, in the thirty days before taking the survey, approximately 22 percent of Americans aged ten to twenty-four years had ridden in a car driven by someone who had been drinking alcohol. The US Centers for Disease Control and Prevention (CDC) reports that, in 2013, 10 percent of teen drivers admitted to drunk driving within the past thirty days.

People who commence heavy or episodic binge drinking before age sixteen years are more than twice as likely as people who start drinking after age eighteen years to develop alcohol dependence. This statistic is often cited as justification for higher drinking ages and for more diligent enforcement of laws against underage drinking. There is some controversy whether this is a matter of cause and effect. Early heavy drinkers usually have parents or siblings who are alcoholics and may be genetically susceptible to alcoholism; also, they probably are subject to environmental influences favoring alcohol misuse.

Rates of both alcohol misuse and alcohol dependence decline steadily after age twenty-five years, a pattern that has been consistent for many decades despite changing social attitudes. Among drinkers with a normal trajectory, work and family responsibilities reduce the opportunities for, and acceptability of, frequent intoxication.

Rates of adolescent and young-adult alcohol misuse in northern Europe are similar to those in the United States, except that the average age of onset of heavy drinking is lower; this is in part due to lower minimum legal drinking ages. A survey of fifteen- to sixteen-year-olds in thirty-four European countries in 2007 showed more than 80 percent had drunk alcohol in the past year and 43 percent had been intoxicated or consumed more than five drinks on one occasion in the past thirty days. There is considerable variation from country to country, with least misuse in southern Europe.

In the United Kingdom and Ireland, which are two European nations with the highest binge drinking rates, drinking among young people is a serious national problem. Up until 1960, persons age sixteen to twenty-four years had the lowest per capita alcohol consumption of any adult group; since 1990, the situation has reversed. Some of this pattern (which is seen to a lesser extent in the United States) may be attributed to the rising age of workforce participation. Fewer sixteen- to eighteen-year-olds are employed full time, and an increasing proportion of eighteen- to twenty-four-year olds are students with more leisure time and fewer responsibilities than working counterparts. In general, high rates of unemployment that are not accompanied by extreme economic privation produce high levels of alcohol misuse. In England, 43 percent of all teenagers aged eleven to fifteen reported consuming at least one drink in 2012. In Ireland, 29 percent of young teenage girls (aged thirteen to fifteen) admitted to binge drinking within the last month.

EFFECTS OF EARLY ALCOHOL USE AND MISUSE

Misuse exacts a heavy toll among young people. According to the NIAAA in 2015, 4,358 people under the age of twenty-one die each year of causes related to alcohol, and about 188,000 visit an emergency room for alcohol-related injuries. Approximately one in four college students report adverse academic consequences due to drinking, such as missing classes, performing poorly on tests or exams, or receiving lower grades. The risks of adolescent binge drinking include alcohol poisoning, accidental injuries, including falls and drowning, drunk driving/motor vehicle accidents, sexual and physical assaults, violence against property and suicide. Alcohol consumption can lead to risky behaviors including unprotected sex resulting in an increased risk of contracting sexually transmitted diseases. Alcohol consumption also makes one susceptible to sexual assaults. There is an increased likelihood of addiction and stress-related issues in adulthood, damage to the brain, liver, and heart over time.

The negative effects on a person's life range from short-lived and inconsequential to profound. Drinking can lead to a massive loss of productivity, both in poor academic performance and in the resources that college administrators and law enforcement divert toward combating alcohol problems on campuses.

Statistics on alcohol use for persons eighteen to twenty-five years of age who are not enrolled in a college or university are not as comprehensive; in general, rates of binge drinking are lower but still significant. For both college and university students and people in the workforce, an early and persistent pattern of alcohol misuse tends to translate into poorer career prospects and family instability, even if the drinker never becomes alcohol dependent or if the drinker later successfully enters a recovery program.

Alcohol can serve as a gateway drug. A high proportion of younger heavy drinkers also use marijuana, and the culture surrounding binge drinking among young people for whom it is illegal provides opportunities for experimenting with more dangerous street drugs. Many methamphetamine addicts report that they began using the drug to counteract the effects of alcohol on the job. Adolescents who drink alcohol are 50% more likely to try cocaine ("coke") than those who never use alcohol.

REDUCING UNDERAGE DRINKING

Federal, state, and local governments devote a great deal of energy to combat underage drinking through education and increased enforcement. Federal law in the United States has mandated a minimum state drinking age of twenty-one years as a condition of receiving federal highway funds since the passage of the National Minimum Drinking Age Act of 1984. This law has reduced the availability of alcohol to middle- and high-school students but has had little effect on levels of consumption among college-aged students.

A comparison of the United States with European countries, where a drinking age of sixteen or eighteen years is typical, calls into question whether the approach in the United States is effective. In no European country is the level of binge drinking among eighteen- to twenty-one-year-olds higher than in the United States. It can be argued that turning any level of alcohol consumption into a criminal activity increases the chances of excessive use and alcohol-associated risky behaviors. According to the CDC,

approximately 90 percent of the alcohol consumed by young people in the United States is consumed during a binge-drinking session. Revenue considerations often complicate efforts to curtail alcohol misuse among young people. Underage drinkers comprise a major market sector. Advertising campaigns continue to target this demographic despite government regulation. Flavored alcoholic beverages are of particular concern to regulators and to opponents of alcohol use among youth. Also, in college and university towns, the revenue stream generated by youth alcohol consumption tends to undermine efforts at truly effective enforcement of liquor laws.

If statistics on traffic accidents are any indication, efforts made toward curbing underage drinking and reducing alcohol misuse among high school and college students do seem to have had a significant effect on driving behavior, but not on consumption. The CDC reports that the percentage of high-school students who drink and drive declined by 54 percent between 1991 and 2012. The agency also reported that graduated driver license programs, zero tolerance laws, and increased parental involvement help into increase teen safety when drinking.

Martha A. Sherwood, PhD;
Updated by Charles L. Vigue, PhD

FOR FURTHER INFORMATION

"10 Facts about Teen Drug Use". Newport Academy. https://www.newportacademy.com/resources/substance-abuse/10-facts-teen-drug-abuse/. Accessed July 19, 2018.

"Alcohol Facts and Statistics". *National Institute on Alcohol Abuse and Alcoholism.* Natl. Inst. of Health, March 2015. Web. 5 Nov. 2015.

Bellenir, Karen, and Amy Sutton. *Alcoholism Sourcebook.* Detroit: Omnigraphics, 2007. Print.

"College Drinking." *National Institute of Alcohol Abuse and Alcoholism.* Natl. Inst. of Health, n.d. Web. 15 Dec. 2014.

"Facts and Statistics on Alcohol Abuse in Teens". Teen Rehab. https://www.teendrugrehabs.com/facts-and-stats/. Accessed July 19, 2018.

Fell, J. C., M. Scherer, and R. Voas. "The Utility of Including the Strengths of Underage Drinking Laws in Determining Their Effect on Outcomes." Alcoholism: Clinical and Experimental Research 39.8 (2015): 152837. Print.

Grant, Bridget, et al. "The 12-Month Prevalence and Trends in DSM-IV Alcohol Abuse and Dependence, United States, 1991–1992 and 2001–2002." *Drug and Alcohol Dependence* 74.3 (2004): 223–34. Print.

Hingson, Ralph W., Wenxing Zha, and Elissa R. Weitzman. "Magnitude and Trends in Alcohol-Related Mortality and Morbidity among U.S. College Students Ages 18–24, 1998–2005." *Journal of Studies on Alcohol and Drugs* 16 (2009): 12–20. Print.

Kann, Laura, et al. "Youth Risk Behavior Surveillance—United States, 2013." *MMWR* 63.4 (2014): 1–168. PDF file.

Monti, Peter M., Suzanne M. Colby, and Tracy O'Leary, eds. *Adolescents, Alcohol, and Substance Abuse: Reaching Teens through Brief Interventions.* New York: Guilford, 2001. Print.

Silveri, Marisa M. "Adolescent Brain Development and Underage Drinking in the United States: Identifying Risks of Alcohol Use in College Populations." *Harvard Review of Psychiatry* 20.4 (2012): 189–200. Print.

"Teen Drug and Alcohol Statistics and Information". Project Know. https://www.projectknow.com/research/teen-drug-addiction-statistics-alcoholism-statistics/. Accessed July 19, 2018.

The Recovery Village. https://www.therecoveryvillage.com/teen-addiction/high-school-drug-use/#gref. Accessed July 19, 2018.

The TEDS Report: Age of Substance Use Initiation among Treatment Admissions Aged 18 to 30. Rockville, MD: Substance Abuse and Mental Health Services Administration. Center for Behavioral Health Statistics and Quality, July 17, 2014. https://archive.samhsa.gov/data/2k14/TEDS142/sr142-initiation-age-2014.htm. Accessed July 19, 2018.

"Underage Drinking." *National Institute of Alcohol Abuse and Alcoholism.* Natl. Inst. of Health, Sept. 2015 Web. 5 Nov. 2015.

United States. Dept. of Health and Human Services. "A Developmental Perspective on Underage Alcohol Use." *Alcohol Alert* 78 (2009). Print.

Adolescents and drug misuse

CATEGORY: Social issues

DEFINITION: Drug use interferes with normal brain communication mechanisms leading to changes in behavior and often to addiction.

OVERVIEW

Adolescents from all socio-economic backgrounds are susceptible to using both legal and illegal drugs. Drug use continues even though many anti-drug campaigns have been running for many years. Many different drugs are used by teens. Teens use drugs for a variety of reasons, and the drugs can have various behavioral and physical effects through their effect on brain communication pathways. Drug use prevention programs have been developed with varying results. Many drug addiction treatment programs have been successful.

COMMONLY USED DRUGS

Excluding tobacco, the most commonly used drugs are marijuana (tetrahydrocannabinol, THC), alcohol, stimulants (amphetamines, methamphetamine, ecstasy and cocaine), opioids such as heroin (morphine), inhalants (solvents, gases, sprays, nitrites) and hallucinogens such as psychedelics [lysergic acid diethylamide (LSD), mescaline, psilocybin, N,N-Dimethyltryptamine (DMT)] and dissociatives [ketamine, methoxetamine (MXE), phencyclidine (PCP), dextromethorphan (DXM), nitrous oxide, salvinorin A].

The 2017 Monitoring the Future survey reported that in the past month 19.9% of 8th, 10th and 12th graders used alcohol. 14.5%, 12%, 2.2%, 0.8% and 0.2% had, respectively, used marijuana, vaping products, amphetamines, LSD and heroin in the past month. 24.9% of 12th graders, 17.2% of 10th graders, and 7% of 8th graders reported using an illicit drug within the past month. The use of nicotine and tobacco have been steadily declining.

REASONS FOR DRUG USE

Adolescents cite many reasons for drug use. The results of a 2013 Partnership for Drug-free Kids Attitude Tracking Survey indicate that 50% of teens use marijuana "to have fun" while 48% use it "to relax" and 45% use it "to feel good". Other reasons cited are "to forget about troubles" (37%), "to experiment" (36%), "to relieve boredom" (33%), "to deal with pressure/stress from school" (30%), "to fit in with friends" (29%) and "to deal with problems at home" (27%). Although results of a 2013 Partnership for Drug-free Kids Attitude Tracking Survey specifically studied marijuana use, it is likely that similar results would be found for other drugs.

The probability that a teen will use or try drugs increases if his/her parents use drugs and/or condone drug use. Stress and genetic factors have also been cited as increasing the probability that a teen will use drugs. Studies have shown that teens start to use and try drugs as they are transitioning from elementary school to middle school and from middle school to high school.

Although the initial decision to use drugs is voluntary, repeated use of drugs causes changes in the brain that affect one's self-control and ability to make sound decisions. Drugs also cause the brain to send intense impulses that compel the user to take more drugs resulting in addiction.

Addiction most often begins while a teenager. In 2011, the National Center on Addiction and Substance Abuse reported that 90% of Americans who are addicted to drugs or are drug misusers began using alcohol and/or other drugs before the age of 18 years.

EFFECTS OF DRUG USE

Adolescents and young adults who misuse drugs often exhibit behavioral changes such as poor academic performance. Teen drug users may show changes in physical appearance and health. They may be susceptible to physical violence and have an increased risk of being sexually assaulted. Continued use can affect judgement, learning, decision-making and memory. Since the brain continues to develop until about 25 years of age, drugs use by teens can have a permanent, life-long effect. The developing brain of a teen makes them more susceptible to addiction.

Drugs produce their effects through a variety of mechanisms. Many drugs interfere with the brain's communication system and change the way nerve cells normally send, receive, and process information. Drugs often interfere with the brain's signaling pathways by disrupting normal neurotransmitter mechanisms. Normal brain signaling occurs when a neuron (the pre-synaptic neuron) releases a neurotransmitter

such as dopamine, serotonin, and acetylcholine, glutamate, which diffuses across the synapse and combines with a receptor on the post-synaptic neuron. Depending on the neurotransmitter involved, a signal may be generated or inhibited in the post-synaptic neuron after which the neurotransmitter is removed from its receptor and recycled to prevent further signal generation or inhibition. Drugs can interfere with any aspect of this normal signaling pathway.

Some drugs (such as marijuana and heroin) have a structure resembling a neurotransmitter. This similarity allows the drugs to interact with neurotransmitter receptors and initiate signals that otherwise would not be initiated. Marijuana and heroin also stimulate the release of the neurotransmitter dopamine. Other drugs, such as cocaine and methamphetamine, prevent the re-uptake (recycling) of certain neurotransmitters leading to a local increased concentration of neurotransmitters (mainly dopamine). Increased dopamine has profound effects on the brain, especially on the reward/pleasure centers. Overstimulation of this pathway produces euphoric effects and sets in motion a reinforcing pattern where the drug misuser needs more drug. Hallucinogenic drugs such as LSD bind to receptors for the neurotransmitter serotonin and interfere with normal serotonin signaling.

As a person continues to misuse drugs, the brain adapts to the overwhelming surges in dopamine by producing less dopamine and/or by reducing the number of dopamine receptors in the reward/pleasure circuit. The result is a lessening of dopamine's effect on the reward/pleasure circuit, which reduces the misuser's ability to enjoy the drugs, as well as the events in life that previously brought pleasure. This decrease compels the addict to keep abusing drugs. Larger amounts of the drug are required to achieve the same dopamine high—an effect known as tolerance.

No single factor determines whether a person will become addicted to drugs. It is estimated that the overall risk for addiction is affected equally by both genetics and environment. Thus, addiction can be influenced by gender, ethnicity, a person's developmental stage, and the surrounding social environment (such as conditions at home, at school, and in the neighborhood).

PREVENTION AND TREATMENT

Many alcohol, tobacco, and illicit drug use prevention programs aimed at teens and pre-teens have been developed over the past several years. One of the most visible programs is D. A. R. E. (Drug Abuse Resistance Education) which had very limited success in its early years. Its curriculum and focus were revamped and introduced in 2009, and the success is now being evaluated. Other newer drug use prevention programs claim that they have been able increase the age of first drug use. Although drug misuse is difficult to treat, many effective treatments available. Severe drug misuse usually requires residential treatment, in which the patient temporarily resides at the treatment center.

Claudia Daileader Ruland, MA;
Updated by Charles L. Vigue, PhD

FOR FURTHER INFORMATION

"10 Facts about Teen Drug Abuse". Newport Academy. August 17, 2017. https://www.newportacademy.com/resources/substance-abuse/10-facts-teen-drug-abuse/. Accessed July 24, 2018.

"Age of Substance Use Initiation among Treatment Admissions Aged 18 to 30". Substance Abuse and Mental Health Services Administration, Center for Behavioral Health Statistics and Quality. (July 17, 2014). *The TEDS Report: Age of Substance Use Initiation among Treatment Admissions Aged 18 to 30.* Rockville, MD.: https://archive.samhsa.gov/data/2k14/TEDS142/sr142-initiation-age-2014.htm. Accessed July 24, 2018.

"Drug Use in High School". The Recovery Village. https://www.therecoveryvillage.com/teen-addiction/high-school-drug-use/#gref. Accessed July 24, 2018.

Graham, A. W. and T. K. Shultz, eds. *Principles of Addiction Medicine.* 3rd ed. Chevy Chase: American Society of Addiction Medicine, 2003. Print.

"Monitoring the Future 2017 Survey Results". National Institute on Drug Abuse, https://www.drugabuse.gov/related-topics/trends-statistics/infographics/monitoring-future-2017-survey-results Accessed July 24, 2018.

National Institute on Drug Abuse. *Drugs, Brains, and Behavior: The Science of Addiction.* Bethesda: NIDA, 2010. Print.

Sherman, Carl. "The defining features of drug intoxication and addiction can be traced to disruptions in neuron-to neuron signaling". National Institute of Drug Abuse (NIDA), *NIDA Notes,* March 9, 2017. https://www.drugabuse.gov/news-events/nida-notes/2017/03/impacts-drugs-neurotransmission. Accessed July 24, 2018.

Tackett, Brittany. "Teen Drug Abuse: The Warning Signs". https://drugabuse.com/teen-drug-abuse-signs/. Accessed July 24, 2018.

"Teen Drug and Alcohol Abuse Facts and Statistics". Teen Rehab. https://www.teendrugrehabs.com/facts-and-stats/. Accessed July 24, 2018.

"Teen Drug and Alcohol Statistics and Information". Project Know. https://www.projectknow.com/research/teen-drug-addiction-statistics-alcoholism-statistics/. Accessed July 24, 2018.

United States. National Institute on Drug Abuse (NIDA). "DrugFacts: High School and Youth Trends." December 2017. https://www.drugabuse.gov/publications/drugfacts/monitoring-future-survey-high-school-youth-trends. Accessed July 24, 2018.

Adolescents, young adults and smoking

CATEGORY: Social issues

DEFINITION: Tobacco smoking typically begins early in the teenage years—usually around age eleven to thirteen years—although many start earlier. Tobacco smoking includes the use of cigarettes (the primary form of smoked tobacco), cigars, pipes, hookahs, and e-cigarettes.

PREVALENCE OF SMOKING

According to the Centers for Disease Control and Prevention (CDC), in 2016, roughly 2 percent of middle school students and 8 percent of high school students reported smoking cigarettes in the past 30 days. Among high school students in 2016, 11.3 percent said that they had smoked an e-cigarette within the last month (CDC, 2018). For e-cigarettes, the number of American middle- and high-school students who regularly used electronic cigarettes tripled between 2013 and 2014. Among adolescents, smoking increased with age; 2.5 percent of middle schoolers who smoke cigarettes and the 3.9 percent who smoke e-cigarettes. Smoking hookah is another popular form of tobacco use for adolescents and young adults. According to the CDC, between 22 and 40 percent of college students smoked a hookah in 2014. According to the American Lung Association, the general perception is that hookah smoking is less harmful than cigarette smoking, however, the amount of nicotine absorbed by smoking a water pipe is comparable to that absorbed from cigarettes making smoking hookah a health risk as well.

INITIATION AND CONTINUATION
Tobacco smoking typically begins around age eleven to thirteen years, although many youths start earlier. An increasing number of young adults are starting to smoke when they enter college. Many factors influence whether a nonsmoking teen will experiment with cigarettes, ranging from genetics, parents' smoking habits beliefs about tobacco use, media/marketing, and individual mental health and coping skills. Research indicates that the strongest predictors of a person's continuing to smoke and eventually becoming addicted are a relaxed, dizzy, or light-headed sensation after the first puff or two on a cigarette; being impulsive and seeking novelty; feeling depressed; smoking being permitted in the home; familiarity with tobacco marketing (for example, having a favorite cigarette advertisement); and believing that smoking helps a person "fit in."

BECOMING ADDICTED
A medical diagnosis of tobacco dependence or addiction can be made when the number of symptoms reaches a threshold specified by either the *Diagnostic and Statistical Manual of Mental Disorders* or the *International Classification of Diseases* (ICD). The earlier a person begins to smoke, the greater the likelihood of that person becoming dependent and the worse the addiction. Most people who smoke more than a few cigarettes in their lifetime go on to develop symptoms of diminished autonomy. They find it difficult to quit or to cut down their smoking because they experience unpleasant symptoms. A sizeable percentage of adolescents experience one or more symptoms of

diminished autonomy after smoking fewer than five cigarettes in their lives, and more than 75 percent of adolescents experienced symptoms while smoking only a cigarette or two each week.

Nicotine (the major ingredient in tobacco smoke), even in low doses, causes the brain to remodel itself. The first few doses of nicotine (the first few cigarettes) sensitize the brain so that it becomes more susceptible to later doses. Thus, the effects of nicotine make it easier for the brain to become accustomed to nicotine, which makes it more difficult for a person to remove nicotine from the body by cutting down or quitting smoking.

RISKS OF SMOKING
Cigarette smoking is considered the primary preventable cause of death. The diseases caused by smoking produce chronic disability in many people and are estimated to cost almost $170 billion per year in health care expenses and lost productivity in the United States alone. For young women, smoking can impact the ability to become pregnant, and place an infant at risk of sudden infant death syndrome (SIDS). Young adults who smoke risk reductions in lung function, and increases asthma-related symptoms. Avoiding smoking is one of the best steps a person can take to remain healthy, and that quitting smoking if one has started is also beneficial.

CESSATION
There are many effective ways to stop smoking. Every US state and every Canadian province has a free telephone "quitline," and many offer help online. Hospitals and other health care facilities offer support groups and one-on-one help, and school and college health services usually provide information and support. For persons who need additional help, various over-the-counter nicotine-replacement products and prescription medications are available.

Robert J. Wellman PhD;
Updated by Michelle L. Holliday-Stocking, PhD.

FOR FURTHER INFORMATION
American Lung Association (2018). "Hookah Smoking." Retrieved 23 June 2018 from http://www.lung.org/assets/documents/tobacco/hookah-policy-brief-updated.pdf
Centers for Disease Control and Prevention. (2016). "Health Effects of Cigarette Smoking." Retrieved

22 July 2016 from https://www.cdc.gov/tobacco/data_statistics/fact_sheets/health_effects/effects_cig_smoking/index.htm

Centers for Disease Control and Prevention. (2018). "Youth and Tobacco Use." Retrieved May 29, 2018 from http://www.cdc.gov/tobacco/data_statistics/fact_sheets/youth_data/tobacco_use/

DiFranza, Joseph R., et al. (2007). "Susceptibility to Nicotine Dependence: The Development and Assessment of Nicotine Dependence in Youth-2 Study." *Pediatrics* 120.4, 974–83

DiFranza, Joseph R. (2007). "Symptoms of Tobacco Dependence after Brief Intermittent Use: The Development and Assessment of Nicotine Dependence in Youth-2 Study." *Archives of Pediatrics and Adolescent Medicine* 161.7, 704–10.

Horton, Allison. (2016). "Think E-Cigs Are Safe for Kids? You'll Think Twice After Reading This." *Miami Herald.* Retrieved 22 July 2016 from https://www.miamiherald.com/living/health-fitness/article91033197.html

U.S. Department of Health and Human Services. (2016). "Adolescents and Tobacco: Trends." Retrieved 20 October 2017 from www.hhs.gov/ash/oah/adolescent-development/substance-use/drugs/tobacco/trends/index.html.

U.S. Department of Health and Human Services. (2014). "The Health Consequences of Smoking—50 Years of Progress." Retrieved 22 July 2016 from, https://www.surgeongeneral.gov/library/reports/50-years-of-progress/index.html

US Dept. of Health and Human Services. (2010). "How Tobacco Smoke Causes Disease: The Biology and Behavioral Basis for Smoking-Attributable Disease—A Report of the Surgeon General." Atlanta: DHHS, 2010.

Adult children of alcoholics

CATEGORY: Psychological issues

DEFINITION: According to estimates by the nonprofit Children of Alcoholics Foundation (CAF), there are more than 26.8 million adult children of alcoholics (ACOA) in the United States in the early twenty-first century. Children brought up in alcoholic or otherwise dysfunctional homes often are exposed to emotional, psychological, or physical abuse, and the scars left by an alcoholic parent can last long into adulthood.

THE EFFECTS OF ALCOHOLISM ON FAMILIES

Adult children of alcoholics (ACOA) suffer from a wide range of negative effects because of their disrupted family backgrounds, including a fourfold increase in the likelihood of suffering from alcohol misuse or alcoholism themselves, higher rates of mental disorders, higher rates of marrying into alcoholic families, and higher rates of becoming separated or divorced from their spouses. Typical ACOA tendencies can affect critical elements of life, including interpersonal relationships, parenting style, career goals, and finances.

Trust and security, two necessities for successful long-term relationships, do not come easily for many ACOAs, who typically grew up in insecure or chaotic homes and may choose to isolate themselves from others. In addition, because many alcoholic parents were often more preoccupied with drinking than with caring for their children, ACOAs may have suffered from neglect during their childhoods and may have a strong need for affection, which can manifest itself as possessiveness, jealousy, and oversensitivity. The strong desire to be loved can lead ACOAs to inspire dependency in their own children. ACOAs' need for approval can also lead them to overspend or pay beyond their means to please others. Also, many ACOAs had to mature early and assume the responsibilities that the alcoholic parent could not fulfill, which can create an overdeveloped sense of responsibility in ACOAs and contribute to feelings of inadequacy and loss of control.

FINDING HELP

The depth to which alcoholism affects ACOAs' daily lives depends on a wide range of variables, from their own personalities and coping skills to the extent to which their parent's alcoholism affected their early developmental years. All ACOAs can benefit from learning strategies that will help them overcome negative behaviors and chart courses for healthy futures, but no single method works best for everyone. Options include:

Reading. Find the latest books and research, both in print and online, about alcohol misuse and the way it can affect family life.

Talking. Confide in a close friend or family member who can understand your feelings and respect your privacy without judgment.

Counseling. Meet with a psychologist or certified social worker who can help you focus on your future, not the pains of the past. Sometimes talking with a stranger can be more therapeutic than talking with a friend.

Joining. Become a part of a free support group that meets in person or in a private online chat forum to find out how other ACOAs have overcome barriers to happiness. Twelve-step programs, such as Al-Anon and Adult Children of Alcoholics (ACA), can be particularly empowering.

Elissa Sonnenberg MSEd

For Further Information

Dayton, Tian. "Adult Children of Alcoholics and Trauma." *The Huffington Post*, 13 Feb. 2015. Web. 27 Oct. 2015.

Ketcham, Katherine, William F. Asbury, Mel Schulstad, and Arthur P. Ciaramicoli. *Beyond the Influence: Understanding and Defeating Alcoholism.* New York: Bantam, 2000. Print.

Ludwig, Arnold. *Understanding the Alcoholic's Mind: The Nature of Craving and How to Control It.* New York: Oxford UP, 1989. Print.

Martin, Scott C. *The SAGE Encyclopedia of Alcohol: Social, Cultural, and Historical Perspectives.* Thousand Oaks: Sage, 2015. Print.

Miller, William R., and Kathleen M. Carroll, eds. *Rethinking Substance Abuse: What the Science Shows, and What We Should Do about It.* New York: Guilford, 2010. Print

Rothenberg, William A., Andrea M. Hussong, and Laurie Chassin. "Modeling Trajectories of Adolescent-Perceived Family Conflict: Effects of Marital Dissatisfaction and Parental Alcoholism." *Journal of Research on Adolescence*, vol. 27, no. 1, 2017, pp. 105–21. *Psychology and Behavioral Sciences Collection*, search.ebscohost.com/login.aspx?direct=true&db=pbh&AN=121443306&site=ehost-live&scope=site. Accessed 17 Oct. 2017.

Taite, Richard. "6 Signs of Addiction in Adult Children of Alcoholics." *Psychology Today*. Sussex, 28 Aug. 2015. Web. 27 Oct. 2015.

See also: Families and substance misuse; Marriage/partnership and alcoholism; Parenting and alcoholism

Advertising for alcohol

Category: Social issues

Definition: Advertising for alcohol involves the use of various media in stores, shops, newspapers, and magazines, and on billboards, television, radio, websites, film, and clothing to entice and persuade persons to buy and consume products containing alcohol. Certain venues, particularly sporting events and concerts, also promote alcohol products because these venues are commonly sponsored by distributors of alcohol. Alcohol advertising especially influences youth.

Alcohol as Image

Since the ancient Greeks celebrated Dionysus, the god of wine, theater, and ecstasy, a connection has endured among alcohol, media, and sensuality. In addition to sharing a profound appeal to the senses, alcohol, theater, and ecstasy offer an escape from the mundane and a sense of liberation. The view of intoxication as a celebration and a rite of passage continues to this day, anchored by the many messages modern society reflects in its depictions of alcohol through advertising.

Echoes of Dionysus reverberate throughout much modern advertising for alcohol, which often touts youth, sexual prowess, beauty, and athleticism. Initiation into manhood, quite often involving male bonding through modern-day sporting events, is rarely viewed as complete without alcohol. Alcohol advertisers carefully create their own myths about alcohol normalcy, portraying a world where the successful people drink and all drinkers are rewarded.

Through advertising, young people in particular learn to associate alcohol with social acceptance. Those who abstain are promptly left behind and dismissed. Young people are especially susceptible to the lure of alcohol advertising. The images depicting alcohol's social benefits are wildly exaggerated and distorted by alcohol advertising, and many young people tend to accept the misconception that drinking will somehow improve their lives.

Instead of finding the advertised camaraderie and companionship, many will find themselves, years later, abusing alcohol alone. Alcohol advertising frequently sells one reality but delivers another.

ALCOHOL ADVERTISING AND YOUTH

The legal age to buy alcohol in all fifty US states is twenty-one years. Many people argue that some alcohol advertising campaigns are designed specifically to appeal to the youth market, despite the legal barriers to consumption. One such compelling argument was frequently made about the advertising mascot Spuds McKenzie, a highly appealing 1980s ad image of a bull terrier dog, the original "party animal."

Wearing sunglasses, a bandana, a Hawaiian shirt, and headphones, and holding a Bud Light beer, Spuds was depicted in tropical locales and surrounded by beautiful, scantily clad young women. First appearing to acclaim in a 1987 Bud Light commercial during the broadcast of the Super Bowl, Spuds, throughout the late 1980s, rode skateboards, raced horses, drove convertibles, maneuvered surfboards, played Frisbee, and combed beaches.

Sales of Bud Light beer soared during the Spuds ad campaign, which not only marketed the alcoholic beverage but also sold millions of dollars of Spuds paraphernalia: everything from T-shirts to caps to plush toys. Antidrinking groups responded by arguing that the campaign targeted children and teenagers. In 1989, Mothers Against Drunk Driving claimed that Anheuser-Busch, the maker of Bud Light, was deceptively marketing alcohol to children and demanded that Spuds ads cease promoting the beer. An investigation of the ad campaign by the Federal Trade Commission (FTC) ensued, and although the FTC found no wrongdoing by Anheuser-Busch, the company nevertheless terminated the campaign in 1989.

Anheuser-Busch again ignited controversy in the 1990s with its Budweiser Frogs ad campaign. First appearing as a Super Bowl television commercial in 1995, the Budweiser Frogs depicted three frogs, Bud, Weis, and Er, who lived on a log in a swamp behind a bar and croaked "Budweiser" rhythmically. In 1996, a study revealed that considerable numbers of nine- to eleven-year-old children could easily identify the Budweiser Frogs and associate them with beer, but were unable to recognize or identify various children's

This advertisement for Jim Beam bourbon uses a smoking Bette Davis as a spokesperson. (Stanford School of Medicine via Wikimedia Commons)

cartoon figures. Antidrinking groups again accused the alcohol industry of targeting children.

Shortly thereafter, another study revealed that when asked to name US presidents, most eight- to twelve-year-old children could name few but had no difficulty naming a variety of brands of beer. In spite of these negative reports, the Budweiser Frogs campaign continued for many years; it is recognized in the adverting industry as one of most successful marketing campaigns in history.

A 2015 study published in *JAMA Pediatrics* found that exposure to alcohol ads predicted onset of underage drinking as well as binge and hazardous drinking in young people between the ages of fifteen and twenty-three. However, the same year, a study from the University of Texas at Austin found that while alcohol advertising increased 400% between 1971 and 2011, overall alcohol sales did not do so significantly, suggesting a weaker link between advertising and alcohol consumption. A 2016 study in the *Journal of Studies on Alcohol and Drugs* set out to find out whether alcohol ads influenced how much alcohol underage drinkers consumed; the study found that underage drinkers who had not been exposed to alcohol ads consumed about fourteen drinks per month, while those who had seen an average amount of alcohol ads consumed thirty-three drinks in the same time period.

ALCOHOL AND SPORTING EVENTS

The alcohol industry is a frequent sponsor and promoter of sporting events, many of which appeal to a large percentage of fans who are minors. From the Super Bowl to the World Series to auto racing to college basketball, the alcohol industry spends billions of sponsorship and advertising dollars each year, specifically targeting an audience of sports fans, many of them younger than twenty-one years.

The alcohol industry provides a lucrative source of funding for collegiate sports, especially the National Collegiate Athletic Association's (NCAA) annual basketball championships (known as March Madness), but some critics argue that the price for this funding is too high, owing to the toll it levies in the form of underage drinking. The NCAA's playoff and championship games, for instance, welcome millions of children and minors as viewers each year, who are subjected to the same degree of intense alcohol advertising as adults. Although the alcohol industry maintains that it is advertising its products so rigorously during such sporting events only to establish brand loyalty among adults who already drink, March Madness nonetheless draws millions of underage viewers.

According to the National Institute on Alcohol Abuse and Alcoholism (NIAAA), studies reveal a greater propensity among young people to initiate drinking at a younger age if they are heavily exposed to alcohol advertising. Moreover, the NIAAA cites evidence demonstrating that the younger a person begins to drink, the greater the likelihood that he or she will become an alcoholic. For example, statistically, the NIAAA reports that a person who begins drinking by age fifteen years is four times as likely to become a heavy drinker and dependent on alcohol than a person who begins drinking at age twenty-one years.

Children, drawn to watch their favorite sports teams and athletes, are ill equipped to decipher the deceptive messages of alcohol advertising. Youths often come away from watching such sporting competitions with a false sense of normalcy, believing that alcohol consumption as portrayed by advertising is ubiquitous, harmless, fun, and inconsequential, regardless of age or circumstance. Fans attending both collegiate and professional sporting events sponsored by alcohol companies have recently become increasingly dismayed and alarmed at the escalation of public drunkenness and violence occurring among fans, an environment that is growing increasingly unsafe for children.

Mary E. Markland MA

FOR FURTHER INFORMATION

Bryant, Jennings, and Mary Beth Oliver. *Media Effects: Advances in Theory and Research.* 3rd ed. New York: Routledge, 2009. Print.

Lankford, Ronnie. *At Issue: Alcohol Abuse.* Farmington Hills: Greenhaven, 2007. Print.

Martin, Scott C. *The SAGE Encyclopedia of Alcohol: Social, Cultural, and Historical Perspectives.* Thousand Oaks: Sage, 2015. Print.

Naimi, Timothy S., et al. "Amount of Televised Alcohol Advertising Exposure and the Quantity of Alcohol Consumed by Youth." *Journal of Studies on Alcohol and Drugs*, vol. 77, no. 5, 2016, pp. 723–29.

Richards, Katie. "Alcohol Ads Increased 400% over 40 Years, but Americans Aren't Drinking More." *Adweek.* Adweek, 25 Mar. 2015. Web. 27 Oct. 2015.

Sheehan, Kim. *Controversies in Contemporary Advertising.* Thousand Oaks: Sage, 2004. Print.

Tanski, Susanne E., et al. "Cued Recall of Alcohol Advertising on Television and Underage Drinking Behavior." *JAMA Pediatrics* 169.3 (2015): 264–71. Print.

Tardiff, Joseph. *Teen Alcoholism.* Farmington Hills: Greenhaven, 2008. Print.

Wechsler, Henry, and Bernice Wuethrich. *Dying to Drink: Confronting Binge Drinking on College Campuses.* Emmaus: Rodale, 2002. Print.

See also: Advertising for tobacco products; Media and substance misuse

Advertising for tobacco products

CATEGORY: Social issues

DEFINITION: Tobacco companies advertise their products, namely cigarettes, cigars, and smokeless tobacco, in newspapers and magazines, on billboards, in retail stores, and at sporting events. Advertising in the United States for tobacco products is banned, however, from television, radio, and the web by the Federal Trade Commission, but motion pictures still promote tobacco products through what is called product placement.

THE "JOE CAMEL" CAMPAIGN

Of all the advertising campaigns launched by the tobacco industry, R. J. Reynolds Tobacco Company's marketing for Camel brand cigarettes was by far the most notorious and controversial. In 1988, in an attempt to create "replacement smokers" for those long-term smokers who were sick and dying, R. J. Reynolds introduced the enormously popular and youth "friendly" animated character Joe Camel. An engaging, wisecracking, and easygoing character, "Old Joe" was an instant success among young people. Few people realize that R. J. Reynolds's Joe Camel was a nod to the Durham bull, a similarly popular anthropomorphic character at the turn of the twentieth century. The Durham bull advertised roll-your-own cigarettes by rebelliously kicking up its heels and making humorous remarks.

Through R. J. Reynolds's marketing campaign, Joe Camel was popularized on billboards and in magazines and newspapers, which became saturated with the Joe Camel image. The character was selling not only Camel cigarettes but also a huge amount of Joe Camel paraphernalia—everything from T-shirts, to baseball caps, to underwear.

In 1991, the American Medical Association sparked debate when it published a study revealing that 90 percent of six-year-old children who were surveyed could recognize and identify Joe Camel, roughly the same percentage who could recognize and identify Mickey Mouse. By contrast, only 67 percent of adults surveyed could identify Joe Camel and directly associate the character with cigarettes.

After filing a lawsuit against R. J. Reynolds for deceptive advertising practices and liability, a San Francisco law firm later revealed an astronomical spike of several hundred percent in revenue from youth market shares between 1988 and 1992 that was specifically attributable to the Joe Camel advertising campaign. In 1997, following public outcry and after the US Congress threatened stricter legislation, R. J. Reynolds settled the lawsuit, agreeing to terminate Joe Camel-related advertisements and agreeing to pay the State of California $10 million to fund antismoking education for youth.

Shortly thereafter, R. J. Reynolds changed its ad campaign by replacing Joe Camel the cartoon character with an image of a true camel, an image that was designed to appeal to adults and an image that still represents Camel cigarettes.

In the end, though, it was the phenomenal success of the Joe Camel advertising campaign that did more than anything else to incense and inflame the public. The ad campaign encouraged public, school, and legislative support for subsequent antismoking campaigns around the United States.

A Marlboro billboard uses cowboys to advertise cigarettes. (via Wikimedia Commons)

LEGISLATING DECEPTIVE TOBACCO ADVERTISING

In 1900, only one in 100 Americans smoked, but that percentage soon rose. During World War I, smoking became immensely popular in both the United States and in Europe, in part because the US military distributed free branded cigarettes to its troops. By the 1930s, the Federal Trade Commission began regulating the false advertising claims made by tobacco companies. Throughout the nineteenth and early twentieth centuries, it had been commonplace for tobacco products to be advertised by doctors and surgeons, who claimed that smoking had all-around health benefits.

Beginning in 1920, tobacco brands, especially Lucky Strike, began advertising campaigns that targeted women, appealing to American women's newfound status as "liberated" voters after the passage of the Nineteenth Amendment to the US Constitution (1920). The ads promised women that smoking would make them more slender, trim, and attractive, a claim repeated fifty years later with the branding of Virginia Slims cigarettes.

The 1930s witnessed en masse the first detrimental fallout of smoking's ever-growing popularity, as doctors began treating huge numbers of patients for lung cancer, a disease otherwise rarely seen. Increasing numbers of medical reports and studies worldwide began to draw direct correlations between the upsurge in smokers and the spike in certain kinds of cancer.

Smoking was further popularized during World War II, when free cigarettes were provided to the troops, as they were during World War I. Also, tobacco companies continued to deny medical reports, and their ads continued to portray smoking as healthy. Hollywood similarly intensified the glamorous appeal of smoking in its films. Consequently, by 1950, approximately 50 percent of American adults smoked cigarettes.

After more than a decade of continued research that further linked smoking and cancer, the US Office of the Surgeon General (in 1964) proclaimed smoking to be hazardous to one's health and to be a direct cause of lung cancer. In 1965, Congress passed the Cigarette Labeling and Advertising Act, which required cigarette manufacturers to place a warning label on each pack of cigarettes. The first label warned consumers that cigarette smoking "might" be hazardous to their health; in 1969, Congress passed additional legislation, the Public Health Cigarette Smoking Act, which required the warning label on cigarettes packs to be more definitive: "Warning: The Surgeon General Has Determined That Cigarette Smoking Is Dangerous to Your Health." The act also banned all advertising for cigarettes on television and radio.

BIG TOBACCO MASTER SETTLEMENT AGREEMENT

Throughout the 1970s and 1980s, scientific studies continued to confirm the harm of tobacco products, yet the tobacco industry continued to deny this fact in its advertising. By the 1990s, with escalating numbers of lawsuits against the tobacco industry for fraudulent misrepresentation, wrongful death, criminal negligence, and criminal liability, an increasing number of cases were decided in favor of injured and, oftentimes, deceased smokers. Moreover, as enormous amounts of taxpayer dollars were being used to treat sick and dying smokers, state attorneys general began to sue tobacco companies to recoup lost revenue from state budgets. As juries awarded plaintiffs ever larger settlements, the tobacco industry began to search for a way to stop the increasing litigation.

Finally, in 1998, R. J. Reynolds, Brown and Williamson, and Philip Morris (three major entities of what came to be called Big Tobacco) were bound to the Master Settlement Agreement (MSA), the largest financial settlement in US history. In addition to severely restricting tobacco advertising, the MSA mandated annual Big Tobacco payments of millions of dollars to state governments for ongoing governmental efforts to control tobacco use, especially among youths. The MSA also led to widespread antismoking advertising campaigns, such as the Truth campaign, which encouraged youth to stop or avoid smoking.

The MSA also made illegal all advertising and selling of tobacco products to any person younger than age eighteen and made it illegal to use any cartoon or animation to advertise tobacco products. This provision would ensure against the recurrence of any marketing campaign reminiscent of the Joe Camel campaign that had targeted children in earlier decades. The MSA additionally placed Big Tobacco advertising under the regulation and control of the US Food and Drug Administration, a provision later reinforced with congressional legislation.

E-cigarettes, which deliver nicotine by vaporizing a liquid solution containing it, are not covered by the laws restricting tobacco advertising, and the age restrictions also do not apply. The debate about advertising nicotine products to young people has therefore continued into the 2010s, with a 2015 study finding that adolescents age thirteen to seventeen were more likely to express an intention to try e-cigarettes after exposure to e-cigarette advertising. Another study, from the University of Pennsylvania, found that e-cigarette advertising was also likely to make smokers and former smokers crave tobacco.

Mary E. Markland MA

FOR FURTHER INFORMATION

Califano, Joseph, Jr. *High Society: How Substance Abuse Ravages America and What to Do About It.* New York: Public Affairs, 2007. Print.

Crawford, Elizabeth Crisp. *Tobacco Goes to College: Cigarette Advertising in Student Media, 1920–1980.* Jefferson: McFarland, 2014. Print.

"E-Cigarette Advertising Makes One Crave... Tobacco? Surprising Findings by Penn Researchers." *Annenberg School for Communication.* U of Pennsylvania. Web. 27 Oct. 2015.

Farrelly, Matthew C., et al. "A Randomized Trial of the Effect of E-cigarette TV Advertisements on Intentions to Use E-cigarettes." *American Journal of Preventive Medicine* 49.5 (2015): 686–93. Print.

Hudson, David, Jr. *Smoking Bans.* Philadelphia: Chelsea House, 2004. Print.

Hyde, Margaret. *Know About Smoking.* New York: Walker, 1995. Print.

White, Larry. *Merchants of Death: The American Tobacco Industry.* New York: Random House, 1991. Print.

Williams, Rodger. *At Issue: Teen Smoking.* Farmington Hills: Greenhaven, 2009. Print.

See also: Advertising for alcohol; Media and smoking

Aerosols addiction

CATEGORY: Substance misuse

ALSO KNOWN AS: Dusters; whippets

DEFINITION: Aerosols are inhalants that use propellants to release a substance from a pressurized container into the air. Examples of aerosols include computer and electronic duster sprays, air fresheners, spray paint, whipped-cream dispensers, whipped-cream dispenser chargers (whippets), and cooking, hair, and deodorant sprays. The propellants and solvents in these devices can be misused like other volatile substances, such as nitrites, and solvents, such as paint thinners and correction fluid.

STATUS: Legal in the United States and worldwide

CLASSIFICATION: Noncontrolled substance

SOURCE: Aerosols are sold in cans that contain propellants such as nitrous oxide or solvents such as toluene.

TRANSMISSION ROUTE: Inhalation

HISTORY OF USE

Aerosols make up a unique category of misused substances, as they are not drugs and were not formulated to produce intoxicating effects. Aerosols are, however, easily obtained and, as such, are more commonly misused by children and adolescents. Most users are adolescents (ages twelve to seventeen years), and in the United States, users are more likely to be poor and to live in impoverished communities, where aerosols are inexpensive and easy to obtain.

Aerosol misuse remains a significant problem, a fact contradicting the results of three surveys in the United States that tracked aerosol and inhalant misuse. The surveys had reported a declining trend in aerosol misuse since the late 1990s, but they also had relied on self-reporting and focused on specific age ranges, so they may provide an incomplete picture of abuse trends.

Reported misuse rates are higher among Hispanics, Native Americans, and Caucasians in the United States, and while national survey data does not show significant gender differences in overall use of inhalants, males are more likely to misuse inhalants over a sustained period of time. Information from the National Poison Data System indicates that nearly 75 percent of cases reported to poison control centers involve boys. Whereas boys and girls report use equally, boys are more likely to have severe incidents requiring immediate medical intervention. Other studies have shown an association between eating disorders and inhalant misuse, and have shown an increased likelihood of misuse among persons living in rural areas or small towns.

Historically, inhalant misuse became a widespread problem in the United States during Prohibition, when ether was inhaled as a substitute for drinking alcohol. misuse shifted mainly to the inhalation of glue, gasoline, and paint fumes during the 1950s. Aerosol spray misuse did not become common until the 1980s, as propellants in products produced before the 1980s generally contained chlorinated fluorocarbons (CFCs), which, based on their properties as refrigerator coolants, froze the lungs of a person who inhaled the fumes. Manufacturers' replacement of CFCs with more environmentally friendly propane and butane led to an increase in the number of people abusing the products. Later data indicated that computer dusters and spray paint are two aerosol products with the highest misuse rates.

EFFECTS AND POTENTIAL RISKS

Inhalation of aerosol propellants leads to effects similar to those of alcohol intoxication. Symptoms include loss of coordination, slurred speech, euphoria, dizziness, and lightheadedness. Some people also experience hallucinations or delusions. The effects do not last as long as alcohol intoxication, however, and they generally subside after a few minutes. This leads users to repeatedly inhale the substance to attempt to extend the effects. Repeated inhalation can lead to headaches, nausea and vomiting, and loss of inhibitions. Addiction can occur, but is not common.

One study found that toluene, a solvent contained in spray paint, can activate the dopamine system in the brain, however. As this system plays a role in the rewarding effects of most drugs of misuse, this particular type of aerosol misuse may be more likely to lead to addiction.

A major concern with aerosol misuse is that the products displace air in the lungs and can lead to oxygen deprivation or hypoxia. Brain cells are particularly sensitive to hypoxia, and repeated misuse of such substances can lead to memory loss, learning difficulties, and conversational problems. Long-term

misuse can destroy myelin, the protective fatty tissue surrounding nerve fibers. Myelin destruction eventually leads to muscle spasms, tremors, and difficulty with walking and other motor activities.

In addition, inhaling highly concentrated amounts of solvent or propellant from aerosol sprays can lead to heart failure and to a condition referred to as sudden sniffing death, which can occur within minutes of inhalation. Death also can occur from severe hypoxia, which leads to suffocation; the chances of this occurring are increased when the substance is inhaled in a closed area or from a paper or plastic bag.

Certain substances also can lead to unique irreversible effects. Hearing loss, central nervous system damage, and brain damage can result from sniffing the toluene component of spray paint. Peripheral neuropathies and limb spasms can result from sniffing the nitrous oxide contained in whipped-cream dispensers. Toluene also can lead to kidney and liver damage.

Although aerosol and other inhalant misuse remains a problem, no clear treatment guidelines exist. This may due to the fact that aerosol dependence and misuse are not generally recognized by clinicians and because treatment is focused on other substances of abuse. Also, most misusers are adolescents who may not wish to seek treatment; also, age limits keep adolescents from enrolling in clinical trials, which could lead to intervention.

Karen Nagel Edwards PhD

FOR FURTHER INFORMATION

Konghom, Suwapat, et al. "Treatment for Inhalant Dependence and Abuse." *Cochrane Database of Systemic Reviews* 12 (2010). Web. 30 Jan. 2012. A review of the treatment methods available for inhalant dependence and abuse. No studies met the authors' inclusion criteria; this was believed to be because inhalant abusers do not wish to seek treatment and tend to abuse many substances. Any substance abuse treatment they receive tends to focus on other substances of abuse.

Marsolek, Melinda R., Nicole C. White, and Toby L. Litovitz. "Inhalant Abuse: Monitoring Trends by Using Poison Control Data, 1993–2008." *Pediatrics* 125 (2010): 906–13. Print. A comprehensive overview of poison control data as it relates to inhalant abuse; focuses on demographic and geographic trends, particularly among teenagers.

Perron, Brian E., and Matthew O. Howard. "Adolescent Inhalant Use, Abuse, and Dependence." *Addiction* 104 (2009): 1185–92. Print. A research report comparing adolescents with documented psychiatric inhalant-use disorders to inhalant users without a diagnosis and to nonusers.

See also: Gateway drugs; Inhalants misuse

Age and addiction

CATEGORY: Social issues

DEFINITION: There is no age limit for addictions. Babies are born addicted to the illicit drugs and prescription medicines that their mothers abused while pregnant, and addiction to a wide range of substances and behaviors is endemic among teenagers and young adults. Although not as widely recognized, older adults also suffer addictions.

A HIDDEN PROBLEM

A nationwide survey in the United States revealed that between 2000 and 2008, admissions for addiction treatments for people age fifty years and older increased by 70 percent, while overall this age group grew by only 21 percent. About 60 percent of these addiction-treatment admissions included persons seeking treatment for alcohol abuse, about 16 percent were for heroin addiction, and about 11 percent were for cocaine addiction.

A study released by the Substance Abuse and Mental Health Services Administration (US Department of Health and Human Services) in 2010 showed that the aging of the baby-boom generation (made up of persons born from 1946 through 1964) has led to a sharp increase in the abuse of illicit drugs by adults older than age fifty years. Researchers concluded that the need for addiction-treatment services for Americans age fifty years and older would double by 2020.

The scope of the problem of addiction among older adults is unknown, largely because many cases go unreported. In addition, the elderly and their families often deny the problem. For example, family members might excuse an older relative's gambling addiction as a harmless hobby, or they might argue that heavy alcohol use is an entitlement for a relative

after a long, hard life. Also, many older people rarely admit they have a problem. They rationalize that they are experienced and wise and able to handle any situation. This way of rationalizing is especially true for people addicted to prescription medications. The symptoms of addiction are often less evident in older people than they are in younger people. For example, many older adults addicted to alcohol or drugs indulge at home, so they are less likely to drive a vehicle and to risk arrest while intoxicated. Also, many elderly persons live alone, making it difficult for others to notice problems with drinking or with drug misuse. Furthermore, many elderly persons are retired, so common determiners of addiction, such as work absenteeism or poor job performance, are poor determiners of addiction in the elderly.

Addiction in older adults often goes unrecognized, even by health professionals. Symptoms of addictions are mistaken for diseases common to old age, such as high blood pressure, dementia, stroke, Parkinson's disease, and sleep disorders. Moreover, most of the medical and psychological screening tests for addiction are designed for younger people, making the tests inadequate for older adults.

SUBSTANCES AND BEHAVIORS

Using a working definition of *addiction* as "a physiological or psychological dependence on a substance or behavior to the extent that its withdrawal causes extreme distress to the user," addictions in older adults are the same as those in younger people. However, two substances, alcohol and prescription medications, and two behaviors, gambling and watching television, appear to be particularly troublesome for older adults.

Alcohol is the drug most often misused by older adults. In a survey of adults between ages sixty years and ninety-four years, some 62 percent reported drinking alcohol regularly and 13 percent admitted to heavy use of alcohol. In many cases, alcohol addiction leads to other problems for the elderly. Older adults addicted to alcohol are three times more likely to already have or to develop another mental disorder.

Prescription medications rank as the second most commonly misused substance among older adults and include sedatives, antidepressants, sleeping pills, and pain relievers, especially the narcotic analgesics. The National Institute on Drug Abuse (NIDA) reported that people age sixty-five years and older received about 33 percent of all medications prescribed by doctors in the United States, yet this group makes up only 13 percent of the US population. According to NIDA, some 18 percent of adults age sixty years and older misuse prescription drugs. Older adults take prescription medications three times more frequently than the general population and are more likely to disregard dosing directions, often choosing to self-medicate instead. To compound the problem, NIDA reported that, in general (for some drugs), older adults receive prescriptions with higher doses and with longer dosage times than younger adults receive.

Gambling has become a popular pastime of older adults. In one survey, 73 percent of study participants said they had engaged in some form of gambling in the previous year. Studies have revealed that throughout North America, about 4 percent of all adult gamblers are addicted to gambling, about the same percentage as older gamblers. However, considering that the older adult segment is the fastest growing segment of gamblers, the actual number of addicted gamblers (known as pathological gamblers) is greater than ever. Researchers in New Jersey found that 4 percent of gamblers age fifty-five years and older are problem gamblers and that 2 percent are pathological gamblers. Nearly 11 percent of persons age sixty-five and older in primary care facilities in Pennsylvania are at-risk gamblers. In Missouri, 4 percent of participants in that state's compulsive gamblers program are older than age sixty-five years.

Television watching, too, can become an addiction, according to many mental health professionals. About 97 percent of older adults watch television regularly, more so than any other age group. For many older adults, especially those living alone or with limited mobility, television is a companion and watching television is an activity that helps them cope with their problems. Watching television is considered an addiction when a viewer cannot stop watching at a chosen time, when he or she wants to but cannot watch less, when he or she complains that watching replaces other activities and takes up too much time, and when he or she is uneasy and experiences withdrawal symptoms when not watching for a time.

AGE-RELATED FACTORS

Some adults carry an addiction into their later years. Most baby boomers with an addiction to illicit drugs,

for example, continue a pattern of misuse that began for them in the 1960s and 1970s. However, not many drug addicts, or alcoholics, live to old age because of the devastating physical effects of lifelong addiction.

Other adults switch addictions when they get older. Studies of the chemistry of addiction are helping to explain why some people and not others become addicted. A seminal study prepared for the National Academy of Sciences in 1983 identified certain personality traits that can contribute to the onset of addiction. A person with an addictive personality, for example, might have been addicted to heroin when young but may have switched to prescription drugs later in life.

Other adults become addicted only in their later years. Many elderly persons turn to substances and behaviors that become addictions as a way to cope with growing older. The factors that contribute to addiction, at any age, are complex, but certain circumstances and elements are unique to older people.

In general, as people reach their sixties they are more vulnerable to compulsive behaviors such as gambling. Older people experience many more types of loss than do younger people—loss of physical and mental capabilities; loss of older family members, of spouses, and of friends in the same age group; loss of earning power; and loss of status in society, especially following retirement and particularity in a society that reveres youth. Older adults deal with more serious medical conditions, such as heart disease, Parkinson's disease, hearing loss, and dementia. Following retirement, many people are unsure how to spend their time and are unaware of social opportunities and community resources. Boredom and loneliness plague many older people.

The consequences of addiction are, in many cases, more serious for older people than for younger people. The aging body processes substances differently than the young body. The level of alcohol or drug use, for example, considered light or moderate in the younger body, is often dangerous to the organs and systems of the older body. Recovery from substance misuse takes longer in the older body. Older people, on average, are more likely to be taking more medications than younger people and, thus, risk serious problems when combining medications with alcohol or illicit drugs. Finally, financial losses are more difficult to recoup for persons, such as the elderly, who often live on fixed incomes.

Addiction affects a person's self-esteem, coping skills, and relationships, which, when combined with the other losses common in later life, can lead to other serious mental illnesses. Clinical depression, although not specifically a disease of age, afflicts many older people. The link between clinical depression and addiction is well established.

Treatment for addictions in older people is similar to treatment for younger people, with the exception that most older addicts receive treatment for co-occurring disorders (two or more diseases present at the same time). On the positive side, health professionals report that once older adults enter treatment, they achieve greater success than any other age group.

Wendell Anderson BA

FOR FURTHER INFORMATION

Bamberger, Peter A., and Samuel B. Bacharach. *Retirement and the Hidden Epidemic: The Complex Link between Aging, Work Disengagement, and Substance Misuse and What to Do About It.* New York: Oxford UP, 2014. Print.

Colleran, Carol, and Debra Jay. *Aging and Addiction: Helping Older Adults Overcome Alcohol or Medication Dependence.* Center City: Hazelden, 2002. Print.

Elinson, Zusha. "Aging Baby Boomers Bring Drug Habits into Middle Age." *Wall Street Journal.* Dow Jones, 16 Mar. 2015. Web. 27 Oct. 2015.

Gurnack, Anne, Roland Atkinson, and Nancy Osgood. *Treating Alcohol and Drug Abuse in the Elderly.* New York: Springer, 2002. Print

Nakken, Craig. *The Addictive Personality: Understanding the Addictive Process and Compulsive Behavior.* Center City: Hazelden, 1996. Print.

Ruiz, Pedro, and Eric C. Strain. *The Substance Abuse Handbook.* 2nd ed. Philadelphia: Wolters, 2014. Print.

See also: Addiction; Substance misuse and addiction in the elderly; Gender and addiction; Risk factors for addiction; Socioeconomic status and addiction

Alcohol misuse

CATEGORY: Substance misuse

DEFINITION: Alcohol misuse is a disorder characterized by a desire for alcohol and the continuation of drinking despite alcohol-related occupational, legal, health, and family problems. Alcohol misuse can progress to alcohol dependence or alcoholism. Alcoholism is a condition in which a person becomes physically dependent on alcohol and drinks to avoid withdrawal symptoms.

CAUSES

According to a 2017 epidemiological study published in the journal *JAMA Psychiatry*, one in eight American adults, or 12.7 percent of the U.S. population (approximately 32 million people over the age of eighteen) qualify for a diagnosis of alcohol use disorder (AUD). This disorder is classified by the National Institute on Alcohol Abuse and Alcoholism (NIAAA) as problem drinking that becomes severe. AUD includes alcohol misuse, alcohol dependence, or hazardous drinking. Alcohol problems are highest among young adults, age eighteen to twenty-nine, and lowest among adults age sixty-five and older. According to the NIAAA, an estimated 623,000 Americans aged twelve to seventeen (2.5 percent of this age group) also qualified for a diagnosis of AUD in 2015. Several factors contribute to alcohol misuse and alcoholism, including genetics, brain chemistry, social pressure, emotional stress, chronic pain, depression or other mental health problems, and problem drinking behaviors learned from family and friends.

RISK FACTORS

A risk factor is anything that increases one's likelihood of contracting or developing a disease or condition. It is possible to develop alcoholism without any of the risk factors listed below. However, the more risk factors an individual has, the greater the likelihood of developing AUD. The following factors can increase the risk of alcoholism:

Gender. Alcohol misuse is five times more likely in men than in women. Men are more likely to binge drink and misuse alcohol than women. The NIAAA defines "binge drinking" as a pattern of drinking, usually within about 2 hours, that brings the blood alcohol concentration (BAC) levels to 0.08 g/dL (typically occurs after 4 drinks for women and 5 drinks for men). However, the incidence of AUD in women has been on the rise in the past thirty years. Women tend to develop an AUD later in life than men, but the condition has a faster progression in women.

Family history. Alcohol misuse tends to run in families. The rate of AUD in men with no alcoholic parents is approximately 11 percent. For men with one alcoholic parent, the rate of alcoholism is approximately 30 percent. A family history of AUD is also seen in women, although the link is somewhat weaker. Adult children of alcoholics may have learned problematic drinking habits from observing their parents' behavior or they may inherit a genetic vulnerability to developing an AUD.

Genetic factors. Studies suggest that genetic factors affect the way a person's body processes and responds to alcohol. This may also influence an individual's risk of developing an AUD. AUD is thought to have a substantial heritable basis, however, the patterns of AUD inheritance are not simple. Although children of parents with alcohol use disorder are at a two-to-four higher risk for AUD, less than half of the children of alcoholics eventually develop AUD.

Cultural and social factors. Alcohol misuse is more of a problem in some cultures than in others. For example, rates of alcohol misuse are high in Europe and the United States where alcohol consumption is common and socially acceptable. In American culture, alcohol is often used as a social lubricant and a means of reducing tension. Among religious groups that abstain from drinking alcohol, such as Mormons or Muslims, the incidence of alcohol misuse is minimal. Higher rates of alcohol misuse are also related to peer pressure and easy access to alcohol. Individuals who work long hours also have elevated incidence rates of alcohol misuse.

Psychological vulnerability. Researchers have found that certain psychological factors increase an individual's risk for alcohol use disorder. These factors include having high self-expectations, having a low frustration tolerance, feeling inadequate and unsure of one's roles, needing an inordinate amount of praise and reassurance, and tending to be impulsive and aggressive. Military personnel with combat exposure are also at a greater risk of developing an AUD compared to non-deployed personnel, likely due to the trauma experienced during combat.

Alcohol

Alcohol is a colorless liquid made up of a hydroxyl derivative of hydrocarbons. Common alcohols include ethanol (used in alcoholic beverages), methanol, and propanol (used as a solvent and an antiseptic). Consumption of ethanol can lead to behavioral changes and addiction. Alcohol, particularly ethanol, is produced by microorganisms, predominantly yeast that ferments sugar-containing plant matter. To make alcoholic beverages that contain higher alcoholic contents, these fermented materials are subjected to distillation.

The euphoric effects of ethanol are triggered by the inhibition of glutamate and GABA receptors and by the concomitant activation of the dopamine- and serotonin-based reward systems in the brain. Alcohol has both short- and long-term effects. Short-term effects include dehydration and intoxication. Consumption of large amounts of alcohol in a short time usually leads to coma, life-threatening respiratory depression, or death. Intake of ethanol by pregnant women can harm the fetus. Long-term heavy drinking can cause liver cirrhosis, neuropathology, immune system problems, and increased susceptibility to cancer. Alcohol addiction is also a leading cause of homicide and suicide.

There exist some benefits from low to moderate consumption of alcohol over longer periods of time. These benefits include lower risk of heart attack and ischemic strokes, and increased levels of HDL (good) cholesterol.

Debra Wood, RN;
Updated by Michael A. Buratovich, PhD

Psychiatric disorders. Researchers have found high rates of AUDs among people with anxiety disorders, post-traumatic stress disorder, depression, antisocial and other personality disorders, schizophrenia, and other substance use disorders, such as smoking and illicit drug use. People with attention deficit hyperactivity disorder (ADHD) also have a higher rate of AUDs (and other substance use disorders); adults with AUD suffer from ADHD five to ten times more frequently than the general population. People suffering from psychological disorders may begin using alcohol to manage their symptoms; repeated use can then develop into dependence.

A "Standard" Drink	
Alcoholic beverage	**Quantity consumed**
Beer (about 5 percent alcohol)	12-fluid ounce glass
Malt liquor (about 7 percent alcohol)	7-9-fluid ounce glass
Table wine (about 12 percent alcohol)	5-fluid ounce glass
80-proof distilled spirits (approximately 40 percent alcohol)	1.5-fluid ounce shot

SYMPTOMS

In the United States, a "drink" of alcohol contains 0.6 fluid ounces or 14 g of 100 percent ethanol. The table below shows the quantities of each type of alcoholic beverage that constitutes a drink.

A nationwide study conducted by the National Institutes of Health that surveyed 43,000 U.S. adults showed that 2 of 100 U.S. adults engaged in "low-risk" drinking patterns. For men, low-risk drinking patterns consist of drinking no more than four drinks on any day and no more than 14 drinks per week, and for women, no more than three drinks on any day, and no more than seven drinks per week. It must be emphasized that low-risk drinking patterns are not risk-free, since people may drink too quickly, have additional health problems, or may be older; men and women over the age of 65 are advised to have no more than three drinks a day and no more than seven drinks per week. For men, "heavy" or "at-risk" drinking consists of drinking more than four drinks on any day or 14 drinks per week, and for women, more than three drinks per day or seven drinks per week. Women will begin to have alcohol-related problems at lower drinking levels than men, since women weigh less than men and, pound for pound, have less water in their bodies than do men. Since alcohol disperses in body water, a woman's blood alcohol concentration will be higher than a man's after drinking the same amount of alcohol. Roughly seventy percent of U.S. adults either abstain from alcohol or always drink within low-risk limits. Approximately nineteen percent of U.S. adults drink more than either the single-day or the weekly limit, and nine percent of U.S.

adults drink more than both the single-day and weekly limits.

According to the fifth edition of the American Psychiatric Association's *Diagnostic and Statistical Manual of Mental Disorders* (DSM-5), published in 2013, an individual who meets two of eleven criteria over the last twelve-month period qualify for AUD. The severity of a person's AUD, whether mild, moderate, or severe, depends on the number of criteria he or she meets. Diagnostic criteria for AUD include drinking more or for longer than intended; wanting or trying to cut down or stop drinking but not being able to; spending a lot of time drinking or recovering from the effects of drinking; experiencing cravings for alcohol; drinking or being sick from drinking that interferes with taking care of home or family or that causes problems at work or school; continuing to drink even though it has caused problems with family or friends; giving up or cutting back on activities that were once important, interesting, or pleasurable in order to drink; getting into situations while or after drinking that increase the chances of getting hurt, such as drunk driving or engaging in unsafe sex; continuing to drink even though it causes feelings of depression or anxiety or exacerbates other health problems; needing to drink much more than once was needed in order to feel the same effects (tolerance); and experiencing withdrawal symptoms such as sleep disturbances, irritability, anxiety, depression, or restlessness when cutting back or stopping drinking. Denial that an alcohol problem exists is common.

Alcohol misuse can progress to alcohol dependence. AUD involves a craving, or a powerful, uncontrollable desire for alcohol. This craving overrides the desire to stop drinking. Symptoms of alcohol dependence include craving a drink of alcohol, the inability to stop or limit drinking of alcohol, and the need for greater amounts of alcohol to feel the same effect. Withdrawal symptoms if alcohol consumption is stopped include nausea, sweating, shaking, anxiety, and increased blood pressure. Seizures are an extreme symptom of withdrawal.

AUD may also lead to physical symptoms caused by the destructive effects of alcohol on the body. Once absorbed into the bloodstream, ethanol is oxidized by liver-specific enzymatic systems into acetaldehyde.

These enzyme systems include cytochrome p450 2E1 (CYP2E1), alcohol dehydrogenase (ADH), and a peroxisomal enzyme called catalase. Ethanol oxidation converts the co-factor nicotinamide adenosine dinucleotide (NAD) into its reduced form (NADH). High NADH:NAD ratios increase endogenous fat production and decrease fat oxidation. Fat accumulation in the liver turns the liver yellow and enlarges it, causing "fatty liver," also known as steatosis of the liver. Acetaldehyde production generates reactive oxygen species (H_2O_2, •OH, O_2^-) that damage cell proteins and nucleic acids. Acetaldehyde itself is also very reactive, and derivatizes intracellular molecules to form "acetaldehyde adducts." The immune system recognizes acetaldehyde adducts as foreign, and white blood cells called neutrophils invade the liver to dispose of acetaldehyde adducts, causing alcoholic hepatitis. The death of hepatocytes (liver cells) causes the leakage of liver enzymes into the bloodstream, and scarring in the liver. Symptoms include enlargement of the liver (hepatomegaly), liver tenderness and pain, high blood pressure, yellowing of the whites of the eyes and/or skin (jaundice), flushed face, spidery veins showing through the skin around the umbilicus and on the face, dyspepsia and ulcers, low numbers of platelets in the blood (thrombocytopenia), and easy bruising or bleeding. Other physical symptoms that may result include general shakiness, weakness of the wrists and ankles, numbness and tingling, impaired memory, fast heart rate, shrunken testicles and erectile dysfunction, and increased susceptibility to infections and cancer.

There is a myriad of other risks associated with AUD. Alcohol misuse can increase the risk of accidents and injury, and is a significant factor in approximately 60 percent of fatal burn injuries, drownings, and homicides, about 50 percent of severe trauma injuries and sexual assaults, and approximately 40 percent of fatal automotive accidents, falls, and suicides. Alcohol misuse also compromises relationships with family and friends, and significantly contributes to domestic violence, family dysfunction and failed relationships, job and income loss, legal problems, and depression. In addition to alcoholic liver disease, heavy alcohol consumption also increases the risk of heart disease, stroke, sleep disorders, stomach bleeding, sexually transmitted infections from unsafe sex, and several types of cancer, including cancer of the head and neck, esophagus, liver, breast, and gastrointestinal tract. Women who drink during pregnancy can subject their babies to irreversible brain damage leading to a condition called fetal alcohol syndrome.

Drug interactions are also of concern when dealing with alcohol, since multiple classes of prescription medications can interact with alcohol, including many different types of antibiotics, antidepressants, antihistamines, barbiturates, benzodiazepines, histamine H2 receptor antagonists, muscle relaxants, nonnarcotic pain medications and anti-inflammatory agents, opioids, and the anticoagulant warfarin.

The excessive use of alcohol also increases the risk of nerve damage; sexual disorders, including impotence and reproductive problems; postoperative complications (infections, bleeding, and delayed healing); neurological problems and brain damage (in long-term use); liver damage, including heart and circulatory problems; pneumonia and acute respiratory distress syndrome; osteoporosis; peripheral neuropathy; hormonal problems in both sexes; malnutrition; disorders of the immune system; and infections.

SCREENING AND DIAGNOSIS

It is often difficult for an individual to accept the fact that he or she needs help for an alcohol problem. Nevertheless, the sooner help is provided, the better the chances for a successful recovery. Some people may perceive alcohol problems as a sign of moral weakness. As a result, one may feel that to seek help is to admit some type of shameful defect in oneself. However, taking steps to identify a possible drinking problem has an enormous payoff: a chance for a healthier, more rewarding life.

The purpose of screening is early diagnosis and treatment of AUD. Screening tests are usually administered to people without current symptoms but who may be at high risk for certain diseases or conditions. Screening tests for alcohol misuse usually involve simple questionnaires, either verbally administered by a doctor or given in written form. Several of the most commonly used tests include the CAGE questionnaire, the Michigan Alcoholism Screening Test (MAST), Self-Administered Alcoholism Screening Test (SAAST), the Alcohol Dependence Scale (ADS), the AUDs Identification Test (AUDIT), and the T-ACE Test.

Some healthcare providers use a single question for screening: "When was the last time you had more than five drinks (for men) or four drinks (for women) in one day?" About 50 percent of all individuals who have a problem with drinking alcohol will answer "within three months" to this question.

A diagnosis of alcohol use disorder is often based on an initial assessment, physical examination, and psychological evaluation. Typically, a doctor will ask several questions about alcohol use to determine whether the patient is experiencing problems related to drinking. A physical examination may include blood tests to determine the size of red blood cells; to check for a substance called carbohydrate-deficient transferrin (CDT), a measure of alcohol consumption; and to check for alcohol-related liver disease and other health problems by measuring blood levels of liver-specific enzymes, such as alanine transaminase (ALT), aspartate transaminase (AST), gamma-glutamyltransferase (GGT).

A patient may also be evaluated for psychiatric disorders that often co-occur with AUD, such as anxiety disorders and depression. He or she may be evaluated by their primary care physician; an attending physician, physician's assistant, or nurse practitioner; or referred to a mental health professional.

TREATMENT AND THERAPY

The type of treatment one receives depends on the severity of the AUD and the resources that are available in the community. Treatment may be on an inpatient or outpatient basis and may include detoxification (the process of safely getting alcohol out of one's system), medications to help prevent a relapse once drinking has stopped, individual or group counseling, and referral to community resources, including support groups.

To manage the disease, a patient will have to make some permanent lifestyle changes. The following strategies can help an individual stay away from alcohol and reduce the risk of relapse: socializing without alcohol, including avoidance of bars; refraining from keeping alcohol in the home; avoiding situations and people that encourage drinking; befriending nondrinking individuals and engaging in activities that do not involve alcohol consumption; attending support groups such as Alcoholics Anonymous; identifying potential relapse triggers; and developing coping strategies for difficult situations. Eating a healthful diet and

Mixing Different Types of Alcohol

Is there any truth to the saying, "beer before liquor, never been sicker; liquor before beer, you're in the clear?" Beliefs about the sequence of drinking may stem from the rate at which the body processes alcohol. The liver can efficiently process one standard-sized alcoholic drink per hour only, although men can process more alcohol per hour than can women. What constitutes one drink? Twelve ounces of beer, five ounces of wine, and one shot (1.5 ounces) of hard liquor are generally equivalent in their alcohol content.

The amount of alcohol in the blood rises more quickly after drinking liquor than after drinking beer. If a person drinks liquor before beer, he or she is likely to feel the effects of the alcohol sooner. This may encourage one not to consume as much, decreasing the chances of getting sick from overdoing it. Drinking beer before liquor, on the other hand, may make one feel ill because, having had little or no immediate effect from the beer, a person may be motivated to consume higher concentrations of alcohol by drinking shots or stronger mixed drinks.

A potential scientific explanation for this common belief is that different types of alcohol contain different amounts of compounds called congeners. Congeners consist of the side products produced during the fermentation process that contribute to the taste and aroma (bouquet) of some distilled alcoholic beverages. Congeners consist of phenolic compounds (tannins), esters, acetone, acetaldehyde, fusel alcohols (mixed alcohols), and sundry aldehydes. Drinks that contain high quantities of congeners seem to increase hangover symptoms. Clear beverages like vodka, gin, and white wine contain fewer congeners than darker drinks like brandy, whisky, rum, and red wine. Mixing congeners can increase stomach irritation.

Nevertheless, the quantity that you drink remains the most important factor, regardless of the order in which you drink various alcoholic beverages or how you mix them. Additionally, the rate at which you consume such drinks also matters. Pacing yourself is of pivotal importance, since drinking too much too quickly can make you sick, regardless of what types of alcohol you drink, or the order in which you drink them.

Robin L. Wulffson MD;
Updated by Michael A. Buratovich, PhD

learning stress reduction techniques, such as deep breathing, meditation, and yoga, are also helpful, along with basic rest and relaxation.

Ethanol causes addiction by affecting regulation of a brain network called the mesolimbic, or reward, pathway. The reward pathway connects the ventral tegmental area (in the midbrain) to the nucleus accumbens and olfactory tubercle (in the ventral striatum). Dopamine release from the mesolimbic pathway into the nucleus accumbens regulates motivation and desire and reinforces reward-based behavior. It also plays a role in the subjective perception of pleasure. Mesolimbic pathway dysregulation in the nucleus accumbens plays a significant role in the development and maintenance of addiction. Ethanol activates the mesolimbic dopaminergic pathway by releasing dopamine-producing neurons in the ventral tegmental area from inhibition by the neurotransmitter gamma-aminobutyric acid (GABA).

Certain FDA-approved medications can help alleviate symptoms of alcohol withdrawal and help to prevent relapse by restoring proper regulation in the reward pathway. Medications are usually prescribed alongside counseling or other psychosocial treatment. Also, alcohol use disorder is usually treated with a combination of medications, rather than just one medication. Treatment varies on a case-by-case basis.

Naltrexone antagonizes opioid receptors in the brain and prevents endogenous opioids from activating dopamine release in the nucleus accumbens. Naltrexone can reduce the cravings for alcohol and help individuals stay away from alcohol, but is not a cure for addiction. Naltrexone is available as a pill (*ReVia*) and an injectable form (*Vivitrol*).

Acamprosate (*Campral*) enhances the effects of the inhibitory neurotransmitter GABA on GABA receptors. Because chronic alcohol consumption desensitizes GABA receptors, it takes higher than normal levels of GABA to reduce dopamine release in the ventral tegmental area. Acamprosate potentiates the effects of GABA so that normal levels of GABA inhibit dopamine release. Thus, acamprosate reduces alcohol craving and decreases the relapse rate of AUD patients and the number of drinking days in patients who do relapse. Possible side effects include diarrhea and headache, and acamprosate cannot be used in patients with compromised kidney function.

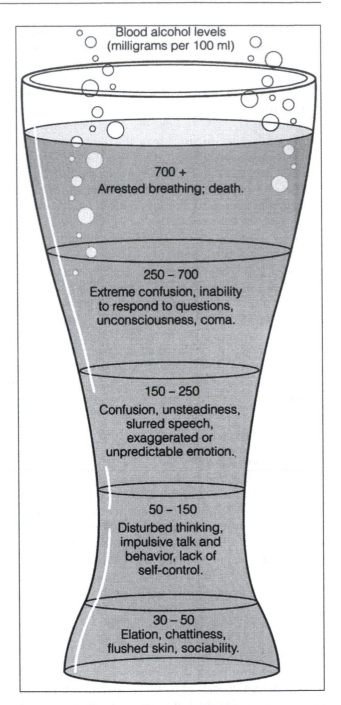

Blood alcohol levels (milligrams per 100 ml)

700 +
Arrested breathing; death.

250 – 700
Extreme confusion, inability to respond to questions, unconsciousness, coma.

150 – 250
Confusion, unsteadiness, slurred speech, exaggerated or unpredictable emotion.

50 – 150
Disturbed thinking, impulsive talk and behavior, lack of self-control.

30 – 50
Elation, chattiness, flushed skin, sociability.

The presence of 30-50 milligrams of alcohol per every 100 milliliters of blood represents one average drink (a glass of beer or wine or an ounce of hard liquor). People who misuse alcohol may not stop drinking until much higher levels result in confusion, unconsciousness, coma, or even death. (Hans & Cassidy, Inc.)

Disulfiram (*Antabuse*) helps overcome a drinking problem by making the individual very sick if they drink alcohol. Like other medications, it is not a cure for AUD. Disulfiram interferes with the metabolism of acetaldehyde, causing rapid acetaldehyde accumulation. If any alcohol is imbibed within 12 hours of taking disulfiram, the patient experiences intense facial flushing 5-15 minutes after drinking, followed by a throbbing headache, rapid heartbeat, heavy breathing and sweating. Consumption of high doses of alcohol while on disulfiram causes nausea and vomiting within 30-60 minutes, which leads to dizziness, and even fainting in some cases. This unpleasant reaction can occur for up to three hours. While this medicine is being taken, and for fourteen days before an individual begins taking it, he or she should not drink even the smallest amount of alcohol. They should also not use any foods, products, or medicines that contain alcohol (e.g., tinctures, elixirs, some over-the-counter cough and cold medicines), nor should they come into contact with any chemicals that contain alcohol while using this medicine. Because the evidence for the efficacy of disulfiram is poor, its use is limited. Adherence is poor with this drug and it works best in combination with social support.

Topiramate (*Topamax*) is an anticonvulsant that is FDA-approved for the treatment of seizure disorders. Topiramate heightens the biochemical effects of GABA receptors and inhibits excitatory glutamate receptors, which suppresses ethanol-induced dopamine release from the nucleus accumbens. Topiramate dulls the mental reward associated with drinking and decreases the effects of alcohol withdrawal. Clinical trials have established that topiramate is safe and decreases the number of drinking days, heavy drinking days, and drinks per day. It is not FDA-approved for AUD, but is used off-label for this indication.

Other medications that have been used off-label to treat AUD patients include: 1) the anticonvulsant gabapentin (*Neurontin*), which reduces alcohol ingestion but has not been studied extensively; 2) antidepressants like sertraline (*Zoloft*), and fluoxetine (*Prozac*), which only decrease alcohol use in persons with co-existing mood disorders; and 3) the antiemetic medication ondansetron (*Zofran*), which antagonizes serotonin receptors in the brain and decreases alcohol craving and consumption, but only seems to do so in specific patient populations.

In addition to medications, alcoholism treatment programs use counseling and group therapy to help a person stop drinking. Most people with an AUD need help to recover from their disease. With support and treatment, many people can stop drinking and rebuild their lives.

Self-help groups are the most commonly sought source of help for alcohol-related problems. Alcoholics Anonymous (AA) is one of the most well-known self-help groups. AA emphasizes person-to-person relationships, group support, and commitment to recovery. Meetings consist mainly of discussions about the participants' problems with alcohol and testimonials from those who have recovered. AA outlines twelve consecutive activities, or steps, that an individual should achieve during the recovery process. Alternative social support groups for patients with AUD include LifeRing Secular Recovery or SMART Recovery that use different strategies for dealing with AUD.

Psychotherapy is also an option, as several cognitive and behavioral therapies may be beneficial in the treatment of alcohol misuse. These approaches target thoughts and behaviors that may contribute to the misuse of alcohol. Cognitive behavioral therapy (CBT) is a form of psychotherapy that reshapes the patient's present modes of thinking to elicit changes in their behavior patterns. CBT has an excellent empirical evidence base and improves mood and reduces substance misuse, particularly in women who are treated with a variant of CBT tailored to women. Aversive conditioning is a behavioral approach in which the consumption of alcohol is associated with a wide range of noxious stimuli. Another approach, self-control training, can help to reduce the intake of alcohol without totally abstaining. A variety of coping skills and stress management techniques may also be used.

Motivational enhancement therapy (MET) assumes that one has the responsibility and capacity for change. A therapist begins by providing individualized feedback about the effects of drinking. Working closely together, the patient and the therapist will explore the benefits of abstinence, review treatment options, and design a plan to implement treatment goals. Often, it is helpful to involve a spouse or significant other in a treatment program. This can increase the likelihood that the patient will complete therapy and continue to abstain after treatment ends.

Behavioral-marital therapy (BMT) combines a focus on drinking with efforts to strengthen marital relationships. BMT involves shared activities and the teaching of communication and conflict evaluation skills. Couples therapy may also be combined with learning and rehearsing a relapse prevention plan. Among those with severe marital and drinking problems, the combination approach produces improved marital relations and higher rates of abstinence.

Brief interventions involve counseling from primary care doctors or nursing staff during five or fewer standard office visits. In brief interventions, the patient will receive information on the negative consequences of alcohol misuse. They will also learn about strategies and community resources to help achieve moderation or abstinence. Most brief interventions are designed to help individuals if they are abusing alcohol and are at risk for developing alcoholism. They are designed to help reduce alcohol consumption. If they are already alcohol-dependent, however, they are encouraged to enter specialized treatment with the goal of complete abstinence. There are no surgical treatments indicated for the treatment of alcoholism.

Amy Scholten, MPH;
Updated by Michael A. Buratovich, PhD

FOR FURTHER INFORMATION

Brown, Stephani, Lewis, Virginia M., Brown, Stephanie, & Lewis, Virginia. (2002). *The alcoholic family in recovery: A developmental model.* New York: Guilford. This book provides recovery strategies designed for the whole family, since recovery from alcoholism can adversely affect the entire family for years.

Elkin, Chris. (2018, April 20). "Alcohol-related diseases & disorders." *DrugRehab.com.* Retrieved from https://www.drugrehab.com/addiction/alcohol/diseases-and-disorders/. A health journalist accurately summarizes the long-term effects of alcoholism in plain language.

Ethen, M. K., Ramadhani, T. A., Scheuerle, A. E., Canfield, M. A., Wyszynski, D. F., Druschel. C. M., "National Birth Defects Prevention Study. (2009). Alcohol consumption by women before and during pregnancy." *Maternal and Child Health Journal,* 13, 274–285. A troubling study that shows that alcohol consumption during pregnancy is rather common.

Grant, Bridget F., Chou, S. Patricia, Saha, Tulshi D., Pickering, Roger P., Kerridge, Bradley T., Ruan, W. June, Hasin, Deborah S. (2017). "Prevalence of 12-month alcohol use, high-risk drinking, and DSM-IV alcohol use disorder in the United States, 2001-2002 to 2012-2013: Results from the national epidemiologic survey on alcohol and related conditions." *JAMA Psychiatry,* 74(9), 911-923. A landmark epidemiological study by scientists from the National Institute on Alcohol Abuse and Alcoholism that showed that alcoholism rose by 49 percent in the first decade of the 2000s.

Jones, Keith. (2015). *Alcoholism sourcebook.* Detroit, MI: Omnigraphics. A reliable source of consumer health information that covers AUD, addiction, and related health effects.

Korsmeyer, Pamela, & Kranzler, Henry R. (Eds.). (2008). *Encyclopedia of drugs, alcohol & addictive behavior.* Detroit, MI: Macmillan Reference. A very useful resource that covers the psychiatric and legal aspects of drug and alcohol addiction.

MacKillop, James, Kenna, George, A., & Leggio, Lorenzo. (Eds.). (2017). *Integrating psychological and pharmacological treatments for addictive disorders: An evidence-based guide.* Abingdon, United Kingdom: Routledge. A comprehensive, but surprisingly concise resource for psychologists, physicians, social workers, and other mental health professionals that explicates addiction treatment practices.

Melton, Sarah T. (2015, October 1). "Topiramate in the treatment of alcohol use disorders." *Medscape.* Retrieved from https://www.medscape.com/viewarticle/851686. Professional pharmacist summarizes the clinical evidence for the efficacy of the anticonvulsant topiramate (*Topamax*) as a treatment for AUD.

Middelton-Moz, Jane, & Dwinell, Lorie. (2010). *After the tears: Helping adult children of alcoholics heal their childhood trauma.* Deerfield Beach, FL: Health Communications, Inc. A sensitively written book that addresses the multidimensional needs of children of alcoholics.

Virtanen, Marianna, Jokela, Markus, Nyberg, Solja T., Madsen, Ida E. H., Lallukka, Tea, Ahola, Kirsi, & Kivimäki, Mika. (2015). "Long working hours and alcohol use: Systematic review and meta-analysis of published studies and unpublished individual participant data." *British Medical Journal,* 350, g7772. A meta-analysis of many different studies that establish an association between working long hours and an increase in alcohol use.

See also: Alcohol misuse; Alcohol poisoning; Alcohol's effects on the body

Alcohol misuse: The Michigan Alcoholism Screening Test (MAST)

CATEGORY: Diagnosis and prevention

DEFINITION: The MAST, the Michigan Alcoholism Screening Test, was developed in 1971 and is one of the oldest alcohol dependence questionnaires in existence.

OVERVIEW

More than fifteen different questionnaires exist to screen patients for alcohol dependence. The three most well-known questionnaires are the CAGE questionnaire, Alcohol Use Disorders Identification Test (AUDIT), and the Michigan Alcoholism Screening Test (MAST). Each screening test has advantages and disadvantages. Although quick to administer, the CAGE questionnaire may not be as accurate for the older population, women, and college students. The AUDIT, created in 1993, including the AUDIT-C (shortened form), continues to be accurate in both reliability and consistency in the diagnosis of alcohol use disorders among diverse populations, at least among the English-speaking ethnic groups. Although effective and accurate, the AUDIT is not often used in the initial screening for alcohol use disorder.

The MAST, developed in 1971, is one of the oldest alcohol dependence questionnaires in existence. It continues to rival the AUDIT in accuracy. The MAST also focuses on lifetime use of alcohol use instead of the acute use disorders. It should be noted that the MAST is more sensitive than specific, 0.92 versus 0.83. It has good internal consistency with a test-retest reliability between one and two weeks. It is the length of MAST (22 questions), versus the AUDIT (10 questions), that hinders its use today.

HISTORY

The MAST has undergone several iterations but specifically, the Brief Michigan Alcoholism Screening Test (bMAST), created in 1972, has ten questions, similar to the AUDIT, and its validity has been studied multiple times in the last two decades. The bMAST is good at evaluating the perception of drinking and its consequences. The bMAST and AUDIT measured similarly across multiple dependence-severity indices. It can be both reliable and efficient in screening for alcohol dependence and is applicable to many situations, including the emergency setting. The bMAST is beneficial in patients seeking treatment as its components of perception and consequences is more relevant than the AUDIT. The bMAST could help elucidate the patients' readiness to change.

FUTURE TRENDS

Whether the CAGE questionnaire, AUDIT, or bMAST is used to screen for alcohol use disorder, it is best interpreted by a trained individual. It should be used in all adults aged eighteen and older, a grade B recommendation by the United States Preventive Services Task Force.

Van Nguyen, MD and Miriam Schwartz, MD, PhD

FOR FURTHER INFORMATION

Connor JP, Grier M, Feeney GF and Young RM. " The Validity of the Brief Michigan Alcohol Screening Test (bMAST) as a Problem Drinking Severity Measure." *Journal of Studies on Alcohol and Drugs.* (2007) Volume 68:771-779. Print.

Dhalla S and Kopec JA. "The CAGE questionnaire for alcohol misuse: a review of reliability and validity studies." *Clinical and Investigative Medicine.* (2007). Volume 30(1):33-41. Print.

Hsueh YJ, Chu H, Huang CC, Ou KL, CHen CH and Chou KR. "Psychometric Properties of the Chinese Version of the Michigan Alcoholism Screening Test (MAST-C) for Patients with Alcoholism." *Perspectives in Psychiatric Care.* (2014). Volume 50(2):83-92. Print.

Reinert DF and Allen JP. "The alcohol use disorders identification test: an update of research findings." *Alcoholism, Clinical and Experimental Research.* (2007). Volume 31(2):185-99. Print.

U.S. Preventive Services Task Force. "Alcohol Misuse: Screening and Behavioral Counseling Interventions in Primary Care." https://www.uspreventiveservicestaskforce.org/Page/Document/UpdateSummaryFinal/alcohol-misuse-screening-and-behavioral-counseling-interventions-in-primary-care. Accessed on August 13, 2018.

See also: Alcohol misuse; Rehabilitation programs for addiction; Treatment methods and research; Twelve-step programs for addicts; Twelve-step programs for family and friends

Alcoholics Anonymous: The Twelve Steps

CATEGORY: Treatment

DEFINITION: Alcoholics Anonymous is a worldwide voluntary association that promotes a program of total abstinence, adherence to a step program for personal reformation, attendance at meetings, volunteer service to recover from alcoholism, and volunteer service to help others achieve recovery.

DATE: Established June 1935

OVERVIEW

The Twelve Steps of Alcoholics Anonymous, commonly referred to simply as "The Steps" or "The Twelve Steps," are a set of steps that individuals follow as part of their recovery from alcohol and substance use. The Steps are considered one of the fundamental pillars of Alcoholics Anonymous (AA). They were first introduced in *Alcoholics Anonymous: The Story of How More Than One Hundred Men Have Recovered from Alcoholism* and are typically displayed in every AA meeting. The primary purpose of the Steps is to aid an individual's recovery by helping an individual live without the use of alcohol and mind-altering substances. Working and completing the Steps are not a requirement of being a member of Alcoholics Anonymous, but since AA is a step program, individuals whom identify as members of AA are strongly encouraged to work through the steps as a part of their recovery. The Twelve Steps of Alcoholics Anonymous are these:

1. We admitted we were powerless over alcohol—that our lives had become unmanageable.
2. Came to believe that a Power greater than ourselves could restore us to sanity.
3. Made a decision to turn our will and our lives over to the care of God as we understood Him.
4. Made a searching and fearless moral inventory of ourselves.
5. Admitted to God, to ourselves, and to another human being the exact nature of our wrongs.
6. Were entirely ready to have God remove all these defects of character.
7. Humbly asked Him to remove our shortcomings.
8. Made a list of all persons we had harmed, and became willing to make amends to them all.
9. Made direct amends to such people wherever possible, except when to do so would injure them or others.
10. Continued to take personal inventory and when we were wrong promptly admitted it.
11. Sought through prayer and meditation to improve our conscious contact with God as we understood Him, praying only for knowledge of His will for us and the power to carry that out.
12. Having had a spiritual awakening as the result of these steps, we tried to carry this message to alcoholics, and to practice these principles in all our affairs.

HISTORY OF THE TWELVE STEPS

The fellowship of Alcoholics Anonymous was founded in 1935 by Bill Wilson and Dr. Bob Smith in Akron, Ohio. AA was originally based on the Oxford Group, and borrows heavily from its procedures and principles such as group sharing, mutual aid, and rigorous honesty in one's dealings. Fundamental in the creation of the Twelve Steps was the influence of The Oxford Group's four practices. These are the following:

1. The sharing of our sins and temptations with another Christian.
2. Surrender our life past, present and future, into God's keeping and direction.
3. Restitution to all whom we have wronged directly or indirectly.
4. Listening for God's guidance, and carrying it out.

The creation of the twelve steps that AA follows did not occur until the publication of Bill W's *Alcoholics Anonymous: The Story of How More Than One Hundred Men Have Recovered from Alcoholism* in 1939. Before this, early AA groups followed six steps:

1. We admitted that we were licked, that we were powerless over alcohol.
2. We made a moral inventory of our defects or sins.
3. We confessed or shared our shortcomings with another person in confidence.
4. We made restitution to all those we had harmed by our drinking.

5. We tried to help other alcoholics, with no thought of reward in money or prestige.

6. We prayed to whatever God we thought there was for power to practice these precepts.

The idea to add more steps stemmed from Bill Wilson's belief that more steps were needed in order to make the purpose of going through the steps easier to understand and to make the steps themselves easier to follow. This expansion first appeared in the chapter "How it Works" where it has remained in all subsequent editions.

After the publication of the Big Book and the overwhelming popularity of the twelve steps as a crucial part of recovery, Bill Wilson created a separate book that focused specifically on the twelve Steps and twelve Traditions of Alcoholics Anonymous. In 1953, *Twelve Steps and Twelve Traditions* was published as a way to further clarify the meaning of the Steps and Traditions and offer guidance on how to best work through them. This book has become one the principle sources for individuals wishing to work the steps. The book contains a short synopsis on the principles behind each step, and each chapter focuses on a specific step or tradition further elaborating on the practice and understanding of them. Periodically a desire to update the language of the *Twelve Steps and Twelve Traditions* arises due to a belief that the outdated language is hard to understand and connect with. The 2002 General Service Conference released a statement addressing this saying "The text in the book *Twelve Steps and Twelve Traditions*, written by bill W., remain as is, recognizing the Fellowship's feelings that Bill's writing be retained as originally published."

PURPOSE OF THE TWELVE STEPS

The purpose of the Twelve Steps is to aid an individual's efforts to remain sober. The *Twelve Steps and Twelve Traditions* describes the Steps as "A group of principles, spiritual in their nature, which, if practiced as a way of life, can expel the obsession to drink and enable the sufferer to be- come happily and usefully whole." Each step has an overall purpose, and when followed in order, is meant to give an individual a basis for a happy, healthy life in sobriety. The specific purposes can be found in the "Contents" section of the *Twelve Steps and Twelve Traditions*.

STARTING THE TWELVE STEPS

There is no specific or perfect way to work through the Twelve Steps. This means that there are many different approaches and attitudes towards the Steps. It is highly important to remember that when looking at or viewing any material relating to the Steps or AA as a whole, including this article, nothing published outside of AA approved materials should be taken as law.

The actual work that goes into the steps usually involves a combination of internal reflection; reading AA literature about the steps and AA; personalized writing that discuses or answers questions and prompts; and speaking to another person about the steps, reflections, readings and writings. This does not encapsulate all the work that an individual either can or will do when working on the steps, there are many different methods of completing the steps that involve some, all, or none of these practices. How an individual chooses to work on the steps is a decision that the guide and the individual decide together.

Alcoholics Anonymous is considered a program of suggestions which is expressed in its statement, "The only requirement for membership is a desire to stop drinking." This means that it makes no demands of its members, and this policy extends towards the working of the Steps. The practice and the effort put into the working the Steps is entirely up to the individual, there is no timetable to complete the Steps nor internal pressure to work on them in a specific way. Despite this, there are some suggestions and some common practices that most AA members follow before beginning them.

One suggestion is to work on the Steps with someone else serving as a guide. That person is normally a sponsor, though it is not uncommon for the guide to be a professional counselor or spiritual advisor. The reason a sponsor is normally suggested as the guide is the sponsor has either already completed the Steps or is further along than the person just starting, and uses that valuable experience to help navigate the individual. The sponsor is the one who normally suggests how the person should work on the Steps and serves as a resource to help the individual get the most out of them.

Another suggestion is to prepare to work through the Steps thoroughly and honestly. AA is a program of honesty and individuals reveal personal information about themselves they may not wish to make public in other forums. The Steps are similar in this, the work done is not usually shared with anyone outside of a sponsor. As the Steps require internal reflection and admission of difficult information, the individual is responsible for how much effort and honesty go into working on them. The stress on thoroughness and honesty is ultimately for the individual to achieve the maximum benefits the steps offer.

The Steps are meant to be worked on in order, and it is recommended that they be done in the order presented. The reason for this is many of the steps build upon the work done in prior steps. Making amends to people harmed in Step Nine is one of the more difficult steps that AA members go through. That is why it is recommended to first go through Step Eight, where a person creates a list of people harmed and becomes willing to make amends to them, in order to aid the work of Step Nine. AA advises trying to avoid "two-stepping," a common practice where an AA member practices only two of the Steps without having gone through them all. Spreading the message of AA (Step Twelve) is more effective if a person is able to show how all the Steps have helped them.

A final suggestion is that once started, to work through all twelve steps. As stated earlier, there is no timetable to complete the Steps. Many people even re-start the Steps for various reasons, such as a change in sponsorship, a desire to work through them again or making a new start in AA. Like many different aspects of AA, the Steps are an individual undertaking and vary greatly from person to person. Some people finish the Steps early on in their sobriety and others take years. The benefits of the Steps is believed to be greatest when all twelve of the steps are completed.

TWELVE STEPS RESOURCES

While some of the steps may at first seem straightforward, they should not be worked on without consulting other sources. There are three traditional resources that most individuals consult as they work through the Steps: AA meetings, AA literature, and other members of AA.

While most AA meetings mention or display the Steps, Step Meetings are a type of AA meeting that focus on the practice and understanding of the Steps. Some common features of Step Meetings are a reading of a specific step, an AA member speaking for an extended period of time on members' experience working and practicing a step or steps, and the group sharing their own experiences with a step. Beginner Meetings expose new members to the Twelve Steps and are meant to help individuals whom are new to the program learn the core fundamentals.

Alcoholics Anonymous has valuable literary resources that further expand upon the Twelve Steps. The General Service Office of Alcoholics Anonymous (GSO) has an approved list of literature that deals specifically with the Twelve Steps, with the two primary sources being *Alcoholics Anonymous* and *Twelve Steps and Traditions*. The *Alcoholics Anonymous* chapter "How it Works" contains many suggestions on how to work on specific steps, such as a moral inventory template for working on Step Four and a prayer for Step Three. *Twelve Steps and Traditions* "proposes to broaden and deepen the understanding of the Twelve Steps," and seeks to answer many questions people working on the Steps may have. It also contains comprehensive information on the benefits and rewards of working the Twelve Steps and the best ways to share the Steps with others. There are also various other non-GSO approved literature and worksheets that deal with the Twelve Steps available online.

Other members of AA are pivotal in helping an individual throughout the process of working on the Steps. A sponsor is the most valuable resource as the sponsor has experience working on the Steps and is able to guide the individual through the process. The sponsor can also serve the direct role of being the person the individual confides in, examples being for Steps One and Four. AA members can offer their own experiences with the Steps, give support, or provide more direct assistance when asked.

Michael Moglia, BA

FOR FURTHER INFORMATION

Alcoholics Anonymous. New York: Alcoholics Anonymous World Services, 2013. Print.

Alcoholics Anonymous Comes of Age: A Brief History of AA. New York: Alcoholics Anonymous World Services, 1985. Print.

Dick B. *The Oxford Group and Alcoholics Anonymous.* Seattle: Glen Abbey, 1992. Print.

Wilson, William. *Twelve Steps and Twelve Traditions.* New York: Alcoholics Anonymous World Services, 1952. Print.

Alcohol poisoning

CATEGORY: Health issues and physiology

ALSO KNOWN AS: Binge drinking; ethanol poisoning; isopropyl alcohol poisoning; methanol poisoning

DEFINITION: Alcohol poisoning is an illness caused by consuming a large amount of alcohol in a short time. It usually occurs after binge drinking, in which a person rapidly ingests five or more drinks in sequence. Alcohol poisoning also can result in coma and death. The amount of alcohol in the body is usually measured as blood alcohol content (BAC) and is expressed as the percentage of alcohol per liter of blood. Alcohol consumption is also measured by the number of drinks a person consumes.

CAUSES

Most alcohol poisoning cases are caused by ethanol (C_2H_5OH), which is a component of alcoholic beverages, namely beer, wine, and hard liquor. Ethanol has been produced by the fermentation of sugar since antiquity. Other alcohol poisoning cases are caused by methanol (CH_3OH) or isopropyl alcohol (C_3H_8O). Methanol is primarily used in the production of other chemicals; it is sometimes used as an automotive fuel. Isopropyl alcohol is a component of rubbing alcohol and is widely used as a solvent and a cleaning fluid.

All forms of alcohol are flammable and colorless, and all are readily available in the marketplace. Although the purchase of alcoholic beverages in the United States is generally restricted to adults age twenty-one years and older, minors often obtain the product through a third party, sometimes even their parents, without difficulty.

RISK FACTORS

A number of factors increase the risk of becoming ill through alcohol poisoning. They include the following:

- *Rate of drinking.* The more rapidly a person consumes a given amount of alcohol, the more likely the risk of alcohol poisoning. One to two hours are required to metabolize one drink.
- *Gender.* Young men age eighteen through twenty-five years are the most likely to experience alcohol poisoning; however, women are more susceptible to alcohol poisoning than men because they produce less of an enzyme that slows the release of alcohol from the stomach.
- *Age.* Teenagers and college-age youth are more likely to engage in binge drinking; however, the majority of these drinking-related deaths occur in persons age thirty-five to fifty-four years. This older age group often does not metabolize alcohol as readily as younger persons and is more likely to have an underlying health problem that increases the risk.
- *Body mass.* A heavier person can drink more alcohol than a lighter person and still register the same BAC. For example, a 240-pound man who drinks two cocktails will have the same BAC as a 120-pound woman who consumes one cocktail.
- *Overall health.* Persons with kidney disease, liver disease, heart disease, or other health problems may metabolize alcohol more slowly. A person with diabetes, for example, who binge drinks might experience a dangerous drop in blood sugar level.
- *Food consumption.* A full stomach slows the absorption of alcohol, so drinking on an empty stomach increases the risk.
- *Drug use.* Prescription and over-the-counter drugs might increase the risk of alcohol poisoning. Ingestion of illegal substances, such as cocaine, methamphetamine, heroin, and marijuana, also increases the risk.

SYMPTOMS

Alcohol poisoning symptoms include confusion, stupor, or unconsciousness; respiratory depression (slow breathing rate); irregular breathing (a gap of more than ten seconds between breaths); slow heart rate; low blood pressure; low body temperature (hypothermia); vomiting; seizures; and pale or blue skin.

SCREENING AND DIAGNOSIS

The BAC is a definitive test for alcohol poisoning. Persons with alcohol poisoning often have a BAC of 0.35 to 0.5 percent. By way of comparison, a person is considered to be driving under the influence in all US states if his or her BAC is 0.08 percent or higher. Other blood tests include those that check a person's complete blood count (CBC) and those that check levels of glucose, urea, arterial pH (acid), and electrolytes.

Hangover

A hangover is the body's way of indicating that over-indulging in alcoholic beverages is unhealthy. An effective treatment for hangovers would undermine the body's own defense system against drinking too heavily. It is important to understand how alcohol consumption and hangovers are related.

After a person stops drinking, his or her blood alcohol concentration (BAC) begins to drop. Hangover symptoms peak around the time the BAC is 0.0. Alcohol acts as a diuretic (increases urine output), leading to dehydration and the loss of electrolytes. Although alcohol initially acts as a sedative, drinking actually disrupts the sleep cycle, causing a person to wake up fatigued. Finally, acetaldehyde, a toxic byproduct of the body's breaking down of alcohol, causes many hangover symptoms.

There is no scientific evidence to support any method to rid the body of hangover symptoms. However, hangover remedies remain well known and often used, despite the evidence. Strong black coffee, for example, is a favorite among persons with a hangover, who reason that a jolt of caffeine will restore energy to their body. However, caffeinated beverages, like alcohol, are diuretics and only worsen dehydration.

Additionally, the modest benefits of acetaminophen (Tylenol) may not be worth the increased risk of liver toxicity that can occur in the presence of alcohol. Ibuprofen and aspirin are safer for the liver, but they may worsen any stomach irritation caused by drinking excesses. One should not expect to recover by drinking more alcohol. The additional alcohol will be metabolized, and the unavoidable hangover will return as the person's BAC drops.

TREATMENT AND THERAPY

Treatment consists of supportive measures until the body metabolizes the alcohol. This includes insertion of an airway (endotracheal tube) to prevent vomiting and aspiration of stomach contents into the lungs; close monitoring of vital signs (temperature, heart rate, and blood pressure); provisions of oxygen; medication to increase blood pressure and heart rate, if necessary; respiratory support, if necessary; maintenance of body temperature (blankets or warming devices); and administration of intravenous fluids to prevent dehydration. In such cases, glucose should be added if the person is hypoglycemic, that is, if the person has low blood sugar (also, thiamine is often added to reduce the risk of a seizure). Another form of treatment is hemodialysis (blood cleansing), which might be needed for a dangerously high BAC (of more than 0.4 percent). Hemodialysis also is necessary if methanol or isopropyl alcohol has been ingested.

PREVENTION

The best prevention against binge drinking is education, especially of persons who participate in at-risk activities. Young men make up the group with the highest risk of alcohol poisoning. Often, young men have a sense of invincibility and they may disregard helpful advice from any source. Peer pressure is probably the best deterrent; however, it also is a factor that can encourage binge drinking. Furthermore, children with a good parental relationship are less likely to drink to excess.

Robin L. Wulffson, MD

FOR FURTHER INFORMATION

Fisher, Gary, and Thomas Harrison. *Substance Abuse: Information for School Counselors, Social Workers, Therapists, and Counselors.* 5th ed. Upper Saddle River, NJ: Merrill, 2012. Incorporating clinical examples with solid research, this text provides counselors and social workers with a detailed overview of alcohol and other drug addictions.

Ketcham, Katherine, and William F. Asbury. *Beyond the Influence: Understanding and Defeating Alcoholism.* New York: Bantam, 2000. The authors define *alcoholism* as "a genetically transmitted neurological disease," and not something that results from a character defect or from moral weakness. Explains in detail the effects of "the drug alcohol" on the human body and brain in both alcoholics and non-alcoholics.

Miller, William R., and Kathleen M. Carroll, eds. *Rethinking Substance Abuse: What the Science Shows, and What We Should Do about It.* New York: Guilford, 2010. Reviews what is known about substance misuse and offers overviews of biological, psychological, and social factors involved in the treatment of substance misuse. It also anticipates developments and evaluates them for their potential impacts on prevention and treatment.

Olson, Kent R., et al., eds. *Poisoning and Drug Overdose.* 6th ed. New York: McGraw-Hill, 2012. A resource for poison control centers, toxicologists, and health care practitioners for the diagnosis, treatment, and management of poisonings caused by exposure to industrial, therapeutic, illicit, and environmental chemicals.

See also: Alcohol's effects on the body; Blood alcohol content (BAC); Intoxication

Alcohol's effects on the body

CATEGORY: Health issues and physiology

DEFINITION: Ethanol, the type of alcohol found in alcoholic beverages, is a colorless, flammable substance with psychoactive (mind-altering) properties. The amount of alcohol in the body is usually measured as the blood alcohol content (BAC), expressed as the percentage of alcohol per liter of blood. Moderate intake of alcohol can have some health benefits; however, excessive or prolonged use has many detrimental effects on the body.

SHORT-TERM EFFECTS

Alcohol is absorbed into the bloodstream through the lining of the stomach, so measurable amounts can be present within five minutes of ingestion. If alcohol is consumed after eating a heavy meal, its absorption is slowed. Alcohol is metabolized (broken down) in the liver. One to two hours are required to metabolize one drink.

Alcohol is a central nervous system (CNS) depressant; small amounts can produce euphoria and relaxation while large amounts can result in coma or death. Furthermore, moderate alcohol intake (a maximum of one or two drinks per day) may have some health benefits although some research suggests that even moderate drinking may increase the risk of hippocampal atrophy, a form of brain damage associated with dementia, a neurocognitive disorder. Likewise, Alzheimer's is a progressive neurodegenerative disease, so calling it a memory loss condition isn't entirely accurate. Excessive and regular alcohol consumption can be severely detrimental to one's health.

Different degrees of BAC produce different effects, including euphoria, lethargy, mental confusion, stupor, vomiting, and coma. These effects are outlined here.

Euphoria (BAC of 0.03 to 0.12 percent). Symptoms include improved mood, increased sociability, increased self-confidence, increased appetite, inhibited judgment, impaired fine-muscle coordination, and flushed appearance. At this level, the person may laugh more readily, be friendlier, become more socially aggressive, or do things he or she would not normally do. Of note, a BAC of 0.08 percent, the threshold for driving under the influence, is set for every US state.

Lethargy (BAC of 0.09 to 0.25 percent). Symptoms include impaired comprehension and memory, sedation, slowed reflexes, blurred vision, and ataxia (lack of coordination), which is manifested by difficulties in balancing and walking. At this level, the person may forget phone numbers, addresses, or where he or she has parked a car. Driving or operating machinery could result in serious injuries or fatalities. If walking, the person could trip or fall.

Mental confusion (BAC of 0.18 to 0.30 percent). Symptoms include pronounced confusion, labile emotions (abrupt mood changes, laughing or crying readily), increased ataxia, decreased pain sensation, slurred speech, staggering, sensory impairment (sight, hearing, and touch), vomiting, and dizziness, which is often associated with nausea. This level is sometimes referred to as falling-down-drunkenness, and the person at this level of intoxication is severely impaired.

Stupor (BAC of 0.25 to 0.40 percent). Symptoms include severe ataxia, vomiting, unconsciousness (may be intermittent), slowed heart rate, slowed respirations, and urinary incontinence. At this level, death can occur from respiratory depression or from vomiting (if while unconscious, the person aspirates vomit into his or her lungs).

Coma (BAC of 0.35 to 0.50 percent). Symptoms include unconsciousness, markedly depressed reflexes (for example, pupils do not respond to light), severe respiratory depression, and severely slowed heart rate. At this level the drinker has alcohol poisoning, and death at this point is not uncommon.

Aftereffects from an acute drinking episode persist for up to twenty-four hours. Consumption of alcohol within several hours before going to sleep results in the drinker falling asleep more promptly. Consumption of one alcoholic beverage may increase total hours of sleep and may decrease awakening during the night. Higher consumption, however, results in the disruption of sleep patterns and prevents a restful night's sleep. The person falls asleep promptly; however, once most of the alcohol has been metabolized, the person experiences (because of a rebound effect) episodes of wakefulness and light, unproductive sleep. The following morning, the person who consumed two or more alcoholic beverages awakens fatigued and may experience a hangover, which can include headache, nausea, thirst, sensitivity to light and noise, diarrhea, and dysphoria (depression, anxiety, and irritability). Some of these symptoms are caused by dehydration, which can occur even with moderate alcohol consumption.

A single episode of drinking at the euphoric level (BAC of 0.03 to 0.12 percent) can have long-term consequences. Inappropriate comments or behavior while under the influence can result in the breakup of a relationship or the loss of a job. Driving under the influence—even if below the legal limit of 0.08 percent—can result in a traffic accident, which might cause serious injuries.

LONG-TERM EFFECTS

In general, regular misusers of alcohol fall into two categories of use: alcoholism and alcohol misuse . Alcoholism is a chronic condition in which a person depends on regular ingestion of alcoholic beverages. Alcoholics are unable to control their drinking and continue to drink even when doing so interferes with their health, interpersonal relationships, and work.

Alcohol misuse is excessive drinking—enough to cause problems in daily life—without the person having complete dependence on alcohol. The long-term effects of regularly consuming more than one or two alcoholic beverages are profound and include medical, neuropsychiatric, and social problems. Both alcoholics and alcohol misusers are more susceptible to the long-term effects of alcohol misuse. These are caused by the direct effects of alcohol on the body and by resultant poor nutrition. Heavy drinkers may have a poor diet because much of their caloric intake often comes from alcoholic beverages.

Long-term alcohol misuse has medical, neuropsychiatric, and social consequences. Medical effects include diabetes, an impaired immune system, kidney infections and kidney failure, pneumonia, gastritis (inflammation of the stomach) and esophagitis (inflammation of the esophagus), and the following, all of which are common in alcoholics:

Cancer. Includes many forms of cancer, such as throat, esophagus, stomach, colon, rectum, liver , and kidney cancers. The combination of tobacco and alcohol markedly increases the risk of cancer, particularly cancers of the mouth and throat.

Cardiovascular disease. Hypertension (high blood pressure), heart failure, cardiomyopathy (damage to the heart muscle), and stroke.

Pancreatitis (inflammation of the pancreas). Acute pancreatitis is the sudden onset of inflammation, which may result in death. Chronic pancreatitis can continue for many years and can ultimately lead to death.

Ulcers of the stomach or duodenum (upper portion of the stomach). A perforated ulcer is a life-threatening situation.

Cirrhosis of the liver. This condition can lead to liver failure and death. Cirrhosis can produce portal hypertension (increased blood pressure in the venous system within the liver). Portal hypertension can produce esophageal varices (dilated blood vessels in the esophagus). Esophageal varices are prone to rupture and can result in a fatal hemorrhage.

Vitamin deficiencies. Vitamin deficiencies, which are usually caused by a poor diet, can result in a number of severe health problems.

Obesity. The appetite-stimulating effect of alcohol coupled with the calories in alcohol can result in obesity in some alcohol misusers.

Long-term neuropsychiatric effects of alcohol-misuse include confusion; impaired memory; dementia; antegrade amnesia (also known as blackouts, the loss of memory following an episode of heavy drinking); tremors; peripheral neuropathy (numbness of the feet and hands); hallucinations (auditory and visual); fear, anxiety, and a sense of impending doom; an obsession with drinking; sexual dysfunction, including decreased libido and erectile dysfunction (inability for a male to get an erection); and delirium tremens, or DTs (tremors or convulsions). DTs occur during an episode of withdrawal from alcohol.

Long-term social effects of alcohol misuse include traffic fatalities or injuries to self or others, dysfunctional home life, spousal battery, child abuse, disruption of interpersonal relationships outside the home, injury or accidents at work, loss of a job or promotion, and codependency (a condition in which an alcoholic manipulates or controls others, such as his or her spouse, children, friends, and coworkers).

Fetal Alcohol Spectrum Disorder

Fetal alcohol spectrum disorder (FASD) is a general category for the long-term effect of alcohol consumption on the fetus of a pregnant woman who also is an alcoholic . FASD involves varying degrees of physical and mental abnormalities. The best known and most thoroughly researched form of FASD is fetal alcohol syndrome (FAS).

Children with FAS are often born with a low birth weight and have varying degrees of facial abnormalities, mental retardation, CNS disorders, skeletal abnormalities, and heart defects. The facial abnormalities include microcephaly (small head and brain), small eyes, thin upper lip, and a small, upturned nose. The CNS disorders include vision and hearing problems, poor coordination, learning disabilities, and sleep problems. The skeletal abnormalities include deformities of the limbs, joints, and fingers. The heart defects include atrial septal defects (defects in the wall separating the upper heart chambers) and ventricular septal defects (defects in the wall separating the lower heart chambers).

Two other forms of FASD are alcohol-related neurodevelopmental disorder (ARND) and alcohol-related birth defect (ARBD). Persons with ARND may have intellectual, behavioral, and learning disabilities. During childhood, they tend to perform poorly in school and have difficulties with mathematics, attention, judgment, memory, and impulse control. Persons with ARBD have abnormalities that include hearing problems and problems of the heart, skeletal system, and kidneys.

Affected children cannot be cured; however, the following factors can improve a child's quality of life: early recognition of the disorder (before the age of six years); enrollment in special education programs; and a nurturing, stable, home environment. FASD is preventable if a woman stops drinking when she learns that she is pregnant.

A February 2011 study found that counseling about alcohol use during pregnancy is often inadequate. A study of 12,611 women who delivered infants from 2001 through 2008 found that, despite the substantial number of women who continue to consume alcohol during pregnancy, health care providers do not routinely assess alcohol consumption or counsel all women about alcohol's harmful effects. As with other alcohol-related disorders, nutrition and other factors (such as misuse of prescription drugs or illegal substances) play a role in the development of FASD.

A safe level of alcohol consumption, which will prevent FASD, is not known; however, no cases of FASD have been reported in which the pregnant woman consumed an occasional alcoholic beverage or even consumed a larger amount on a few occasions. A large study (11,513 children) published by researchers at University College London in October 2010 found that children at age five years who were born to women who drank one or two alcoholic beverages per week during pregnancy were not at increased risk for any behavioral or cognitive problems. However, a study published in *JAMA* in 2017 showed an association between all levels of prenatal alcohol exposure and the minor changes in the shapes of the newborns' faces when measured at twelve months. This study concluded that avoiding all alcohol by mothers is the safest option.

Alcohol Combined with Other Substances

Many msusers of alcohol also misuse other substances. Sometimes, the combination has a synergistic effect—the combined effect is significantly more harmful than either substance alone. These harmful effects can occur with both short- and long-term use of alcohol plus another substance or substances. These substances include tobacco, marijuana, CNS depressants, CNS stimulants, prescription drugs, and over-the-counter (OTC) medications.

Tobacco. The combination of alcohol and tobacco greatly increases the risk of many types of cancers. The risk of oral (mouth and tongue) cancer is extremely high in smokers (or tobacco chewers) who also drink alcohol in excess. Smoking is a particularly difficult habit to quit. For example, studies have found that heroin addicts who had given up the drug for more than one year found it more difficult to quit smoking than breaking a heroin habit. Other studies have found that it is more difficult to quit smoking than to quit using cocaine.

Marijuana. Marijuana is a commonly used recreational drug and is frequently used with alcohol. The combination of the two can be particularly lethal. Vomiting after having overindulged in alcohol removes some of the alcohol from the stomach, but this reflex is suppressed with marijuana. As a result, more alcohol remains in one's system, increasing the chance of alcohol poisoning. Even small amounts of alcohol and marijuana increase the risk of a traffic accident. Alcohol slows reaction time and alertness, and marijuana further impairs the driver. For example, marijuana reduces the frequency of a driver's visual searches (that is, of looking right and left before entering an intersection or before changing lanes).

CNS depressants. Alcohol is a CNS depressant. Co-ingestion (mixing) of alcohol and other CNS depressants, such as heroin, barbiturates, tranquilizers, analgesics (pain relievers), and sedatives, is particularly harmful. Reports have shown that more than 70 percent of fatal heroin overdoses are caused by the co-ingestion of heroin and another depressant, such as alcohol. The drug interaction can lead to depressed breathing and slowed heart rate, resulting in unconsciousness. The unconscious state can progress to coma and death. While unconscious, the person may vomit and aspirate the vomitus into his or her lungs, which frequently causes death.

CNS stimulants. CNS stimulants, such as cocaine, methamphetamine, and caffeine, interact with alcohol. Researchers have found that cocaine and alcohol combine in the liver to produce cocaethylene, which intensifies the euphoric effect of cocaine. Cocaine by itself has been associated with sudden death; however, cocaethylene is associated with a greater risk of sudden death than cocaine alone.

Methamphetamine is a potent stimulant. Studies have suggested that when combined with alcohol, it increases the risk of alcohol poisoning. Caffeine is a mild stimulant, compared with cocaine and methamphetamine. However, the combination of alcohol and caffeine has added risks. Not uncommonly, a person who has overindulged is offered a cup of coffee to "sober up." However, the caffeine in the coffee does not improve sobriety—it merely produces a state of wide-awake drunkenness. The increased alertness coupled with the augmented self-confidence from alcohol increases the risk of unsafe activity, such as driving an automobile.

Prescription or nonprescription medication. Many prescription drugs, such as antipsychotics and antidepressants, interact with alcohol. In addition, some OTC products, such as sleep aids and cold remedies, also may have an interaction. It is prudent for one taking any medication to read the label of the medication before consuming alcohol.

MODERATE ALCOHOL INTAKE

Moderate drinking (up to three drinks per occasion or seven drinks per week) may have some health benefits. This level of drinking might reduce the risk of heart disease, of dying from a heart attack, and of developing gallstones, and it might possibly reduce the risk of stroke and diabetes. Drinking red wine might be particularly beneficial. The so-called French paradox observes that the French have a relatively low incidence of coronary artery disease, despite high rates of smoking, low rates of exercise, and high rates of diets that are relatively high in saturated fat. The answer to this paradox might lie in the consumption of red wine by the French.

Red wine contains resveratrol, which is an antioxidant. Experimental evidence shows that resveratrol may have anti-inflammatory, anticancer, and blood-sugar-lowering properties, all of which promote cardiovascular health. Despite the positive evidence, the health benefits of resveratrol are subject to controversy. In one 2015 study comparing moderate drinkers with nondrinkers and published by the *British Medical Journal*, alcohol has been linked to a small increased risk of cancer.

The appetite-stimulating properties of alcohol have been found to benefit the elderly, whose health can suffer from a lack of appetite. A variety of tonics containing alcohol are on the market, and they often improve appetite. They also often improve sleep patterns.

Robin L. Wulffson MD

FOR FURTHER INFORMATION

"Alcohol Use and Your Health." *Centers for Disease Control and Prevention.* CDC, 7 Nov. 2014. Web. 28 Oct. 2015.

Fisher, Gary, and Thomas Harrison. *Substance Abuse: Information for School Counselors, Social Workers, Therapists, and Counselors.* 4th ed. Boston: Allyn & Bacon, 2008. Print.

Ketcham, Katherine, and William F. Asbury. *Beyond the Influence: Understanding and Defeating Alcoholism.* New York: Bantam, 2000. Print

Ludwig, Arnold. *Understanding the Alcoholic's Mind: The Nature of Craving and How to Control It.* New York: Oxford UP, 1989. Print.

Miller, William R. *Rethinking Substance Abuse: What the Science Shows, and What We Should Do about It.* New York: Guilford, 2010. Print.

Siple, Molly. *Eating for Recovery: The Essential Nutrition Plan to Reverse the Physical Damage of Alcoholism.* Da Capo Press, 2008.

Thompson, Dennis. "Health Benefits of Moderate Drinking Overblown: Report." *HealthDay.* HealthDay, 10 Feb. 2015. Web. 28 Oct. 2015.

Walton, Alice G. "Study Suggests People Start Drinking Alcohol for Health Benefits: Should We Believe It?" *Forbes.* Forbes.com, 17 Jan. 2015. Web. 28 Oct. 2015.

See also: Alcohol's effects on the body; Birth defects and alcohol; Drunk driving; Parenting and alcoholism; Stress and alcohol; Substance misuse; Support groups

Alternative therapies for addiction

CATEGORY: Treatment
DEFINITION: Alternative therapies are therapies other than prescription medication, behavioral therapy, or other types of conventional therapy to treat addiction.

INTRODUCTION

Many types of alternative therapies have historically helped persons who suffer with substance addiction. Generally, these therapies are not scientifically proven, but anecdotal evidence and some scientifically based studies show they can ease cravings and the side effects of withdrawal. Alternative therapies work in different ways with different types of people and with different kinds of addictions. Alternative therapies usually can be safely used as part of a comprehensive addiction relief program.

ACUPUNCTURE

Acupuncture is part of the whole-body treatment program of traditional Chinese medicine. It treats addiction and addictive tendencies as an imbalance of qi, the body's life energy. By correcting the imbalance of qi, the body can use its natural energy to ease withdrawal symptoms, such as headaches, depression, nausea, sweating, and insomnia. With qi restored, the body may even be able to achieve the balance it needs to overcome an addiction.

- Some studies using acupuncture for different types of addiction have shown success rates as high as 50 percent. It is thought that acupuncture increases the amount of endorphins in the body, thus easing the cravings that accompany addiction and even removing the need for the addictive substance.
- Auriculotherapy, which is a form of acupuncture that uses points on the ears to treat the entire body, is usually the type of therapy used for addiction treatment. Five points on the ear are stimulated, and if a person does not need treatment daily, small pellets may be taped over the acupressure points. The patient is given instructions on how to press on the points to stimulate them frequently to help deal with addictive desires.
- Acupuncture is a long-term treatment, often spanning several months, and it is usually used with other therapies, such as counseling. One study showed that in people with severe alcohol addiction, those who received a placebo acupuncture treatment had twice the number of relapses than those who received true acupuncture treatment. Studies with acupuncture therapy also have shown success with nicotine addiction and cocaine addiction. In one hospital where acupuncture was used with methadone treatment for heroin addicts, acupuncture treatment alone was so well received that the methadone portion of the treatment was discontinued. Acupuncture also can be helpful with other addictions, such as overeating.

HOMEOPATHY

Homeopathic remedies have been used historically to combat cravings and desires, to minimize general addictive tendencies, and to counteract the negative side effects of substance misuse. Homeopathy is a whole-body type of treatment. Before recommending a remedy, practitioners consider the substance to which a patient is addicted, whether the patient has addictive tendencies, the patient's symptoms, and the patient's personality traits.

For example, a person who has an addiction to opium, morphine, or alcohol and who also has insomnia may be helped by a remedy involving Avena sativa (oat), while someone with an alcohol addiction who is anxious and irritable may fare better with carboneum sulphuratum. Another time-honored homeopathic remedy for addiction is white bryony, which is used for eating addiction accompanied by insecurity.

Homeopathy is considered by some to be a pseudoscience, but some studies show that it is at least as successful as a placebo, and with some types of addiction it is more successful than a placebo. Homeopathy is assumed to be generally harmless and, thus, may be recommended as an alternative therapy.

MEDITATION

Meditation practices, including yoga and qigong, attempt to help alleviate withdrawal symptoms. These practices can reduce anxiety, improve concentration, ease depression, and promote a sense of calmness and peace that may help an addict regain a sense of control. These practices encourage a deep interior and exterior self-awareness that may help a person face difficulties and challenges, both in dealing with addiction and withdrawal and in dealing with life challenges. A religious or spiritual component may be involved with meditation, so this type of therapy may appeal to certain persons and not to others. Meditation is often used with traditional or other alternative therapies to boost success in overcoming addictions.

A common type of meditation used in addiction treatment is Vipassana meditation, which attempts to help a person avoid the blame that may accompany thoughts about an addictive substance and, rather, to accept the reality of the thought or thoughts. One is taught that when an addictive thought or craving arises, one should observe and accept the thought but not act upon it and then refocus energy and attention more positively. Meditation helps with self-esteem and provides positive affirmations to improve confidence, both of which can help a person overcome addictive tendencies.

OTHER ALTERNATIVE THERAPIES

Nutritional therapy. Persons with addictions are often malnourished and suffer damage to major body organs, such as the liver. Nutritional therapy—adding dietary supplements such as vitamins and minerals to the body—attempts to overcome or correct some of these deficiencies and to aid in detoxifying the body. Supplements that have shown nutritional promise

are zinc, vitamin C, beta-carotene, vitamin E, selenium, calcium, magnesium, and the B vitamins, particularly thiamine. Some persons believe that nutritional therapy can restore balance to the brain, and that this balance eliminates the need for an addictive substance.

Herbal medicine. Herbal medicine is another type of therapy that may help ease withdrawal symptoms and reduce cravings. Some helpful herbs for addiction include catnip, chamomile, peppermint, skullcap, and St. John's wort. These herbs are thought to work with the nervous system to provide relief. They may also calm the brain and help with any depressive tendencies. Herbs must be used carefully, as many can have serious side effects.

Hypnotherapy. Hypnotherapy is a controversial alternative therapy for addiction, with many people claiming good results while others dismissing this type of therapy as a sham. It seems that the best results are obtained with less serious addictions, such as nicotine and behavioral addictions. It also seems that results depend heavily on the type of person with the addiction. Persons who are receptive to hypnotic suggestion and who believe that the therapy works generally have the most success.

Hypnotherapists attempt to find the root of the addiction in "buried" thoughts and actions. By

---

Passionflower

The herb passionflower is thought to have mild sedative properties and has been suggested as an aid to drug withdrawal. A 14-day, double-blind trial enrolled 65 men addicted to opiate drugs and compared the effectiveness of passionflower combined with the drug clonidine and with clonidine alone.

Clonidine is used widely to assist in narcotic withdrawal. It effectively reduces physical symptoms, such as increased blood pressure. However, it does not help emotional symptoms, such as drug cravings, anxiety, irritability, agitation, and depression. These symptoms can be severe, and they often cause addicts in drug treatment programs to end participation.

In this 14-day study, the use of passionflower with clonidine significantly eased the emotional aspects of withdrawal compared with the use of clonidine alone. However, more research is necessary to prove this treatment's effectiveness.

confronting the thoughts and behaviors that cause the addiction, one can, theoretically, recover from it. Hypnotherapists use post-hypnotic suggestion to help persons with addiction avoid addictive substances, overcome the need for the substance, and ease cravings.

Other types of alternative therapies thought to help with addiction-related cravings and to possibly address some of the underlying issues that led to the addiction include relaxation, breathing exercises, progressive muscle relaxation, biofeedback training, massage, and chiropractic treatment.

Marianne Moss Madsen, MS, BCND

FOR FURTHER INFORMATION

Hoffman, Jeffrey A. *Living in Balance: 90 Meditations for Recovery from Addiction.* Center City: Hazelden, 2011. Print.

Pruett, J., Nishimura, N., & Priest, R. (2011). "The Role of Meditation in Addiction Recovery." *Counseling and Values,* https://onlinelibrary.wiley.com/doi/abs/10.1002/j.2161-007X.2007.tb00088.x.

Wu, Sharon LY; Leung, Albert Wing-Nang and Yew, David Tai-Wai. "Acupuncture for detoxification in treatment of opioid addiction [online]." *East Asian Archives of Psychiatry,* Vol. 26, No. 2, Jun 2016: 70-76. Availability:<https://search.informit.com.au/documentSummary;dn=170546030151901;res=IELHEA> ISSN: 2078-9947.

Zgierska, A., Rabago, D., Zuelsdorff, M., Coe, C., Miller, M., & Fleming, M. (2008). "Mindfulness Meditation for Alcohol Relapse Prevention: A Feasibility Pilot Study." *Journal of Addiction Medicine,* 2(3), 165–173.

See also: Addiction medications; Behavioral therapies for addiction; Treatment methods and research

Amphetamine misuse

CATEGORY: Substance misuse

DEFINITION: Amphetamine misuse is the repeated, high-dose, nonmedical use of amphetamines, which are potent, highly addictive central nervous system stimulants. Misuse continues despite the user's inability to function normally at home, school, and work.

CAUSES

Amphetamines are rapidly absorbed once ingested. When they reach the brain, they cause a buildup of the neurotransmitter dopamine. This leads to a heightened sense of energy, alertness, and well-being that misusers find to be pleasurable and productive for repetitive tasks. Tolerance develops rapidly, leading to the need for higher doses.

Amphetamines are easy to obtain, often through diversion from legal use, and they are relatively inexpensive. Using them does not carry the social stigma or legal consequences associated with the use of other stimulants, such as methamphetamines and cocaine.

RISK FACTORS

Amphetamine misuse is widespread and has been present almost since their introduction for medical use in the 1930s. Amphetamines were widely misused by soldiers during World War II to maintain alertness during long hours on duty. They are still used by some military personnel in combat settings.

After the war, amphetamines became popular among civilians, especially students who used them to keep awake for studying and as appetite suppressants and recreational drugs. By the 1960s, about one-half of all legally manufactured amphetamines were diverted for illegal use. With greater control over distribution of commercially manufactured amphetamines, manufacture by clandestine laboratories increased dramatically. In addition, the Internet has become a popular source for nonprescription amphetamines.

Misuse now occurs primarily among young adults (age eighteen to thirty years). A common venue for their misuse is the rave, an all-night music and dance concert or party. Use among males and females is evenly divided, except for intravenous use; in this case, males are three to four times more likely to use the drug intravenously. Misusers can rapidly become both physically and psychologically dependent on amphetamines, with a compulsive need for the drug.

SYMPTOMS

Physical symptoms of amphetamine misuse include euphoria, increased blood pressure, decreased or irregular heart rate, narrowing of blood vessels, dilation of bronchioles (the breathing tubes of the lungs), heavy sweating or chills, nausea and vomiting, and increases in blood sugar. High doses can cause fever, seizures, and cardiac arrest.

Frequent, high-dose misuse can lead to aggressive or violent behavior, ending in a psychotic state indistinguishable from paranoid schizophrenia. Features of this state include hallucinations, delusions, hyperactivity, hypersexuality, confusion, and incoherence. One such delusion is formication, the sensation of insects, such as ants, crawling on the skin. Long-term use can result in permanent memory loss.

SCREENING AND DIAGNOSIS

Routine blood and urine testing do not detect amphetamines in the body. Misusers who use pills or who snort amphetamine leave no outward signs of the misuse. Smokers may use paraphernalia to use the drug. Misusers who inject the drug will have needle marks on their skin.

A change in behavior is the primary clue to amphetamine misuse. The misuser develops mood swings and withdraws from usual activities and family and friends. Basic responsibilities and commitments are ignored or carried out erratically. The misuser becomes hostile and argumentative. Any change in a person's appearance, such as sudden weight loss, or in behavior, such as agitation or change in sleep patterns, should be addressed. Such changes may indicate amphetamine misuse. Experts recommend that parents focus their concern with the youth's well-being, and not on the act of misuse.

TREATMENT AND THERAPY

Symptoms of amphetamine withdrawal can develop within a few hours after stopping use. Withdrawal symptoms include nightmares, insomnia or hypersomnia (too much sleep), severe fatigue or agitation, depression, anxiety, and increased appetite. Severe depression can produce suicidal thoughts. Withdrawal symptoms usually peak within two to four days and resolve within one week.

No specific medications are available for directly treating amphetamine misuse. However, antidepressants can be helpful in the immediate and post-withdrawal phases.

The National Institute on Drug Abuse recommends psychotherapeutic intervention utilizing a cognitive behavioral approach. Such an approach helps the misuser learn to identify counterproductive thought patterns and beliefs and to change them so that his or her emotions and actions become more manageable. The misuser is also taught how to improve coping skills to address life's challenges and stresses. Narcotics Anonymous and amphetamine-specific recovery groups are also helpful.

PREVENTION

As there are medical indications for amphetamines, experts recommend that prescription formulations be kept from potential misusers. Pill counts should be taken regularly. Young people should be taught the differences between medical use and illegal misuse. Parents should ensure that their children are not attracted to social settings or activities where amphetamine misuse is or might be encouraged or tolerated.

Ernest Kohlmetz MA

FOR FURTHER INFORMATION

Abadinsky, Howard. *Drug Use and Abuse: A Comprehensive Introduction.* 7th ed. Belmont: Wadsworth, 2011. Print.

Julien, Robert M. *A Primer of Drug Actions.* 11th ed. New York: Worth, 2008. Print.

Kuhn, Cynthia, Scott Swartwelder, and Wilkie Wilson. *Buzzed: The Straight Facts about the Most Used and Abused Drugs from Alcohol to Ecstasy.* 3rd ed. New York: Norton, 2008. Print.

Lowinson, Joyce W., et al., eds. *Substance Abuse: A Comprehensive Textbook.* 4th ed. Philadelphia: Lippincott, 2005. Print

Rogge, Timothy. "Substance Abuse—Amphetamines." *MedlinePlus.* US Natl. Lib. of Medicine, 21 May 2014. Web. 28 Oct. 2015

See also: Controlled substances and precursor chemicals; Recreational drugs; Stimulant misuse; Stimulant's effects on the body

Anabolic steroids

CATEGORY: Substances

DEFINITION: Anabolic steroids are synthetic formulations structurally related testosterone, the male sex hormone. The steroids are used illicitly to increase muscle size and strength.

STATUS: Legal in the United States for specific medical applications. Nonmedical use is illegal.

CLASSIFICATION: Schedule III controlled substance in the United States (possession, buying, and selling are illegal); schedule IV controlled substance in Canada (buying and selling are illegal); legal in Mexico

SOURCE: Diversion from medical and veterinary practices and suppliers, produced in clandestine laboratories, and smuggled. Sold at gyms, in schools, and the web.

TRANSMISSION ROUTES: Intramuscular injection, pills, creams, and gels

HISTORY OF USE

Although commonly called anabolic steroids, these drugs are more correctly identified as anabolic-androgenic steroids. They have both anabolic properties, which promote the growth of skeletal muscle, and androgenic properties, which promote the development of male sexual characteristics.

Synthetic testosterones were first developed in the 1930s in Europe. After World War II they were used by sports officials in the Soviet bloc, especially East Germany, to enhance athletic strength and performance in both males and females. In 1956, John Ziegler, a US Olympic Team physician, developed methandrostenolone, which in 1958 became the first anabolic steroid licensed in the United States for medical use. Eventually, the danger and long-term risk of the use of anabolic steroids as muscle enhancers became apparent. The steroids were banned from use in Olympic competitions in 1976.

The US Anabolic Steroids Control Act was passed in 1990, making anabolic steroids a schedule III controlled substance in the United States. Anabolic steroids now are used in medicine primarily to treat men with hypogonadism (low production of testosterone by the testes) and to treat boys with delayed puberty. The steroids also are used to facilitate tissue regrowth in persons with severe burns and to treat severe weight loss in persons with acquired immune deficiency syndrome.

The illegal use of anabolic steroids, including among professional athletes, remains a major problem. Newer formulations based on molecules not screened by existing tests are always being developed. These newer steroids are popular among teenage boys, especially those participating in competitive sports, most notably wrestling, football, and weightlifting. Although anabolic steroids are banned by virtually all major amateur and professional sports organizations, there have been numerous cases of

high-profile athletes revealed to have used the drugs to enhance their performance. Within Major League Baseball (MLB) especially, steroid use was rampant among players throughout the 1980s and 1990s, affecting the way baseball was played and leading to a public scandal. The US Drug Enforcement Administration has also noted a relatively high rate of steroid misuse among law enforcement officials, particularly police officers. Misusers take doses of anabolic steroids in quantities ten to one-hundred times greater than those doses used in medicine.

Anabolic steroids, including formulations of bolderone and nandrolone, are usually injected. Methandrostenolone, oxymetholone, and stanozole are taken as pills. Steroid gels, creams, and transdermal patches are less effective when used alone, but many misusers employ a "stacking" regimen, in which topical, oral, and injectable formulations are combined to increase the total effect and to avoid detection of high levels of any one steroid in testing. New formulations of anabolic steroids that are not specifically restricted or that are not detectable using current screening methods are being developed and distributed. Well over fifty anabolic steroids have been identified as controlled substances in the United States.

EFFECTS AND POTENTIAL RISKS

Unlike most other misused drugs, anabolic steroids do not cause immediate euphoria or other pleasurable feelings. They are used to promote rapid muscle growth and weight gain (also called bulking up) and to increase strength and sports prowess over time. A common adverse effect of high, prolonged dosing is "roid rage," in which one experiences mood swings, anxiety, irritability, and aggressiveness. Other psychological effects such as depression and psychosis may be observed, and some evidence suggests that the risk of suicide may be increased by prolonged steroid use.

Misusers do not become physically addicted to anabolic steroids, but they can develop a compulsive reliance on them. Depression, headache, fatigue, loss of appetite, and insomnia may result if the drugs are discontinued. Depression may be long-lasting and can lead to suicidal thoughts and actions. In males, long-term misuse suppresses the sex drive, lowers or halts sperm production, and causes shrinking of the testicles. Severe acne may develop. In general these adverse effects are reversible. Feminine characteristics, including breast development, may occur

Former Major League Baseball player Barry Bonds was convicted on one count of obstruction of justice in relation to his use of performance enhancing drugs. (Jim Accordino via Wikimedia Commons)

because some of the excess testosterone produced is converted into the female hormone estradiol. Such changes cannot be reversed.

In females, misuse leads to the emergence of masculine characteristics, including extra muscle deposits, deeper voice, thicker and coarser body hair, male-pattern baldness, disruption of the menstrual cycle, and enlargement of the clitoris. Some of these changes are irreversible. Among younger misusers, high testosterone levels in the body can prematurely signal bones to stop growing and, thus, can stunt growth. In both males and females, steroid misuse contributes to the risk of heart attack and stroke. High levels of testosterone negatively impact cholesterol levels. Levels of bad cholesterol (low-density lipoprotein, or LDL) are increased, while those of good cholesterol (high-density lipoprotein, or HDL)

are decreased. This causes a buildup of plaque in the arteries (atherosclerosis), which decreases or eventually blocks blood flow to the heart, leading to a heart attack, or blood flow to the brain, leading to a stroke. Liver disease too is a rare but potential risk of steroid abuse. Blood-filled cysts that develop in the liver may rupture and cause life-threatening internal bleeding. Kidney failure also can occur. Misusers who share or use contaminated needles are at risk of infection with HIV (human immunodeficiency virus) or with the hepatitis B or C viruses. Anabolic steroids are also considered likely carcinogens by the International Agency for Research on Cancer (IARC), a branch of the World Health Organization (WHO).

Ernest Kohlmetz MA

FOR FURTHER INFORMATION

"Anabolic Steroids." *Center for Substance Abuse Research.* U of Maryland, 29 Oct. 2013. Web. 28 Oct. 2015.

"Anabolic Steroids." *MedlinePlus.* US National Library of Medicine, 18 Sept. 2015. Web. 28 Oct. 2015.

"Anabolic Steroids." *National Institute on Drug Abuse,* Mar. 2016, www.drugabuse.gov/publications/drugfacts/anabolic-steroids. Accessed 17 Oct. 2017.

Gold, Mark S., ed. *Performance-Enhancing Medications and Drugs of Abuse.* Binghamton, NY: Haworth, 2007. Print

Kuhn, Cynthia, Scott Swartwelder, and Wilkie Wilson. *Buzzed: The Straight Facts about the Most Used and Abused Drugs from Alcohol to Ecstasy.* 3rd ed. New York: Norton, 2008. Print.

Minelli, Mark J. *Drug Abuse in Sports: A Student Course Manual.* 7th ed. Champaign, IL: Stipes, 2008. Print.

Rosen, Daniel M. *Dope: A History of Performance Enhancement in Sports from the Nineteenth Century to Today.* Westport, CT: Praeger, 2008. Print

Yasalis, Charles E., ed. *Anabolic Steroids in Sport and Exercise.* Champaign, IL: Human Kinetics, 2000. Print.

See also: Controlled substances and precursor chemicals; Steroid misuse; Substance misuse

Anesthesia misuse

CATEGORY: Substance misuse

DEFINITION: Anesthesia misuse is the intentional use of anesthetic agents for recreational and nonmedical purposes. Anesthetic agents are potent medications with mind-altering effects and include inhaled gases such as nitrous oxide, intravenous medications such as propofol, and local anesthetics such as cocaine.

CAUSES

As with any addiction, biological and environmental factors contribute to anesthesia misuse. Addicts have a genetic predisposition and a chronic, compulsive need for the substance of choice. For the anesthesia misuser, these substances include a variety of potentially addictive agents. Generally, insatiable cravings compel chronic use (misuse) of a particular drug, which results in damage to internal organs. However, because many anesthesia drugs have the potential to cause apnea or paralysis within seconds, misuse of anesthetic agents can lead to death.

RISK FACTORS

Although laypersons misuse anesthesia drugs, the most frequently cited anesthesia misusers are anesthesia providers such as certified registered nurse anesthetists, medical residents, and anesthesiologists. Easy access to anesthetic medications enables anesthesia providers to experiment with controlled substances such as fentanyl and other opioids, which are highly addictive.

Anesthesia providers often work long and irregular hours under stressful conditions with access to anesthetic agents. Propofol misuse is increasingly popular because the substance has a short half-life and is quickly eliminated from the body. Nitrous oxide, commonly known as laughing gas, is an inhaled anesthetic that also is misused. The primary risk of inhaled nitrous oxide is hypoxia, which results from inadequate oxygen supply to the body's tissues and particularly the brain.

SYMPTOMS

A variety of symptoms occur from using common anesthetic medications. These symptoms (and their symptom-producing medications) include amnesia and anxiolysis (midazolam), pain relief (opioids), and sedation and apnea (opioids and propofol).

Misusers experience impaired functioning because of these drugs. The dose associated with misuse is often less than that required for general anesthesia. However, the effects of anesthetic medications are dose dependent and may also lead to dysphoria and mood changes. Therefore, misusers may exhibit behavioral changes; may appear fatigued, irritable, euphoric, dysphoric, drowsy, or depressed; or may simply appear out of character. Recognition of these signs is imperative to protect the misuser and to aid health care providers who have a legal responsibility to report colleagues known or suspected of chemical dependency. This not only protects the misusers but also the patients under their care.

SCREENING AND DIAGNOSIS

The screening test commonly used to confirm drug use is typically a urine drug screen. However, many anesthetic medications (such as fentanyl, propofol, naltrexone, and ketamine) are not included in standard drug screens and must be specifically requested. Because of the short half-lives of these anesthesia drugs, many are quickly eliminated from the body and, therefore, are difficult to detect. In some cases, the metabolites of these drugs can be detected in urine samples, while hair samples fulfill other testing needs. Although more expensive than urine testing, hair-sample testing can detect chronic exposure to certain drugs; urine drug screens are limited to detecting drug use only within hours or days of use.

TREATMENT AND THERAPY

The American Association of Nurse Anesthetists and the American Society of Anesthesiologists are two national organizations that govern the practice of anesthesia providers. These organizations and many others not affiliated with medical and nursing personnel recommend inpatient treatment for persons with chemical dependency.

Short- and long-term therapy combined with support-group attendance and abstinence monitoring offer the highest success rates. Various peer assistance groups are available to monitor and assist those undergoing treatment. Narcotics Anonymous offers a twelve-step program that protects anonymity and offers the addict a structured plan for recovery that includes admitting loss of control over the compulsion (the repeated use of anesthetics) and the aid of a sponsor to evaluate mistakes made by the addict. In

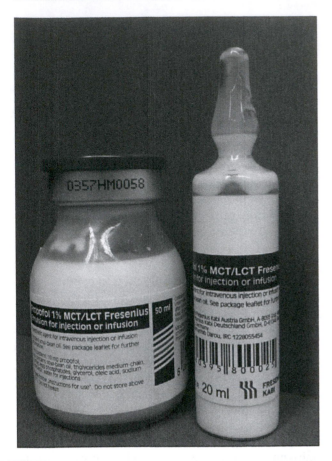

A bottle of the anesthetic Propofol. (via Wikimedia Commons)

return, the addict offers help to others who have the same type of addiction.

PREVENTION
The US Drug Enforcement Administration (DEA) establishes standards and substance schedules and enforces these standards to prevent and control drug misuse. The DEA has plans to treat propofol as a controlled substance, and doing so would institute more accountability and address the overwhelming availability of the drug to anesthesia providers. Random drug screening in accordance with the US Substance Abuse Mental Health Services Administration's guidelines and employing the proper chain of custody are two methods that various organizations use to deter and detect drug misusers, including anesthesia misusers.

Virginia C. Muckler CRNA, MSN, DNP

FOR FURTHER INFORMATION
Bryson, Ethan O., and Jeffrey H. Silverstein. "Addiction and Substance Abuse in Anesthesiology." *Anesthesiology* 109.5 (2008): 905–17. Print. An excellent overview that covers manifestations, legal issues, diagnosis and treatment, prognosis, prevention, and testing methodologies.

Sinha, Ashish C. "The Drug-Impaired Anesthesia Provider." *Audio-Digest Anesthesiology* 50.7 (2007). Print. Through use of several studies, discusses incidence, influencing factors, reasons for suspicion, intervention, treatment, and therapy.

See also: Barbiturates; Fentanyl; Ketamine; Nitrous oxide; Opioid misuse

Anhedonia

CATEGORY: Health issues and psychology

DEFINITION: Anhedonia is the failure or inability to feel pleasure from activities that are pleasurable for most people. Some of these activities are eating, sports, listening to music, sexual activity, and interacting with other people.

CAUSES
Anhedonia is associated with substance misuse, depression, schizophrenia, and some neuroses. It is thought that anhedonia reflects a problem in the dopamine pathways of the brain. Research has used functional magnetic resonance imaging to examine the brains of persons with depression and anhedonia. This research showed less activity in the ventromedial prefrontal cortex, ventral striatum, and amygdala of the brain. These areas of the brain are involved in reactions to pleasant and unpleasant occurrences.

Clinical depression is often associated with anhedonia. However, not all persons with depression have anhedonia, although it is common. Persons with anhedonia often have a flat affect; have a loss of interest in eating, sexual activity, and other normal daily activities; avoid eye contact; and withdraw or isolate themselves. With schizophrenia, it is thought that the chemical imbalance that causes this condition also causes anhedonia.

Anhedonia is fairly common in drug addicts withdrawal, particularly from cocaine and amphetamines.

Withdrawal appears to deplete dopamine, serotonin, and other neurotransmitters involved with feeling pleasure. Also, chronic substance misuse causes changes in the functioning of the brain. These changes affect emotions and are more likely to occur in persons whose substance withdrawal, called protracted withdrawal, has taken longer than usual. A person with long-term addictions appears to have permanent damage to the pleasure pathways in his or her brain, damage that is characterized by apathy.

Serious losses that cause depression also can trigger anhedonia. These losses include the loss of a loved one; physical trauma; serious illness; extreme stress, such as living through a disaster; and other life-altering happenings. In these instances, the anhedonia will pass eventually, as will the depression.

TREATMENT

The most common treatments of anhedonia are antidepressant medications, cognitive-behavioral psychotherapy, and group milieu therapy. Other treatments for anhedonia include regularly scheduled exercise, setting goals, spending time with other people, yoga, art and music therapy, and sunlight and fresh air. The antidepressants most commonly used are the selective serotonin reuptake inhibitors and the selective serotonin and norepinephrine reuptake inhibitors.

The therapist working with a withdrawing substance misuser should inform the patient that he or she may continue to have withdrawal symptoms after the acute withdrawal period or detoxification. If necessary, the patient's doctor should prescribe medications to counter these symptoms.

Ideally, the therapist should encourage his or her patient to be active both physically and mentally, and should suggest that the patient join an appropriate support group. Many recovering addicts need to relearn good sleep habits. The therapist should assist them with this as well.

Christine M. Carroll RN, BSN MBA

FOR FURTHER INFORMATION

Brynie, Faith. "Depression and Anhedonia." *Psychology Today*, 21 Dec. 2009.
Hatzigiakoumis, D. S., et al. "Anhedonia and Substance Dependence: Clinical Correlates and Treatment Options." *Frontiers in Psychiatry* 2 (2011). Web. http://www.frontiersin.org/addictive_disorders/10.3389/fpsyt.2011.00010/full

Substance Abuse and Mental Health Services Administration, Center for Substance Abuse Treatment. "Substance Abuse Treatment Advisory: Protracted Withdrawal." Web. http://hap.samhsa.gov/products/manuals/advisory/pdfs/SATA_Protracted_Withdrawal.pdf.

See also: Depression; Schizophrenia and addiction; Stress and drug misuse; Substance misuse; Withdrawal

Antabuse

CATEGORY: Treatment
ALSO KNOWN AS: Disulfiram
DEFINITION: Antabuse (disulfiram) is classified as an aldehyde dehydrogenase (ALDH) inhibitor and is considered an alcohol-aversive drug. Persons taking disulfiram while also ingesting alcohol will experience a disulfiram-ethanol reaction. This reaction involves a multitude of symptoms, including flushing, sweating, and nausea. Even small amounts of alcohol can produce this pharmacologic response. It is important to remind persons taking disulfiram that alcohol can be absorbed by the body even from common substances such as mouthwash or topical toners. This absorption can lead to a disulfiram-ethanol reaction, also known as acetaldehyde syndrome.

HISTORY OF USE

Disulfiram was discovered in the United States in 1937 by E. E. Williams when employees for the chemical plant Williams worked at were exposed to disulfiram and later experienced physical discomfort upon ingesting alcohol. One of the first medications specifically indicated for alcohol misuse, disulfiram was approved by the US Food and Drug Administration in 1951. Disulfiram was first used in high doses, up to 3,000 milligrams (mg), and was regularly used in the treatment of persons with alcohol dependence or misuse. These high dosages often led to undesired, adverse effects and, on rare occasions, deaths.

Dosing recommendations now are much more conservative. Patients should start with 500 mg as a single daily dose. After one to two weeks, depending on response, the dose may be decreased to a range of 125 to 250 mg daily. Therapy should continue until the patient and the patient's caregiver decide that a full recovery has been achieved; this may take up to a few years in some patients. These dosing requirements represent the minimum drug concentration necessary to achieve the amount of physical discomfort targeted, should the patient ingest alcohol.

Initially used in persons with alcohol dependence, disulfiram also has shown potential benefit in persons addicted to cocaine. Multiple clinical trials on the use of disulfiram for the treatment of cocaine dependence and methamphetamine dependence are in various stages of completion. Disulfiram is estimated to be used by about two hundred thousand alcoholics in the United States. The number of persons treated with disulfiram is far fewer than the estimated seventeen million or more persons with alcohol dependence or misuse in the United States.

EFFECTS AND POTENTIAL RISKS

Disulfiram inhibits aldehyde dehydrogenase (ALDH), the enzyme that converts acetaldehyde to acetate in the liver during the metabolism of alcohol. In the absence of disulfiram, acetaldehyde is quickly converted to acetate. Acetaldehyde levels are increased because of the inhibition of ALDH, which leads to the constellation of adverse effects. The adverse effects occur immediately and can include, at a mild level, headache, facial flushing, and sweating. Effects experienced in a moderate reaction can include nausea, tachycardia, hyperventilation hypotension , and respiratory difficulties. In the most severe reactions, persons can experience serious cardiovascular decomposition, which could lead to death. The severity of the reaction depends on both the dose of disulfiram and the amount of alcohol ingested.

This medication should not be given to anyone without their knowledge and should not be given less than twelve hours after alcohol ingestion because of the risk of an unintended disulfiram-ethanol reaction. Even upon discontinuation of disulfiram treatment, the drug can remain in circulation for up to fourteen days, and alcohol must be avoided during this whole period.

Adherence is another hurdle to success with disulfiram. Studies have shown that supervised medication ingestion or other incentives to take the medication may result in higher rates of adherence. Side effects that occur even without ingestion of alcohol, although generally mild, include drowsiness, headache, and taste disturbances and can lead patients to stop taking the medication.

Disulfiram is available in tablet form and may be crushed and mixed with liquids. Disulfiram use can increase liver function tests into abnormal values and should be monitored before therapy initiation and again a few weeks after beginning therapy. Often, patients with alcohol dependence have underlying liver dysfunction.

Allison C. Bennett PharmD

FOR FURTHER INFORMATION

Pani, P. P., et al. "Disulfiram for the Treatment of Cocaine Dependence." *Cochrane Database of Systematic Reviews* 20.1 (2010): CD007024. Web. 8 Feb. 2012.

Soghoian, Samara, Sage W. Wiener, and Jose Eric Diaz-Alcala. "Toxicity, Disulfiram." *WebMD*. Aug. 2008. Web. 9 Mar. 2011.

Suh, Jesse J., et al. "The Status of Disulfiram: A Half of a Century Later." *Journal of Clinical Psychopharmacology* 26 (2006): 290–302. Print.

Wright, Curtis, and Richard D. Moore. "Disulfiram Treatment of Alcoholism." *American Journal of Medicine* 88 (1990): 647–55. Print.

See also: Addiction medications; Alcoholics Anonymous: The Twelve Steps; Baclofen; Naltrexone

Anticholinergics

CATEGORY: Substances

ALSO KNOWN AS: Angel's trumpet; crazy tea; devil's seed; devil's snare; devil's trumpet; ditch weed; Jamestown weed; Jimson weed; locoweed; madhatter; stinkweed; thornapple

DEFINITION: Anticholinergics, such as Jimson weed, are plants that contain euphoria- and delirium-inducing properties.

STATUS: Legal in the United States

CLASSIFICATION: Noncontrolled substance

SOURCE: Jimson weed is the common name for the plant *Datura stramonium,* a member of the family Solanacea. It is native to most of the United States.

TRANSMISSION ROUTE: All parts of Jimson weed contain anticholinergic compounds. The plant is misused by smoking the dried leaves, ingesting the seeds, or drinking teas made from its leaves.

HISTORY OF USE

Anticholinergic medications, directly derived from plants such as *Datura* species, are used for treating asthma, gastrointestinal disorders, diarrhea, bedwetting, and motion sickness. Such anticholinergic plants contain the alkaloids atropine, hyoscyamine, and scopolamine, all potent inhibitors of the neurotransmitter acetylcholine.

The anticholinergic plant Jimson weed has been used for hundreds of years by Native Americans as a medicine and in religious and social rituals. The ingestion of *Datura* species of plants in Jamestown, Virginia, reportedly caused British soldiers during the Revolutionary War to behave bizarrely.

In modern times, Jimson weed is misused mostly by teenagers and adolescents, and it is usually used one time because of its unpleasant adverse effects. Other anticholinergic plants and medications have the potential for misuse, but most people who routinely use these agents have a significant history of drug misuse, personality disorders , or schizophrenia . In many cases, the overuse and inappropriate use of anticholinergic medications are attempts to treat adverse effects of certain antipsychotic agents. Sometimes, anticholinergic medications are combined with other illegal street drugs, such as heroin, to enhance the effect of the illicit drug.

EFFECTS AND POTENTIAL RISKS

Symptoms of anticholinergic toxicity, which may appear within minutes of ingestion of plant extracts, include increased heart rate, dry mouth, agitation, nausea, vomiting, incoherence, disorientation, auditory and visual hallucinations, dilated pupils, slurred speech, urinary retention, and high blood pressure. High doses may cause seizures, paralysis, coma, or death. Anticholinergic toxicity also may cause damage to liver and muscle tissues, and it can cause cardiac arrhythmias. The anticholinergic effects may last for several days.

Jennifer L. Gibson PharmD

FOR FURTHER INFORMATION

Centers for Disease Control and Prevention. "Jimsonweed Poisoning Associated with a Homemade Stew: Maryland, 2008." *Morbidity and Mortality Weekly Report* 59.4 (2010): 102–4. Print.

Graeme, Kimberlie A. "Anticholinergic Plants (Tropane Alkaloids)." *Wilderness Medicine*. Ed. Paul S. Auerbach. 5th ed. Philadelphia: Mosby, 2007.

Wiebe, Tannis H., Eric S. Sigurdson, and Laurence Y. Katz. "Angel's Trumpet (*Datura stramonium*) Poisoning and Delirium in Adolescents in Winnipeg, Manitoba: Summer 2006." *Paediatric and Child Health* 13.3 (2008): 193–96. Print.

See also: Hallucinogen misuse; Hallucinogen's effects on the body; Psychosis and substance misuse

---

Anxiety

CATEGORY: Psychological issues and behaviors

DEFINITION: Many people feel anxious when faced with a challenge, and for some, that anxiety can help them to better perform a given task. Anxiety also can be useful when it alerts people to potential threats or dangers. In these situations, anxiety can help a person to be aware of his or her surroundings, and to act accordingly. However, for some people, anxiety can become overwhelming and interfere with their everyday lives, manifesting as anxiety disorder. Common anxiety disorders include generalized anxiety disorder, generalized anxiety disorder, panic disorder, panic disorder, obsessive-compulsive disorder, obsessive-compulsive disorder, post-traumatic stress disorder, post-traumatic stress disorder, and social anxiety disorder, social anxiety disorder.

INTRODUCTION

The paradoxical nature of anxiety is perhaps best understood by the Yerkes-Dodson law. The law states that there is a relationship between arousal and performance on a task. On a graph where the x-axis represents performance on a given task and the y-axis represents arousal level, an inverted "u" shape was noted. This observation indicates that at a marginal level of arousal, performance potential is minimal, at a moderate level of arousal, performance is maximized, and at a high level of arousal performance again is minimal. One can ascertain from this law that a moderate degree of arousal, or anxiety, actually maximizes performance; however, elevated (or minimal) anxiety actually decreases performance. As such, not all anxiety is inherently unhealthy and maladaptive. As our distant ancestors who trekked across the land in search of food and shelter would attest, a healthy level of anxiety would aid in either avoiding potential predators, or help in finding the necessary strength and will to find food to survive.

However, for some individuals, the threat level associated with novel or ambiguous stimuli can be misinterpreted, and an over exaggerated avoidance response may occur. The anxious reaction can become so overwhelming that the person is unable to function as they desire, such as being unable to engage in routine daily activities. The development of such disordered behavior can take the form of several anxiety disorders, such as: Generalized Anxiety Disorder, Panic Disorder, Agoraphobia, specific phobia, and Social Anxiety Disorder. Post-traumatic stress and Obsessive-Compulsive Disorder, while classified as anxiety disorders in previous editions of the DSM, were given their own separate chapters ("Trauma and stressor-related disorders and Obsessive-Compulsive and related disorders, respectively) in the DSM 5, and will therefore not be discussed within this article. Although, Separation Anxiety Disorder and Selective Mutism have been re-classified into the diagnostic category of anxiety disorders, they will not be described here as they typically present in childhood.

ANXIETY DISORDERS

Anxiety disorders are the most commonly diagnosed psychiatric illness in the United States of America. Recent estimates indicate that at least 40 million adults in the U.S. are diagnosed with an anxiety disorder. Symptoms of each anxiety disorder may vary, and understanding the diagnostic criteria of each can aid in understanding how anxiety may lead to addiction, and how addiction may lead to the development of anxiety.

Generalized anxiety disorder (GAD). GAD is characterized by persistent, excessive, unrealistic worry about things that is disproportional to the stimulus. A diagnosis of GAD is made when this form of excessive worry regarding common stressors is present for a minimum of six months. Additional symptoms of GAD may include physical symptoms such as muscle tension, fatigue, restlessness, and difficulty obtaining quality sleep on a consistent basis; as well as gastrointestinal symptoms such as stomach discomfort, vomiting, and diarrhea.

Panic disorder. Panic disorder is characterized by intense fear, bodily discomfort (such as elevated heart rate, sweating, bodily uneasiness, difficulty breathing, chills or flushed face and dizziness), and feelings of impending doom or demise. These symptoms often present without warning, and are typically overwhelming and debilitating. Those with chronic panic episodes often live in fear of when their next attack may occur. Typically, panic episodes last at least several minutes, however may last for a half an hour or more for some individuals.

Agoraphobia. Agoraphobia is characterized by an intense fear related to large crowds, open spaces, or any place that the person perceives to be unsafe, often with an absence of clear escape. Agoraphobia was previously classified as co-occurring with panic disorder, however the disorder has been given its own diagnostic category in the DSM 5. Typically, those with agoraphobia avoid locations that would trigger an anxious reaction, such as grocery stores, airports, shopping malls and public spaces.

Specific phobia. The hallmark of a specific phobia is an intense and irrational fear related to an object, creature, item, situation, etc. The fear reaction often leads to an avoidance of the object, or place or situation wherein the perceived threat may be or occur. When the situation or item is presented, an immediate feeling of fear or overwhelming nervousness is present. Several hundred specific phobias have been documented, ranging from more common (e.g. arachnophobia, the fear of spiders; acrophobia, the fear of heights), to more obscure (e.g. anthophobia, the fear of flowers; arachibutyrophobia, the fear of peanut butter being stuck to the roof of one's mouth).

Social anxiety disorder. Social anxiety disorder is characterized by an excessive and irrational fear of social situations. Those with social anxiety disorder often anticipate they will behave in a way that evokes embarrassment and/or humiliation when in a social setting. In general, the classic symptom of social anxiety disorder is the avoidance of situations in which the individual will be forced to interact socially. Additional symptoms may include: elevated heart rate, bodily discomfort and uneasiness, and possible gastro-intestinal distress such as upset stomach or diarrhea. The individual may consciously or unconsciously evoke those symptoms of anxiety as a means of avoiding social situations.

ANXIETY AND SUBSTANCE USE

Although the disorders described vary in terms of diagnostic criteria, a common thread amongst anxiety disorders is an excessive or irrational level of arousal. To manage this intense emotional reaction, individuals may steer towards the use of substances. Substances that suppress arousal of the Central Nervous System (i.e. alcohol, marijuana, opioids, etc.) are commonly used for this purpose; their long term use, however, may lead to the development of addiction.

The long-term, sustained use of these substances often leads to the development of tolerance, which requires the user to increase the frequency or intensity of use. A person who is legally prescribed an opiate for chronic pain, for example, may initially use the substance as prescribed; however the continuation of physical pain may lead to an increase in use, ultimately leading to addiction. A person who uses marijuana to unwind following a stressful day at work may soon feel the need to increase the quantity and use of the substance to cope with prolonged stress. What initially may begin as self-medicating can, therefore, develop into long-term, chronic substance misuse.

Additionally, the use of substances may also lead to the development of anxiety. For example, the use of stimulating substances (e.g. cocaine, amphetamines, etc.) may cause psycho-physiological symptoms (e.g. elevated heart rate, sweating, nervousness, worry, panic and difficulty obtaining quality sleep on a consistent basis), that may elucidate an anxious reaction. The user may then increase the frequency and intensity of substance use to manage the symptoms, leading to an unhealthy cycle of self-created anxiety and self-medication. The longer this cycle persists untreated, the more difficult it becomes to break.

Robert S. Cavera, PsyD

FOR FURTHER INFORMATION

Buckner, J. D. (2014). "Dual Diagnosis Cases: Treating Comorbid Social Anxiety Disorder and Substance Abuse or Dependence." In *The Wiley Blackwell Handbook of Social Anxiety Disorder*, J. W. Weeks (Ed.).

Milosevic, I., Chudzik, S. M., Boyd, S., & McCabe, R. E. (2017). "Evaluation of an integrated group cognitive-behavioral treatment for comorbid mood, anxiety, and substance use disorders: A pilot study." *Journal of anxiety disorders*, *46*, 85-100.

Vázquez, G. H., Forte, A., Camino, S., Tondo, L., & Baldessarini, R. J. (2017). "Treatment implications

for bipolar disorder co-occurring with anxiety syndromes and substance abuse." *The Treatment of Bipolar Disorder: Integrative Clinical Strategies and Future Directions.*

See also: Addiction; Anxiety medication misuse; Obsessive-compulsive disorder (OCD); Panic disorders and addiction; Post-traumatic stress and addiction; Self-medication; Valium

Anxiety medication misuse

CATEGORY: Substance misuse
ALSO KNOWN AS: Anxiolytic medication misuse; Anxiolytic medication misuse
DEFINITION: Anxiolytic medications are typically prescribed to reduce the symptoms of anxiety and panic attacks. Anxiety medication misuse occurs when these drugs are used for reasons other than what is instructed by a health care provider. In some instances, individuals seeking anxiety relief may take more than their prescribed amount, which may lead to feelings of euphoria. These medications are taken more frequently, at a greater dose, or for a longer period of time than directed to produce changes in one's mental or physical state. This combined feeling of relief of emotional stressors with a compounded "high-like" sensation can lead to misuse of these medications.

OVERVIEW

Clinically significant anxiety that requires treatment is defined as generalized anxiousness or worry that is difficult to control, causes stress that impairs an individual's ability to function or perform activities of daily living, and occurs on a majority of days over a span of at least six months. Pharmacologic relief for these symptoms is typically prescribed by myriad specialists including physicians, physician assistants, nurse practitioners, naturopaths, podiatrists and dentists. The specialists most often prescribing anti-anxiety medication are psychiatrists.

The most commonly misused class of anxiety medications are benzodiazepines, and the most frequently misused benzodiazepine is alprazolam (Xanax), believed to be due to the increasing frequency with

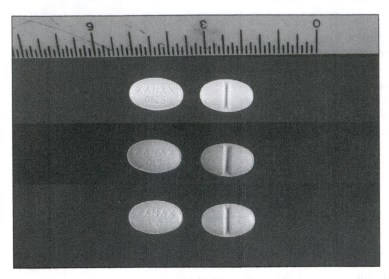

The most frequently misused benzodiazepine is alprazolam (Xanax) because of the frequency with which physicians prescribe this medication. (United States Department of Justice, via Wikimedia Commons)

which physicians are prescribing this medication. Other common types of benzodiazepines are clonazepam (Klonopin), diazepam (Valium), and lorazepam (Ativan). Additional classes of anxiety medications, such as selective serotonin reuptake inhibitors (SSRIs), are not as popular with misusers, although there have been reports of recreational use of SSRIs and other anxiety drugs. Tolerance and physical dependence may occur after a short time of misuse, causing people to use larger quantities of medication to produce the same effects and to avoid withdrawal symptoms.

RISK FACTORS

The adolescent Caucasian population is most often affected by anxiety medication misuse although all ethnicities, ages, and genders have affected by anxiolytic drug misuse. Adolescents are at particularly high risk because of the ability to obtain the substance from a friend or from a family member who is prescribed the medication.

Alcohol misusers and persons with a psychiatric diagnosis are also at high risk for anxiety medication misuse. Those who are contemplating suicide are more likely to add benzodiazepine medications to alcohol. Misusers of illegal drugs, such as opiates (heroin and methadone), marijuana, and cocaine,

may also misuse anxiolytic drugs. Within the substance use disorders population, it is more likely for an illicit substance misuser to secondarily misuse a benzodiazepine than it is for a benzodiazepine misuser to secondarily begin abusing other illegal substances.

SYMPTOMS

While these drugs are typically considered safe and effective when taken at the prescribed dosage, they may lead to significant and life-threatening symptoms when misused. Benzodiazepines are intended to produce a calming and drowsy sensation to reduce anxiety or panic attacks by depressing the central nervous system. Persons who misuse the drug seek the euphoria and extreme sleepiness that occurs when taken in excess quantity. When combined with other illegal substances, especially opiates, the benzodiazepines often enhance or extend the other drug's high. Additionally, anxiety medication may counteract the unwanted effects of abusing other illegal substances.

Adverse effects of misuse include confusion, lack of coordination, impaired memory, tachycardia, hallucinations, and coma. Although rare, case reports of death have also been documented. Some publications in the medical literature report that when compared with other benzodiazepines, the greatest risk for death is with alprazolam misuse. Withdrawal symptoms, such as nausea, tremors, abdominal cramps, sweating, and seizures, may also result from sudden discontinuation of the drugs.

SCREENING AND DIAGNOSIS

A urine drug-screen will detect the presence of benzodiazepines. Because anxiety medication misuse often occurs in conjunction with other illegal substance or alcohol misuse, physicians often screen patients for concurrent disorders before prescribing anxiety medications. Inquiring about other psychological diagnoses also helps to identify misuse potential in prospective patients.

TREATMENT AND THERAPY

As with many substances of misuse, a gradual tapering of medication is involved in the process of detoxification and done in an effort to minimize withdrawal symptoms. Persons who misuse anxiety medications seek treatment less frequently than those who misuse illegal substances or alcohol; those who have an addiction may be referred to Narcotics Anonymous or Pills Anonymous to complete their accredited and peer reviewed program. Individual or group inpatient or outpatient therapy has proven effective for treating underlying anxiety, coexisting mental health disorders, or substance use disorder problems.

PREVENTION

When prescribing medications, physicians review the risks and benefits for their patients, including the medication's misuse potential. Additionally, pharmacists and physicians often verify that a patient is not filling excessive prescriptions for the same medication. There are many gatekeepers to avoid medication misuse, but knowledge of misuse potential by the physician and by the patient can help prevent the problem before it occurs.

Janet Ober Berman MS, CGC;
Updated by Zachary Sax, DPM

FOR FURTHER INFORMATION

"Anxiety or Substance Use Disorder: Which Comes First?" Anxiety and Depression Association of America. Jan 2018. Web 20 July 2018.

Lader, Malcolm. Anxiolytic drugs: dependence, addiction and abuse. European Neuropsychopharmacology , Volume 4 , Issue 2 , 85 - 91.

Schmitz, Allison. "Benzodiazepine use, misuse, and abuse: A review." Mental Health Clinician, 6, 3, (120), (2016).

Smith JP, Book SW. Anxiety and Substance Use Disorders: A Review. The Psychiatric times. 2008;25(10):19-23.

Substance abuse and mental health services association. What is substance abuse treatment: A book for families Department of Health and Human Services, 2014.

See also: Anxiety; Benzodiazepine misuse; Panic disorders and addiction; Valium

Autoerotic asphyxiation

CATEGORY: Behavioral addictions
ALSO KNOWN AS: Hypoxphilia
DEFINITION: Autoerotic asphyxiation , also known as hypoxyphilia, is an act of reducing the flow of oxygen to the brain to heighten sexual arousal and orgasm. The blood flow to the brain is reduced by self-hanging, intentional strangling, or suffocation. Autoerotic asphyxiation is most commonly practiced by males and is usually a solitary act. Autoerotic asphyxiators use cords, belts, ropes, neckties, scarves, or plastic bags to strangle or suffocate themselves while masturbating. Autoerotic asphyxiation is also practiced with a partner as a form of sexual masochism .

CAUSES

There is no known cause for autoerotic asphyxiation. Some experts believe the practice may be related to childhood trauma, such as sexual abuse. Others believe it may stem from an anxiety about death. The anxiety is relieved, and sexual gratification is obtained, by repeatedly "cheating death."

RISK FACTORS

There are no known factors that predispose a person to engage in autoerotic asphyxiation. People who practice autoerotic asphyxiation are often involved in otherwise healthy relationships. However, there are some comorbidities that can be associated with the practice of autoerotic asphyxiation, including mood disorders, anxiety disorders, and other forms of masochism, sadism, and fetishism .

People who play the choking game as adolescents or teenagers also may be predisposed to practicing autoerotic asphyxiation. The choking game is "played" by depriving the brain of oxygen through strangulation or by hugging a person from behind until he or she passes out. The choking game produces a feeling of euphoria and, therefore, is used as a means of getting high.

SYMPTOMS

Autoerotic asphyxiation is a dangerous practice that can end in death. Because it is normally a solitary act that is practiced behind locked doors, it may be difficult to determine if a person is at risk. However, there are some signs and symptoms, including the following: unexplained bruises on the neck; bloodshot eyes; bed sheets, belts, ties, or ropes tied in strange knots and found in unusual places; frequent, severe headaches; disorientation after being alone; wearing high-neck shirts or scarves in warm weather; locked bedroom or bathroom doors; and wear marks on bed posts or closet rods. Aside from death, there are some potential complications that are associated with autoerotic asphyxiation, including heart attack and permanent brain damage.

SCREENING AND DIAGNOSIS

Each year, as many as one thousand people in the United States are found dead—naked or partially naked—hanging by their necks in their bedroom closets (or in similar positions). Sexual paraphernalia is often found nearby.

People who practice autoerotic asphyxiation do not intend to kill themselves. They often devise some sort of safety mechanism that is intended to prevent accidental death in case they lose consciousness. Safety mechanisms may include slip knots or hanging from something that is shorter than they are. These safety mechanisms often fail because the person becomes disoriented and is unable to take the necessary steps to restore the flow of oxygen. Many people also mistakenly believe that autoerotic asphyxiation with a partner is safe because they assume that the partner can remove the object that is cutting off the flow of oxygen after the person who is being asphyxiated loses consciousness.

It is difficult to diagnose autoerotic asphyxiation because it often goes undetected until it results in death. People who practice autoerotic asphyxiation tend to go to great lengths to keep it a secret; most do not discuss it with peers, parents, or clinicians.

Screening for autoerotic asphyxiation requires that clinicians be knowledgeable about autoerotic asphyxiation, its signs and symptoms, and other related risky behaviors, such as the choking game. It may be helpful for clinicians to begin a discussion about autoerotic asphyxiation with people who are assumed to be engaging in the practice by approaching the subject in a nonsexual way. Instead of focusing on the sexual aspects or autoerotic asphyxiation, the clinician could focus on the dangers of getting high by self-hanging, strangulation, or suffocation.

TREATMENT AND THERAPY

Treatment for autoerotic asphyxiation may include a combination of cognitive behavior therapy and medication. Common medications for the treatment of autoerotic asphyxiation include selective serotonin reuptake inhibitors and antiandrogens .

PREVENTION

Education is key to the prevention of autoerotic asphyxiation. Education about the dangers of the choking game and about autoerotic asphyxiation may take place both at home and as part of sex education classes at school.

Once the behavior has started, many children begin looking for a way to perform autoerotic asphyxiation safely, so they need to be told that there is no safe way to do it. Clinicians should also be educated about autoerotic asphyxiation. Education could be incorporated into medical, nursing, and psychology curricula, and into primary care, psychiatry, and emergency medicine residency programs.

Julie Henry

FOR FURTHER INFORMATION

Cowell, Daniel. "Autoerotic Asphyxiation: Secret Pleasure, Lethal Outcome." *Pediatrics* 124.5 (2009): 1319–24. Print.

Hucker, Stephen. "Hypoxphylia/Auto-Erotic Asphyxia." Web. 13 Feb. 2012. http://www.forensic-psychiatry.ca/paraphilia/aea.htm.

"Paraphilias." Web. 13 Feb. 2012. http://www.medicinenet.com/paraphilia/article.htm#.

Sheleg, Sergey, and Edwin Ehrlich. *Autoerotic Asphyxiation: Forensic, Medical, and Social Aspects.* Tucson, AZ: Wheatmark, 2006. Print.

Warner, Jennifer. "Some Docs in the Dark about Choking Game." Web. 13 Feb. 2012. http://www.webmd.com/parenting/news/20091214/some-docs-in-the-dark-about-choking-game

See also: Anxiety; Behavioral addictions: Overview; Choking game; Marriage/partnership and behavioral addictions

B

Baclofen

CATEGORY: Treatment

ALSO KNOWN AS: Lioresal

DEFINITION: Baclofen is a skeletal-muscle relaxant, primarily administered for the treatment of reversible muscle spasticity and mobility impairments associated with spinal cord injury, multiple sclerosis, cerebral palsy, or various neuralgias. It has been investigated as a treatment for addiction and dependence disorders.

HISTORY OF USE

Baclofen was developed to control seizures in persons with epilepsy ; however, its effectiveness for this treatment has been inadequate. Instead, baclofen has evolved into a treatment of choice for spasticity related conditions.

Baclofen was introduced as a possible addiction treatment when physician Olivier Ameisen self-treated his alcohol addiction with high-dose baclofen. His results were published in a self-case study report in the journal *Alcohol and Alcoholism* in 2005, prompting the public and the medical community to evaluate the use of baclofen to treat addiction.

EFFECTIVENESS

According to research, baclofen suppresses symptoms and cravings associated with alcohol dependence and reduces symptoms of alcohol withdrawal. Baclofen works by activating the gamma amino-butyric acid (B) receptors in the central nervous system. Baclofen is safe and effective, even in persons with alcohol-related liver damage. Baclofen possesses no misuse potential, has limited drug interactions, and causes fewer side effects than traditional medications used to treat alcohol dependence.

Baclofen is also being investigated as a treatment for cocaine- and opioid-dependence and misuse disorders. Large-scale clinical trials are needed to prove the long-term safety and effectiveness of baclofen in the treatment of substance misuse disorders.

PRECAUTIONS

High doses of baclofen can cause excessive drowsiness, dizziness, psychiatric disturbances, and decreased muscle tone that may impair daily function. Overdoses of baclofen may precipitate seizures, slowed breathing, altered pupil size, and coma . Abrupt discontinuation of baclofen can result in withdrawal symptoms, including hallucinations, disorientation, anxiety, dizziness, memory impairments, and mood disturbances.

Owing to increased publicity regarding baclofen as a potential treatment for addictions, some people have turned to illegally buying baclofen over the Internet in an attempt to control their addictions. As with any medication, baclofen should be used only under the guidance and supervision of a trained medical professional.

Jennifer L. Gibson PharmD

FOR FURTHER INFORMATION

Ameisen, Olivier. "Complete and Prolonged Suppression of Symptoms and Consequences of Alcohol-Dependence Using High-Dose Baclofen: A Self-Case Report of a Physician." *Alcohol and Alcoholism* 40.2 (2005): 147–50. Print.

---. *The End of My Addiction.* New York: Farrar, 2008. Print.

Leggio, Lorenzo, J. C. Garbutt, and G. Addlorato. "Effectiveness and Safety of Baclofen in the Treatment of Alcohol Dependent Patients." *CNS and Neurological Disorders Drug Targets* 9.1 (2010): 33–44. Print. /

Swift, Robert, and Lorenzo Leggio. "Adjunctive Pharmacotherapy in the Treatment of Alcohol Dependence." *Evidence-Based Addiction Treatment.* Ed. Peter M. Miller. New York: Academic, 2009. Print.

See also: Addiction medications; Alcohol misuse; Self-medication; Treatment methods and research; Withdrawal

Barbiturates

CATEGORY: Substances

ALSO KNOWN AS: Central nervous system depressants; sedative-hypnotics

DEFINITION: Barbiturates are a family of central nervous system depressant drugs with considerable potential for harm. Historically, they have played important roles in the treatment of sleep disorders, anxiety, anesthetics, and seizures. Largely replaced by benzodiazepines, they retain clinical usefulness mainly as anticonvulsants and anesthetics.

STATUS: Prescription drugs

CLASSIFICATION: Schedule II, III, or IV controlled substances

SOURCE: Barbiturates are synthetic compounds with no natural sources.

TRANSMISSION ROUTE: Routes of administration include by tablet and oral elixir (common) and intravenous (infrequent).

HISTORY OF USE

In 1903, Emil Fischer and Joseph von Mering discovered an effective sedative, diethylbarbituric acid or barbital, which entered medicine under the trade name Veronal. Another barbiturate, phenobarbital (Luminal), was introduced in 1912 and continues to be used as an anticonvulsant. By the mid-twentieth century, barbiturates became the most widely used sedative-hypnotic medication and the most popular substances of misuse. Collectively referred to as "downers" because they were effective in depressing the central nervous system, barbiturates were taken alone or with alcohol (ethanol) to produce a feeling of relaxation and euphoria. In the United States, barbiturate misuse and addiction markedly increased in the 1950s and 1960s. The drugs became especially popular with people who experienced high levels of stress, anxiety, or panic attacks.

The beginning of the twenty-first century saw a modest increase in usage of barbiturates as substances of misuse. Some drug specialists attribute this increase to the desire of drug users to seek out the relaxing, calming, and disinhibiting effects of barbiturates as a means to counteract stimulant drugs such as cocaine and methamphetamines. According to a national survey on drug use and health by the US Substance Abuse and Mental Health Services Administration, an estimated 3.1 million people (approximately 9%) age twelve years and older had misused barbiturates.

Barbiturates today are used clinically for treatment of seizures that last longer than five minutes or occur close together before a person regains consciousness (status epilepticus). Barbiturates are also used for anesthesia, pediatric sedation, migraines and insomnia. One particular barbiturate, pentobarbital, is the drug of choice for veterinary anesthesia and euthanasia.

PHARMACOLOGICAL AND PSYCHOLOGICAL EFFECTS

Barbiturates are classified according to their duration of action. The effects of ultra-short-acting drugs, such as Pentothal (used in surgical settings as an anesthesia), last less than one hour. Short-acting barbiturates (such as Nembutal and Seconal) act for three to four hours and are more likely to be taken for recreational purposes. The effects of intermediate-acting barbiturates (such as Amytal) last for six to eight hours, and the effects of long-acting barbiturates (such as Veronal and Luminal) that are taken as anticonvulsants last approximately twelve hours. Like other sedative-hypnotic drugs, barbiturates produce relaxation or sleep. Barbiturates are not analgesic. If an individual is experiencing moderate or high levels of pain, they will be less effective in producing sedation or sleep. The mechanism underlying their effect is thought to be an enhancement of the neural inhibition induced by the neurotransmitter gamma-aminobutyric acid (GABA) at the receptor. Additionally, barbiturates directly open the chloride channel on cell membranes without GABA.

Although barbiturates can produce sleep, the quality of sleep can be far from normal. The stage of sleep referred to as rapid eye movement (REM) is markedly suppressed. Since this stage is associated with dreaming, the frequency of dreams can be dramatically reduced. For individuals experiencing withdrawal, dreaming can become excessive and more vivid during this period where the brain attempts to make up for lost time spent in REM. The term "REM rebound" is used to describe this phenomenon and it can frequently bring on insomnia. However, more significant and noticeable changes brought on by barbiturates include their capacity to act as a cognitive inhibitor. Memory functioning can be compromised along with alterations of judgment, decision making, insight, and planning. An above-regular dosage of barbiturates induces a state of intoxication similar to that caused by alcohol. Mild intoxication is characterized by drunk-like behavior with slurred speech, unsteady gait, lack of coordination, abnormal eye movements, and an absence of alcohol odor. Driving prior to the drug being completely metabolized and eliminated is considered dangerous.

At regular doses, the effects of barbiturates vary depending on the user's previous experience with the drug, the setting of use, and the mode of administration. A particular dose taken in the evening, for example, may induce sleep, whereas it may produce relaxed contentment, euphoria, and diminished motor skills during the day. Some users report sedation, fatigue, unpleasant drowsiness, nausea, vomiting, and diarrhea. A paradoxical state of excitement or rage also can occur. Users may experience a "hangover" phenomenon the day after drug administration. Hypersensitivity reactions, sensitivity to sunlight (photosensitivity), decreased sexual function, and impaired memory also have been reported.

POTENTIAL RISKS, DRUG MISUSE AND DEPENDENCE

Although barbiturates have been around for over 100 years, there has been a steep and rapid decline in their clinical uses. Compared to the number of prescriptions written for barbiturates during the 1970s, today, they are rarely used. Two primary factors are responsible for the change. First, safer drug alternatives have been developed. An example of this would be the use of benzodiazepines in the treatment of anxiety disorders. Secondly, barbiturates, overall, have been found to be extremely dangerous to use effectively. They have become associated with numerous deaths, widespread dependency and misuse, and have been found to interact deleteriously with many other drugs. Barbiturates are extremely dangerous when combined with alcohol since both drugs are central nervous system depressants and they produced a synergistic, exaggerated effect when taken together.

One reason these drugs pose a significant risk is due to the fact the therapeutic dosage of any barbiturate is close to its lethal dose. Because of this narrow therapeutic window, severe intoxication or drug-induced death can easily occur. Intentional or accidental overdose results in extreme drowsiness, respiratory depression (with slow breathing), hypotension, hypothermia, renal failure, decreased reflexes, and, ultimately, coma and death. In addition, taking barbiturates over a period of months can induce tolerance

---

Medicines Classified as Barbiturates

- Amytal sodium
- Butisol sodium
- Luminal
- Nembutal sodium
- Phenobarbital
- Seconal sodium

---

whereby the sedative effects (not so much the depressant effects on respiration) diminish over time. This requires higher dosages to achieve the same clinical benefits. Eventually, the therapeutic window mentioned above is narrowed even further making barbiturate usage unacceptably dangerous.

Both physical and psychological dependence can result with normal clinical doses. This potential for misuse, particularly for short and intermediate acting barbiturates, contributed to the medical communities' movement away from using barbiturates if other drug alternatives were available. Physical dependence is characterized by withdrawal symptoms during periods of drug cessation. Withdrawal symptoms may include restlessness, disorientation, hallucinations, hyper-excitability, delirium, convulsions, and possibly death. Barbiturate dependency, followed by abrupt termination of drug use, can be extremely dangerous. Persons who want to stop taking these drugs should do so under medical supervision only.

The amount of barbiturates needed to reach a toxic dose which causes an overdose can vary considerably. However, in most circumstances, a dose of one gram of the majority of barbiturates leads to serious poisoning. Ingesting two to ten grams frequently causes death. A person with suspected barbiturate overdose should be seen by a physician without delay. In a 2016 study published about 277 people admitted to a hospital emergency room for drug overdose, investigators found that 19.5% had taken barbiturates. It was also found that these individuals needed to be monitored more closely since they had a higher risk for incurring additional medical implications. In some instances, the overdose was a deliberate attempt to die. Among advocates of euthanasia and among those who commit suicide, barbiturates remain one of the most commonly employed drugs.

Mihaela Avramut MD, PhD;
Updated by Bryan C. Auday, PhD

FOR FURTHER INFORMATION

Advokat, Claire D., Joseph E. Comaty, and Robert M. Julien. *Julien's Primer of Drug Action: A Comprehensive Guide to the Actions, Uses, and Side Effects of Psychoactive Drugs.* 13th ed. New York: Worth, 2014. This guide will not only address the topic of barbiturates, but it will place the topic within a broader context of additional drugs used as medicines for psychological and psychiatric disorders.

Hori, Satoshi and Kosaku Kinoshita. "Clinical characteristics of patients who overdose on multiple

psychotropic drugs in Tokyo." *The Journal of Toxicological Sciences.* Vol.41, No.6, (2016) 765-773. This article takes a close look at the specific drugs which caused an overdose and led to the admission to an emergency room.

Howard, Sherrel. "Benzodiazepines and Barbiturates." *Drugs of Abuse: Pharmacology and Molecular Mechanisms.* Ames: Wiley, 2014. 77–92. This chapter provides in-depth material regarding how barbiturates interact with the central nervous system.

Jones, Keith. (Ed.). *Drug Abuse Sourcebook (Health Reference Series)* 5th ed. Detroit: Omnigraphics Inc., (2016). This book is an excellent resource for learning about drugs that are commonly misused.

Marion, Nancy E., and Willard M. Oliver. *Drugs in American Society: An Encyclopedia of History, Politics, Culture, and the Law.* Santa Barbara: ABC-CLIO, 2014. This resource places the topic of drugs within a broader historical and cultural context.

Weaver, Michael F. "Prescription Sedative Misuse and Abuse." *Yale Journal of Biology and Medicine* 88.3 (2015): 247–56. This article addresses the use of barbiturates, as well as other drugs, for the purpose of a sleeping aid.

See also: Anesthesia misuse; Controlled substances and precursor chemicals; Depressants misuse; Prescription drug addiction: Overview; Stress and drug misuse

Behavioral addictions: Overview

CATEGORY: Psychological issues and behaviors, psychological issues and behaviors, behavioral addictions overview

DEFINITION: Behavioral addictions are patterns of behavior that follow a cycle similar to that of substance dependence. Behavioral addictions begin when a person experiences pleasure in association with a behavior, initially as a way of enhancing his or her experience of life and, later, as a way of coping with stress. The process of seeking out and engaging in the behavior becomes more frequent and ritualized, until it becomes a significant part of the person's daily life. The person experiences urges or cravings to engage in the behavior that intensifies until he or she carries out the behavior again; these urges or cravings usually lead to relief and elation. Someone who cannot control or stop an activity, even after experiencing adverse consequences, has become a person with a behavioral addiction.

TYPES OF BEHAVIORAL ADDICTIONS

Compulsive Gambling Addiction

A person is said to have a gambling addiction, gambling addiction when they feel compelled to gamble and do so regardless of monetary loss. The person takes game-playing, in which a person has a chance to win, to an extreme level. Compulsive gamblers feel a rush or a high from gambling that further motivates them.

Causes. People who have a family history of addiction may be more likely to become addicted to gambling themselves. Some research points to a biological component. People with gambling addiction may have a deficiency of the neurotransmitter serotonin in the brain. Other causes of gambling addiction include emotional immaturity, having friends and associates who are involved in gambling, having low self-esteem, and experiencing stress without an outlet.

Symptoms. Persons with a gambling addiction may exhibit several behavioral symptoms, including becoming defensive if someone expresses concern about their gambling habits, borrowing money or selling belongings so they can continue to gamble, feeling anxious or depressed when they are unable to gamble, lying about how much they are betting and how much they have lost, and taking time from work or family life to gamble.

Consequences. People with gambling addiction will likely have financial, relational, and, in some cases, legal problems. They may be unable to pay their bills. Relational problems may develop because a loved one or a family member may have a problem with his or her excessive gambling and spending. Gamblers desperate for money may resort to illegal activities to support their addiction.

Treatment and therapy. The first step in getting help is acknowledging the symptoms and admitting that there is a problem. A program such as Gamblers Anonymous can be effective. Staying in recovery involves avoiding places that offer gambling and finding friends who do not gamble. Those who are struggling with this addiction are supported in finding new strategies for dealing with stress because stress can act as a trigger and cause a relapse.

Sex Addiction

Sex addiction, sex addiction is a compulsive need or desire to have sex, to masturbate, to participate in one-time sexual affairs, to regularly use prostitutes, to engage in voyeurism, or to obsessively think about sex. A person with sex addiction uses sex to get a rush, to deal with stress, or to escape from negative feelings. For them, sexual activities interfere with their everyday lives.

Causes. Family history may influence whether a person becomes addicted to sex. Having a parent who acted out sexually increases the likelihood that a child will grow up thinking the behavior is appropriate. Growing up in a home with distant or abusive parents also may lead to sexual addiction. Another cause may lie in brain chemistry. Antidepressant medications help to control symptoms, indicating that the problem has to do with insufficient levels of certain neurotransmitters in the brain. The act of having sex and an orgasm releases a powerful feeling of euphoria, prompting continuance of the behavior.

Symptoms. Individuals with sex addiction may have much sex, but not necessarily enjoyable sex. They use sex as a coping mechanism instead of a way to interact with a partner. Some of their behaviors may involve looking at pornography, excessive masturbation, exhibitionism, extramarital affairs, multiple sexual partners, voyeurism, phone sex, and inordinate viewing of Internet pornography.

Consequences. The negative consequences of sex addiction include arrest and criminal charges; debts from buying pornography, paying for prostitutes, or phone sex; sexually transmitted diseases; and relationship problems, including separation and divorce.

Treatment and therapy. The first step in treatment is to stop the behavior. A period of abstinence gives the person time to focus on finding the cause of the addiction. Treatments can include individual or group therapy sessions at a rehabilitation center. He or she must learn new coping skills and learn how to have healthy sexual relationships. Lifelong abstinence is not the goal. Support groups such as Sex Addicts Anonymous may be helpful, and prescribed medications such as Prozac or Anafranil can help to deal with the obsessive-compulsive aspect of the addiction.

Pornography Addiction

A person is considered to be addicted to pornography, pornography addiction (porn) if that person's interest in looking at pornographic images goes from something that is a casual part of life to the focus of a good portion of their time and energy. A person addicted to porn uses this medium as a way to deal with stress, worries, or emotional upset and to get a high from seeing images that feed into their sexual fantasies. Individual with pornography addiction accumulate large collections of porn or spend a great deal of time viewing Internet porn.

Causes. For some, the cause of their addiction can be traced to childhood. He or she may have been exposed to inappropriate images as a child and may have then fixated on and fantasized about what they had seen. Others may have begun using porn as a way to cope with physical, emotional, or sexual abuse experienced in childhood.

Symptoms. A person who is addicted to porn may devote a large amount of time to thinking about pornographic images and to planning porn viewing. They spend much time watching porn in secret or they visit strip clubs or adult bookstores excessively, while lying about their activities. These persons may even forgo sexual relations in favor of looking at porn. Persons addicted to porn may be unable to have successful sexual relationships because their views of sex have become skewed by this addiction.

Consequences. Being addicted to porn can have several negative consequences, both for the one addicted and for the spouse or partner. Relationships are often strained if one person is addicted to porn and the other is repulsed by it. A person with pornography addiction also may have sexual performance problems, preferring porn over physical sex. This can result in significant problems for those with a partner.

Treatment and therapy. Help can come from a therapist who works with clients individually with cognitive-behavior therapy, or they can investigate rehabilitation centers that provide treatment programs. A person who has "quit" porn needs follow-up care and support from others who have struggled with this addiction to avoid returning to former patterns of addiction.

Compulsive Eating Disorder: Food Addiction

For a person addicted to food, the obsession goes well beyond enjoying a good meal. A food obsessed person is out of control, even when he or she understands the dangers associated with eating too much. When not actually eating, these individuals are thinking about their next snack or meal. Food is their "drug" of choice, and many food eat much more food then they need as a form of self-medication.

Causes. Food addicted individuals often eat to improve their mood and to deal with negative feelings. They may suffer from low self-esteem and depression. Some eat because they associate certain foods with comfort. A person who is feeling depressed or stressed may turn to foods containing high amounts of sugar or fat because of the effect these ingredients have on the brain. These foods act in the same way as endorphins, the body's "feel good" hormones. Someone with food addiction gets a kind of high after eating. However, after the effect has worn off, the person feels guilty and more depressed. Brain scans reveal that the mere sight or smell of favorite foods triggers a spike in dopamine, a brain chemical linked to reward and motivation.

Symptoms. Those with food addiction may display a number of signs that point to a problem with their relationship with food. These signs can include cravings for certain kinds of foods, eating in secret or hiding food, eating when not hungry, eating past the point of feeling full or even to the point of feeling sick, feeling guilty about what and how much they eat, spending much time thinking about what they ate or what they plan to eat next, and turning to food to relieve stress or to deal with unpleasant emotions.

Consequences. The effects of food addictions are serious. Food addicted people may develop eating disorders such as bulimia, which involves binging and purging. They might also gain unhealthy amounts of weight, putting them at risk for a host of health problems and diseases, including high blood pressure, heart disease, and diabetes. The most prominent complications of food addiction are weight gain, obesity, and chronic illness, all of which can lead to death.

Treatment and therapy. A therapist can help avoid the cycle of eating food for comfort. The addiction may be a symptom of an underlying condition, such as abuse, which needs to be addressed to help the client learn to have a more healthy relationship with food and discover how to stop compulsive overeating. A support group such as Overeaters Anonymous or Food Addicts in Recovery Anonymous also can be part of the treatment process. As most food addicted individuals tend to have low self-esteem and depression, a group such as Emotions Anonymous also might help the person learn how to have a better relationship with food.

Exercise Addiction

Exercise, exercise addiction can be a great way to stay in shape, release stress, and fight disease. However, exercising, or working out, excessively, especially when not overweight, can quickly become a problem. Exercise addiction and extreme fixation on physical fitness are compulsive behaviors that may be quite difficult to stop without appropriate treatment.

Causes. People may develop an exercise addiction if they have a poor body image. To a person addicted to exercise, what matters is not weight but how he or she perceives his or her own body. Many are fit and may not be considered by others to be overweight. One of the positive effects of engaging in exercise is the release of endorphins. These hormones give a feeling of euphoria after exercising. The individual may fall into a pattern of continuing to exercise to excess to try to experience these sensations. It also is possible that he or she turns to physical activity to cope with the stresses of everyday life.

Symptoms. Exercise addicted persons may have various motivations for their behavior, including a desire to control their body weight or shape, a feeling of inexplicable dread if exercise is not performed, or feeling the need to achieve an exercise-induced high. They may have rigid fitness schedules to which they always adhere. They may compulsively exercise alone to avoid attracting the attention of trainers and gym staff. People with exercise addiction will exercise even when they are sick or injured. They may miss social obligations in order to exercise and may choose exercise over spending time with friends and family. They may feel guilty when unable to exercise, may experience withdrawal symptoms when unable to exercise, may repeatedly exercise for more than two hours daily, may fixate on weight loss or calories burned, or may suffer frequent injury from over-exercising.

Consequences. A person can exercise so much that they lose too much weight, become undernourished, and develop nutrition-related health problems. Women may lose so much weight that they stop menstruating. Psychological and social effects also occur. They may always be tired or irritable because of the demands of their fitness routines, and they might isolate themselves socially because they are preoccupied with exercising.

Treatment and therapy. Recovering individuals need to learn how to limit their level of physical activity to moderate levels. Therapy and medications for obsessive-compulsive disorder may help them deal with the urge to exercise to excess. Counseling with a psychologist or psychiatrist can help uncover and address deeper problems. The goal of treatment is to learn how to exercise enough to stay healthy, without becoming obsessed again.

Compulsive Shopping Addiction

Shopping addiction, shopping addiction, also known as oniomania, is considered to be an impulse control disorder. Shopping addiction involves the uncontrolled urge to spend. Shopping addicted people may feel compelled to buy items they do not need or want, and they get a rush from the experience itself. They use shopping as a way to cope with anxiety or stress, and they may not feel fulfilled or happy unless they have made a purchase. Despite efforts to stop reckless spending, the person addicted to shopping is unable to change his or her behavior.

Causes. A shopping addiction may be caused by low self-esteem. A person may seek to compensate by spending money. Social pressure to keep up with the spending of others also might be a factor. For some, shopping becomes a way to self-medicate; the person might go shopping to improve his or her mood or to soothe hurt feelings. Other reasons why a person

may turn to shopping as a coping mechanism include attempting to deal with symptoms of depression, difficulty handling intense emotions such as anger, lacking impulse control, and needing acceptance.

Symptoms. Some people get a rush from spending money. They will hide their purchases from loved ones and attempt to cover their actions to hide their addiction. They will likely have money problems. They may be unable to pay their bills and may have to borrow and go into debt to finance their addiction.

Consequences. Compulsive spending continues for a certain time only before one has to deal with the consequences. Shopping addicted individuals often will find themselves in financial trouble. Foreclosure and even bankruptcy can be consequences of a severe shopping addiction, a situation that can result in marriage and relationship problems.

Treatment and therapy. If the shopping addicted individual is depressed or has obsessive-compulsive disorder, medications may be prescribed as part of a treatment plan. Seeing a therapist is another part of treatment. The goal is to get to the root of the addictive behavior. Cognitive-behavioral counseling can help them avoid shopping as a way to deal with other issues. Shopping addiction treatment also needs to deal with the financial fallout of excessive spending.

Internet and Online Gaming Addiction

As we evolve into a more technology filled world, we're introduced to new relationships and behaviors in conjunction with computers, smartphones, social media, and gaming. Many fear addictions are forming to these devices, apps, and outlets, but internet/online gaming is by far the most researched currently. While for most individuals it's easy to enjoy a simulating and interactive computer game on the occasion, various intra and interpersonal risk factors may attract certain users to computer gaming as a way to cope with individual problems or as an excuse to isolate from others or responsibilities. Although currently there is no officially recognized internet/online gaming disorder, the most recent DSM-5 listed the issue under its Section III, a section reserved for conditions that require further research. Developments of new online technologies continue to progress and the corresponding psychological impacts have peeked interest and further research among clinicians and professionals. As we wait for further research findings on the issue, some symptoms have been expressed to date as instructive to look out for: binging for excessive hours without stopping (5-10 hours), neglecting family or friends, lying to others about time they've spent playing, decreased interest or performance in school or work related duties, poor physical hygiene, frustration and/or anxiety when unable to play the game, and/or eating or sleeping while gaming or skipping meals entirely.

Gerald W. Keister, MS; Updated by Kelly Owen, Esq.

FOR FURTHER INFORMATION

American Psychiatric Association. (2013). *Diagnostic and statistical manual of mental disorders* (5th Ed.). Washington, DC: Author.

Ascher M, Levounis P. *The Behavioral Addictions.* Arlington, VA, US: American Psychiatric Publishing, Inc.; 2015. Print. Overview of behavioral addictions and case studies on established and newly proposed behavioral addictions.

Ebert, M. H., P. T. Loosen, and B. Nurcombe. *Current Diagnoses and Treatment in Psychiatry.* New York: McGraw-Hill, 2000. A comprehensive reference for answering day-to-day questions on psychiatric diseases and disorders. Clearly describes behavioral addictions.

Karim R, Chaudhri P. Behavioral addictions: An overview. *Journal of Psychoactive Drugs.* [serial online]. January 2012;44(1):5-17.

Paulus F, Ohmann S, von Gontard A, Popow C. Internet gaming disorder in children and adolescents: A systematic review. *Developmental Medicine & Child Neurology* [serial online]. July 2018; 60(7):645-659.

Sadock B, Sadock V, Ruiz P. *Kaplan and Sadock's Synopsis of Psychiatry: Behavioral Sciences/Clinical Psychiatry. 11Th Ed.* US: Wolters Kluwer Health; 2015. Print. Contains detailed descriptions of various behavioral addictions and overview of psychiatry for clinicians and students, but also comprehensible to the general reader.

See also: Body modification addiction; Children and behavioral addictions; Cleanliness addiction; Compulsions; Exercise addiction; Food addiction; Gaming addiction; Internet addiction; Marriage/partnership and behavioral addictions; Media and behavioral addictions; Men and behavioral addictions; Parenting and behavioral addictions; Pornography addiction; Sex addiction; Shopping/spending addiction; Television addiction; Trends and statistics: Behavioral addictions; Women and behavioral addictions; Work issues and behavioral addictions

Behavioral addictions: Treatment

CATEGORY: Treatment

ALSO KNOWN AS: Compulsive behavior: process addictions; psychological addictions

DEFINITION: A behavior or activity becomes an addiction when it interferes with daily functioning and causes emotional, social, or physical harm. The most common behavioral addictions are compulsive shopping, workaholism, pathological gambling, overeating, and exercise (most often bodybuilding and running). Other common behavioral addictions are sex, Internet, tanning, and computer gaming. Sometimes a person will present more than one addiction, as is often the case with gambling and alcohol misuse. Behavioral addictions are also commonly tied to another mental disorder, as obsessive compulsive disorder and eating disorders.

OVERVIEW AND ASSESSMENT

As behavioral addictions share similarities with drug and alcohol addictions, obsessive-compulsive disorders (OCDs), and impulse control disorders (ICDs) such as kleptomania and pyromania, their treatment plans can be similar. Unlike a treatment goal for substance misuse addictions, however, behavioral addictions do not usually require total abstinence, as clients must still eat, work, shop, exercise, and so forth. The one exception to the nonabstinence rule is pathological gambling, as it is usually treated as a substance addiction, with recovery tied closely with abstinence. In other cases, a period of temporary abstinence might be required until the client can resume the activity normally. In all cases, the primary goal of most behavioral addiction treatment plans is the formation of healthy behaviors and habits.

Mental health experts do not know the causes of most behavioral addictions, although most agree that they stem from some combination of physiologic, social, genetic, and psychological etiologies, and thus their treatment plans vary greatly. The selection of an effective treatment plan for an addictive behavior begins with an initial assessment of the client.

Examples of commonly used diagnostic and screening tools include the workaholism battery, Minnesota impulsive disorder interview, compulsive buying scale, sexual addiction screening test, Massachusetts gambling screen, exercise dependence questionnaire, bodybuilding dependency scale, Internet addiction test, and online cognition scale. As research is still being conducted on behavioral addictions, tests and surveys are devised regularly, such as the Yale food addiction scale and the Dutch work addiction scale.

The American Psychiatric Association's *Diagnostic and Statistical Manual of Mental Disorders* (DSM) is the standard starting point for the diagnosis of pathological gambling, currently classified as an OCD not elsewhere classified; however, experts have proposed that gambling be moved in the revised DSM to a new category— addiction and related disorders—along with substance addictions. Other psychological addictions are either not included in the DSM or fall under a miscellaneous category, as with sexual disorders not otherwise specified.

As a high comorbidity exists between behavioral addictions and substance dependence and other mental disorders, clients are often tested also for depression, anxiety, post-traumatic stress disorder, and other disorders. Treatment plans are personalized and may involve individual, couples, group, and family therapy; a twelve-step program; or pharmacological intervention. Most clients are treated as outpatients, but some may require treatment at an inpatient facility or a hospital. In either case, successful treatment depends on the willingness of the client to be treated.

Therapy

Cognitive-behavioral therapy (CBT) now represents the most common approach to treating process addictions, as neither cognitive therapy nor behavioral therapy proved to be completely effective by itself. There are as many different approaches to CBT as there are addictions, although these schools and approaches tend to share more similarities than differences, including the ultimate goal of empowering the client to take charge of his or her life in a healthy manner.

Most CBT treatment plans are administered in steps or phases over a period of usually no less than two months, although intensive residential programs might be shorter and include both individual and group sessions, with couples or family therapy when relevant. Flexibility and personalization are key to the most successful therapy programs.

CBT focuses on the client's thoughts because cognitions, rather than external influences or stimuli, are believed to be the primary sources for the addiction. This focus is also the foundation for the highly popular rational-emotive behavior therapy school, a precursor of CBT.

In CBT, while listening to the client discuss his or her behavior, the therapist can help the client to identify the thoughts that tend to trigger the behavior or trigger the emotions that cause the behavior. The therapist also helps the client to overcome any negative personality issues, such as low self-esteem or antisocial attitudes; irrational or distorted thoughts, such as overconfidence (which is common among pathological gamblers); or the belief that a person's worth is based on ownership of consumer goods, which is common among compulsive shoppers. The therapist then suggests alternative activities, deterrents to the behavior, and strategies to avoid the places, people, or objects associated with the behavior. The therapist also teaches relevant skills, including problem solving, critical thinking, stress management, or social skills, and introduces such techniques as deep breathing and mindfulness to help ground the client.

Drawing upon behavioral therapy, CBT also might include covert sensitization techniques, in which a patient learns to associate the undesirable behavior with an aversive image that usually elicits a strong, negative reaction. For example, an exercise addict who thinks about working out should, instead of visualizing a physically fit body, try to visualize a black widow spider spinning a web across a treadmill.

Behavioral interventions also make up a typical part of treatment. For example, a compulsive shopper might be asked to destroy all credit cards, perhaps keeping a bank card for emergencies, and entrust that card to another family member. A sex addict might be required to move his or her computer into the kitchen or another busy room of the house, where a lack of privacy might inhibit the person from viewing pornography.

CBT is especially goal-oriented and structured, and it relies heavily on homework, with reading assignments, self-monitoring exercises, and practice scenarios. Clients might be asked to keep a log or journal that details the time and place when they entered into the addictive behavior, along with their moods and other contributing factors.

Insight-oriented therapy, a type of psychotherapy that might be combined with cognitive therapy or CBT, attempts to uncover the unconscious conflicts that might be causing the behavioral addiction. Such conflicts could be responsible not only for the addiction but also for problems with relationships, work, and other aspects of life. Once uncovered, the client gains control over his or her life and is able to assume full responsibility for his or her behavior. Hypnosis may be used to draw out unconscious thoughts or events that could be contributing factors to the addiction. By using special induction techniques, the therapist can encourage the client to fall into a trance, or a heightened state of relaxation. Once in this state, the therapist can make positive suggestions intended to replace negative thoughts or memories.

Couples therapy involves the spouse or partner of the addicted client and may resemble marriage counseling in that communication and sexuality are often primary topics, or it might focus on developing specific skills, such as effective budgeting, particularly relevant to shopping addicts, or house cleaning and organizational skills, especially relevant to hoarders. Family counseling, which can involve the client's children, siblings, parents, grandparents, or other relatives, is an especially important component of a treatment plan when relationships have become dysfunctional.

Group therapy can be similar to couples or individual therapy but offers the added benefit of peer support and the opportunity to learn from others. The most common type of group therapy is the twelve-step program devised by Alcoholics Anonymous (AA). AA's model has been adopted for use by Sex Addicts Anonymous, Gamblers Anonymous, Debtors Anonymous, Shopaholics Anonymous, and other organizations. Twelve-step therapies also are considered types of CBTs, as they engage the client in the active process of identifying and changing his or her behavior.

The first steps in this model involve getting the client to admit that he or she is unable to control his or her behavior and then recognizing a higher power can give one the strength to change. The client then asks for help and forgiveness, and through a spiritual awakening learns new behaviors while also receiving the benefits of a support group and the positive feelings that come with helping others overcome their addictions.

Secular programs, such as Rational Recovery's Addictive Voice Recognition Technique program, require a person to assume responsibility rather than placing oneself in the hands of a higher being. Related to the twelve-step programs is SMART Recovery's Four-Point Program, which is used to treat pathological gambling.

Successful therapy also involves relapse-prevention planning. The therapist will ensure that the client is well equipped to monitor and assess his or her behavior and to deal with moments of weakness and the general hurdles of life that sometimes cause setbacks. Planning might simply involve compiling a list of affirmations, alternative activities, or people that the client can call upon if needed, or a more elaborate course of action.

PHARMACOLOGICAL INTERVENTION

Drugs are administered as part of a treatment plan for behavioral addictions when therapy alone is insufficient and when other mental disorders are present. While research on the effectiveness of pharmacological interventions in treating behavioral addictions is limited, most of the medications prescribed are associated with treating substance addictions or OCD, and they have been documented as useful in treating some behavioral addictions.

The most commonly prescribed medications for treating addictions are the opioid receptor antagonists, such as naltrexone (Revia, Depade, Vivitrol), which is known to reduce cravings in recovering alcoholics and to block the "pleasure-feeling" effects of opioids (heroin, cocaine, oxycodone). For this reason, naltrexone has proven useful also in treating pathological gambling and sex and shopping addictions (as well as other behavioral addictions).

Antidepressants, particularly the selective serotonin reuptake inhibitors (SSRIs) such as fluoxetine (Prozac, Sarafem), paroxetine (Paxil, Pexeva), sertraline (Zoloft), and citalopram (Celexa), are often prescribed to treat depression, which tends to have a high comorbidity with compulsive buying, eating disorders, and some other addictions. Mood stabilizers such as lithium (Lithobid), commonly prescribed for treating bipolar disorder, a mental illness often present in substance misusers, may be prescribed for some process addictions too.

Antiandrogen drugs, prescribed for clients with a paraphilia disorder (pedophilia, zoophilia, necromania, and others), can lower the levels of or inhibit production of testosterone and androgens (male sex hormones) and have some demonstrative success in treating nonparaphilic sex addictions as well. Antiandrogens tend to be prescribed only after SSRIs have proven ineffective. Other medications also might be prescribed when a client is experiencing suicidal thoughts, anxiety, or another mental or medical condition.

ALTERNATIVE TREATMENTS AND SELF-HELP

Alternative, or holistic, therapies and techniques can complement a traditional treatment plan or be undertaken instead of medicine or psychotherapy. Alternative treatments are often an important part of residential treatment-center programs, where clients undergo a full daily schedule of therapy sessions. The expressive therapies—dance, music, art, creative writing, and drama—are especially useful in treating children, young adults, seniors, and persons with limited verbal communication skills. These creative therapies allow addicts to explore deep emotions and thoughts; they also teach new skills that can build self-esteem and support personal growth.

Alternative medicine therapies include laser, acupuncture, biofeedback, homeopathy, and herbal medicine. As with yoga, tai chi, qigong, massage, meditation, drumming, and laughter and humor therapy, these types of activities help people relax and decrease stress, while they simultaneously teach new skills and provide healthy diversions from the negative behavioral addiction.

Any healthy activity or diversion that offers positive rewards can help with recovery from an addiction. These activities include nature walks, taking care of a pet, and taking a vacation away from the source of the addiction. Most addicts also will benefit from exercise and nutritional programs.

Self-help is another form of alternative therapy, although only the most motivated addicts will find success with this type of treatment. The best books are written by mental health experts with extensive experience treating a particular addiction, and they are structured to follow the CBT model used to treat their own clients. Personal experience with a particular addiction also can prove insightful. In general, the best books emphasize goal setting, include exercises for self-reflection, and teach a variety of skills.

Sally Driscoll, MLS

FOR FURTHER INFORMATION

Benson, April Lane, ed. *I Shop, Therefore I Am: Compulsive Buying and the Search for Self*. Northvale, NJ: Aronson, 2000. This collection of essays includes a variety of treatment plans for shopping and spending addictions.

Collins, George, and Andrew Adleman. *Breaking the Cycle: Free Yourself from Sex Addiction, Porn Obsession, and Shame*. Oakland, CA: New Harbinger, 2010. This self-help book for men offers insights into the nature and recovery of sex addictions from a former addict turned mental health expert.

Dobson, Keith S., ed. *Handbook of Cognitive-Behavioral Therapies*. 3rd ed. New York: Guilford, 2009. This standard reference text includes chapters on Addictions and Substance Abuse Behavioral therapies for addictions • 73 treating couples, children, and teenagers, and has been updated to include newer types of CBT.

Duarte, Garcia Frederico, and Florence Thibaut. "Sexual Addictions." *American Journal of Drug and Alcohol Abuse* 36.5 (2010): 254–60. Print. Discusses the classification of excessive nonparaphilic sexual behavior and pharmacological treatment.

Grant, Jon E. *Impulse Control Disorders: A Clinician's Guide to Understanding and Treating Behavioral Addictions*. New York: Norton, 2008. Examines the etiology, assessment, and treatment of impulse control disorders and how they are related to substance addictions.

Grusser, Sabine M., Ulrike Albrecht, and Nina Ellen Kirschner. "Diagnostic Instruments for Behavioural Addiction: An Overview." *GMS Psycho- Social-Medicine* 4 (2007). Web. 18 Apr. 2012. http://www.ncbi.nlm.nih.gov/pmc/articles/ PMC2736529. This article discusses various tools for assessing sex, exercise, shopping, work, and Internet addictions.

Hartston, Heidi. "The Case for Compulsive Shopping as an Addiction." *Journal of Psychoactive Drugs* 44.1 (2012): 64–67. Print. Discusses the similarities between compulsive shopping and substance addictions on dopamine levels in the brain and argues for similar treatment plans.

Ladouceur, Robert, and Stella Lachance. *Overcoming Pathological Gambling: Therapist Guide.* Treatments that Work Series. New York: Oxford UP, 2007. Although this book is intended for mental health experts, students and general readers will appreciate the examples of diagnostic tools and other information.

Yapko, Michael D. *Trancework: An Introduction to the Practice of Clinical Hypnosis.* 4th ed. East Sussex, England: Brunner, 2012. This standard, updated work can be used as an entry point for students or referred to by professionals.

Young, Kimberly S., and Christiano Nabuco de Abreu. *Internet Addiction: A Handbook and Guide to Evaluation and Treatment.* Hoboken, NJ: Wiley, 2010. Two internationally known mental health experts offer the latest research on online gambling, cybersex, and gaming addictions.

See also: Addiction medications; Gamblers Anonymous; Group therapy for behavioral addictions; Overeaters Anonymous; Screening for behavioral addictions; Support groups; Treatment methods and research

Behavioral Disorders in the *DSM-5*: Disruptive, Impulse-Control and Conduct Disorders

CATEGORY: Diagnosis and prevention

DEFINITION: Behavioral addictions are behaviors that a person feels compelled to complete even if those behaviors result in long-term negative consequences. Behavioral addictions are not substance related but have a compulsive quality. These behaviors are often focused on gambling, stealing, food intake, Internet or web use, pornography and sex, and self-mutilation.

INTRODUCTION

In the most recent edition of the American Psychiatric Association's Diagnostic and Statistical Manual of Mental Disorders (DSM-5), published in 2013, Behavioral Disorders are classified within the chapter entitled "Disruptive, Impulse-Control and Conduct Disorders." In the previous edition of the *DSM (DSM-IV-TR)*, Behavioral addictions were included within the impulse control disorders classification. The chapter in the *DSM-5*, however, further specifies disorders that are behavior based, and separates out addiction-related disorders, which are classified in the chapter titled "Substance-Related and Addictive Disorders."

Disorders included within the *DSM-5* chapter of "Disruptive, Impulse-Control and Conduct Disorders" include those which were previously encapsulated in other chapters of the *DSM-IV-TR*. These include Oppositional Defiant Disorder and Conduct Disorder, which were previously classified in the chapter "Disorders Usually First Diagnosed in Infancy, Childhood, or Adolescence;" and Intermittent Explosive Disorder, Pyromania, and Kleptomania, which were previously classified as "Impulse-Control Disorders Not Otherwise Specified" in the *DSM-IV-TR*. The underlying tie for these disorders, which led to them being classified together in the *DSM-5*, is difficulty with emotional or behavioral self-control. Also of note for this chapter, Antisocial Personality Disorder is described in both this chapter, as well as the chapter on personality disorders. The *DSM-5* eliminated the multi-axial diagnostic system which was present in the *DSM-IV-TR* (as well as many previous editions), in favor of listing disorders based more so on their degree of impact on the psycho-social functioning of the individual. Attention Deficit/Hyperactive Disorder (ADHD), which is often comorbid with many of the disorders in this chapter, is classified under the *DSM-5* chapter titled "Neurodevelopmental Disorders."

Oppositional Defiant Disorder (ODD): Oppositional Defiant Disorder is marked by a pattern of angry/irritable mood (e.g. often loses temper, is often touchy or easily annoyed, is often angry and resentful), argumentative/defiant behavior (e.g. often argues with authority figures, or, for children and adolescents, with adults; often actively defies or refuses to comply with requests from authority figures or with rules; often deliberately annoys others, often blames others for his or her mistakes or misbehaviors), or vindictiveness (e.g. has been spiteful or vindictive at least twice within the previous six months). The behaviors must be present for a minimum of six months, and be observable through interactions with others (who are not siblings of the individual).

Of note, the frequency and intensity of these behaviors should be used to differentiate between behaviors that are within normal limits developmentally, and those that are pathological. For example, for a child who is less than 5 years old, the behavior should generally occur on most days for a minimum period of six months. For children older than 5 years of age, the behaviors should occur at least weekly for a minimum period of six months. Additional considerations, including gender and culture should also be taken into account prior to assigning a diagnosis.

Further criteria for diagnosis include the determination that the disturbance in behavior is associated with clinically significant distress within the social context of the individual (e.g. peers, family members), and/or the behaviors negatively impact essential areas of functioning (e.g. social, education, occupational). The behaviors must not occur exclusively during the course of a psychotic, substance use, depressive or bipolar episode or disorder. The diagnostic criteria for disruptive mood dysregulation disorder, a newly created diagnosis in the *DSM-5* which is defined by frequent and extreme irritability, anger, and intense temper outbursts, supersedes a diagnosis when symptoms go beyond those described in the diagnostic criteria.

The severity of the disorder is specified based on the following criteria: **Mild:** the symptoms are present in only one context (e.g. at school, with peers, at work, at home); **Moderate:** the symptoms are present in at least two settings; **Severe:** the symptoms are present in three or more settings.

Intermittent Explosive Disorder: Intermittent Explosive Disorder is characterized by recurrent behavioral outbursts representing a lack of control over aggressive impulses. The disorder is demonstrable by either (or both): verbally aggressive behavior (e.g. being verbally argumentative, frequent temper tantrums); physically aggressive behavior (directed towards property, animals, or others), and/or three behavioral outbursts that involve damage or destruction of property (within a 12-month period).

Additional diagnostic criteria include: the degree to which the expressed aggressiveness is present during outbursts is significantly disproportionate to the precipitating stressor; the recurrent aggressive outbursts are not premeditated or committed in pursuit of obtaining something tangible, and/or cause marked distress in the individual or impairment(s) in functioning (e.g. social, occupational) or are associated with consequences (e.g. legal, financial). In order to make a diagnosis of Intermittent Explosive Disorder, the individual must be at least six years old, and the recurrent aggressive outbursts are not better explained by another psychiatric disorder (e.g. a personality disorder, a depressive disorder, an anxiety disorder, a psychotic disorder) or the psycho-physiological effects of a substance (e.g. illicit substance, medication side effect or misuse). Lastly, when frequent and intense displays of aggressive behaviors are present in excess of those typically observed in other disorders (e.g. Autism Spectrum Disorders, Attention Deficit/Hyperactive Disorders), a diagnosis of Intermittent Explosive Disorder may also be made in addition to further and more accurately hone the focus of the treating clinician.

Conduct Disorder: Conduct Disorder is diagnosable when there is the presence of persistent behavior that intentionally violates or disregards the rights of others, or is significantly age-inappropriate and is defiant of the norms of society. Symptoms are classified under four categories: 1) Aggression towards other people or animals, such as engaging in bullying, or physically threatening behavior (with or without a weapon); being physically cruel to other people or animals; engagement in criminal behavior (such as stealing, extortion, etc.); or forcing someone into unwanted sexual activity. 2) Destruction of Property, including fire setting with the intention of causing significant damage; or the intentional destruction of another person's property. 3) Deceitfulness or Theft, including breaking into another person's property (e.g. car, place of business); lying to trick or manipulate another person in order to obtain a desirous object or situation; theft of objects of minimal value without directly victimizing an individual (e.g. petty shoplifting, forgery). 4) Serious Violation of Rules, such as intentionally breaking a pre-established curfew (beginning before age 13); running away from home; and truancy from school (beginning before age 13). All of the behaviors noted must cause clinically significant distress in social, academic or occupational functioning.

Several specifiers to further describe the disorder are available for a diagnosis of Conduct Disorder. For example, the diagnosis for a child who demonstrates the symptoms prior to age 10 may be specified as "Childhood-onset type." An individual who does not present with the previously noted symptoms prior to age 10 may be classified with "Adolescent-onset type." When a determination of symptom onset is unable to be made, a specification of "Unspecified onset" may be given.

To further detail the exact nature of the disorder, an additional specifier is available to pinpoint the area(s) of clinical focus. The specifier "With limited prosocial emotions" may be added when the individual presents with at least two of the following (within the most recent 12 month period): Lack of remorse or guilt (e.g. does not demonstrate a sense of guilt or remorse for wrongdoing, excluding remorse when anticipating being caught or punished); a callous lack of empathy (e.g. a complete and total disregard for the feelings of others); Unconcerned about performance (e.g. demonstrates a lack of concern or worry regarding poor outputs in work or at school, and often blames others for their performance); Shallow or deficient affect (e.g. is emotionally expressive in ways that seem insincere, superficial, and generally disingenuous).

The severity of the disorder is characterized as: **Mild** (at least three symptoms present, the minimum number to make a diagnosis), **Moderate** (more than three symptoms are present, and the intensity of the behavior is of moderate degree), and **Severe** (a substantial amount of the symptoms noted are present, and their degree of intensity results in extreme harm to others).

Antisocial Personality Disorder: The diagnostic criteria for Antisocial Personality Disorder are located in the chapter "Personality Disorders." However, as the disorder is intimately connected to the disorders in this chapter, it is simultaneously listed in this. The *DSM-5* removed the multiaxial system present in its previous editions of the DSM; and as such disorders are now listed in order of degree of impact on functioning, and not on the corresponding diagnostic axis.

Pyromania: Pyromania is defined by an intentional fire setting on multiple occasions, with a degree of psychophysiological tension or arousal prior to action. The individual demonstrates an intense curiosity, intrigue and/or attraction to fire and related objects. The person also gains pleasure, satisfaction or relief when fires are set, or there is involvement in any

process following the setting of the fire. The fire setting is not done for any type of gain (e.g. monetary), for protest (e.g. ideological reasons), in the presence of another disorder (e.g. psychosis, substance use), as a cover up (e.g. to destroy evidence), or in a responsive (e.g. vengeful) manner. The fire setting behavior should also not be better explained by another disorder (e.g. conduct or antisocial personality disorder).

Kleptomania: Kleptomania is diagnosable when the individual presents with a persistent inability to resist the impulse to steal items not for their use or value. Similar to Pyromania, the person experiences a degree of psychophysiological tension or arousal prior to action, and they gain a sense of enjoyment, satisfaction or relief at the time of committing the act. The act of theft is not committed as an expression of anger or revenge, and not in response to a psychotic event (e.g. delusion or hallucination). The theft is not better explained by another disorder (e.g. conduct or antisocial personality disorder).

The chapter titled "Disruptive, Impulse-Control and Conduct Disorders" concludes with two additional disorders which encompass symptoms not accounted for by the previously described disorders. "Other Specified Disruptive, Impulse-Control and Conduct Disorder" can be diagnosed when the individual presents with clinically significant distress that impacts multiple areas of functioning, however the symptoms do not meet the necessary threshold for diagnosis of any other disorder in the chapter. This diagnosis is used when the clinician decides to convey the specific reason the individual's symptoms do not meet the criteria for a specific disorder in the chapter. Conversely, when a clinician does not wish to explain the reason(s) for why the individual does not meet the diagnostic criteria for a specific disruptive, impulse-control or conduct disorder, a diagnosis of "Unspecified Disruptive, Impulse-Control and Conduct Disorder" may be made. This diagnosis may be of particular clinical utility when there is inadequate information to make a more definitive diagnosis.

Robert S. Cavera, PsyD

FOR FURTHER INFORMATION
American Psychiatric Association. *Diagnostic and Statistical Manual of Mental Disorders.* 5th ed. Washington, DC: Author, 2013. Print.

Coccaro, E. F. (2018). "DSM-5 intermittent explosive disorder: Relationship with Disruptive Mood Dysregulation Disorder." *Comprehensive psychiatry, 84,* 118-121.

Coccaro, E. F., & Grant, J. E. (2017). *The Wiley Handbook of Disruptive and Impulse-Control Disorders,* John J. Wiley & Sons Ltd., Hobroken, N.J., 2018.

Fernandez, E., & Johnson, S. L. (2016). "Anger in psychological disorders: Prevalence, presentation, etiology and prognostic implications." *Clinical psychology review, 46,* 124-135.

Frick, P. J. (2016). "Current research on conduct disorder in children and adolescents." *South African Journal of Psychology, 46*(2), 160-174.

Frick, P. J., & Matlasz, T. M. (2018). "Disruptive, impulse-control, and conduct disorders." In *Developmental Pathways to Disruptive, Impulse-Control and Conduct Disorders* (pp. 3-20).

Behavioral therapies for addictions

CATEGORY: Treatment

ALSO KNOWN AS: Behavior therapy; cognitive-behavioral therapy

DEFINITION: Behavioral therapies, which have their roots in learning principles, focus on observable antecedents to behavior and on the consequences of the actions on the self and others. Cognitive-behavioral therapies add a person's thoughts as factors in maintaining and causing behavior.

THE BEHAVIORAL PERSPECTIVE

From the behavioral perspective, an addiction is a maladaptive way to cope with difficulties and to satisfy unmet needs in life. Behaviorally, the person who is addicted to drugs or alcohol is experiencing a learned sequence of behaviors acquired over time in response to problems or circumstances in life.

An addiction is a learned behavior that may have resulted from observing other persons coping with stressors through the use of substances. An addiction also can develop after a person has a rewarding experience with the physiological effects of alcohol or drugs. Once a person finds that the depressive or stimulating properties of drugs or alcohol have desirable effects, that person will use the substances to cope with stressors and other negative states. Substance misuse can become a preferred coping behavior, as substances work fairly rapidly. Also, ingesting these substances usually takes little effort. Repeatedly using a substance to cope with personal or situational problems leads to an addictive pattern of misuse.

Addiction from the behavioral perspective can be summarized as follows: a stressor triggers the need for coping, a substance is obtained and used, its effects are experienced, the negative feelings from the stressor are blunted, and, consequently, the substance is used in greater quantities to mitigate personal or situational problems. This learned pattern then becomes an addiction from which the person is unwilling or unable to break.

LEARNING THEORY FOUNDATIONS

The behavioral therapies for addictions are based upon the early research conducted by Ivan Pavlov and B. F. Skinner . Pavlov studied the concept of classical conditioning, in which a neutral stimulus that previously did not evoke any positive or negative response could be conditioned to produce a positive or negative response. This classical conditioning paradigm involved the pairing of the neutral stimulus with a reward or punishment. When associated with a rewarding stimulus, a positive response to the neutral stimulus emerged. A negative or punishing stimulus when paired with the neutral stimulus would produce a negative or avoidance response.

Skinner is known for his work with operant conditioning, which showed the power of positive reinforcement or reward in producing and maintaining responses. Skinner showed that a person will learn behavior that has been positively reinforced and will keep responding to earn the reward.

The foundations of classical and operant conditioning demonstrate that the pattern of addiction can be explained through the application of learning principles. Neutral settings may become classically conditioned to promote substance use and misuse through the power of rewards. Operant conditioning strengthens the behaviors associated with addictions, as the substance may initially manage stressors in a person's life and then reward the person for engaging in the addictive actions. The behavioral therapies focus on reversing the previous patterns of classical and operant conditioning that produced the addiction patterns.

TREATMENT FROM THE BEHAVIORAL PERSPECTIVE

The behavioral therapies for addictions focus on the emotional or situational factors that promote episodes of substance use and on the underlying factors that maintain the behaviors. These therapies seek to break the learned pattern that promotes addiction and to replace the maladaptive pattern with new adaptive behaviors. The triggers for the learned pattern are identified as the antecedents for the maladaptive addiction. This helps a therapist determine the occasions or reasons for the substance use.

A number of antecedents to the pattern of maladaptive substance use exists, so therapists seek to identify what has produced the pattern of addiction. Some common triggers or antecedents are social pressures, interpersonal conflicts, depressive moods, anger or frustration in life, chronic pain, poor role models, or settings where substances are routinely abused. Once a pattern has been learned, a number of factors can contribute to its maintenance.

The addictive pattern can continue because of the physiological effects of a substance, because of a reduction in anxiety, or because of social reinforcement from others with similar addictions. For each person affected, treatment involves identifying the most common and powerful triggers or antecedents and developing behavioral strategies to learn effective ways to manage the triggering factors that had created the learned pattern of addiction.

Treatment can be difficult because each person may have significant behavioral deficits to overcome. Some persons may never have learned the coping skills or behaviors that would help them to handle personal or situational distress. Behavioral therapies not only try to break the pattern of addiction but also try to overcome skill deficits that keep a person from facing problems in an adaptive fashion.

COPING SKILLS

To overcome the detrimental long-term consequences of addictive behavior, treatment includes coping-skills training, a behavioral therapy designed to achieve abstinence and to learn adaptive behaviors. This training involves an initial functional analysis to determine the role of the addiction in the person's life. Functional analysis shows what skills are lacking in the person's behavioral repertoire, especially those skills needed to cope with situational or personal stressors, and shows how addictive behaviors have been used as ways to cope.

The clinical interview is used for the functional analysis in conjunction with a variety of assessment instruments. These instruments provide objective measures to identify the extent of the addiction behaviors. It has often been found in the functional analysis that a person's emotional state is closely tied to the addiction. Feelings of depression, anxiety, loneliness, inadequacy, estrangement, and weakness are often inadequately managed because the person lacks effective coping skills. Substance use and abuse or some other behavioral addiction become conditioned responses to unpleasant emotional states.

With the completion of the functional analysis, behavioral therapy then enters a treatment planning phase that focuses on skills to overcome addictive behavior. Two major categories of skills make up the treatment planning phase: intrapersonal and interpersonal.

Intrapersonal skills involve the person's decision-making patterns and problem-solving capabilities. Intrapersonal-skills training helps to improve a person's ability to think through stressor situations (and anticipate problems) and then to select adaptive ways of coping with the situation or feeling. New ways of acting and thinking about problems or feeling states can be reinforced, resulting in a new pattern of behavior learned through the assistance of a behavioral therapist.

Interpersonal-skills training seeks to overcome problems with familial and social interactions. Behavioral therapies attempt to refresh or teach the skills needed for effective interpersonal relationships. The person with a substance abuse problem needs to learn how to refuse invitations from others to take substances and to avoid the social contexts that may reinforce addictive behaviors.

Having inadequate social skills also can contribute to feelings of loneliness and inadequacy. Interpersonal-skills training can bolster self-esteem and enhance a person's resistance to addiction.

TRAINING IN ACTION

Coping-skills training begins with the establishment of specific behavioral goals that focus on the elimination and management of the triggers for substance abuse or behavioral addictions. Behavioral goals, which are regularly reviewed at the beginning of each therapy session, can be covered in an individual, group, or family format. Contingency management, the major technique used in behavioral therapy, attempts to modify a behavioral response by controlling the consequences of that response. Patients are rewarded when their adaptive behavior adheres with their behavioral goals. Failure to adhere to the behavioral goals in a treatment plan leads to a loss of reinforcement or reward. Contingency management is based upon the basic principles of operant conditioning, which predict that if a good or desirable behavior is rewarded, it is more likely to be repeated.

A component of contingency management is stimulus control. This is a procedure that is used to help a patient avoid or leave a situation that leads to substance misuse or behavioral addictions. Stimulus control is basically learning to pay attention to characteristics in the environment that can promote or trigger the pattern of addiction. Behavioral therapy is expanded for individual patients to whatever areas can promote adaptive function; it can include skill development in the areas of communication, parenting, time management , and occupational training.

Frank J. Prerost PhD

FOR FURTHER INFORMATION

Azrin, Donahue, et al. "Family Behavior Therapy for Substance Abuse and Other Associated Problems: A Review of Its Intervention Components and Applicability." *Behavior Modification* 33 (2009): 495–519. Print.

Hougue, Aaron, et al. "Family Based Treatment for Adolescent Substance Abuse: Controlled Trials and New Horizons in Services Research." *Journal of Family Therapy* 31 (2009): 126–54. Print.

Potenza, March, et al. "Neuroscience of Behavioral and Pharmacological Treatments for Addictions." *Neuron* 69 (2011): 695–712. Print.

Witkiewitz, Katie, et al. "Behavioral Therapy across the Spectrum." *Alcohol Research* 33 (2010): 313–19. Print.

See also: Alternative therapies for addiction; Cognitive behavioral therapy; Treatment methods and research

Benzodiazepine misuse

CATEGORY: Substance misuse
DEFINITION: Benzodiazepine misuse involves the misuse of benzodiazepine, an anti-anxiety, controlled sedative, often leading to dependence.

CAUSES

Benzodiazepines ("benzos") such as Valium, Xanax, Ativan and Klonopin are primarily used as anti-anxiety and anti-insomnia sedatives (tranquilizers) because of their rapid inhibitory effect. They bind to receptors for the inhibitory neurotransmitter gamma-aminobutyric acid (GABA) receptors in the central nervous system (CNS) resulting in enhancement of GABA activity. Benzodiazepines provide relaxation and hypnotic effects therapeutically and can be misused to get high or to come down from the effects of stimulants. Benzodiazepine misuse may be acute (for example, illegal use or accidental overdose from prescription) or may be chronic (for example, repeatedly and deliberately combining with cocaine or alcohol to get high or to self-medicate during alcohol withdrawal). Also, chronic misuse of prescribed benzodiazepines by increasing the dose, duration, or number of prescriptions can result in drug dependency.

Although newer CNS agents for anxiety treatment, such as selective serotonin reuptake inhibitors, are available, benzodiazepines can be taken as needed for sporadic anxiety-inducing circumstances and to quickly relieve acute anxiety. However, these uses can cause benzodiazepine misuse. The widespread availability of the drug makes accessibility for nonprescription users easier. Benzodiazepines have been used as date rape drugs, which impair function and, thus, resistance to sexual assault, especially since the drug is difficult to taste when dissolved in a drink.

RISK FACTORS

Although benzodiazepines have lower misuse potential than do older psychotropic drugs, opioids, and stimulants, benzodiazepines remain popular for misuse in combination. Benzodiazepines with rapid onset, such as diazepam, are the most likely to be misused, although short- or intermediate-acting agents, such as alprazolam or lorazepam, may be misused too. Longer-acting agents, such as clonazepam, are associated with fewer cases of rebound anxiety or misuse.

Longer duration of prescription use (more than four weeks) and higher prescribed dosages (greater content or multiple daily doses) both increase the risk of physical dependence and withdrawal symptoms upon drug discontinuation. As tolerance develops to the prescribed dosages, abusive self-medicating behaviors such as increasing the number of pills or increasing the times a pill is taken without consulting a physician can occur.

Additional risk factors for misuse of a benzodiazepine prescription are combining controlled substance prescriptions, particularly prescribed drugs that have similar CNS activity, and having a history of legal or illegal drug use. For example, methadone users often combine diazepam with methadone to increase the effect of the latter drug.

SYMPTOMS

Acute symptoms of benzodiazepine misuse are less likely to be fatal than benzodiazepine misuse in combination with alcohol. Prominent acute symptoms of misuse are mood changes, increased sleep with trouble awakening, unusual behaviors, and poor focus. With high doses, possible symptoms include confusion, blurred vision, dizziness, weakness, slurred speech, poor coordination, shallow breathing, and even coma.

Chronic symptoms of benzodiazepine use disorder are more difficult to identify. Signs of addiction to a prescribed product include requests for increased doses to provide the same anxiety-relieving effects (drug tolerance) and the use of multiple prescriptions and doctors for the same drugs (drug-seeking behavior). Persons who misuse benzodiazepines chronically may have a changed appearance, changed behaviors, or changed mood, and they may regularly display poor performance at work or home. At times, these symptoms may mimic anxiety disorders themselves.

Long-term benzodiazepine use may lower cognition permanently with only partial recovery of cognitive abilities upon discontinuation of the benzodiazepine. Seizure risk exists during withdrawal especially with drugs (such as alprazolam) in the class that have short half-lives.

SCREENING AND DIAGNOSIS

Except for acute overdose presenting in an emergency room, screening for benzodiazepine use disorder requires subtle observation by family and health care providers. Chronic misuse may lead users to stop performing their normal duties at home and work. Those struggling with benzodiazepine use disorder will increasingly neglect themselves and others. Misusers may take benzodiazepines even in unsafe circumstances, such as before driving a vehicle, and may experience legal or family problems. Repeated requests for prescriptions, early pharmacy refills, and hiding medications in different locations are signs of addiction and drug-seeking behavior.

Dependence may be identified as an aid to diagnosing benzodiazepine use disorder. When benzodiazepines are used regularly for more than two to three weeks, even at low doses, they begin to lose their inhibitory GABA effects, and higher doses are required to relieve anxiety or to obtain a high. Once this tolerance develops, withdrawal symptoms upon drug discontinuation are also likely and may occur within days of stopping the benzodiazepine.

Withdrawal symptoms also may contribute to a diagnosis of benzodiazepine use disorder because they differ from rebound anxiety symptoms and appear similar to the symptoms of alcohol withdrawal. Tremor, insomnia, sweating, and nausea and vomiting are possible. Sensitivity to light and sound are common and directly distinguish withdrawal from symptoms of an underlying anxiety disorder. More severe withdrawal symptoms include agitation, confusion, myoclonic jerks, and seizures.

TREATMENT AND THERAPY

Acute overdose treatment in an emergency room depends upon the amount of time passed since the benzodiazepine was ingested. Within one to two hours of a lethal dose, gastric lavage may be used to flush the stomach. Alternatively, one dose of activated charcoal can be given within four hours of ingestion to bind the drug in the stomach. Severe cramps and nausea are possible, and vomiting is a risk. Flumazenil provides an antidote to the sedative effects of benzodiazepines in cases of severe overdose and coma risk; however, its use may cause seizures when given to people who misuse benzodiazepines chronically and who may have become dependent.

Treating chronic benzodiazepine use disorder is multifactorial and gradual. A slow tapering of dosage is key to avoiding rebound anxiety or withdrawal symptoms which may take three to four days after

Common Benzodiazepines

The following common benzodiazepines are used to treat acute mania, alcohol dependence, seizures, anxiety, insomnia, and muscular disorders:

Trade Name : Generic name

- Ativan : lorazepam
- Dalmane : flurazepam
- Dormicum : midazolam
- Halcion : triazolam
- Klonopin: clonazepam
- Lexotanil : bromazepam
- Librium : chlordiazepoxide
- Loramet : lormetazepam
- Mogadon : nitrazepam
- ProSom : estazolam
- Restoril : temazepam
- Rohypnol : flunitrazepam
- Sedoxil : mexazolam
- Serax : oxazepam
- Valium : diazepam
- Xanax : alprazolam

and to minimize tolerance or misuse, which are likely with higher dosages, without sacrificing anti-anxiety therapy.

PREVENTION

The key to prevention of acute or chronic benzodiazepine misuse is to lower its availability in prescribed and nonprescribed forms. The drug should be replaced as a prescription with safer and newer anti-anxiety agents. Physical dependence and acute misuse are less likely to occur if longer-acting or alternatively acting agents are prescribed for short time periods with careful physician supervision.

Nicole M. Van Hoey PharmD,
Updated by Charles L. Vigue Ph.D.

FOR FURTHER INFORMATION

"Drug Abuse and Addiction: Benzodiazepines." *Cleveland Clinic: Current Clinical Medicine.* 2nd ed. Cleveland: Elsevier, 2010. Print.

Goldman, Lee, and Dennis Ausiello. "Drugs of Abuse: Benzodiazepines and Other Sedatives." *Cecil Medicine.* Eds. Lee Goldman and Dennis Ausiello. 23rd ed. Philadelphia: Elsevier, 2007. Print.

Kaye, Alan David, Nalini Vadivelu, and Richard D. Urman, eds. *Substance Abuse: Inpatient and Outpatient Management for Every Clinician.* New York: Springer, 2015.

O'Brien, Charles P. "Benzodiazepine Use, Abuse, and Dependence." *Journal of Clinical Psychiatry* 66 (2006): 28–33. Print.

Ruiz, Pedro, and Eric C. Strain. *The Substance Abuse Handbook.* Philadelphia: Wolters, 2014. Print.

United States. Department of Health and Human Services. Substance Abuse and Mental Health Services Administration. *The DAWN Report: Benzodiazepines in Combination with Opioid Pain Relievers or Alcohol: Greater Risk of More Serious ED Visit Outcomes.* Rockville: SAMHSA, 2014. PDF file.

See also: Anxiety; Anxiety medication misuse; Date rape drugs; Panic disorders and addiction; Prescription drug addiction: Overview; Temazepam; Valium

drug discontinuation to begin. At the physician's discretion, a short-acting benzodiazepine such as triazolam may be replaced with longer-acting agents in the class, such as chlordiazepoxide (Librium), or with a prescription agent from another class with a similar mechanism, such as gabapentin (an antiseizure drug). Either replacement may be more safely tapered and stopped.

In some persons with chronic anxiety disorder, benzodiazepines cannot be fully discontinued. These persons may remain on very low dosages of the misused drug or another benzodiazepine, under strict observation, to avoid withdrawal and rebound risks

Betty Ford Center, The Hazelden Betty Ford Foundation

CATEGORY: Treatment

DEFINITION: The Hazelden Betty Ford Foundation is a nonprofit alcohol- and drug-addiction treatment foundation with 17 locations in the United States. The Betty Ford Center, Rancho Mirage, California, is the most comprehensive service location.

DATE: The Betty Ford Center was established in October 1982 and merged with the Hazelden Foundation in 2014

BACKGROUND

The Betty Ford Center was founded in 1982 to provide treatment services for alcoholism and other substance use disorders. With the 2014 merger with the Hazelden Foundation, the newly combined Hazelden Betty Ford Foundation has 17 sites in the United States and 14 are alcohol and drug addiction treatment centers. The center offering the most comprehensive service capabilities remains the original Betty Ford Center in Rancho Mirage, California.

The Betty Ford Center, which sits adjacent to the Eisenhower Medical Center, has 160 inpatient beds available on its campus and additional lodging for clients in its residential day-treatment program. Accommodations are in two person rooms. Services are often covered by insurance plans. The center's mission from the start has been to provide low-cost treatment usually unobtainable in acute-care hospitals. The original founders utilized the natural resources available in the area of Rancho Mirage. In a 2011 interview, Ford said, "Leonard Firestone and I realized we wanted a recovery hospital that would be less institutionalized and more of a relaxed setting in these mountains with their serenity and the beauty of them where people would be able to reach a spiritual feeling about their recovery."

The Betty Ford Center is accredited by The Joint Commission and is licensed by the State of California as an addiction treatment hospital with 24/7 medical coverage. There is an on-campus detoxification center and special expertise is available related to addiction due to chronic pain. Specialties are available for LGBTQ individuals. Gender specific interventions are employed. The length of treatment varies by individual situations. Upon completion of treatment, an 18 month continuing care plan is implemented. Programs for the entire family, including children discuss educational and prevention needs of the patient and family. Over 100,000 alumni of the program are available to support patients upon return home.

Inpatient treatment, residential day-treatment, and intensive outpatient treatment form the core of the nonprofit center's therapy. The licensed recovery hospital facilitates a structured program including daily lectures, group therapy, and counseling sessions. Physicians, nurses, psychologists, spiritual care counselors, activity therapists, registered dietitians, and other staff work together to create individualized treatment plans for each patient and to evaluate their progress.

There are 17 sites throughout the United States under the name Hazelden Betty Ford Foundation. Each Hazelden Betty Ford Foundation facility is also accredited by The Joint Commission, the organization that sets the standards for quality and safety of patient care. Fourteen sites are alcohol and drug addiction centers. Services vary by site and may include Inpatient, Outpatient and Sober Living Programs. Sober Living homes are located near treatment centers. With one in ten Americans over the age of 12 experiencing addiction to drugs and alcohol, educational programs for family members are key. The Intensive Family Program is three days and the Children's Program for boys and girls age 7-12 is four days in length.

A list of locations and services available may be found at https://www.hazeldenbettyford.org/locations.

VISION AND MISSION

The vision of the Foundation states that "together, we will overcome addiction." Centers around the country provide alcohol and drug treatment and rehabilitation for individuals suffering from alcohol, narcotic and chemical dependency, provides support for family members and interacts with the community at large. Treatment is based on the spiritual principles embodied in the twelve-step recovery program and is integrated with the latest medical and therapeutic treatments.

The Hazelden Betty Ford Foundation is a nonprofit organization. Services may be paid for by an individual's insurance plan. Medicare and Medicaid

First Lady Betty Ford founded the Betty Ford Center after dealing with her own struggle with alcoholism. (Library of Congress)

do not cover services at the Hazelden Betty Ford Centers at present. Financial case managers are available to assist patients in determining if their insurance company provides coverage and will also determine if patient aid is available to be used in combination with the patient's insurance benefits.

FOR FURTHER INFORMATION

Bergman BG, Hoeppner BB, Nelson LM, Slaymaker V, Kelly JF. "The effects of continuing care on emerging adult outcomes following residential addiction treatment." *Drug Alcohol Depend.* 2015 Aug 1; 153: 207–214. Retrieved from: https://www.ncbi.nlm.nih.gov/pmc/articles/PMC4510025/ on June 14, 2018.

"Betty Ford Center at Rancho Mirage." *Psychology Today.* Retrieved from: https://www.psychology-today.com/us/treatment-rehab/betty-ford-center-at-rancho-mirage-rancho-mirage-ca/196734 on June 14, 2018.

"Betty Ford Center merges with Hazelden Foundation." *USA Today.* Retrieved from https://www.usatoday.com/story/news/nation/2013/09/24/betty-ford-center-merges-with-hazelden-foundation/2865931/

Fessier, Bruce. "History of the Betty Ford Center." *Desert Sun,* 8 Jul. 2011. Web. 6 Mar. 2012. http://www.mydesert.com/article/20110708/NEWS01/110708022/History-Betty-Ford-Center.

Ford, Betty. *Healing and Hope: Six Women from the Betty Ford Center Share Their Powerful Journeys of Addiction and Recovery.* New York: Putnam, 2003.

Hazelden Betty Ford Foundation. Retrieved from: https://www.hazeldenbettyford.org/ on June 14, 2018

West, James W. *The Betty Ford Center Book of Answers.* New York: Pocket, 1997.

Camillia King; Revised by Patricia Stanfill Edens, MS, MBA, PhD, RN, LFACHE

See also: Alcohol misuse; Alcoholics Anonymous: The Twelve Steps; Treatment methods and research; Twelve-step programs for addicts; Twelve-step programs for family and friends

Binge drinking

CATEGORY: Substance misuse
ALSO KNOWN AS: Heavy episodic drinking
DEFINITION: The National Institute on Alcohol Abuse and Alcoholism (NIAAA) defines binge drinking as a pattern of drinking that brings blood alcohol concentration (BAC) levels to 0.08 g/dL. This typically occurs after four drinks for women and five drinks for men—in about two hours. The Substance Abuse and Mental Health Services Administration (SAMHSA), which conducts the annual National Survey on Drug Use and Health (NSDUH), defines binge drinking for men as drinking five or more alcoholic drinks on the same occasion on at least one day in the past 30 days. SAMHSA defines binge drinking for women

as drinking four or more alcoholic drinks on the same occasion on at least one day in the past 30 days.

BACKGROUND

The term "binge" originated as a clinical description of a pattern of problematic alcohol use characterized by a period of heavy use followed by a period of abstinence. In the mid-1990s, as part of the *College Alcohol Study,* conducted by the Harvard School of Public Health, the definition of binge drinking was modified to five or more drinks for men and four or more drinks for women on a single occasion within the past two weeks. The different thresholds selected for men and women reflect different alcohol metabolism rates between the sexes. The thresholds also represent the number of drinks that tend to place individuals at an increased risk for experiencing various alcohol-related social, economic, legal, and health consequences such as violence, engagement with law enforcement, and physical injuries.

In 2004, the National Institute of Alcohol Abuse and Alcoholism (NIAAA) proposed the following definition for binge drinking: "a pattern of drinking alcohol that brings BAC to 0.08 gram percent or above. For the typical adult, this pattern corresponds to consuming five or more drinks (male), or four or more drinks (female), in about two hours." This definition recognizes different thresholds for men and women and defines a specific period of time in which the drinking occurs.

Peer pressure may be the number one factor in binge drinking. Teenagers and young adults who have never consumed alcohol, or who have consumed only an occasional alcoholic beverage, may succumb to peer pressure in a party environment and engage in binge drinking through drinking games (e.g., "beer pong").

RISK FACTORS

Excessive alcohol use, including underage drinking and binge drinking, may increase a person's risk of developing serious health problems, including brain and liver damage, heart disease, and hypertension. The following factors increase one's risk of binge drinking:

Rate of drinking. Rapid consumption of a given amount of alcohol increases the risk of alcohol poisoning. One to two hours are required to metabolize one drink.

Gender. Young men from age eighteen through twenty-five years are the most likely group to engage in binge drinking; thus, they are at the highest risk for alcohol poisoning. However, young women also engage in binge drinking and are more susceptible to alcohol poisoning because women produce less of an enzyme that slows the release of alcohol from the stomach than men.

Age. Teenagers and college-age youth are more likely to engage in binge drinking; however, the majority of deaths from binge drinking occur in people ages thirty-five to fifty-four. The persons in this age group often do not metabolize alcohol as readily and are more likely to have underlying health problems that increase their risk.

Body mass. A heavier person can drink more alcohol and still register the same blood alcohol content (BAC). For example, a 240-pound man who drinks two cocktails will have the same BAC as a 120-pound woman who consumes one cocktail.

Overall health. Persons with kidney, liver, or heart disease, or with other chronic health problems, may metabolize alcohol more slowly. Persons with diabetes who binge drink might experience a dangerous drop in blood sugar level.

Food consumption. A full stomach slows the absorption of alcohol; thus, drinking on an empty stomach increases the risk.

Drug use. Prescription and over-the-counter drugs might increase the risk of alcohol poisoning. Ingestion of illegal substances, such as cocaine, methamphetamine, heroin, and marijuana, also increase the risk.

SYMPTOMS

Symptoms of alcohol poisoning include respiratory depression (slow breathing rate); confusion, stupor, or unconsciousness; slow heart rate; low blood pressure; low body temperature (hypothermia); vomiting; seizures; irregular breathing (a gap of more than ten seconds between breaths); and blue-tinged skin or pale skin.

SCREENING AND DIAGNOSIS

The BAC test is the definitive measure of alcohol in the blood. Persons with alcohol poisoning often have a BAC of 0.35 to 0.5 percent. By comparison, the BAC level that marks driving under the influence is 0.08 percent. Other screening tests include complete

College binge drinking

Binge drinking, or heavy episodic drinking, represents one of the most serious problems on college campuses. According to the National Institute on Alcohol Abuse and Alcoholism (NIAAA), "Harmful and underage college drinking are significant public health problems, and they exact an enormous toll on the intellectual and social lives of students on campuses across the United States." Binge drinking not only leads to alcohol overdose (poisoning) but also leads to drunk driving, accidents, poor school performance, risky sexual activity, property damage, illicit drug use, and death. Furthermore, studies suggest that heavy drinking in adolescence is strongly associated with heavy drinking in young adult life. Rather than "growing out" of binge drinking behavior, many young persons "grow into" a pattern of alcohol dependence or misuse.

Binge drinking among adolescents and young adults—both within and outside of college settings—is of great concern given the severity of the associated consequences.

blood count and other tests that check levels of glucose, urea, arterial pH, and electrolytes in the blood.

TREATMENT AND THERAPY

Acute treatment consists of supportive measures until the body metabolizes the alcohol. Acute treatment includes the insertion of an airway (endotracheal tube) to prevent vomiting and aspiration of stomach contents into the lungs; close monitoring of vital signs (temperature, heart rate, and blood pressure); oxygen administration; medication to increase blood pressure and heart rate, if needed; respiratory support, if needed; and maintenance of body temperature (blankets or warming devices). Acute treatment also includes the administration of intravenous fluids to prevent dehydration (glucose should be added if the person is hypoglycemic, and thiamine is often added to reduce the risk of a seizure). Further treatment includes hemodialysis (blood cleansing), which might be needed for dangerously high BAC levels (more than 0.4 percent).

Follow-up treatment for binge drinking requires the aid of a health care professional skilled in alcohol use disorder treatment. A treatment plan includes behavior-modification techniques, counseling, goal setting, and use of self-help manuals or online resources. Counseling on an individual or group basis is an essential treatment component. Group therapy, which is particularly valuable because it allows interaction with others who misuse alcohol, helps a person become aware that his or her problems are not unique. Family support is a significant component of the recovery process, so therapy may include a spouse or other family member. Binge drinking may be a component of other mental health disorders. Treatment for depression or anxiety also may be a part of follow-up care.

Care also may include long-term pharmaceutical treatment, including the oral medications disulfiram, acamprosate, and naltrexone. Disulfiram (Antabuse) produces unpleasant physical reactions to alcohol ingestion, which may include flushing, headaches, nausea, and/or vomiting. Disulfiram, however, does not reduce the craving for alcohol. One drug that can reduce craving is acamprosate (Campral). Another drug, naltrexone (ReVia), may reduce the urge to drink, and it blocks the pleasant sensations associated with alcohol consumption.

Although death can occur from binge drinking, most alcohol-related fatalities occur in automobile accidents caused by driving under the influence. Repeated episodes of binge drinking can result in permanent physical injury and in reduced quality of health. Brain and liver damage is common in repetitive binge drinkers. A young adult who binge drinks often progresses to problematic drinking or alcoholism in adulthood.

PREVENTION

The best way to prevent binge drinking is to educate persons who partake in at-risk behaviors. The highest risk for binge drinking occurs among young men, who often have a sense of invincibility and who often disregard advice from any source. While peer pressure is probably the best deterrent, it is also a significant risk factor for binge drinking.

According to the NIAAA, people who drink socially and possess certain risk factors for alcohol use disorder (AUD), self-administer more alcohol at a faster rate during a single session of alcohol consumption than people at low risk for developing AUD. Participants with all three risk factors evaluated in the study—being male, having a family history of

AUD, and having higher impulsivity behaviors—had the highest rates of binge drinking. These findings suggest that people at risk for AUD have different drinking patterns than those at low risk.

A wide-range of risk factors for AUD are known, but many people with risk factors for AUD do not develop the disease. Binge drinking may be an early indicator for risk of developing AUD. Examining drinking behavior during individual drinking sessions may provide more clues for identifying individuals at risk for AUD.

To determine whether the three AUD risk factors examined in the study could predict the rate of binge drinking, 159 social drinkers between the ages of 21 and 45 completed assessments about family history of problem drinking, behavioral impulsivity, and level of response to alcohol. They then participated in a laboratory session in which they self-administered alcohol intravenously to mimic a typical drinking session with friends. The participants' BAC was continuously estimated by computer and confirmed by breathalyzer every 15 minutes.

Participants who were identified as being at a higher risk for AUD administered alcohol faster, reaching a binge-like BAC more quickly than those at a lower risk for developing AUD. Having a family history of AUD was most strongly associated with a faster rate of binge drinking. Participants with all three risk factors had the fastest rates of intravenous alcohol administration—five times faster—during a session compared to the lowest risk group. Although more research is needed, the results suggest that assessing binge drinking during individual drinking sessions as part of a clinical exam may help identify individuals in need of early intervention.

Robin L. Wulffson, MD;
Updated by Duane R. Neff, PhD, MSW

FOR FURTHER INFORMATION

"Alcohol Overdose: The Dangers of Drinking Too Much." *National Institute on Alcohol Abuse and Alcoholism.* Natl. Inst. of Health, Apr. 2015. Web. 26 Oct. 2015.

"Binge Drinking: Terminology and Patterns of Use." *Substance Abuse and Mental Health Services Administration.* SAMHSA, 22 Nov. 2016. Web. 2 Jul. 2018.

Gowin, JL, Sloan ME, Stangl BL, Vatsalya V, Ramchandani VA. "Vulnerability for Alcohol Use Disorder and Rate of Alcohol Consumption." *Am J Psychiatry.* 2017 Nov 1;174(11):1094-1101. PMID:28774194

Kanny, D, Liu, Y, & Brewer, RD (2011, Jan. 14). Binge drinking – United States, 2009. *MMWR, Vol. 60.* 101-104.

Martin, Scott C. *The SAGE Encyclopedia of Alcohol: Social, Cultural, and Historical Perspectives.* Thousand Oaks: Sage, 2015. Print.

Olson, Kent R., et al., eds. *Poisoning and Drug Overdose.* 6th Ed. New York: McGraw-Hill, 2012. Print.

Patrick, Megan E., and John E. Schulenberg. "Prevalence and Predictors of Adolescent Alcohol Use and Binge Drinking in the United States." *Alcohol Research: Current Reviews* 35.2 (2015): 193–200. Print.

See also: Alcohol poisoning; Peer pressure; Adolescents and alcohol misuse

Bipolar disorder and addiction

CATEGORY: Psychological issues and behaviors

DEFINITION: Bipolar disorder is a mental illness characterized by cycles of depression and mania. This disease, earlier known as manic-depressive disorder, affects nearly six million American adults, about 2.5 percent of the adult population. Persons with bipolar disorder are at high risk of substance misuse and suicide. This disease has a high rate of recurrence and, if untreated, has a 15 percent increased risk of death by suicide than if treated.

BACKGROUND

Bipolar disorder and addiction frequently coexist. As many as 60 percent of people with bipolar disorder also will misuse an addictive substance during their lifetime, according to the National Alliance on Mental Illness.

A person in the manic phase of bipolar disorder may turn to alcohol or drugs to try to stabilize his or her condition. An addiction to alcohol or drugs might come about because the person is trying to slow down his or her thought processes long enough to get some rest. Addiction may be the result of, and not the reason for, the manic phase of the illness.

In the depressive stage of the illness, a person is vulnerable to addiction because he or she is looking for something that will help with feelings of hopelessness, isolation, and worthlessness. Alcohol or drugs may be considered a type of anesthetic to help the person escape from these kinds of feelings.

CAUSES

Persons with bipolar disorder are subject to overwhelming forces that are largely beyond their conscious control, which explains why so many persons with the disorder turn to drugs and alcohol for support and relief. Often, persons with bipolar disorder will use alcohol or drugs to numb their painful and difficult symptoms and to help them cope with their intense feelings. This can lead to a pattern of misuse that can quickly spiral into dependency and addiction.

People suffering with bipolar disorder are three to seven times more likely than others to misuse alcohol or drugs, such as sleeping pills and stimulants (including cocaine and methamphetamines). Drugs and alcohol are misused to increase the natural high of the mania and to self-medicate during depressive episodes.

SYMPTOMS

Bipolar disorder is characterized by drastic mood swings—extreme highs and devastating lows. Some of the symptoms exhibited during manic episodes include an extremely elated, happy mood or an extremely irritable, angry, unpleasant mood; increased physical and mental activity and energy; racing and uncontrolled thoughts; increased talking (speech more rapid than normal); ambitious, often grandiose plans; inflated self-esteem; risk taking; and impulsive activity such as spending sprees; sexual indiscretion; and decreased sleep without experiencing fatigue.

Symptoms of depressive episodes include loss of energy; prolonged sadness; decreased energy and activity; restlessness and irritability; inability to concentrate or make decisions; increased worry and anxiety; less interest or participation in, and less enjoyment of, activities normally enjoyed; feelings of guilt and hopelessness; change in appetite; change in sleep patterns; and thoughts of suicide.

People with bipolar disorder often have difficulty in the workplace. Many of their symptoms can interfere with their ability to show up for work, to do their job, and to interact productively with others.

The consequences of addiction for persons with bipolar disorder are many and include taking drugs

Pop singer Mariah Carey was diagnosed with bipolar disorder in 2001, but she told People *magazine she "lived in denial and isolation" for years. She said she finally sought treatment after a series of professional and romantic issues.* (via Wikimedia Commons)

or consuming alcohol to regulate, stabilize, or improve their mood. Drugs and alcohol can provide temporary symptom relief, but in time, they worsen the symptoms, resulting in ever-increasing drug or alcohol use. Alcohol and drugs can reduce the effectiveness of bipolar medications and can reduce compliance for bipolar treatment. Stimulant drugs, such as cocaine or methamphetamines, can induce mania and then deep depression, exacerbating symptoms. Withdrawal symptoms can worsen depression.

SCREENING AND DIAGNOSIS

Having a diagnosis for substance use disorder in persons with bipolar disorder is known as having a dual diagnosis. In such cases, the substance misuse can occur during both the manic and the depressive phases.

No diagnostic laboratory tests exist for bipolar disorder. Thus diagnosis occurs through standardized diagnostic criteria to rate and evaluate the person's behavior.

TREATMENT AND THERAPY

Treatment for addiction includes psychiatric care and medication. Because bipolar disorder and alcohol and drug addiction often appear together, the symptoms of each disorder overlap, making it difficult to recognize the coexistence of both. The two conditions must be treated in tandem, making dual diagnosis critical to the recovery process.

Residential substance use disorder treatment programs may be effective in treating co-occurring disorders. This treatment typically includes individual and group counseling, cognitive-behavior therapy, dialectical behavior therapy, twelve-step programs, and other mental health services. Research has shown that the most effective treatment combines supportive psychotherapy and the use of a mood-stabilizer (either lithium, carbamazepine, or divalproex/valproic acid), often with an antipsychotic medication. No research exists to show that any form of psychotherapy is an effective substitute for medication.

PREVENTION

The best recoveries are achieved when individuals with bipolar disorder get effective treatment and faithfully follow that treatment for a lifetime. The patient should regularly see a supportive physician who is knowledgeable about the psychiatric management of this disorder, should learn what symptoms predict the return of this illness and what additional "rescue" medication can be taken, and should learn to trust the warnings given by family and friends when they see early signs of relapse.

Gerald W. Keister;
Updated by Marianne Moss Madsen, MS

FOR FURTHER INFORMATION

Bacciardi, Silvia, et al. "Drug (Heroin) Addiction, Bipolar Spectrum, and Impulse Control Disorders." *Heroin Addiction and Related Clinical Problems* 15.2 (2013): 29–36. Print.

Basco, M. R., and A. J. Rush. *Cognitive-Behavior Therapy for Bipolar Disorder.* 2nd Ed. New York: Guilford, 2007. Print.

Goodwin, F. K., and K. R. Jamison. *Manic-Depressive Illness: Bipolar Disorders and Recurrent Depression.* 2nd Ed. New York: Oxford UP, 2007. Print

Johnson, C., et al. "Convergent Genome-Wide Association Results for Bipolar Disorder and Substance Dependence." *American Journal of Medical Genetics B: Neuropsychiatric Genetics* 150.2 (2009): 182–90. Print.

Mondimore, Francis Mark. "Alcoholism and Drug Abuse." *Bipolar Disorder: A Guide for Patients and Families.* 3rd ed. Baltimore: Johns Hopkins UP, 2014. 174–92. Print.

Perkinson, Robert R., Arthur E. Jongsma, and Timothy J. Bruce. "Bipolar Disorder." *The Addiction Treatment Planner.* 5th ed. Hoboken: Wiley, 2014. 90–103. Print.

See also: Addiction; Depression; Mental illness; Suicide and addiction

Birth defects and alcohol

CATEGORY: Health issues and physiology

DEFINITION: Fetal alcohol exposure is one of the leading causes of birth defects and developmental disorders. Estimates from the Centers for Disease Control and Prevention (CDC) in 2015 place the number of children in the United States affected by fetal alcohol exposure at approximately 0.2 to 1.5 infants for every 1,000 live births.

THE DANGERS OF DRINKING FOR TWO

When a pregnant woman drinks alcoholic beverages, the alcohol in her blood crosses the placenta easily and enters the embryo or fetus through the umbilical cord. Children affected by prenatal exposure to alcohol may suffer lifelong consequences, including intellectual impairment, learning disabilities, and serious behavioral problems.

All drinks containing alcohol can hurt an unborn baby. A standard twelve-ounce can of beer has the same amount of alcohol as a four-ounce glass of wine or a one-ounce shot of straight liquor. In addition, some alcoholic drinks, such as malt beverages, wine coolers, and mixed drinks, often contain more alcohol than a twelve-ounce can of beer. Studies have not been done to establish a known safe amount of alcohol that a woman can drink while pregnant.

Any time a pregnant woman participates in regular drinking increases her chance of having a miscarriage and puts her unborn child at risk for growth deficiencies, learning disabilities, and behavioral problems. Birth defects associated with prenatal exposure to alcohol can occur in the first eight weeks of pregnancy, before a woman even knows that she is pregnant.

Between 2011 and 2013, one in ten pregnant women surveyed reported alcohol use, and one in thirty-three reported binge drinking within thirty days of the survey, according to the CDC.

FETAL ALCOHOL SYNDROME

Fetal alcohol syndrome (FAS) is caused by alcohol consumption during pregnancy and is one of the leading known causes of mental disability and birth defects. It is characterized by abnormal facial features including: small head size, narrow eye slits, abnormalities of the nose and lip areas, growth deficiencies, and problems with the central nervous system (CNS).

Children with FAS may have problems with learning, memory, attention span, problem solving, speech, and hearing. These problems often lead to difficulties in school and in getting along with others. FAS is an irreversible condition that affects every aspect of a child's life and the lives of his or her family. FAS is preventable if a woman abstains from alcohol while she is pregnant.

FETAL ALCOHOL EFFECTS

In the past, the term fetal alcohol effects (FAE) was generally used to describe children who did not have all of the clinical signs of FAS, but who had various problems, including growth deficiency, behavioral problems, or problems with motor and speech skills. FAE has also been used to describe children who have all of the diagnostic features of FAS, but at mild levels. Because experts in the field were unable to agree on a single definition for FAE, the Institute of Medicine (IOM) proposed the terms alcohol-related neuro-development disorder (ARND) and alcohol-related birth defects (ARBD). ARND describes the functional

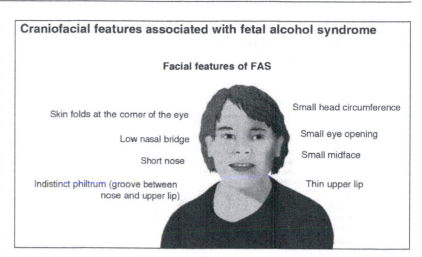

Craniofacial features associated with fetal alcohol syndrome

Facial features of FAS

Skin folds at the corner of the eye

Low nasal bridge

Short nose

Indistinct philtrum (groove between nose and upper lip)

Small head circumference

Small eye opening

Small midface

Thin upper lip

Fetal Alcohol Syndrome (FAS) causes abnormalities in facial structure to occur during prenatal development. (National Institute on Alcohol Abuse and Alcoholism)

or mental impairments linked to prenatal alcohol exposure, such as behavioral or cognitive abnormalities. These include learning difficulties, poor school performance, poor impulse control, and problems with mathematical skills, memory, attention, and judgment. ARBD describes malformations of the skeletal system and major organ systems. Such malformations may include defects of the heart, kidneys, bones, and auditory system.

TREATMENT AND PREVENTION

There is no cure for either fetal alcohol syndrome or fetal alcohol effects. They are irreversible, lifelong conditions that affect every aspect of a child's development. With early identification and diagnosis, a child with FAS can receive services that can help to maximize his or her potential.

The easiest way to prevent FAS is to abstain from alcohol use during pregnancy. Any amount of alcohol consumed during pregnancy is potentially dangerous to an unborn baby. If a pregnant woman is drinking during pregnancy, it is never too late for her to stop. The sooner a woman quits drinking, the better it will be for both her and her baby. If a woman is not able to quit drinking, she should contact her local social service agency or health plan for alcohol misuse treatment, if needed. If a woman is not yet pregnant, she should use an effective form of birth control until her drinking is under control.

Levels of Intellectual Disability

Mild

- IQ 50–70
- Slower than normal in all areas
- No unusual physical signs
- Can acquire practical skills
- Reading and math skills up to grades 3–6
- Can conform socially
- Can acquire daily-task skills
- Integrated in society

Moderate

- IQ 35–49
- Noticeable delays, particularly with speech
- May have unusual physical signs
- Can learn simple communication
- Can learn elementary health and safety skills
- Can participate in simple activities and self-care
- Can perform supervised tasks
- Can travel alone to familiar places

Severe

- IQ 20–34
- Significant delays in some areas; may begin walking later than normal
- Little or no communication skills, but some understanding of speech with some response
- Can be taught daily routines and repetitive activities
- May be trained in simple self-care
- Need direction and supervision socially

Profound

- IQ <20
- Significant delays in all areas
- Congenital abnormalities present
- Need close supervision
- Require attendant care
- May respond to regular physical and social activity
- Not capable of self-care

Mothers are not the only ones who can help prevent FAS, however. Significant others, family members, schools, social organizations, and communities alike can help to prevent FAS through education and intervention. Also, emerging research suggests that long-term alcohol use disorder among men may alter sperm cells in ways that introduce defects to the fetus at conception. Continued research will help to clarify this link and improve prevention efforts.

Celeste M. Krauss, MD;
Updated by Christine Gamble, MD, MPH

FOR FURTHER INFORMATION

Chaudhuri, J. D. "Alcohol and the Developing Fetus—A Review." *Medical Science Monitor* 6.5 (2000): 1031–41. Print.

"Drinking Alcohol during Pregnancy." *March of Dimes.* March of Dimes Foundation, Apr. 2016. Web. 29 Mar. 2012.

"Drinking and Your Pregnancy." *NIAAA.* Natl. Inst. on Alcohol Abuse and Alcoholism, May 2012. Web. 10 July. 2018.

"FASD: What Everyone Should Know." *NOFAS.* Natl. Org. on Fetal Alcohol Syndrome, 2014. Web. 11 Jul. 2018.

"Fetal Alcohol Spectrum Disorders (FASDs): Data and Statistics." *Centers for Disease Control and Prevention.* CDC, 27 Mar. 2018. Web. 10 Jul. 2018.

Nayak, Raghavendra B., and Pratima Murthy. "Fetal Alcohol Spectrum Disorder." *Indian Pediatrics* 45.12 (2008): 977–83. Print

"Prenatal Exposure to Alcohol." *Alcohol Research & Health* 24.1 (2000): 32–41. Print.

Thackray, Helen M., and Cynthia Tifft. "Fetal Alcohol Syndrome." *Pediatrics in Review* 22 (2001): 47–55. Print.

Warren, K. R. (2015), A Review of the History of Attitudes toward Drinking in Pregnancy. Alcohol Clin Exp Res, 39: 1110-1117. doi:10.1111/acer.12757

Williams, J. F., & Smith, V. C. (2015, November). Fetal Alcohol Spectrum Disorders. *American Academy of Pediatrics,* e1395-e1406.

See also: Alcohol's effects on the body; Birth defects and drug use; Birth defects and smoking; Fetal alcohol syndrome; Newborn addicts; Pregnancy and alcohol

Birth defects and drug use

CATEGORY: Health issues and physiology

ALSO KNOWN AS: Congenital anomalies and substance use disorder; developmental defects and substance misuse

DEFINITION: Birth defects or developmental defects refer to problems that develop in the fetus during the course of prenatal development. Birth defects are physical abnormalities that are present at birth regardless of the cause. One of the common causes of birth defects is drug use during pregnancy.

DRUGS AS TERATOGENS

Teratogens (teratogenic substances) are environmental substances that cause birth (or developmental) defects. Thousands of teratogenic substances exist, and a large number of them are drugs, including over-the-counter (OTC) drugs, prescription drugs, and illegal drugs of misuse.

Nearly all teratogens are most detrimental during the embryonic period (the second to eighth week of pregnancy). It is during this period in which organs form. Exposure to teratogenic substances may interfere with this normal organ formation. While drugs that are taken beyond the eighth week of pregnancy are not likely to cause actual birth defects, they may interfere with normal functioning of organs or may interfere with normal growth, causing intrauterine growth retardation. Drugs, like most other teratogens, affect the fetus when they cross the placenta along with oxygen and nutrients. Aspirin is one of the OTC drugs that is teratogenic, potentially causing bleeding in the pregnant woman and the fetus.

The use of prescription drugs may be necessitated because of a medical condition in the pregnant woman. If this is the case, it is essential for the medical professional to prescribe a drug that is not teratogenic or one that is unlikely to harm the fetus. One formerly common prescription drug, the broad-spectrum antibiotic tetracycline, caused discoloration of primary and secondary teeth in utero. Today, another broad-spectrum antibiotic is used to treat infection, decreasing the likelihood of a resultant birth defect.

Generally, when speaking of birth defects and drug use, one more commonly attributes defects to tobacco (smoking), alcohol, marijuana, stimulants, sedatives, addictive substances (like heroin or cocaine), and hallucinogens, most of which are teratogenic. Smoking tends to cause heart defects and intrauterine growth retardation. Alcohol exposure most typically causes fetal alcohol syndrome. This condition generally involves growth retardation and other physical and cognitive problems. No definite evidence exists about the teratogenic effects of marijuana, although the drug has been implicated in cases of small head circumference, neurological problems, and learning deficiencies. Investigations are ongoing into the effects of marijuana on prenatal development, especially because marijuana is the single most common illicit drug used by pregnant women.

Stimulants (including amphetamines) and sedatives (including phenobarbital) seem to cause developmental defects within the nervous system. Cocaine has been found to cause placental abruptions, causing death of pregnant woman and baby, or premature delivery. Opioids like heroin often cause intrauterine growth retardation and cause infants to be born addicted. Also, newborns addicted to heroin or other opioids are likely to have learning disabilities later in life.

Hallucinogens (like LSD or belladonna) differ from the other categories of drugs in that they can cause birth defects even if they are taken years before pregnancy. Hallucinogens have been found to cause chromosomal damage at the time of use. Because chromosomes in egg cells (ova) and in spermatogenic cells may be damaged, a wide variety of birth defects can occur. Similarly, if hallucinogens are used during early pregnancy, chromosomal damage may occur, leading to various types of birth defects. Many pregnant drug-users use more than one type of drug. This complicates the situation in that drugs may interact to have a significantly different and greater effect on the fetus.

DRUG TREATMENT FOR PREGNANT WOMEN

Pregnant women who use heroin or other opioids are often treated with methadone. While this is an effective immediate treatment, it does not prevent a fetus from being born addicted. Suboxone (also known as buprenorphine) is drug used since the 1980s to treat opioid addiction (first used in the United States for this purpose in 2002). According to the National Institute on Drug Abuse, the findings of a 2012 clinical trial suggest that buprenorphine may be a safe and effective alternative to methadone, the standard treatment for opioid dependence during pregnancy.

Infants born to mothers on heroin, methadone, or Suboxone are evaluated using the neonatal abstinence (Finnegan) scale. The use of this scale determines the course of treatment in stopping the use of these substances.

Robin Kamienny Montvilo, PhD;
Updated by Christine Gamble, MD, MPH

For Further Information

Bandstra, E. S. (2012), "Maternal Opioid Treatment: Human Experimental Research (MOTHER) Study: maternal, fetal and neonatal outcomes from secondary analyses." *Addiction*, 107: 1-4.

Boyd, Susan C., and Leonora Marcellus. *With Child: Substance Use During Pregnancy—A Woman-Centered Approach.* Halifax: Fernwood, 2007. Print.

Chabarria, K., Racusin, D. A., Antony, K. M., Kahr, M., Suter, M. A., Mastrobattista, J. M., et al. (2016, October). "Marijuana Use and its effects in Pregnancy." *American Journal of Obstetrics and Gynecology*, 506.e1-506.e7.

Forray, A. (2016). "Substance use during pregnancy." *F1000Research*, 5, F1000 Faculty Rev–887.

Huestis, Marilyn A., and Robin E. Choo. "Drug Abuse's Smallest Victims: In Utero Drug Exposure." *Forensic Science International* 128 (2002): 20–30. Print.

Hui, K., Angelotta, C., and Fisher, C. E. (2017) "Criminalizing substance use in pregnancy: misplaced priorities." *Addiction*, 112: 1123–1125.

Huizink, Anja C., and Eva J. Mulder. "Maternal Smoking, Drinking, or Cannabis Use During Pregnancy and Neurobehavioral and Cognitive Functioning in Human Offspring." *Neuroscience Biobehavioral Review* 30 (2006): 24–41. Print.

Mark, K., A. Desai, and M. Terplan, "Marijuana use and pregnancy: prevalence, associated characteristics, and birth outcomes." *Arch Womens Ment Health*, 2016. 19(1): p. 105-11.

Rayburn, William, F. "Maternal and Fetal Effects from Substance Use." *Clinical Perinatology* 34 (2007): 559–71. Print.

Whitten, Lori. "A Multisite Clinical Trial Lays Groundwork for Improving Care for Mothers and Babies Affected by Opioid Dependence." *Natl. Inst. on Drug Abuse.* NIH NIDA, July 2012. Web. 08 Jul. 2018.

See also: Birth defects and alcohol; Birth defects and smoking; Hallucinogen's effects on the body; Narcotics' effects on the body; Pregnancy and drug use; Simulants' effects on the body

Birth defects and smoking

Category: Health issues and physiology

Definition: It is estimated that between 10 and 25 percent of women smoke during their pregnancies. Incidence rates are especially high among women who are young, single, or poor. Prenatal exposure to nicotine results in many negative effects on the developing fetus, including physical and cognitive problems evident at birth and throughout the lifespan.

Mechanism of Action

The pharmacologically active ingredient in cigarettes is nicotine. When a woman smokes during pregnancy, the nicotine passes into the bloodstream of her fetus. After nicotine crosses the placenta, the level of nicotine in the fetus exceeds that of the level in the pregnant woman. Nicotine also can constrict blood vessels in the umbilical cord, which decreases the amount of oxygen available to the fetus. The effect of nicotine on fetal development appears to be dose-dependent: the more cigarettes a woman smokes during her pregnancy, the greater the risk to her fetus.

Prenatal Exposure to Nicotine: Physical Effects

Fetuses exposed to nicotine are less likely to survive pregnancy than are fetuses not exposed. Smoking increases the likelihood of ectopic pregnancy, spontaneous abortion, and placental abruption (in which the placenta detaches from the uterine wall), which can lead to perinatal mortality (death during the end of pregnancy or within the first month after birth).

Fetuses exposed to nicotine prenatally are at a greater risk of being born prematurely, of having a low birth weight (an average weight reduction of 200 grams), of showing heightened tremors and startles, and of having respiratory problems. Prenatal exposure to nicotine also increases the risk of stillbirth and infant mortality. The rate of sudden infant death syndrome is three to four times higher among exposed infants than it is among infants who were not exposed to nicotine before birth.

Research on the relationship between maternal smoking and the risk of congenital birth defects has produced mixed results. While some researchers suggest a link between maternal smoking and, for example, cleft palate, this result is not found in all studies. There is evidence to support an increased risk of cardiovascular anomalies and neural tube defects in infants who were exposed to nicotine before birth. Data from the National Birth Defects Prevention Study also reveals an increase in craniosynostosis (in which the bones in the skull of a fetus close too early) in fetuses carried by women who smoked more than fifteen cigarettes per day while pregnant.

The problems associated with prenatal exposure to nicotine continue beyond infancy. Children who had been prenatally exposed to nicotine continue to be at risk for poor respiratory function during childhood and are more likely to be diagnosed with asthma and wheezing than are children who were not exposed. Children born to women who smoked during their pregnancies are also at an increased risk for developing all types of childhood cancer.

While most of the research in this field has focused on pregnant women who smoke, some new work looking at secondhand smoke suggests that exposure to secondhand smoke may increase fetal risk at a rate that is similar to that seen in women who smoke less than one-half a pack per day while pregnant.

PRENATAL EXPOSURE TO NICOTINE: COGNITIVE EFFECTS

When women smoke during pregnancy, their children have (when tested at three and four years of age), on average, poorer language skills and lower cognitive functioning than children not exposed. Many studies report that children prenatally exposed to nicotine are at an increased risk for intellectual impairment. Furthermore, controlled studies have documented a 50 percent increase in idiopathic intellectual disability (in which a low intelligence quotient is not associated with a chromosomal defect).

Children whose mothers smoked during pregnancy also are more likely to be diagnosed with attention deficit hyperactivity disorder than are their peers who were not exposed. In addition to having academic difficulties, children whose mothers smoked during their pregnancies are also more likely to have disruptive behavior disorders. Finally, children exposed to nicotine before birth are at an increased risk of being diagnosed with a psychiatric disorder during childhood, especially if their mothers were heavy smokers.

PATERNAL SMOKING

Although most studies focus on maternal smoking, some researchers have explored the effect of paternal smoking on fetuses and found evidence that men who smoked for years before conceiving a child had children who were at increased risk for developing brain tumors and cancer before the age of five years. Other researchers have reported an increased risk of anencephalus (the absence of a large part of the brain and skull) and of spina bifida (in which some vertebrae are not fully formed, preventing their closure around the spinal cord) in the offspring of fathers who smoked.

Monica L. McCoy, PhD;
Updated by Christine Gamble, MD, MPH

FOR FURTHER INFORMATION

Centers for Disease Control and Prevention. "Reproductive Health: Tobacco Use and Pregnancy." *CDC.gov*. CDC, 28 Jun. 2018. Web. 04 Jul. 2018.

Cnattingius, Sven. "The Epidemiology of Smoking during Pregnancy: Smoking Prevalence, Maternal Characteristics, and Pregnancy Outcomes." *Nicotine and Tobacco Research* 6.2 (2004): 125–40. Print.

Grice, D. E. (2016). "Prenatal Maternal Smoking and Increased Risk for Tourette's Disorder and Chronic Tic Disorder." *Journal of the American Academy of Child & Adolescent Psychiatry*: 784-791. Print.

Huizink, Anja, and Eduard Mulder. "Maternal Smoking, Drinking, or Cannabis Use During Pregnancy and Neurobehavioral and Cognitive Functioning in Human Offspring." *Neuroscience and Biobehavioral Reviews* 30.1 (2006): 24–41. Print.

Kaneshiro, Neil K. "Intellectual Disability." *MedlinePlus*. US Natl. Lib. of Medicine, 10 May 2013. Web. 28 Oct. 2015.

Shea, Alison, and Meir Steiner. "Cigarette Smoking During Pregnancy." *Nicotine and Tobacco Research* 10.2 (2008): 267–78. Print.

Perez da Silva Pereira, Priscilla, Fabiana A. F. Da Mata, Ana Claudia Godoy Figueiredo, Keitty Regina Cordeiro de Andrade, Maurício Gomes Pereira. "Maternal Active Smoking During Pregnancy and Low Birth Weight in the Americas: A Systematic Review and Meta-analysis." *Nicotine & Tobacco Research*, Volume 19, Issue 5, 1 May 2017, Pages 497–505, https://doi.org/10.1093/ntr/ntw228

Reitan, Therese and Callinan, Sarah. "Changes in Smoking Rates among Pregnant Women and the General Female Population in Australia, Finland, Norway, and Sweden." *Nicotine & Tobacco Research*, Volume 19, Issue 3, 1 March 2017, Pages 282–289, https://doi.org/10.1093/ntr/ntw188

Shisler, Shannon, Eiden, Rina, Molnar, Danielle S., Schuetze, Pamela, Huestis, Marilyn, Homish, Gregory (Grice, 2016); "Smoking in Pregnancy and Fetal Growth: The Case for More Intensive Assessment."*Nicotine & Tobacco Research*, Volume 19, Issue 5, 1 May 2017, Pages 525–531,https://doi.org/10.1093/ntr/ntx018

Woods, Scott E., and Uma Raju. "Maternal Smoking and the Risk of Congenital Birth Defects: A Cohort Study." *Journal of the American Board of Family Practice* 14.5 (2001): 330–34. Print.

See also: Birth defects and alcohol; Birth defects and drug use; Pregnancy and smoking; Smoking's effects on the body

Blood alcohol content (BAC)

CATEGORY: Diagnosis and prevention

ALSO KNOWN AS: Blood alcohol concentration

DEFINITION: Blood alcohol content is a measurement of the amount of alcohol in a person's circulatory system at a given time. This measurement is commonly obtained by law enforcement officers in the field, who check drivers for operating a vehicle under the influence of alcohol. Blood alcohol content is less often used as a measure in medical treatment.

BACKGROUND

Blood alcohol content (BAC) is a measure of the amount of ethanol (or ethyl alcohol) in a person's bloodstream. In the United States, BAC is measured in grams of alcohol per 100 milliliters (ml) of blood. If a person has 0.10 grams of alcohol in his or her bloodstream for every 100 ml of blood, the BAC for that person would be 0.10. Another way to think of BAC is that it is the percentage of a person's blood that is composed of alcohol.

BAC is most often measured to determine if a person is impaired by alcohol while driving . Because drawing blood is an invasive procedure, law enforcement officers usually use a breath analyzer (or breathalyzer) in the field to estimate a person's BAC. Breathalyzer results accurately reflect blood-alcohol levels. In the United States (all states), the legal blood-alcohol limit for drivers who are old enough to legally drink alcohol is 0.08. Some states have stiffer penalties for drivers whose BAC is 0.17 or higher. The legal blood-alcohol limit for persons younger than age twenty-one years is 0.02 in most states, rather than 0.0 because some legal drugs or mouthwashes contain small amounts of ethyl alcohol, which could register as alcohol in one's BAC.

RELATIVITY OF BAC LEVELS

Although blood alcohol levels are directly proportional to the amount of alcohol consumed, BAC levels vary significantly from person to person and from situation to situation for the same amount of alcohol. Factors that affect BAC are a person's weight and gender, the length of time in which the alcohol was consumed, the presence or absence of food in the stomach at the time of alcohol consumption, and a person's genetic makeup.

Women's bodies generally contain less water than do men's bodies, so alcohol has a greater relative impact on women. Also, the greater a person's weight, the more that person can consume alcohol before feeling its effects. For instance, a 200-pound man who drank two 12-ounce beers in one hour would likely have a BAC of 0.04, whereas a 120-pound woman drinking the same two beers in the same amount time would likely have a BAC of 0.08.

Food in the stomach at the time of alcohol consumption can keep a person's BAC lower because the alcohol makes its way into the bloodstream at a slower rate. One factor that does not affect BAC is caffeine , which can mask the depressant effects of alcohol but does not improve impaired judgment or increase a person's reaction time while, for example, driving. Finally, a physician may be interested in a patient's BAC if the physician suspects acute alcohol poisoning or when making a diagnosis of alcoholism.

Cathy Frisinger MPH

FOR FURTHER INFORMATION

"The ABCs of BAC." *National Highway Traffic Safety Administration.* US Dept. of Transportation, n.d. Web. 27 Oct. 2015.

"Alcohol-Impaired Driving." *Insurance Institute for Highway Safety.* Insurance Institute for Highway Safety, 2013. Web. 27 Oct. 2015.

Dasgupta, Amitava. *The Science of Drinking: How Alcohol Affects Your Body and Mind.* Lanham, MD: Rowman, 2011. Print.

"Drunk Driving Laws." *Governors Highway Safety Association.* Governors Highway Safety Assn., Oct. 2015. Web. 27 Oct. 2015.

Hingson, R., T. Heeren, and M. Winter. "Lower Legal Alcohol Limits for Young Drivers." *Public Health Reports* 109.6 (1994): 738–44. Print.

"Impaired Driving: Get the Facts." *Injury Prevention and Control: Motor Vehicle Safety.* Centers for Disease Control and Prevention, 19 May 2015. Web. 27 Oct. 2015.

Shults, R. A., et al. "Association Between State-Level Drinking and Driving Countermeasures and Self-Reported Alcohol-Impaired Driving." *Injury Prevention* 8 (2002): 106–10. Print.

See also: Alcohol's effects on the body; Diagnosis methods; Drunk driving

Body modification addiction

CATEGORY: Health issues and physiology; Psychological issues and behaviors

DEFINITION: Body modification is the intentional physical altering of one's body, often for aesthetic reasons, by means of piercing and tattooing, for example. Personal modification is mediated by numerous psychological and social constructs (such as religion, culture, self-esteem, and identity development). Literature on body modification addiction is predominantly focused on how to understand, balance, and differentiate issues of self-mutilation versus issues of self-empowerment and identity formation, in the context of a person's unique cultural background.

HISTORY

Body modification's long history is rooted in the practice of more clearly marking or imposing meaning upon a particular person by physically changing their appearance. The practices of body piercing and tattooing, for example, have enabled cultures to more closely monitor religious affiliation, social groups, and social status for thousands of years.

Body modification occurs across the world today in various forms and reasons Other examples of body modifications from around the world include neck elongation in Thailand and Africa, henna tattooing in Southeast Asia and the Middle East, tooth filing in Bali, lip piercing and earlobe stretching in Africa, and female and male circumcision in many areas of the world.

Modern understandings of body modification have evolved in nuanced ways. While some cultures continue to use modification rituals in the ways of predecessors, other cultures have seen body modification practices take a more provocative turn, away from tenets of group affiliation or rite-of-passage and toward self-expression and identity formation.

The latter part of the twentieth century and the beginning of the twenty-first century have seen a steep increase in body modification (in both the number of people choosing to modify their body and in the larger cross-section of society engaging in the practice). Body modification has become so popular that it has become difficult to assign a person to a particular subgroup (or subculture) based solely on the chosen modification. Historically, this was the principal reason why people chose to modify their body.

The most common motivators behind the practice of body modification include art and fashion, individuality (control), group affiliation, and personal transformation. As such, the tenor of body modification research has shifted slightly over the years, away from issues of self-mutilation and toward a greater appreciation for and understanding of how such practices align with one's self-structures and ongoing personal narrative.

Finally, a powerful undercurrent to these motivators is that of addiction. A question that remains is this: What exactly is a person becoming addicted to when his or her body modification rituals intersect with obvious patterns of addictive behavior?

TRANSITIONAL RESEARCH

Sociological research on issues related to body modification has been largely replaced with research aimed at identifying existing personality structures that make body modification more likely. This transition has been made, in part, because issues of body modification have become so prevalent in society. Body modification is now a mainstream practice, so drawing lines between specific social groups and exploring their derivations has become something of an antiquated notion.

Psychological research has instead taken up the issue of underlying motivational factors and existing personality structures that make it more likely for someone to pursue specific body modification (body piercing, tattooing, and plastic surgery, in particular). Additionally, while there is a dearth of research focused exclusively on body modification addiction, valuable research is available to help one better understand the mechanisms that lead to addictive behavior. Of particular importance is research that values pluralism and examines body modification addiction through several, competing theoretical modalities.

Today research continues to be is far more collaborative and inclusive when it comes to understanding body modification and treating body modification addiction. Research now considers traditional, well-accepted medical underpinnings of addiction, long-standing sociological precedents inherent to all body modification, and the complex self-processes and personality structures that may predispose people to body modification, all of which has helped advance research in this area. As such, what may have once fallen into the realm of psychopathology is now considered more broadly and more carefully.

MOTIVATORS AND ADDICTIVE BEHAVIOR

An addiction, by definition, is a behavior that persists despite negative consequences. In the case of body modification addiction, the negative consequences can include infections (sometimes severe), the perpetuation of unhealthy coping mechanisms, and potential pathological stigma, among others. Underlying these consequences are complex representations and expressions of the self, including prevalent cultural dynamics and experiences in one's early history that led to a specific self-identity. Dieting, bodybuilding, tanning, ear piercing and cosmetic surgery have long been common in the United States, and practices such as tattooing, body piercing and scarification are becoming increasingly popular. Cosmetic surgery is also a form of body modification that may be compared to previous examples and is becoming increasingly popular.

According to the American Society for Aesthetic Plastic Surgery (ASAPS), in 2008, Americans underwent 10.2 million cosmetic procedures, paying out just under $12 billion. While the more recent general economic downturn has led to a slight decrease in such procedures, cosmetic surgery has increased dramatically in the last decade. In fact, while the majority of procedures are performed on women, men's use of cosmetic procedures has increased 20 percent since the year 2000. Several different motivation factors could exist for all of the modification methods described. For example, people may seek to control, "correct" or "perfect" some aspect of their appearance, or to use their bodies as a canvas for creative self-expression. While some seek to improve their body-image, this is not necessarily a motivating factor for everyone who engages in body modification. Additionally, some attempts at body modification can also have unintended negative consequences that might ultimately damage self-esteem. For example, while societal acceptance of tattoos and piercings has increased, there may still be repercussions. In a 2014 survey, 76 percent of 2,700 people interviewed said they believed that a tattoo or piercing had hurt their chances of getting a job.

Considerable research has looked at the most prevalent motivators and personality traits common to people who engage in body modification. This research has helped advance the discussion about how to best identify and treat body modification addiction. It considers, for example, external and internal triggers, conflicts that arise, and factors that interfere with goal-setting and necessary support systems.

Perhaps most important to any treatment of addiction is identifying the motivation in place to help reduce (and ultimately stop) the negative behavior. A preliminary, vital step would be considering why it is that someone is engaged in the behavior in the first place (before even considering why it is that they want to change). Taken together, evaluating motivational factors and personality constructs that contribute to a specific behavior is a crucial first step for any treatment.

Tattooing is a form of body modification where a design is made by inserting ink, dyes and pigments into the dermis layer of the skin to change the pigment. (Photographer: Alexander Kuzovlev; Tattoo artist: Anton Ivkin, via Wikimedia Commons)

With respect to body modification, considerable overlap exists between motivators and personality traits common to those who engage in this behavior. Typically, the average body modifier is one who seeks sensation and control and one who is (often) driven by art and fashion, individuality, group affiliation, and personal transformation. Those addicted to body modification typically strive to hold on to specific memories, experiences, and values (positive and negative).

CURRENT UNDERSTANDINGS

How might one answer a person who asks why he or she cannot stop a child from piercing his or her body? Before answering this question, one may want to consider how body modification addiction differs from other substance-based addictions.

Whereas tracing the derivation of one's substance-based addiction is more "paint-by-numbers" (linear), tracing the derivation of one's body modification addiction is more comparable to a fresco painting, with layers upon layers of factors contributing to the overall portrait. It can be difficult to navigate to a particular place in time, or event, that led to a specific body modification addiction. Instead, it is better to consider the range of factors that can make body modification addiction so complex. This is precisely what modern research is aiming to do.

Discriminative overtones have been largely replaced with questioning and curious inquiry about how (and why) people choose to modify their body, about what is driving their proclivity to do so, and about possible patterns or character traits common to those who modify often. The body has been an artistic canvas for thousands of years. It also has become more than an object. The body has become the vehicle through which people assert control in their lives, transform and heal in the face of trauma, and tell the world how they would like to be identified.

One recent study has suggests that some individuals become addicted to tanning, despite the documented links to skin damage, severe wrinkling, and skin cancer. Others suggest that tanning addiction, what some have called "tanorexia," may be linked to Body Dysmorphic Disorder (BDD). Excessive tanning may be stem from an obsession with perceived physical flaws and the compulsion to "correct" them.

FUTURE TRENDS

Much has been written about the ways in which people use their body to reclaim some aspect of their life, empower themselves, and express themselves in a therapeutic way. As such, a twenty-first-century understanding of body modification has been elevated by research examining theories of the self and embracing pluralism. What is known about body modification addiction has been greatly enhanced by research into motivational factors and personality constructs common to those who engage in this behavior. Future research should continue this trend, examining the powerful representations of the self and cultural factors that shape human identity.

Joseph C. Viola, PhD, Updated by Jeffrey Larson

FOR FURTHER INFORMATION

Eschler, Jordan & Bhattacharya, Arpita & Pratt, Wanda. "Designing a Reclamation of Body and Health: Cancer Survivor Tattoos as Coping Ritual." ACM Digital Library, 2018, https://dl.acm.org/citation.cfm?id=3173574.3174084

Jocelyn Camacho & Wyatt Brown. "The evolution of the tattoo in defiance of the immutable definition of deviance: current perceptions by law enforcement of tattooed arrestees." *Deviant Behavior*, 39:8, 1023-1041, 2018.

Nathanson, Craig, Delroy L. Paulhus, and Kevin M. Williams. "Personality and Misconduct Correlates of Body Modification and Other Cultural Deviance Markers." *Journal of Research in Personality* 40 (2006): 779–802. Print.

Pfeifer, Gail M. MA, RN, "Attitudes Toward Piercings and Tattoos." *AJN, American Journal of Nursing*: May - Volume 112 - Issue 5 - p 15. (2012)

Pitts, V. *In The Flesh: The Cultural Politics of Body Modification*. New York: Palgrave, 2003. Print.

Suchet, Melanie. "The 21st Century Body: Introduction." *Studies in Gender and Sexuality* 10.3 (2009): 113–18. Print.

Winchel, Ronald M., and Michael Stanley. "Self-Injurious Behavior: A Review of the Behavior and Biology of Self-Mutilation." *American Journal of Psychiatry* 148 (1991): 306–17. Print.

Wohlrab, Silke, et al. "Differences in Personality Characteristics Between Body-Modified and Non-Modified Individuals: Associations with Individual Personality Traits and Their Possible Evolutionary Implications." *European Journal of Personality* 21.7 (2007): 931–51. Print.

Wohlrab, Silke, Jutta Stahl, and Peter M. Kappeler. "Modifying the Body: Motivations for Getting Tattooed and Pierced." *Body Image* 4.1 (2007): 87–95. Print.

See also: Behavioral addictions: Overview; DSM-5 Criteria for substance use disorders; Self-destructive behavior and addiction

Brain changes with addiction

CATEGORY: Health issues and physiology

DEFINITION: Continued use of illicit substances and alcohol may lead to positive reinforcement. This activation within the brain leads to continued use given the activation response is strong and pleasurable. The increased release of dopamine, indicates the individual will continue to search-out the same feeling; thus, it is important to pair similar stimuli to trigger this same release when the individual discontinues use of the substance.

OVERVIEW

Neuroimaging techniques provide an understanding as to how the brain is affected in those diagnosed with substance use disorders. In substance use treatment, the focus is often on the behaviors that lead to using, as well as understanding the neurological underpinnings. The *Diagnostic and Statistic Manual, Fifth Edition* reported substance use is often co-occurring with other mental health disorders. It is thought this co-occurrence is due to utilizing substances as a means to cope with life stressors.

Chronic use of substances may lead to changes within the brain. Some of the changes that occur may be reversible others are permanent. Due to utilizing illicit substance and alcohol as a means to cope with life stressors, relapse may be high in this population. This is further complicated by the neuronal changes that occur within the brain when someone uses a substance. There are multiple modalities of treatment, of which the most effective has been found to be treatment that engages a biopsychosocial approach. Pharmaceutical approaches may be appropriate on a case-by-case basis.

MENTAL HEALTH DISORDERS IN THOSE WITH ADDICTION HISTORIES

Addiction differs from dependence. For example, addiction is the repetitive use of a substance, despite negative consequences; where as dependence is the change the body experiences that occurs when the substance is discontinued. For example, someone may continuously utilize cocaine and their family ceases a relationship with them; yet, they do not experience the continued euphoria most individuals crave when using cocaine. The question of did the chicken or egg come first is often sought after in those with substance use histories – there is no one solid answer. For some, the addiction came from using the substance, for others they began using as a maladaptive coping technique (Kuhn, Swartzwelder, & Wilkie, 2014).

The most common mental health disorders that are comorbid with substance use includes schizophrenia, bipolar disorders, conduct disorder, depressive disorders, posttraumatic stress disorder, attention-deficit-hyperactivity disorder, gambling disorder, other substance use diagnoses, and personality disorders (American Psychiatric Association, 2013). When individuals have co-occurring disorders, it is thought their use of the substance is a maladaptive means to cope with life stressors or the mental health disorder. This may proliferate the symptoms of their mental health aliments. Thus, it is important for those assessing and treating individuals diagnosed with a substance use disorder to utilize a multistep approach to treatment.

Researchers found that addiction develops based on a number of factors, including genetics and environment. To illustrate, there are some individuals who utilize alcohol and/or cocaine in moderation or recreationally; yet, there are others who use the substance a few times and the use becomes chronic. The individuals, who use in moderation or recreationally, may not have the genetics or problematic environments that may lead someone to continued use. For those whose use alcohol chronically, it was found that the variations in genes for alcohol dehydrogenase, the mu opiate receptor, the alpha GABA receptor, and the muscarinic acetylcholine receptor all play a role in addiction to alcohol (Carlson, 2010).

BRAIN RESPONSES IN BEHAVIOR

Advancements in neuroimaging show researchers how substances and related images, sounds, taste, or smells affect the brain. In functional-imaging, researchers found that multiple cortical regions are activated in those with addiction disorders, whereas the same areas do not become activated for those who do not have a diagnosis of such. Further, the volume of gray matter may also be depleted in individuals with addiction diagnoses.

Illicit substances and alcohol change the brain's biochemical processes, specifically, there is an alteration of neuroreceptors and how they receive, process, and send information to various areas of the brain and body. This is further complicated when the reward centers of the brain (e.g., amygdala and nucleus accumbens [NA]) are activated. With continued use of a substance and activation of dopamine receptors, the brain begins to believe it needs the substance in order to sustain life. The increased activation in the pleasure centers of the brain, leads to lower activation in the judgment and higher-order thinking that is found within the frontal lobe. Mental health and medical providers may see a decrease in the individual's ability to control pain, anxiety, impulsiveness, and may report lower experiences of euphoria.

Addiction is a complex process that is both physical and behavioral. Those who continue to use a substance will likely need to increase what they are using, in order to obtain the same effects they initially had when they tried the substance. The individual may also report they are using more to avoid experiencing withdrawal symptoms (e.g., lethargy, anxiety, diarrhea, or lack of sleep). Furthermore, depending on how the person delivers the substance to the brain (e.g., injection, insufflation, or oral) this will affect how quickly and how much enters the brain. When one discusses addiction behaviors, they will note the individual describes excitement that begins when they think about when and how they will obtain their next high. This excitement will continue through obtaining the substance, prepping to use, and then using. After using, the individual may feel sad, anxious, guilty, or numb. These feelings may be quickly replaced by the thought of using again. As previously described, this is why treatment of addiction needs to include both medical and psychological intervention, depending on the substance. For example, someone with an addiction to a barbiturate will need medical assistance in order to safely discontinue the substance. The individual will then need psychological treatment to focus on the behavioral aspects of addiction. It is ostensible the behavioral treatment will be utilized throughout the person's life, as there may be situations, scents, or images, that ignite the pleasure center's in the brain that suggest the person should use again (Carlson, 2010).

PHYSICAL BRAIN EFFECTS

As described in the previous section, substances influence the synaptic transmissions within the brain.

This activation increases the amount of certain neurotransmitters, most often dopamine as this neurotransmitter is known for increasing the perception of pleasure. The area of the brain that is initially affected is the ventral tegmental area (VTA), which is located in the midbrain. As changes occur in the VTA area of the brain, including the n-acetylcysteine (NAC), the areas of the brain responsible for compulsive behaviors are changed with continued use of the substance. More specifically, the area affected is the dorsal striatum, which is involved in conditioning. Initially, the individual enjoys the pleasurable effects they feel from the substance. This pleasure ensures reinforcement, as the person enjoys the feeling and the routine they develop with using the substance. As the routine continues, the individual may need to increase the amount of the substance they are using, as they may begin to build a tolerance. When tolerance occurs, this means the brain is not being rewarded the same way it was when the individual first began using. The individual is not feeling the same sense of pleasure, so they begin to increase either the amount used, or the number of times they use throughout the day. The habitual nature of addiction changes the dorsal striatum. Neuroimaging research found neural changes in the brain are responsible for addiction. Further, researchers found a connection between the striatum and the VTA, which appears to continue the cycle of addiction (Carlson, 2010).

Depending on the substance used, certain neurotransmitters and areas of the brain are affected differently. For example, neurotransmitters that are affected by alcohol are known as GABA and glutamate. These neurotransmitters are important in forming new memories and higher-order thinking. This is often why individuals evidence memory deficits from the previous day or evidence poor judgment while intoxicated. Another example is opiates affect on the brain. Specifically, opioids act on receptors of endogenous neurotransmitters within the brain that control involuntary movement or mood, and act on the reward system of the brain. These types of neurotransmitters are found naturally in the body, so when someone takes a synthetic opiate, the endogenous opioid receptors are activated so the individual feels a rush of pleasure (Kuhn et al., 2014).

TREATMENT

Currently, there are many different treatments for those with addiction problems. More specifically, treatment modalities that focus on the following aspects of recovery have been found to be most effective: cognitive-behavioral treatment to educate the individual on cycle of addiction; contingency management, when the client is provided positive reinforcement for healthy behaviors; motivational enhancement therapy, which helps to build motivation, create a plan, engage in the plan, and seek recovery; and 12-step programs, as described below (Substance Abuse and Mental Health Services Administration [SAMHSA], 2018). Additionally, providers will assess, and treat as needed, for a reduction of the primary substance and increased functioning in employment, education, interpersonal relationship, overall medical health, legal status, mental health aliments, and reduction in disease(s) (Springer, McNeece, & Arnold, 2003).

The treatment that has found to be most promising is the Transtheoretical Model of Change (TTM). In this treatment, the provider utilizes a biopsychosocial lens, encompassing the identified client as a whole. The biopsychosocial lens includes utilization of people and entities at the individual (e.g., person, or community), micro (e.g., nuclear family, peers, or immediate connections), mezzo (e.g., organizations, neighborhoods, or cultural groups), and macro (e.g., societal perspectives) (Springer et al., 2003). In 1992, Prochaska, DiClemente, and Norcross created the TTM, and Shorkey and DiNitto applied this theory to addiction in 1995 and coined the treatment Individuals, Families, Organizations, and Communities in an Ecological Context Model (IFOCECM) (Springer et al., 2003). The first stage is Precontemplation when the client is not aware they have a problem and they are not seeking treatment. Stage 2 is Contemplation, when the client is aware of their problem, begins to think about change, but has yet to commit to the process. The third stage is Preparation. In this stage, the client begins to set goals and identifies what needs to be changed in the near future. During Stage 4, the client is in Action, indicating they are making effort to change and identifying barriers to sobriety. In the fifth stage, Adaption/Maintenance, the client is adapting to the change in order to maintain the new way of living. Finally, the last stage is Evaluation. The client assesses the results of the different stages and obtains feedback from others. The process does not stop with Stage 6, as the client will continue to work towards maintaining sobriety long-term (Springer et al., 2003).

There is community-based treatment, Alcoholics Anonymous, Narcotics Anonymous, AL-ANON, and SMART Recovery. These types of programs are found to be helpful, given they hold the individuals accountable, as well as provide a supportive system for those outside the individual's family and friend unit. Another option is pharmaceutical therapies. For alcohol use disorder, individuals may be prescribed Acamprosate, which reduces the symptoms of withdrawal and may help individuals maintain abstinence. Another medication for alcohol use is called Naltrexone, which blocks the effects of opioids, which in turn reduces the craving for alcohol. Disulfiram is a medication that alters the way the body metabolize alcohol. When the individual takes Disulfiram and consumes alcohol, they will experience unpleasant bodily reactions (e.g., flushing or nausea). The other substance that has medications to assist with decreasing use is opioids. The common treatments are Methadone or Buprenorphine, which reduce the withdrawal effects and cravings of opioid use. In utilizing these medications, research evidenced that individuals are more likely to remain in treatment and decrease risky-behaviors (e.g., needle-sharing). There is also an injectable medication, Extended-Release Naltrexone, which reduces the risk of relapse and decreases cravings for opioids. This medication is often provided to those who are incarcerated, in a residential setting, or when maintenance with Methadone or Buprenorphine is contraindicated (as it either is not appropriate or not available) (SAMHSA, 2018).

The treatment protocol the client chooses to use is one that they will make with their mental health and medical providers. Treatment, when completed from a team standpoint, can be effective in maintaining sobriety. When treatment includes a focus on mental health, the cycle of addiction, and, if appropriate, pharmaceutical therapies will assist the client in long-term recovery. One aspect all involved in treatment with individuals who use illicit substance or alcohol must remember is that while relapses may occur, this does not mean the individual does not want help or does not want to become healthy again.

Lindsey L. Wilner, Psy.D.

FOR FURTHER INFORMATION

American Psychiatric Association. (2013). *Diagnostic and Statistical Manual of Mental Disorders – Fifth Edition (DSM-5)*. Arlington, VA: American Psychiatric Association.

Carlson, N. R. (2010). *Physiology of behavior* (10th Ed.). Boston, MA: Allyn & Bacon.

Kuhn, C., Swartzwelder, S., & Wilson, W. (2014). *Buzzed: The straight facts about the most used and abused drugs from alcohol to ecstasy* (4th Ed.). New York, NY: W. W. Norton & Company, Inc.

Springer, D. W., McNeece, C. A., & Arnold, E. M. (2003). *Substance abuse treatment for criminal offenders: An evidenced-based guide for practitioners*. Washington, DC: American Psychological Association.

Substance Abuse and Mental Health Services Administration. (2018, June 13). *Treatments for substance use disorders*. Retrieved from https://www.samhsa.gov/treatment/substance-use-disorders

See also: Alcohol's effects on the body; Dopamine and addiction; Genetics and substance misuse; Narcotics' effects on the body; Science of addiction

Bupropion

CATEGORY: Treatment

ALSO KNOWN AS: as: Wellbutrin; Zyban

DEFINITION: Bupropion is an antidepressant, but it is also prescribed to help people quit smoking. It can be used in combination with a nicotine replacement product. Bupropion appears to affect two brain chemicals that may be related to nicotine addiction: dopamine and norepinephrine. Bupropion reduces the cravings for cigarettes that smokers experience when they try to quit. The drug also seems to reduce many of the nicotine withdrawal symptoms, including irritability, frustration, and anger.

HISTORY OF USE

Bupropion is a widely prescribed antidepressant, at one time the fourth-most prescribed antidepressant in the United States. It was invented in 1969 by GlaxoSmithKline (then Burroughs Wellcome) and was designed and synthesized by Nariman Mehta. It was approved as an antidepressant in 1985 by the US Food and Drug Administration, withdrawn in 1986 because of concerns over seizures, and reintroduced to the market in 1989, after the maximum dosage was adjusted. Bupropion was approved in 1997 as an aid for smoking cessation (under the name Zyban). Under the name Wellbutrin XL, it has also been approved to treat seasonal affective disorder, a mood disorder prevalent in either the winter or the summer months.

TREATMENT

Patients are instructed to start taking bupropion one week before they plan to stop smoking. It takes about one week for this medication to reach adequate levels in a person's system, and patients are instructed to target a specific quit date during the second week that they are taking bupropion. If a dose is missed, patients are instructed to skip it and to stay with their regular dosing schedule. Taking too much bupropion at one time can cause seizures.

EFFECTS AND POTENTIAL RISKS

Most people do not have side effects from taking bupropion for smoking cessation. If side effects do occur, they can usually be minimized. In addition, side effects are most often temporary, lasting only as long as one is taking the medication.

There are rare but serious side effects that patients should be aware of. In some people, medications like bupropion may cause severe mood and behavior changes, including suicidal thoughts. Young adults may be more at risk for these side effects.

Other side effects include anxiety; buzzing or ringing in the ears; headache (severe); and skin rash, hives, or itching. Side effects that may occur frequently or become bothersome include abdominal pain, constipation, decrease in appetite, dizziness, dry mouth, increased sweating, nausea or vomiting, trembling or shaking, insomnia, and weight loss.

Symptoms of an overdose may be more severe than side effects seen at regular doses, or two or more side effects may occur together. They include fast heartbeat, hallucinations, loss of consciousness, nausea or vomiting (or both), and seizures.

Bupropion should not be combined with other medications that lower the threshold for seizures. These medications include theophylline, antipsychotic medications, antidepressants, Tramadol

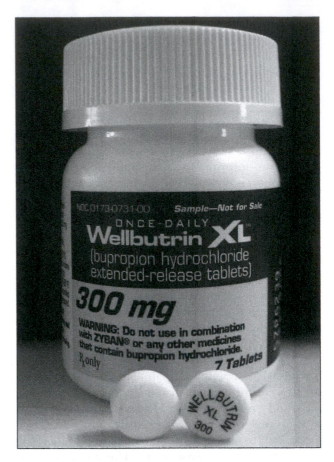

Wellbutrin XL. (via Wikimedia Commons)

(Ultram), Tamoxifen, steroids, diabetes drugs, and Ritonavir.

Karen Schroeder Kassel MS, RD, Med

FOR FURTHER INFORMATION

Cahill, Kate, Sarah Stevens, and Tim Lancaster. "Pharmacological Treatments for Smoking Cessation." *Journal of the American Medical Association* 311.2 (2014): 193–4. Print.

Fiore, M. C., et al. "Treating Tobacco Use and Dependence: 2008 Update." Tobacco Use and Dependence Guideline Panel. Rockville, MD: Department of Health and Human Services, 2008. Print.

Hong, Arthur S., Muhamad Y. Elrashidi, Darrell R. Schroeder, and Jon O. Ebbert. "Depressive Symptoms among Patients Receiving Varenicline and Bupropion for Smoking Cessation." *Journal of Substance Abuse Treatment* 52 (2015): 78–81. Print.

Hughes, J. R., L. F. Stead, and T. Lancaster. "Antidepressants for Smoking Cessation." *Cochrane Database of Systematic Reviews* 1 (2007): CD000031. Print.

McDonough, Mike. "Update on Medicines for Smoking Cessation." *Australian Prescriber* 38.4 (2015): 106–11. Print.

Wu, P., et al. "Effectiveness of Smoking Cessation Therapies: A Systematic Review and Meta-Analysis." *BMC Public Health* 6 (2006). Print.

See also: Addiction medications; Smoking cessation; Treatment methods and research

---

Bureau of Alcohol, Tobacco, Firearms and Explosives (ATF)

CATEGORY: Social issues, social issues, Bureau of Alcohol, Tobacco, Firearms and Explosives (ATF)

DEFINITION: The US Bureau of Alcohol, Tobacco, Firearms and Explosives, Bureau of Alcohol, Tobacco, Firearms and Explosives, U.S. is a federal law enforcement agency within the US Department of Justice. Among other tasks, the bureau regulates interstate trade and illegal trafficking, drug trafficking of alcohol and tobacco products, helping to prevent substance misuse, particularly among minors and young adults.

DATE: Established in its present form in 2003

BACKGROUND

The roots of the US Bureau of Alcohol, Tobacco, Firearms and Explosives (ATF) go back to the earliest days of the United States. In 1789, the first Congress under the US Constitution imposed a tax on imported spirits (alcoholic beverages). This tax was followed in 1791 by a tax on domestic production of alcoholic beverages. Collection of these taxes became the responsibility of the Department of the Treasury. In 1862, Congress created the Office of Internal Revenue within the Treasury. Among its duties were the collection of taxes on distilled alcohol and on tobacco. The following year, three federal agents (called revenuers) were appointed to aid in the prevention, detection, and punishment of tax evaders. During Prohibition (1919–1933), revenuers had a prominent role in combating the illicit importation, production, and sale of alcoholic beverages.

In 1942, responsibility for enforcing federal firearms regulations was transferred to the Alcohol Tax Unit (ATU) of the Bureau (or Office) of Internal Revenue (BIR). In 1952, when the BIR was renamed the Internal Revenue Service (IRS), the ATU expanded to become the Alcohol and Tobacco Tax Division of the BIR. With the passage of the Gun Control Act of 1968, the ATF became responsible for explosives. In 1972, the ATF gained federal jurisdiction over alcohol, tobacco, firearms, and explosives, effectively severing ties to the IRS. In 1982, the ATF was assigned responsibility for investigating commercial arsons.

In 2003, under the Homeland Security Act, the ATF was reorganized into two separate divisions. The tax and trade functions of the agency remain within the Treasury Department as the Alcohol and Tobacco Tax and Trade Bureau (TTB). The law-enforcement functions of the agency were transferred to the Department of Justice as the Bureau of Alcohol, Tobacco, Firearms and Explosives (ATF) in its current form.

MISSION AND GOALS

The mission of the ATF is to enforce laws against violent crimes, criminal organizations, the illegal use and trafficking of firearms, the illegal use and storage of explosives, acts of arson and bombings, acts of terrorism, and the illegal diversion of alcohol and tobacco products. The ATF's motto is At the Frontline Against Violent Crime.

The alcohol and tobacco diversion mission of the ATF is to disrupt and eliminate criminal and terrorist organizations by identifying and arresting offenders who traffic in contraband cigarettes and illegal liquor; to conduct financial investigations in conjunction with alcohol and tobacco diversion investigations to seize and deny further access to assets and funds utilized by criminal enterprises and terrorist organizations; to prevent criminal encroachment on the legitimate alcohol and tobacco industries by organizations trafficking in counterfeit and contraband cigarettes and illegal liquor; and to assist local, state, and other federal law enforcement and tax agencies investigating interstate trafficking of contraband cigarettes and liquor.

SUBSTANCE MISUSE CONCERNS

Although the ATF is not directly involved in combating substance misuse, by regulating interstate trade of alcohol and tobacco and prosecuting those who divert them, the agency contributes to preventing misuse, particularly among minors and young adults. The ATF regulates the content and distribution of all alcoholic beverages in the United States.

One major concern regarding potential misuse, especially among minors and young adults, is the availability of flavored alcoholic beverages (FABs) and alcohol and caffeine energy-drinks, energy drinks. Both have become popular "entry-level" alcoholic drinks for minors and young adults. FABs, or "alcopops," combine fruit juices or other flavorings with beer, wine, or other alcoholic beverages, such as vodka and rum. These drinks appeal to young people because they do not taste or smell like alcohol and users think they do not carry the risk of misuse or serious adverse effects associated with alcohol consumption. Alcohol-caffeine energy drinks also are popular because users believe the caffeine will counter sedation and other adverse effects of alcohol while providing a different and safer high. The US Food and Drug Administration (FDA) has taken action against several brands of such energy drinks that effectively removes them from store shelves.

Another concern of the ATF is online sales of cigarettes, cigarettes, online sales. Vendors of these products disregard their responsibility to collect taxes from their customers. They also do not fulfill their obligation to avoid selling to minors. Prosecuting vendors for not fulfilling their tax obligations ends their role as suppliers of tobacco products to minors. In 2005, the major credit card companies were persuaded to no longer accept payments for tobacco products bought online, effectively putting many online cigarette merchants out of business.

A new concern that the ATF may have to address is electronic cigarettes, electronic cigarettes (e-cigarettes), which are battery-operated devices that deliver vaporized, flavored nicotine to the smoker. E-cigarettes are not under ATF jurisdiction, as they are a nicotine by-product rather than a tobacco product. As of September 2010, the FDA had banned e-cigarette machines sold by five companies because of the excessive amount of nicotine and carcinogens that e-cigarettes released in their vapors.

Ernest Kohlmetz MA

For Further Information

Howland, Jonathan, et al. "The Acute Effects of Caffeinated versus Noncaffeinated Alcoholic Beverage on Driving Performance and Attention Reaction Time." *Addiction* 106 (2010): 335–41. Print. A scientific study that shows that consuming a caffeinated beverage after drinking an alcoholic beverage does not counter the adverse effects of alcohol.

Kurian, George T., ed. *Historical Guide to the US Government.* New York: Oxford UP, 1998. Presents detailed information of the early history of the ATF and its predecessors.

Tedeschi, Bob. "E-Commerce Report: Trouble for Online Vendors of Cigarettes." *New York Times* 4 Apr. 2005. Web. http://www.nytimes.com/2005/04/04/technology. Explains how pressuring major credit card companies to not accept payments for tobacco products purchased on the web affected sales of those products.

See also: Caffeinated alcoholic drinks; Cigarettes and cigars; Crime and substance misuse

C

Caffeinated alcoholic drinks

CATEGORY: Substances

DEFINITION: A caffeinated alcoholic beverage, or CAB, contains alcohol with caffeine as an additive. It is sold in this combined form. Alcoholic beverages that contain caffeine as a natural constituent, such as a coffee flavoring, are not part of the CAB category.

STATUS: Illegal in some US states and in Canada

CLASSIFICATION: Non-controlled substance

SOURCE: Premixed beverage, usually with a malt or distilled-spirits base

TRANSMISSION ROUTE: Ingested orally

HISTORY OF USE

In 2008, a group of state attorneys general successfully pressed two manufacturers of caffeinated alcoholic beverages (CABs) to stop production of the drinks because of concern for public safety. The attorneys general asked the US Food and Drug Administration (FDA) to review the safety of the drinks, because the FDA had not approved the use of caffeine in any alcoholic beverages. Several states have since banned or restricted the drinks.

The FDA and the Federal Trade Commission warned manufacturers that the marketing and sale of CABs could be considered deceptive and unfair. Additional manufacturers have withdrawn their products from the market.

Hypercaffeinated energy drinks entered the United States market in 1997, with the market value of energy drinks growing to $5.4 billion in 2006. Looking to expand their profits and customer base, manufacturers began experimenting with caffeine-alcohol energy drink formulas. After many CAB-related hospitalizations of college students and underage drinkers in the fall of 2010, the FDA issued warning letters to manufacturers, leading several states to ban the products. Legislation has been initiated in some states to remove CABs from convenience stores and to require that they be sold in liquor stores.

EFFECTS AND POTENTIAL RISKS

The caffeine in a CAB masks the consumer's sense of inebriation, leading to a state of intoxication known as wide-awake drunkenness. In this physical state, a person may drink to the point of alcohol poisoning, putting him or her in danger of blackouts, seizures, acute mania, stroke, impaired driving, sexual assault, or even death.

Caffeine intoxication can lead to high blood pressure, restlessness, insomnia, tremors, rapid heartbeat, psychomotor agitation, major depression, and panic disorder. Users can develop a tolerance for and dependence on alcohol and caffeine. Addiction specialists view this combination as a gateway for other forms of drug dependence. Research shows at least one-quarter of college students mix alcohol and caffeinated energy drinks on their own.

Merrill Evans MA

The FDA launched an investigation into the safety of Four Loko, a fruit flavored malt beverage in 2010. (Austin Uhler via Wikimedia Commons)

FOR FURTHER INFORMATION

Benac, Nancy. "United States Food and Drug Administration Signals Crackdown on Caffeinated Alcohol Drinks." *Canadian Medical Association Journal* 183 (2011): E47–48. Print.

O'Brien, Mary Claire, et al. "Caffeinated Cocktails." *Academic Emergency Medicine* 15 (2008): 453–60. Print.

Reissig, Chad J., Eric C. Strain, and Roland R. Griffiths. "Caffeinated Energy Drinks: A Growing Problem." *Drug and Alcohol Dependence* 99 (2009): 1–10. Print.

See also: Bureau of Alcohol, Tobacco, Firearms and Explosives (ATF); College and substance misuse; Adolescents and alcohol misuse

---

Caffeine addiction

CATEGORY: Substance misuse

DEFINITION: Caffeine addiction is indicated by physiological and psychological disturbances due to the absence of the drug. When an individual's normal functioning is impaired when caffeine intake is reduced or stopped, addiction has occurred.

OVERVIEW

Caffeine acts as a central nervous system stimulant and is a mood-altering substance. Caffeine blocks adenosine, a neurotransmitter that increases sleepiness and decreases inflammation, and increases the catecholamines (dopamine, norepinephrine, epinephrine), which have energizing and arousing effects. Addiction occurs when the absence of the drug leads to an increase of adenosine and a decrease of the catecholamines resulting in headaches, drowsiness, fatigue, and irritability.

Caffeine addiction is marked by the development of withdrawal symptoms if caffeine is not ingested. The *Diagnostic and Statistical Manual of Mental Disorders* of the American Psychiatric Association (5th Ed.; *DSM-5*) does not classify a caffeine use disorder; however, it does present diagnostic criteria for caffeine intoxication, caffeine withdrawal, and other caffeine-related disorders. Criteria for withdrawal symptoms, a key component of addiction are: a) headaches, b) fatigue and/or drowsiness, c) mood disturbances, d) difficulty concentrating, and e) flu-like symptoms.

Three or more of the symptoms are necessary for a diagnosis.

CAUSES

People ingest caffeine to stay alert, combat drowsiness and fatigue, and because its use is socially encouraged (e.g., coffee breaks). Long-term use of caffeine increases the number of adenosine receptors, which leads to increased presence of neural adenosine, resulting in sleepiness. Moreover, continual release of the catecholamines leads to decrease in these chemicals causing adrenal exhaustion, tiredness, difficulty concentrating, and emotional disturbances. The adverse symptoms of caffeine withdrawal motivate individuals to ingest caffeine to alleviate those symptoms.

Caffeine also decreases blood flow to the brain. When habitual caffeine users decrease or stop use of the drug, vascular blood flow to the head increases, usually resulting in a headache. According to the *DSM-5*, approximately half of habitual caffeine users suffer headaches upon caffeine cessation.

RISK FACTORS

The more caffeine consumed, the greater the possibility of developing a caffeine addiction; however, how much caffeine is necessary to produce addiction is dependent on several factors. Biologically, numerous studies have identified genetic predispositions to addiction (e.g., a thrill-seeking personality). Addiction decreases activity in the medial prefrontal cortex, a neural area involved in impulse control, emotional regulation, and higher order thinking, such as problem solving. Smokers, those struggling with alcohol, and misusers of other drugs are more likely to be heavy users of caffeine. Those with psychological disorders, such as depression, anxiety, problematic eating, and propensity toward violence are a greater risk for caffeine addiction.

Socially, ubiquitous advertising, social media, and group pressure reinforce the consumption of caffeine. Caffeine is typically presented as an innocuous drug and the high prevalence of its use – nearly 90% of Americans are regular users – makes it difficult for people to think they have a problem with the drug, let alone decrease its use.

SYMPTOMS

The effects of caffeine are observable within thirty to sixty minutes of consuming caffeinated foods or

Caffeine

A plant alkaloid from numerous sources, caffeine is a central nervous system stimulant used recreationally more than therapeutically. It is found in different concentrations from myriad sources worldwide. Perhaps the best-known sources of caffeine are cacao from Brazil and West Africa, *Camellia sinensis* (green tea) and other tea leaves from Asia and India, and *Coffea arabica* or other coffee bean varieties from the African and South American continents. Some shrub-like plants also contain caffeine.

Caffeine improves mood and alertness, but exacerbates anxiety and insomnia with long-term and/or high intake. These effects are principally caused by caffeine's action in antagonizing adenosine receptors and increasing dopamine, epinephrine, and adrenaline. It constricts cerebral vasculature but decreases peripheral blood flow. Caffeine increases heart rate and blood pressure, stimulates muscle contractions, can cause tremors, increases gastric secretions, and relaxes stomach muscles causing heartburn.

Caffeine is an addictive and reinforcing drug that encourages habitual use. More than 90 percent of adults in the United States ingest caffeine by consuming an average of one to two cups of caffeinated beverages per day. This daily number of caffeine users totals more than that for alcohol or nicotine. Withdrawal symptoms start 12-24 hours after consumption cessation and can last for upwards of three weeks. As little as 100 mg of caffeine each day may lead to withdrawal symptoms including headache, poor performance, drowsiness, fatigue, impaired concentration, anxiety, and depression.

drinks. When ingested in moderate doses, caffeine produces the desired effects of increased alertness and decreased lethargy. Many people do not experience symptoms of excess caffeine intake because they develop a tolerance to the substance. However, overconsumption still may lead to insomnia, nausea, restlessness, mental confusion, and tremors. It also may induce cardiac arrhythmias, seizures, respiratory failure, gastrointestinal irregularities, and even, but rarely, death.

Caffeine withdrawal symptoms usually occur 12-24 hours after cessation of the drug. Symptoms can last for up to three weeks, with a peak severity occurring one to two days after stopping caffeine use.

Withdrawal symptoms dissipate within 30-60 minutes after caffeine is re-ingested.

SCREENING AND DIAGNOSIS

Many individuals addicted to caffeine are unaware of their condition because of misattribution to other problems (e.g., migraines) or misdiagnosis (e.g., anxiety disorder). Thus, even though research suggests that approximately 75% of people experience caffeine withdrawal symptoms, the prevalence of caffeine addiction is unclear.

According to the *DSM-5*, diagnosis of caffeine withdrawal disorder criteria include: a) prolonged caffeine use, b) withdrawal symptoms, c) impairment of functioning due to the absence of the drug (e.g., unable to work adequately). Changes in brain wave patterns (e.g., increased theta and decreased beta waves), abnormal neural activity (e.g., ventral striatum & and nucleus accumbens), and reduced gray matter (e.g., medial prefrontal cortex) are associated with caffeine addiction.

TREATMENT AND THERAPY

Recognizing there is a problem is the first step in overcoming caffeine addiction. Strong societal promotion of caffeine make this first step the most difficult one. As with any substance of addiction, a gradual tapering off of caffeinated substances may help to minimize withdrawal symptoms. Switching from drinking or eating caffeinated to decaffeinated beverages or foods will facilitate overcoming caffeine addiction. Some people may benefit from outpatient therapy or support groups to treat caffeine addiction or underlying issues, such as depression, anxiety disorders, or sleep disorders, which may predispose them to addiction. People who have additional substance misuse problems should be treated for the co-occurring addiction issues.

PREVENTION

The primary means of preventing a caffeine addiction is to abstain from consuming products that contain the substance. To prevent addiction among children and adolescents, parents and caretakers should be educated about caffeine's effects and should be aware of products, such as energy drinks that contain large amounts of caffeine. Government regulations on energy drinks and other caffeinated products can help deter overconsumption of caffeine, particularly among children and teenagers. Soda taxes reduce consumption of those, mostly caffeinated, beverages. On the other hand, the proliferation of coffee shops has led to an increase in the consumption of caffeine in the first quarter of the twenty-first century. Companies that sell caffeinated products not only encourage their use, they also fund research promoting the supposed benefits of caffeine. Being a wise consumer of food and beverage products and of research may help to prevent the overuse of caffeine.

Janet Ober Berman MS, CGC;
Updated by Paul J. Chara Jr, PhD

FOR FURTHER INFORMATION

Allday, Erin. "Caffeine Dependence Tied to Physical, Emotional Problems." *SFGate*. Hearst Communications, 5 Mar. 2014. Web. 26 Oct. 2014.

American Academy of Sleep Medicine. "New Algorithm Determines Ideal Caffeine Dosage and Timing for Alertness: Algorithm-Based Caffeine Dosing Strategy Provides Customized Guidance to Counter Sleep Loss." *ScienceDaily*. ScienceDaily, 4 June 2018. Web. July 19, 2018. www.sciencedaily.com/releases/2018/06/180604093116.htm.

Carpenter, Murray. "Generation Jitters: Are We Addicted to Caffeine?" *Guardian*. Guardian News and Media, 8 Mar. 2014. Web. 26 Oct. 2015.

Dews, P., C. O'Brien, and J. Bergman. "Caffeine: Behavioral Effects of Withdrawal and Related Issues." *Food and Chemical Toxicology* 40 (2002): 1257–61. Print. Details the concepts and controversies of tolerance of, withdrawal from, and dependence on caffeine.

Elsevier Health Sciences. "Increased Education Could Help Adolescents Limit Caffeine Consumption: Negative Outcomes of Caffeine Consumption Could be Curbed with More Instruction, According to a New Study." *ScienceDaily*. ScienceDaily, 8 March 2016. Web. 19 Jul. 2018. www.sciencedaily.com/releases/2016/03/160308084928.htm.

Evatt, D., L. M. Juliano, and R. R. Griffiths. "A Brief Manualized Treatment for Problematic Caffeine Use: A Randomized Control Trial." *Journal of Consulting and Clinical Psychology* Feb, 84(2) (2016): 113-121. Print. DOI: 10.1037/ccp0000064.

Kushner, Mariana. "The Truth about Caffeine." Miami, FL: SCR Books, 2015. Kushner summarizes the short- and long-term effects of health issues associated with the consumption of caffeine and presents the case that caffeine is a highly addictive drug. Print.

Meredith, S. E., L. M. Juliano, J. R. Hughes, and R. R. Griffiths. "Caffeine use Disorder: A Comprehensive Review and Research Agenda. *Journal of Caffeine Research* September, 3(3) (2013): 114-130. Print. DOI: 10.1089/jcr.2013.0016.

Satel, Sally. "Is Caffeine Addictive? A Review of the Literature." *American Journal of Drug and Alcohol Abuse* 32 (2006): 493–502. Print. Satel argues that caffeine should not be classified as a substance of addiction and reviews the literature supporting this argument.

Smith, Fran. "The Addicted Brain." *National Geographic* September (2017): 30-51. Print. Provides an overview of addiction statistics and recent scientific findings on addiction and treatment approaches in overcoming it.

See also: Caffeine's effects on the body; Coffee; Physiological dependence; Stimulant misuse; Stimulants' effects on the body

Caffeine's effects on the body

CATEGORY: Health issues and physiology
ALSO KNOWN AS: Caffeinism
DEFINITION: Caffeine, a derivative of methylxanthine found in certain plants worldwide, is a central nervous system stimulant that causes short- and long-term effects on the body, by blocking the release of the neurotransmitter adenosine and stimulating the release of the catecholamines (dopamine, norepinephrine [noradrenaline], and epinephrine [adrenaline]). Adenosine is critical in inducing sleep and the catecholamines all have an arousing effect on the body; consequently, caffeine has an energizing effect on the mind and body.

OVERVIEW

Most of the world's population consumes caffeine daily in beverages, such as coffee, tea, sodas and energy drinks, and food products, such as chocolate. Higher daily intake and long-term moderate use can have adverse effects on the health of numerous body systems, and psychological well-being.

Caffeine is a stimulant drug that causes short- and long-term effects on the central and peripheral nervous systems, the majority of which ultimately lead to adverse effects throughout the body. Although generally regarded as safe as a food additive by the US Food and Drug Administration, caffeine also is a drug with the capacity to cause diverse physiological and psychological harmful effects and to worsen medical and psychological problems.

SHORT-TERM EFFECTS

The effects of caffeine are observable within 30 minutes of its ingestion. By blocking adenosine and increasing catecholamines, the most immediate effect in is a decrease in drowsiness and fatigue, and an increase in alertness and concentration. However, at higher dosage levels it can lead to insomnia, irritability, worsen psychological problems (e.g., anxiety, depression) and cause panic attacks. Side effects, particularly mild effects like stomach upset and insomnia, can begin with moderate caffeine doses as low as 50 milligrams (mg). Caffeine circulates in the body within five to thirty minutes and may cause acute effects for up to twelve hours. Its half-life in adults ranges from roughly four to six hours but is shorter in smokers because of enhanced liver metabolism. The half-life increases to five to ten hours in women taking oral contraceptives, nine to eleven hours in pregnant women, and thirty hours in newborns.

Caffeine constricts blood vessels to the head, easing symptoms of vasodilating headaches, such as migraines, and increases gastric secretions and smooth muscle relaxation in the stomach resulting in heartburn pain. The drug relaxes the renal vasculature causing increased urination. Intake during evening hours may result in low energy levels and excessive fatigue the next day.

Caffeine also is an ingredient in many over-the-counter and prescription headache medications because of its own symptom relief and its amplification of other pain-relieving drugs. Some short-term studies suggest that caffeine can improve certain types of memory and attention span; however, higher doses generally have detrimental effects and long-term studies suggest caffeine may worsen cognitive functioning. Dry mouth, poor appetite, and dizziness are possible directly after large caffeine intake, and

---

Soda drinks

A soda drink is a sweetened, nonalcoholic, carbonated beverage that consists of various flavoring additives, among other ingredients. There are many different classifications of soda drinks, including regular (with sugar and caffeine), regular decaffeinated, diet (sugar-free), diet decaffeinated, and highly caffeinated. The arousing effects of caffeine paired with the high amounts of sugar make many sodas stimulatory beverages.

Short-term effects of drinking sodas include tooth decay and heartburn from soda's acidic properties. Other short-term effects include developing caffeine addiction, which can lead to irregular heartbeat, high blood pressure, insomnia, and numerous physiological and psychological abnormalities. Withdrawal during caffeine addiction can result in headaches, anxiety, depression, fatigue, and drowsiness, depending on the severity of the addiction.

Drinking sugary sodas can lead to the consumption of too many calories and, thus, obesity. However, since the brain does not adequately regulate artificial sweeteners, animals and people put on more weight with so-called diet sodas than those sweetened with sugar. Obesity increases the likelihood of cancer, heart disease, diabetes, miscarriage, and birth defects. Caffeinated sodas have been linked to metabolic dysfunction, poor cognition, neurological abnormalities, and accelerated aging.

The combination of carbonation, sugar/or artificial sweeteners, and caffeine is deleterious to one's health and, ultimately, a deadly brew.

---

caffeine acutely worsens existing ulcers and anxiety disorders. Within one hour of ingesting caffeine, some people may feel edgy and have increased heart rate and blood pressure because of caffeine's effects on heart muscle and rhythm. Caffeine presence in the mother's breast milk may cause a nursing infant to become jittery and experience sleep disturbances.

CYP 450, 1A21, and 2C19 metabolize caffeine, and both metabolites are active in the body as well. The latter two enzymes also metabolize Selection Serotonin Reuptake Inhibitors (SSRIs); therefore, the combination of caffeine and SSRI drugs may lead to a deficit of these enzymes. Several cups of coffee may provide a serum level of 5 to 10 micrograms per milliliter (microg/mL).

LONG-TERM EFFECTS FROM CHRONIC USE

Some chronic effects of caffeine are simply extensions of short-term effects of use. The fifth edition of the *Diagnostic and Statistical Manual of Mental Disorders* (DSM-5, 2013) recognizes several caffeine-related disorders, such as caffeine intoxication, caffeine-induced anxiety disorder, caffeine-induced sleep disorder, caffeine withdrawal, and other caffeine-related disorders.

In 2018, a large British study (Loftfield et al.) involving nearly a half million participants suggested that coffee drinkers had a lower risk of death than non-coffee drinkers. This study supposedly reinforced a spate of studies purporting that caffeine has beneficial health effects. However, in the study, those whose bodies eliminated caffeine the fastest lived the longest and there was no statistically significant difference between those who drank caffeinated versus non-caffeinated coffee. One interpretation of this study is that the critical variable may be more the type of person who drinks coffee than what is in the coffee. Some studies do suggest beneficial effects of caffeine for the elderly with cognitive problems or people with Parkinson's disorder; however, the benefits may be more attributable to simply decreasing drowsiness and fatigue than direct effects on the underlying issues. Feeling tired is not conducive to feeling happy or healthy.

The harmful effects of caffeine identified by researchers are numerous and serious. Psychologically, caffeine increases anxiety, panic attacks, irritability, and exacerbates mood disorders, such as depression. Physiologically, caffeine increases heart rate and blood pressure, and high dosage levels lead to diarrhea, excess urination, muscle stiffness and muscle cell breakdown, gastroesophageal reflux disorders, peptic ulcers, and tremors. Long-term usage can lead to decreased bone mineral density, impaired blood-sugar regulation, worsened symptoms associated with senility, adrenal exhaustion, and renal failure. Neurologically, caffeine blocks calcium channels necessary for the release of neurotransmitters and decreases blood flow to the brain, which deprives the brain of oxygen and glucose. Caffeine use during pregnancy causes excessive weight gain of the offspring, and 200 mg of daily caffeine while pregnant doubles the risk of miscarriage.

Caffeinism, a diagnosis similar in part to panic disorder or generalized anxiety disorder, acknowledges the dangers of caffeine in high amounts, particularly with repeated use. High levels of caffeine intake leading to this diagnosis cause anxiety, rapid heart rate and breathing, diarrhea and excess urination, tremors, and increased blood pressure. Irritability and agitation from Caffeinism are often indistinguishable from anxiety disorders in the physician's office, so the disorder is best identified by discussing caffeine use during symptom review. Prescribed antianxiety medications are unlikely to improve symptoms of Caffeinism if caffeine use continues.

Caffeine that remains in the body leads to adrenal exhaustion and, hence, tolerance. With tolerance, the body requires even more caffeine to obtain the same mood- and performance-heightening effects. Thus, caffeine is reinforcing, and users will ingest increasing amounts to experience alertness and concentration. Abrupt caffeine discontinuation causes physiologic withdrawal even with only moderate chronic use (e.g., two cups of coffeee per day). Studies report that approximately 75% of regular caffeine users will experience withdrawal symptoms with reduction or discontinuation of caffeine. Headache is the primary withdrawal symptom and may be throbbing at first; poor performance and depression over time may occur as a result of the sudden changes in catecholamine levels. Other reported symptoms include reduced concentration and lethargy. Renewing caffeine intake relieves withdrawal symptoms temporarily but continues the habitual cycle of caffeine-induced symptoms, tolerance, and withdrawal symptoms.

ACUTE INTOXICATION

Overdose, or acute intoxication, is rare from social use. At doses of 5 to 50 grams or serum levels of 100 to 200 mg per kilogram of body weight, caffeine is potentially lethal, although some individuals may experience severe overstimulation with daily dosages as low as 200 mg. Cases have been recorded of fatal cardiac arrhythmia caused by caffeine toxicity, usually in combination with a preexisting medical condition exacerbated by particularly high caffeine intake.

Moderate toxicity from overdose (for example, the use of large quantities of energy drinks) causes vomiting, muscle stiffening, and heart muscle irritation. When caffeine levels in the blood are extremely high, intoxication causes metabolic changes in the body, including low potassium levels, high sugar levels, and ketosis. The central nervous system musculoskeletal effects can include repeated seizures, muscle posturing and hypertonicity, and ventricular fibrillation or tachycardia. Severe acute overdose effects can cause pulmonary edema, resulting in life-threatening blocked airways and hypoxia.

Nicole M. Van Hoey, PharmD;
Updated by Paul J. Chara Jr, PhD

FOR FURTHER INFORMATION

Allday, Erin. "Caffeine Dependence Tied to Physical, Emotional Problems." *SFGate.* Hearst Communications, 5 Mar. 2014. Web. 26 Oct. 2014.

American Academy of Neurology. "Caffeine Level in Blood May Help Diagnose People with Parkinson's Disease." *ScienceDaily.* ScienceDaily, 6 January 2018. Web. 27 Jul. 2018 www.sciencedaily.com/releases/2018/01/180106185435.htm.

Baeta-Corral, R., B. Johansson, and L. Giménez-Llort. "Long-term Treatment with Low-Dose Caffeine Worsens BPSD-Like Profile in 3xTg-AD Mice Model of Alzheimer's Disease and Affects Mice with Normal Aging." *Frontiers in Pharmacology,* 2018. Web 27 Jul. 2018. 9. doi: 10.3389/fphar.2018.00079.

BMJ. "Fetal Exposure to Moderate/High Caffeine Levels Linked to Excess Childhood Weight Gain: Should Moms-to-be Cut Out Caffeine Altogether, Ask the Researchers?" ScienceDaily. ScienceDaily, 24 April 2018. Web. 27 Jul. 2018. www.sciencedaily.com/releases/2018/04/180423190544.htm.

Brodwin, Erin, and Kevin Loria. "What Caffeine Does to Your Body and Brain." *Business Insider.* Business Insider, 23 Apr. 2015. Web. 26 Oct. 2015.

Carpenter, Murray. "Generation Jitters: Are We Addicted to Caffeine?" *Guardian.* Guardian News and Media, 8 Mar. 2014. Web. 26 Oct. 2015.

Lande, R. G. "Caffeine-Related Psychiatric Disorders." *Emedicine Health,* 1 Aug. 2011. Web. 13 Apr. 2012. http://emedicine.medscape.com/article/290113-overview.

Olini, N., Salomé K., and R. Huber. "The Effects of Caffeine on Sleep and Maturational Markers in the Rat." *PLoS ONE,* 2013; 8 (9): e72539. Web. 27 Jul. 2018. Papadopoulou, E., J. Botton, A. Brantsæter, M. Haugen, J. Alexander, H. M. Meltzer, J. Bacelis, A. Elfvin, B. Jacobsson, and V. Sengpiel. "Maternal Caffeine Intake During Pregnancy and Childhood Growth and Overweight: Results from a Large Norwegian Prospective Observational Cohort Study." *BMJ Open,* 2018, 8 (3): e018895. Web. 27 Jul. 2018.

Wilson, Perry F. "Study: The More Coffee You Drink, the Longer You Live." *Medpage Today,* 5 July, 2018. Web. 27 Jul. 2018.

See also: Caffeine addiction; Coffee; Physiological dependence; Stimulant misuse; Stimulants' effects on the body

Canada's drug strategy (CDS)

CATEGORY: Diagnosis and prevention
ALSO KNOWN AS: National Anti-Drug Strategy
DEFINITION: Canada's Drug Strategy (CDS) was an initiative developed and funded by the federal government of Canada to address the harmful effects of substance misuse and the supply and demand of illicit drugs. The principles of this strategy were based on four pillars: education and prevention, treatment and rehabilitation, harm reduction, and enforcement and control. CDS is now called the National Anti-Drug Strategy.
DATE: Established 1992

BACKGROUND

The National Drug Strategy in Canada was launched by the Canadian government in 1987 as a five-year program with a $210 million budget (Canadian dollars). In 1992, this program was merged with the National Strategy to Reduce Impaired Driving, thus creating the initiative Canada's Drug Strategy (CDS). An additional $270 million was allocated to reduce the harmful effects of substance misuse on individuals, families, and communities and to reduce the supply and demand of addictive substances. The strategy focused on balancing drug supply reduction and drug demand reduction.

CDS was developed as a collaborative effort between federal, provincial, and territorial governments, and law enforcement, community groups, addiction agencies, and the private sector. Consultation between government and nongovernment organizations determined seven important components that would need to be applied to create an effective framework for the strategy. The seven components were research and knowledge development; knowledge dissemination; prevention programming; treatment and rehabilitation; legislation, enforcement, and control; national coordination; and international cooperation.

Health Canada provided national coordination and leadership for CDS and was required to report to Parliament and the Canadian public every two years about the direction, advancement, and developments of the program. The CDS provided policy makers and researchers with valuable information, raising the level of understanding about the prevalence and effects of substance misuse in Canada.

In 2001, reports began to emerge that were highly critical of the CDS and its policies, use of funding, and effectiveness. It appeared that there were no measurable outcomes to report and that the total impact of the program was uncertain. This unflattering feedback prompted Canada's Prime Minister, Stephen Harper, to announce the new National Anti-Drug Strategy (NADS) in October 2007. CDS was transitioned to NADS in 2008.

MISSION AND GOALS

In addition to the four pillars (education and prevention, treatment and rehabilitation, harm reduction, and enforcement and control efforts), the strategy acknowledged that for interventions to be effective for individuals, several factors had to be recognized. These factors were gender, age, and culture; involvement and buy-in of target groups; attention to the needs of drug users; and the underlying causes associated with substance misuse.

Between 1992 and 1998 the focus of CDS was on school-based drug-prevention programs, although reports from the Canadian Centre on Substance Abuse indicated that illicit drug use among youth increased during this time. When the CDS was renewed in 1998, its primary objective was to reduce the harm associated with alcohol and other drug misuse to families and communities.

The NADS continues to operate on three principle goals: preventing illicit drug use, treating persons with illicit drug dependencies, and combating the production and distribution of illicit drugs.

April D. Ingram BSc;
Updated by Marianne Moss Madsen, MS, BCND

FOR FURTHER INFORMATION

DeBeck, Kora, Evan Wood, Julio Montaner, and Thomas Kerr. "Canada's new federal 'National Anti-Drug Strategy': An informal audit of reported funding allocation." *International Journal of Drug Policy*, Vol 20, Issue 2, March 2009, pp. 188-191. https://www.sciencedirect.com/science/article/pii/S0955395908001308. Review of how monies are spent in this program; concludes that evidence-based drug policies need more attention.

Department of Justice Canada, Youth Justice and Strategic Initiatives, "National Anti-Drug Strategy Annual Performance Report 2012-13," http://www.justice.gc.ca/eng/rp-pr/other-autre/nads201213-sna201213/index.html. Overview of Canada's anti-drug program.

Webster, Paul Christopher. "U.S. drug strategy runs counter to Canada's." *CMAJ*, v. 185(11); 2013 Aug 6, PMC3735758, https://www.ncbi.nlm.nih.gov/pmc/articles/PMC3735758/. Compares and contrasts the US and Canadian drug strategies.

See also: Education about substance misuse; Harm reduction; Law enforcement and drugs; Prevention methods and research

Cancer and substance misuse

CATEGORY: Health issues and physiology

DEFINITION: Certain substances, such as tobacco, have an associated cancer risk. Illegal substances can contain carcinogenic additives. Some persons with cancer become addicted to illegal substances and prescription medications during the course of their disease. An estimated 526,000 people in the United States die each year from cancer, most commonly from cancers of the breast, colon, and lung.

CANCER RISKS

Certain substances of misuse, including tobacco, marijuana, alcohol, methamphetamine, cocaine, and heroin, present special risks for the development of cancer.

TOBACCO

Tobacco is a well-known carcinogen, and its use is the leading cause of preventable illness and death in the United States. In addition to causing lung, throat, and mouth cancer, it has been associated with cancers of the nasal cavity, esophagus, stomach, pancreas, breast, kidney, bladder, and cervix. Nicotine, which is contained in tobacco leaves, is highly addictive; however, it is not known to be carcinogenic. Nicotine is a vasoconstrictor (blood vessel constrictor), so it increases the risk of cardiovascular disease.

The National Cancer Institute has revealed the following statistics related to cancer and tobacco use in the United States:

- Cigarette smoking causes an estimated 443,000 deaths each year, including approximately 49,400 deaths from exposure to secondhand smoke.
- Lung cancer is the leading cause of cancer-related death among both men and women; 90 percent of lung cancer deaths among men and approximately 80 percent of lung cancer deaths among women are caused by smoking.
- Persons who smoke are up to six times more likely to have a heart attack than are nonsmokers, and the risk increases with the number of cigarettes smoked. Smoking also causes most cases of chronic lung disease.
- In 2009, about 21 percent of adults were cigarette smokers.
- Nearly 20 percent of high school students smoke cigarettes.

Smoking (or chewing) tobacco markedly increase the risk of cancers of the oral cavity (mouth, lips, and tongue). One of the effects of tobacco is that it weakens the immune system, which not only increases the risk of cancer but also increases the risk of infection. Aside from its relationship to cancers of the oral cavity, chewing tobacco also increases the risk of many other cancers and health problems.

MARIJUANA

Smoked marijuana and smoked tobacco are chemically similar; thus, like cigarettes, the greatest health hazard of marijuana is from smoking the substance. The psychoactive component of marijuana leaves, delta-9-tetrahydrocannabinol (THC), is a relatively safe drug.

Smoked marijuana, however, is a health risk. Thorough scientific analyses have identified at least six thousand of the same chemicals in marijuana smoke present in tobacco. The chief difference between the two plants is that marijuana contains THC and tobacco contains nicotine. Moreover, one of the most potent carcinogens in tobacco smoke, benzo[a]-pyrene, is present in larger quantities in marijuana smoke.

Another factor increasing the carcinogenic risk of marijuana is in the way it is inhaled; marijuana smokers frequently inhale and hold the smoke in their lungs, which increases the amount of tar deposited in the respiratory tract by a factor of about four. Approximately 20 percent of regular marijuana smokers (those who smoke three to four joints a day) have problems with chronic bronchitis, coughing, and excess mucus.

An alternative to smoking marijuana is ingesting it in pastries, drinks, and lollipops. Marijuana leaves also can be baked into brownies and other desserts. Ingested marijuana has no known carcinogenic effect; however, it still has a psychoactive effect, which can result in myriad problems, including social problems, traffic accidents, and dependence.

A problem with ingesting rather than smoking marijuana is that the digestive process markedly slows the onset of psychoactive effects. This makes ingesting less attractive to users of the substance; furthermore, because the onset of marijuana's effect is slowed through ingestion, a large amount of the substance must be consumed, ultimately resulting in an unusually high level of THC in the body.

ALCOHOL

The combination of alcohol abuse and tobacco use markedly increases the risk of cancers of the oral cavity. Approximately 50 percent of cancers of the mouth, pharynx (throat), and larynx (voice box) are associated with heavy drinking. Even in nonsmokers, a strong association exists between alcohol abuse and cancers of the upper digestive tract, including the esophagus, the mouth, the pharynx, and the larynx.

Alcohol abuse, either alcoholism or binge drinking, also has been linked to pancreatic cancer, particularly in men. The risk has been reported to be up to six times greater than in men who do not abuse alcohol. A possible association may exist between alcohol abuse and other cancers, such as liver, breast, and colorectal cancers. It has been estimated that 2 to 4 percent of all cancer cases are caused either directly or indirectly by alcohol abuse. Alcohol abuse, like cigarette smoking, suppresses the immune system, which in turn increases the risk of developing cancer. These persons often do not seek treatment until the cancer is well advanced.

METHAMPHETAMINE

A number of different chemical processes can be used to make methamphetamine; most of the processes include the use of volatile organic compounds, which are emitted gases, some of which have carcinogenic effects. Also, other toxic substances can be produced through the production of methamphetamine. Some of these substances are carcinogenic. Specifically, pancreatic cancer has been associated with methamphetamine use.

COCAINE AND HEROIN

Cocaine itself is not associated with a cancer risk; however, substances added to cocaine are carcinogenic. One example is phenacetin, which not only can cause cancer but also can induce kidney damage. Heroin and other opiates have no known carcinogenic properties. However, like cocaine, heroin may contain additives that are carcinogenic.

SUBSTANCES USED AND ABUSED BY PERSONS WITH CANCER

Cancer, particularly in advanced stages, can cause extreme pain; thus, persons with cancer are often prescribed opiates to lessen their pain. Marijuana too is used by persons with cancer for pain relief and to reduce the side effects of chemotherapy.

OPIATES

An opiate is a drug derived from opium, which is the sap of the opium poppy (*Papaver somniferum*). Opium has been used by humans since ancient times. Many opiates are on the market, including morphine, meperidine hydrochloride (Demerol), hydromorphone hydrochloride (Dilaudid), hydrocodone (Vicodin), and oxycodone (Oxycontin). Heroin is an excellent analgesic, but it is not prescribed for pain relief because of its highly addictive properties compared

The Union Minister for Health and Family Welfare, Dr. Harsh Vardhan (third from left) released the Report on "Economic Burden of Tobacco Related Diseases in India" on the occasion of the World No Tobacco Day 2014 commemoration, in New Delhi. More than 1 in 10 Indians, or an estimated 140 million people, use 'pan,' a preparation of tobacco wrapped in a leaf, and other forms of smokeless tobacco, according to Healis, a Mumbai-based public health research institute. Its widespread use has given India the highest rate of oral cancer. (Ministry of Health and Family Welfare, via Wikimedia Commons)

with other opiates. Another property of opiates is tolerance, which results in the need for increasingly higher doses to achieve the same effect.

Tolerance and addiction are not a major concern for a terminally ill person with cancer but they are a concern for persons with cancer that is in remission or cured. Some of these persons have "exchanged" their cancer for a drug addiction. After completing a drug rehabilitation program, these persons are at high risk to resume the use of opiates. Researchers believe that drug relapse is caused by the stress associated with cancer, combined with the ready availability of psychoactive drugs, both prescription and illegal.

MARIJUANA

Cancer and its treatment with chemotherapy is associated with side effects such as nausea, vomiting, anorexia (loss of appetite), and cachexia (muscle wasting). Marijuana is effective in reducing these symptoms; therefore, it has been recommended for persons with cancer.

The opinion of scientists at the National Cancer Institute, however, is that pharmaceuticals are available that are superior to marijuana in their effects. These pharmaceuticals include serotonin antagonists such as ondansetron (Zofran) and granisetron (Kytril), used alone or combined with dexamethasone (a steroid hormone); metoclopramide (Reglan) combined with diphenhydramine and dexamethasone; methylprednisolone (a steroid hormone) combined with droperidol (Inapsine); and prochlorperazine (Compazine).

Medical marijuana legislation is a controversial topic in the United States. Despite the controversy, medical marijuana outlets (dispensaries) are increasing in number throughout the country. Their incidence depends on state and federal regulations. Many states have adopted marijuana statutes that are much more liberal than federal statutes.

Although there are legitimate medical uses for marijuana for persons with cancer and other conditions (such as glaucoma), many of the medical marijuana outlets supply the product to almost anyone for any reason.

Robin L. Wulffson MD

FOR FURTHER INFORMATION

Barclay, Joshua S., Justine E. Owens, and Leslie J. Blackhall. "Screening for Substance Abuse Risk in Cancer Patients Using the Opioid Risk Tool and Urine Drug Screen." *Supportive Care in Cancer* 22.7 (2014): 1883–8. Print.

Earleywine, Mitch. *Understanding Marijuana: A New Look at the Scientific Evidence.* New York: Oxford UP, 2005. Print.

Fisher, Gary, and Thomas Harrison. *Substance Abuse Information for School Counselors, Social Workers, Therapists, and Counselors.* 4th ed. Boston: Allyn, 2008. Print.

Granata, Roberta, Paolo Bossi, Rossella Bertulli, and Luigi Saita. "Rapid-Onset Opioids for the Treatment of Breakthrough Cancer Pain: Two Cases of Drug Abuse." *Pain Medicine* 15.5 (2014): 758–61. Print.

Miller, William. *Rethinking Substance Abuse: What the Science Shows, and What We Should Do about It.* New York: Guilford, 2010. Print.

O'Neill, Siobhan, et al. "Associations between DSM-IV Mental Disorders and Subsequent Self-Reported Diagnosis of Cancer." *Journal of Psychosomatic Research* 76.3 (2014): 207–12. Print.

See also: Alcohol's effects on the body; Esophageal cancer; Laryngeal cancer; Lung cancer; Opioid misuse; Respiratory diseases and smoking; Smoking; Smoking's effects on the body

---

Cannabis-induced psychosis

CATEGORY: Psychological issues and behaviors

DESCRIPTION: Marijuana use is an established risk factor for acute psychotic episodes and chronic psychotic disorders, such as schizophrenia. Psychotic episodes induced by the consumption of marijuana or synthetic cannabinoids are known as "cannabis-induced psychosis."

KEY TERMS WITH DEFINITIONS:

Cannabis – psychoactive drug derived from flowering plants of the genus *Cannabis*

Cannabidiol – CBD; a cannabinoid with anti-psychotic properties

Cannabinoid hyperemesis – bouts of intractable vomiting that result from chronic cannabis use and do not respond to typical antiemetics

Cannabinoids – psychoactive compounds specific to *Cannabis* plants

Positive symptoms – psychological or physiological symptoms that occur in a person with a mental disorder but not in the unaffected population

Psychosis – a psychiatric symptom characterized by delusions and hallucinations

Sinsemilla – marijuana derived from unpollinated *Cannabis* plants that contains very high THC levels; also known as "skunk"

Synthetic cannabinoids – laboratory-made cannabinoids that are more potent than THC; street names include K2, Spice, Black Mamba, Bombay Blue, Genie, Zohai, Banana Cream Nuke, Krypton, Lava Red and many others

Δ⁹–Tetrahydrocannabinol – THC; the most psychoactive of the cannabinoids

PREVALENCE

The number of cases of cannabis-induced psychosis (CIP) in the U.S. is unknown. Surveys from 2015 show that cannabis is the most commonly used illicit drug in the U.S.; over 11 million young adults, ages 18 to 25, used marijuana in the past year.

Easier access to cannabis, due to increased legalization of medicinal and recreational marijuana, has increased the number of cannabis-related emergency department visits, some of which are for CIP. In Colorado (one of the first two states to legalize both medical and recreational use of marijuana), emergency department (ED) visits for cannabis use grew 50.4 percent between 2007 and 2012. Other states, both those with legal cannabis use for medicinal purposes and those in which all cannabis use is illegal, also showed significant increases in cannabis-related ED visits during the same period. The reasons for ED visits for cannabis included pediatric ingestion, acute cannabis intoxication, cannabinoid hyperemesis, butane hash oil burns, and CIP.

In Colorado, from 2012 to 2014, there were 4,693,173 ED visits for mental health conditions, 38,301 (0.8%) of which had concomitant cannabis use, and of these, 1,136 (2.97%) presented with schizophrenia or some other psychotic disorder.

With respect to synthetic cannabinoids, during 2010-2015, 456 patients were admitted to EDs for synthetic cannabinoid intoxications.

CAUSES AND HISTORY

The *Cannabis* plant is subdivided into three species: *Cannabis sativa*, *Cannabis indica*, and *Cannabis ruderalis*. Each species has differences in the concentration of various chemical compounds.

Chemicals specific to the *Cannabis* plant are known as cannabinoids. The most common of these cannabinoids are Δ^9–tetrahydrocannabinol (THC), Δ^9–tetrahydrocannabivarin (THCV), cannabidiol (CBD), cannabinol (CBN), cannabigerol (CBG), and cannabichromene (CBC). The two cannabinoids of the most interest to psychiatry are THC and CBD. In *Cannabis* plants, THC, CBD, and CBC are all produced from the same precursor. The *B* locus encodes an enzyme that converts cannabigerolic acid (CBGA) to either Δ^9–tetrahydrocannabinolic acid, cannabidiolic acid, or cannabichromenic acid. The specific catalytic activity of this enzyme depends upon the precise amino acid sequence encoded by the allele of the *B* locus. The T allele of the *B* locus encodes an enzyme that predominantly catalyzes the synthesis of Δ^9–tetrahydrocannabinolic acid from CBGA. The D allele of the *B* locus encodes an enzyme that mostly catalyzes the synthesis of cannabidiolic acid from CBGA. Heating *Cannabis* plant material readily converts Δ^9–tetrahydrocannabinolic acid to THC and cannabidiolic acid to CBD. The T and D alleles of the *B* locus are codominant, which means that the traits specified by these alleles are expressed whether there are one or two copies of these alleles in the plant. The THC:CBD ratio of the plant is determined by its genetic composition. Some plants are rich in T alleles and make large amounts of THC and very small amounts of CBD, but other plants have a balance of T and D alleles and make roughly equal amounts of THC and CBD. Because THC is the most psychoactive of these compounds, most street forms of *Cannabis* are enriched for the T allele and make high amounts of THC and relatively low amounts of CBD.

The human central nervous system makes its own cannabinoids called "endocannabinoids." This endocannabinoid system plays integral roles in learning and memory, neuronal communication, and neuroplasticity. The main receptor in the brain for the endocannabinoid system in called CB1. The two main molecules in the brain that bind CB1 and activate it are anandamide and 2-arachidonoylglycerol (2-AG). THC elicits its psychoactive effects by binding to CB1. Normally the endocannabinoid system is tightly controlled. However, cannabis use causes THC to flood CB1 receptors, which disrupts neural network function, resulting in disturbances of information processing and memory.

Laboratory experiments with animals have shown that the interaction of THC with the CB1 receptor is inhibited by CBD. Clinical trials with human subjects have demonstrated that THC administration can induce psychosis and worsen memory, but co-administering CBD with THC counteracts the psychotic and adverse memory effects of THC. Thus, THC induces psychotic episodes, but CBD attenuates the adverse psychological effects of THC.

Whereas THC partially activates the CB1 receptor, synthetic cannabinoids completely activate the CB1 receptor and cause even greater psychological effects. Synthetic cannabinoids were originally made in research laboratories in the 1980s. Two synthetic cannabinoids, HU-210 (1,1-dimethylheptyl- 11-hydroxytetrahydrocannabinol) and JWH-018 (1-pentyl-3-(1-naphthoyl)indole) are components of illicit drugs that are known as "K2" or "spice." Fifteen different synthetic cannabinoids are Schedule I controlled substances. These compounds are remarkably powerful psychoactive compounds.

RISK FACTORS

Cannabis use is a risk factor for schizophrenia (chronic psychosis). A longitudinal study of 45,000 Swedish military conscripts showed that those who had smoked cannabis by the age of conscription had double the risk of developing schizophrenia in the following 15 years, and those who had smoked cannabis on at least 50 occasions by the age of conscription had a six-fold increased risk of developing schizophrenia in the 15 years following conscription. A follow-up study in 2002 confirmed these observations and excluded other drugs as the cause of increased risk of schizophrenia. A host of other epidemiological studies have confirmed the link between cannabis use and the risk of schizophrenia.

Genetic studies have established that some people have an increased risk of cannabis-induced psychosis. The *COMT* gene encodes the enzyme catechol-O-methyltransferase, which degrades a group of neurotransmitters in the brain known as catecholamines (e.g., norepinephrine, epinephrine, and dopamine). Specific genetic polymorphisms of COMT, specifically the *COMT Val*^{158} *Met* allele, increase the risk of hallucinations from cannabis use, and may be associated with an increased risk of psychotic illness from cannabis use.

The more potent the cannabis consumed by the patient, the greater their risk for developing psychosis disorders. The potency of *Cannabis* plants is augmented if the female plants remain unpollinated. Pollinated *Cannabis* plants devote enormous amounts of energy into seed production. Unpollinated plants, however, use that energy to produce vast quantities of cannabinoids. Cannabis produced from unpollinated female *Cannabis* plants is called "sinsemilla," which is Spanish for "without seeds," although the term sinsemilla can also refer to the unpollinated plants themselves. Today, T-allele dominant sinsemilla cannabis, very high in THC but virtually devoid of CBD, dominates the *Cannabis* market in the United Kingdom and other places in the world. Whereas traditional *Cannabis* may have a THC content of four to five percent, sinsemilla can have a THC content greater than 15 percent. Also, traditional *Cannabis* contains cannabidiol (CBD), but sinsemilla contains no cannabidiol, and is a very potent, unbalanced product.

Cannabis use, particularly heavy, daily patterns of use beginning in adolescence, is a significant risk factor for developing chronic psychotic illness, and those who use sinsemilla or synthetic cannabinoids are at the highest risk.

ASSESSMENT

To assess psychosis, the Revised Behavior and Symptom Identification Scale (BASIS-R) instrument is a 24-item self-reporting instrument that identifies psychosis in patients and measures its severity. Two other validated instruments include the Symptom Checklist-90-Revised (SCL-90-R), a 90-item self-assessment tool that measures paranoid ideation, psychotic symptoms, and other symptoms, and the Brief Symptom Inventory (BSI), which is a 53-item self-administered scale that is a shorter, acceptable alternative to the SCL-90-R. For cannabis-induced psychosis, recent cannabis use must be established.

DIAGNOSIS

The fifth edition of the *Diagnostic and Statistical Manual of Mental Disorders* (*DSM-5*) classifies cannabis-induced psychotic disorder as a substance-induced psychotic disorder. To distinguish between cannabis-induced psychosis and other psychotic disorders, recent use of high-potency cannabis or synthetic cannabinoids must be established. Cannabis-induced psychosis commonly occurs when cannabis users increase the quantity of their cannabis consumption or the potency of the cannabis they consume.

Sudden mood changes and paranoid symptoms that appear within one week or as early as 24 hours after heavy cannabis use are two reproducible features of cannabis-induced psychosis. Other transient symptoms persist beyond the effects of cannabis intoxication and include positive symptoms (paranoia, grandiosity, and perceptual alterations), mood symptoms (anxiety), and cognitive deficits (problems with verbal recall, working memory, and attention).

Synthetic cannabinoid toxicity produces rigid positioning of the body for long periods of time (catatonic posturing), bizarre behaviors, grandiosity, persecutory ideation, disinhibition and aggression. Synthetic cannabinoids also cause cardiac symptoms that include a very fast heart rate (tachycardia); hard, fast and irregular heartbeats that the patient is aware of (palpitations); and chest pain. Since such cardiac symptoms rarely accompany other psychotic diseases, they can help identify synthetic cannabinoid toxicity. Unfortunately, synthetic cannabinoids are not detected in standard urine screens, and they may overwhelm the effects of any antipsychotic drugs used to treat the psychotic episodes they cause.

TREATMENT

Cannabis or synthetic cannabinoid abstinence is the definitive treatment that prevents recurrence of cannabis-induced psychosis. For recalcitrant cases, second-generation antipsychotic drugs, specifically haloperidol or olanzapine, effectively treat psychosis. The antiepileptic medication carbamazepine is an effective adjunct treatment that works rapidly to offset the delayed onset of activity associated with antipsychotic treatments and improves the tolerability of antipsychotic mediations.

FUTURE TRENDS

Cannabis legalization leads to increased cannabis use among young people. Since earlier and heavier cannabis use increases the risk of chronic psychotic diseases, increased cannabis use resulting from legalization will probably increase the prevalence of schizophrenia.

Edibles, food items imbued with cannabis, are attractive to children, and have THC dissolved in their fatty components. Poison center calls for pediatric marijuana exposure increased by 30% after legalization and emergency department visits for pediatric marijuana exposure increased significantly after legalization. Early exposure to marijuana increases the risks of chronic psychotic disorders.

In the United Kingdom, surveys of South London patients who presented with psychosis showed that those who used high-potency cannabis were five times more likely to suffer from psychosis and that those who used sinsemilla showed the highest risk of psychosis. Researchers estimated that 25% of all new psychosis cases in South London were due to sinsemilla, which is probably an underestimate, since sinsemilla dominates the U.K. cannabis market.

Michael A. Buratovich, PhD

FOR FURTHER READING

"A brave new weed." (2016, November 2). *Wall Street Journal*, editorial page. https://www.wsj.com/articles/a-brave-new-weed-1478043007. A distressing editorial from the *Wall Street Journal* on the deleterious social effects of marijuana legalization.

Brauser, Deborah. (2014, December 16). "Cannabis-related ED visits rise in states with legalized use." *Medscape*. Retrieved from https://www.medscape.com/viewarticle/836663. The emergency medical consequences of cannabis legalization.

Crow, Timothy J. (2015). "Cannabis and psychosis." *The Lancet Psychiatry*, 2(5), 381-382. Psychiatrists and other public health researchers discuss the significance of the South London surveys conducted by Marta Di Forti and her group.

Gettman, Jon. (2018, January 25). "Why are people going to the emergency room because of pot?" *High Times*. Retrieved from https://hightimes.com/health/people-going-emergency-room-pot/. A summary of the reasons for marijuana-caused hospital emergency departments visits that suspiciously omits cannabis-induced psychosis.

Grewal, Ruby S., & George, Tony P. (2017). "Cannabis-induced psychosis: A review." *Psychiatric Times*, 34(7). Retrieved from http://www.psychiatrictimes.com/substance-use-disorder/cannabis-induced-psychosis-review. A very readable albeit technical review of the psychiatric aspects of cannabis-induced psychosis.

Knight, Victoria. (2017, August 14). "133% leap in children admitted to ER for Marijuana, study finds." *CNN*. https://www.cnn.com/2017/08/14/health/marijuana-intoxication-children-france-study/index.html. A report of the increase in marijuana-caused emergency room visits in states that have legalized marijuana that focuses on the effects on children.

Celebrities and substance misuse

CATEGORY: Social issues

DEFINITION: The news media has documented a number of cases of substance misuse among celebrities, with negative impacts ranging from career loss to relationship problems to death.

PREVALENCE

Although there have been no scientific studies of how often addictions occur among celebrities, popular news sources frequently report celebrity arrests for drunk driving, drug possession, public intoxication, and other criminal offenses related to substance misuse. Many celebrities and public figures, including Betty Ford, Elizabeth Taylor, Melanie Griffith, Drew

Barrymore, Keith Urban, Eminem, and Ben Affleck, to name just a few, have openly shared their personal stories of struggle with addictions in interviews and autobiographies.

Substance misuse also has been linked to the deaths of many celebrities. Whitney Houston, Michael Jackson, Amy Winehouse, Elvis Presley, Dorothy Dandridge, Marilyn Monroe, John Belushi, Anna Nicole Smith, Janice Joplin, and Heath Ledger are a few examples of celebrities whose deaths involved drug or alcohol overdoses or otherwise harmful combinations of legal and illegal substances.

Other celebrities, such as Lindsay Lohan, Mel Gibson, Robert Downey Jr., and Charlie Sheen, have been in the public eye because of their addictions and substance-misuse-related behaviors. One television reality show, *Celebrity Rehab with Dr. Drew* (which aired from 2008 to 2012), documented the lives of celebrities seeking inpatient hospital treatment for a variety of addictions. The show ended after its sixth season following the death of a fifth former cast member.

POSSIBLE CAUSES

By the nature of their work, celebrities are subject to public attention and scrutiny. Often, this attention and scrutiny extends beyond celebrities' work into their personal lives. In 1972 psychologists Thomas Duval and Robert Wicklund proposed self-awareness theory, a framework that may explain why some celebrities misuse substances to cope with excessive attention.

According to self-awareness theory, when persons engage in activities that draw attention to themselves, they often evaluate themselves negatively because their actual lives do not live up to some high internal standard. When this happens, these persons are likely to experience a drop in self-esteem. Researchers who tested self-awareness theory found that people who are more self-focused, as many celebrities can be, are at increased risk for depression, anxiety, and substance misuse. Persons with higher degrees of self-focus also are more likely to have long-lasting negative moods. People may cope with this discomfort by trying to behave in ways that match their internal standards, or they may look for ways to avoid or escape a focus on the self. Some of these escapes include substance use, gambling, sex, shopping, and other addictive behaviors.

Celebrity Lindsay Lohan, whose fight with substance misuse has kept her in the spotlight, was ordered by a court to attend substance misuse treatment classes. (Rafael Amado Deras via Wikimedia Commons)

Psychologists Jay Hull and Richard Young documented this phenomenon in a 1983 study in which they asked one hundred twenty men age twenty-one years and older to complete a fake IQ test and a real measure of self-consciousness. The researchers then gave the men fake feedback about their IQ test results, telling them that they had scored poorly on the test.

Afterward, the men were asked to participate in a wine-tasting experiment in which they could moderate the amount of wine they consumed. The researchers found that men who were highly self-conscious and received negative feedback on the fake IQ test drank larger quantities of wine than did men who were less self-conscious. These findings support the theory that highly self-conscious people's alcohol consumption increases in response to a reduction in their self-esteem. It follows that celebrities, whose life experiences force them to be highly self-conscious, also may engage in heavy substance use after receiving negative feedback, such as poor reviews or seeing oneself featured in a tabloid.

Additionally, researchers Lynne Cooper, Michael Frone, and Marcia Russell conducted an online survey and found that both adolescents and adults reported using alcohol both to cope with negative emotions and to increase positive emotions. Additionally, psychological research studies have found that people report increased or inflated self-esteem after consuming alcohol. This research suggests that celebrities may misuse substances as a means to artificially increase their self-perception.

Celebrities also may be likely to misuse substances because of norms of substance use and misuse in celebrity culture. Anthropological research indicates that throughout the world, persons more often than not tend to conform to the accepted social practices and behaviors of their cultures; celebrities are no exception. Young or emerging celebrities may be socialized into a culture in which substance misuse is common, and these celebrities may then later take part in that cultural norm and encourage other celebrities to do the same.

NEGATIVE SOCIAL EFFECTS

Several research studies have documented that people imitate behaviors they observe in others. In a famous study of observational learning, psychologist Albert Bandura and his colleagues Dorothea Ross and Sheila Ross showed children a film of an adult punching, kicking, beating, and insulting a doll. Children who had observed this aggressive behavior were significantly more likely to engage in aggressive play with the doll, imitating the behaviors of the adult and engaging in new aggressive behaviors.

Many other psychological studies have replicated these results, showing that people learn behaviors, both desirable and undesirable, through watching others. Observing celebrities engage in substance misuse increases the likelihood that members of the general public will imitate this behavior.

Other research in psychology suggests that celebrities are particularly influential role models because they have many of the factors that increase the likelihood of others selecting them as models for observational learning. These factors include attention, high social status, attractiveness, and in some cases, similarity in age, gender, or other characteristics. Additionally, celebrities who misuse substances often face less serious legal and financial consequences for their behavior than do noncelebrities. Therefore, those who are observing celebrity behaviors may be more likely to misuse substances themselves, as they do not see their role models experiencing significant negative consequences for their behavior.

Tracy Ksiazak PhD

FOR FURTHER INFORMATION

Bandura, Albert, Dorothea Ross, and Sheila A. Ross. "Transmission of Aggression through Imitation of Aggressive Models." *Journal of Abnormal and Social Psychology* 63.3 (1961): 575–82. Print.

Cooper, M. Lynne, et al. "Drinking to Regulate Positive and Negative Emotions: A Motivational Model of Alcohol Use." *Journal of Personality and Social Psychology* 67.5 (1995): 990–1005. Print.

Duval, Thomas S., and Robert A. Wicklund. *A Theory of Objective Self-Awareness.* New York: Academic, 1972.

Hull, Jay G., and Richard D. Young. "Self-Consciousness, Self-Esteem, and Success-Failure as Determinants of Alcohol Consumption in Male Social Drinkers." *Journal of Personality and Social Psychology* 44.6 (1983): 1097–109. Print.

Ingram, Rick E. "Self-Focused Attention in Clinical Disorders: Review and a Conceptual Model." *Psychological Bulletin* 107.2 (1990): 156–76. Print.

or, Nilly, and Jennifer Winquist. "Self-Focused Attention and Negative Affect: A Meta-Analysis." *Psychological Bulletin* 128.4 (2002): 638–62. Print.

Spradley, James, and David W. McCurdy, eds. *Conformity and Conflict: Readings in Cultural Anthropology.* 13th ed. Boston: Allyn & Bacon, 2008.

See also: Media and substance misuse; Promises Treatment Centers; Substance misuse

Center for Substance Abuse Prevention (CSAP)

CATEGORY: Diagnosis and prevention

DEFINITION: The Center for Substance Abuse Prevention, a branch of the Substance Abuse and Mental Health Services Administration, aims to improve behavioral health through evidence-based prevention approaches. CSAP works with federal, state, public, and private organizations to develop comprehensive prevention systems by providing national leadership in the development of policies, programs, and services to prevent the onset of illegal drug use, prescription drug misuse, alcohol misuse, and underage alcohol and tobacco use.

DATE: Established 1988

BACKGROUND

The Anti-Drug Abuse Act of 1988 established the Center for Substance Abuse Prevention (CSAP), originally named the Office for Substance Abuse Prevention (OSAP). CSAP has the task of coordinating drug prevention initiatives nationwide. Before becoming part of OSAP, CSAP was a center within the Alcohol, Drug Abuse, and Mental Health Administration (ADAMHA), under the US Department of Health and Human Services. ADAMHA has since been renamed the Substance Abuse and Mental Health Services Administration (SAMHSA).

MISSION AND GOALS

The mission of the Center for Substance Abuse Prevention (CSAP) is to improve behavioral health through evidence-based prevention approaches. The early mission of CSAP was to bring effective substance misuse prevention to every community in the U.S. CSAP's new mission more closely aligns with that of SAMHSA by focusing to reduce the impact of substance use disorder and mental illness on communities in the U.S.

For both CSAP and SAMHSA, the prevention of substance use disorder and mental illness involves supporting community efforts that promote emotional health and that work to reduce the rates of mental illness, suicide, and drug use. Additionally, CSAP provides national leadership in the prevention of problems related to alcohol, tobacco, and other drug use. CSAP's mission is "to improve behavioral health through evidence-based prevention approaches."

In 2015, SAMHSA established six Strategic Initiatives that provide a roadmap for how CSAP will navigate its goals and focus its work. In addition to prevention of substance misuse and mental illness, CSAP's initiatives address issues related to trauma and justice; workforce development; recovery support; health care and health systems integration; and health information technology.

CSAP's reorganization reflects an emerging trend in the field of substance misuse prevention, treatment, and recovery that attempts to address the wide array of issues involved in the development of substance use disorder and other mental disorders.

Julie A. Hogan, PhD;
Updated by Duane R. Neff, PhD, MSW

FOR FURTHER INFORMATION

"About us." *Substance Abuse and Mental Health Services Administration.* SAMHSA. Web. 10 Jul. 2018.

"Center for Substance Abuse Prevention." *Substance Abuse and Mental Health Services Administration.* SAMHSA, 11 Sept. 2014. Web. 28 Oct. 2015.

Fisher, Gary, and Nancy Roget. *Encyclopedia of Substance Abuse Prevention, Treatment, and Recovery.* Thousand Oaks: Sage, 2009. Print.

See also: Center for Substance Abuse Treatment (CSAT); Prevention methods and research; Substance Abuse and Mental Health Services Administration (SAMHSA)

Center for Substance Abuse Treatment (CSAT)

CATEGORY: Treatment

DEFINITION: CSAT is a US government organization that supports the research work of the US Substance Abuse and Mental Health Services Administration by providing substance use disorder treatment services, especially for children and adolescents.

DATE: Established 1992

BACKGROUND

For 18 years, the Center for Substance Abuse Treatment (CSAT) was a program of the National Institute on Drug Abuse (NIDA), which was responsible both for overseeing research related to substance use disorders and for delivery of services to patients. When NIDA became part of the National Institutes of Health in 1992, its focus shifted entirely to research. CSAT and the Center for Substance Abuse Prevention became responsible for delivering services to patients.

MISSION AND GOALS

CSAT's initiatives and programs are based on research findings and the general consensus of experts in the field of addiction. For most people, treatment and recovery work best in a community-based, coordinated system of comprehensive services. Because no single treatment approach is effective for everyone, CSAT supports efforts to provide multiple treatment modalities, evaluate treatment effectiveness, and use evaluation results to enhance treatment and recovery approaches.

ADVISORS

CSAT's national advisory council was established under Section 502 of the Public Health Service Act (1944) and was originally chartered on December 9, 1992, in keeping with public law. The council advises, consults with, and offers recommendations to the US Secretary of Health, the SAMHSA (Substance Abuse and Mental Health Services Administration) administrator, and the CSAT director concerning issues relating to the activities done by and through the center and to the policies related to such events.

The advisory council can, on the basis of evidence provided, make recommendations to the director of CSAT concerning actions conducted there. The council reviews applications submitted for grants and cooperative agreements for activities requiring council permission; it also recommends for approval applications for projects that show promise of making valuable contributions to CSAT's mission. Furthermore, the council can consider any grant proposal made by the organization itself.

The advisory council collects material about studies and services that are ongoing in the United States or other countries that relate to the issues of substance misuse and mental illness. The council also examines material on issues linked to diseases, disorders, or other aspects of human health that relate to the mission of SAMHSA and its programs.

The director of CSAT permits the council to make such information available through publications for the benefit of public and private health entities, health professions personnel, and the general public. The council may appoint subcommittees and convene workshops and conferences. Management and support services for the council are provided by the center.

PROGRAMS

CSAT programs include a treatment helpline (1-800-662-HELP) and National Recovery Month, which promotes the societal benefits of treatment for substance use and mental disorders, celebrates people in recovery, lauds the contributions of treatment providers, and promotes the message that recovery is possible. National Recovery Month spreads the message that behavioral health is essential to overall health, that prevention works, that treatment is effective, and that people can and do recover.

Another CSAT service is the Behavioral Health Treatment Services Locator, an online resource for locating drug and alcohol use disorder treatment programs. The locator lists private and public facilities that are licensed, certified, or otherwise approved for inclusion by their respective state's substance use disorders agency. It also lists treatment facilities administered by the US Department of Veterans Affairs, the US Indian Health Service, and the US Department of Defense.

Margaret Ring Gillock, MS;
Updated by Marianne Moss Madsen, MS

FOR FURTHER INFORMATION

"Center for Substance Abuse Treatment." *Substance Abuse and Mental Health Services Administration.* SAMHSA. https://www.samhsa.gov/about-us/who-we-are/offices-centers/csat

SAMHSA. *Leading Change 2.0: Advancing the Behavioral Health of the Nation 2015-2018.* https://store.samhsa.gov/product/PEP14-LEADCHANGE2.

SAMHSA. *National Recovery Month.* https://www.recoverymonth.gov/

See also: Prevention methods and research; Substance Abuse and Mental Health Services Administration (SAMHSA)

Centre for Addiction and Mental Health (CAMH)

CATEGORY: Diagnosis and prevention

ALSO KNOWN AS: Centre de toxicomanie et de santé mentale

DEFINITION: CAMH is the largest mental health and addiction teaching hospital in Canada. It is an internationally renowned research center in the field of addiction and mental health. CAMH is affiliated with the University of Toronto and is a collaborating center of the Pan American Health Organization and the World Health Organization.

DATE: Established 1998

BACKGROUND

CAMH was formed in 1998 following the merger of the Clarke Institute of Psychiatry, the Addiction Research Foundation, the Donwood Institute, and Queen Street Mental Health Centre. CAMH combines clinical care, research, education, policy, and health promotion to transform the lives of people affected by mental health and addiction issues.

The organization is focused on the assessment and treatment of schizophrenia and mood, anxiety, and personality disorders and of addictions to alcohol, drugs, and pathological gambling. CAMH also includes the Law and Mental Health Programme, which provides forensic psychiatry and forensic psychology services. This program serves as a major research center for these disciplines.

The central facilities of CAMH are located in Toronto. It also includes 26 satellite facilities within the province of Ontario. CAMH offers practical, research-based publications and online resources for professionals and the general public. Journals, newsletters, documents, and websites provide updated information in the areas of substance use and addiction, mental health, concurrent disorders, trauma, policy research, clinical tools, and health promotion.

Research at CAMH is an integral part of the organization and features four areas of scientific focus: clinical research, neuroscience, positron emission tomography (PET), and social and epidemiological research. The research laboratories include a wet lab, an animal facility, two PET scanners, and a cyclotron.

A number of scientists associated with CAMH hold prestigious positions as Canadian research chairs, endowed university chairs, or professorships. Research is conducted in collaboration with national and international neural and social scientists to address global issues related to addiction and mental health.

MISSION AND GOALS

The goal of CAMH is to provide a national leadership network for better awareness, prevention, and care of substance misuse and mental health issues. The research generated and the publications produced promote the discovery, sharing, and application of new knowledge that helps to improve the lives of those affected by addiction and mental health problems.

The major mission of CAMH is to conduct research and develop adequate services. Its research findings and developments are widely disseminated in Canada and internationally. CAMH also ensures that people in Ontario and the rest of Canada are able to access effective and appropriate services as required in a client-centered practice. In addition to the operation of numerous facilities, CAMH provides reliable, easily accessible online resources for the general public regarding addiction and mental health.

CAMH promotes continuous learning and evaluation, diversity, collaboration, and accountability. The mission of client-based care incorporates a holistic view of health and recognizes the unique social, physical, psychological, and spiritual needs of each patient and works to incorporate these preferences, needs, aspirations, and cultural beliefs into more effective prevention and treatment programs.

April D. Ingram, BSc;
Updated by Marianne Moss Madsen, MS

FOR FURTHER INFORMATION

CAMH Monitor eReport 2015: *Substance Use, Mental Health and Well-being among Ontario Adults.* https://www.camh.ca/-/media/files/pdfs---camh-monitor/camh-monitor-2015-ereport-final-web-pdf.pdf?la=en&hash=A4490B23075FEA9ADF9E3F899B8F62DD90440DB0

Centre for Addiction and Mental Health, http://www.camh.ca/.

Giesbrecht, Norman, Andrée Demers, and Evert Lindquist. *Sober Reflections: Commerce, Public Health, and the Evolution of Alcohol Policies in Canada, 1980–2000.* Toronto: McGill-Queen's UP, 2006.

Moran, James, and David Wright. *Mental Health and Canadian Society: Historical Perspectives.* Toronto: McGill-Queen's UP, 2006.

See also: Canada's Drug Strategy (CDS); Education about substance misuse; Mental illness

Children and behavioral addictions

CATEGORY: Social issues

ALSO KNOWN AS: Soft addictions

DEFINITION: A behavioral addiction is defined as compulsive, repetitive participation in any activity not related to the use of illicit substances to the point that such behavior dominates a person's life, disrupting normal behavior patterns and potentially causing physical, mental, or social harm. Common behavioral addictions among all age groups include those related to gambling, sex, technology, shopping, eating, and exercise. Common behavioral addictions among children include addictions to video gaming, the Internet and computers, exercise, food, sex, and exercise.

BEHAVIORAL ADDICTIONS

Though the cause or causes of behavioral addictions have not been established, some studies have suggested that behavioral addictions, like physical addictions, may be rooted in brain chemistry. Many researchers believe that the act of engaging in certain activities results in an increase in the production of beta-endorphins in the brain, an increase that leads to a feeling of euphoria. In the case of behavioral addictions, it is thought that repetitive engagement in an activity for the purpose of achieving this euphoric feeling may, in turn, cause a person to become trapped in a cycle of addiction.

Experts also have suggested that the development of behavioral and physical addictions may be related to hereditary factors or environmental influences. For example, in the case of behavioral addictions in children, a child with a parent or parents who engage in some form of addictive behavior may be more likely than other children to engage in the same or similar behaviors at some point in their lives.

Regardless of the cause of their condition, people who suffer from behavioral addictions often exhibit certain characteristics that suggest they have become addicted to a particular activity. Many behavioral addicts become obsessed with the activity and find themselves unable to stop thinking about it. They often continue the activity without regard to how it may be affecting their own lives or the lives of others.

In many cases, the addict's engagement in the activity becomes compulsive, meaning that the addict is driven to continue the activity. Some addicts also experience a loss of control over when or to what degree they will engage in an addictive activity. Other characteristics of behavioral addictions include a tendency to deny that the behavior is causing personal problems. Some addicts also attempt to conceal their behavior from family members or friends.

Some behavioral addicts also encounter physical and mental symptoms related to their condition. Many claim to black out during the activity and are thus unable to remember their actions. In some cases, withdrawal symptoms, such as irritability or restlessness, result when the behavioral addict cannot engage in the addictive behavior. Many behavioral addicts also have depression and low self-esteem.

CHILDREN AND ADOLESCENTS

Children and adolescents are equally prone to developing behavioral addictions as adults. Many children also suffer from the same types of behavioral addictions as adults. Most commonly, children and adolescents struggle with behavioral addictions related to eating, exercise, sex, gambling, and technology, including Internet use.

Behavioral addictions related to eating and diet among children and adolescents often manifest as eating disorders, including binge eating, bulimia, and anorexia nervosa. If left untreated, these eating disorders can lead to serious health consequences and even death.

Exercise-related behavioral addictions are often triggered by the importance placed on sports in the lives of many young people. Some adolescents who are involved in a team or individual sport can easily become obsessed with their performance and may engage in excessive physical training to improve their skills. This, in turn, can lead to the development of anorexia athletica, an exercise addiction wherein the addict feels the need to exercise continually in order to feel normal.

As older children and young teens enter puberty, they become increasingly aware of their sexuality and begin to engage in sexual behaviors. During this period, some teens may come to rely on sex to relieve stress or to cope with other emotional issues. This reliance can, in some cases, lead to sex addiction. Persons who develop such addictions may be unable to control their sexual behavior.

Gambling may seem like a problem faced only by adults, but adolescents are susceptible to gambling addictions too. Much like adults, adolescents become addicted by playing games of chance. Some resort to selling off their personal possessions or securing money from their parents to fund their addiction.

Increasingly, however, the most commonly occurring behavioral addiction among children and adolescents is addiction to video games and the Internet, especially social media. For children and young adults in particular, the Internet has become a vital part of their everyday lives, providing nearly constant access to social networks and a wealth of information and entertainment. This widespread use of computer technology also presents a serious risk of addiction.

Children and adolescents with computer and Internet addictions often spend excessive amounts of time online or engage in other computer activities. Many experts agree that spending more than twenty hours per week on the Internet may indicate an addiction. Other factors that suggest addiction include obsessive preoccupation with the Internet, decreased interest in non-Internet-related social activities, and the onset of withdrawal symptoms when Internet access is not available.

Internet addictions also frequently lead to obsessive behaviors. Many young Internet addicts spend an inordinate amount of time building and maintaining online relationships while disregarding real-life relationships. Others may simply find themselves compulsively surfing the web.

In some cases, technological addictions also can intersect with other common addictions, such as sex addiction. Many adolescents turn to adult chat rooms or online pornography, which is often a highly addictive form of sexual behavior. While more common among adults, the frequent use of online gambling websites also can lead to the development of a gambling addiction.

For many young people, playing video games can become as addictive as Internet use. According to a 2009 Harris Poll, 8.5 percent of video-game players between the age of eight and eighteen years showed signs of addiction. And, according to a May 2016 poll by Common Sense Media, 50 percent of teens polled reported that they felt they were addicted to mobile devices, such as smartphones. Addiction to video games, online games, and the Internet in general is often driven, among other factors, by the opportunity these technologies provide for escape from reality and retreat into a virtual world where they feel more self-confident.

The consequences of addiction to computers, the Internet, or video games can vary in scope and severity. Excessive use of technology can lead to weight issues caused by skipping meals or eating poorly, by a lack of sleep, and by a decrease in physical activities away from the computer or game console. Technological addictions often also result in a reduction in the amount of time students spend studying, which, in turn, leads to poor academic performance. In some cases, such as viewing content that users must pay to access, technological addictions can result in financial problems. Finally, the continual use of a computer or other technology also can lead to physical health problems, such as carpal tunnel syndrome, eye strain, or back and neck pain.

SOLUTIONS

All forms of addiction have negative consequences for children and adolescents. Parents should be watchful for signs of any behavioral addiction. A variety of treatment options are available for children and adolescents with behavioral addictions. Medical treatments or other forms of therapy can help break the cycle of addiction and encourage the resumption of a normal, healthy lifestyle.

FOR FURTHER INFORMATION

Bruner, Olivia, and Kurt D. Bruner. *Playstation Nation: Protect Your Child from Video Game Addiction.* New York: Hachette, 2006. Print.

Choo, Hyekyung, et al. "Parental Influences on Pathological Symptoms of Video Gaming among Children and Adolescents: A Prospective Study." *Journal of Child and Family Studies* 24.5 (2015): 1429–41. Print.

Felt, Laurel J., and Michael B. Robb. *Technology Addiction—Concern, Controversy, and Finding Balance*, Common Sense Media, 2016, www.commonsensemedia.org/sites/default/files/uploads/research/csm_2016_technology_addiction_executive_summary_red_0.pdf. Accessed 9 Oct. 2017.

Gullotta, Thomas P., Robert W. Plant, and Melanie A. Evans, eds. *Handbook of Adolescent Behavioral Problems: Evidence-Based Approaches to Prevention and Treatment*. 2nd ed. New York: Springer, 2015. Print.

Gupta, Rupal Christine. "Gambling Addiction." *TeensHealth*, The Nemours Foundation, Mar. 2015, kidshealth.org/en/teens/gambling.html#, pp. 1–5. Accessed 9 Oct. 2017.

Peele, Stanton. *Addiction Proof Your Child: A Realistic Approach to Preventing Drug, Alcohol, and Other Dependencies*. New York: Crown, 2007. Print.

Pontes, Halley M., Mark D. Griffiths, and Ivone M. Patrao. "Internet Addiction and Loneliness among Children and Adolescents in the Education Setting: An Empirical Pilot Study." *Revista de Psicologia, Ciències de l'Educació i de l'Esport* 32.1 (2014): 91–8. Print.

Young, Kimberly S., and Cristiano Nabuco De Abreu. *Internet Addiction: A Handbook and Guide to Evaluation and Treatment*. Hoboken: Wiley, 2011. Print.

See also: Behavioral addictions: Overview; Families and behavioral addictions; Parenting and behavioral addictions

China white

CATEGORY: Substances
DEFINITION: China white is a common name for a number of illegally manufactured fentanyl derivatives. These substances, considered designer drugs, are highly potent narcotic analgesics with opiate-like properties.
STATUS: Illegal in the United States and worldwide
CLASSIFICATION: Schedule I controlled substance
SOURCE: China white consists of various synthetic fentanyl derivatives. Most China white is smuggled into the United States from Mexico or is manufactured in illegal clandestine laboratories.
TRANSMISSION ROUTE: China white exists in powder form and resembles street heroin. It can be inhaled, smoked, snorted, or injected.

HISTORY OF USE

Fentanyl was first synthesized in the 1950s by Janssen Pharmaceuticals of Belgium as a fast-acting narcotic analgesic. The modification of the fentanyl molecule by clandestine chemists produced analogs known as designer drugs that are similar to, but more potent than, heroin. In the 1970s, the first fentanyl designer drug created and labeled as China white was alpha-methylfentanyl, a simple derivative with twice the potency of fentanyl. China white gained popularity as a recreational drug among heroin users because it was a cheaper and more potent synthetic alternative.

China white is one of the most addictive, unpredictable, and lethal illegal drugs available. It is more dangerous than legal opioids because of its high potency and unknown purity. It is frequently combined with low quality heroin to increase potency. By the 1980s, China white was responsible for numerous overdose deaths in the United States. As a result, the fentanyl forms of China white are now classified as schedule I controlled substances under the US Controlled Substances Act (1970). Schedule I controlled substances are drugs with high misuse potential and no legitimate medical use. Despite numerous efforts to curb the illegal manufacture of China white, its misuse continues to be a concern.

EFFECTS AND POTENTIAL RISKS

Similar to other opiates, China white acts through opioid receptors to alter the brain's response to pain. It lessens pain sensations and elevates levels of dopamine, the neurotransmitter linked to pleasurable experiences.

China white pharmacologically mimics the effects of heroin but has a quicker onset and a shorter duration. Its short-term effects include a rush of euphoria followed by feelings of peacefulness and physical relaxation. Negative short-term effects include drowsiness, nausea, dizziness, fatigue, and headache.

Many people who use China white do so to achieve greater heroin-like highs. The most immediate and intense "rush" typically occurs through intravenous injection; the high is fast and intense, but brief. However, there is little distinction between a dose that leads to euphoria and one that leads to death.

China white is highly addictive, and physical and psychological tolerance and dependence develop quickly. Long-term use can lead to anxiety and paranoia and can cause many physical problems, including painful constipation, muscle rigidity, tremors, paralysis, and respiratory depression. Accidental overdose and death also are prevalent.

Rose Ciulla-Bohling PhD

FOR FURTHER INFORMATION

Clayton, Lawrence. *Designer Drugs.* New York: Rosen, 1998.

Gahlinger, Paul M. *Illegal Drugs: A Complete Guide to Their History, Chemistry, Use, and Abuse.* New York: Plume, 2004.

Goldberg, Raymond. *Drugs across the Spectrum.* Belmont, CA: Wadsworth, 2010.

Olive, M. Foster. *Designer Drugs.* Philadelphia: Chelsea House, 2003.

See also: Controlled substances and precursor chemicals; Designer drugs; Fentanyl; Narcotics misuse

Choking game

CATEGORY: Psychological issues and behaviors

ALSO KNOWN AS: Airplaning; American dream; black out game; breath play; California high; choke out; cloud nine; fainting; fainting game; flatline; flatliner; gasp; ghost; hanging; Hawaiian high; knock out; natural high; pass out game; purple dragon; rising sun; space cowboy; space monkey; suffocation roulette

DEFINITION: The choking game is an activity in which, most frequently, children, teenagers, and young adults use strangulation to reduce the flow of oxygen to the brain. This reduction in oxygen flow leads to a temporary state of euphoria, or a "high." There are two ways to play the choking game. The first is to apply pressure to the neck using the hands or a ligature, such as a belt, necktie, scarf, or other device, until the person faints or nearly passes out. The second is for one person to take a deep breath and hold it while another grips him or her in a "bear hug" from behind until the first person passes out. The choking game is most commonly "played" by two people, but it can also be played alone.

CAUSES

There is no known reason why some people participate in the choking game while others do not. Many adolescents mistakenly believe that the game is a safe way to get high because it does not involve drugs or alcohol.

The Internet may also give children a false sense of security about the game. One can find numerous instructional videos on the web that teach how to participate in the choking game, but these videos most often do not include information about the activity's dangers.

Many people also mistakenly believe that if they play the choking game with another person, doing so will be safe. The other player is trusted to remove the object cutting off the oxygen after the person being asphyxiated loses consciousness.

RISK FACTORS

There are no known factors that predispose a person to begin playing the choking game. Many children who play the game do not otherwise engage in risky activities, such as drug and alcohol use. However, some factors are common to those who play the game, including age and peer pressure. The choking game is most often played by children and young adults age nine to twenty years, and most children learn about the game from other children.

SYMPTOMS

Because many parents have never heard of the choking game, they are not likely to know the signs that their child may be participating. Symptoms that one is playing the game include the following: having unexplained bruises on the neck; having bloodshot eyes; leaving bed sheets, belts, ties, or ropes tied in strange knots and in unusual places; having frequent, severe headaches; being disoriented after being alone; wearing high-neck shirts or scarves, even in warm weather; locking one's bedroom or bathroom doors; leaving marks of wear on bed posts or closet rods; and showing curiosity about the choking game or asphyxiation in general. The choking game is a dangerous practice that can lead to seizures, fractures, retinal hemorrhages, brain damage, stroke, and death.

SCREENING AND DIAGNOSIS

The choking game often goes undetected until the person who has been playing the game dies. It is unknown how many people die each year from playing the game, because many cases are likely classified as suicides. However, most people who play the game do not intend to kill themselves. Those persons who play it alone often devise some sort of safety mechanism that is intended to prevent accidental death in case they lose consciousness. Safety mechanisms may include the use of slip knots or arranging to hang from something that is shorter than themselves. These safety mechanisms often fail because the person becomes disoriented and is unable to take the necessary steps to restore the flow of oxygen.

At minimum, physicians and other clinicians trying to determine whether or not their patients have been playing the choking game need to be knowledgeable about the game and its warning signs. Screening for evidence of the choking game can take place during routine physical examinations or when a patient presents with symptoms. Diagnosis is based on the patient's symptoms and medical history.

TREATMENT AND THERAPY

Treatment for choking game participants may include a combination of cognitive-behavioral therapy and education about the dangers of asphyxiation.

PREVENTION

Education is key to preventing children from playing the choking game. Once the behavior has started, many children begin looking for a way to play the game safely, so they need to be told that there is no safe way to do it.

Parents also should be educated about the choking game, including learning the warning signs. Parents who believe their child may be participating in the game should discuss the dangers with their child and then seek treatment for the child. The child's physician may be able to provide a referral. Even if parents do not believe their child is playing the game, they still should discuss the dangers of the game with their children.

Many clinicians remain unaware of the choking game. Education about the game could be included in continuing education programs. It also could be incorporated into medical, nursing, and psychology curricula and into primary care, psychiatry, and emergency medicine residency programs.

Julie Henry

FOR FURTHER INFORMATION

Hitti, Miranda. "CDC Warns of Choking-Game Deaths." *WebMD.com.* 14 Feb. 2008. Web. http://children.webmd.com/news/20080214/cdc-warns-of-choking-game-deaths.

McClave, Julie L., et al. "The Choking Game: Physician Perspectives." *Pediatrics* 125.1 (2010): 82–87. Print.

Parker-Pope, Tara. "'Choking Game' Deaths on the Rise." *New York Times.* New York Times, 14 Feb. 2008. Web. 28 Oct. 2015.

Re, Laura, et al. "The Choking Game: A Deadly Game. Analysis of Two Cases of 'Self-Strangulation' in Young Boys and Review of the Literature." *Jour. of Clinical Forensic and Legal Medicine* 30 (2015): 29+. Print.

"Unintentional Strangulation Deaths from the 'Choking Game' among Youths Aged 16–19 Years—United States, 1995–2007." *Morbidity and Mortality Weekly Report* CDC, 15 Feb. 2008. Web. 28 Oct. 2015.

See also: Autoerotic asphyxiation; Behavioral addictions: Overview; Children and behavioral addictions

Chronic bronchitis

CATEGORY: Health issues

DEFINITION: Chronic bronchitis is a condition in which the airways in the lungs become inflamed. The condition persists for a long time or continues to recur following periods of remission. Chronic bronchitis, along with emphysema, is a form of chronic obstructive pulmonary disease (COPD).

CAUSES

With chronic bronchitis, the airways in the lungs become inflamed. When these airways become irritated, thick mucus forms inside the airways, making it difficult to breathe.

The most common causes of chronic bronchitis include cigarette smoking and exposure to secondhand cigarette smoke. Air pollution, infections, and allergens worsen the symptoms of bronchitis.

RISK FACTORS

Cigarette smoking is the single greatest risk factor for developing chronic bronchitis. The more a person smokes and the longer he or she smokes, the greater the risk is of developing chronic bronchitis. Frequent and long-term smoking also increases the risk that the chronic bronchitis will be severe.

Other factors that may increase the chance of developing chronic bronchitis include long-term exposure to chemicals, dust, and other substances that have been inhaled; long-term cigar or marijuana smoking; uncontrolled asthma; and long-term exposure to air pollution.

SYMPTOMS

Symptoms of chronic bronchitis include coughing up mucus, coughing up mucus streaked with blood, and shortness of breath (difficulty breathing). Difficulty breathing may especially occur after mild activity or exercise. Other symptoms include recurring respiratory infections that cause symptoms to worsen; wheezing when breathing; fatigue; swelling of the ankles, feet, and legs; and headaches.

SCREENING AND DIAGNOSIS

To diagnose chronic bronchitis, symptoms of productive cough must have been present for three or more months in at least two consecutive years, and not have been caused by another condition. A doctor will ask about symptoms and medical history and perform a physical examination.

Tests may include breathing tests to check lung function, arterial blood gas tests, chest X-ray (a test that uses radiation to take a picture of structures inside the chest), blood tests to determine complete blood count and oxygen saturation of the blood, exercise stress testing to test lung function, and a CT scan of the chest (a type of X-ray that captures 3-D images of the internal organs).

TREATMENT AND THERAPY

There is no cure for chronic bronchitis, but there are treatments that can reduce symptoms and improve lung function. The best way to reduce symptoms is to stop smoking. Short-acting bronchodilator medications may be prescribed to help open the airways in the lungs and improve breathing. Long-acting bronchodilator medication may be prescribed as well, and steroids may be prescribed to help improve breathing.

Antibiotics are rarely prescribed to treat bronchitis. However, they may be needed to treat a lung infection that often accompanies the illness. A small percentage of patients may need chronic antibiotic therapy.

Oxygen therapy can restore oxygen to parts of the body depleted because of chronic bronchitis. Exercise can also help. Breathing exercises can help to improve lung function, and are usually done under the supervision of a respiratory therapist. A regular exercise program can reduce symptoms and improve lung function.

PREVENTION

The best way to prevent chronic bronchitis is to stop smoking, or avoiding smoking altogether for nonsmokers. Early diagnosis and treatment of the condition will preserve lung function and reduce symptoms.

Diana Kohnle

FURTHER READING

Halbert, R. J., et al. "Global Burden of COPD: Systematic Review and Meta-Analysis." *European Respiratory Journal* 28.3 (2006): 523–532. Quantifies the prevalence of chronic obstructive pulmonary disease (COPD) through a systematic review and random effects meta-analysis.

Lopez, A.D., et al. "Chronic Obstructive Pulmonary Disease: Current Burden and Future Projections." *European Respiratory Journal* 27.2 (2006): 397–412. Uses the results from a global burden of disease study to provide estimated and projected statistics about the prevalence of COPD. Also estimates and projects mortality rates resulting from the disease.

Mayo Clinic Staff. "Bronchitis." *Mayo Clinic.* Mayo Foundation for Medical Education and Research. 2012. Web. 29. Mar. 2012. Information about bronchitis, including its definition, symptoms, causes, risk factors, complications, diagnosis, treatment, lifestyle, home remedies, and prevention.

See also: Chronic obstructive pulmonary disease (COPD); Nicotine addiction; Respiratory diseases and smoking; Smoking's effects on the body; Tobacco use disorder

Chronic obstructive pulmonary disease (COPD)

CATEGORY: Health issues

DEFINITION: Chronic obstructive pulmonary disease (COPD) is a progressive illness that makes it increasingly difficult to breathe. In COPD, the airways and air sacs of the lungs become inelastic and inflamed, making it more difficult for oxygen to reach the bloodstream. COPD includes emphysema, which is caused by damage to the air sacs, and chronic bronchitis, a lung disorder of the large airways. Changes to lung tissue differ between the two diseases. However, their causes and treatment are similar.

CAUSES

COPD develops due to inhaling toxins or other irritants. In fact, smoking cigarettes is the leading cause of COPD. A genetic predisposition may make a person's lungs more susceptible to damage from smoke or pollutants (including alpha-1-antitrypsin deficiency), increasing the chances of developing COPD.

RISK FACTORS

Factors that increase the chance of developing COPD include smoking cigarettes, long-term exposure to secondhand smoke, and exposure to pollutants. Other factors include having family members with COPD and having a history of frequent childhood lung infections. Because COPD develops over a long period of time, the risk increases for people fifty years or older.

SYMPTOMS

Early symptoms of COPD include coughing in the morning, coughing up clear sputum (mucus from deep in the lungs), wheezing, and shortness of breath with physical activity. As the disease progresses, symptoms may include increased shortness of breath, a choking sensation when lying flat, fatigue, trouble concentrating, and heart problems. Other progressive symptoms may include weight loss, breathing through pursed lips, desire to lean forward to improve breathing, and more frequent flare-ups (periods of more severe symptoms).

Nutrition in the Treatment of COPD

There are several ways to treat COPD with nutrition and proper eating:

- Maintain a normal weight; excess weight causes the lungs and heart to work harder.

- Eat a healthy diet that is low in saturated fat and rich in fruits, vegetables, and whole grain foods.

- Eat several small meals during the day; doing so makes breathing easier.

- Avoid gas-producing foods; large meals and excess gas swell the stomach, which pushes up on the diaphragm.

- Drink fluids to keep mucus thin.

SCREENING AND DIAGNOSIS

A diagnosis from a doctor will include questions about a patient's symptoms and medical history. A physical exam will also be conducted. Tests may include a chest X-ray (X-rays of the chest may detect signs of lung infection), CT scan (a type of X-ray that uses a computer to generate pictures of the structures inside the chest), blood tests to assess the amount of oxygen and carbon dioxide in the blood, and a lung function test.

TREATMENT AND THERAPY

There is no treatment to cure COPD. Instead, treatment aims to ease symptoms and improve the patient's quality of life. Such treatments include smoking cessation, environmental management (limiting the number of irritants in the air), and medication. Drugs used to ease COPD may work by opening airways, relaxing the breathing passages, decreasing inflammation, and thinning secretions to bring up mucus from the lungs. Chronic and mild to moderate COPD may require antibiotics. One study found that shorter antibiotic treatment (five days or less) is as effective as longer treatment (more than five days). Additionally, the flu vaccine may help to reduce COPD flare-ups.

A few people can benefit from receiving oxygen. Oxygen is given to improve the air breathed in and to increase the amount of available oxygen. This can improve energy levels and heart and brain function. Special exercises can strengthen chest muscles and make breathing easier. Physical activity builds endurance and improves quality of life. Yoga is an example of an exercise routine that may offer benefits for people with COPD.

A small number of patients may benefit from surgery, such as lung transplants.

PREVENTION

Steps taken to reduce the risk of developing COPD include quitting smoking, avoiding exposure to second-hand smoke, avoiding exposure to air pollution or irritants, and wearing protective gear when exposed to irritants and toxins at the workplace.

Debra Wood, RN

FURTHER READING

COPD Foundation. The COPD Foundation. 2012. Web. 29 Mar. 2012. The COPD Foundation develops and supports programs for research, education, diagnosis, and therapy for those affected by COPD. Their website has educational resources that outline the preventability and treatability of COPD.

COPD Learn More Breathe Better. National Heart, Lung, and Blood Institute. 2012. Web. 29 Mar. 2012. The "COPD Learn More Breathe Better" campaign has resources to increase the awareness of COPD and how to treat it. The campaign encourages those at risk to talk to their health care providers about COPD.

Eisner, Mark D., et al. "Lifetime Environmental Tobacco Smoke Exposure and the Risk of Chronic Obstructive Pulmonary Disease." *Environmental Health: A Global Access Science Source.* Biomed Central Ltd. 12 May 2005. Web. 29 Mar. 2012. Examines the association between lifetime exposure to environmental tobacco smoke (ETS) and the risk of developing COPD.

See also: Chronic bronchitis; Nicotine addiction; Respiratory diseases and smoking; Smoking's effects on the body; Tobacco use disorder

Cigarettes and cigars

CATEGORY: Substances

DEFINITION: A cigarette is a cylinder of cured and finely cut tobacco wrapped in paper. The paper is ignited and the smoke is inhaled through the mouth into the lungs. A cigar is a larger cylinder of dried and fermented tobacco wrapped in whole-leaf tobacco that is also ignited. Cigar smoke is drawn into the mouth, and nicotine is absorbed through the oral membranes. Because of its alkalinity, cigar smoke irritates inner mucous membranes, and is typically not inhaled.

STATUS: Legal in the United States and most countries for adults. In some Canadian provinces, the legal age is nineteen years. In Japan, the legal age is twenty years. In Kuwait, the legal age is twenty-one years. In Austria, Belgium, France, and the Netherlands, the legal age is sixteen years.

CLASSIFICATION: Regulated by the U.S. Food and Drug Administration as a nicotine delivery system.

SOURCE: The United States grows about 10 percent of the world's tobacco and is the fourth largest global producer of tobacco (4.5 percent); the major tobacco-growing countries are China (40 percent), India (8 percent), Brazil (7 percent), and Turkey (4 percent). Two-thirds of the American tobacco crop is grown in the states of Kentucky and North Carolina.

TRANSMISSION ROUTE: The nicotine in cigarette smoke is absorbed in the lungs and rapidly acts on the brain to activate pleasure centers and stimulate an adrenaline rush. Small amounts of nicotine in the smoke may be absorbed through the mucous membranes of the nose and mouth. The nicotine in cigar smoke is absorbed slowly through the mucous membranes of the mouth because the smoke is too harsh to be inhaled.

HISTORY OF USE

Tobacco use has a long history in the New World and tobacco cultivation sites in Mexico date to 1400–1000 BCE. Tobacco smoking among Native Americans had important social, ceremonial, and religious significance, and tobacco was also grown for trade.

Smoking tobacco was introduced in Europe in the sixteenth century and in the United States in the seventeenth century. Matches and cigarettes were first commercially produced in the nineteenth century, facilitating the habit of smoking. By 1901, 80 percent of American men smoked at least one cigar a day; that same year, 6 million cigars and 3.5 million cigarettes were sold in the United States.

In 1913, the R. J. Reynolds Tobacco Company introduced Camel cigarettes, and ten years later, Camels were smoked by 45 percent of American smokers. By 1940, the number of cigarette smokers had doubled from that of 1930. The advertising and marketing of tobacco products in the twentieth century especially targeted military personnel and women.

In 1950, the first evidence linking lung cancer and tobacco smoking was published in a British medical journal. In 1965, a U.S. federal law mandated that a warning from the U.S. surgeon general be placed on all packages of cigarettes and all cigarette advertising, stating the risks of smoking tobacco. In 1971, cigarette advertising was banned from television. In 1972, Marlboro cigarettes became the best-selling brand of cigarettes in the world, and it remains the best-selling brand. In 1988, the U.S. surgeon general determined that nicotine, the chief active constituent of tobacco, was an addictive substance. Nine years later, a U.S. federal judge ruled that the U.S. Food and Drug Administration could regulate tobacco as a drug.

Globally, the total number of cigarettes smoked is decreasing. The largest markets for tobacco consumption are populous Asian countries. China, whose people smoke more than 40% of all cigarettes, remains the largest consumer of tobacco products, even though cigarette use in China has begun to decrease. Indonesia is set to increase the number of tobacco smokers by 24 million from 2015 to 2025. Africa and the Eastern Mediterranean show the fastest growth of tobacco use. Nigeria, for example, is set to increase the number of tobacco smokers by seven million from 2015 to 2025.

Worldwide, there are an estimated 1 billion smokers and approximately 6.5 trillion cigarettes are sold, globally, each year. In terms of supply and demand, the tobacco industry makes much of its money off the world's poorest people, since lower socioeconomic groups tend to smoke more. In 2016, 7.1 million people died from tobacco-related illnesses, including heart disease, stroke, and cancer. For every smoker who dies of a smoking-related disease, twenty others are living with a serious smoking-related disease. On average, men who do not smoke live 13.2 years longer than men who smoke, and women who do not smoke live 14.5 years longer than women who smoke.

The U.S. is the top cigar-consuming country. From 2000 to 2012, cigar consumption increased by 101 percent while cigarette consumption declined by 41 percent. According to data from the 2012 National Youth Tobacco Survey, cigar use is most common among young people; an estimated 12.6 percent of high school students had smoked at least one cigar in the past 30 days. The CDC's national Adult Tobacco Survey for 2009-2015 showed that cigar smoking prevalence among adults was highest among 18–24 years (15.9 percent).

EFFECTS AND POTENTIAL RISKS

Tobacco smoking usually leads to nicotine addiction. Upon entry into the brain, nicotine binds to receptors that usually bind the neurotransmitter acetylcholine and increases the release of several neurotransmitters, the most important of which is dopamine. Nicotine induces dopamine release in the mesolimbic pathway; in particular, the nucleus accumbens and the ventral tegmental area (VTA) of the midbrain. Dopamine-based activation of the mesolimbic pathway is integral to drug-induced reward and drug addiction. When dopamine levels in the brain drop, the smoker feels depressed and lights the next cigarette or cigar to regain the heightened sense of pleasure and well-being. Nicotine withdrawal symptoms include irritability, depressed mood, restlessness, anxiety, relational problems, difficulty concentrating, increased hunger and eating, insomnia, and tobacco craving.

Tobacco smoking has multiple deleterious health effects. Women who smoke have an increased risk of miscarriage, premature labor, and giving birth to an underweight baby. Tobacco smoke also contains multiple toxins including carbon monoxide, which reduces the blood's ability to carry oxygen to cells. The harmful health effects of tobacco smoking are cataloged in the table below.

Organ	Health effects
Eyes	Cataracts, blindness (macular degeneration), stinging, excessive tearing and blinking
Brain and Psyche	Stroke, addiction, altered brain chemistry, anxiety about tobacco
Hair	Odor and discoloration
Nose	Cancer of nasal cavities and paranasal sinuses, chronic rhinosinusitis, impaired sense of smell
Teeth	Discoloration and staining of teeth, periodontal disease, loose teeth, tooth loss, root-surface caries, plaque
Mouth and Throat	Cancers of the lips, mouth, throat, larynx, and pharynx, sore throat, impaired sense of taste, bad breath
Ears	Hearing loss, ear infection
Lungs	Lung, bronchi, and tracheal cancer, chronic obstructive pulmonary disease and emphysema, respiratory infections, shortness of breath, asthma, chronic cough, excessive sputum production
Heart	Coronary thrombosis (heart attack), atherosclerosis (damage and occlusion of coronary artery)
Chest and Abdomen	Esophageal cancer, gastric, colon, and pancreatic cancer, abdominal aneurysm, peptic ulcer, possible increased risk of breast cancer
Liver	Liver cancer
Male Reproduction	Infertility, loss of sperm motility, low sperm counts, impotence, prostate cancer
Female Reproduction	Cervical and ovarian cancer, premature ovarian failure, early menopause, reduced fertility, painful menstruation
Urinary System	Bladder, kidney, and ureter cancer
Hands	Peripheral circulation disease, poor circulation, resulting in cold fingers
Skin	Psoriasis, loss of skin tone, wrinkling, premature aging
Skeletal System	Osteoporosis, hip fracture, susceptibility to back problems, bone marrow cancer, rheumatoid arthritis
Wounds and Surgery	Impaired wound healing, poor post-surgical recovery, burns from cigarettes and from fires caused by cigarettes
Legs and Feet	Peripheral vascular disease, cold feet, leg pain and gangrene, deep vein thrombosis
Circulatory system	Buerger's disease (inflammation of arteries, veins, and nerves in legs), acute myeloid leukemia
Immune system	Impaired resistance to infection, possible increased risk of allergies
Others	Diabetes, sudden death

Adapted from *The Tobacco Atlas*, p. 24.

Cigar smoking is not a safe alternative to cigarette smoking. Cigar smoking has been credibly linked to an increased risk of gum disease and tooth loss, as well as cancers of the lung, esophagus, tongue, larynx, lips, mouth, and throat. Heavy cigar smoking can also increase the risk for lung diseases and coronary heart disease.

Nonsmokers who breathe environmental, or secondhand cigarette or cigar smoke are also exposed to the toxins and carcinogens contained in it. Children exposed to tobacco smoke suffer from higher incidence of Sudden Infant Death Syndrome, asthma, pneumonia, and middle ear disease. Nonsmoking adults routinely exposed to cigarette smoke show significantly higher incidence of coronary heart disease, lung cancer, nasal irritation, stroke, and, in women, low birth weight. Epidemiological evidence suggests that exposure to secondhand smoke may also increase the risk of chronic obstructive pulmonary disease, asthma, impaired lung function, atherosclerosis, cancer of the nasal sinuses, pharynx, and larynx, and, in women, increased risk of breast cancer and preterm delivery. Exposure to secondhand smoke is highest in Asia.

Bethany Thivierge, MPH;
Updated by Michael A. Buratovich, Ph.D.

FOR FURTHER INFORMATION

Bellenir, Karen. (2010). *Tobacco information for teens: Health tips about the hazards of using cigarettes, smokeless tobacco, and other nicotine products.* Aston, PA: Omnigraphics. A comprehensive, easy-to-read reference book for middle school and high school students.

Boonn, Ann. (2017). *The rise of cigars and cigar-smoking harms.* Washington, DC: Campaign for Tobacco-Free Kids. Retrieved from https://www.tobaccofreekids.org/assets/factsheets/0333.pdf. A free resource that focuses on the statistics and consequences of cigar smoking among the younger generation.

Carr, Allen. (2010). *The easy way to stop smoking: Join the millions who have become non-smokers using Allen Carr's easy way method.* New York: Sterling. This book helps smokers discover the underlying reasons for smoking and discusses how to handle nicotine withdrawal and avoid the temptation to relapse.

Drope, Jeffery, & Schluger, Neil W. (Eds.). (2018). *The tobacco atlas* (6th Ed.). Atlanta: The American Cancer Society and Vital Strategies. Retrieved from https://tobaccoatlas.org/. A free resource that graphically catalogues the societal costs of tobacco use.

Jamal, Ahmed, Gentzke, Andrea, Hu, S. Sean, Cullen, Karen A., Apelberg, Benjamin J., Homa, David M., & King, Brian A. (2017). Tobacco use among middle and high school students — United States, 2011–2016. *Morbidity and Mortality Weekly Report* 66, 597–603. DOI: http://dx.doi.org/10.15585/mmwr.mm6623a1. A summary of the statistics of tobacco use among secondary school students.

Rose, Jed E., Behm, Frédérique M., Drgon, Tomas, Johnson, Catherine, & Uhl, George R. (2010). Personalized smoking cessation: Interactions between nicotine dose, dependence, and quit-success genotype score. *Molecular Medicine* 16, 247–253. Discussion of a study that found that the reduction of carbon monoxide levels with nicotine replacement therapy increases the likelihood of successful smoking abstinence.

See also: Nicotine addiction; Smoking's effects on the body; Tobacco use disorder

Cirque Lodge

CATEGORY: Treatment

DEFINITION: Cirque Lodge is a private drug and alcohol rehabilitation facility located in the mountains of Utah. Based on the 12-step treatment model of Alcoholics Anonymous (AA), Cirque Lodge offers drug and alcohol treatment through a 30-day residential program.

DATE: Established in 1999

HISTORY

Cirque Lodge was founded in 1999 by entrepreneur Richard Losee, a native of Provo, Utah, and the center's chief executive officer. Losee became interested in drug and alcohol treatment because of his own experience with a family member.

Cirque Lodge is located in Sundance, Utah, in the Wasatch Range of the Rocky Mountains. The name of the treatment center derives from the nearby glacier-carved Cascade Cirque.

Cirque Lodge expanded to include Cirque Studio in 2002. Located in Orem, Utah, this 110,000-square foot facility was built in the 1970s as a television studio for the Osmond family and their television variety show. It has been turned into a unique and original treatment center, with horse arenas, gardens, and an indoor challenge course. The studio and lodge are accredited by the Joint Commission on Accreditation of Health Care Organizations.

Because treatment costs at Cirque Lodge may exceed $1,000 per day per person, it has gained the reputation as an exclusive and private treatment center for the rich and famous. Although some celebrities have been associated with Cirque Lodge, most of the center's clients are not celebrities. The center offers some scholarships for clients who cannot afford treatment.

The model of drug and alcohol treatment used by Cirque Lodge can be traced back to 1949. Abstinence-based treatment was first developed at Willmar State Hospital and the Hazelden Treatment Center in Minnesota. Borrowing from the 12-step meetings of AA, which were developed in the 1930s, these alcoholic treatment centers added residential treatment that included lectures, open discussions, small group therapy, and peer interaction.

Abstinence-based treatment centers became the predominant model for treating both alcohol and drug misuse in the 1980s. Private treatment in 28-day residential centers dominated the treatment landscape but was affected by cost-cutting managed health care in the 1990s.

Most abstinence-based treatment now is provided in outpatient settings. Treatment focuses on individualized treatment plans, family involvement, and frequent use of group meetings such as AA, Narcotics Anonymous, and Al Anon. Studies show that more than 90 percent of drug and alcohol treatment programs in the United States are abstinence-based programs that use the 12 steps of AA as a core principle.

MISSION AND GOALS

Cirque Lodge's premise is that addiction to drugs or alcohol is caused by an uncontrollable impulse in the brain caused by an imbalance of brain chemicals. Center staff acknowledge that heredity and life experiences also contribute to addiction. As the brain becomes accustomed to addictive substances, physical changes in the brain lead to the mental and social symptoms of addiction.

The treatment philosophy at Cirque Lodge is to use the most effective therapies available. This includes learning coping skills from the 12 steps of AA, cognitive behavioral therapy, independent counseling, lectures, group therapy, and peer support. Family involvement is also seen as important, and families are invited to spend four days at the facility to attend a special program. Family members are integrated into group classes and group therapy during this program.

Before beginning the actual residential treatment program, all clients must go through detoxification, if needed. This treatment is offered through a separate licensed detoxification facility. Upon arrival at Cirque Lodge, staff assess the clients and then develop individualized treatment programs. Cirque Lodge also treats co-occurring eating disorders and mood disorders.

In addition to therapy sessions and 12-step meetings, clients are offered programs in exercise, meditation, journaling, working with horses, hiking, climbing, and organic gardening. Clients can take part in a ropes course and can use a fully equipped art room. The former soundstage at the Cirque Studio houses the indoor ropes challenge course, and it also has an archery range and a lecture hall.

Cirque Lodge staff believe that addiction is a chronic condition and that relapse is a common reality. To address this, they provide an active aftercare program, an alumni program, and a guesting program. Clients who have completed treatment at the facility may return without charge for a few days of additional care if needed.

Christopher Iliades, MD;
Updated by Marianne Moss Madsen, MS

FOR FURTHER INFORMATION

Hoffman, John, et al. *Addiction: Why Can't They Just Stop?* New York: Rodale, 2007. A companion book to the HBO television documentary of the same name. Provides a human face to the hidden problem of addiction in the United States and breaks through the myths and misunderstandings that surround addiction and its treatment.

Ries, Richard K., et al., Eds. *The ASAM Principles of Addiction Medicine.* 5th ed. Philadelphia: Wolters, 2014. A respected text for physicians and mental health professionals covering all aspects of drug and alcohol addiction. A text from the American Society of Addiction Medicine.

Spicer, Jerry. *The Minnesota Model: The Evolution of the Multidisciplinary Approach to Recovery.* Center City, MN: Hazelden, 1993. Describes how the blend of behavioral science and the philosophy of Alcoholics Anonymous became the treatment model for all abstinence addiction treatment.

See also: Abstinence-based treatment; Hazelden Foundation; Minnesota Model; Rehabilitation programs; Twelve-step programs for addicts

Cleanliness addiction

CATEGORY: Psychological issues and behaviors

ALSO KNOWN AS: Contamination OCD; germaphobia

DEFINITION: Cleanliness addiction is a type of obsessive compulsive disorder (OCD), which consists of unwanted thoughts (obsessions) accompanied by repetitive behaviors (compulsions) intended to reduce the anxiety caused by the unwanted thoughts. Typical obsessions involve contamination, aggression, religious concerns, sexual concerns, and the need for exactness or symmetry. More than one-half of all persons with OCD experience contamination fears. For some persons, cleaning obsessively is the main symptom. A person may develop an obsession with contamination, bodily functions, and illness; this obsession manifests as cleanliness addiction.

CAUSES

Researchers do not understand the genetic mechanisms of obsessive compulsive disorder (OCD), though they suspect multiple genes are involved. Genetic links are being investigated. OCD often runs in families, and identical twins have a 70 percent chance of sharing the disorder (fraternal twins have a 50 percent chance of sharing the disorder). Later studies have shown that a streptococcal infection may trigger OCD in children; the infection is known as PANDAS (pediatric autoimmune neuropsychiatric disorders associated with streptococcal infections).

RISK FACTORS

The onset of OCD is usually gradual. It most often begins in adolescence or early adulthood and is surprisingly common. Most people at some time in their lives exhibit some obsessive and compulsive symptoms.

A recent study suggests that fluctuating hormones may trigger OCD symptoms during pregnancy. The same study reports OCD in 30 percent of women observed. A woman may also sometimes develop OCD or see a mild condition worsen in the postpartum stage. Illness may intensify fears about health and cleanliness and increase the compulsive activities associated with those fears. Major life changes and problems at work or school may trigger worries, fears, and obsessions.

SYMPTOMS

Those with contamination OCD have compulsions, intrusive thoughts, or rituals related to cleaning. Cleaning must be done in a certain order or frequency. Worry overwhelms the person, who might think, for example, that a critical spot may have been missed during cleaning. A person with contamination OCD may wash their hands repeatedly until their hands are chapped and even bleeding. This may expose the person to infection.

Washing behaviors are rarely confined to the hands and may include excessive bathing and showering. Rituals might also involve washing clothing and utensils, and house cleaning. Cleanliness addicts may also insist that others adopt the same extreme cleaning behaviors.

OCD can interfere with one's ability to concentrate, and it is not uncommon for a person with OCD to avoid certain situations. For example, someone with cleanliness addiction may be unable to use public restrooms. That person also may have panic attacks when faced with certain situations; they may avoid shaking another person's hand or may avoid public transportation.

People with OCD often miss work or appointments because of compulsions and may even become housebound. Sometimes their pattern of behaviors is confusing to others because it may seem inconsistent. For example, they may have a contamination concern about one specific thing, such as not touching bruised fruit, but be unconcerned about other things (such as gardening manure) that may seem more of a contamination concern to many others.

Unlike adults, children with OCD do not realize that their obsessions and compulsions are excessive. Some experts believe that OCD that begins in childhood may be different from OCD that does not manifest until adulthood.

SCREENING AND DIAGNOSIS

A psychiatrist, psychologist, primary care physician, or nurse with mental health training will usually make a diagnosis of OCD. Many health care professionals use a tool called a structured clinical interview, which contains standardized questions about the nature, severity, and duration of various symptoms. For OCD to be diagnosed, the obsessions and compulsions must demand from the person a minimum of one hour every day or must interfere with normal routines, occupational functioning, social activities, or relationships.

People with contamination obsessions and washing compulsions are sometimes mistaken for hypochondriacs. However, a hypochondriac fears that he or she is already ill and a person with cleanliness addiction fears that he or she may become contaminated (and later, ill). Furthermore, OCD should not be confused with obsessive-compulsive personality disorder (OCPD), which involves, in the case of a cleanliness addict, obsessive concern with cleanliness but a concern that does not cause distress; thus, OCPD is not considered an anxiety disorder.

Dermatologists are often alerted to a cleanliness addiction because of chapped skin or other skin problems that excessive washing can cause. In many cases, family members and friends will urge a cleanliness addict to get help when they see the obsession interfering with the addict's life and the lives of those around him or her.

TREATMENT

Recovery is a process, not a discrete event. There is no cure for this addiction, but cleanliness addiction can be managed. Cognitive-behavioral therapy and antidepressant medications are used to treat the disorder, usually in combination. Cognitive-behavioral therapy involves exposure with response prevention and cognitive therapy.

Exposure involves imagined or actual exposure to things (for example, touching a pet or taking off shoes) that triggers the obsessions and anxiety. Eventually, such exposure will cause little anxiety, if any. This process is called habituation. Response refers to the ritual behaviors that people with cleanliness addiction perform to reduce anxiety. Patients learn to resist the compulsive behaviors. Cognitive therapy focuses on how the person interprets the obsessions. A destructive belief will be objectively challenged and reinterpreted.

Some medication, such as selective serotonin reuptake inhibitors, can increase the levels of serotonin available to transmit messages in the brain, and they have been shown to alleviate the symptoms of 40 to 60 percent of persons with OCD. In cases extremely resistant to treatment, brain surgery may be considered.

PREVENTION

There is no known prevention for OCD. However, by adhering to therapy, it can be managed and relapse can be avoided.

Stephanie Eckenrode BA, LLB

FOR FURTHER INFORMATION

American Psychiatric Association. *Diagnostic and Statistical Manual of Mental Disorders*. 5th ed. Arlington: 2013. Print.

Grayson, Jonathan. *Freedom from Obsessive Compulsive Disorder: A Personalized Recovery Program*. New York: Penguin, 2004. Print.

March, John S., and Karen Mulle. *OCD in Children and Adolescents: A Cognitive-Behavioral Treatment Manual*. New York: Guilford, 1998. Print.

Penzel, Fred. *Obsessive Compulsive Contamination Fears*. Boston: International OCD Foundation, 2010. PDF file.

"What Is OCD?" *Beyond OCD*. Beyond OCD, 2015. Web. 28 Oct. 2015.

See also: Addiction; Behavioral addictions: Overview; Obsessive-compulsive disorder (OCD)

Closing the Addiction Treatment Gap (CATG)

CATEGORY: Treatment

DEFINITION: Closing the Addiction Treatment Gap (CATG), is a private, nonprofit initiative aimed at addressing the gap between those who need substance use treatment and those who receive it. The initiative aims to expand access to quality substance use treatment and to increase knowledge about addiction as a disease. Under CATG sponsorship, millions of dollars have been invested across the United States in the development of state and local substance use treatment. CATG strives to increase awareness of the wide disparity between the number of people in need of alcohol and substance use treatment and the number who ultimately receive treatment.

DATE: Established 2008

BACKGROUND

The origin of the addiction treatment gap stems, in part, from stigma and the erroneous, but common belief that addiction is a moral failing or choice rather than a chronic, treatable disease. Despite these beliefs, alcohol and substance use disorders can develop in any person, regardless of age, gender, or ethnicity, and the impact of alcohol and substance use disorders extends beyond the user to impact their entire community.

However, even though alcohol and substance use disorders impact all demographic groups, the addiction treatment gap effects low income populations most noticeably. This is because they face a greater number of obstacles to receiving care, such as limited access to transportation, childcare, and access to insurance coverage. Additionally, people with alcohol and substance use disorders are more likely to receive Medicaid, as opposed to private health insurance. Given that Medicaid often has more limited provider networks access to care can be delayed. Surveys have also shown that people with alcohol and substance use disorders are also likely to believe that addiction treatment is inaccessible or unaffordable, in addition to also having a limited knowledge of the treatment systems or provider referral options available. People of color also experience a disparate impact of the addiction treatment gap, both because they are more likely to also be low income, and because they face additional barriers to receiving culturally competent healthcare.

The benefits of addressing the addiction treatment gap are numerous. Evidence based alcohol and substance use treatment literally saves lives, and can help people live more productive lives. Additionally, the costs of providing treatment are substantially lower than the costs of healthcare in emergency rooms, prisons, and chronic-disease management programs. Alcohol and substance use disorder care is not a burden on the health care system, but rather a tactic of cost-effective preventive medicine.

MISSION & GOALS

The CATG program was established in 2008 by the Open Society Institute, a private organization for global health and social initiatives. CATG was a one-time, three-year grant program that also offered literature and public outreach. Efforts by CATG to close the treatment gap comprised three tenets: increasing insurance coverage for treatment, increasing public funding for treatment programs, and increasing access to programming by improving its quality and positive outreach. Addiction programs are expanding and their stigma is decreasing because of better healthcare provider communication and better quality of professional education.

The CATG program sought to stimulate community- and medical-based efforts on multiple fronts by advocating for local treatment programs in hospitals and public health settings. Programs funded by or inspired by CATG are part of a long-term solution to encourage both public and private engagement to close the addiction treatment gap. CATG provided grants to businesses, communities, public health entities, and healthcare centers at the state and local level. Eight sites within the United States received grants to implement and model bridging strategies; each grant provided about $600,000 in three years to foster successful practices to minimize the treatment gap.

Grantee programs and efforts led to treatment for addiction as a covered item in basic insurance plans in the state of Wisconsin, added Medicaid programs in multiple states to cover addiction treatment for pregnant women and their children, increased the numbers of medication-assisted treatment programs, provided referrals to community treatment programs, and certified treatment centers to obtain Medicaid or insurance reimbursements. Additionally, in Puerto Rico it let to Medicaid covering Suboxone as an approved medication to treat opioid dependence. Documented benefits of these CATG programs include dramatically lower overall health care costs and reduced numbers of hospital visits.

Research funded by CATG documented how the healthcare costs of people with substance use disorders were more than twice as high as those without. The study looked at Medicaid beneficiaries in Puerto Rico, and found that on nearly half of the additional medical costs were for treatment of co-morbid physical conditions. Other studies worked to develop performance measures for substance use disorder treatment to promote quality care.

Future directions to close the addiction treatment gap remain broad, as states develop programs founded on the initiative principles. Opportunities continue to involve new federal and state regulations, better definitions of treatment benefits, integrations of addiction care services into existing health care infrastructures, monitoring of community-based programs to maintain quality and certification, expanded coverage of community-based programs by public and private health insurance, and the reintegration of recovering persons with addiction into all levels of society.

Nicole M. Van Hoey, PharmD;
Updated by Brandy Henry, PhD (Cand.), LICSW

FOR FURTHER INFORMATION

Barnes, Michael C., and Stacey L. Worthy. "Achieving Real Parity: Increasing Access to Treatment for Substance Use Disorders under the Patient Protection and Affordable Care Act and the Mental Health and Addiction Equity Act." *UALR L. Rev.* 36 (2013): 555.

Deren, Sherry, et al. "Addressing the HIV/AIDS epidemic among Puerto Rican people who inject drugs: the need for a multiregional approach." *American journal of public health* 104.11 (2014): 2030-2036.

Jordán, Héctor M. Colón, et al. "Medical Costs of Persons with Drug Use Disorders among Medicaid Managed Care Beneficiaries in Puerto Rico." *The Journal of Behavioral Health Services & Research* 43.2 (2016): 293-304.

Lipari, Rachel N., and Struther L. Van Horn. "Trends in substance use disorders among adults aged 18 or older." *The CBHSQ Report. Substance Abuse and Mental Health Services Administration* (US), 2017.

NIDA. *Principles of Drug Addiction Treatment: A Research-Based Guide* (Third Edition). (2018, January 17). Retrieved from https://www.drugabuse.gov/publications/principles-drug-addiction-treatment-research-based-guide-third-edition on 2018, May 25

Open Society Institute. *Closing the Addiction Treatment Gap: Early Accomplishments in a Three-Year Initiative.* Baltimore: OSI, 2010. Retrieved from https://www.opensocietyfoundations.org/sites/default/files/early-accomplishments-20100701.pdf on 2018, May 31

Shidhaye, Rahul, Crick Lund, and Dan Chisholm. "Closing the treatment gap for mental, neurological and substance use disorders by strengthening existing health care platforms: strategies for delivery and integration of evidence-based interventions." *International journal of mental health systems* 9.1 (2015): 40.

See also: Alcohol misuse: Treatment; Education about substance misuse; Insurance for addiction treatment; Rehabilitation programs

---

Club drugs

CATEGORY: Substances

ALSO KNOWN AS: Designer drugs

DEFINITION: Club drug is a term for a wide variety of substances that generally are used in social situations, such as at clubs or dance parties. Common club drugs include methylenedioxymethamphetamine (MDMA), gamma-hydroxybutyrate (GHB), ketamine, and methamphetamine. Club drugs often have hallucinogenic properties and may have either excitatory or sedative effects.

STATUS: Illegal in the US and worldwide.

CLASSIFICATION: Controlled substances

SOURCE: Illegally manufactured in illicit laboratories or diverted from legitimate pharmaceutical sources

TRANSMISSION ROUTE: Ingested orally, snorting, rectally and intravenous injection.

USE AND SYMPTOMS

Club drugs are often less expensive and more accessible than other controlled substances, making them particularly attractive to young people who want to experiment with drugs at a rave, dance party, or bar with

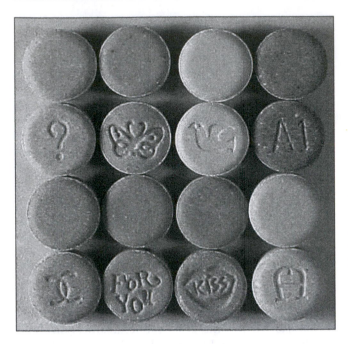

Ecstasy tablets often have an image pressed into one side. (DEA via Wikimedia Commons)

friends. This desire, combined with a false belief that club drugs are safer than other drugs, can lead people to try drugs and sometimes begin using them regularly. Club drugs are often first used at dance clubs or with friends. Because the drugs are psychedelic, reactions of individual users will vary significantly depending on the user's emotional state, concurrent use of other substances, underlying psychiatric conditions, personality, and past experience with the drugs. Additionally, because these substances are street drugs, their contents are usually subject to some variability, such as being mixed with less expensive drugs, and their quality may vary substantially.

Club drugs include a wide variety of different drug classes. GHB (aka Georgia home boy) is a medication used to treat sleep disorders like narcolepsy, it has a reputation as a date rape drug and is misused for its sedating properties. Ketamine (aka special K) is a pharmaceutical sedative-hypnotic misused for its powerful hallucinogenic and dissociative effects. Lysergic acid diethylamide (LSD, acid, blotter) is a powerful synthetic hallucinogen with complex visual and perceptual hallucinations. Methylenedioxymethamphetamine (MDMA, Adam, ecstasy, X, Molly) is a synthetic drug with hallucinogenic and stimulatory properties.

Common stimulants include methamphetamine. Novel drug analogs are continuously formulated and sold which are used to bypass legal restrictions. These especially include the emerging class of cathinones, often called bath salts, which are frequently sold in the club scene for their hallucinatory and stimulatory effects.

The effects of club drugs vary as they have diverse pharmacological profiles. As a group, they are used for a number of desired reactions, including euphoria, feelings of well-being, emotional clarity, a decreased sense of personal boundaries, and feelings of empathy and closeness to others. However, they can also cause significant negative reactions, including panic, impaired judgment, amnesia, impaired motor control, insomnia, paranoia, irrational behavior, flashbacks, hallucinations, rapid heartbeat, high blood pressure, chills, sweating, tremors, respiratory distress, convulsions, and violence. It is not uncommon for individuals to mix these drugs with alcohol, prescription drugs, or other illegal drugs. When drugs are taken in combination, the drugs can interact and cause dangerous and unexpected reactions.

TREATMENT AND THERAPY

The effects of club drugs vary by substance and the treatment for drug misuse varies by substance as well. In general, club drugs tend to be seen more in emergency care settings than in primary health care settings. This is because some of the problems that they cause are often critical and require emergency care. For instance, overdose, strokes, allergic shock reactions, blackouts, loss of consciousness, and accidents related to these conditions may require emergency care. Similarly, dehydration and heat exhaustion can result from prolonged periods of dancing or other physical exertion, as can occur in rave situations. Date rapes have been known to occur with these drugs, particularly Rohypnol and GHB, and injuries due to sexual assault may also require emergency care.

The long-term impact of problems, such as those described above, may require psychotherapy. In addition, problems related to the misuse of or dependence upon club drugs will be addressed in much the same manner as for other substances of misuse. General addiction treatment is advised.

PERSPECTIVE AND PROSPECTS

The dangers of club drugs underscore the continuing need for social awareness of these substances that may otherwise seem harmless. While the therapeutic use of psychedelic substances for psychotherapeutic work may prove to have clinical benefit to certain groups of patients, the illicit use and misuse of these drugs can be highly dangerous.

Nancy A. Piotrowski, PhD; Updated by Denis Folan, DO

FOR FURTHER INFORMATION

Bhatia, S C, and A Hassan. "Ecstasy Substance Use Disorder." *Substance and Non Substance Related Addiction Disorders: Diagnosis and Treatment*, Bentham Science Publishers, 2017, pp. 121–127.

Holland, Julie, ed. *Ecstasy: The Complete Guide—A Comprehensive Look at the Risks and Benefits of MDMA*. Rochester: Inner Traditions International, 2001. Print.

Jansen, Karl. *Ketamine: Dreams and Realities*. Ben Lomond: Multidisciplinary Association for Psychedelic Studies, 2004. Print.

Kuhn, Cynthia, Scott Swartzwelder, and Wilkie Wilson. *Buzzed: The Straight Facts about the Most Used and Abused Drugs from Alcohol to Ecstasy*. Rev. 4th Ed. New York: Norton, 2014. Print.

Moore, Karenza, et al. "Do novel psychoactive substances displace established club drugs, supplement them or act as drugs of initiation? The relationship between mephedrone, ecstasy, and cocaine." *European addiction research* 19.5 (2013): 276-282.

National Institute on Drug Abuse. "Research Reports: MDMA." NIDA, 2018, www.drugabuse.gov/publications/research-reports/mdma-ecstasy-abuse/Introduction.

O'Neill, John, and Pat O'Neill. *Concerned Intervention: When Your Loved One Won't Quit Alcohol or Drugs*. Oakland: New Harbinger, 1992. Print.

Stafford, Peter. *Psychedelics*. Berkeley: Ronin, 2003. Print.

Substance Abuse and Mental Health Services Administration. "Hallucinogens" SAMHSA, 2018. https://www.samhsa.gov/atod/hallucinogens.

Substance Abuse and Mental Health Services Administration. "Stimulants" SAMHSA, 2018. https://www.samhsa.gov/atod/stimulants.

See also: Adolescents and drug misuse; Designer drugs; Ketamine; LSD; MDMA; Rohypnol

Cocaine Anonymous

CATEGORY: Treatment

DEFINITION: Cocaine Anonymous (CA) is a nonprofit recovery program that was developed for men and women addicted to crack cocaine or any other mind-altering substance, including alcohol. CA aims to provide a community for discussion and bonding in support of the goals of abstinence and longstanding addiction recovery.

DATE: Established 1982

BACKGROUND

Cocaine Anonymous (CA) was established in Los Angeles in November of 1982 by a member of Alcoholics Anonymous (AA). From the charter region, or service area, CA has since spread across the United States into Canada and throughout many European countries. By 1996, two thousand service groups with thirty thousand members existed worldwide. CA World Services, or CAWS, has become the overarching global board that provides services and oversees individual service areas, both physical and virtual. CA has a defined online presence that began with the first CA website in 1995. CA Online (CAO) meetings were established in 1997 and were expanded in 1999, receiving full service-area status by CAWS in 2000. In 2010, audio Internet discussion meetings were initiated too, making six online meeting groups available for members worldwide. Cocaine Anonymous Online offers online meetings presented as email meetings that run twenty-four hours per day, seven days a week. Voice meetings are held once per week via Skype. These meetings are similar in format to the in-person CA meetings.

CA was formed on the basis of principles from AA (which was established in 1935) for coping with the misuse of cocaine and other illicit substances. The inclusion of all types of substances is validated in part because people addicted to cocaine and other abusive drugs of choice face similar addiction and recovery challenges; in addition, addicts often interchange substances or replace cocaine with new drugs during their struggles for abstinence. CA relies on the group lessons of shared recovery experiences and mutual understanding among longtime and new participants within the community.

The CA program, like AA, models a twelve-step recovery. During the recovery process, group participants progress through steps of acknowledgement, forgiveness, and resolve. The addict begins abstinence by letting go of his or her sense of fault for the addition, continues by asking and accepting forgiveness for past actions, and ultimately identifies a greater spiritual authority.

CA tenets also include twelve traditions, which provide a moral code of themes based on faith, forgiveness, and autonomy to supplement the twelve-step process. The traditions are directives for the individual members and for the larger group, including the CAWS board.

Although initial recovery relies on the CA steps and traditions, CA participation does not end when the twelfth step is completed. Instead, the social network of a person's local recovery group continues to provide positive reinforcement to sustain recovery after the twelve-step process and after any other treatment programs have ended. Leadership roles or simple comfort zones exist in the physical and virtual settings without a time line or defined conclusion; recovery from substance misuse addiction is lifelong, and so too is CA support.

CA meetings are separated by regional service areas, and each regularly scheduled group is identified as a service unit. Each unit is independently supported by contributions from its members and is not affiliated with business or political organizations. Although the meetings follow a traditional format outlined by AA and by CAWS, each unit is autonomous in its decision making and particular needs. Service units are available in rural, suburban, and urban areas; numerous district sites also are often available within a major city. Home groups are the unit meetings at which the addict should feel most comfortable, uninhibited, and open to participation.

To be fully participatory, a member should attend one meeting each day for the first month as an immersive recovery experience. In addition, participants are encouraged to identify a member who has already completed the twelve-step recovery process; sponsorship by a member with a minimum of a one-year history of sobriety in the service unit can guide the new member on his or her own recovery path and promote abstinence on an individual level. In addition, a sponsor can build a close relationship with the new member and can provide deeper guidance and more thorough discussions than the group meetings permit.

MISSION AND GOALS

The primary goal of CA is to provide a local, accessible, and comfortable community for substance misuse addicts to start and maintain their addiction-free lives. One mission of the CA unit for each member through the recovery period is to encourage self-supporting discipline, community involvement, and re-entry into active society after suffering from the disease of substance misuse. CA supports a goal of freedom from addiction as one of its traditions; related tenets focus on God, spirituality, and personal inventory to further support the CA mission of addiction-free living.

To bolster each unit's goal of unity through community outreach, CAWS publishes "Newsgram" each quarter; it is available in print and digital versions. A newsletter subscription can be purchased by members or any website visitors; single copies also can be obtained at service units. Similarly, CAWS released a two-volume series that presents the CA principles through literature and fellowship stories. The first volume, *Hope, Faith, and Courage*, was followed by a second volume of the same title about recovery experiences. CAWS also holds a yearly convention. The CA organization has also released a number of video public service announcements (PSAs) in a number of languages that are accessible on the web and linked through their website. These short clips identify problems of addiction and encourage addicts to get help by contacting CA. The Hope, Faith, Courage motto is now part of the organization's logo and summarizes the qualities that each member learns to depend on to sustain an addiction-free goal.

Nicole M. Van Hoey PharmD

FOR FURTHER INFORMATION

Cocaine Anonymous World Services. *Hope, Faith, and Courage*. 2 vols. Los Angeles: CAWS, 1993, 2007. Relates the shared experiences of CA members during their recovery to encourage and inspire current recovering members or other readers, such as family and friends.

Kampman, K. M. "What's New to Treat Cocaine Addiction?" *Current Psychiatric Report* 12.5 (2010):

441–47. Print. Discusses medical and behavioral treatment options, which can be administered before or during a twelve-step program, for people addicted to cocaine.

National Institute on Drug Abuse. *Principles of Drug Addiction Treatment: A Research-Based Guide.* 2nd ed. National Institutes of Health Publication No. 09-4180. Bethesda, MD: NIDA, 2009. An evidence-based guide to treating addiction and recovery.

Seeking Drug Abuse Treatment: Know What to Ask. National Institutes of Health Publication No. 12–7764. Bethesda, MD: NIDA, 2011. Provides the top five questions a person seeking substance abuse treatment for self or another should consider when evaluating treatment options. Considers twelve-step programs as crucial to treatment and recovery success.

See also: Abstinence-based treatment; Cocaine use disorder; Group therapy for substance misuse; Sponsors; Support groups; Twelvestep programs for addicts

Cocaine use disorder

CATEGORY: Substance misuse

ALSO KNOWN AS: Cocaine addiction; cocaine dependency

DEFINITION: Cocaine use disorder is diagnosed when the repeated use of cocaine harms a person's health or social functioning, or when a person becomes physically dependent on cocaine. Powdered cocaine can be snorted or dissolved in water and injected, while crack, which a rock crystal form, can be heated and its vapors smoked. Cocaine use disorder is treatable, but recovery is often difficult and may require professional care.

CAUSES

Cocaine is a powerful central nervous system stimulant that causes the brain to release large amounts of the hormone dopamine. Dopamine, a neurotransmitter associated with feelings of pleasure, floods the brain's reward pathways and results in the euphoria commonly reported by cocaine users. As a person continues to use cocaine, a tolerance is developed. This means that more frequent use and higher doses are required to achieve the same feeling of euphoria. Repeated use of cocaine can result in long-term disruptions to the brain's dopamine levels and reward circuitry.

When a cocaine user stops using abruptly, he or she experiences a crash or withdrawal. This results in an extremely strong craving for more cocaine. It also may result in fatigue, loss of pleasure in life, depression, anxiety, irritability, and paranoia. These withdrawal symptoms often prompt the user to seek more cocaine.

RISK FACTORS

Being male and being aged eighteen to twenty-five years are factors that increase one's chances of developing cocaine use disorder.

SYMPTOMS

The short-term effects associated with cocaine use include euphoria, increased energy, mental alertness, decreased need for food and sleep, dilated pupils, increased temperature, increased heart rate, increased blood pressure, erratic or violent behavior, vertigo, muscle twitches, paranoia, restlessness, irritability, and anxiety. A cocaine overdose can result in a dangerous elevation of blood pressure, leading to stroke, heart failure, or even sudden death

The long-term effects include uncontrollable or unpredictable cravings; increased tolerance; increased dosing; increasing irritability, restlessness, and paranoia; paranoid psychosis; and auditory hallucinations.

Medical complications that may result from cocaine use disorder include heart rhythm abnormalities, heart attack, chest pain, respiratory failure, stroke, seizure, headache, abdominal pain, and nausea.

SCREENING AND DIAGNOSIS

A doctor who suspects cocaine use disorder will ask the patient about symptoms and medical history. He or she will also perform a physical examination. The doctor will ask specific questions about the cocaine use, such as how long the patient has been using the drug and how often.

TREATMENT AND THERAPY

A medical professional should be consulted to develop the best treatment plan for an individual with cocaine use disorder. Treatment programs may be inpatient or outpatient. Treatment programs may require the patient to have already stopped using cocaine prior to treatment, or they may involve a supervised detoxification program.

Medications can be used to help manage the symptoms of withdrawal, but there are no medications that have been approved to specifically treat cocaine use disorder. Medications that have shown some promise include modafinil (Provigil), N-acetylcysteine, topiramate (Topamax), disulfiram, agonist replacement therapy, and baclofen. Antidepressants may also be helpful for people in the early stages of cocaine abstinence. A 2015 study from the Yale School of Medicine also found that progesterone may be effective as a treatment for cocaine use disorder in women.

Behavioral therapies to help people quit using cocaine are often the only effective treatment for cocaine use disorder. These therapies use contingency management. With this program, people receive positive rewards for staying in treatment and remaining cocaine-free. Additionally, cognitive-behavioral therapy helps people to learn the skills needed to manage stress and prevent relapse.

Recovery programs such as Cocaine Anonymous provide community support for people seeking to recover from cocaine addiction. In rehabilitation programs, people with cocaine use disorder stay in a controlled environment for six to twelve months. During this time, they may receive vocational rehabilitation and other support to prepare them to return to society.

PREVENTION

The best way to prevent cocaine use disorder is to never use cocaine because the drug is highly addictive. Education programs on the dangers of cocaine use have helped to lower rates of cocaine use in the United States since the 1990s.

Krisha McCoy MS and Theodor B. Rais MD

FOR FURTHER INFORMATION

DiGirolamo, Gregory J., David Smelson, and Nathan Guevremont. "Cue-Induced Craving in Patients with Cocaine Use Disorder Predicts Cognitive Control Deficits toward Cocaine Cues." *Addictive Behaviors* 47 (2015): 86–90. Print.

DuPont, Robert L. *The Selfish Brain: Learning from Addiction.* Center City.: Hazelton, 2000. Print.

Cocaine

Cocaine is a powerful central nervous system stimulant that causes the brain to release large amounts of the hormone dopamine. Dopamine, a neurotransmitter associated with feelings of pleasure, floods the brain's reward pathways and results in the euphoria commonly reported by cocaine users. As a person continues to use cocaine, a tolerance is developed. This means that more frequent use and higher doses are required to achieve the same feeling of euphoria. Repeated use of cocaine can result in long-term disruptions to the brain's dopamine levels and reward circuitry.

Cocaine's easy availability and strong addictive potential make it a popular drug of misuse. Additionally, cocaine is rapidly absorbed by and eliminated from the body, leading to a short duration of effects; this prompts cocaine misusers to rapidly repeat doses of cocaine until their supply is exhausted. Cocaine misuse is prevalent across all gender, demographic, and socioeconomic lines.

Julien, Robert M., Claire D. Advokat, and Joseph Comaty. *A Primer of Drug Action: A Comprehensive Guide to the Actions, Uses, and Side Effects of Psychoactive Drugs.* 12th ed. New York: Worth, 2010. Print.

Shorter, Daryl, Coreen B. Domingo, and Thomas R. Kosten. "Emerging Drugs for the Treatment of Cocaine Use Disorder: A Review of Neurobiological Targets and Pharmacotherapy." *Expert Opinion on Emerging Drugs* 20.1 (2015): 15–29. Print.

Sosinsky, Alexandra. "Progesterone Reduces the Use of Cocaine in Postpartum Women with Cocaine Use Disorder." *MGH Center for Women's Mental Health.* Massachusetts General Hospital, 4 Feb. 2015. Web. 29 Oct. 2015.

Sussman, Steven, and Susan L. Ames. *Drug Abuse: Concepts, Prevention, and Cessation.* New York: Cambridge UP, 2008. Print.

Weil, Andrew, and Winifred Rosen. *From Chocolate to Morphine: Everything You Need to Know About Mind-Altering Drugs.* Rev. ed. Boston: Houghton Mifflin, 2004.

See also: Cocaine Anonymous; Crack; Dopamine and addiction; Withdrawal

Codeine

CATEGORY: Substances

ALSO KNOWN AS: Methylmorphine; morphine methylester; 3-methylmorphine

DEFINITION: Codeine is a drug used primarily as an analgesic, but it also is used in antidiarrheal and antitussive medications.

STATUS: Legal by prescription in the United States; legal outside the United States without a prescription if combined with other drugs in relatively small dosages

CLASSIFICATION: Controlled substance: schedule I (derivatives of codeine), II (codeine alone), III (with other analgesics), or V (in cough preparations with other drugs)

SOURCE: Milky fluid of immature seed capsules of the opium poppy plant (*Papaver somniferum*); also synthesized from morphine

TRANSMISSION ROUTE: Oral, intramuscular, subcutaneous, and intravenous

HISTORY OF USE

Codeine was isolated from opium by French chemist Pierre-Jean Robiquet in 1832 and was used in the nineteenth century for pain relief and diabetes control. Near the end of the nineteenth century, codeine was used to replace morphine , another substance found in the opium poppy, because of the highly addictive properties of morphine. Codeine has effects similar to, albeit weaker than, morphine and was not thought to be addictive. Codeine was subsequently used in treatment for withdrawal from morphine.

The first detailed report of codeine addiction is thought to be from 1905, and reports by others followed. In the 1930s, concern over the widespread misuse of codeine in Canada was noted. Codeine misuse in the United States was evaluated more fully in the 1960s, leading to inclusion of codeine as a schedule II controlled substance. Schedule II drugs have a high potential for misuse.

Subsequently, among substance misusers, prescription cough syrups containing codeine began to be mixed with soft drinks and candy (in a combination known as lean syrup, sizzurp, or purple drank). The combination remains a substance of concern.

EFFECTS AND POTENTIAL RISKS

Codeine primarily exerts its medicinal effects by being metabolized by liver enzymes to substances that bind to specific receptors in the central and peripheral nervous systems. One of the most potent of these substances is morphine. The codeine metabolites can effectively block the transmission of pain signals to the brain and can inhibit the cough reflex. The metabolites also contribute to the usefulness of codeine in treating diarrhea by affecting, among other things, the contraction of gastrointestinal tract muscles.

Short-term use of codeine provides pain relief and euphoric effects. Some of the more common side effects of codeine ingestion include itching, constipation, dizziness, sedation, flushing, sweating, nausea, vomiting, and hives.

Long-term use of codeine can lead to tolerance, necessitating higher doses to achieve the same euphoric effect. Endorphin (natural painkiller) production may be slowed or stopped, causing increased sensitivity to pain if codeine is not used. More serious side effects include respiratory depression, central nervous system depression, seizures, and cardiac arrest.

Jason J. Schwartz PhD

FOR FURTHER INFORMATION

Amer. Soc. of Health-System Pharmacists. "Codeine." *MedlinePlus.* US Natl. Lib. of Medicine, 15 Sept. 2015. Web. 27 Oct. 2015.

McCoy, Krisha. "Opioid Addiction." Ed. Michael Woods. *Health Library.* EBSCO, Jan. 2014. Web. 27 Oct. 2015.

Manchikanti, Laxmaiah, et al. "Therapeutic Use, Abuse, and Nonmedical Use of Opioids: A Ten-Year Perspective." *Pain Physician* 13 (2010): 401–35. Print.

Parker, James N., and Philip M. Parkers, eds. *Codeine: A Medical Dictionary, For Further Information, and Annotated Research Guide to Internet References.* San Diego: Icon, 2003. Print.

Parker, Philip M., ed. *Codeine: Webster's Timeline History, 1888-2007.* San Diego: Icon, 2010. Print.

See also: Controlled substances and precursor chemicals; Painkiller misuse; Prescription drug addiction: Overview

Codependency

CATEGORY: Psychological issues and behaviors

ALSO KNOWN AS: Relationship addiction

DEFINITION: No single definition exists for codependency, but available definitions describe a pattern of unhealthy learned behaviors that generally result from a psychologically unhealthy and dysfunctional family situation. Codependents are often focused on others, rather than themselves, and are unable to communicate or take action in a healthy, productive way about their situation, the relationship, or themselves.

CAUSES

Common causes of codependency include being a child of a drug or alcohol misuser or coming from a home that is dysfunctional in other ways.

RISK FACTORS

Persons who were exposed to a dysfunctional family situation as a child are at risk for developing codependency. This risk is attributed to the difficult realities and premature responsibilities that made it challenging for the child to cope. This risk also is attributed to the lack of role models to demonstrate the appropriate management of emotions and behavior.

SYMPTOMS

There is no universally accepted list of symptoms of codependency; symptoms can vary from person to person and are described differently by different sources. A key characteristic of many codependent persons is caretaking, or feeling responsible for other people and feeling excessively compelled to help other people solve their problems. This can result in overcommitment and a feeling of being constantly under pressure.

Even though codependent persons will take on excessive responsibilities, they also often blame others for their own negative feelings and for their situation. Conversely, some participants in codependent relationships may become extremely irresponsible.

Codependent persons often have feelings of low self-esteem, will generally blame themselves for many situations, and will have trouble receiving compliments or praise. Low self-worth is often associated with feelings of guilt as well.

Codependent persons can engage in denial, or "pretending" that uncomfortable situations or feelings are not happening. They also can seem to be rigid and controlled; this can be a result of not wanting to deal with uncomfortable emotions, such as fear and guilt.

It is not uncommon for codependent persons to obsess about specific people or problems and to perceive themselves as unable to get things done or have a "normal" life because of these people or problems. They also tend to feel unable to be comfortable or happy with themselves and, as a result, seek happiness from external sources. They often worry that they will be left alone or abandoned and may tolerate misuse in relationships because of this fear. A term often used in association with codependence is *poor boundaries*, meaning that people who are codependent may allow others to treat them inappropriately or to hurt them.

Codependent persons often feel unable to trust themselves or others. They have not learned effective ways to communicate and may use such manipulative strategies as blaming and begging to get what they want from others. They often are uncomfortable with angry emotions.

Codependent persons often are described as engaging in "enabling" behavior, meaning that they allow and support the person with whom they are in an unhealthy relationship to continue behaviors that are harmful for both of them. For example, an enabler might continue to "cover" for an alcoholic who frequently engages in binge drinking. In such as case, the codependent person might contact the person's place of employment to call in sick for that person or to otherwise lie to help him or her avoid the consequences of the behavior.

People who struggle with codependency for a long period of time may feel withdrawn and depressed and may even consider suicide. They also may become addicted to alcohol, drugs, or other harmful behaviors, such as compulsive or binge eating.

Authors on codependency have identified several ways to broadly categorize patterns that are typical of the condition. For example, the three dimensions of the personality of an addict, as identified by C. Robert Cloniger, are described as novelty seeking, harm-avoidance, and reward-dependence. Codependent persons may gravitate toward either extreme of these dimensions.

Enabling

Enabling describes any behaviors by family members, partners, therapists, coworkers, or friends of addicts that allow the addicted person to continue engaging in substance misuse or other self-destructive behavior without facing negative consequences. Enabling is one of the hallmarks of codependency.

A person often begins engaging in enabling behavior because he or she cares about the addict and wants to be helpful and kind. However, enabling actually allows the addict to increase the severity of his or her substance misuse or other self-destructive behavior. Without negative consequences, the addict can continue engaging in denial that he or she has a problem.

Additionally, the addict's tolerance for the drug of choice increases, requiring more of the drug of choice to achieve the same physical and psychological effects. As the addict uses increasingly more of the drug of choice, members of his or her family system engage in more frequent, more severe, and more consequential forms of enabling. Thus, the family system or social system that includes the addict engages in a negative cycle of enabling and addictive behavior.

In the case of novelty seeking, codependent persons can be high novelty-seeking, exhibiting impulsive behaviors, or low novelty-seeking, with a rigid style of coping. In the reward-dependence dimension, codependent persons can be either eager to help others or appear socially detached and self-willed. In the harm-avoidance dimension, codependent persons can be either excessively pessimistic or anxious, or they can be overconfident and eager to take risks.

Codependent behaviors also have been explained, originally by Sharon Wegscheider-Cruse, in terms of "survival roles" in the family or relationship that arise from a dysfunctional environment. Survival roles include the "family hero," who takes on tremendous responsibilities; the "family scapegoat," who accepts blame; the "lost child," who remains removed from most people; and the "mascot," who attracts attention by acting inappropriately.

SCREENING AND DIAGNOSIS

The diagnosis of codependency is not listed in the *Diagnostic and Statistical Manual of Mental Disorders,* which is used by psychiatrists and other mental health professionals as a diagnostic guide.. However, several personality disorders in the manual contain elements recognized by authors on codependency as being part of the condition.

Many who write about codependency encourage the codependent person to examine his or her own behaviors to determine if he or she is codependent. Self-help groups, including Co-Dependents Anonymous (CoDA) and Nar-Anon, provide checklist-style guidelines for identifying patterns of thought and behavior that indicate codependency. For example, the CoDA patterns of codependency list includes thoughts and behaviors indicative of patterns of denial, low self-esteem, compliance, and control. Nar-Anon lists twelve common characteristics of codependency. Many mental health care professionals, particularly those who work in the area of substance misuse and addiction, are familiar with the characteristics of codependency and can help persons identify dysfunctional patterns and behaviors.

TREATMENT AND THERAPY

Mental health professionals can work with codependent persons in individual or group therapy sessions with the goal of modifying dysfunctional patterns and adopting healthy coping skills. Although much of the focus of treatment for codependency tends to be on the caretaker, it is important to note that the addict or substance misuser in the relationship is also considered to be codependent.

Experts thus suggest that the problems of misuse and addiction cannot be fully resolved if the codependency is ignored. Programs designed to address addiction often involve education for the patient and family on codependency.

Self-help programs including CoDA and Nar-Anon provide support and instruction to aid the person in monitoring and modifying his or her own behaviors based on the same twelve-step model that is often employed by substance misusers and addicts in programs such as Alcoholics Anonymous and Narcotic Anonymous.

The twelve steps identified by CoDA begin with "We admitted we were powerless over others—that our lives had become unmanageable" and progress to a final step of carrying the messages learned through the twelve steps to other codependent persons. CoDA also provides examples of patterns of recovery that can, over time, replace patterns of codependency that most likely developed over many years.

PREVENTION

Literature regarding the prevention of codependency is limited. However, it has been suggested that codependency might be prevented or mitigated by the early employment of healthy coping strategies to deal with dysfunctional behaviors such as drug or alcohol misuse.

Katherine Hauswirth RN, MSN

FOR FURTHER INFORMATION

Beattie, Melody. *Codependent No More*. San Francisco: HarperCollins, 1987. Print.

Co-Dependents Anonymous. "Patterns and Characteristics of Codependence." 2010. Web. 16 Apr. 2012. http://www.coda.org/tools4recovery/patterns-new.htm.

---. "The Twelve Steps of Co-Dependents Anonymous." 2010. Web. 16 Apr. 2012. http://www.coda.org/tools4recovery/twelve-steps.htm.

Cruse, Joseph R. *Painful Affairs: Looking for Love through Addiction and Co-dependency*. Deerfield Beach: Health Communications, 1989. Print.

See also: Families and substance misuse; Psychological dependence

Coffee

CATEGORY: Substance
DEFINITION: Coffee, coffee is a commonly consumed beverage and one of the most common sources of the stimulant caffeine.
STATUS: Legal in the United States and worldwide
CLASSIFICATION: Stimulant, stimulants, coffee
SOURCE: Coffee bean
TRANSMISSION ROUTE: Coffee is consumed through oral ingestion.

HISTORY OF USE

Coffee has been consumed for centuries and has played a critical role in many societies. The coffee bean originally came from a berry of an Ethiopian shrub. Coffee drinking was believed to have started in Sufi monasteries in Yemen in southern Arabia during the fifteenth century. Coffee's ability to deter sleep made it popular among Sufi monks, who used it to keep themselves alert during nighttime devotions. Coffee was initially banned for secular consumption and also for its stimulating effects, but bans were eventually overturned because of coffee's popularity.

Coffee drinking first spread through the Middle East, then to Europe, Indonesia, and the Americas. Coffeehouses, or their equivalents, became popular first in the Middle East, then in Europe and later in the United States. In the 1950s, the idea of a coffee break was popularized. Specialty coffeehouses arose during the 1970s.

Coffee is the most commonly consumed mood-altering substance worldwide and is the leading source of caffeine in the United States. More than 80 percent of the adults in the United States consume behaviorally active doses on a daily basis. Until recently, coffee was rarely considered an addictive stimulant.

EFFECTS AND POTENTIAL RISKS

Although once thought harmless, coffee consumption, according to numerous studies, can have adverse effects. Physiological effects begin within ten to twenty minutes of consumption, with maximum effects coming within thirty to sixty minutes. Effects substantially diminish after about three hours. Coffee, through the effects of caffeine, has been shown to alter mood, stamina, and heart rate, and it can lead to gastric disturbances, such as heartburn. Caffeine increases heartbeat, respiration, metabolic rate, and stomach acid and can result in tension, irritability, and insomnia.

Risks associated with coffee overconsumption include liver, heart, and pancreatic problems. Coffee drinking also is associated with infertility, birth defects and disorders, sudden infant death syndrome, and the development of fibrocystic breasts.

The typical caffeine in a cup of coffee, approximately 155 milligrams, is enough to produce measurable metabolic effects. Caffeine affects the body similarly regardless of a person's body size or age, but effects are much more pronounced in children than in adults.

C. J. Walsh PhD

FOR FURTHER INFORMATION

Cherniske, Stephen. *Coffee Blues: Wake up to the Hidden Dangers of America's #1 Drug.* New York: Warner, 1998.

Hanson, Dirk. *The Chemical Carousel: What Science Tells Us about Beating Addiction.* Charleston, SC: Book-Surge, 2008.

Pendergrast, Mark. *Uncommon Grounds: The History of Coffee and How It Transformed Our World.* New York: Basic, 2010.

See also: Caffeine addiction; Caffeine's effects on the body; Physiological dependence; Stimulants' effects on the body

Cognitive-behavioral therapy for addictions & substance misuse

CATEGORY: Treatment

ALSO KNOWN AS: Relapse-prevention coping skills

DEFINITION: Cognitive-behavioral therapy (CBT) is a form of psychotherapy in which a person works with a therapist to identify, challenge, and rethink any misperceptions or negative thoughts and their associated undesirable behaviors. The term cognitive-behavioral therapy applies not to one specific type of therapy but rather to a group of therapy types that share a similar approach. These therapy types include rational-emotive behavior therapy, rational behavior therapy, rational living therapy, cognitive therapy, and dialectical behavior therapy (DBT).

HISTORY AND DEVELOPMENT

Early work by researchers including Ivan Pavlov, John B. Watson, and B. F. Skinner was based on classical behavioral theory, which states that learning begins with an individual's interactions with the environment and that behaviors form from exposure to stimuli in the environment. In the 1960s theorist Aaron T. Beck emphasized the impact of each person's thoughts and emotions on behavior, referring to therapy that addressed both thoughts and behaviors as cognitive-behavioral therapy (CBT).

GENERAL USES

CBT has been used widely in the field of psychiatry for disorders including those of mood, thought, personality, and addiction. CBT can occur in either a one-to-one therapist-patient setting or in a group therapy setting. In the area of addictions and substance misuse, research by G. Alan Marlatt and J. R. Gordon published in the 1980s incorporated CBT concepts into a specific strategy for preventing relapse of negative addictive behaviors. Experts note that CBT may be one of the most studied treatments for addiction, and research has confirmed that this approach, especially when used in a group setting, has a generally modest but positive effect in persons who have misuse or addiction diagnoses.

The use of CBT with either medication or other psychosocial approaches may provide an added benefit in some cases as compared with CBT alone. While CBT differs in many ways from popular twelve-step programs such as Alcoholics Anonymous and Narcotics Anonymous that are often used by people struggling with addictive behaviors, both CBT and twelve-step approaches encourage participants to pursue activities that are incompatible with the addictive behavior and to find ways to combat negative thinking.

Persons who participate in CBT to cope with an addiction or misuse problem work with the therapist to understand repeated patterns that promote ongoing substance misuse and addiction. Persons in therapy learn to identify factors that can trigger relapse of abusive or addictive behaviors and learn how to successfully refuse the substance or behavior of misuse.

CBT participants explore the consequences of continued substance misuse behaviors. Scrutiny of even seemingly small decisions that may affect thoughts, emotions, or behavior, as in the case of an alcoholic who may pass a favorite bar on the way to or from work, is strongly encouraged. CBT emphasizes the successful use of coping skills and the adoption of new activities that are completely unrelated to the addictive behavior.

An important aspect of CBT is identifying thoughts that support continued substance misuse or other addictive behaviors (often referred to as cognitive distortions) and learning to replace these thoughts with more beneficial ones. This process is called reframing. Patients engage in role play or rehearsal that is intended to help them cope with cravings for the addictive substance or behavior, or with high-risk situations, such as being invited to an occasion at which the substance of misuse will be available. Patients are often assigned homework, during which they can practice new thought patterns or skills learned during therapy sessions. Treatment goals are usually well defined in CBT, and sessions are structured, brief in duration, and often limited to twelve to twenty-four weeks.

LIMITATIONS

While experts have identified many benefits associated with CBT, one potential disadvantage of this approach is the need for specialized and fairly complex training of therapists so that they can use CBT techniques effectively with patients. CBT may have limited usefulness in patients who have higher levels of cognitive impairment or in those who are not prepared to undertake the work that is required for learning new thoughts and behaviors.

Katherine Hauswirth RN, MSN

FOR FURTHER INFORMATION

Ball, Samuel A. "Psychotherapy Models for Substance Abuse." *Psychiatric Times* 20 (2003): 171. Print.

Bennett-Levy, James, et al. *Experiencing CBT from the Inside Out: A Self-Practice/Self-Reflection Workbook for Therapists.* New York: Guilford, 2015. Print.

Carroll, Kathleen M. "Cognitive-Behavioral Therapies." *The American Psychiatric Publishing Textbook of Substance Abuse Treatment.* Ed. Marc Galanter and Herbert D. Kleber. 4th ed. 2011. Web. 16 Apr. 2011.

Kobak, Kenneth A., et al. "Web-Based Therapist Training on Cognitive Behavior Therapy for Anxiety Disorders: A Pilot Study." *Psychotherapy* 50.2 (2013): 235–47. Print.

Larimer, Mary E., Rebekka S. Palmer, and G. Alan Marlatt. "Relapse Prevention: An Overview of Marlatt's Cognitive-Behavioral Model." *Alcohol Research and Health* 23 (1999): 151–60. Print.

Magill, Molly, and Lara A. Ray. "Cognitive-Behavioral Treatment with Adult Alcohol and Illicit Drug Users: A Meta-Analysis of Randomized Controlled Trials." *Journal of Studies on Alcohol and Drugs* 70 (1999): 516–27. Print.

Natl. Assn. of Cognitive-Behavioral Therapists. "What Is Cognitive-Behavioral Therapy?" *NACBT.org.* Natl. Assn. of Cognitive-Behavioral Therapists, n.d. Web. 16 Apr. 2012.

Wells, Adrian. *Cognitive Therapy of Anxiety Disorders: A Practice Manual and Conceptual Guide.* New York: Wiley, 2013. Print.

Winerman, Lea. "Breaking Free from Addiction." *American Psychological Association.* American Psychological Assn., June 2013. Web. 26 Oct. 2015.

Wright, Jesse, Michael Thase, and Aaron Beck. *Cognitive-Behavior Therapy.* Washington: Amer. Psych., 2014. Print.

See also: Addiction medications; Alcoholics Anonymous: The Twelve Steps; Behavioral addictions: Treatment; Behavioral therapies for addiction; Treatment methods and research

College and substance misuse

CATEGORY: Psychological issues and behaviors

DEFINITION: College students make up one of the largest groups of drug misusers in the nation. In fact, young adults enrolled in a full-time college program are twice as likely to misuse drugs and alcohol as those who are not. Alcohol is the substance most misused by college students. In fact, about 80% of college students drink alcohol. Furthermore, 40% of U.S. college students binge drink (five or more drinks per occasion at least once in the past two weeks). Drinking, and binge drinking in particular is a problem because of the high frequency of associated negative incidents such as assault, motor vehicle accidents, and violations of college policies. Additionally about 25% of college students report suffering academic consequences related to drinking too much, such as missing class, falling behind in class, lower test scores, and lower grades. College students also use other drugs including marijuana, opioids and stimulants.

BACKGROUND

College students make up one of the largest groups of drug misusers in the nation. In fact, young adults enrolled in a full-time college program are twice as likely to misuse drugs and alcohol as those who are not. Young adults (defined as those aged 17-25 years) who leave home to live at a college or university are presented with many new experiences, and are often faced with making major decisions independently for the first time. One of the biggest challenges and decisions for college students is how to deal with the alcohol and drug culture rampant on college campuses. Parties, Greek organizations, bars and dance clubs are common places for college students to gather, and provide easy access to alcohol and other substances. A combination of academic stress, unstructured time, curiosity, social pressure, and widespread availability of alcohol and other substances particularly at parties and Greek organizations leads to experimentation with recreational, stress-relieving, and/ or performance-enhancing drugs. For some students, experimentation leads to eventual misuse of alcohol and/ or drugs.

TYPICAL SUBSTANCES OF MISUSE

Alcohol is, by far, the drug most misused by college students. In fact, about 80% of college students drink alcohol. Furthermore, according to the most recent Monitoring the Future national survey (a long term epidemiological survey studying trends in drug use among American adolescents and adults) released in 2017, 4 in every 10 U.S. college students (about 40%) binge drink (defined as defined as having five or more drinks per occasion at least once in the past two weeks.) A Harvard University study found that among fraternity and sorority members, 8 out of 10 (80%) regularly binge drink in comparison to the 40% among college students overall. These higher rates of binge drinking among Greek members compared to their peer counterparts do not end with college graduation; in fact, they continue through age 35. Binge drinking is a significant problem because of the high frequency of negative consequences and other incidents that occur in conjunction with binge drinking, such as assault, drunk driving, and violations of college policies. About 25% of college students report suffering academic consequences related to drinking too much, such as missing class, falling behind in class, lower test scores, and lower grades. College students also die from alcohol-related unintentional injuries, including motor-vehicle crashes. Many students are assaulted by another student who has been drinking. Other consequences include suicide attemps, health problems, vandalism and involvement with the police. Drinking, and binge drinking in particular, is commonly part of the pledging process for Greek organizations and part of the initiation (hazing) process for

new athletes. It is also seen as a means to fit in and to deal with social and academic stress.

Though drinking has long been the most common form of substance misuse in college, according to the National Institute on Drug Abuse, use of marijuana/ hashish, ecstasy, cocaine, and illicit drugs in general, is on the rise. In fact, Marijuana use among U.S. college students in 2016 was at the highest level seen in the past three decades, according to the most recent findings from the national Monitoring the Future follow-up study. In 2016, 39% of full-time college students aged 19-22 indicated that they used marijuana at least once in the prior 12 months, and 22% indicated that they used at least once in the prior 30 days. Both percentages are the highest found since 1987, and represent a steady increase since 2006, when they were 30 and 17 percent, respectively.

College students also commonly misuse prescription drugs including opioids (such as Percocet, Vicodin, and OxyContin), stimulants (such as Ritalin and Adderall), and anabolic steroids. These legal drugs are used to get high and, depending on the drug, to stay awake for studying, to enhance athletic ability, to lose weight, or to self-medicate for anxiety, depression, and related mental stresses. Students obtain these substances through valid prescriptions for pain, from friends or family, and even from street dealers.

Date rape drugs are drugs used to facilitate sexual assault. The most common date rape substance is alcohol; in fact, over 97,000 students between 18 and 24 years of age are victims of alcohol-related sexual assault or date rape. Other common date rape drugs include GHB, ketamine, and Rohypnol. These drugs are often slipped into drinks or given to people who ingest them unknowingly, and cause that person to become physically incapacitated, judgment-impaired and/ or unable to refuse sex.

COLLEGE OFFICIALS' RESPONSE

Colleges and universities are acutely aware of substance misuse and how it affects both the individual and the college community. Because of their missions to educate, institutions across the United States are making efforts to address substance misuse from the moment students first arrive on campus during orientation until they graduate. Many colleges and universities are trying to develop alternatives to the bar and party scenes, and educating students about the possibilities of recreation without using substances. Colleges and universities are also reviewing and revising their policies about substance use and misuse, aiming to educate and prevent substance misuse rather than using punishment. Specific information about the drug and alcohol policies of a particular college or university can be obtained from that institution.

Mary Frances Stuck, PhD;
Updated by Shiliang Alice Cao, BA

FOR FURTHER INFORMATION

"Binge Drinking in College - The Impact of Alcohol in Higher Education." *AddictionCenter*, 2018, www.addictioncenter.com/alcohol/binge-drinking/.

Borsari, Brian, and Kate B. Carey. "Peer Influences on College Drinking: A Review of the Research." *Journal of Substance Abuse* 13.4 (2001): 391–424. Print.

"College Drinking." *National Institute on Alcohol Abuse and Alcoholism.* NIAAA, Apr. 2015. Web. 28 Oct. 2015.

"Drinking and Drug Abuse in Greek Life." *Addiction-Center*, Mar. 2018, www.addictioncenter.com/college/drinking-drug-abuse-greek-life/.

Harrington, Cleveland H., et al., eds. *Substance Abuse Recovery in College.* New York: Springer, 2010.

Lewis, Beth A., and H. Katherine O'Neil. "Alcohol Expectancies and Social Deficits Relating to Problem Drinking among College Students." *Addictive Behaviors* 25.2 (2000): 295–299. Print.

McCabe, Sean Esteban, et al. "Non-Medical Use of Prescription Stimulants among US College Students: Prevalence and Correlates from a National Survey." *Addiction* 100.1 (2005): 96–106. Print.

Miech, Richard A., et al. "The Influence of College Attendance on Risk for Marijuana Initiation in the United States: 1977 to 2015." *American Journal of Public Health*, vol. 107, no. 6, 2017, pp. 996–1002., doi:10.2105/ajph.2017.303745.

Perkins, H. Wesley, Ed. *The Social Norms Approach to Preventing School and College Age Substance Abuse: A Handbook for Educators, Counselors, and Clinicians.* San Francisco: Jossey-Bass, 2003.

"Results from the 2013 National Survey on Drug Use and Health: Summary of National Findings." *SAMHSA*. SAMHSA, Sept. 2014.

Sharma, Manoj, et al. "Predictors of Responsible Drinking or Abstinence Among College Students Who Binge Drink: A Multitheory Model Approach." *The Journal of the American Osteopathic Association*, American Osteopathic Association, 1 Aug. 2018, jaoa.org/article.aspx?articleid=2687950.

Schulenberg, John E, et al. "National Survey Results on Drug Use, 1975-2016: Volume II, College Students and Adults Ages 19-55." *Monitoring the Future*, 2017, doi:10.3998/2027.42/139710.

U.S. National Library of Medicine. (2008). Health Behavior and College Students: Does Greek Affiliation Matter? 2018, http://www.ncbi.nlm.nih.gov/pmc/articles/PMC2430938/

See also: Adolescents and alcohol misuse; Adolescents and drug misuse; Club drugs; Designer drugs; Prescription drug addiction: In depth; Stimulant misuse;

Compulsions

CATEGORY: Psychological issues and behaviors

DEFINITION: Compulsions are strong, irresistible, and often persistent impulses to perform an act that can be irrational or that can conflict with self-will. Compulsions are distinct from habits and addictions.

COMPULSIVE BEHAVIOR

Compulsions are repetitive behaviors or mental acts to prevent or reduce anxiety rather than to provide pleasure or gratification. The most common compulsive behaviors include washing and cleaning, hoarding, checking, requesting or demanding assurance, and ordering. The acts can last a few minutes or an entire day, often disrupting the compulsive person's work, family, or social roles. Some compulsive acts also can cause physical harm. For example, harm can occur when a person repetitively washes his or her hands so that they become raw or when a person repetitively bites his or her fingernails.

COMPULSIONS VERSUS HABITS

Although people normally perform tasks repetitively, these tasks are not necessarily compulsive. Daily routines and practices are not compulsions; instead, they are normal habits. The difference between compulsions and habits can be recognized contextually.

Habits bring efficiency to one's life and compulsions tend to disrupt one's life.

Researchers sometimes distinguish between habits and compulsions as normal compulsions and abnormal compulsions; habits are considered normal compulsions. As such, normal and abnormal compulsions are often similarly diagnosed as compulsive behavior and are distinguished only contextually. That is, if the behavior is detrimental, it is considered an abnormal compulsion.

COMPULSION VERSUS ADDICTION

The use of both *compulsion* and *addiction* in everyday language is the most likely cause of confusion between the terms. Common and analogous use has led to the terms *compulsion* and *addiction* being both misused and misunderstood. A history of the change in the use of the word *addiction* can also be to blame, as *compulsion* was sometimes substituted for *addiction* to add legitimacy to the treatment of addiction.

Since the 1990s, research by scientists and clinicians has looked into differentiating and disentangling these behaviors. The American Psychological Association, for example, substitutes the term *dependency* for *addiction* to reflect the change in the definition of addiction to include behavioral addiction. Nevertheless, the difference between compulsion and addiction can be simplified. Compulsion is the repetitive behavior or mental act that prevents or reduces anxiety; addiction is a repetitive compulsive condition. Compulsion, or repetitive behavior, is a part of addiction, or repetitive compulsion. Although new research is expanding the definition of the two terms, the complexity of these disorders makes it difficult to propose a single model that could account for all their characteristic features.

COMPULSIVE DISORDERS

The basic mechanisms underlying compulsive and addictive disorders overlap in their phenomenology, their genetics and family history, and in their co-morbidity and pathophysiology. Compulsion is most often coupled with obsession to form obsessive-compulsive disorder (OCD).

OCD is characterized by obsessions and compulsions. Obsessions are unwanted persistent thoughts that produce distress and compulsions are repetitive behaviors that prevent or reduce distressing situations. Persons with OCD often use compulsive behaviors to rid themselves of obsessive thoughts; however, the relief is often temporary.

Symptoms of OCD include excessive washing or cleaning, extreme hoarding, repetitive checking, and preoccupation with limited but specific thoughts, such as sex or violence. According to the Anxiety and Depression Association of America in 2014, approximately 1 percent, or 2.2 million adults, in the United States have the disorder. Many people with OCD often remain undiagnosed because of their ability to cope with and function with the disorder.

There is considerable overlap in the co-occurrence of compulsion and addiction. Addiction is a recurring and persistent compulsive condition in which a person engages in a specific activity or uses a substance despite its negative or dangerous effects. Moreover, compulsion is the behavioral aspect of addiction, while further characterization of addiction includes dependency and changes in brain chemistry. A person becomes initially addicted to a substance or behavior as it provides pleasure. Through continued use of the substance or performance of the behavior, the person develops a dependency. Soon after, involvement with the substance or procedure is necessary for the person to provide relief, thereby developing a compulsion. Studies have found that 27 percent of people under treatment for OCD also met the criteria for substance use disorder.

Multiple studies have linked compulsive behavior to dysregulation of frontostriatal neurocircuitry in the brain and the associated monoamine systems. The pathological neurochemistry underlying these disorders is caused by dysfunction in serotonin-, dopamine-, and glutamate-dependent neurotransmission. Therefore, first-line pharmacologic treatment involves the use of selective serotonin reuptake inhibitors and clomipramine. Cognitive behavioral therapy is another popular approach. It is being extensively investigated for dealing with different aspects of this disorder. However, the clinical picture for persons with compulsive disorder is complex, as it is marked with wide heterogeneity of the presenting symptoms.

Poonam Bhandari PhD

FOR FURTHER INFORMATION

Abramowitz, Jonathan S., Dean McKay, and Steven Taylor, eds. *Obsessive-Compulsive Disorder: Subtypes and Spectrum Conditions*. Boston: Elsevier, 2008. Print.

"Facts & Statistics." *Anxiety and Depression Association of America*. ADAA, Sept. 2014. Web. 28 Oct. 2015.

Fontenelle, Leonardo F., et al. "Obsessive-Compulsive Disorder, Impulse Control Disorders, and Drug Addiction." *Drugs* 71 (2011): 827–40. Print.

Franklin, Martin E., and Edna B. Foa. "Treatment of Obsessive Compulsive Disorder." *Annual Review of Clinical Psychology* 7 (2011): 229–43. Print.

Hyman, Steven E., and Robert C. Malenka. "Addiction and the Brain: The Neurobiology of Compulsion and Its Persistence." *Nature Reviews Neuroscience* 2 (2001): 695–703. Print.

Markarian, Yeraz, Michael J. Larson, and Mirela A. Alde. "Multiple Pathways to Functional Impairment in Obsessive-Compulsive Disorder." *Clinical Psychology Review* 30 (2010): 78–88. Print.

See also: Addiction; Anxiety; Behavioral addictions: Overview; Obsessive-compulsive disorder (OCD)

Compulsive gambling

CATEGORY: Psychological issues and behaviors

ALSO KNOWN AS: Compulsive gambling; disordered gambling; pathological gambling; problem gambling

DEFINITION: Gambling is an activity that involves a degree of risk and an expenditure of money or goods with the hope of an increased return but with the possibility of a total loss. Some people gamble for pleasure and in a nonaddictive fashion, and they suffer no ill effects from gaming activities. Others have a problem with gambling, which is manifested by their increasing desire to gamble, regardless of whether their gambling creates hardships in their lives or the lives of their loved ones. These hardships can include money and debt problems, difficulties at work or at concentrating on tasks, relationship problems, or other negative consequences.

CAUSES

Problem gambling has a familial component because parents with a gambling addiction tend to socialize their children into the gambling world. Many of these young people, in turn, develop disordered gambling behavior. Neuroscientific and genetic research, which includes research with twins, has also determined that compulsive gambling runs in families and is often a co-occuring disorder with other addictions and/or mental health issues. Cultural components have also been associated with problem gambling.

RISK FACTORS

Greater numbers of men typically experience gambling addiction, although women are also at risk. People with gambling addictions often have other mental health issues (including personality, mood, and/or anxiety disorders) and other addictive disorders, which increase the challenge in determining what effects were caused by gambling and what were caused by other comorbidities. Problem gamblers often consume alcohol, nonprescription drugs, and tobacco in unhealthy ways, which also contributes to dysfunctional behavior.

Prevailing research suggests that approximately.02 to 5.3 percent of adults worldwide experience gambling disorders, according to the US National Institutes of Health. The disordered gambling figures for adolescents in locations where such research has been completed are much higher, with the implication that gambling-addiction numbers will rise as adolescents age and as increasing means to gamble become available. The growth of online gaming, which includes online gambling, is particularly challenging for local authorities to license, control, or measure. Particular concerns with these web-based services are that young players are difficult to identify and thus cannot be prevented from accessing these sites, even when local laws do not permit children to gamble. The National Council on Problem Gambling offers risk education on their web site to educate athletes about the problems and risks of sports gambling. The organization provides resources on gambling addiction and recovery, responsible gaming, and links to certified gambling counselors. They also offer training and certification in gambling counseling. In 2012 they developed the first US Internet Responsible Gaming Standards to guide stakeholders on internet gambling.

SYMPTOMS

According to the fifth edition of the *Diagnostic and Statistical Manual of Mental Disorders* (*DSM-5*), published in 2013 by the American Psychiatric Association (APA), gambling disorder is considered to be an addictive disorder similar to substance use disorder (SUD). As with SUD, gambling disorder affects the brain's reward system in ways similar to the affects of abusing drugs or alcohol. Additionally, problem gamblers report cravings for gambling and getting a "high" as a result of the stimulus of gambling. The previous edition of this manual, the *DSM-IV-TR* published in 2000, categorized gambling disorder as an impulse control disorder, not an addiction disorder, and labeled the condition "pathological gambling." The *DSM-5* not only reclassified problem gambling as an addictive disorder but also renamed it "gambling disorder", which was welcomed by clinicians, researchers, and those suffering from the condition. The word "pathological" has negative connotations, and many feel it reinforced the stigma associated with the problem, thus potentially inhibiting sufferers of gambling disorder from seeking help.

Gambling disorder is defined operationally by the *DSM-5* as the presence of at least four of nine criteria that the individual experiences within a twelve-month period. The measures focus on the negative effects of gambling (such as a preoccupation with gambling, using gambling as a way to escape problems, and difficulty cutting back on, or stopping gambling despite repeated attempts) and the negative consequences or problems that result from gambling (such as lying to hide the degree of gambling, deteriorating personal and/or professional relationships, loss of educational or employment opportunities as a result of gambling, and financial hardship and increasing debt to cover gambling losses). The *DSM-5* also removed the criterion from the *DSM-IV-TR* that states that problem gamblers commit illegal acts such as fraud, theft, or forgery. Research has shown that there is a low prevalence of this behavior among problem gamblers, and this stand-alone symptom did not help to distinguish those with gambling disorder from those without.

A person may manifest a gambling addiction for a period of time and then gain some control over his or her behavior, only to relapse and begin the cycle yet again. This is common among other addictive disorders, and this cyclical progression is challenging for the person suffering from this disorder as well as for persons in his or her family and social circles.

SCREENING AND DIAGNOSIS

There are many screening and diagnostic tools to measure or assess problem gambling. Many of these are based on the *DSM-5* criteria for measuring gambling disorder. Two common tools are the Brief Biosocial Gambling Screen (BBGS) and the modified NORC diagnostic screen, which also has a self-administered version titled "NODS-SA." Although often criticized for producing too many false positives, the South Oaks Gambling Screen is often used to assess problem gambling and has also been adapted to assess problem gambling in youth.

Diagnosis typically occurs using the *DSM-5* criteria for gambling disorder. The criteria are used by mental health professionals and by insurance companies to reimburse for treatment. Diagnosis typically places the person along a continuum of increasingly disordered behavior. At the lowest levels are people who have never gambled, who do not gamble excessively, or who do not cause harm to themselves or others because of gambling behavior. Gamblers who display symptoms of gambling disorder are diagnosed according to the level of severity. Those with mild severity have displayed four to five of the nine *DSM-5* criteria for gambling disorder during the previous twelve months. Those with moderate severity display six to seven criteria, and those with severe symptoms display eight to nine criteria. Individuals with gambling disorder are also referred to as compulsive gamblers, disordered gamblers, excessive gamblers, intemperate gamblers, or problematic gamblers.

TREATMENT AND THERAPY

Treatment traditionally involves cognitive and cognitive behavioral therapy (CBT) as well as family therapy, although more recent approaches have focused on pharmacological interventions, especially antidepressants or other drugs that treat the often co-occurring mental health issues such as anxiety and bipolar disorder. The change in classification of problem gambling to now be included as an addiction-based disorder forces insurance companies to cover treatment and medication. Free Gamblers Anonymous groups are found in most urban centers, which is helpful for this client group.

In addition to methodological problems with studies that make it difficult to identify the most promising treatment options, there are conceptual issues. Generally, people with gambling addictions have been considered to be a fairly uniform subject group by researchers; however, there are many differences within the group in terms of comorbidity and other factors, which might influence treatment outcomes. Also, there are many problem gamblers who manage to recover without treatment.

Treatment efforts also have focused on spouses and other family members of problem gamblers. Because the gambling addict negatively affects others with his or her addiction, therapists have suggested that family members could benefit from some intervention. Gam-Anon is an organization that provides help to families and friends of compulsive gamblers.

PREVENTION

It can be argued that the best prevention for gambling addiction is to avoid gambling, since most people do not realize their propensity for unhealthy and problematic gambling until they have a problem. Generally, government dollars have been spent on treatment rather than on prevention, but there are strong public health arguments that support greater efforts in prevention. Many groups lobby against legalizing gambling in the United States.

Susan J. Wurtzburg PhD

FOR FURTHER INFORMATION

American Psychiatric Association. *Diagnostic and Statistical Manual of Mental Disorders: DSM-5*. Washington: American Psychiatric Assoc., 2013. Print.

Denis C., M. Fatséas, and M. Auriacombe. "Analyses Related to the Development of DSM-5 Criteria for Substance Use Related Disorders: An Assessment of Pathological Gambling Criteria." *Drug and Alcohol Dependence* 122.1–2 (2012): 22–27.

Kaminer, Yifrah, and Oscar G. Bukstein, eds. *Adolescent Substance Abuse: Psychiatric Comorbidity and High-Risk Behaviors*. New York: Routledge, 2008. Print.

Ladouceur, Robert, and Stella Lachance. *Overcoming Pathological Gambling: Therapist Guide*. New York: Oxford UP, 2006. Print.

Leeman, Robert F., and Marc N. Potenza. "Similarities and Differences Between Pathological Gambling and Substance Use Disorders: A Focus on Impulsivity and Compulsivity." *Psychopharmacology* 219.2 (2012): 469–90. Print.

Nathan, Peter E., and Jack M. Gorman, eds. *A Guide to Treatments That Work*. 3rd ed. New York: Oxford UP, 2007.

Newman, Stephen C., and Angus H. Thompson. "The Association between Pathological Gambling and Attempted Suicide: Findings from a National Survey in Canada." *Canadian Journal of Psychiatry* 52.9 (2007): 605–12. Print.

Petry, Nancy M. *Pathological Gambling: Etiology, Comorbidity, and Treatment*. Washington: American Psychological Association, 2005. Print.

Williams, Robert J., and Rachel A. Volberg. "The Classification Accuracy of Four Problem Gambling Assessment Instruments in Population Research." *International Gambling Studies* 14.1 (2014): 15–28. Print.

Wong, Irene Lai Kuen. "Internet Gambling: A School-Based Survey among Macau Students." *Social Behavior and Personality* 38.3 (2010): 365–72. Print.

See also: Behavioral addictions: Overview; Gaming addiction; Internet addiction; Social media addiction

Computer addiction

CATEGORY: Psychological issues and behaviors

ALSO KNOWN AS: Internet addiction disorder (IAD), pathological computer use; computer addiction, video game addiction; video game overuse, Internet overuse, pathological computer use, and problematic computer use.

DEFINITION: Obsessive use of computer programs, especially video games, has been proposed as a behavioral addiction similar to compulsive gambling. Disregarding Internet use, computer addiction is a concern of industries that lose productivity, and of parents and teachers who see a decrease in the academics and social skills of children and teenagers, especially boys, who are more likely to develop a computer addiction.

HISTORY

With personal computers becoming commonplace in the 1990s came an increase in the numbers of children who appeared to be obsessive computer users, primarily focused on video games. Children and teenagers moved from non-electronic fantasy games to video arcades to home computers and smartphones, dramatically increasing the numbers of children and teens playing video games.

Over the last 15 years, research into various online addictions has greatly increased. Obsessive use of computer programs, especially video games, has been proposed as a behavioral addiction similar to compulsive gambling. Disregarding Internet use, computer addiction is a concern of industries that lose productivity and of parents and teachers who see a decrease in the academics and social skills of boys especially, who are more likely to develop a computer addiction.

The latest edition of the *Diagnostic and Statistical Manual of Mental Disorders (DSM-5)* actually includes computer addiction as a disorder however it continues to need further study and research. In a publication on the National Center for Biotechnology Information website, the study, which was conducted by the Department of Adult Psychiatry in the Poland Medical University, showed that Internet addiction was seen to be quite popular and common among young people, especially those who were only children. In fact, every fourth child is addicted to the Internet.

CAUSES

With personal computers becoming commonplace in the 1990s came an increase in the numbers of children who appeared to be obsessive computer users, primarily focused on video games. Children and teenagers moved from non-electronic fantasy games to video arcades to home computers and smartphones, dramatically increasing the numbers of children and teens playing video games.

These games are purchased or are resident programs in desktop computers, laptop computers, smartphones, and dedicated video gaming units, or consoles. Many games may also be available with live streaming, allowing the users to interact with other players worldwide and in real time. While some video games are available over the Internet, many are sold in packaged software for use with a general purpose computer or

a dedicated computer unit; other computers are designed and advertised as gaming computers.

Whenever a person with computer addiction feel overwhelmed, stressed, depressed, lonely or anxious, they often use the Internet to seek solace and escape. Studies from the University of Iowa show that Internet addiction is quite common among males ages 20 to 30 years old who are suffering from depression.

Certain people are predisposed to having a computer or Internet addiction, such as those who suffer from anxiety and depression. Their lack of emotional support means they turn to the Internet to fill this need. There are also those who have a history of other types of addiction, such as addictions to alcohol, drugs, sex and gambling. Even being stressed and unhappy can contribute greatly to the development of a computer or Internet addiction. People who are overly shy and cannot easily relate to their peers are also at a higher risk of developing a computer or Internet addiction.

Computer addiction and particularly video game addiction continues to expand as electronic media use increases and as more computers come in smaller and more portable sizes, such as tablets and smartphones. A 2016 report by Common Sense Media reported that teens spend almost nine hours per day

Customers flood an Apple store after the launch of the MacBook Pro. (Emmelie via Wikimedia Commons)

on electronic devices viewing entertainment media (watching videos, gaming, or using social media). Preteens (aged eight to twelve) consume approximately six hours of content. That does not include the additional time that children spend using media for school or homework.

Students have been able to extend their electronic life by several hours by multitasking with electronic devices. Tasks that tend to take more of their time on the phone include texting (text messaging), watching other media, and video gaming. According to a 2016 survey from the Centers for Disease Control and Prevention, 84 percent of American households contain at least one smartphone. Eighty percent of households own a desktop or laptop computer, 68 percent contain a tablet, 39 percent contain a streaming media device such as Apple TV, Google Chromecast, or Amazon Fire TV.

Also problematic is video gaming in the workplace. Depending on the availability of computers, work time and productivity lost to video games and other non-work-related computer use can exceed 10 percent.

RISK FACTORS

Researcher Douglas A. Gentile published a survey of eight- to eighteen-year-olds in the United States and found that 12 percent of boys were addicted to video games. Only 3 percent of girls were addicted to video games. Also, insofar as computers require a level of affluence, computer addiction is a problem mainly for developed and advanced-developing countries.

A Kaiser Family Foundation survey found that while daily use of all electronic media did not vary much by gender (eleven hours and twelve minutes for boys versus ten hours and seventeen minutes for girls), girls lost interest in computer video games and played less as teenagers, averaging only three minutes per day. Some researchers suggest that computer addiction is a major cause of the worldwide "boy problem," in which boys are dropping out of academics and girls predominating in the higher levels of education. The decline in boys in academics parallels the rise of personal computer technology. As previously noted, males ages 20 to 30 years old who are suffering from depression and or anxiety may be predisposed to having a computer or Internet addiction.

SYMPTOMS

Researcher Margaret A. Shotton was the first to extensively document computer addiction and dependency, although primarily through anecdotal cases and with references to early video arcade games. Ricardo A. Tejeiro Salguero proposed a problem video-game-playing (PVP) scale in 2002. Because problematic video gaming is a behavioral addiction (in contrast with a chemical addiction), video gaming was more closely associated with compulsive gambling. Gentile developed a similar scale of eleven self-reported negative factors. Having a minimum of six symptoms of the eleven on the scale was set as the threshold for addiction.

The correlation between computer addiction as determined by Gentile's scale and poorer grades in school, for example, could have been an indication of comorbidity; that is, a child might spend more time on the computer and get poor grades because of a separate but common factor.

Proof that pathological video game addiction causes a decline in academics was established by Robert Weis and Brittany C. Cerankosky. After establishing a group of boys' academic baseline achievement, they gave one-half of the boys access to computer video games and saw their academics decline. The control group continued on with solid schoolwork.

An extensive Kaiser Family Foundation survey found an inverse relationship between electronic media use and good grades, with 51 percent of heavy users getting good grades versus 66 percent of light users getting good grades. Heavy users were less likely to get along with their parents, were less happy at school, were more often bored, got into trouble at twice the average rate, and were often sad or unhappy compared with light users.

Internet gaming disorder has been proposed as a "Condition for Further Study" in the fifth edition of the *Diagnostic and Statistical Manual of Mental Disorders* published by the American Psychiatric Association (*DSM-5*), and centers to treat individuals who display symptoms of excessive internet use are opening in the United States signaling a response to a perceived problem.

According to Oberlin College of Computer Science, aside from being dependent on the Internet, persons who are addicted may develop technostress wherein they internalize how a computer works, such as accelerated time and perfect results. It can also cause social withdrawal, feeling more at ease interacting with people online rather than in person. Individuals who have an Internet addiction may also experience physical symptoms that could include:

- Strained vision
- Sleep problems
- Carpal tunnel syndrome
- Significant weight loss or weight gain
- Severe headaches

SCREENING AND DIAGNOSIS

Salguero and Gentile both proposed a multiple-factor scale to designate pathological computer video gaming. Extensive time spent playing computer games is not a sufficient indicator of addiction. However, when combined with risk factors of low social competence and higher impulsivity, there is a greater chance of pathological gaming that can result in anxiety, depression, social phobia, and poor school performance. There may be a correlation of computer addiction and attention deficit hyperactivity disorder that may be related to a child's difficulty relating normally in social settings, but these are a minority of cases.

Presently there are numerous studies and surveys being conducted to measure the extent of this type of addiction. Dr. Kimberly S. Young created a questionnaire based on other disorders to assess levels of addiction.

It is the Internet Addict Diagnostic Questionnaire or IADQ. Answering positively to five out of the nine questions may be indicative of an online addiction.

1. Are you preoccupied with using the Internet?
2. Do you think about your previous or future online activity?
3. Do you have the need to be online longer to be satisfied?
4. Have you made repeated but unsuccessful attempts to cut back, stop or control your Internet use?
5. Do you become moody, restless, irritable or depressed when you stop or decrease your Internet use?
6. Is your time spent online longer than what you originally planned?
7. Did your online use negatively affect a significant relationship, education, career or job?
8. Do you conceal the extent of your Internet usage from your therapist, family or others?
9. Does the Internet serve as an escape from problems or relief from a bad mood?

TREATMENT AND THERAPY

At the public policy level, Western countries appear little concerned with computer addiction beyond lost workplace productivity. The main societal concerns are in Asia, where there is much more focus on the pool of intellectual talent and more concern with children's academic success. Several Asian nations have attempted to place limits on the amount of time that teenagers can spend on computers per day; most indications are that these limits are easily circumvented by tech-savvy students.

Modeled on summer camps for overweight children are China's experimental summer camps for weaning students from computer addiction. Programs beginning in the United States attempt to use counseling to treat, for example, the psychological problems and antisocial feelings that may coexist with computer addiction. Other programs use outdoor wilderness experiences. Limited evidence exists of the success of these types of programs.

Computer addictions may be triggered by underlying emotional disorders such as depression and anxiety. Therefore, medications used for those conditions can be given in the hope that treating the underlying cause will cause a cessation of the Internet or computer addiction. These medications are antidepressants and anti-anxiety drugs. Escitalopram is a drug option that has been shown to be effective for Internet addiction, according to studies by Mount Sinai School of Medicine.

PREVENTION

Because computers, tablets, e-readers, smart phones, and other media that are primarily small computers are presumed to be technical advances, little likelihood to date exists of establishing regulatory measures or controls on the availability of computers and video games. In 2011, the US Supreme Court rejected regulation of violent computer video games in the United States. There is a rating system developed by the Entertainment Software Rating Board (ESRB) similar to that used in the entertainment industry that suggests age appropriateness, content descriptors, and interactive elements present in apps and video games, and rated on a scale. But this leaves the control of children's access in the hands of teachers and parents. Surveys show many parents have a low level of concern about or have little desire to regulate their children's computer activities although that may continue to be revised as more studies are conducted.

John Richard Schrock, PhD,
Updated by Jeffrey Larson

FOR FURTHER INFORMATION

Chiu, Shao-I, Jie-Zhi Lee, and Der-Hsiang Huang. "Video Game Addiction in Children and Teenagers in Taiwan." *Cyberpsychology and Behavior* 7 (2004): 571–81. Print.

Gentile, Douglas A. "Pathological Video-Game Use among Youths Ages 8 to 18: A National Study." *Psychological Science* 20 (2009): 594–602. Print.

Gentile, Douglas A., et al. "Pathological Video-Game Use among Youths: A Two-Year Longitudinal Study." *Pediatrics* 127 (2011): 319–29. Print.

Griffiths MD, Pontes HM (2014) "Internet Addiction Disorder and Internet Gaming Disorder are Not the Same." *J Addict Res Ther* 5:e124.

Madden, Mary, et al. "Teens and Technology 2013." *Pew Research Center.* Pew Research Center, 13 Mar. 2013. Web. 3 Nov. 2015.

M'hiri K, Costanza A, Khazaal Y, Khan R, Zullino D, et al. (2015) "Problematic Internet use in Older Adults, A Critical Review of the Literature." *J Addict Res Ther* 6:253.

Nielsen. "An Era of Growth: The Cross-Platform Report Q4 2013." *Nielsen.* Nielsen, 5 Mar. 2014. Web. 3 Nov. 2015.

PsychGuides.com. "Computer/Internet Addiction Symptoms, Causes and Effects." (2018) https://www.psychguides.com/guides/computerinternet-addiction-symptoms-causes-and-effects/

Rideout, Victoria J., Ulla G. Foehr, and Donald F. Roberts. "'Generation M2': Media in the Lives of 8- to 18-Year-Olds—A Kaiser Family Foundation Study." Jan. 2010. Web. 16 Apr. 2012.

Salguero, Ricardo A. Tejeiro, and Rosa M. Bersabe Moran. "Measuring Problem Video Game Playing in Adolescents." *Addiction* 97 (2002): 1601–6. Print.

Shotton, Margaret A. *Computer Addiction? A Study of Computer Dependency.* New York: Taylor, 1989. Print.

Shotton, Margaret A. "The Costs and Benefits of 'Computer Addiction.'" *Behaviour and Information Technology* 10 (1991): 219–30. Print.

Weis, Robert, and Brittany C. Cerankosky. "Effects of Video-Game Ownership on Young Boys' Academic and Behavioral Functioning: A Randomized, Controlled Study." *Psychological Science* 21 (2010): 463–70. Print.

See also: Behavioral addictions: Overview; Gaming addiction; Internet addiction; Social media addiction

Conduct disorders

CATEGORY: Psychological issues and behaviors

ALSO KNOWN AS: Disruptive behavior disorders; juvenile delinquency

DEFINITION: Conduct disorders are psychiatric disorders based on different types of callous and aggressive behaviors: physical harm to others, substantial damage to property, pervasive dishonesty or stealing, and breaking rules or defying authority. Substantial evidence suggests that conduct disorders have both neurobiological and environmental causes.

BACKGROUND

Conduct disorder (CD) is characterized by pervasive dishonesty, aggression, and callous disregard for others and for rules. These behaviors are more intense and longer-lasting than the occasional rule-breaking behavior associated with young people, for example. As of 2009, the Institute of Medicine estimated that 3.5 percent of the child population in the United States has CD. National Survey of Children's Health data from 2007 and 2012 suggest that CD is twice as common in boys than in girls.

The disorder exists in a continuum with two closely related disorders, one of which—oppositional defiant disorder (ODD)—tends to appear in younger children and the other of which—antisocial personality disorder—is not strictly diagnosable until adulthood. It is believed that some children with ODD "grow into" CD in their teenage years; later, some teens with CD demonstrate an antisocial personality when they become adults.

In practical terms, some children with high levels of irritability, developmentally inappropriate tantrum-like behaviors, and defiance of adults may demonstrate (as they age) a continuing lack of empathy, increasing callousness, and difficulty in restraining from cruel impulses. If these tendencies manifest in three or more different types of serious misbehavior that are repeated multiple times for more than one year, clinicians may consider a diagnosis of CD. Even in this case, the behaviors must be substantially worse than occasional acts of petty cruelty or vandalism and the behaviors cannot be caused by underlying mood problems, attention deficit hyperactivity disorder, or post-traumatic stress disorder. Usually, the earlier the problem behaviors appear, the more severe the disorder is likely to be.

CAUSES

Most mental illnesses emerge from the interaction of internal and external causes. Traditionally, some of the internal causes for aggressive behavior are believed to be low self-esteem, aberrant moral judgment, low frustration tolerance, low IQ, and concomitant low school achievement. CD is highly heritable. A person with a sibling or parent with conduct, hyperactivity, or substance misuse problems is more likely to have a CD.

Other studies have pointed to neurological dysfunctions as important in CD. One study of extremely violent men has offered evidence that the neural pathways associated with recognizing and interpreting facial cues are not particularly effective in these men. Although the data are arguable, it is possible that persons with CD may be similarly unable to correctly interpret facial cues and are therefore more likely to believe that neutral persons are hostile.

Other neurologic studies suggest that the brains of antisocial persons experience difficulty with regulating stress and maintaining appropriate levels of certain neurotransmitters, including serotonin and norepinephrine. Low levels of these brain chemicals have been associated with depression. Persons who experience increased levels of serotonin and norepinephrine after engaging in risky behaviors may increasingly seek out those behaviors to avoid low moods. Other studies have examined problems in neural pathways linking those parts of the brain responsible for overall decision making with other parts of the brain associated with rewards and with learning.

Even someone prone to aggression or dishonesty may not demonstrate significant behavioral problems without environmental stress. Among the more commonly accepted environmental contributors to CD

are poor parenting, especially ineffective monitoring or inappropriate discipline; family problems, including conflict between parents or other disruptions in family life; economic problems like family poverty and poor and crime-ridden neighborhoods; and school problems, including schools that are plagued with high rates of criminal or deviant behavior among students. Not all who experience these environmental issues demonstrate conduct problems, however.

Typically a diagnosis of CD will be based on extensive problems with aggression, property destruction, dishonesty, and rule-breaking behaviors. These problems are discussed here.

TYPES

Aggression Toward People and Animals. The first group of behaviors associated with CD has to do with repetitive viciousness toward people and animals. These behaviors indicate deep unconcern with the basic rights of others to be safe from physical harm. Hence, persons with CD may enjoy bullying or threatening. Beyond just threats, however, many will start fights and may use whatever weapons are available to wound or kill others. Other vicious behaviors in this group include the perpetration of other serious criminal acts in the course of physically harming or threatening others. Armed robbery, rape, and extortion are some examples.

Destruction of Property. Those with little regard for others' physical well-being frequently demonstrate even less respect for others' property. This second group of behaviors associated with CD involves arson, vandalism, and other forms of property destruction. However, this group does not include vandalism that is better explained as thrill-seeking behavior; instead, it includes vandalism for the purpose of destruction and to deprive others.

Dishonesty and Stealing. When confronted with their behavior, many with CD either minimize the severity of their actions or project the blame onto the victim. This basic dishonesty characterizes the third group of behaviors used to diagnose CD. These behaviors include house breaking, lying, forgery, writing worthless checks, and stealing when victims are not present.

Rule-Breaking Behaviors. As the previous sets of behaviors demonstrate, someone diagnosed with CD may often perceive others as unimportant, so rules developed in society to protect others will be likewise unimportant. However, this fourth group of diagnostically significant behaviors involves the transgression of rules designed to maintain the safety of the young person with CD him- or herself. These behaviors include eloping from school or from home multiple times, especially overnight and often before age thirteen years.

There are other deviant or dangerous behaviors associated with CD that are not diagnostically definitive but nonetheless important. Persons with CD are more likely to engage in several risky behaviors, including risky sexual behaviors, substance misuse, and other criminal behaviors.

TREATMENT

Persons with CD do not appear to respond well to medications. At its most basic level, no medication can help someone who refuses to take it, and with persons who have problems with honesty, compliance can be difficult to determine. Moreover, although they may help with mood lability or poor impulse control, medications are unlikely to help a person unlearn aberrant behavior patterns.

The more effective forms of treatment for children or adolescents with CD involve the entire family. Parents or other caregivers are taught to set appropriate limits, to encourage and reward good choices, and to use sensible and consistent discipline. Sometimes caregivers are taught the importance of spending more time with their children with CD, involving them in socially appropriate activities to lessen the amount of time they can spend with bad influences. Other therapies emphasize the importance for the person with CD of learning impulse control and stress management skills.

Michael R. Meyers PhD

FOR FURTHER INFORMATION

Boat, T. F., and J. T. Wu, editors. "Prevalence of Oppositional Defiant Disorder and Conduct Disorder." *Mental Disorders and Disabilities Among Low-Income Children.* National Academies Press, 2015. *NCBI,* www.ncbi.nlm.nih.gov/books/NBK332874. Accessed 5 Oct. 2017.

Diagnostic and Statistical Manual of Mental Disorders. 4th ed. Arlington, VA: American Psychiatric Association, 2000.

Finger, E. C., et al. "Disrupted Reinforcement Signaling in the Orbitofrontal Cortex and Caudate in Youths with Conduct Disorder or Oppositional Defiant Disorder and a High Level of Psychopathic Traits." *American Journal of Psychiatry* 168.2 (2011): 152–62. Print.

Murray, Joseph, and David P. Farrington. "Risk Factors for Conduct Disorder and Delinquency: Key Findings from Longitudinal Studies." *Canadian Journal of Psychology* 55.10 (2010): 633–42. Print.

"Options for Managing Conduct Disorder." *Harvard Mental Health Letter* 27.9 (2011): 1–3. Print.

Scheepers, Floortje E., Jan K. Buitelaar, and Walter Matthys. "Conduct Disorder and the Specifier Callous and Unemotional Traits in the DSM-5." *European Child and Adolescent Psychiatry* 20.2 (2011): 89–93. Print.

Van Goozen, Stephanie, et al. "The Evidence for a Neurobiological Model of Childhood Antisocial Behavior." *Psychological Bulletin* 133.1 (2007): 149–82. Print.

See also: Children and behavioral addictions; Crime and behavioral addictions; Pyromania

Controlled Substances Act

CATEGORY: Social issues

DEFINITION: The United States Congress passed the Controlled Substances Act (CSA) as part of the Comprehensive Drug Abuse Prevention and Control Act of 1970. The CSA regulates the production, importation, distribution, use, exportation, and possession of certain drugs and substances.

DATE: Effective October 27, 1970

BACKGROUND

The Controlled Substances Act (CSA), Title II of the Comprehensive Drug Abuse Prevention and Control Act of 1970, is the federal U.S. drug policy under which regulates the manufacture, importation, possession, use and distribution of certain narcotics, stimulants, depressants, hallucinogens, anabolic steroids and other chemicals.

President Richard Nixon signed the CSA on October 27, 1970. The DEA implements the CSA and may prosecute violators of these laws at both the domestic and international level. The Controlled Substances Act (CSA) places all substances that were in some manner regulated under existing federal law into one of five schedules based upon the substance's medical use, potential for misuse, and safety or dependence liability.

In determining into which schedule to place a drug or other substance, or whether to decontrol or reschedule a substance, requires the consideration of certain factors:

(1) Its actual or relative potential for misuse.
(2) Scientific evidence of its pharmacological effect, if known.
(3) The state of current scientific knowledge regarding the drug or other substance.
(4) Its history and current pattern of misuse.
(5) The scope, duration, and significance of misuse.
(6) What, if any, risk there is to the public health.
(7) Its psychic or physiological dependence liability.
(8) Whether the substance is an immediate precursor of a substance already controlled under this subchapter.

Schedule I drugs have no medical use, have a high potential for misuse, and have no accepted safety levels. Prescriptions may not be written for schedule I drugs (e.g., cannabis, heroin, 3,4-methylenedioxymethamphetamine, lysergic acid diethylamide, mescaline, and methaqualone).

Schedule II drugs have a high potential for misuse, have either no medical use or may have a medical use in certain conditions, and have a high potential for addiction (e.g., cocaine, opium, morphine, methamphetamine, methylphenidate, and methadone).

Schedule III drugs have less potential for misuse, legitimate medical use, and have a moderate risk for addiction (e.g., anabolic steroids, ketamine, and dihydrocodeine).

Schedule IV drugs are much less likely to be misused, have a medical use, and are less likely to lead to addiction (e.g., benzodiazepines, modafinil, zolpidem, and meprobamate).

Schedule V drugs are even less likely to be misused, have a medical use, and are unlikely to lead to addiction (e.g., diphenoxylate, pregabalin, and cough suppressants with codeine).

The CSA also has provisions related to drug use. Individuals who order, handle, store, and distribute controlled substances must register with the DEA to perform these functions. They must also maintain accurate inventories, records, and security of the controlled substances. In addition, the CSA discusses penalties for misuse of controlled drugs, procedures for importing and exporting controlled drugs, procedures for producing controlled drugs, and the provision for the taking of the violator's assets.

MISSION AND GOALS

The CSA's mission aims to regulate the production, importation, use, possession, and distribution of certain drugs and substances. This mission enables the United States to meet its obligations under international treaties. Additionally, the CSA's mission and goals classify drugs according to their addiction potential and whether they have a medical use; protect the public safety; create a closed system of distribution for those authorized to handle controlled substances; and identify key officials in international and national drug enforcement.

Christine M. Carroll, RN, BSN, MBA;
Updated by Duane R. Neff, PhD, MSW

FOR FURTHER INFORMATION

"Controlled Substances Act (1970)." *National Substance Abuse Index.* National Substance Abuse Index, n.d. Web. 29 Oct. 2015.

Marion, Nancy E., and Willard M. Oliver. *Drugs in American Society: An Encyclopedia of History, Politics, Culture, and the Law.* Santa Barbara: ABC-CLIO, 2014. Print.

Steel, Brent S., ed. *Science and Politics: An A-to-Z Guide to Issues and Controversies.* Thousand Oaks: Sage, 2014. Print.

"Title 21 United States Code (USC) Controlled Substances Act." *Office of Diversion Control.* Drug Enforcement Administration, 2012. Web. 29 Oct. 2015.

Van Dusen, Virgil, and Alan R. Spies. "An Overview and Update of the Controlled Substances Act of 1970." 1 Feb. 2007. Web. 14 Apr. 2012.

Yeh, Brian T. *Drug Offenses: Maximum Fines and Terms of Imprisonment for Violation of the Federal Controlled Substances Act and Related Laws.* Rep. Washington, DC: Congressional Research Service, 2015. PDF file.

See also: Controlled substances and precursor chemicals; Drug Enforcement Administration (DEA); Legislation and substance misuse

Controlled substances and precursor chemicals

CATEGORY: Substances

DEFINITION: Controlled substances are drugs that are regulated by the US Controlled Substances Act and by state laws. The laws aim to interdict the trafficking of illegal drugs and to minimize the danger of misuse and addiction to drugs that have valid medical uses. Precursor chemicals are used in the manufacture of controlled substances.

CONTROLLED SUBSTANCES AND THE LAW

The Controlled Substances Act (part of the Comprehensive Drug Abuse Prevention and Control Act of 1970), consists of many laws regulating the manufacture and distribution of substances that are illegal or that can become addictive or abusive. The term *substance* is used in the act rather than the term *drug* because *substance* is a more encompassing term.

Substances listed in the act are classified into five schedules. Schedule I substances have a high potential for misuse and have no accepted medical use. They are therefore illegal drugs and cannot be sold or used; violators of schedule I are prosecuted.

Schedules II through V substances have acceptable medicinal uses and are progressively less likely to be misused or to cause physical or psychological dependence. The rules for prescribing and dispensing of controlled drugs by physicians and pharmacists are most rigorous for schedule I drugs and are progressively less rigorous for schedule II to V substances.

Physicians must be registered with the US Drug Enforcement Administration to prescribe controlled substances, and they must maintain detailed records of all transactions. The number of authorized refills (if any) must be stated and adhered to. The act has been modified several times since its enactment in 1970, and the classification of specific substances is subject to change.

CONTROLLED SUBSTANCES ACT: SCHEDULE CHARACTERISTICS

Schedule I includes a large number of substances classified as opioid drugs and hallucinogens and also a few depressants and stimulants. Opioid drugs have a chemical structure and physiological activity similar to opium that are derived from the poppy plant. Opioid drugs also are known as narcotic drugs or narcotics.

Opioid drugs such as heroin and several morphine and codeine drugs are useful in treating moderate to severe pain, but these drugs are listed in schedule I because of their potential for misuse and dependence.

Hallucinogens include the synthetic compound LSD (lysergic acid diethylamide) and also peyote and mescaline, which are found naturally in certain cacti. Marijuana is a popular drug of misuse, whose classification is controversial. Although as of 2015 four US states and Washington, DC, have legalized recreational use of marijuana, and twenty other states have legalized the use of medical marijuana, it is still listed as a Schedule I substance.

Schedule II drugs include the opium poppy and the purified opium derived from the poppy. Other opioid drugs in schedule II include cocaine, methadone, oxycodone, hydrocodone, hydromorphone, and natural coca leaves. Oxycodone, sold under the trade name OxyContin, is a valuable drug for relieving chronic pain, but the drug has become popular with misusers.

Included in schedule II are the amphetamines, which act as stimulants. Methamphetamine is a synthetic compound made from amphetamine. Short-acting barbiturates, such as pentobarbital, also are in this schedule.

Schedule III substances include anabolic steroids, stimulants, and depressants. Drugs that have a depressant effect on the central nervous system act as sedatives. Intermediate-acting barbiturates are included in this category. Drugs that have a stimulant effect on the central nervous system include amphetamines and methamphetamines. Also included are drug formulations or preparations that have a limited quantity of narcotics.

Schedule IV drugs act as central nervous system depressants and produce sedation, induce sleep, and reduce anxiety. The most common drugs in this group are the barbiturates, including barbital, phenobarbital, and methylphenobarbital. Also included in this schedule are other drugs that have a similar effect, such as chloral betaine, meprobamate, and ethchlorvynol.

Schedule V drugs include formulations containing limited quantities of narcotic drugs in combination with other medically active drugs. The levels of narcotic drugs allowed are less than those in schedule III.

Many prescription drugs are controlled substances, and the diversion of these drugs for nonmedical uses is increasing rapidly. Opioids are by far the most common prescription drugs that are diverted to illicit uses. Some professionals in the medical community believe pain is actually undertreated. This belief is controversial because increased prescriptions for opioid drugs increases the supply for diverted uses. The overall effectiveness of opioids for pain relief remains a topic of debate.

The diversion of prescription drugs can occur by persons who sell or give their drugs to friends or associates. Diversion also can occur by theft or by what is called doctor shopping, visiting several doctors to obtain multiple prescriptions. The White House Office of National Drug Control Policy, established in 1989, addresses problems in illicit drug supply and use and coordinates efforts to control the problem.

PRECURSOR CHEMICALS

Precursor chemicals are chemicals used in the synthesis and manufacture of controlled substances. They become part of the drug's chemical structure. It is difficult to regulate these precursor chemicals because they also have valid commercial uses.

Also of concern to drug enforcement officials are essential chemicals. These chemicals are used in the extraction, purification, and concentration of drugs from natural sources. Essential chemicals do not become part of the molecular structure of a drug. Methamphetamine precursors such as pseudoephedrine, phenylpropanolamine, and ephedrine are most problematic.

The US Chemical Diversion and Trafficking Act (1988), which amended the Controlled Substances Act of 1970, regulates forty chemicals as list 1 and list 2 chemicals in the US Code of Federal Regulations. In addition to administering regulatory controls, the act administers criminal sanctions that control the diversion of precursor chemicals; the act permits, however, access to chemicals necessary for legitimate commerce.

David A. Olle MS

FOR FURTHER INFORMATION

United States. Drug Enforcement Administration. "Drug Info: Drug Scheduling." *DEA.gov.* US DEA, Dept. of Justice, n.d. Web. 29 Oct. 2015.

Manchikanti, Laxmaiah. "National Drug Control Policy and Prescription Drug Abuse: Facts and Fallacies." *Pain Physician* 10 (2007): 399–424. Print.

"Marijuana and the Controlled Substances Act." *Congressional Digest* 93.8 (2014): 2–6. *Academic Search Complete.* Web. 29 Oct. 2015.

Sevick, James R. "Precursor and Essential Chemicals in Illicit Drug Production: Approaches to Enforcement." Washington, DC: Department of Justice, 1993. Print.

"Where Is Pot Legal?" *CNN Money.* Cable News Network, 2015. Web. 29 Oct. 2015.

See also: Anabolic steroids; Barbiturates; Codeine; Controlled Substances Act (CSA); Gateway drugs; Hydrocodone; Methadone; Methamphetamine

Co-occurring disorders

CATEGORY: Psychological issues and behaviors

ALSO KNOWN AS: Chemical misuse and mental illness; comorbid disorder; co-occurring psychiatric and substance disorders; dual diagnosis

DEFINITION: Co-occurring disorders (CODs) refer to diagnoses of one or more mental disorders with the use of alcohol and drugs of misuse. A COD diagnosis applies when one or more of each of the two types of disorders can be established independently of the other. Comorbidity of substance misuse disorders and mental illness is common, although individual conditions may vary in terms of severity, chronicity, disability, and degree of impairment in functioning.

OVERVIEW

Persons who have been diagnosed with a substance use disorder are twice as likely to also have a serious mental illness, compared with the general population. The reverse also holds true—people diagnosed with a serious mental illness are twice as likely to also have a substance use disorder. When two (or more) separate disorders occur simultaneously or concomitantly in the same person, they are said to be comorbid or co-occurring, although one illness does not directly cause the other.

Despite this, the two disorders do interact, and each can affect the course and outcome of the other. Substance use disorders and serious mental illnesses are caused by overlapping factors, such as underlying deficits in the brain and genetic vulnerabilities, and both affect similar neurotransmitters and signaling pathways. Substance misuse can exacerbate or trigger psychosis and mood and affective disorders; worsening or untreated mental illness can intensify the drug or alcohol problem.

Experience has shown that mental health issues tend to surface before the onset of substance misuse, which then becomes a conscious or subconscious form of self-medication to alleviate symptoms of mental anguish. People with COD have a poorer prognosis and higher rates of drug relapse, and they are more prone to treatment noncompliance and violent behaviors. Risk factors for having CODs include family history of substance use; multidrug use; antisocial personality disorder; being a young, single, adult male; having a lower level of education; homelessness; incarceration; and limited access to treatment.

Evolving Evidence

The association between substance use disorder and serious mental illness has been well established, supported by several major studies first conducted during the late 1990s. These studies include the landmark Epidemiologic Catchment Area Study and the National Comorbidity Survey, both sponsored by the National Institute of Mental Health. Also, the Substance Abuse and Mental Health Services Administration (SAMHSA), part of the US Department of Health and Human Services, issues its annual National Survey on Drug Use and Health (NSDUH), which provides data on health and the use of tobacco, alcohol, and illicit drugs in the United States.

According to the NSDUH for 2015, 8.1 million adults aged eighteen years or older had some form of mental illness co-occurring with a substance use disorder during the past year, and 2.3 million had a serious mental illness co-occurring with substance use disorder. About 18.6 percent of adults who had any mental illness in the past year, and 23.8 percent of adults with a serious mental illness, had also had a substance use disorder during that period, compared to 5.8 percent of adults with no mental illness. In addition, adults with any past-year mental illness (both serious and nonserious) had higher rates of past-year illicit drug use (32.1 percent versus 14.8 percent), past-year tobacco use (41.8 percent versus 28.7 percent), past-month heavy alcohol use (8.6 percent versus 6.7 percent), and past-month binge alcohol use (30.2 percent versus 26.1 percent) compared to those with no mental illness.

The 2015 NSDUH also reported that of the approximately three million adolescents between the ages of twelve and seventeen who had experienced an MDE in the past year, 11.6 percent had a substance use disorder during that time, compared to 4.0 percent of adolescents without an MDE. Adolescents with a past-year MDE also had higher rates of past-year illicit drug use (31.5 percent versus 15.3 percent), past-month daily cigarette use (1.8 percent versus 0.7 percent), and past-month heavy alcohol use (1.7 percent versus 1.8 percent), compared with those without an MDE.

Treatment Approaches

Researchers now have a better understanding of the prevalence of CODs, of the specific issues related to CODs, and of how CODs affect treatment and treatment outcome. Of the 8.1 million adults with COD in 2015, 48.0 percent received treatment for either mental illness or substance use at a specialty facility, but only 6.8 percent received both mental health care and specialty substance use treatment. However, efforts to provide targeted treatment for both disorders concurrently are gaining favor, as mental health professionals realize the need to address the interrelationships among the two disorders and begin to focus more attention on their shared neurobiological aspects.

Integrated treatment involves combining COD treatment with a primary treatment relationship or service setting. The intention is to treat the whole person. SAMSHA states that integrated COD treatment "is an evidence-based approach to care, which recognizes that individuals go through different stages on their way to recovery." These stages include engagement (establishing a working alliance), persuasion (forming a trusting relationship), active treatment (seeing the problem and making positive changes), and relapse prevention (creating a relapse prevention plan and building on positive behaviors). Such practices as integrated screening and assessment techniques, treatment planning strategies, motivational interviewing, cognitive behavioral therapy, and peer support are part of the treatment program. Integrated stage-wise treatment is proving to be a viable path to recovery and is helping individuals with COD improve the quality of their lives.

Barbara Woldin BS

FOR FURTHER INFORMATION

Atkins, Charles. *Co-occurring Disorders: Integrated Assessment and Treatment of Substance Use and Mental Disorders.* Premier Publishing and Media, 2014.

Choi, Sam, et al. "Gender Differences in Treatment Retention among Individuals with Co-occurring Substance Abuse and Mental Health Disorders." *Substance Use and Misuse,* vol. 50, no. 5, 2015, pp. 653–63.

Galanter, Marc, and Herbert D. Kleber, editors. *Psychotherapy for the Treatment of Substance Abuse.* American Psychiatric Publishing, 2011.

Hendrickson, Edward L. *Designing, Implementing, and Managing Treatment Services for Individuals with Co-occurring Mental Health and Substance Use Disorders: Blueprints for Action.* Haworth Press, 2006.

Mignon, Sylvia I. *Substance Abuse Treatment: Options, Challenges, and Effectiveness.* Springer Publishing, 2015.

Smith, John. *Co-occurring Substance Abuse and Mental Disorders: A Practitioner's Guide.* Jason Aronson, 2007.

Substance Abuse and Mental Health Services Administration, Center for Behavioral Health Statistics and Quality. *Key Substance Use and Mental Health Indicators in the United States: Results from the 2015 National Survey on Drug Use and Health.* HHS Publication No. SMA 16-4984, NSDUH Series H-51, US Department of Health and Human Services, 2016. *SAMHSA,* www.samhsa.gov.

See also: Depression; Mental illness; Risk factors for addiction; Substance Abuse and Mental Health Services Administration (SAMHSA)

Cough and cold medications addiction

CATEGORY: Substance misuse

ALSO KNOWN AS: Dextromethorphan; DXM; poor man's PCP; red devils; robo; skittles; triple C; tuss

DEFINITION: Dextromethorphan hydrobromide (DXM HBr) is an active ingredient (cough suppressant) in a variety of over-the-counter (OTC) cough and cold medications sold under such trade names as Robitussin, NyQuil, Dimetapp, and Coricidin. DXM also can be purchased on the Internet in pure powder form. In high doses, DXM is a dissociative hallucinogen that produces effects similar to those of ketamine and phencyclidine, or PCP.

STATUS: OTC medications containing DXM are legal worldwide; some US states require proof of age to purchase

CLASSIFICATION: Noncontrolled substance

SOURCE: Synthetic compound

TRANSMISSION ROUTE: Oral

HISTORY OF USE

Dextromethorphan (DXM) was developed by the US Navy in the early 1950s as a nonaddictive substitute for codeine. It was patented in 1954 and approved by the US Food and Drug Administration for over-the-counter (OTC) sale as an antitussive (cough suppressant) in 1958.

DXM has been widely used since as an active ingredient in cough and cold medications. More than 140 OTC medications containing DXM are sold in the United States. DXM in powder form can be purchased on the Internet in 1 gram multiples.

DXM use was first noted in the 1960s with the use of Romilar, an OTC tablet form of DXM. Romilar was taken off the market in the United States in 1973. Misuse of DXM in liquid and capsule forms of cough and cold medications was first observed among teenagers in the 1990s. These preparations are appealing to adolescents because they are inexpensive (compared with other drugs of misuse) and are easy to purchase (or shoplift). In addition, many teenagers think DXM is safe because it can be obtained without a prescription; websites promote its misuse and offer recipes for extracting the substance from cold tablets.

Between 1999 and 2004, the number of reported cases of DXM misuse among adolescents increased tenfold; some experts consider it the most commonly misused dissociative drug in North America. About 10 percent of teenagers in the United States report abusing cough and cold medications. On average, fifty-five hundred adolescents are taken to emergency rooms each year in the United States because of a DXM overdose.

The average age of DXM misusers is fifteen years, although there are also reported cases of middle-aged adults abusing the drug. Most teenagers, however, stop using DXM in their early twenties because harder drugs are readily available to young adults.

EFFECTS AND POTENTIAL RISKS

DXM in therapeutic doses (15–30 milligrams) suppresses coughing by acting on the area in the brain that controls coughing rather than directly on the respiratory tract. It can cause drowsiness or dizziness at the therapeutic level.

Because it affects the brain, it can cause hallucinations, blurred vision, feelings of unreality, out-of-body sensations, loss of sense of time, excitement, euphoria, and distortions of perception when taken in high doses (between thirteen and seventy-five times the normal therapeutic dose). DXM also can cause paranoia, high blood pressure, heavy sweating, nausea, fever, vomiting, headache, skin rash or itching, seizures, loss of consciousness, and death.

DXM is unusual among dissociative drugs of misuse in that users experience its effects in a series of distinct stages or plateaus rather than in a gradual fashion. Users at the first plateau typically experience DXM as a stimulant, while those at the second plateau are more likely to feel a dreamlike state and be detached from reality. Misusers at the third plateau may report serious disruptions of cognitive function (such as inability to perform simple arithmetic) and other frightening experiences.

Several specific risks are associated with DXM misuse. First, teenagers who use it in the form of OTC preparations are taking it in combination with antihistamines, pain relievers (usually acetaminophen), and fever reducers. These other ingredients considerably increase the risk of overdose or damage to the liver from the acetaminophen. DXM also is dangerous when taken in combination with ecstasy because of the risk of overheating and dehydration, particularly when taken at raves or in hot weather.

Second, about 5 percent of Caucasians are genetically unable to metabolize the drug normally, which leads to the rapid development of toxic levels of DXM in the bloodstream. Third, because DXM affects an misuser's sense of reality and awareness of his or her surroundings, it can lead to impaired driving, risk-taking, and fatal accidents.

DXM in OTC medications is safe for use by most persons when the products are taken as directed. It

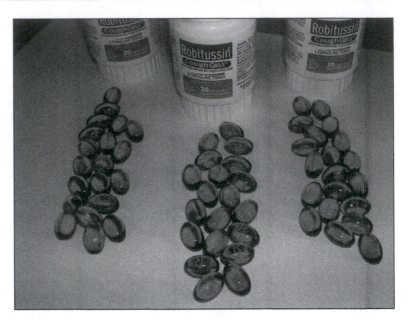

Cold medicines containing dextromethorphan are offered for sale at a retail store. According to reports, between 1999 and 2004 the misuse of over-the-counter cough medicines, many containing dextromethorphan, has risen 50% a year, mostly among youths. (via Wikimedia Commons)

should not, however, be taken by persons using monoamine oxidase inhibitors or selective serotonin reuptake inhibitors because it has potentially dangerous interactions with these drugs.

Rebecca J. Frey PhD

FOR FURTHER INFORMATION

Bryner, Jodi K., et al. "Dextromethorphan Abuse in Adolescence." *Archives of Pediatric and Adolescent Medicine* 160.12 (2006): 1217–22. Print. An account of recent trends in abuse of cough and cold medications by teenagers in the United States that includes descriptions of the effects of DXM abuse and overdose symptoms.

Finn, Robert. "Easy Availability Driving Dextromethor-phan Abuse: Hallucinations, Dystonia." *Pediatric News* 38.5 (2004): 24. Print. Brief overview of DXM abuse that includes descriptions of the various experienced plateaus.

Miller, S. C. "Dextromethorphan Psychosis, Dependence, and Physical Withdrawal." *Addiction Biology* 10.4 (2005): 325–27. Print. A brief article on the potential for addiction to DXM and its long-term complications.

Shannon, Joyce Brennfleck, ed. *Drug Abuse Sourcebook.* 3rd ed. Detroit: Omnigraphics, 2010. A comprehensive standard reference work for college students about all known drugs of abuse, including OTCs, prescription medications, and illegal substances.

See also: Adolescents and drug misuse; Controlled substances and precursor chemicals; Dextromethorphan; Over-the-counter drugs of misuse

Crack

CATEGORY: Substances

ALSO KNOWN AS: Rock

DEFINITION: Crack is a solid form of cocaine made by dissolving powdered cocaine in a mixture of baking soda or ammonia with water. The mixture is boiled into a solid form and then broken into chunks. Crack is a powerful stimulant that reaches the brain in about eight seconds and produces an intense high that lasts between five and ten minutes.

STATUS: Illegal in the United States, Canada, and Europe

CLASSIFICATION: Schedule II drug in the United States because of its high misuse potential; has medicinal purposes (as an anesthetic). Crack and cocaine are considered the same drug. Canada classifies crack as a schedule I drug. Since 1961, the United Nations has identified cocaine as a schedule I drug. In the United Kingdom, crack is a class A drug, and in the Netherlands it is a list 1 drug under that country's opium law.

SOURCE: A chemically altered form of cocaine, which is derived from the leaves of the coca plant, commonly found in South America. Cocaine also can be biosynthesized in a laboratory.

TRANSMISSION ROUTE: Inhalation; intravenous (of the liquid form of crack, also called freebase)

HISTORY OF USE

Crack first appeared in the US cities of Los Angeles, San Diego, and Houston in the early 1980s, reportedly as a means of moving a large amount of cocaine that was available in the United States in the 1970s. The major crack epidemic, as it came to be called, took place between 1984 and 1990, mostly in poor, urban areas in the United States. By 2002, the United Kingdom reported a crack epidemic, and today, crack is used worldwide.

Since about 2000, the use of crack has decreased substantially, though it has not disappeared. Young adults (at levels as high as 65 percent) report having tried crack at least once; however, repeat-usage percentages are significantly lower. Arrest rates for crack possession are also dramatically lower than those of the 1980s and 1990s, with some cities showing crack-arrest percentages in the single digits. In 2010 the National Institute on Drug Abuse reported that according to the National Survey on Drug Use and Health, there were an estimated 359,000 US crack cocaine users in 2008.

There are several explanations for these lowered rates, including higher prices for cocaine and also changes in how the law handles charges for crack possession. However, the most significant cause for the decrease in the use of crack is the dramatic rise in methamphetamine use. Methamphetamine's low cost, easy availability, and extremely addictive nature make it popular among drug misusers.

EFFECTS OF USE

Crack is a stimulant that artificially increases the levels of dopamine released from the brain. Also, crack prevents dopamine from being "recycled" by the body, leading to an excess of dopamine with repeated use. This excess causes an overamplification of the dopamine-receptor neurons and leads to a disruption of normal neural communications. For example, the brain loses the ability to properly respond to pleasurable stimuli, which causes the drug user to seek more drugs to feel any pleasure. While the initial response of the brain to this massive dopamine buildup is a drug-induced euphoria, an increase in self-confidence, and increased high energy, these effects become harder and harder to attain as the dopamine system becomes damaged, leading to addiction and tolerance.

RISKS OF USE

Crack affects not just the brain but also almost every system in the body. One of the most strongly affected is the pulmonary system. Because crack is inhaled using high temperatures (90 degrees Celsius, or 194 degrees Fahrenheit), users often suffer burned lips, tongue, and airways. Another common side effect of crack use is a cough with black sputum, which is caused by the butane torches used to heat the smoking pipes. Other crack-related respiratory illnesses include pulmonary edema (also known as crack lung), asthma, and adult respiratory distress syndrome.

Sudden death from cardiac arrest is another danger to crack users, especially those who drink alcoholic beverages while using crack. (Any polydrug use increases the risk of sudden cardiac arrest.) Psychiatric trauma also is common in crack users and may include severe paranoia, violent behavior, and hallucinations (including delusional parasitosis, or Ekbom's syndrome, the belief that one is infested with parasites; this can cause a person to violently scratch themselves).

Crack users are especially at risk for infections with the human immunodeficiency virus and hepatitis virus. Shared needles are one source; the other source is the exchange of sex for drugs. This often places women at an especially high risk. Another danger is tuberculosis and other saliva-borne diseases, which are passed by sharing a common crack pipe.

The so-called crack-babies epidemic has been weighted by myth and misinformation, leading people to believe that a generation of children became an essentially lost generation. Studies show that the stereotype of the crack baby, born addicted to crack and facing insurmountable developmental issues and an inability to bond, is simply false. The reality is more complicated. Independent of other issues, such as alcohol and tobacco misuse and poor physical environment, many of these babies are living normal lives.

Further research shows that the area of the body most affected in these children is the dopamine system that develops early in the fetal cycle; the system may show long-term effects of crack and cocaine exposure. A child also may have a mild behavioral disorder or a subtler developmental phenotype that resembles attention deficit hyperactivity disorder. Cognitive and attention systems may be affected, and these children may require help from a special-needs program.

S. M. Willis MS, MA

FOR FURTHER INFORMATION

Laposata, Elizabeth A., and George L. Mayo. "A Review of Pulmonary Pathology and Mechanisms Associated with Inhalation of Freebase Cocaine ('Crack')." *American Journal of Forensic Medicine and Pathology* 14 (1993): 1–9. Print.

Lejuez, C. W., et al. "Risk Factors in the Relationship between Gender and Crack/Cocaine." *Experimental and Clinical Psychopharmacology* 15 (2007): 165–75. Print.

Palamar, Joseph J., et al. "Powder Cocaine and Crack Use in the United States: An Examination of Risk for Arrest and Socioeconomic Disparities in Use." *Drug and Alcohol Dependence* 149.(2015): 108–116. *PsycINFO*. Web. 29 Oct. 2015.

Natl. Inst. on Drug Abuse. "Cocaine: What Is the Scope of Cocaine Use in the United States?" *National Institute on Drug Abuse*. NIH, Sept. 2010. Web. 29 Oct. 2015.

United Nations. Office on Drugs and Crime. *World Drug Report 2014*. Vienna: UNODC, 2014. Digital file.

Thompson, Barbara L., Pat Levitt, and Gregg D. Stanwood. "Prenatal Exposure to Drugs: Effects on Brain Development and Implications for Policy and Education." *Nature* 10 (2009): 303–12. Print.

See also: Cocaine use disorder; Dopamine and addiction; Recreational drugs

---

Crime and behavioral addictions

CATEGORY: Social issues

DEFINITION: Behavioral addictions involve the compulsive repetition of negative behaviors independent of the ingestion of drugs and alcohol. While far less prevalent than substance misuse addictions, behavioral addictions, when they involve criminal acts, can be equally destructive to the addict, the addicts' family, and society in general. Several particular facets of behavioral addiction commonly result in criminal activity; they include gambling addiction, sex addiction, kleptomania, and pyromania. However, not all behavioral addictions are attributable to criminal behavior.

INTRODUCTION

Behavioral addictions are closely related to maladapted impulse-control abilities as defined by the repeated failure or inability to resist harmful behavior or impulsive actions. Behavioral addictions involve a variety of both common behaviors and peculiar activities.

Many behavioral addicts become hooked on activities that other persons engage in only occasionally, such as shopping, sexual activity, eating, or gambling. According to the American Association for Marriage and Family Therapy in 2015, nearly 12 million Americans suffer from sexual addiction. Additionally, research published in the *American Journal on Addictions* in 2015 showed that an estimated 6 to 7 percent of Americans may shop compulsively, while prevailing research suggests that approximately .02 to 5.3 percent of adults worldwide experience gambling disorders, according to the US National Institutes of Health. Behavioral addictions to food, shopping, technological devices, exercise, and appearance are conventionally only harmful to the addicts themselves. Several addictions, however, result in criminal activity.

CRIMINAL BEHAVIOR AND COMPULSIVE GAMBLING

Compulsive gambling is a behavioral addiction that manifests itself as an obsession with placing financial wagers for the possibility, however scant, of a profitable return. Gambling addiction spans the entire gamut of games of chance, from sports betting and card games to billiards, casino gaming, and lotteries. Legalized gambling has been one of the fastest growing industries in the United States for several decades, while illegal wagering has maintained a cultural presence so large for so long that law enforcement agencies can only contain it rather than try to prevent it.

Conventionally, compulsive gamblers resort to criminal behavior only after all other avenues of potential income are no longer available. This behavior includes the sale of personal property, the sale of property of friends and family, or petty theft from spouses and family.

Aside from engaging in such illicit acts as petty and grand theft, compulsive gamblers, according to researchers, also engage in a variety of other criminal activities. These activities range from fabricating auto accident claims to health insurance fraud, arson, and making false claims about thefts, fires, and property damage. Data indicate that compulsive gambling also can lead to involvement in drug trafficking, assault, and prostitution. Many parallels can be made between gambling addicts and substance addicts, because each addiction lends itself to the erratic tendencies, poor judgment, and violent behavior that often can result in criminal activity.

Gambling disorder is listed as a substance-related and addictive disorder in the American Psychiatric Association's *Diagnostic and Statistical Manual of Mental Disorders, Fifth Edition*. The listing reflects growing evidence that gambling disorder is similar to substance use disorders in terms of its effects on the brain's reward system.

CRIMINAL BEHAVIOR AND SEX ADDICTION

Research indicates that as much as 6 percent of all adults in the United States have some form of sex addiction. Sex addiction can range from the constant desire for sexual activity or stimulation to an inability to control sexual urges, behaviors, and thoughts.

Sex addiction enters the realm of criminal behavior when it involves the improper coercion, exploitation, or duress of other persons. It also involves forcing others to act out sexual behaviors in a public forum without discretion or respect for societal norms.

Not all sex addicts partake in criminal activities or are addicted to perverse sexual behaviors, but some sex addicts are involved in criminal behaviors including sexual assault and rape, prostitution, incest, pedophilia, harassment, voyeurism, and exhibitionism. Like many other behavioral and substance addictions, sex addiction may be related to the effect of dopamine on the brain.

The rise of the internet with its perceived anonymity has been linked with the growth of illegal sexual behaviors such as viewing child pornography, soliciting sex with minors, and engaging in cybersex.

KLEPTOMANIA

Kleptomania, or compulsive stealing, is by definition an addiction to a criminal behavior. While petty thieves and shoplifters customarily steal for want of items they cannot afford or steal for profit, kleptomaniacs impulsively steal from all locations and for any reason; they steal for the sake of stealing. According to 2007 statistics from researchers at Stanford University, nearly 1.2 million Americans have this behavioral addiction. The cause of kleptomania is unknown and widely debated among both medical and sociological professionals. While some experts believe it is related to the release of dopamine during the act of theft, others believe it also may be a behavior symptomatic of other underlying psychological or social development problems. The *DSM-5* lists kleptomania as one of several disruptive, impulse-control, and conduct disorders.

PYROMANIA

Pyromania is an extremely rare but potentially lethal behavioral addiction involving the compulsive starting of fires. According to a study in the *British Journal of Criminology*, pyromaniacs account for only about 1 to 4 percent of all arsonists in the United States each year. In 2011 the *Oxford Handbook of Impulse Control Disorders* reported that the US population had a lifetime prevalence of 1 percent for fire setting. Unlike arsonists, who ignite fires for personal or financial gain or as an act of assault, pyromaniacs achieve euphoria from creating fire as a destructive force. Pyromaniacs also take pleasure in surveying the damage left behind from fires.

Much like kleptomania, pyromania is believed to be rooted in underlying psychological trauma or impaired social development of some kind. This trauma often includes a childhood history of psychological, physical, or sexual abuse. Experts believe that pyromania may be caused by an aggression rooted in childhood abuse and by poorly developed problem-solving skills and cognitive maladjustment. The *DSM-5* lists pyromania as one of several disruptive, impulse-control, and conduct disorders.

STRATEGIES FOR TREATMENT

Although persons with behavioral addictions have several similarities with persons with substance misuse addictions, there remains a great deal of debate on whether behavioral addictions can be classified as addictive behavior. A wide sociological and scientific gap exists between the concepts of addiction and impulse control disorders.

Research indicates that the neurological patterns between substance misusers and behavioral addicts have many similarities, but not enough is known about these neurological functions to present a clear delineation between the two. It is perhaps because of these similarities that the treatment strategy for behavioral addictions closely mirrors that of substance misuse recovery.

Treatment for gambling, sex, shopping, and other compulsive behaviors often involves cognitive therapy to attempt to highlight the underlying psychological factors that lead a person to act on such impulses. This connection has been further established by the effective use of substance misuse treatments such as group therapy and by the use of antidepressant medications in persons with impulse control disorders.

Individualized therapy coupled with immersion in support groups also has shown to be beneficial for impulse control addicts. Like their substance misuse counterparts, behavioral addiction support groups strive to deconstruct the common repetitive cycle of isolation and shame inherent in addictive behavioral patterns. These programs also focus on the development of new coping skills with which to combat the anxieties that may lead to compulsive behaviors.

Much of the debate lies in the neurological function in the brain of pleasure-inducing chemicals such as beta-endorphins and serotonin. Scientific research has shown that persons on medications that boost production of such chemicals are more likely to develop addictive behavioral patterns.

A major disruption to the development of early screening, treatment, and prevention of impulse control behaviors is the lack of agreement in determining what behaviors constitute the diagnosis of addiction and where behavioral addictions land on this spectrum. Another source of disruption is determining the relationship between these disorders and criminal behavior.

John Pritchard

FOR FURTHER INFORMATION

Amer. Psychiatric Assn. *Highlights of Changes from DSM-IV-TR to DSM-5*. N.p.: APA, 2013. Digital file.

Bailey, C. Everett, and Brian Case. "Sexual Addiction—AAMFT Therapy Topic." *AAMFT*. Amer. Assn. for Marriage and Family Therapy 2002–15. Web. 2 Nov. 2015.

Banks, James. *Gambling, Crime and Society*. MacMillan, 2017.

Chambers-Jones, Clare. *Financial Crime and Gambling in a Virtual World: A New Frontier in Cybercrime*. Edward Elgar Publishing Limited, 2014.

DiClemente, Carlo. *Addiction and Change: How Addictions Develop and Addicted People Recover*. New York: Guilford, 2003. Print.

Gaita, Paul. "20 Million Americans May Be Compulsive Shoppers." *Fix*. Fix, 13 Apr. 2015. Web. 2 Nov. 2015.

Grant, Jon E. *Impulse Control Disorders: A Clinician's Guide to Understanding and Treating Behavioral Addictions*. New York: Norton, 2008. Print.

Grant, Jon E., and Marc N. Potenza, eds. *The Oxford Handbook of Impulse Control Disorders*. New York: Oxford UP, 2012. Print.

Jabr, Ferris. "How the Brain Gets Addicted to Gambling." *Scientific American*. Scientific American, 15 Oct. 2013. Web. 2 Nov. 2015.

See also: Behavioral addictions: Overview; Crime and substance misuse; Socioeconomic status and addiction

---

Crime and substance misuse

CATEGORY: Social issues

DEFINITION: Alcohol and illicit drugs are involved in approximately 80 percent of all criminal offenses leading to arrest and incarceration in the United States. Common crimes involving substance misuse are domestic violence, driving under the influence, assault and battery, and property offenses such as theft and burglary.

BACKGROUND

The precise relationship between substance misuse and crime is difficult to define. First, the cultivation, manufacturing, possession, and sale of illicit drugs are each crimes in their own right. This fact is aligned with numerous studies that have connected the propensity of persons who misuse illicit drugs to commit crimes. Similarly, laws dictating the appropriate distribution and consumption of alcoholic beverages exist throughout the United States. While these statutes themselves are often violated, there exists a well-established parallel between abusive alcohol use and criminal behavior.

It is widely accepted that the behavior of persons impaired by illicit drug and alcohol misuse are prone to erratic tendencies, poor judgment, impulsivity, and violence that lends itself to criminal activity. Repeated misuse of alcohol and drugs also decreases the self-control and inhibitions that distinguish criminals from law-abiding citizens.

Data acquired from the prison population in the United States illustrates that a considerable number of criminals and prison inmates were under the influence of drugs or alcohol, or both, when committing offenses of all kinds. According to a 2009 survey of ten metropolitan areas in the United States by the Office of National Drug Control Policy, the number of criminals who tested positive for at least one controlled substance during their arrest was as high as 82 percent in some locales. The most prevalent drugs of choice for arrestees included marijuana, cocaine, heroin, morphine, and methamphetamine. Fifty percent of jail and prison inmates have clinical addictions.

CRIME AND ALCOHOL MISUSE

Motor vehicle violations make up the majority of alcohol-related crimes in the United States. The National Partnership on Alcohol Misuse and Crime (NPAMC) reports that more than 1 million Americans are arrested for driving while intoxicated each year, cases that result in 780,000 criminal convictions. NPAMC findings also note that alcohol-related automobile accidents cost taxpayers more than $100 billion in law enforcement expenses annually. In 2015, 10,265 died in alcohol-impaired driving accidents, accounting for nearly 29 percent of all traffic-related deaths in the United States, according to the Centers for Disease Control and Prevention (CDC).

While decades of public interest campaigns led by national law enforcement agencies like the National Highway Traffic Safety Administration (NHTSA) and nonprofit organizations such as Mothers Against Drunk Driving (MADD) and the DUI Foundation have kept the dangers of drunk driving in the public eye, alcohol misuse is also ubiquitous in a wide variety of non-vehicle-related crimes. Domestic violence, underage drinking, and assault are the most frequently occurring non-vehicle-related but alcohol-related crimes in the United States.

While research has uncovered a recurring coexistence between domestic violence and alcohol misuse, not all domestic abusers are alcoholics and not all alcoholics are domestic abusers. A contrary rationale is that while alcohol misuse is regularly a contributing factor in many acts of domestic violence, there also are cases in which alcohol misuse is used as an excuse or an avoidance of accountability by its perpetrators.

There is a less scholarly gray area between alcohol use and criminal behavior by underage people. Consumption of alcohol by persons younger than age twenty-one years is itself a commonly perpetrated crime. According to the CDC, underage drinkers consume 11 percent of all the alcohol consumed in the United States each year, despite the illegality of doing so. In 2015, the CDC reported that 90 percent of this illegal alcohol consumption is binge drinking. CDC data also indicate that underage alcohol misuse leads to higher rates of school absence and reckless sexual behavior, and to brain development and memory problems.

Like their adult counterparts, abusive underage drinkers also have a higher propensity to violate laws against drunk driving and to engage in or be victimized by physical assault. The risk of criminal behavior appears to follow underage drinkers into adulthood, according to a 2011 study by the University of Miami that linked abusive underage alcohol consumption with a greater probability of committing property crimes like theft or predatory crimes like assault later in adulthood.

In 2015, the National Council on Alcoholism and Drug Dependence (NCADD) reports that alcohol is more closely associated with violent crime more than any other drug, with the exception of robbery. It is a factor in 40 percent of all violent crimes and 37 percent of almost two million offenders currently in jail report that they were drinking at the time of their arrest. A 2008 report by the Pew Center on the States reported that more than 5 million incarcerated adults were drinking at the time of committing their offense, a group that constitutes 36 percent of the entire US prison population. The research also showed trends indicating that the more violent a crime, the more likely alcohol was involved.

CRIME AND DRUG MISUSE

Drug-related offenses are broken down into three categories by the National Institute on Drug Abuse (NIDA): drug possession and sales, offenses committed to support preexisting drug misuse, and drug-related involvement in criminal activities not related to drugs. In 2016, the US Federal Bureau of Investigation estimated 1,572,579 arrests for drug law violations. In 2011, thirty-one thousand people were arrested in the United States on federal drug charges. The US Drug Enforcement Administration (DEA) arrests more than twenty-six thousand people for possession each year, and has done so every year since 1986.

A majority of illicit drug misusers rely on petty crimes to support their habit. These crimes range from petty theft to burglary to grand theft auto. Data from the US Bureau of Justice Statistics (2007) indicates that there were approximately 1,841,200 arrests at the state and local levels for drug misuse violations

and that number has been increasing. NIDA research also ties drug use to several other felony convictions, including money laundering, grand theft, and counterfeiting.

While a majority of drug-related crimes can be attributed to the illegality of drugs themselves, research shows that a majority of criminal acts are carried out by persons acting under the influence of or in the pursuit of many types of illicit drugs. That said, the relationship between drugs and crime remains extremely difficult to determine from a research perspective and remains a topic of debate among criminologists and sociologists.

YOUTH-ORIENTED PREVENTION

Federal, state, and local law enforcement agencies have developed numerous systems and processes aimed at reducing the appeal of drug use in hopes of simultaneously halting the various criminal activities that accompany that use. Aimed largely at school-age children and young adults, the agencies' primary goals have been to prevent persons from entering into the culture of drugs. These programs, which involve coursework and demonstrations of the negative aspects of drug use, have met with varying degrees of success.

The Drug Abuse Resistance Education program (D.A.R.E.) is an example of a failed nationwide effort to curtail drug use and violence. Founded in 1983 by former Los Angeles Police Department chief Daryl Gates, the program was widely utilized in public schools in the United States to explicitly educate young people on the dangers of drug use and activity through lecture-style lessons, drug identification demonstrations, and attempts at building trusting relationships with local police officers through in-school interactions.

By the late 1990s research began to show that the D.A.R.E. program not only was ineffective in decreasing drug use in the majority of communities in which it was utilized but also contributed to a rise in alcohol and drug use among its participants. Evaluation studies demonstrating the program's ineffectiveness were made by several federal agencies, including the US Office of the Surgeon General and US Department of Education (DE). The program's widespread reputation for ineffectiveness led the DE to prohibit schools from utilizing federal funds for the program in 1998.

Data acquired from the prison population in the United States illustrates that a considerable number of criminals and prison inmates were under the influence of drugs or alcohol, or both, when committing offenses of all kinds. (Peter Strescino via Wikimedia Commons)

New strategies fostered by the National Youth Anti-Drug Media Campaign in online campaigns, such as TheAntiDrug.com and AboveTheInfluence.com, detract from the communal, schoolroom-oriented strategies of previous programs like D.A.R.E.. The AntiDrug.com program emphasizes positive parental influence as a crucial dissuasion from the temptations of drug-related activity, while AbovetheInfluence. com seeks to tear down the status of illegal drug use as a popular counterculture. New models in Europe that emphasize teaching youth to get high naturally through music, dance, or other self-improvement classes, as well as an outdoor nightly curfew for anyone aged thirteen to sixteen, have seen dramatic results in curbing underage misuse of drugs and alcohol, but the United States has not adopted their national models.

John Pritchard

FOR FURTHER INFORMATION

"Alcohol, Drugs and Crime." *National Council on Alcoholism and Drug Dependence.* NCADD, 27 June 2015. Web. 29 Oct. 2015.

Andrews, D. A. *The Psychology of Criminal Conduct.* Cincinnati: Anderson, 2010. Print.

Belenko, Steven, and Cassia Spohn. *Drugs, Crime, and Justice.* Thousand Oaks: Sage, 2015. Print.

Galanter, Mark, ed. *Alcoholism and Violence: Epidemiology, Neurobiology, Psychology, Family Issues.* Recent Developments in Alcoholism 13. New York: Springer, 1997. Print.

Galvin, Emily V. "How Treatment Courts Can Reduce Crime." *Atlantic.* Atlantic Monthly, 29 Sept. 2015. Web. 29 Oct. 2015.

Hammersley, Richard. *Drugs and Crime.* London: Polity, 2008. Print.

Hanson, Glen, Peter J. Venturelli, and Annette E. Fleckenstein. *Drugs and Society.* 11th ed. Sudbury: Jones, 2012. Print.

US Department of Justice. "The Systems Approach to Crime and Drug Prevention: A Path to Community Policing." *Bulletin— Bureau of Justice Assistance* 1.2 (Sept. 1993). PDF file.

See also: Crime and behavioral addictions; Prison and substance misuse; Socioeconomic status and addiction

---

Cross-addiction

CATEGORY: Health issues and physiology

ALSO KNOWN AS: Addiction transfer

DEFINITION: Cross-addiction involves the transfer of an addiction from one harmful substance or behavior to another. It also involves the misuse of more than one mind-altering substance at a time.

CAUSES

Scientists now understand that addiction is a physiological problem caused both by nature and by nurture. A person who becomes an addict often inherits a sensitive brain and develops behavioral habits that lead to chemical changes in the brain. These changes, in turn, lead the person to use toxic substances against his or her will.

Research confirms that all drugs of misuse, including alcohol, marijuana, nicotine, amphetamines, barbiturates, opiates, and heroin, work on the same neurological pathways in key areas of the brain—in particular, dopamine receptors and the limbic system, a primitive area focused on meeting basic needs. Dopamine is a "feel-good" chemical that tricks the limbic system into equating drugs with pleasure or relief, and even with survival.

In people who are genetically predisposed to addiction, the release of dopamine is more intense, and it unleashes what is known as the phenomenon of craving. Such persons cannot limit their intake of an addictive drug because of this craving. People who do not come from a family of addicts or alcoholics can, through force of habit, still become addicted to toxic drugs and experience the same phenomenon.

Often when a person attempts to quit a drug of choice, he or she will use another drug to satisfy the craving and essentially keep the reward pathways of the brain in hypersensitive mode. Alternatively, cross addicts who have no desire to quit will mix a cocktail of drugs to get a desired effect.

RISK FACTORS

The dopamine hypothesis suggests that if a person is addicted to one drug, they are at higher risk of becoming addicted to another. For people who are trying to quit a particular drug, cross-addiction can lead to a relapse of the original drug-taking behavior because of the sustained craving and because of impaired decision-making abilities.

SYMPTOMS

The symptoms of addiction feature three characteristics: chemical dependency, drug-taking habits, and denial of dependency and habits. Chemical dependency involves four components: craving, or the compulsion to ingest a mood-altering substance; impaired control of the amount ingested on any given occasion; physical dependence, which produces a period of withdrawal when the drug is discontinued; and tolerance, or the need for more of the drug to feel its effects.

Cross addicts are often in extreme denial. They tend to be more secretive than alcoholics and will hide their behavior from friends and family members. Because most drugs are illegal, cross addicts often suffer from paranoia.

SCREENING AND DIAGNOSIS

Cross-addictions are far more dangerous than alcoholism alone, because mixing drugs and alcohol can lead to death sooner. As with alcoholism, cross-addiction requires a certain amount of self-diagnosis to be treatable.

Dependence can be diagnosed when the person admits to three or more of the following: taking substances in greater amounts than intended; a persistent desire to cut down or stop using fails to change the behavior; frequent intoxication or presence of withdrawal symptoms that interfere with functioning; spending significant amounts of time acquiring drugs or dealing with the consequences of use; giving up activities in order to use drugs; persistent use despite adverse consequences; marked tolerance; withdrawal symptoms; and the use of drugs to treat withdrawal symptoms.

TREATMENT AND THERAPY

Intensive therapy and treatment are required to break an addiction without transferring that addiction. The first step is building self-awareness and an understanding of the nature of addiction. Sobriety must be the first priority, and it should be affirmed and nurtured daily.

If a person transfers an addiction from one substance to another, the brain remains in addictive mode; the neural associations and pathways have no opportunity to become disabled and dormant. Thus, the cycle of cross-addiction can be broken only by stopping the drug-taking and by remaining totally abstinent from all mind-altering drugs.

Acute withdrawal symptoms, such as sweating and nausea, can last a couple of weeks. Postacute withdrawal symptoms can happen for two years. These bouts tend to last three or four days and produce irritability, mood swings, variable energy, low enthusiasm, disturbed sleep, and difficulty concentrating. The first two years are the most difficult; after five years of abstinence, relapse is uncommon.

PREVENTION

Recovery is a lifelong process that requires new coping skills. Relaxation is chief among them; rigorous honesty and avoiding high-risk situations also will help prevent a relapse.

People who have been addicted to one drug must be vigilant, because cross-addiction can occur by happenstance. A recovering alcoholic, for example, may go to the dentist and be prescribed pain medicine, to which he or she develops a chemical dependency.

Without thinking about it, the patient begins to increase the dosage and frequency of the pain medication and may seek unnecessary refills. Not all doctors learn about the physiology of addiction, so to protect oneself, a recovering addict must be wary when taking prescription medications.

Laura B. Smith

FOR FURTHER INFORMATION

Christopher, James. *How to Stay Sober: Recovery without Religion.* New York: Prometheus, 1988. Print.

Johnson, Marlys C., and Phyllis Alberici. *Cross-Addiction: The Hidden Risk of Multiple Addictions.* New York: Rosen, 1999. Print.

Kipper, David, and Steven Whitney. "Cross-Addiction." *The Addiction Solution: Unraveling the Mysteries of Addiction through Cutting-Edge Brain Science.* New York: Rodale, 2010. Print.

Ries, Richard, and Shannon C. Miller. *Principles of Addiction Medicine.* Philadelphia: Lippincott, 2009. Print.

See also: Addiction; Addictive personality; Co-occurring disorders; Relapse

Cutting and self-mutilation

CATEGORY: Psychological issues and behaviors
ALSO KNOWN AS: Self-injury
DEFINITION: Cutting and self-mutilation are behaviors in which a person injures his or her own body; this behavior is often called non-suicidal self-injury, or NSSI. Some examples of self-injury are cutting, burning, hair pulling, and head banging.

RISK FACTORS AND RELATED CONDITIONS

Although self-injury can occur at any age, it usually begins in adolescence. It was originally thought that women were more likely than men to engage in self-injury, but later research indicates that the incidence is equal among women and men. Statistically, women are more likely to cut, while men are more likely to engage in other forms of self-harm, such as burning or hitting. According to the US National Library of Medicine, every one in one hundred people inflicts self-injury.

Persons who self-injure commonly have a history of abuse, including sexual, physical, or emotional abuse. Self-injury is often associated with other mental health problems, such as eating disorders, substance misuse, obsessive-compulsive disorders, schizophrenia, depression, bipolar disorder, borderline personality disorder, anxiety disorders, post-traumatic stress disorder, dissociative disorders, panic disorder, and phobias.

Persons who engage in self-injury often come from homes where expressing anger and other emotions is (or was) forbidden. They frequently have low self-esteem and exhibit perfectionism. Also, they are likely to be impulsive and to have poor problem-solving skills. However, self-injury does not indicate the severity of mental illness or the ability of the person to function and lead a relatively normal life.

WHY PERSONS SELF-INJURE

There are many reasons for self-injury. One is using the behavior to provide a way to deal with overwhelming feelings, such as anger, extreme sadness, anxiety, depression, stress, sense of failure, self-hatred, or the helplessness of a trauma. Persons who self-injure have difficulty coping with severe emotional pain.

Self-injury can serve as a distraction from emotional pain, a way to express feelings that the person is unable to describe, or a way to feel a sense of control over something that is uncontrollable. Persons who self-injure often describe a feeling of calmness and relief of their intense feelings after they have injured themselves. Other self-injurers describe feeling emotionally numb and empty. For these persons, the self-injury allows them to feel something. Some are communicating their distress and expressing a need for help through self-injury. Others are punishing themselves for some imagined wrong.

Other persons use self-injury to prevent something worse from happening to them. A person may justify his or her behavior through the belief that if something bad is happening to him or her now, nothing else bad can happen. Others use self-injury to separate themselves from their feelings, which fade in the face of the physical pain. Though research has not conclusively proven it, a prevalent theory is that self-injury leads to the release of endorphins in the brain. Endorphins are chemicals found in the body that act as natural pain relievers and tranquilizers. Endorphin release produces a natural high that can temporarily mask emotional or physical pain.

It is thought that some persons self-injure to seek attention and to manipulate others. This is unlikely because most self-injurers are ashamed of the injuries that they cause, and they will hide their self-inflicted injuries. It is common for self-injurers to wear shirts with long sleeves and full-length pants in all types of weather to hide their injuries. The exceptions to this are persons who are developmentally or otherwise mentally disabled, such as those with autism. They are likely to engage in self-injury without also trying to hide the injury or the behavior. In this context, self-harm is called self-injurious behavior (SIB) and can have a number of causes. Someone with autism, for example, may exhibit SIB as a result of biochemical imbalances, sensory issues, to distract from other sources of physical pain, or in response to social or environmental triggers.

Symptoms and Treatment

No single therapy exists to treat persons who self-injure, and there is no consensus as to the most effective treatment. Typically, treatment must be developed based on the needs and other mental health conditions of the self-injurer. Possible helpful medications include antidepressants, antipsychotic drugs, and minor tranquilizers.

Often-used psychotherapeutic approaches include cognitive-behavioral therapy, dialectical-behavior therapy, and psychodynamic psychotherapy. The type of psychotherapy also depends on the other psychological illnesses of the client. In severe cases of self-injury, the person may be hospitalized to exert some control over the behavior.

Psychotherapy usually begins with an exploration of why the person self-injures. The therapist will teach alternative behaviors to use when the person feels like self-injuring. These alternatives include physical activities, journaling, and talking with friends or family members. Alternative actions also may be taught, such as snapping an elastic band that is wrapped around the self-injurer's wrist. While this action does cause some pain, it does not cause injury. Biofeedback may be used to help the person identify the feelings that lead to the urge to self-injure.

It is important that the person understands that treatment, especially self-treatment, takes time, hard work, and motivation. If the self-injurer is an adolescent or child, family therapy may be necessary to identify what triggers the self-injuring behavior. Group therapy also may be used to provide the person with supportive relationships with others who are dealing with similar issues. Self-injurers who are developmentally disabled can be taught how to accomplish goals without using self-harming behaviors.

Christine M. Carroll RN, BSN MBA

For Further Information

Hollander, Michael. *Helping Teens Who Cut: Understanding and Ending Self-Injury*. New York: Guilford, 2008.

Peterson, John, et. al. "Nonsuicidal Self Injury in Adolescents." *Psychiatry* 5.11 (2008): 20–26. Print.

Smith, Melinda, and Jeanne Segal. "Cutting and Self-Harm." Jan. 2012. Web. 17 Apr. 2012. http://www.helpguide.org/mental/self_injury.htm.

Strong, Marilee. *A Bright Red Scream: Self-Mutilation and the Language of Pain*. New York: Virago, 2005.

Sutton, Jan. *Healing the Hurt Within: Understanding Self-Injury and Self-Harm, and Heal the Emotional Wounds*. 3rd ed. Oxford, England: How to Books, 2007.

See also: Behavioral addictions: Overview; Body modification addiction; Self-destructive behavior and addiction

D

D.A.R.E. (Drug Abuse Resistance Education)

CATEGORY: Diagnosis and prevention

DEFINITION: Drug Abuse Resistance Education (D.A.R.E.) is a world-wide, K-12, drug prevention program of law enforcement agencies and school systems that educates children and adolescents about the consequences of drug use, gang membership, and violent behavior.

DATE: Established in 1983

BACKGROUND

The Drug Abuse Resistance Education (D.A.R.E.) program was established by the Los Angeles Police Department (LAPD) and the Los Angeles Unified School District in 1983 as a drug prevention program to address drug use among elementary school children. Its American headquarters are in Inglewood, California. The program received early support from the Robert Wood Johnson Foundation and many private donors. In its early days, D.A.R.E., under its cofounders, LAPD officers Glenn Levant and Daryl Gates (who later became LAPD chief), focused both on demand reduction (decreasing the desire for drugs by making students aware of the physical, personal, and social consequences of drug use) and, with law enforcement agencies, on supply reduction (decreasing drug availability to potential misusers of all ages).

D. A. R. E. is now a world-wide, K-12, drug prevention program of law enforcement agencies and school systems that educates children and adolescents about the consequences of drug use and teaches them how to avoid drug use, gang membership, and violent behavior so that they will lead productive drug-free and violence-free lives.

Police officers and teachers participating in the program undergo 80 and 40 hours of training, respectively. The programs differ depending on the age and grade level of the students. The D. A. R. E. programs are taught in grades K through 12 and now operates in every state in the United States and nearly fifty other countries. The program involves over 26 million children in the U. S. and over 40 million children world-wide. In the U. S., the program has been funded by several government agencies.

A 2009 study by the U. S. Bureau of Justice Assistance that reviewed thirty evaluations of D.A.R.E.'s effectiveness concluded that there was no significant

The D.A.R.E. program, sponsored by the Combat Center Provost Marshal's Office, graduated a class of elementary school students at Twentynine Palms Elementary School Nov. 12, 2013. (Lance Cpl. Charles J. Santamaria via Wikimedia Commons)

long-term effect on the participants' drug use. These studies resulted in a decrease in operating revenue in the U. S. from $10 million in 2002 to $3.7 million in 2010.

In the early 1980s, before the existence of programs like D.A.R.E., 66 percent of high school students had used illegal drugs. In 2008, illegal drug use among high school students had decreased to about 47 percent, although the impact of D.A.R.E. on this decline is thought to be negligible. The D.A.R.E. program was revamped in 2001 and again in 2008 and has altered its curriculum to improve its effectiveness. In 2009, D.A.R.E. introduced its "Keepin' It REAL" program, which focuses less on drugs and more on improving students' decision-making skills. (REAL stands for refuse, explain, avoid, and leave.) Early evaluations of Keepin' It REAL's effectiveness show that it reduces substance misuse and maintains antidrug attitudes in its participants. Reviews of the effectiveness of D. A. R. E. and related programs are continuing.

MISSION, VISION AND GOALS

The original (pre-2009) mission of D.A.R.E. was to "implement and support drug abuse resistance education and crime prevention programs". The mission now is to "teach students good decision-making skills to help them lead safe and healthy lives". The vision of D. A. R. E. is "a world in which students everywhere are empowered to respect others and choose to lead lives free from violence, substance abuse, and other dangerous behaviors". While the program originally targeted drug prevention, it has been expanded to include Internet safety and the prevention of cyberbullying, and its focus has shifted to improving communication and decision-making skills. D.A.R.E. also attempts to establish positive relationships between police officers and school children by having officers visit schools and speak to students in a friendly, approachable, non-threatening manner.

All officers have mentors who are senior D.A.R.E. officers. Mentors teach the classroom officers how to effectively present material to children, inform them of helpful interactive activities, and provide further tips on teaching about drugs, gang membership and violent behavior. D.A.R.E. officers provide students with skills to help them make informed decisions in and out of the school environment. This helps students build self-esteem, stand firm against peer pressure, and develop the courage to refuse drugs, gang membership and participation in violent or dangerous activities.

Robin Kamienny Montvilo, PhD;
Updated by Charles L. Vigue, PhD

FOR FURTHER INFORMATION

Bergman, Greg, and Aubrey Fox. *Lessons from the Battle over D.A.R.E.: The Complicated Relationship between Research and Practice.* Washington, DC: U. S. Bureau of Justice Assistance, 2009. PDF file.

Cima, Rosie. "DARE: The Anti-Drug Program That Never Actually Worked." *Priceonomics.* December 19, 2016. Accessed on June 29, 2018 https://priceonomics.com/dare-the-anti-drug-program-that-never-actually/.

D. A. R. E. https://dare.org/. Accessed June 29, 2018.

Ennett Susan T., et al. "How Effective Is Drug Abuse Resistance Education? A Meta-Analysis of Project D.A.R.E. Outcome Evaluations." *American Journal of Public Health* 84 (1994): 1394–401. Print.

Hecht, Michael L., et al. "Culturally Grounded Substance Use Prevention: An Evaluation of the Keepin' It R.E.A.L. Curriculum." *Prevention Science* 4 (2003): 233–48. Print.

Kanof, Marjorie E. "Youth Illicit Drug Use Prevention: D.A.R.E. Long-Term Evaluations and Federal Efforts to Identify Effective Programs." Washington D.C.: GAO, January 15, 2003.

Nordrum, Amy. "The New D.A.R.E. Program—This One Works." *Scientific American 10* (2014). Web. 26 Oct. 2015.

Rosenbaum, Dennis P., and Gordon S. Hanson. "Assessing the Effects of School-Based Drug Education: A Six-Year Multilevel Analysis of Project D.A.R.E." *Journal of Research in Crime and Delinquency* 35.4 (1998): 381–412. Print.

West, Steven L., and K. K. O'Neal. "Project D.A.R.E. Outcome Effectiveness Revisited." *American Journal of Public Health* 94 (2004): 1027–29. Print.

See also: Education about substance misuse; Just Say No campaign; Law enforcement and drugs; Prevention methods and research; Schools and substance misuse

Date rape drugs

CATEGORY: Substances

ALSO KNOWN AS: Club drugs; ecstasy; flunitrazepam; gamma hydroxybutyrate; ketamine; Rohypnol

DEFINITION: Date rape drugs are typically odorless, colorless, and tasteless substances that are often combined with alcohol and other drinks to sedate and incapacitate an unsuspecting person to facilitate a sexual assault.

COMMON DATE RAPE DRUGS

Alcohol used voluntarily is the most commonly used date rape drug. Alcohol affects judgment and behavior and may place a person at risk for sexual assault or risky sexual activity.

Benzodiazepines such as Valium, Xanax and Librium are sedatives, tranquilizers and depressants that are used to treat sleeping disorders but are often used as date rape drugs. The most commonly used benzodiazepines are Rohypnol (flunitrazepam), gamma hydroxybutyrate (GHB), and ketamine. Midazolam and temazepam are benzodiazepines that are also used to treat sleeping disorders, but they are used less commonly as date rape drugs.

Rohypnol use began to gain popularity in the United States in the early 1990s. Rohypnol is illegal in the United States but legal in Europe and Mexico where it is prescribed for sleep disorders and used for anesthesia. It is exported to the United States illegally. Rohypnol is a pill that dissolves in liquid. Some of these pills are small, round, and white. Newer pills are oval and green-gray in color that when placed in a drink turns a clear drink bright blue and turns a dark drink cloudy. However, this color change is often difficult to see in a dark drink, such as cola or dark beer or in a darkened room. Pills with no dye are still available. The pills can be ground into a powder.

GHB (Xyrem), a metabolite of gamma-aminobutyric acid (GABA), an inhibitory neurotransmitter, is a central nervous system depressant that was originally used as a general anesthetic. It was removed from the market in 1990 by the U. S. Food and Drug Administration (FDA), but since 2002, the FDA has allowed its use but restricted it to the treatment of narcolepsy (a sleep disorder). The FDA requires that it be monitored through a patient registry. GHB exists naturally in the brain, but at much lower concentrations than those found when GHB is misused. GHB is available as a liquid with no odor or color, as a white powder, and as a pill. It can make a drink taste slightly salty.

Ketamine is legal in the United States for use as an anesthetic for humans and animals. It is mostly used with animals. Veterinary clinics are sometimes burglarized for their ketamine supplies. Ketamine is available as a liquid and as a white powder.

Zolpidem (Ambien) along with Zopiclone and zaleplon (Sonata) are hypnotic, sedative agents used to treat insomnia. These "Z drugs" are some of the most commonly used date rape drugs.

Methaqualone is sold under the name Quaalude and acts as a hypnotic, sedative agent. It is often used as a date rape drug.

MDMA (3,4-methylenedioxy-methamphetamine, also known as ecstasy or Molly) is also used to commit sexual assaults.

EFFECTS ON THE HUMAN BODY

The sedative-hypnotic effects of date rape drugs are powerful. The drugs can affect a person quickly and without that person's knowledge which makes them especially appealing to potential perpetrators of sexual assault. The length of time that the effects last varies and depends on how much of the drug is taken and whether the drug is mixed with other drugs or alcohol. Alcohol makes the drugs even stronger and can cause serious health problems, even death.

The effects of Rohypnol occur within thirty minutes of ingestion and can last for several hours. A victim may look and act like someone who is drunk. He or she may have trouble standing, may have slurred speech, or might pass out. GHB takes effect in about fifteen minutes and can last three or four hours. Ketamine is fast-acting, and the victim may be aware of what is happening but unable to move. Ketamine also causes lapses in memory. A victim may not remember what occurred while drugged.

It is often difficult for a person to know if he or she has been drugged and assaulted. Most victims do not remember details of the incident. The victim may not be aware of the attack until eight or twelve hours after when the effects of the drug wear off.

Date rape drugs can leave the body quickly. By the time a victim receives help, the drug has likely been cleared from the person's system. However, there are other indications that a person may have been drugged, including feeling drunk although no alcohol has been consumed, waking up feeling hung over and disoriented, and having no memory of recent events.

Persons who have ingested a date rape drug should get medical treatment immediately. As with any sexual assault, it is important that the victim not urinate, douche, bathe or shower, brush teeth, wash hands, change clothes, or eat or drink before seeing a medical professional. Doing so may destroy evidence of the assault. The hospital will use a rape kit to collect evidence. A urine sample can be analyzed for the presence of drugs.

Claudia Daileader Ruland, MA;
Updated by Charles L. Vigue, PhD

FOR FURTHER INFORMATION

Albright, J. A., S. A. Stevens, and D. J. Beussman. "Detecting Ketamine in Beverage Residues: Application in Date Rape Detection." *Drug Testing and Analysis* 4.3–4 (2011). Print.

"Commonly Abused Drugs Chart." *National Institute on Drug Abuse.* NIH, Oct. 2015. Web. 29 Oct. 2015.

Conley, Kate, *Date Rape Drugs (Drugs in Real Life).* Edina, Minnesota: Essential Library (ABDO Publishing). (2018). Print.

"DrugFacts: MDMA (Ecstasy or Molly)." *National Institute on Drug Abuse.* NIH, Sept. 2013. Web. 29 Oct. 2015.

Methamphetamine and date rape drugs: a new generation of killers, United States Congress and United States House of Representatives (2018). Print.

Németh, Z., B. Kun, and Z. Demetrovics. "The Involvement of Gamma-Hydroxybutyrate in Reported Sexual Assaults: A Systematic Review." *Journal of Psychopharmacology* 24.9 (2010): 1281–87. Print.

Shoup, Kate, *Rohypnol (Dangerous Drugs).* New York: Cavendish Square Pub. (2015). Print.

See also: Club drugs; GHB; Ketamine; Rohypnol; Sexual assault and drug use

Debtors Anonymous

CATEGORY: Treatment
DEFINITION: Debtors Anonymous is a twelve-step recovery program modeled on Alcoholics Anonymous, which helps people overcome the accumulation of unmanageable, unsecured debt.
ESTABLISHED: April 1976

BACKGROUND

Debtors Anonymous (DA) owes its inception to a group of recovering alcoholics in New York City who, in 1968, organized an informal support group, under the leadership of John H., to explore members' self-destructive behavior with money. After trying various approaches (at one time the group called itself Penny Pinchers and emphasized thrift, and it later called itself Capital Builders, emphasizing savings and income maximization), group members concluded that the central problem was accumulating unmanageable, unsecured debt.

In April of 1976 the group formally inaugurated DA, a program based on the twelve-step recovery model of Alcoholics Anonymous (AA). The early, central aim of DA was to help its members avoid accumulating additional unsecured debt and clearing up past debts through negotiations with creditors and repayment, when feasible.

The organization grew slowly. By 1982, five meetings were being held, all in Manhattan. At this time the founders established a board of trustees and a general service conference. DA now provides about five hundred meetings in twelve countries, but it remains concentrated in urban areas in the United States.

The organization has published the book *A Currency of Hope* (1999), a compendium of thirty-eight stories about recovery from debt through DA participation, and also a number of pamphlets, mainly on the mechanics of working the program. For general information on twelve-step programs, members are referred to AA literature, to which DA publications are considered supplemental.

Most of DA's growth occurred before 1996. A number of explanations have been offered concerning why interest in DA has leveled off or even declined since the mid-1990s. One possibility is that it treats the act of incurring debt as if it were an addiction, a model that remains questionable. Indebtedness often accompanies addictive behaviors, as prudent financial management is overcome by compulsion; the act of borrowing itself is secondary. As long as the bulk of DA membership was drawn from the ranks of alcoholics, who were accustomed to using the twelve-step model to combat a "real" addiction, people would accept the type of program (like DA) that demanded total abstinence and strenuous efforts to clear up old debts, because it had worked for them. An increase in the number of people without twelve-step experience who expected general financial management support and rejected abstinence in favor of moderation, has shifted DA's focus, and that shift introduced terms such as *self-debting, financial anorexia,* and *situational debting.* There is a movement within DA to return to a more strict concentration on monetary debt.

MISSION AND GOALS

The aim of DA is twofold. First, it provides recovery tools for people who are struggling with debt, and second, it provides a support structure within which recovering members can share their experiences with newcomers.

A key feature of the program is awareness, both of individual finances and of the climate in which people operate. Members are encouraged to keep a daily journal in which they note every expenditure and keep receipts. Although the organization does not lobby publicly against the often-deceptive practices of the credit industry (one of DA's traditions, borrowed from AA, is avoiding politics), it does play an active role in educating members about how the industry encourages people to incur debt.

A person wishing to receive help from DA should first start attending meetings, or, if none are available, should explore meetings online or by telephone. Upon joining, a debtor will connect with a sponsor, a more experienced member who guides him or her through the twelve steps. The new member will then be asked to join a pressure relief group, comprising three people who have gone a minimum of ninety days without accumulating unsecured debt. The new member will work with other group members to formulate a spending and action plan. Ideally, a spending plan allocates funds to meet needs, retire debt, and save for the future, and it also includes ways to increase income.

People become financially indebted for many reasons, not all under personal control. One pattern of behavior that has addictive characteristics and can lead to spiraling credit card debt is compulsive spending disorder. The *Diagnostic and Statistical Manual of Mental Disorders* of the American Psychiatric Association (APA) includes compulsive spending under the diagnostic category of impulse control disorders not specified, but the APA may recognize the disorder as distinct in revised manuals. DA addresses spending compulsion indirectly, through a strict program of budgeting and prohibition against credit card use for consumer purchases.

Since the collapse of the housing market in the United States and the ensuing global recession beginning in 2007/2008, the availability of consumer credit has contracted considerably, and the realities of debt in the United States have changed. Overconsumption and lack of impulse control play a smaller role now, while declining income, declining home values, medical debt, and student loans have become more prominent. This shift may be another reason why fewer people are using the services of DA.

DA considers legal bankruptcy proceedings to be an outside issue and has no position for or against it. Declaring bankruptcy would force a debtor into the sort of careful budgeting and economizing that DA encourages. It is often the only realistic option for people with large involuntary, primarily medical, debts.

Martha A. Sherwood PhD

FOR FURTHER INFORMATION

Bill W. *Alcoholics Anonymous.* 4th ed. New York: Alcoholics Anonymous, 2002. The first 168 pages of this oft-referenced text contain a blueprint for twelve-step recovery programs, including Debtors Anonymous.

Debtors Anonymous. *A Currency of Hope.* Needham, MA: Author, 1999. A collection of thirty-eight personal stories of recovery from debt, plus an explanation of the Debtors Anonymous program.

Geisst, Charles R. *Collateral Damaged: The Marketing of Consumer Debt to America.* New York: Bloomberg, 2009. Explains how the United States turned from a nation of savers into a nation of consumers addicted to debt.

Manning, Robert D. *Credit Card Nation: The Consequences of America's Addiction to Credit.* New York: Basic, 2003. A mostly historical look at the problem of consumer debt in the United States.

Morenberg, Adam D. "Governing Wayward Consumers: Self-Change and Recovery in Debtors Anonymous." MA thesis. UP of South Florida, 2004. Print. A sociological analysis of Debtors Anonymous.

See also: Group therapy for behavioral addictions; Self-destructive behavior and addiction; Support groups; Twelve-step programs for addicts

Decriminalization of drugs in the United States

CATEGORY: Social issues

DEFINITION: Decriminalization refers to a reduction in or an elimination of the criminal classification or status of any activity considered a criminal offense. Decriminalization of drugs specifically refers to reducing or eliminating legal restrictions placed on the possession, distribution, and use of illicit substances, most notably marijuana.

OVERVIEW

For much of the twentieth century and into the twenty-first century, the United States has been engaged in a pronounced effort to stop the flow of illicit substances into the country, to curb the use of such substances, and to reduce the number of crimes related to their use. This effort has been characterized as the War on Drugs.

Increasingly, however, many activists have called attention to the belief that this "war" has thus far proved ineffective at best and even counterproductive in reducing drug-related crime. In response, a substantial movement in favor of the decriminalization of drugs has developed and turned the question of the appropriate legal status of illicit substances into a hotly debated issue in contemporary politics.

At the center of this debate is marijuana, one of the most widely used drugs. According to a July 2017 Gallup poll, 45 percent of Americans have experimented with marijuana. (That figure is the highest recorded percentage from Gallup of Americans using the drug.) Proponents of decriminalization argue that marijuana is a largely harmless substance that has been unjustly maligned in the arena of public opinion and should thus be legalized.

Opponents of the decriminalization of marijuana argue that marijuana is potentially as harmful as other drugs and that its legalization would only encourage more drug-related crime and other social problems. Further intensifying this debate is medical marijuana, which has benefits for persons with certain ailments and diseases. To fully understand the debate over the decriminalization of marijuana and other drugs, it is critically important to view the issue from both sides of the argument and carefully study the potential benefits and consequences such legislation would likely have. Early in 2017, the Task Force on Crime Reduction and Public Safety was formed under Attorney General Jeff Sessions to explore options with regard to marijuana policy. Options ranged on a spectrum from a total crackdown on state policies in the for-profit commercial regime in states that have legalized marijuana and medical marijuana, to legalization at the federal level.

ARGUMENTS FOR DECRIMINALIZATION

According to an October 2017 Gallup poll, 60 percent of Americans are in favor of legalizing the use of marijuana, a record number. Those in favor of decriminalizing marijuana argue that the legalization of its use would be beneficial in many ways.

Among the chief and often most persuasive of these arguments is the belief that decriminalization would save governments and law enforcement agencies much money. The enforcement of laws related to marijuana costs states an estimated $3.6 billion annually, according to the American Civil Liberties Union (ACLU). Proponents of marijuana decriminalization argue that legalizing marijuana would eliminate these costs, thus allowing for the reallocation of these funds for other, more useful purposes, including taxpayer savings.

To some extent, this theory of cost reduction has been proven. As of 2015, thirty-five US states have legalized medical marijuana in some capacity, while four states—Colorado, Oregon, Washington, and Alaska—as well as the District of Columbia have legalized recreational use. In November of 2016 California, Massachusetts, Maine, and Nevada all passed measures legalizing the recreational use of marijuana. In California, where the possession of small amounts of marijuana has been partially decriminalized, reports have shown that the state saves close to $30 million annually—funds that would otherwise be used to prosecute small-time marijuana offenders. Legalization has also been shown to bring in revenue. In Colorado, the state brought in $150 million from taxes, fees, and licenses from legal marijuana sales from January to October of 2016 alone, while money from legal sales and marijuana-related tourism poured into the economy during the same period.

In addition to highlighting the potential financial benefits of the decriminalization of marijuana, proponents also frequently target what they see as misconceptions about the drug's use. First and foremost, to counter the claim that decriminalization would likely result in a dramatic upsurge in the number of marijuana users, proponents respond by arguing that marijuana is already a widely used drug, with about 20.3 million people using the drug at least once per month, according to combined 2012 to 2014 data compiled by the National Survey on Drug Use and Health (NSDUH).

Proponents also point out that those who use marijuana often do so responsibly, and without dependence. For example, whereas most people who use alcohol or tobacco generally consume these addictive substances daily, most marijuana users consume marijuana on a monthly or weekly basis only. This, supporters claim, shows that marijuana is not as addictive as alcohol or tobacco and is not as likely to lead to misuse or dependence. In addition, according to a survey conducted by the Pew Research Center in February 2014, 69 percent of Americans questioned said that they thought alcohol was more was worse for health than marijuana.

Another common concern many people have about the decriminalization of marijuana or other drugs is that decriminalizing drugs might lead to an increase in crime. Proponents of decriminalization, however, argue that this concern is based on a misconception, one that is based primarily on the belief that because many people who have committed crimes have also used drugs that drugs must directly cause people to commit criminal acts. Proponents of decriminalization say that drug use is only one of many factors that leads people to crime and should not be considered a sole cause.

In addition, studies have shown that marijuana is the least likely of the major illicit drugs to result in criminal activities of any kind (alcohol, on the other hand, has been implicated in 40 percent of violent crimes in the United States). Persons who are high on marijuana are unlikely to become violent.

Finally, proponents of decriminalizing marijuana also argue that doing so would, to some degree, lighten the workload and general burdens of the criminal justice system. Though the number of marijuana-related crimes is relatively low in comparison with other types of crime, the elimination of these cases would reduce the workload of police and the courts, free up much needed space in correctional facilities, and save the criminal justice system, governments, and taxpayers money. In fact, in Colorado, where recreational marijuana was legalized in 2012, robberies decreased in Denver from 2013 to 2014.

It also is important to note that the proponents of decriminalization support the legalization of marijuana for medicinal purposes. Research has shown that marijuana does improve the painful symptoms of certain illnesses. While medical marijuana has become legal in many states, it is still illegal at the federal level. This leaves many people without access to medical marijuana and those who provide it legally at the state level vulnerable to federal intervention. Marijuana supporters often strongly believe that, even if marijuana were not decriminalized for recreational use, it should be legalized for those with a legitimate medical need for the substance.

OPPOSITION TO DECRIMINALIZATION

For all those who support the decriminalization of marijuana and other drugs in the United States, there are nearly as many people who oppose decriminalization, though according to a 2015 Gallup poll, public opinion is changing rapidly. Opponents cite a variety of reasons why such legislation would fail and, possibly, lead to even larger social concerns.

Opponents of decriminalization argue that legalizing marijuana would lead to a significant increase in drug use across the United States. They also believe that decriminalization would lead to an increase in the number of teenagers who experiment with marijuana, a claim that proponents refute (arguing that only a minimal, if any, increase in use would occur among teens).

Finally, opponents argue that marijuana is a gateway drug and that legal use of the substance would eventually lead to an increase in the use of harder drugs. However, proponents refute this claim also, claiming that statistics show the rate of usage of harder drugs is much lower than the rate of use of marijuana, which suggests that most marijuana users never move on to more dangerous substances.

Another argument made regularly by opponents is that decriminalization would cause a dramatic increase in the crime rate. They believe that the majority of those crimes labeled as drug-related are actually crimes committed by persons under the influence of a mind-altering substance, and are not committed as part of the sale of drugs. There is also the fear that increased availability will lead to an upsurge car accidents with drivers operating under the influence of marijuana. There is not yet a good way to measure marijuana intoxication levels, like there is with alcohol and breathalyzer tests, though studies are underway to create such tests because driving under the influence of marijuana is illegal in all states, including those where consuming the drug is legal. Opponents believe that legalizing a drug will not stop related crimes.

Opponents also argue that drugs should remain illegal because of the medical issues surrounding drug use. In answer to the claim made by proponents of decriminalization that legalization has economic advantages, opponents argue that any financial savings incurred would be offset by increased expenses related to health costs, traffic and industrial accidents, decreased productivity, domestic violence, and other issues. Finally, in regard to medical marijuana, those who oppose decriminalization, even for persons with legitimate medical conditions, argue that there exist safer alternatives to marijuana, some of which use the same ingredients found in marijuana itself.

Jack A. Lasky

FOR FURTHER INFORMATION

Caulkins, Jonathan P., et al. *Marijuana Legalization: What Everyone Needs to Know.* New York: Oxford UP, 2012. Print.
Downes, Lawrence. "The Great Colorado Weed Experiment." *New York Times.* New York Times, 2 Aug. 2014. Web. 29 Oct. 2015.
Fisher, Gary L. *Rethinking Our War on Drugs: Candid Talk about Controversial Issues.* Westport: Praeger, 2006. Print.
Gray, James P. *Why Our Drug Laws Have Failed and What We Can Do about It: A Judicial Indictment of the War on Drugs.* Philadelphia: Temple UP, 2012. Print.
Husak, Douglas N. *Legalize This! The Case for Decriminalizing Drugs.* New York: Verso, 2002. Print.
Martin, Alyson, et al. *A New Leaf: The End of Cannabis Prohibition.* The New Press. 2014.
Motel, Seth. "6 Facts About Marijuana." *Pew Research Center.* Pew Research Center, 14 Apr. 2015. Web. 29 Oct. 2015.
Newton, David E. *Marijuana: A Reference Handbook.* Santa Barbara: ABC-CLIO, 2013. Print.
Regan, Trish. *Joint Ventures: Inside America's Almost Legal Marijuana Industry.* Hoboken: Wiley, 2011. Digital file.

See also: Crime and substance misuse; Law enforcement and drugs; Legislation and substance misuse; Medical marijuana

Dependence

CATEGORY: Substance misuse

ALSO KNOWN AS: Addiction

DEFINITION: Chemical dependence is a primary, progressive, and potentially fatal condition resulting from the chronic use of certain substances such as drugs or alcohol. Repetitive use of a substance leads to a higher tolerance so that more of the drug is needed for the person to feel its effects. Once chemical dependence has developed, suddenly stopping the substance use will produce withdrawal symptoms such as anxiety and other unpleasant physical symptoms.

CAUSES

Substance misuse is caused by a combination of factors, including inherited genes, environmental stressors, and, often, an underlying or preexisting mental health issue, such as depression or anxiety. Social factors, such as peer pressure to experiment, also come into play. Environmental stress, whether at work or home, is also a major contributor to cravings that drive a person to misuse substances.

Physiologically, addictive substances flood the brain's reward circuit, primarily with the hormone dopamine. When these reward pathways are continually overstimulated, the brain produces less of its own hormones and dopamine receptors. Dependence occurs when the user's brain neurons adapt to chronic drug exposure and can function normally only in the presence of the drug. Without the drug, the person experiences a number of withdrawal symptoms, including agitation, anxiety, and insomnia. The person progressively takes greater amounts of the substance to overcome tolerance, which leads to profound chemical changes in neurons and brain circuits that compromise the long-term functioning and health of the brain.

RISK FACTORS

Aside from genetics, risk factors for developing a pharmacological dependence include surviving a disaster or experiencing psychic trauma. Disaster and trauma survivors are prone to stress-related disorders such as post-traumatic stress disorder and depression. Such persons may self-medicate with alcohol or other drugs to relieve unbearable symptoms. People who suffer from drug dependence are about twice as likely to suffer from mood disorders than the general population.

Social factors also may play a role in drug misuse and addiction. The attitudes and beliefs of one's family members, peers, and friends about drug use are a significant factor in initial drug use. Once an individual has begun using a drug, the development of dependence is thought to depend upon that person's genetic traits, and some people may be particularly susceptible with developing dependence

SYMPTOMS

According to the fifth edition of the American Psychiatric Association's *Diagnostic and Statistical Manual of Mental Disorders* (DSM-5), published in 2013, there are eleven diagnostic criteria for substance use disorder organized into four categories: impaired control, social impairment, risky use, and pharmacological dependence. According to the DSM-5, pharmacological dependence is characterized by tolerance to the effects of a substance and symptoms of withdrawal when discontinuing or decreasing use of the substance. The

World Health Organization describe dependence syndrome as "a cluster of physiological, behavioral, and cognitive phenomena in which the use of a substance or a class of substances takes on a much higher priority for a given individuals than other behaviors that once had greater value." Behavioral symptoms of dependence include neglect of other interest and obligations due to substance use, including the time spent attaining the drug and recovering from its use, and repeated substance use despite negative consequences.

SCREENING AND DIAGNOSIS

Toxicology screens, known as drug tests, can be used to determine whether substances are present in the body. The sensitivity of these tests depends on the drug itself, when it was taken, and whether the test is done on blood or urine. Blood tests are more successful at detecting toxic substances, but urine tests are used more often, in part because they can be done at home and are cheaper and less invasive to perform than drawing blood samples.

TREATMENT AND THERAPY

It can be difficult to convince a person with a drug dependence that he or she needs treatment. Denial, a common indicator of addiction, is less of a hurdle when the person is approached and treated with empathy and respect.

Once a problem has been acknowledged, treatment involves stopping the substance use either gradually or abruptly (with a period of detoxification) and providing support for the person to remain drug-free. Dependence is characterized by relapse, as withdrawal from the substance can cause uncomfortable withdrawal symptoms, and many people who want to quit have to try several times. Even after long periods of sobriety, relapses are possible.

The term detoxification refers to a controlled environment in which people may be monitored as their bodily systems return to normal. Medications may be used to control withdrawal symptoms, especially with heavy alcohol use, because suddenly stopping the substance can lead to death in extreme cases of alcohol misuse. Medications are available for treating dependence to nicotine, alcohol, and opiates but not to stimulants or marijuana. Treatment programs exist as in-patient or out-patient services and should be evaluated based on the type of drug misused, the duration of dependence, and whether the goal is to quit entirely or to minimize a habit's deleterious effects.

Twelve-step programs such as Alcoholics Anonymous and Narcotics Anonymous provide networks of support for total abstinence through reliance on a higher power; some people, however, do not respond to the spiritual underpinnings of these programs. Individual and group therapies that employ cognitive-behavioral therapy focus on changing negative thought patterns to alter behaviors, often with the goal of reducing the habit's impact on work and family. Rehabilitation (or rehab) centers exist to separate more seriously dependent patients.

Prevention

Education on drug dependence is important for prevention, as are strategies for coping with stress. These strategies can include meditation, yoga, cognitive-behavioral strategies, physical exercise, and progressive-relaxation techniques. For those who are recovering from dependence, relapse prevention involves avoiding places frequented by people using drugs and developing a new social network that supports the recovering individual in leading a drug-free lifestyle.

Laura B. Smith

For Further Information

American Psychiatric Association. *Diagnostic and Statistical Manual of Mental Disorders.* 5th ed. Washington, DC: Author, 2013. Print.

"Dependence Syndrome." *World Health Organization.* WHO, n.d. Web. 27 Oct. 2015.

Essau, Cecelia A. *Substance Abuse and Dependence in Adolescence: Epidemiology, Risk Factors, and Treatment.* New York: Taylor, 2002. Print.

Kleber, Herbert, et al. "Treatment of Patients with Substance Use Disorders." *American Journal of Psychiatry* 164 (2007): 5–123. Print.

Liptak, John J., Ester Leutenberg, and Amy Brodsky. *The Substance Abuse and Recovery Workbook.* Duluth: Whole Person, 2008. Print.

White, Jason M. *Drug Dependence.* Upper Saddle River: Prentice Hall, 1990. Print.

See also: Codependency; Physiological dependence; Psychological dependence; Science of addiction; Substance misuse

Depressants misuse

Category: Substance misuse

Also known as: Sedative-hypnotic misuse; tranquilizer misuse

Definition: Depressants represent a broad category of substances, with or without clinical use, which reduce the activity of the central nervous system. Included in this category of substances are ethanol, sedative-hypnotics (barbiturates, benzodiazepines), barbiturate-like compounds (chloral hydrate, methaqualone, meprobamate), narcotics (opium, morphine, codeine), marijuana, antihistamines, and some inhalants. Frequently, the term depressants misuse is used in a restricted sense, to designate specifically the nonmedical use of sedative-hypnotic drugs.

Causes

Humans have always sought to alleviate the effects of stress and to reduce anxiety, depression, restlessness, and tension. Alcohol and kava kava are two of the oldest depressant agents. The nineteenth century brought synthetic substances such as bromide salts and chloral hydrate. These were followed by barbiturates and benzodiazepines, which were introduced in the twentieth century.

Depressant misuse is on the rise because of the wide availability of drugs by prescription or through the illicit marketplace. Examples of illegal depressants of misuse include the date rape drugs flunitrazepam (Rohypnol) and gamma-hydroxybutyric acid (GHB, a natural depressant).

Overall, short-acting agents are more likely to be used nonmedically than those with long-lasting effects. Because of their wider margin of safety, benzodiazepines have largely replaced barbiturates. They now constitute the most prescribed central nervous system (CNS) depressants—and the most frequently misused, usually to achieve a general feeling of relaxation. However, barbiturates and barbiturate-like drugs still pose clinical problems, as many young people underestimate the risks these drugs carry. Non-benzodiazepine sedatives, such as zolpidem (Ambien), also can generate misuse and dependence.

Most sedative-hypnotic drugs work by enhancing the inhibitory activity of the neurotransmitter gamma-aminobutyric acid, thus reducing CNS activity and promoting relaxation and sleep. They are usually prescribed to treat sleep disorders, anxiety, acute stress reactions, panic attacks, and seizures. In higher doses, some agents become general anesthetics. Chronic use results in tolerance and dependence (both psychological and physical).

RISK FACTORS

Barbiturate misuse occurs most commonly in mature adults with a long history of use, while benzodiazepines are favored by younger persons (those younger than forty years of age). Two main categories of people misuse depressant drugs. The first category comprises people who receive depressant prescriptions for psychiatric disorders or who obtain them illicitly to cope with stressful life situations. These persons have a high risk of becoming dependent, especially if they receive high doses, take the drug for longer than one month, and have a history of substance misuse or a family history of alcoholism. However, if dose escalation is not evident and drugs are not used to achieve a state of intoxication, chronic benzodiazepine users should not be considered misusers.

A second important category comprises people who use sedative drugs in the context of alcohol or multiple-drug misuse. These people may take benzodiazepines to alleviate insomnia and anxiety (sometimes induced by stimulants), to increase the euphoric effects of opioids, and to diminish cocaine (or alcohol) withdrawal symptoms.

SYMPTOMS

People who misuse depressants often engage in drug-seeking behaviors that include frequently requesting, borrowing, stealing, or forging prescriptions; ordering and purchasing medication online; and visiting several doctors to obtain prescriptions. These behaviors often accompany changes in sleep patterns and irritable mood and increased alcohol consumption. Recreational use and self-medication with depressants may lead to accidental overdoses and suicide attempts. Many persons use a "cocktail" of alcohol and depressant medications for enhanced relaxation and euphoria. This practice is dangerous, as it carries a high risk of overdose.

Sedative-hypnotic drug intoxication resembles alcohol, painkillers, and antihistamine intoxication. It presents with impaired judgment, confusion, drowsiness, dizziness, unsteady movements, slurred speech, and visual disturbances. Young adults attempting to get high may show excitement, loss of inhibition, and even aggressive behavior. Acute GHB intoxication leads to sleep and memory loss. These manifestations occur without alcohol odor on the breath, unless the misuser combined the drug with alcohol. In the case of barbiturates, the behavioral effects of intoxication can vary depending on the time of day, the surroundings, and even the user's expectations.

Tolerance to barbiturates is not accompanied by an increase in lethal dose, as it is with opiates. For this reason, an overdose can be fatal. Signs and symptoms of barbiturate overdose vary, and they include lethargy, decreased heart rate, diminished reflexes, respiratory depression, and cardiovascular collapse.

All sedative-hypnotics can induce physical dependence if taken in sufficient dosage over a long time. Withdrawal from depressant medication results in a "rebound" of nervous system activity. In a mild form, this leads to anxiety and insomnia. In cases of more severe dependence, withdrawal manifests with nausea, vomiting, tremors, seizures, delirium, and ultimately, death. Therefore, discontinuation of prescription drugs necessitates close medical supervision.

SCREENING AND DIAGNOSIS

To evaluate a person who might misuse depressant medication, a doctor will obtain a thorough medical history, ask questions about current and previous drug and alcohol use, and perform a physical examination. A psychiatric evaluation may also be required. The diagnosis of depressant drug misuse relies on evidence of dose escalation, on obtaining multiple prescriptions, and on taking the drug for purposes other than those stated in the prescription.

Multiple tests detect the presence of drugs and also potential medical complications. These include drug screening (urine and blood), electrolyte and liver profiles, an electrocardiogram, and X-ray and magnetic resonance imaging.

TREATMENT AND THERAPY

Therapeutic strategies for depressants misuse vary according to the drug used, the severity of the manifestations, and the duration of drug action. Common therapies include detoxification, which involves the use of agents that reverse the effects of the drug (for example, using Flumazenil for benzodiazepine misuse and using Naloxone for narcotics misuse). Other common therapies include the use of medications that mitigate withdrawal symptoms, counseling in inpatient or outpatient settings, support groups, and relaxation training. When a person receiving treatment has combined a CNS depressant with alcohol or other drugs, all aspects of this addiction have to be addressed and treated.

PREVENTION

Sedative-hypnotic medication should be used only as prescribed. Combinations of CNS depressants (such as alcohol/drug or over-the-counter drug/prescription medication) pose high risks and should be avoided.

People who are unsure of a drug's effects, or who suspect dependence, should consult a pharmacist or a doctor. Those people who are contemplating the discontinuation of a CNS depressant or who are experiencing withdrawal symptoms should seek medical care immediately.

A careful assessment is necessary before prescribing depressant medication in persons with a history of drug misuse. These individuals require close monitoring. Also, caregivers and health care providers should verify that there are no alternative sources for obtaining the drug of misuse.

Mihaela Avramut MD, PhD

FOR FURTHER INFORMATION

Hanson, Glen R., Peter J. Venturelli, and Annette E. Fleckenstein. *Drugs and Society.* 9th ed. Sudbury: Jones, 2006. Print.

Parker, James N., and Philip M. Parker. *The Official Patient's Sourcebook on Prescription CNS Depressants Dependence.* San Diego: Icon, 2002. Print.

Sadock, Benjamin J., and Virginia A. Sadock. *Kaplan and Sadock's Synopsis of Psychiatry: Behavioral Sciences/Clinical Psychiatry.* 10th ed. Philadelphia: Lippincott, 2007. Print.

Sue, David, Derald Wing Sue, and Stanley Sue. *Understanding Abnormal Behavior.* Boston: Wadsworth, 2010. Print.

See also: Prescription drug addiction: Overview; Psychosis and substance misuse; Sedative-Hypnotic misuse

Depression

CATEGORY: Psychological issues and behaviors
DEFINITION: Depression, addiction, and depression, depression, or clinical depression, is a serious mental illness that can lead to self-neglect and self-abuse, including substance misuse, which can lead to addiction.

INTRODUCTION

Severe depression that is acute and of short duration is known as major depression. Seasonal adjustment disorder is a type of acute major depression, and mild chronic depression lasting more than two years is known as dysthymia. Clinical depression is thought to be caused in most cases by a chemical imbalance in the brain. This imbalance can occur among a number of naturally occurring chemicals, including neurotransmitters, vitamins, and amino acids.

Symptoms of depression include loss of interest in normal activities, fatigue, sleeping problems, weight loss or gain, sexual dysfunction, and thoughts of death and suicide.

The National Alliance on Mental Illness estimates that as many as 15 million Americans suffer from depression in a given year. The 2004 *World Health Report* (World Health Organization) reported that major depressive orders affect 6.7 percent of adults in the United States, about 14.8 million people. Depression is the major cause of disability in people age fifteen to forty-four years in the United States and in Canada.

ADDICTION

Addiction is roughly defined as a chronic, relapsing disease that affects both the brain and behavior. Like depression, addiction has a biochemical component and is considered a mental illness. The accepted scientific model of addiction suggests that addiction is involved with the pleasure centers of the brain. Chemicals in these centers are activated when a person ingests certain substances or engages in certain behaviors.

Many pleasure-inducing substances, such as chocolate, and pleasurable behaviors, such as listening to music, cause no harm. However, some substances and behaviors are destructive and can become addictions. Addiction to nicotine, alcohol, and certain illegal and prescription drugs is well documented. People also can become addicted to activities such as gambling, sex, web surfing, pornography, and shopping. People with destructive addictions generally have little or no control over their addiction and spend a great deal of time obsessing over it.

When a person uses a pleasure-inducing substance excessively and repeatedly, his or her body becomes saturated with metabolites, metabolites, the chemicals in a substance that the body converts (metabolizes) into nutrients or energy. Some metabolites, especially those found in alcohol and certain drugs, become trapped in fatty tissue in the body. If a person stops using the substance, the metabolites are released back into the bloodstream, causing the brain to react as if the body were withdrawing from the substance. The pleasure centers in the brain accustomed to dealing with large amounts of the metabolites now must cope with only a small amount of the available chemicals. The brain then calls for, even demands, the substance. This is known as a craving, an uncomfortable and sometimes agonizing biological response accompanied by mental distress. The only way to end the craving is to take more of the substance, and the addictive cycle repeats. In medical terms, the user relapses.

DEPRESSION WITH ADDICTION

Some people suffer from both depression and addiction in varying degrees. This condition is known as a dual diagnosis, dual diagnosis, and depression or a co-occurring disorder, co-occurring disorder, and depression. These terms apply to a condition in which a person has at least one addictive disorder, such as alcoholism, and one major mental disorder, such as depression. Questions then arise: How common are these co-occurring disorders? What is the relationship between depression and addiction? Does one cause or contribute to the other?

As might be expected, the exact number of diagnosed cases of co-occurring disorders for any given period or population is difficult to determine. More studies need to be done. However, a small number of studies conducted since the 1980s reveals some interesting data.

One study found that, when compared with the general population, people with mood disorders like depression were twice as likely to also have an addictive disorder, and people with an addictive disorder were about twice as likely to have a mood disorder. Another study found that about 53 percent of drug misusers and 37 percent of alcohol misusers suffered from at least one serious mental illness. A series of national household surveys on health and drug use conducted by the US Department of Health and Human Services in the early 2000s revealed co-occurring disorders in about 5.2 million adults, 2.4 percent of full-time employed adults, and 31 percent of adults using homeless services. In 2004 an estimated 192,690 persons in emergency rooms for drug-related incidents had co-occurring disorders.

Chemical changes and imbalances are characteristic of both depression and addiction. Studies have shown that depression and other mental illnesses can trigger addiction, that addiction can contribute to depression, and that depression and addiction share common risk factors. It is not clear, however, that one disorder actually causes the other, or which disorder came first.

DEPRESSION AS RISK

A common cause of clinical depression is the imbalance or dysregulation of the chemicals serotonin, serotonin, and depression and dopamine, dopamine, and depression. Among their many functions in the human body, these chemicals are involved with mood, emotions, and the experience of pain and pleasure. They are sometimes called the reward molecules. The lack or dysfunction of either of these chemicals can trigger depression symptoms.

To relieve the symptoms, many people with clinical depression self-medicate, turning to food or drugs or alcohol to boost themselves, as these substances react positively on the pleasure receptors of the brain. This sometimes works for a while. Eventually, however, symptoms return and the addictive cycle continues. Alcohol, in particular, is counterproductive. Because it is a depressant, it can lessen the effect of antidepressant medications (a common treatment for depression).

ADDICTION AS RISK

Addiction can intensify or trigger depression and other mental illness symptoms. Addicts often experience depression and anxiety over their lack of control. A well-documented example is the prevalence of depression among obese people, especially children.

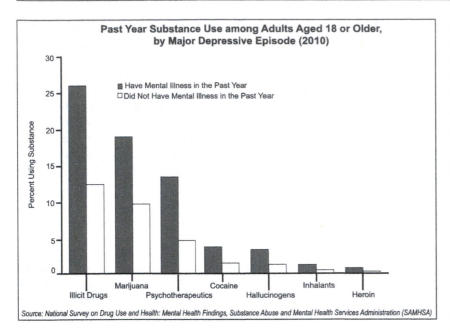

Past Year Substance Use among Adults Aged 18 or Older, by Major Depressive Episode (2010)

■ Have Mental Illness in the Past Year
□ Did Not Have Mental Illness in the Past Year

Source: National Survey on Drug Use and Health: Mental Health Findings, Substance Abuse and Mental Health Services Administration (SAMHSA)

Food is a pleasure-inducing substance, and out-of-control overeaters are as much addicts as are alcoholics.

Many alcoholics have depression because of the harmful effects of alcohol on their relationships, careers, and physical and emotional health. As a drug, alcohol is classified as a depressant. It slows brain activity and the function of the central nervous system, which affects a person's movement, perception, and emotions.

Drug users also risk depression. Marijuana, cocaine, and hallucinogens raise dopamine levels and provide short-lived pleasure. Misusers often "crash," however, and sink into a depression when they stop using. Also, misuse of some of these drugs can result in psychosis and other forms of severe mental illness.

Common Risks

Depression and addiction can stem from the same source separately or simultaneously. Research has found shared risk factors between the two disorders. Genetic factors, for example, make it more likely that some people will develop either disorder or that one disorder will develop once the other has surfaced. Brain development problems can lead an adolescent, or even a child, to early drug use, which can lead to depression later in life. Environmental factors such as trauma and stress can trigger both depression and addiction. Certain regions of the brain, such as the area that handles response to stress, are adversely affected by both depression and addiction.

Treatment

Both depression and addiction can be treated separately, although focusing on one does not mean the other will disappear. Many medical and behavioral professionals maintain that dysthymia (chronic depression) and addiction can only be treated, not cured. Nevertheless, research has found that an integrated approach to treatment for both disorders (that is, treatment that occurs at the same time and in the same setting) can be effective. Successful integrated treatment is individualized, coordinated, and long term.

A specialized team of health care professionals and service providers, working with each patient, creates a personalized illness model and treatment program. In addition to the traditional medications and talk therapy, interventions and services might include detoxification, behavioral modification therapy, pain management, family counseling, diet and wellness counseling, job training, and the teaching of relationship and money-management skills. Family involvement and peer support are important components of integrated treatment. Each patient proceeds at his or her own pace, often taking years to recover. Relapses are common, even expected, because of the complex nature of treating two disorders simultaneously.

A number of integrated treatment centers have formed across the United States. Many centers accept insurance from most providers. This relatively new approach to treating co-occurring disorders shows much promise.

Wendell Anderson BA

For Further Information

Dosh, Tyanne, et al. "Comparison of the Associations of Caffeine and Cigarette Use with Depressive and ADHD Symptoms in a Sample of Young Adult Smokers." *Journal of Addiction Medicine* 4 (2010): 52–54. Print. Report on a study of the relationship between caffeine use and psychiatric symptoms in young adult cigarette smokers.

Schwartz, Thomas L., and Timothy Petersen, eds. "Depression and Addiction." *Depression: Treatment Strategies and Management.* 2nd ed. London: Informa, 2009. This chapter reviews evidence of genetic causes of depression and addiction.

Westermeyer, Joseph J., Roger D. Weiss, and Douglas M. Ziedonis, eds. *Integrated Treatment for Mood and Substance Use Disorders.* Baltimore: Johns Hopkins UP, 2003. Clinicians discuss co-occurring disorders and their treatment.

See also: Co-occurring disorders; Depressants misuse; Mental illness

---

Designated drivers

Category: Social issues

Definition: Designated drivers are sober drivers who are designated to transport people who have consumed alcohol. The concept was spearheaded as a public safety campaign at the national level in the United States.

History

The National Highway Transportation Safety Administration (NHTSA), the US Department of Transportation (DOT), and the Ad Council were the lead agencies in bringing public attention to the dangers of impaired driving in the United States. The Ad Council has worked with relevant US government agencies in using the power of media to enhance awareness and foster action against drinking and driving.

The Friends Don't Let Friends Drive Drunk campaign, formed by the DOT and the Ad Council, effectively illuminated problems associated with drinking and driving. The public service announcement (PSA) campaign called Innocent Victims focused on the victims of alcohol-related automobile accidents. Moving beyond television, PSAs have been delivered through radio, print, and online.

Mission and Goals

Designated driver programs alert the public about designating a driver to remain sober on all outings involving alcohol consumption, so that those who choose to consume alcohol at such outings will not later drive a vehicle while drunk or will not ride in a vehicle driven by an impaired driver. This safe ride concept, which also involves variously funded, alternative transportation, is an important component of community-based, designated-driver programs.

Support for designated-driver programs comes from civic organizations, foundations, community groups, local residents, and businesses. The scope of this support ranges from community-wide efforts to independent programs. Endorsement can come from law enforcement, public health, education, and service groups. The NHTSA's Safe Communities program involves forming coalitions that promote issues associated with traffic, road, highway, and personal safety.

Effectiveness

The NHTSA notes that almost 80 percent of drivers report being influenced by the Friends Don't Let Friends Drive Drunk campaign of the DOT. These drivers took steps to prevent others from driving under the influence of alcohol. In addition, 25 percent of drivers report that the campaign helped them to refrain from drinking and driving. The importance of such campaigns is underscored by data provided in a NHTSA report that about sixteen thousand people die in the United States each year in alcohol-related motor vehicle accidents. Furthermore, a three-component program recently announced by the NHTSA offers the public a program of enhanced law enforcement, offender prosecution and adjudication, and relevant medical and mental health services.

Ronna F. Dillon PhD and Laurel D. Dillon-Sumner BA

For Further Information

DeJong, William, and Jay A. Winsten. "The Use of Designated Drivers by US College Students: A National Study." *Journal of American College Health* 47.4 (1999): 151–56. Print.

Kazbour, Richard R., and Jon S. Bailey. "An Analysis of a Contingency Program on Designated Drivers at a College Bar." *Journal of Applied Behavior Analysis* 43.2 (2010). Print.

Lange, James E., et al. "The Efficacy of Experimental Interventions Designed to Reduce Drinking among Designated Drivers." *Journal of Studies on Alcohol* 67.2 (2006): 261–68. Print.

See also: Drugged driving; Drunk driving; Prevention methods and research

Designer drugs

CATEGORY: Substances

ALSO KNOWN AS: Club drugs; party drugs; recreational drugs

DEFINITION: Designer drugs are illegal synthetic analogs of controlled substances that possess similar pharmacological qualities. Designer drugs encompass a wide range of stimulants, depressants, hallucinogens, and opiates. They are produced and purchased as alternatives to traditional drugs of misuse to bypass regulations on the sale and use of controlled substances.

STATUS: Most are illegal globally, however novel chemical structures sometimes are not covered by current regulations

CLASSIFICATION: Most are Schedule 1 controlled substances

SOURCE: Illicit laboratories distributed globally, frequently manufactured in China, the Netherlands, and the USA.

TRANSMISSION ROUTE: Ingested in a wide variety of ways including orally, nasally, intravenously, inhalation, smoking

HISTORY OF USE

Designer drugs became popular in the 1970s as a way to bypass existing regulations on controlled substances. After the Controlled Substances Act (1970) restricted the availability of illicit substances, clandestine chemists began modifying and manufacturing synthetic alternatives with similar pharmacological effects. Designer-drug production and trafficking became widespread, producing cheaper and stronger alternatives.

Some designer drugs were originally intended for medical use; others were created strictly for recreational use. The first designer drugs included hallucinogens and synthetic substitutes for heroin and amphetamine. By the 1980s, many designer drugs became known as club drugs and gained popularity among young people at underground dance parties, bars, and nightclubs.

During the 1980s, the drugs caused numerous overdose deaths worldwide. By 1986, the widespread manufacture and misuse of designer drugs prompted legislators in the United States to modify the Controlled Substances Act and add the Federal Analog Act to include all chemically similar substances and possible derivatives as controlled substances. As certain formulations are made illegal, novel analogs come onto the market, making it difficult to identify and control their distribution and use.

Designer drugs make up a substantial portion of the illegal drug market. Newer classes of designer drugs such as synthetic cathinones (bath salts), and synthetic cannabinoids (K2, Spice) are continually being developed, marketed, and sold. Despite efforts to curb designer drug production, their misuse and popularity continue to be a concern. Because the chemical structure can be modified to circumvent legal restrictions, these substances have exploded in diversity. They are often found as adulterants to other well-known psychoactive drugs as they are often cheaper with somewhat similar effects. This leads to complex and unpredictable effects to users.

COMMON DESIGNER DRUGS

Common designer drugs include hallucinogens and

Foxy

Foxy is a hallucinogenic drug in the tryptamine family, similar to psilocybin (mushrooms). It is used recreationally as a psychedelic.

Foxy most frequently appears in tablet or capsule form. The drug was first synthesized by Alexander Shulgin, and its chemical creation was reported by him in 1980. With the placement of MDMA (ecstasy) under legal control in the United States in 1985, foxy began to appear in the illicit-drug street trade.

Foxy, named in 1999, was first called Eve to contrast with Adam, a name used occasionally for ecstasy. Foxy soon became more widely known as a designer street drug and became popular in dance clubs and raves and other such venues, where the use of club drugs, particularly ecstasy, was well established.

depressants as well as synthetic substitutes for heroin and amphetamine. The most popular amphetamine or speed analogs include methamphetamine and methylenedioxymethamphetamine (MDMA, or ecstasy).

Methamphetamine, known variously as "meth," "crystal," "ice," "speed," and "crank," is one of the most addictive designer drugs available. It is a commonly misused drug in rural communities as well as in LGBTQ communities. By the 1960s, methamphetamine misuse reached epidemic proportions.

MDMA has both stimulant and hallucinogenic properties and is related to amphetamine and mescaline. MDMA is a drug used for its rush of euphoria followed by heightened sociability and hallucinations. It is common in clubs and raves. Overdose is uncommon but deaths have been attributed due to its ability to cause severe dehydration and hyponatremia. It is commonly co-administered with other drugs or easily adulterated, leading to increased risk of adverse effects.

Hallucinogenic designer drugs include LSD and PCP. LSD, or acid, is the most widely known of the hallucinogenic drugs. It is an extremely potent semi-synthetic psychedelic drug derived from lysergic acid. PCP, or angel dust, derivatives were popular in the 1970s. PCP, originally developed as a surgical anesthetic, is a dangerous and unpredictable hallucinogen; users can experience horrifying and violent hallucinations.

A synthetic heroin alternative is -methylfentanyl (China white), among other similar fentanyl derivatives. Fentanyl is the extremely high potency opiate that has been progressively more common in the illicit market. China white gained popularity as a recreational drug among heroin users as a cheaper and more powerful alternative.

In the last decade, two synthetic drugs have exploded in popularity, cathinones, and cannabinoids. Synthetic cathinones (commonly 'bath salts'), was first sold legally in the early 2010s. Bath salts were made illegal shortly thereafter as the severe and common overdoses appeared in US emergency departments. Synthetic Cannabinoids (K2, Spice) act on the same endocannabinoid system as Tetrahydrocannabinol (THC), the psychoactive component of marijuana.

They were marketed heavily in the late 2000s and sold as a "legal high." High dose misuse is, however, associated with severe effects including marked hallucinations and psychosis. The psychological effects can be permanent. These drugs have progressively been banned by the global drug enforcement agencies, however, their diverse structural modification possibilities have made them difficult to control.

EFFECTS AND POTENTIAL RISKS

Designer drugs have diverse and unpredictable effects for a number of reasons. Firstly, they are developed to circumvent legal restrictions, increase their potency, and change their effects. This complicates our understanding because slight modifications in their chemical structure can create markedly different physiologic effects. They can lack a significant scientific and illicit use history, so their effects can be largely undocumented in humans. Secondly, as they are sold illegally, they are often misrepresented or adulterated leading to unpredictable effects of users. Mixing drugs, both intentionally and unintentionally, leads to synergistic effects, often increasing the harmful and possibly deadly effects.

Stimulants, like methamphetamine, increase brain activity by increasing the neurotransmitter dopamine, producing euphoria, excitement, and increased energy. At higher doses, they cause increased physiologic responses including rapid heartbeat, hyperthermia, and psychomotor agitation. Chronic use can cause severe anxiety, psychosis, anorexia, and disturbed sleep. Methamphetamine has a high addictive potential.

MDMA has both stimulant and hallucinogenic effects via activity on norepinephrine, dopamine, and serotonin. It produces euphoria, sense of well-being, social connectedness, empathy, visual hallucinations. Its negative effects include rapid heartbeat, sweating, tremors, jaw clenching. At high doses it can cause hyperthermia, hyponatremia (low blood sodium), dehydration, marked psychomotor agitation and has rarely led to deaths. Chronic use can cause anxiety, panic attacks, sleep disturbance as well as some psychological dependence. There is current research into the therapeutic possibilities of MDMA use in monitored, guided psychotherapy for the treatment of post-traumatic stress disorder (PTSD).

Hallucinogens, like LSD and PCP, have a well-known misuse history and documented effects. These drugs bind to serotonin receptors in the brain, producing sensory distortions. This leads to complex visual and perceptual hallucinations, thought wandering, and disinhibition. These thought disturbances and mood modifications can be long-term to permanent. LSD by itself has no lethal effects, however, deaths have been recorded that are attributed to accidents like falling or driving while under the influence. PCP has stronger hallucinogenic effects in humans. It may cause extreme and horrifying hallucinations as well as violent and combative behavior.

Opiates act by binding opioid receptors in the brain to alter pain responses. It is misused as it produces euphoria, sense of release, and dulling of sensations. Overdose, due to high doses or re-dosing, is common for users. High doses cause severe respiratory depression leading to death. Overdose can be reversed with the use of the drug naloxone in the emergency department or with auto-injectors. Opiates have an extreme physiologic dependence and addiction potential. Withdrawal is not considered lethal but is extremely difficult for patients and causes severe symptoms. Long-term use leads to depression, irritability, behavioral changes, and infection risk.

Newer synthetic cathinones (bath salts) have little data on human effects and our understanding is mostly based on rat models. Bath salts interact with monoamine transporters causing alterations in norepinephrine, serotonin, and dopamine. Acting on the same mechanisms as cocaine and methamphetamine, acute symptoms include psychosis, hallucinations, agitation, rapid heartbeat, high blood pressure, combative and violent behavior, convulsions and death. They have marked addiction potential in rat models.

Synthetic cannabinoids (K2, spice) bind the same endocannabinoid system in the brain as THC. They cause marijuana-like intoxication. Misuse has been associated with highly prevalent severe effects including hallucinations, agitation, seizures, and permanent psychosis. There is unclear addictive potential.

Rose Ciulla-Bohling, PhD; Updated by Denis Folan, DO

FOR FURTHER INFORMATION

Baumann, Michael, H. et al. "Bath Salts, Spice and Related Designer Drugs: The Science behind the Headlines." 2014, *The Journal of Neuroscience* 34(46):15150-15158.

Clayton, Lawrence. *Designer Drugs*. New York: Rosen, 1998. Print.

Gahlinger, Paul M. *Illegal Drugs: A Complete Guide to Their History, Chemistry, Use, and Abuse*. New York: Plume, 2004. Print.

Goldberg, Raymond. *Drugs across the Spectrum*. 7th ed. Belmont: Wadsworth, 2014. Print.

Hanson, Glen R., Peter J. Venturelli, and Annette E. Fleckenstein. *Drugs and Society*. 12th ed. Burlington: Jones, 2014. Print.

National Institute on Drug Abuse. "Drug Facts: MDMA." National Institute on Drug Abuse, 2018. https://www.drugabuse.gov/publications/drugfacts/mdma-ecstasymolly

National Institute on Drug Abuse. "Research Reports: MDMA." NIDA, 2018, www.drugabuse.gov/publications/research-reports/mdma-ecstasy-abuse/Introduction.

Olive, M. Foster. *Designer Drugs*. Philadelphia: Chelsea House, 2004. Print.

Substance Abuse and Mental Health Services Administration. "Hallucinogens" SAMHSA, 2018. https://www.samhsa.gov/atod/hallucinogens.

Substance Abuse and Mental Health Services Administration. "Stimulants" SAMHSA, 2018. https://www.samhsa.gov/atod/stimulants.

See also: Adolescents and drug misuse; Club drugs; Ketamine; LSD; MDMA; Rohypnol

Detoxification and substance misuse

CATEGORY: Treatment

DEFINITION: Detoxification, also referred to as detox, is the removal of harmful substances from the body with necessary supportive care, which may include the administration of medication or other therapies, such as hemodialysis.

Overview

Detoxification (detox) is applied to chronic situations of substance misuse, such as alcoholism and drug addiction. It also applies to acute conditions such as alcohol poisoning caused by binge drinking and drug overdoses. Detox is only the first step in the resolution of a substance misuse problem. It removes the substance from the body and restores homeostasis (a state of normalcy), but it does not remove the person's desire to ingest the substance again. Follow-up care is essential to reduce the likelihood of continued substance misuse.

Alcohol Detoxification

Alcohol detox is necessary in cases of alcohol poisoning caused by the rapid ingestion of a large quantity of alcohol over a short time and in cases of long-term alcohol misuse (alcoholism). Most cases of alcohol poisoning are caused by ingestion of ethanol (C_2H_5OH), which is a component of beer, wine, and hard liquor. Ethanol is produced by the fermentation of sugar.

Some cases of alcohol poisoning are caused by methanol (CH_3OH) or isopropyl alcohol (C_3H_8O). Methanol is primarily used in the production of other chemicals; it is sometimes used as an automotive fuel. Isopropyl alcohol is a component of rubbing alcohol and is widely used as a solvent and cleaning fluid.

The amount of alcohol in the body is usually measured as the blood alcohol content (BAC). The BAC is expressed as the percentage of alcohol per liter of blood. Alcohol consumption is also measured by the number of drinks consumed.

Alcohol Poisoning. Treatment of alcohol poisoning consists of supportive measures as the body metabolizes the alcohol. These measures include insertion of an airway (endotracheal tube) to prevent vomiting and aspiration of stomach contents into the lungs; close monitoring of vital signs (temperature, heart rate, and blood pressure); oxygen; medication to increase blood pressure and heart rate, if necessary; respiratory support, if necessary; maintenance of body temperature (blankets or warming devices); and intravenous fluids to prevent dehydration. Glucose should be added to fluids if the patient is hypoglycemic (has low blood sugar). Thiamine is often added to fluids to reduce the risk of a seizure. A final measure is hemodialysis (blood cleansing), which might be needed in cases of dangerously high BACs (more than 0.4 percent). Hemodialysis is also necessary if methanol or isopropyl alcohol has been ingested.

Alcoholism. Withdrawal symptoms from long-term alcohol misuse may range in severity from mild tremors to seizures, which can be life-threatening. Approximately 5 percent of patients undergoing alcohol withdrawal have delirium tremens (DTs), which are characterized by shaking, confusion, and hallucinations. DTs also cause large increases in heart rate, respiration, pulse, and blood pressure. These symptoms usually appear two to four days after abstinence from alcohol. Withdrawal may require up to one week. Patients suffering from DTs require inpatient care at a hospital or a treatment center.

Although some patients with less severe symptoms also receive inpatient care, many can be successfully treated as outpatients. Sedatives are administered to control withdrawal symptoms, which range from anxiety to seizures.

Drug Detoxification

A patient in need of detox can be either a long-term substance misuser or a person who has had an acute drug-related episode (for example, an overdose). Drugs requiring detox include both illegal substances such as heroin and cocaine and prescription medications used inappropriately. Most cases of drug misuse involve psychoactive (mood-altering) substances. Psychoactive substances are either central nervous system (CNS) stimulants (cocaine and methamphetamine) or CNS depressants (heroin or barbiturates). Many substance misusers ingest more than one drug with different properties, which complicates detox measures. Drugs are sometimes ingested with alcohol, which is a CNS depressant.

Long-term substance misusers are admitted voluntarily to a health care facility, through the prompting of friends or relatives, or by court order. Initially, health care staff take a complete medical history (with particular attention to substances used). This history is followed by a physical examination and laboratory tests, which check for levels of substances in the bloodstream. A treatment plan is formulated based on the duration of misuse and on the substances involved.

The condition of persons experiencing an acute drug-related episode ranges from euphoric to comatose; furthermore, the status may change rapidly. For example, a relatively alert person may lapse into a coma, have a seizure, or suffer cardiac arrest. For a person with a drug overdose, detox consists of supportive measures similar to those for alcohol poisoning. If a CNS stimulant was ingested, medication may need to be administered to lower the patient's heart rate, blood pressure, and respiration. If a CNS depressant was ingested, medication may need to be administered to raise these parameters.

The first step of detox is to evaluate the patient's physical and mental status and determine the types of substances involved. In some cases, information can be obtained from the person, witnesses, or physical evidence (such as syringes or pill containers). If this information is not available, medical staff conduct laboratory tests to determine the substances (and amount) present in the bloodstream.

If necessary, supportive measures such as oxygen administration, respiratory assistance, and intravenous medication will be initiated. Usually, medication is required to guide the patient through the detox process. Patients will be told of the medications used during treatment. The detox process may take one or two weeks and can be done on an inpatient or outpatient basis, or in combination.

For people with a serious substance misuse problem, inpatient care is often necessary. These programs include detox followed by counseling, group therapy, and medical treatment. A benefit of an inpatient program is that it greatly reduces the risk of a patient gaining access to harmful substances. For anyone who receives inpatient care, regular outpatient follow-up is essential. Many medical centers include treatment for substance misuse. Stand-alone facilities also are present throughout the United States and in other developed nations. Some provide care in a basic, clinical setting while others function in a resort-like setting. One well-known facility is the Betty Ford Center (in Rancho Mirage, California), which was founded by former US First Lady Betty Ford. The one-hundred-bed nonprofit residential facility offers inpatient, outpatient, and day treatment for substance misusers. It also provides prevention and education programs for family members (including children) of substance misusers.

RAPID DETOXIFICATION

Rapid detox is a controversial treatment method for addiction to opiates such as heroin. In rapid detox, the patient is placed under a general anesthetic and is administered drugs such as naltrexone, which block the brain's opiate receptors from any circulating opiates. Additional medications are administered to accelerate the physical reactions to the rapid withdrawal while the patient is unconscious. Proponents of the process state that the procedure not only shortens the withdrawal process but also avoids much of the associated pain, which can be severe. Opponents point to studies that some patients undergo serious complications and death, and to other studies that describe the return of withdrawal symptoms after the patient awakens from the anesthetic. Critics also note that the treatment can be expensive.

NICOTINE DETOXIFICATION

Nicotine , which is contained in tobacco leaves, is highly addictive. In addition, cigarette smoking (or chewing) has pleasurable associations and induces stress relief. This component of smoking markedly increases the likelihood of a relapse. Detox occurs on an outpatient basis with the use of aids such as nicotine patches or gum, which are gradually decreased in amount.

Innumerable resources are available to individuals who desire to quit smoking. These resources include personal physicians, smoking-cessation clinics, and self-help groups. Some people can simply quit smoking on their own and endure the withdrawal symptoms, which include strong cravings for a cigarette, restlessness, and irritability. Withdrawal from nicotine takes one to two weeks after last dose.

Robin L. Wulffson MD

FOR FURTHER INFORMATION

Bean, Philip, and Teresa Nemitz. *Drug Treatment: What Works?* New York: Routledge, 2004. Print.

Fisher, Gary, and Thomas Harrison. *Substance Abuse: Information for School Counselors, Social Workers, Therapists, and Counselors.* 4th ed. Boston: Allyn, 2008. Print.

Liptak, John, et al. *Substance Abuse and Recovery Workbook.* Whole Person, 2008. Print.

Miller, William. *Rethinking Substance Abuse: What the Science Shows, and What We Should Do About It.* New York: Guilford, 2010. Print.

Seixas, Judith. *Children of Alcoholism: A Survivor's Manual.* New York: Harper, 1986. Print.

See also: Addiction medications; Alcohol misuse; Alcohol poisoning; Treatment methods and research

Dextroamphetamine

CATEGORY: Substances

ALSO KNOWN AS: Dexedrine

DEFINITION: Dextroamphetamine is a stimulant used medically for narcolepsy, attention-deficit hyperactivity disorder, and in the treatment of depression.

STATUS: Legal in the United States and in other countries, including Australia and Great Britain

CLASSIFICATION: Schedule II controlled substance

SOURCE: Dextroamphetamine sulfate is the dextroisomer of the compound d,1-amphetamine sulfate. Dextroamphetamine is categorized as an amphetamine and is a sympathomimetic amine of the amphetamine group.

TRANSMISSION ROUTE: Oral ingestion of tablets, capsules, or solution. Crushed tablets can be snorted or injected.

HISTORY OF USE

Dextroamphetamine is classified as a stimulant. The drug was approved by the US Food and Drug Administration (FDA) in 1976 and is available in generic and brand formulations. The misuse of this and other stimulant pharmacologic compounds, and the prescription rates for attention deficit hyperactivity disorder (ADHD) medications, has increased since 2000. Prescription amphetamines, including dextroamphetamine, are misused to enhance focus, to lose weight, and to get high.

EFFECTS AND POTENTIAL RISKS

Dextroamphetamine produces both central nervous system (CNS) and peripheral effects. In the CNS, dextroamphetamine has a stimulant effect; peripherally it raises blood pressure and produces weak brochodilatory and respiratory stimulation. Additionally, stimulants in general are known to increase focus and attention, which can help students during their studies. Dextroamphetamine is misused by teenagers and young adults as a diet aid. The drug suppresses feelings of hunger, leading the user to eat less and lose weight.

Short-term risks associated with dextroamphetamine are similar to those seen with other stimulants. Persons with preexisting hypertension or cardiovascular conditions are at a higher risk for cardiac complications. Increased aggression, hostility, and mixed or manic episodes in people with preexisting psychiatric conditions have been reported. Long-term use can lead to dependence, and abruptly stopping the medication can cause withdrawal symptoms, including fatigue, depression, and sleep abnormalities.

Allison C. Bennett PharmD

FOR FURTHER INFORMATION

Grabowski, John, et al. "Dextroamphetamine for Cocaine-Dependence Treatment: A Double-Blind Randomized Clinical Trial." *Journal of Clinical Psychopharmacology* 21 (2001): 522–26. Print.

Williams, Robert J., et al. "Methylphenidate and Dextroamphetamine Abuse in Substance-Abusing Adolescents." *American Journal of Addictions* 13 (2004): 381–89. Print.

Wu, Li-Tzy, et al. "Misuse of Methamphetamine and Prescription Stimulants among Youths and Young Adults in the Community." *Drug and Alcohol Dependence* 89 (2007): 195–205. Print.

See also: Depression; Prescription drug addiction: Overview; Stimulant misuse; Stimulants' effects on the body

Dextromethorphan

CATEGORY: Substances

ALSO KNOWN AS: CCC; DXM; poor man's PCP; robo; skittles; triple C

DEFINITION: Dextromethorphan is a cough suppressant contained in dozens of over-the-counter medications, and it is increasingly being misused for its dissociative opioid effects.

STATUS: Legal in many countries worldwide

CLASSIFICATION: Unclassified

SOURCE: Widely produced as an additive to cough and cold preparations in the form of liquids, tablets, and capsules

TRANSMISSION ROUTE: Oral ingestion

HISTORY OF USE

Familiar since the 1950s to people with coughs and colds, dextromethorphan (DXM) was originally developed as a safer alternative to the codeine cough syrups that were then common. DXM was long considered devoid of any potential for misuse, even though it is an opioid derivative. When taken at higher than recommended doses, however, DXM produces dissociative hallucinogenic effects. As a result, since the 1990s, misuse of over-the-counter (OTC) medications, including DXM, has grown. In 2011, only alcohol, tobacco, and cannabis were misused more frequently than OTC medications.

EFFECTS AND POTENTIAL RISKS

DXM acts in the brain and spinal cord to inhibit receptors for N-methyl-d-aspartate (NMDA). As such, DXM—along with other NMDA antagonists—alters distribution of the neurotransmitter glutamate throughout the brain, in turn altering the user's perception of pain, the user's understanding of the environment, and the user's memory. Subjective effects include euphoria, hallucinations, paranoid delusions, confusion, agitation, altered moods, difficulty concentrating, nightmares, catatonia, ataxia, and anesthesia. The typical clinical presentation of DXM intoxication involves hyperexcitability, lethargy, ataxia, slurred speech, sweating, hypertension, and nystagmus.

Misusers of DXM describe the following dose-dependent plateaus: mild stimulation at a dosage between 100 and 200 milligrams (mg); euphoria and hallucinations begin at a dosage of between 200 and 400 mg; between 300 and 600 mg, the user will experience distorted visual perception and loss of motor coordination; and between 500 and 1,500 mg, the user will experience dissociative sedation. These effects are experienced only when a person has consumed vastly more DXM than recommended for normal therapeutic use.

This consumptive practice is particularly dangerous when DXM is combined with other active ingredients, such as pseudoephedrine, acetaminophen, or guaifenesin. Health risks associated with abusing these latter substances include increased blood pressure (pseudoephedrine), potential liver damage (acetaminophen), and central nervous system toxicity, cardiovascular toxicity, and anticholinergic toxicity (antihistamines).

Michael R. Meyers PhD

FOR FURTHER INFORMATION

Cherkes, Joseph. "Dextromethorphan-Induced Neurological Illness in a Patient with Negative Toxicology Findings." *Neurology* 66 (2006): 1952–53. Print.

"DrugFacts: Cough and Cold Medicine Abuse." *National Institute on Drug Abuse*. NIH, May 2014. Web. 27 Oct. 2015.

Heller, Jacob L. "Dextromethorphan Overdose." *Medline Plus*. US Nat'l. Lib. of Medicine, 18 Jan. 2014. Web 27 Oct. 2015.

Lachover, Leonard. "Deciphering a Psychosis: A Case of Dextromethorphan-Induced Symptoms." *Primary Psychiatry* 14 (2007): 70–72. Print.

Zawertailo, Laurie A., et al. "Effect of Metabolic Blockade on the Psychoactive Effects of Dextromethorphan." *Human Psychopharmacology* 25 (2010): 71–79. Print.

See also: Cough and cold medications addiction; Over-the-counter drugs of misuse

Diagnosis methods

CATEGORY: Diagnosis and prevention

DEFINITION: Before treating addictions, health practitioners must be sure that the addiction actually exists. They must differentiate between alcohol and drug abuse and alcohol and drug addiction. To do this, health practitioners must complete an initial assessment of their patients' conditions and then make their diagnosis. A diagnosis is the identification of an illness or a condition. After a health practitioner diagnoses a patient, he or she must develop a suggested method of treatment for the patient's condition.

ASSESSMENT METHODS

The diagnosis process is typically initiated by the patient or the patient's loved ones. The patient and his or her family may request the help of their family doctor. Depending on the family doctor's knowledge of and experience with diagnosing alcohol and drug addictions, the doctor may decide to perform the addiction assessment him- or herself or may refer the patient to a specialist or therapist.

Physicians perform addiction assessments to determine whether the patient is abusing or is addicted to drugs or alcohol. Though the general public does not typically differentiate between these two conditions, medical professionals adhere to strict guidelines that define misuse and addiction. This is important, as the treatment that the professional recommends is affected by whether he or she believes the patient is abusing drugs or is addicted to them.

To make this determination, the physician performing the addiction assessment instructs the patient to think about his or her behavior during a twelve-month period. The physician then asks the patient a series of questions based on one of many assessment tools. The most commonly used addiction-assessment tools are surveys known as CAGE, T-ACE, AUDIT, and AA20. While these surveys were initially developed to diagnose alcohol addiction, they can be altered and used to uncover a drug addiction.

CAGE. This short four question survey is meant to identify a drinking problem in the lifetime of the patient. The physician will ask the patient each of the following questions, expecting a yes or no response:

C—Have you ever felt you should **cut down** on your drinking?

A—Have people **annoyed** you by criticizing your drinking?

G—Have you ever felt bad or **guilty** about your drinking?

E—**Eye opener**: Have you ever had a drink first thing in the morning to steady your nerves or to get rid of a hangover?

Answering yes to two of these questions indicates that the patient has a serious drinking problem. CAGE is a popular test because it can be administered in any setting and is useful for persons all of genders, ages, races, and socioeconomic backgrounds.

T-ACE. This survey is based on CAGE and also consists of four short questions; however, it is used to uncover a drinking or drug problem in pregnant women.

This survey helps physicians identify a drinking problem in the woman's lifetime and during pregnancy. The physician will ask the patient to answer the following questions:

T—**Tolerance**: How many drinks does it take to make you feel high?

A—Have people **annoyed** you by criticizing your drinking?

C—Have you ever felt you ought to **cut down** on your drinking?

E—**Eye opener**: Have you ever had a drink first thing in the morning to steady your nerves or to get rid of a hangover?

The physician scores the patient's responses to these questions. If the patient has a score of two or higher, the physician can assume that the patient may have a drinking problem and will need further assessment. The scores attributed to these questions are as follows: 1 point for a positive answer for A, C, or E; 2 points for answering T with a number higher than 2.

AUDIT (Alcohol Use Disorder Identification Test). This survey is favored by medical professionals because it provides more details about the patient's drinking habits than other shorter surveys. It consists of ten questions and presents five answer options for the first eight questions and three answer options for the last two questions. The patient is to select the option that best captures his or her honest answers. Like CAGE, AUDIT can be used to assess patients of all genders, ages, races, and backgrounds. The questions on the AUDIT are the following:

1. How often do you have a drink containing alcohol?

2. How many drinks containing alcohol do you have on a typical day when you are drinking?

3. How often do you have six or more drinks on one occasion?

4. How often during the last year have you found that you were not able to stop drinking once you started?

5. How often during the last year have you failed to do what was normally expected from you because of drinking?

6. How often during the last year have you needed a first drink in the morning to get yourself going after a heavy drinking session?

7. How often during the last year have you had a feeling of guilt or remorse after drinking?

8. How often during the last year have you been unable to remember what happened the night before you had been drinking?

9. Have you or someone else been injured as a result of your drinking?

10. Has a relative or friend, or a doctor or other health worker, been concerned about your drinking or suggested you cut down?

A score of 8 or more on AUDIT tells the physician that the patient may have a drinking problem that needs to be addressed. Scores for the first eight questions can be 0 to 4 points each. Scores for the last two questions are worth 0, 2, or 4 points.

AA20. An assessment survey developed and distributed by Alcoholic Anonymous (AA). As its name indicates, the survey includes twenty questions designed to determine whether a person has a drinking problem. In a clinical setting, the physician asks the patients to answer yes or no to the following questions:

1. Do you lose time from work due to drinking?
2. Is drinking making your home life unhappy?
3. Do you drink because you are shy with other people?
4. Is drinking affecting your reputation?
5. Have you ever felt remorse after drinking?
6. Have you gotten into financial difficulties as a result of drinking?
7. Do you turn to lower companions and an inferior environment when drinking?
8. Does your drinking make you careless of your family's welfare?
9. Has your ambition decreased since drinking?
10. Do you crave a drink at a definite time daily?
11. Do you want a drink the next morning?
12. Does drinking cause you to have difficulty sleeping?
13. Has your efficiency decreased since drinking?
14. Is drinking jeopardizing your job or business?
15. Do you drink to escape from worries or trouble?
16. Do you drink alone?
17. Have you ever had a complete loss of memory as a result of drinking?
18. Has your physician ever treated you for drinking?
19. Do you drink to build up your self-confidence?
20. Have you ever been to a hospital or institution on account of drinking?

Craving

Craving denotes an intense desire or need for a specific substance of misuse (such as alcohol, cocaine, heroin, and nicotine), following a period of abstinence or cessation of substance use. Craving may be elicited by exposure to cues (triggers) associated with that substance, by stress, or by a low (priming) dose of the self-administered drug. Craving may motivate drug-seeking behaviors and is thought to contribute to relapse even in long-abstinent persons.

Many researchers consider drug craving within a Pavlovian conditioning framework of drug addiction, in which the drug is the unconditioned stimulus. Environmental cues paired with drug consumption are conditioned stimuli that come to evoke conditioned responses, one of which is craving. In a 1992 study by Ronald Ehrman and colleagues, men addicted to cocaine but with no history of heroin use reported craving in response to cocaine-related stimuli but not to heroin-related or nondrug stimuli.

Craving also can be elicited by the initial effects of a drug experience that signal a more intense later drug effect. These conditioned cravings make it difficult for addicts to use drugs in moderation.

According to AA, answering yes to three of these questions indicates a serious drinking problem. The physician should order further assessment to determine if the patient is abusing alcohol or is addicted to alcohol.

MISUSE VERSUS ADDICTION

Medical professionals rely on criteria set by the *Diagnostic and Statistical Manual of Mental Disorders* to determine if a patient is combating alcohol or drug misuse or addiction. To make an accurate diagnosis, physicians urge their patients to answer all questions honestly.

A physician may diagnose a patient as a substance or drug misuser if the patient has been in one or more of the following situations within the past year:

- The patient has failed to meet obligations, such as skipping classes at school, missing shifts at work, or neglecting to spend scheduled time with a friend or family member.
- The patient has engaged in reckless activities, such as driving or starting a fight while under the influence of drugs or alcohol.

- The patient has encountered legal troubles, such as being accused of a serious crime, getting arrested, or neglecting to pay fines.
- The patient has continued to drink or take drugs even though he or she has encountered personal difficulties or problems, such as frequent disagreements with family members or coworkers.

A physician may diagnose a patient with a substance or drug addiction if the patient has experienced two specific psychological factors—withdrawal and an increased tolerance for his or her drink or drug of choice—and one or more of the following behavioral patterns:

- Inability to stop once using starts
- Failure to adhere to self-imposed limits
- Limiting time spent on other activities to consume drugs or alcohol
- Spending a disproportionate amount of time consuming drugs or alcohol
- Continuing to use a drug or drink even though the patient is in poor health

Once the physician has diagnosed the patient with either a substance or drug misuse problem or an addiction, the physician can then speak with the patient about the next course of action: treatment. Addictions may require more aggressive treatments, such as medications and various types of therapy. Users will be encouraged to seek help for their problems through group therapy, drug and alcohol counseling, and familial support.

Nicole Frail

FOR FURTHER INFORMATION

American Psychiatric Association. *Diagnostic and Statistical Manual of Mental Disorders.* 4th ed. Washington: APA, 1994.

Hoffman, John, and Susan Froemke, eds. *Why Can't They Just Stop?* New York: Rodale, 2007.

National Institute on Alcohol Abuse and Alcoholism. *Assessing Alcohol Problems: A Guide for Clinicians and Researchers.* 2nd ed. Washington, DC: DHHS, 2003.

Orford, Jim. *Excessive Appetites: A Psychological View of Addictions.* New York: 2nd ed. Wiley, 2001.

See also: Drug testing; Prevention methods and research; Screening for behavioral addictions

DMT

CATEGORY: Substances

ALSO KNOWN AS: Businessman's special; N,N-dimethyltryptamine

DEFINITION: DMT is a naturally occurring compound with hallucinogenic properties. It is also produced synthetically.

STATUS: Illegal except for use in controlled research; no approved medical indication in the United States

CLASSIFICATION: Schedule I controlled substance in the United States; schedule 3 drug in Canada

SOURCE: Found in a number of plants, especially in the American tropics, and in trace amounts in humans and other animals. Its natural function in the human body has not been determined. Structurally, it is analogous to the neurotransmitter serotonin.

TRANSMISSION ROUTE: Ingested as a tea or mixed with marijuana and smoked; also snorted and, when liquefied, injected

HISTORY OF USE

Europeans who first arrived in the Caribbean and in Central and South America came into contact with indigenous peoples who used DMT derived from plants to induce hallucinations as part of their religious experience. The explorers tried to suppress these practices, which persisted, often in secretive settings.

DMT was first synthesized in a laboratory in 1931 by chemist Richard Manske. It gained popularity as a drug of misuse in the counterculture of the 1960s. In 2006, the US Supreme Court ruled in *Gonzales v. O Centro Espirita Beneficente Uniao Do Vegetal* that a Brazilian church in the United States could import and use hoasca, a tea containing DMT, for their religious ceremonies, saying that the practice is protected by the 1993 Religious Freedom Restoration Act. According to the US National Survey on Drug Use and Health, the use of DMT in the United States has increased from roughly 688,000 users in 2006 to more than 1.4 million in 2012. In 2015, some 1.2 million American teenagers and adults were using hallucinogens of any kind, including DMT.

DMT Chemical Structure

| Tryptamine | DMT |

EFFECTS AND POTENTIAL RISKS

DMT is the shortest-acting of commonly misused hallucinogens. Its effects are evident within ten minutes, peak at about thirty minutes, and usually end within an hour. Hence the street name "businessman's special."

Physical effects of DMT misuse include increased blood pressure and heart rate, agitation, dizziness, nystagmus (involuntary rapid eye movement), and loss of coordination. At high doses, seizures and respiratory arrests have occurred. Psychological effects of DMT misuse include intense visual hallucinations, depersonalization, auditory distortions, and altered sense of time and body image. DMT causes anxiety attacks far more frequently than the hallucinogen LSD (acid) does.

Ernest Kohlmetz MA

FOR FURTHER INFORMATION

Abadinsky, Howard. *Drug Use and Abuse: A Comprehensive Introduction.* 8th ed. Belmont: Wadsworth, 2013. Print.

Bose, Jonaki, et al. *Key Substance Use and Mental Health Indicators in the United States: Results from the 2015 National Survey on Drug Use and Health.* Center for Behavioral Health Statistics and Quality, 2016. *SAMHSA,* www.samhsa.gov/data/.

Kuhn, Cynthia, Scott Swartwelder, and Wilkie Wilson. *Buzzed: The Straight Facts about the Most Used and Abused Drugs from Alcohol to Ecstasy.* 4th ed. New York: Norton, 2014. Print.

Ruiz, Pedro, and Eric Strain. *Lowinson and Ruiz's Substance Abuse: A Comprehensive Textbook.* 5th ed. Philadelphia: Lippincott, 2011. Print.

See also: Hallucinogen misuse; Hallucinogens' effects on the body; Psychosis and substance misuse

Domestic violence and addiction

CATEGORY: Social issues

DEFINITION: Domestic violence occurs when a person in an intimate relationship physically, sexually, mentally, emotionally, psychologically, or verbally assaults his or her partner. Family violence occurs when most members of the same household—spouses, children, or the elderly—are abused. Women are more likely than men to be abused. Research has shown that the presence of alcohol or drug addictions in the home increases the likelihood of domestic or family violence.

DOMESTIC VIOLENCE IN THE UNITED STATES

Domestic violence is one of the most underreported and most common crimes in the United States. According to researchers Jennifer P. Schneider and Richard Irons, in the article "When Is Domestic Violence a Hidden Face of Addiction?" (1997), more than one-quarter of women in the United States will be abused in their lifetimes. More than 54 percent of married women in violent households will be sexually assaulted repeatedly. Although an estimated 25 to 35 percent of all women who visit emergency rooms have been abused through acts of domestic or family violence, only 5 percent of these women admit that their partners or spouses are responsible for their injuries.

When a person struggling with an addiction to drugs or alcohol is present in the household, many of these numbers increase. In 2010, *Addiction Treatment* magazine reported that 80 percent or more of all cases of domestic violence are somehow connected to the use of drugs or alcohol. The US Department of Justice (DOJ) has reported that 61 percent of domestic violence offenders are addicted to drugs or alcohol. Schneider and Irons found that 75 percent of women living with addicts have been threatened with violence, while 45 percent have been physically or sexually assaulted by their partners.

Regardless of whether an addiction coexists with violence in a household, women are typically abused thirty-five times or more before they make a formal complaint to police. In addition, 47 percent of men—those with and without a substance misuse problem—who beat their wives do so three times or more each year.

As time passes, violence is likely to escalate in a home where a family member is dealing with an addiction to drugs or alcohol. In extreme cases, this leads to the murder of a spouse. The DOJ estimates that one-half or more of persons accused of killing their spouses admit that they were drunk or high at the time of the murder.

Women are not the only victims of domestic violence; children are victimized too. The National Coalition Against Domestic Violence (NCADV) reported that children living in a home with an addict are more likely to suffer physical, mental, or emotional abuse than those in a household where substance misuse is not present. More than 80 percent of child abuse cases involve an abuser who was under the influence of drugs or alcohol at the time of the abuse.

DOMESTIC VIOLENCE AND ADDICTION

Domestic violence and addiction do not have a causal relationship; throughout the years, experts have established that these problems are closely related, but these same experts have not and cannot prove that domestic or family violence is a direct result of a drug or alcohol addiction. It is true, however, that domestic violence is more likely to occur in homes in which a member of the family has become dependent on a particular substance.

Experts cannot call the relationship between domestic violence and addiction causal because it is unclear what factor is the cause and what is the effect. Questions such as the following remain: Did the abuser commit an act of violence because he or she was drunk? Or did the abuser begin drinking because he or she felt guilty for acting violently?

Even though experts have tried to inform the public that evidence of a causal relationship between addiction and domestic violence does not exist, the general public continues to view this relationship as such. Many people do not consider that violence is present in homes where addictions are not. They take no issue with blaming the violence on alcohol and drug misuse; they view abusers as weak and controlled by their substance or drugs of choice. According to the Center for Substance Abuse Treatment, this view has facilitated a "learned disinhibition." Essentially, society has provided abusers with an excuse for their violence. This view also provides abusers with expectations that they will become violent if they drink or get high.

Although society may continue to view this relationship as causal, experts remain unconvinced. Researchers have discovered, however, that cases of domestic violence and addiction do appear to be connected through behavioral parallels. According to Schneider and Irons, the relationship between an addict and his or her drug of choice is similar to the relationship between an abuser and his or her violent tendencies in the following ways:

- In both substance misuse and domestic violence, the user/abuser experiences a loss of control. The abuser loses control of his or her emotions and anger, while the addict loses control of his or her drinking or drug use.
- Both the addict and the abuser continue their behaviors despite recognizing negative consequences of their actions. The addict and abuser feel remorse or guilt regarding their actions, and abusers are aware that their victims may have experienced emotional, sexual, or physical damage or discomfort because of their behaviors.
- The addict and the abuser develop a preoccupation or obsession with their behaviors. Addicts become obsessed with being drunk or high,

while abusers become obsessed with the idea of controlling their victims—especially in circumstances where the abuse is sexual. This preoccupation often erases all guilt or remorse the addict and abuser may feel about their behaviors.

- Both the addict and abuser become tolerant. The addict requires higher doses of his or her substance of choice to reach a mental state in which he or she is content. The abuser becomes increasingly more violent; the abuse may become more frequent, more intense, or more diverse in nature. The victim, too, becomes more tolerant of and desensitized to the abuse.

Because of these, and a number of other similarities between domestic violence and addiction, it is easy for both of these conditions to present themselves in a single household. In many cases, the person with the addiction is also the abuser; however, the addict also can become the victim. Sober members of the household who are unhappy with the addict's behavior are also capable of losing control. This may lead to abuse of the addict.

TREATING COEXISTING CONDITIONS

When treating a person addicted to drugs or alcohol who is also a domestic violence offender, it is important that both the violent tendencies and the addiction receive attention. In these cases, drug and alcohol counselors, physicians, and domestic violence counselors should work together to determine the proper approach to treatment.

Physicians may prescribe medications to help treat the addiction and eliminate any rage or depression. Therapists and other treatment professionals may recommend one-on-one counseling or group therapy. They may even require their patients to be active in multiple groups, such as a domestic violence group and an addiction group, in addition to taking medication and speaking with a therapist.

Professionals, regardless of the course of treatment chosen, should ensure that both the violence and the addiction are being treated. Because medical professionals do not view addiction as the cause of family violence or vice versa, they should be able to separate each factor and assign specific treatments to each. Many experts agree that once the addiction is under control, the persons who are abused can be part of the treatment process. The abused person might

attend therapy sessions with the patient and are often expected to support the patient as best as they can.

Providing patients with both domestic violence and substance misuse counseling in a single setting is the ideal way to treat these coexisting conditions; however, the number of patients who receive both of these services in one location is quite low across the United States. The DOJ reported that 80 percent of domestic violence programs do not offer services to help their patients deal with substance misuse, though 92 percent of the program directors surveyed wish the programs did. These numbers are low because of a lack of financial resources and the absence of staff members who know how to counsel both family violence and addictions.

THE FUTURE?

Schneider and Irons found that 63 percent of abusive men admitted to seeing their fathers abuse their mothers when they were children. Many of these men were abused by their fathers too. Both witnesses and victims of family violence are more likely to form a dependency on drugs and alcohol than those who did not grow up in violent homes. This increases the likelihood that they will then abuse their own family members.

Children who no longer wish to see their parents abused—in addition to children who wish to escape a household in which they are abused—often run away from home. The NCADV has determined that runaways have a high risk of becoming addicted to drugs and alcohol. This substance misuse, combined with memories of abusive childhoods, may place these persons on destructive paths to violent future homes of their own.

Nicole Frail

FOR FURTHER INFORMATION

Center for Substance Abuse Treatment. *Substance Abuse Treatment and Domestic Violence.* Rockville, MD: SAMHSA, 1997. Print.

Devries, Karen M., et al. "Intimate Partner Violence Victimization and Alcohol Consumption in Women: A Systematic Review and Meta-Analysis." *Addiction* 109.3 (2014): 379–91. Print.

Irons, Richard, and Jennifer P. Schneider. "When Is Domestic Violence a Hidden Face of Addiction?" *Journal of Psychoactive Drugs* 29 (1997): 337–44. Print.

McCollum, Eric E., and Terry S. Trepper. *Family Solutions for Substance Abuse: Clinical and Counseling Approaches.* New York: Haworth, 2001. Print.

McCormick, Cynthia. "Experts: Addiction 'Pervasive' in Domestic Violence." *Cape Cod Times.* Local Media, 8 Oct. 2015. Web. 30 Oct. 2015.

Riger, Stephanie, Larry W. Bennett, and Rannveig Sigurvinsdottir. "Barriers to Addressing Substance Abuse in Domestic Violence Court." *American Journal of Community Psychology* 53.1 (2014): 208–17. Print.

Sanders, Mark. *Slipping through the Cracks: Intervention Strategies for Clients with Multiple Addictions and Disorders.* Deerfield Beach, FL: HCI, 2011. Print.

See also: Children and behavioral addictions; Families and behavioral addictions; Families and substance misuse; Gender and addiction

Dopamine and addiction

CATEGORY: Health issues and physiology

ALSO KNOWN AS: Dihydroxyphenylethylamine

DEFINITION: Dopamine, a catecholamine neurotransmitter, is the brain's reward and anticipation (craving) molecule. It plays an important role in the reinforcing effect of drugs and in the powerful cycle of brain dysfunction they cause.

THE DOPAMINE SYSTEM

In the central nervous system, dopaminergic (dopamine-producing) neurons reside only in a few areas, such as the substantia nigra of the midbrain, but establish connections with numerous brain regions. Dopamine (DA) dysfunctions in Parkinson's disease and schizophrenia, for example, suggest that projections from midbrain to certain brain regions (such as the striatum and frontal cortex) are involved in behavioral reactions controlled by rewards. Extensive studies conducted since the mid-twentieth century revealed that DA is involved in the generation of movement, cognition, attention, mood, reward, reward expectation, addiction, and stress. DA also serves various other functions, including as a hormone helping to stop breast milk flow, as an antipsychotic agent, in the function of the kidneys, and in regulating nausea.

Pleasant behavioral events (natural reinforcers such as eating, drinking, exercising, and sexual activity) stimulate the brain's reward (limbic) circuitry, causing DA release from dopaminergic neuron terminals. The information is relayed to the frontal lobe of the brain and stored in memory. The stored memory leads to behaviors directed at procuring the reward.

DOPAMINE IN ADDICTION

Dopamine involvement in multiple stages of addiction is a complex phenomenon and the subject of intense research efforts. The need for DA and its pleasurable effect can be satisfied by substances that mimic the action of this molecule on its receptor.

These substances (addictive drugs) induce transitory, exaggerated increases in DA outside the cells in a deep brain area called nucleus accumbens, a key component of the reward system. This occurs through enhanced release or decreased recycling of the neurotransmitter. The DA surges mimic or exceed the physiological responses that follow natural rewards. A 2015 article published in the journal *Nature Reviews Neuroscience* suggested that alcohol and stimulants including nicotine, cocaine, and methamphetamine particularly rely on changes in dopamine levels to cause addiction. For other addictive drugs, including heroin, dopamine is thought to be more of a supporting factor in the development of addiction.

Human brain imaging studies demonstrate that the subjective feeling of euphoria occurring during intoxication associated with DA increases in deep brain nuclei. The drug-induced surge of the neurotransmitter is especially rewarding for persons with abnormally low densities of certain DA receptors (such as D2DR). Low receptor availability is associated with an increased risk for misuse of cocaine, heroin, methamphetamine, alcohol, and methylphenidate.

The euphoria triggers a reinforcing pattern that "instructs" the person to repeat the rewarding behavior of abusing drugs. As the misuse continues, long-lasting and significant adaptive decreases in DA brain function occur. These decreased levels reduce the effect of the neurotransmitter on the reward system and force the addicted person to keep abusing drugs in an attempt to normalize DA function.

When larger amounts of the drug are required to achieve the same DA high, desensitization (tolerance) occurs. Chronic drug use ultimately produces cellular and molecular adaptations in higher-processing areas of the brain, leading to disruptions in learning, mood, inhibitory control, and many other functions.

Mihaela Avramut MD, PhD

FOR FURTHER INFORMATION

Brookshire, Bethany. "Dopamine Is. . ." *Slate*. Slate Group, 3 July 2013. Web. 28 Oct. 2015.

Kipper, David, and Steven Whitney. *The Addiction Solution*. New York: Rodale, 2010. Print.

Koob, George F., and Nora D. Volkow. "Neurocircuitry of Addiction." *Neuropsychopharmacology* 35 (2010): 217–38. Print.

Nutt, David J., et al. "The Dopamine Theory of Addiction: 40 Years of High and Lows." *Nature Reviews Neuroscience* 16 (2015): 305–312. Print.

Renner, John A. Jr., and E. Nalan Ward. "Drug Addiction." *Massachusetts General Hospital Comprehensive Clinical Psychiatry*. Eds. Theodore A. Stern et al. St. Louis, MO: Mosby, 2008. Print.

See also: Brain changes with addiction; Drug interactions; Science of addiction; Symptoms of substance misuse

Drug misuse and addiction: Overview

CATEGORY: Substance misuse

ALSO KNOWN AS: Drug dependence

DEFINITION: Drug misuse is a disease characterized by continued misuse of drugs even when faced with drug-related occupational, legal, health, or family difficulties. Problems associated with drug misuse must be present for a minimum of twelve months to meet the diagnosis, according to the fourth edition of the American Psychiatric Association's *Diagnostic and Statistical Manual of Mental Disorders* (DSM-IV). Drug dependence refers to long-term, compulsive drug use, with attempts to stop that end in repeated returns to use. Drug dependence also indicates that the user's body has begun to develop a tolerance to the drug and may require the drug in higher doses to achieve the same effects and to avoid withdrawal symptoms. Drug misuse and drug dependence are not terms that should be used to describe people who are taking appropriate dosages of prescribed drugs (pain medication, for example) and who have become physically dependent on them. Diagnosis of both drug misuse and drug dependence requires the presence of specific behavioral symptoms.

CAUSES

The cause of drug misuse and dependence is unknown, although there are a variety of theories. One theory holds that there may be a genetic component that predisposes a person to developing a drug addiction. Another theory is that drug misuse is a learned behavior and that people begin to use drugs by copying the behavior of those around them. Medical professionals have not been able to target a specific cause. Long-term drug use alters the brain's structure and chemistry, which may reinforce the desire to keep using drugs regardless of the consequences.

RISK FACTORS AND SYMPTOMS

A risk factor is something that increases the chances of getting a disease or condition. For drug misuse and addiction, young males are at a greater risk, as are those who have family members with substance misuse problems. Other risk factors include social and peer pressure, early antisocial behavior, stress, and easy access to drugs. Anxiety, depression, and panic disorders are also risk factors associated with drug misuse and addiction. Denial that a drug problem exists is common. Drug misuse can occur without physical dependence and often progresses to drug dependence. To diagnose drug misuse, the symptoms must have lasted for at least twelve months and may include repeated work, school, or home problems due to drug use; continued use of drugs even though it means risking physical safety; recurring trouble with the law related to drug use, including impaired driving; and continued use of drugs despite drug-related problems in personal relationships.

Symptoms of drug dependence include at least three of the following: craving for the substance; inability to stop or limit drug use; tolerance, or taking greater amounts to feel the same effect; withdrawal symptoms that occur when the drug is stopped; significant amounts of time trying to acquire drugs and recover from their effects; and giving up activities to use drugs or recover from their effects. Drug use continues even when it causes or worsens health and/or psychological problems.

DIAGNOSIS

To help with diagnosis, doctors ask a series of questions regarding drug-related problems, specifically:

- how often the patient uses drugs
- which drugs the patient uses
- what amount and if the patient has increased the amount to receive the same desired effect
- emotional problems that may have occurred while using drugs
- problems with a job, family, or the law Tests may include blood and urine tests to check for the presence of drugs.

TREATMENT

There is no cure for drug misuse or drug dependence. Treatment consists of three main goals: to help patients stop using drugs, to decrease the toxic effects of the drugs being used and to aid in symptoms of drug withdrawal ("detoxification"), and to prevent relapse. Successful treatment depends on the drug user's recognition of the problem and desire to change. Recovery takes a long time and is not an easy process. Patients may need multiple courses of treatment.

Therapies include medications, counseling, and self-help organizations. Drugs may help to alleviate some of the symptoms of withdrawal. In some cases, medication may be ordered to prevent relapse. People addicted to heroin may be given methadone to help taper them off. Methadone may also be given on a long-term basis to improve the chance of staying in treatment. Methadone is a narcotic that blocks cravings as well as the pleasurable effects of heroin and other opiates. Other drugs that are used in treatment are naltrexone (e. g., ReVia, which blocks the effect of opiates) and buprenorphine (e. g., Subutex, which is similar to methadone).

Therapy raises awareness of the underlying issues and lifestyles that promote drug use. Therapy also works to improve coping and problem-solving skills and works to develop other ways of dealing with stress or pain. Through counseling, a person can learn how

Drug-Seeking Behavior

Drug-seeking behavior (DSB) is a symptom of drug misuse and addiction. A person with DSB will continuously try to access narcotic pain medication or tranquilizers even though he or she may have no medical need for these drugs. In order to obtain the desired drug from a pharmacy or doctor, a person with DSB may exhibit the following behavior:

- complaints about severe pain
- repeated requests for "lost" prescriptions
- use of forged prescriptions and false identification
- assertiveness, including demands to see a doctor immediately
- evasiveness in answering questions about medical history and references
- giving exaggerated accounts of textbook symptoms
- becoming violent if requests are denied

to handle situations associated with drug use and replace drug-using activities with other activities that are more meaningful. Family support is encouraged.

There are numerous organizations and support groups dedicated to helping people stop using drugs. Two examples are Narcotics Anonymous and Cocaine Anonymous. These are twelve-step programs. Members of these organizations meet regularly to talk about their drug-related troubles and provide a network of support for each other.

Debra Wood, RN

FOR FURTHER INFORMATION

Fisher, Gary, and Nancy Roget. *Encyclopedia of Substance Abuse Prevention, Treatment, and Recovery.* Thousand Oaks, CA: Sage, 2009. An encyclopedia of key concepts and approaches used in the field of substance abuse.

Shapiro, Harry. *Recreational drugs: A Directory.* London: Collins & Brown, 2004. A compendium of all major recreational drugs, including facts about use, effects, risks, and legal status.

Thombs, Dennis. *Introduction to Addictive Behaviors.* 3rd ed. New York: Guilford Press, 2006. Covers theories of addiction, prevention, comorbidity, motivation enhancement, and harm reduction. Also covers psychoanalytic, cognitive, family, and social/cultural issues.

See also: Addiction; Narcotics misuse; Routes of administration; Substance misuse

Drug misuse and addiction: In depth

CATEGORY: Substance misuse

DEFINITION: Although drug misuse and drug addiction are often related, these conditions are viewed independently by experts. While it is true that drug misuse may lead to drug addiction, many circumstances can cause a person to only experiment with drugs and alcohol and not become addicted. Some people may have a biological predisposition for substance addiction, but there are a number of initiatives that aim to prevent the development of this disease.

CAUSES

The reasons people misuse drugs and alcohol are innumerable. Some become addicted to a drug after the first recreational use. Others find comfort in the escape that the effects of drugs and alcohol provide them: They become numb to any physical or emotional pain and memories of past trauma and are distracted from any thoughts or emotions that may be causing them stress. Still others misuse medications that doctors prescribe for particular ailments or illnesses.

One of the most common reasons people misuse drugs is to escape reality. Research has shown that a high percentage of drug users are survivors of past emotional and/or physical trauma and have resultant PTSD (post-traumatic stress disorder). Many have memories of being physically, verbally, or sexually abused as children or adolescents. Others recall violent households and quarreling parents who were not able to meet their emotional needs as children. Women in physically or sexually abusive marriages are more likely to seek comfort in drugs and alcohol than are women in healthy relationships.

Men who are domestic violence offenders also are more likely to misuse drugs and alcohol—and act violently toward others while intoxicated—than men who are not violent. It is important to note, however, that drug and alcohol misuse is not a proven cause of domestic violence and that domestic violence is not a proven cause of drug and alcohol misuse. These situations are known as correlated rather than causal.

Lesbian, gay, bisexual, and transgendered (LGBT) men and women are more likely to use drugs—and continue to use them throughout their lifetime—than are heterosexual individuals. The drug use is often in response to the frequent and perceived discrimination and abuse that LGBT individuals may face because of their sexual orientation or gender expression.

When a person misuses a drug too frequently, he or she can become addicted to that substance. Another cause of drug addiction is genetics. It is true that some people are predisposed to addiction because of family history and genetics. Misuse also may lead to addiction if the person has a mental illness, such as antisocial personality disorder, bipolar disorder, or schizophrenia. Drugs may ease the symptoms of these conditions or can make living with them more bearable. Thus, people may become addicted to drugs or alcohol as they attempt to self-medicate their disorders.

People also are more likely to misuse drugs if they enjoy the effects the substances have on their brains. Opioids, for example, block the nerve receptors in the brain that help the body to sense pain. Opioids also engage the receptors in the brain that detect pleasure. The drug causes users to enter a euphoric state in which they experience stress relief and a carefree emotional state. People who enjoy this sensation may come to think they need the drug to be happy. Users report feeling an intense desire to use the drug again after their first encounter with it, despite the fact that their body is not physically addicted to it at that point. Repeated and ongoing use of opioids causes significant and detectable changes in the brain and the brain's chemistry. Chronic use requires a period of one to three years of abstinence for the brain to heal.

RISK FACTORS

As discussed, risk factors to drug misuse and addiction, specifically addiction, include a genetic predisposition to addictive behavior. According to the National Association for Children of Alcoholics, children of addicted parents are in the highest risk group of individuals with the potential to become addicted themselves.

Considering the argument of nature versus nurture, both play a crucial role in the development of an addiction. Genetics are extremely important, but so is the environment in which a child is raised. If a child witnesses uncorrected addictive behavior, he or she is more likely to adopt that behavior at a later point in life. However, not all men and women who become drug users and addicts grew up in a household with a drug or alcohol addict. Witnessing a parent with a behavioral addiction, such as to gambling or sex, also may influence a child's later addiction to a substance, and not to a behavior.

Other factors that lead to drug and alcohol misuse and addiction include peer pressure and drug use at a young age. The earlier one starts smoking cigarettes and marijuana or drinking alcohol, the more likely that person will become addicted to those drugs in the future. Also, persons who start abusing drugs during adolescence are more likely to experiment with harder drugs.

The diagnosis of a mental disorder of various types—anything from anxiety to multiple personality disorder—also increases the chances that a person will begin abusing (and possibly become addicted to) drugs or alcohol. Persons who are prescribed medications for mental illnesses or for pain relief may become addicted to their prescriptions. Persons who wish to ignore treatment of their mental conditions may fall into the habit of smoking, injecting, snorting, or drinking substances that offer relief from their present stresses.

Social risk factors for drug and alcohol misuse include being between the ages of eighteen and forty-four years, being of low socioeconomic status, and being single (not married). According to the US Department of Justice, men are more likely than women to misuse or become addicted to drugs and alcohol.

SYMPTOMS

The difference between drug misuse and drug addiction lies within the physical and psychological

---

Drug Abuse Screening Test

Created in 1982 by Harvey Skinner, the drug abuse screening test (DAST) is a self-report questionnaire that assesses problems associated with the lifetime abuse of over-the-counter, prescription, and illicit drugs. The test does not directly assess the specific type, frequency or quantity of drug use, and it does not assess for problems related exclusively to alcohol use.

DAST is a self-administered questionnaire. Items on the test parallel questions on the Michigan alcoholism screening test. Questions require a yes or no response. Each response is assigned one point when answered in a manner consistent with drug use problems. A scoring system recommended by Skinner suggests that scores greater than five indicate problems with drug use.

DAST may be used either for research or for clinical purposes. Because DAST is a screening instrument only, the confirmation of DAST scores with more thorough diagnostic procedures is often necessary for clinical purposes.

---

symptoms of each condition. Medical professionals use guidelines defined by the *Diagnostic and Statistical Manual of Mental Disorders 5* (DSM-5) to diagnose substance use disorder (SUD). When diagnosing SUD, clinicians utilize the criteria put forth in the DSM-5 to diagnose the level of substance use disorder from mild to severe.

The key features of the abuse facet of the disorder are patterns of repeated problems in individual functioning in roles at work, school, or home; legal status; use of the substance in hazardous situations; or the consequences of the use on interpersonal relationships. For the substance dependence category, the key features of the disorder are patterns of repeated problems in several areas that are distinct from those considered for abuse. Diagnosis of dependence relies on factors such as tolerance; withdrawal; new or worsened physical or emotional problems directly resulting from the use of the substance; loss of control over the use of the substance; unsuccessful efforts to cut down or quit coupled with intense desire to quit; excessive periods of time spent obtaining, using, or recovering from using the substance; and the displacement of social or occupational activities to use the substance.

When persons are physically addicted to a substance, they may feel as though they cannot live without that substance in their system. People can become physically ill, and emotionally and mentally unstable, if their bodies crave a substance and do not receive it. This experience is called withdrawal. Withdrawal from alcohol or benzodiazepines is potentially fatal. Individuals withdrawing from these substances should do so under medical supervision. Withdrawal from opiates such as heroin, although extremely painful and long-lasting, is not usually fatal, but individuals have been known to die from dehydration during the withdrawal process.

Symptoms of drug misuse include some or all of the following:

- failure to meet obligations, such as missing a meeting with a family member or friend, purposely skipping classes at school, or neglecting to arrive on time for work or to show up at all
- engaging in reckless activities, such as driving under the influence of drugs or alcohol
- developing legal or financial troubles, such as getting arrested, being accused of a serious crime, or failing to secure or keep track of personal funds
- continuing to use drugs even after encountering personal difficulties or issues or severe consequences, such as imprisonment or fighting with family members, friends, or coworkers

When a person becomes addicted to the substance, he or she will experience withdrawal without the drug and an increased tolerance for the drug in addition to some or all the following behavioral symptoms:

- inability to stop using
- failure to follow self-imposed limits
- decreased time spent on other activities that do not include drugs
- spending an excessive amount of time consuming drugs or alcohol
- continuing to consume a substance despite the presence of other illnesses or poor health

These symptoms will be present along with the symptoms belonging to the individual substances the person is using. If someone is addicted to opioids, for example, that person may exhibit slurred speech, itching, paranoia, depression, confusion, low blood pressure, and excessive sleeping.

SCREENING AND DIAGNOSIS

The first step in treating drug misusers and addicts typically involves their loved ones—people who take notice of their behavioral changes, physical appearance, and drug use. These persons may convince or force the substance misuser to seek treatment, which is usually first in the form of calling call his or her primary physician or family doctor. After an initial screening in which the doctor runs a series of tests and asks the patient questions about his or her drug use, the doctor may refer the patient to a specialist for an accurate diagnosis. If the individual requires detoxification from the substance, they are referred to a medical facility or specialized detox and recovery program.

Another important part of the screening and diagnosis process is the discovery of other physical ailments, coexisting drug addictions or mental health issues, which is referred to as comorbidity. Specific medications and methods used in addiction treatment may counteract other drugs the patient is using or interfere with other conditions the patient may have; it is crucial to discover all illnesses, diseases, and dependencies before treatment begins. Often times, mental health issues cannot be addressed unless and until the individual is free from drugs and alcohol for a period of time.

Diagnosing comorbidity is a critical step in addictions treatment; treating a patient addicted to cocaine requires a different approach than the one taken to treat a patient addicted to prescription painkillers who is simultaneously struggling to overcome depression, anxiety, or a personality disorder. According to SAMHSA's 2014 National Survey on Drug Use and Health (NSDUH), almost 7.9 million adults who had substance use disorders also had a mental illness. A mental illness may be present before a person starts using drugs, or a person might start using drugs before becoming mentally ill. Both conditions also may be the result of similar risk factors, such as genetic predisposition and environmental triggers (such as high stress or trauma).

Through laboratory screenings, medical professionals may discover that vital organs such as the lungs, liver, or heart have been damaged by repetitive drug misuse. They also may discover conditions such as Hepatitis C or HIV, which are common among individuals who share needles used for intravenous drug use.

Research has found that people living with mood disorders have a greater likelihood of becoming addicted to drugs than do individuals without such mental health conditions. In addition, patients with drug disorders are two times as likely to be diagnosed with a mood or anxiety disorder. Men seeking help for drug misuse are often diagnosed with antisocial personality disorders while women are likely to exhibit behavior indicative of depression, anxiety, or post-traumatic stress disorder.

TREATMENT AND THERAPY

Ideally, a person who is abusing or addicted to a substance and who is also dealing with an additional addiction, physical illness, or mental illness should be treated for these issues by the same health professionals at a single facility, often referred to a dual-diagnosis facility. This does not often occur in the United States, however. Patients' conditions are viewed as unrelated, and patients are sent to multiple facilities to speak to a variety of medical professionals, from physicians to psychotherapists to drug and alcohol counselors.

A common course of treatment is to assign an individual to an Individual Outpatient Program (IOP) where they attend group therapy sessions, individual counseling, and psychiatric medicine consultations daily for an average of six hours a day, five days a week for anywhere from three to six weeks, depending upon what the individual's insurance will approve. In group therapy sessions, individuals speak about their drug use in front of other persons who understand what they are going through. If they are uncomfortable with—or are in need of supplementing group therapy, a drug and alcohol counselor or psychologist may counsel them independently. Therapy helps patients learn to deal with their cravings, the issues that led them to drugs in the first place, and to learn to begin to live a drug-free life. It enables them to set goals for the future and to repair strained or broken relationships with friends and family members.

After an addict's body is free of all drugs and alcohol, the patient may begin treatment for his or her conditions. This treatment may be similar to therapies embraced by drug misusers—either group therapy or individual meetings with drug and alcohol counselors. Doctors also can choose to place some patients on medications to help calm cravings, fight depression, or reduce anxiety. Naltrexone, acamprosate,

and disulfiram are common drugs administered to alcohol addicts. Naltrexone also can be distributed to opioid addicts. Even those addicted to nicotine can use bupropion or varenicline in addition to nicotine gum, patches, and nasal sprays.

Each year about 40 percent of people who have become dependent on drugs or alcohol seek help for their problems. Research has found that the majority of those seeking help are men, as women are less likely to admit that they have substance misuse problems. They also, in general, have to ensure their children are cared for, which often keeps them from leaving home and joining treatment groups. Most rehabilitation facilities or drug and alcohol centers are not equipped to care for children and do not offer babysitting or daycare services.

The United States faces an epidemic of opioid addiction. Federal dollars have expanded the access to naloxone (an antidote to opioid overdose) and created a program to track opioid prescriptions. Additional resources are also being allocated to the state's drug courts which allow defendants the option of receiving treatment for their addiction versus going to jail.

To prevent relapse, people recovering from substance misuse and addiction are reminded to pay attention to their bodies and minds and to ask for help when they need it. The relapse process includes three stages: emotional, mental, and physical. If a patient feels anxious, defensive, or angry and misses group meetings or doctors' visits, he or she could be in the first stage of relapse. Combined with poor sleeping and eating habits and mood swings, this first stage may lead a patient to post acute withdrawal. Patients are instructed to reach out to medical professionals, friends, or family members if they feel they are in danger of relapse.

Nicole Frail

FOR FURTHER INFORMATION

"Alcohol and Drug Problem Overview." *DrugFree.org*. Partnership for Drug-Free Kids, 2012. Web. 29 Oct. 2015.

American Psychiatric Association. *Diagnostic and Statistical Manual of Mental Disorders: DSM-5*. Washington: American Psychiatric Association, 2013. Print.

"Drug Facts: Comorbidity: Addiction and Other Mental Disorders." *NIDA*. National InstituteDrug Abuse, Mar. 2011. Web. 5 Nov. 2015.

Ghodse, Hamid. *Ghodse's Drugs and Addictive Behaviour: A Guide to Treatment.* New York: Cambridge UP, 2010. Print.

Gwinnell, Esther, and Christine A. Adamec, eds. *The Encyclopedia of Addictions and Addictive Behaviors.* New York: Infobase, 2005. Print.

Hoffman, John, and Susan Froemke, eds. *Why Can't They Just Stop?* New York: Rodale, 2007. Print.

Kaufmann, Christopher N., Lian-Yu Chen, Roas M. Crum, and Ramin Majtabai. "Treatment Seeking and Barriers to Treatment for Alcohol Use in Persons with Alcohol Use Disorders and Comorbid Mood or Anxiety Disorders." *Social Psychiatry and Psychiatric Epidemiology.* (2013). Print.

Ries, Richard K., ed. *Principles of Addiction Medicine.* Philadelphia: Lippincott, 2009. Print.

See also: Anxiety medication misuse; Gateway drugs; Hallucinogen misuse; Narcotics misuse; Opioid misuse; Painkiller misuse; Recreational drugs; Substance misuse

Drug Enforcement Administration (DEA)

CATEGORY: Social issues

DEFINITION: The Drug Enforcement Administration, Drug Enforcement Administration, U.S. (DEA) is an agency of the US government that enforces the controlled substances laws and regulations of the United States.

DATE: Established in July 1973

BACKGROUND

The enforcement of federal drug laws in the United States began in 1915 within the Bureau of Internal Revenue (now the Internal Revenue Service). By the 1960s, two agencies were responsible for drug law enforcement: the Bureau of Drug Abuse Control within the Department of Health, Education, and Welfare and the Federal Bureau of Narcotics within the Treasury Department. In 1968, these agencies were combined as the Bureau of Narcotics and Dangerous Drugs (BNDD) within the Department of Justice, giving the US attorney general full authority and responsibility for enforcing all federal laws on narcotics and dangerous drugs.

The Drug Enforcement Administration (DEA), which superseded the BNDD, was created by US president Richard M. Nixon, Richard M. Nixon by executive order in July 1973, to establish a single, unified command to enforce federal drug laws and to consolidate and coordinate the government's drug control activities. Nixon called on the new agency to launch a global "war" on drugs, war on drugs, beginnings.

In 1982, jurisdiction over drug investigations was coordinated between the DEA and the Federal Bureau of Investigation, greatly expanding the number of agents and technical support focused on this effort. The DEA also works closely with Immigration and Customs Enforcement. In 1984, the DEA was given expanded authority to work with parents, teachers, and other concerned citizens on drug education and prevention strategies.

The DEA is headed by an administrator of drug enforcement, who is appointed by the president and confirmed by the US Senate. The president also appoints the DEA's deputy administrator. All other DEA officials are career government employees. Those directly involved in drug-law enforcement outside the legal branch are special agents, diversion investigators, and intelligence research specialists.

Special agents are the primary criminal investigation and enforcement officers of the DEA. Most are assigned to regional or international offices. They enforce the controlled substances laws and regulations of the United States, identify and immobilize drug traffickers, and seize and dismantle the financial assets of drug traffickers.

Diversion investigators conduct investigations of the illicit sales and misuse of controlled substances. They work within the Office of Diversion Control of the DEA. A relatively new concern and area of investigation for this office is the rise of Internet sites offering controlled substances openly or with little pretense of control. Many of these sites are based in Canada. Diversion investigators are authorized to take administrative, civil, and criminal actions against people and organizations in violation of controlled substances regulations.

Intelligence research specialists work closely with special agents to conduct major drug investigations, both in the United States and abroad. Areas in which intelligence research specialists conduct and manage research projects include drug cultivation and production, methods of transportation, trafficking routes, and the structure and working operations of trafficking organizations.

MISSION AND GOALS

The mission of the DEA is to enforce the controlled substances, controlled substances, law enforcement and laws and regulations of the United States and to bring to the appropriate criminal and civil justice system those organizations and principal members of organizations involved in the growing, manufacture, or distribution (including smuggling, smuggling, drugs, and law enforcement) of controlled substances within or destined for illicit traffic in the United States. Additionally, the DEA is empowered to recommend and support educational and training programs aimed at reducing the availability of illicit controlled substances on the domestic and international markets.

The DEA has a number of primary responsibilities, starting with the investigation and preparation for prosecution of two types of offenders: major violators of controlled substances laws operating at interstate and international levels and criminals and drug gangs who perpetrate violence in local communities. The DEA manages a national drug intelligence program in cooperation with federal, state, local, and foreign officials that collects, analyzes, and disseminates strategic and operational drug intelligence information. It is mandated to seize and divest assets derived from, traceable to, or intended to be used for illicit drug trafficking. The DEA enforces the provisions of the Controlled Substances Act (1970) as they pertain to the manufacture, distribution, and dispensing of legally produced controlled substances.

The DEA coordinates the work of federal, state, and local law enforcement officials on mutual drug enforcement efforts. It works with foreign governments in developing and carrying out programs designed to reduce the availability of illicit abuse-type drugs in the United States through such methods as crop eradication and substitution, and through training foreign officials. Under the policy guidance of the US secretary of state and US ambassadors, the DEA is responsible for all programs associated with drug counterparts in foreign countries. The DEA acts as a liaison with the United Nations, with Interpol, and with other organizations on matters relating to international drug control programs.

Ernest Kohlmetz MA

FOR FURTHER INFORMATION

Clifford, Tom. *Inside the DEA*. Bloomington, IN: Authorhouse, 2006. The narrative of a former DEA agent who began working with the agency in 1971.
Robbins, David. *Heavy Traffic: 30 Years of Headlines and Major Ops from the Case Files of the DEA*. New York: Chamberlin, 2005. Presents the history of the agency through 2005 and examines possible future challenges.

See also: Controlled Substances Act (CSA); Education about substance misuse; Law enforcement and drugs ; Legislation and substance misuse

---

Drug interactions

CATEGORY: Health issues and physiology

DEFINITION: Drug interactions occur when two or more medications or drugs are taken simultaneously or near simultaneously, causing interference with the metabolism of one or both agents. Drug interactions can cause the concentrations of one or both agents to either increase or decrease, potentially resulting in unforeseen negative reactions, including fatalities.

INTERACTIONS AND DRUG METABOLISM

Medications and recreational drugs are metabolized in the body into pharmacologically active chemical components; nonpharmacologically active chemical moieties are then excreted from the body. Most medications are either metabolized by the kidney (renal metabolism) or by the liver (hepatic metabolism).

Within the liver and intestines exist multiple enzymes and pathways responsible for breaking down medications. Some of the enzymes that are most commonly involved in drug metabolism are the cytochrome P450 (CYP) enzymes. Of the CYP enzymes, CYP3A4 is most commonly involved in drug metabolism. It has been estimated that this enzyme is at least partly responsible for the metabolism of almost 50 percent of medications. The rate and amount of drug that can be metabolized depends on a number of factors, including the amount of enzyme present and the speed at which these enzymes are working.

When a person ingests multiple medications metabolized through the same pathway, the enzymes may not be able to metabolize all the medications simultaneously, leading to elevated, possibly toxic, levels of the drugs. For example, alprazolam (Xanax) is metabolized through CYP3A4. If a patient taking alprazolam is prescribed clarithromycin (Biaxin) for sinusitis and takes the two medications together, the clarithromycin, a CYP3A4 inhibitor, will effectively slow the breakdown of alprazolam, leading to increased sedation and central nervous system (CNS) depression. If the patient continues to take alprazolam, unaware that drug levels are building up in his or her system, dangerous consequences can occur.

DRUG-FOOD INTERACTIONS

In addition to the medications that may interact with one another, drugs also can have interactions with food. Milk and other calcium- and magnesium-containing products can interact with certain medications, including fluoroquinolone antibiotics such as ciprofloxacin (Cipro) and levofloxacin (Levaquin). Divalent cations such as calcium and magnesium can bind the antibiotic, keeping it from being absorbed by the body. Citrus juices, especially grapefruit juice, are also known to strongly interact with various drugs.

Another example of drug and food interactions is the heightened CNS depressant effects of alcohol when combined with medications that already produce CNS depressant effects, such as benzodiazepines (alprazolam, or Xanax, and lorazepam, or Ativan) and morphine or morphine derivatives (such as the hydrocodone products Vicodin, Norco, and Loratab and the oxycodone products Percocet and Percodan).

CNS depressant medications and substances, such as alcohol, slow down certain brain processes. This can lead to decreased motor function and coordination, drowsiness, confusion, and respiratory depression. CNS effects are cumulative, which is why the addition of alcohol to the system of a person taking either chronic or recreational (and legal) CNS depressants can be so dangerous. These medications and the resulting sensations can have addictive properties, leading the user to purposely combine the two in an unsafe and potentially fatal manner.

DRUG AND HERBAL SUPPLEMENTS INTERACTIONS

Herbal medications are often assumed to be more natural and, therefore, safer than pharmacologically produced medications. The use of these agents has continued to increase, although the exact number of people using supplements is hard to gauge because these agents are available without a prescription (over the counter).

Some of the most popular supplements have serious interactions with common medications. These supplements include St. John's wort, *Ginkgo biloba*, ginseng, and garlic. St. John's wort, which is used to treat many ailments, most commonly depression, is metabolized through CYP 3A4 and 2E1 and, therefore, can be unsafe when used with some anticoagulants, including warfarin, and with some medications used to treat human immunodeficiency virus (including protease inhibitors and non-nucleoside reverse transcriptase inhibitors). Ginkgo is commonly used for memory enhancement. There have been numerous reports of bleeding in patients taking ginkgo while also taking anticoagulants, and in patients with clotting disorders.

It is important that patients understand that herbal supplements, although generally safe, can dangerously interact with over-the-counter and prescription medications. Patients should alert their doctors, pharmacists, and other providers about what supplements they are taking to help prevent serious interactions.

Allison Armagan PharmD

FOR FURTHER INFORMATION

"Drug Interactions: What You Should Know." *FDA.* US Food and Drug Administration, 25 Sept. 2013. Web. 27 Oct. 2015.

Izzo, Angelo, and Edzard Ernst. "Interactions between Herbal Medicines and Prescribed Drugs." *Drugs* 61.15 (2001): 2163–75. Print.

"Medication Interaction: Food, Supplements, and Other Drugs." *American Heart Association.* American Heart Assn., 15 Oct. 2014. Web. 27 Oct. 2015.

Saito, Mitsuo, et al. "Undesirable Effects of Citrus Juice on the Pharmacokinetics of Drugs." *Drug Safety* 28.8 (2005): 677–94. Print.

Wallace, Allison W., Jennifer M. Victory, and Guy W. Amsden. "Lack of Bioequivalence When Levofloxacin and Calcium-Fortified Orange Juice Are Coadministered to Healthy Volunteers." *Journal of Clinical Pharmacology* 43 (2003): 539–44. Print.

See also: Brain changes with addiction; Dopamine and addiction; Science of addiction

Drug paraphernalia

CATEGORY: Substance misuse

DEFINITION: Drug paraphernalia encompasses any product, device, or material that enables illicit drug use, concealment, or manufacturing. Most drug paraphernalia are illegal. The most common drug paraphernalia include hypodermic needles and syringes, bongs, pipes, spoons, roach clips, mirrors, razor blades, and scales.

HISTORY OF USE

Drug paraphernalia have a long history of use. By the 1970s in the United States, recreational drug use reached epidemic proportions, giving rise to drug paraphernalia stores known as head shops. These stores, which often also sold music, sold a variety of specialized drug-related items. These items, which included water pipes called bongs and marijuana cigarette holders known as roach clips, catered to, enhanced, and glamorized drug use. Head shops openly displayed other items that advertised and promoted drug culture, including clothing, jewelry, tattoo designs, posters, and publications.

The commercial distribution of drug paraphernalia and the growing drug problem prompted antiparaphernalia laws. In 1979, the US Drug Enforcement Administration (DEA) enacted the Model Drug Paraphernalia Act to help states prohibit the sale and possession of any article used to prepare and consume illicit drugs. The act defined drug paraphernalia, listed criteria to determine the presence of drug paraphernalia, and prohibited advertisements for drug paraphernalia. By the 1980s, many states required businesses to obtain a license to sell drug paraphernalia, forcing many head shops to close.

To further restrict access to drug paraphernalia, the DEA drafted the Federal Drug Paraphernalia Statute as part of the Controlled Substances Act (1970) to regulate the possession, selling, offering, and transport of illegal drug paraphernalia. Many US states enacted their own regulations prohibiting drug paraphernalia.

Drug paraphernalia are frequently designed with bright and colorful logos to attract teenagers and young adults. Various drug paraphernalia can be acquired on the Internet, through mail-order businesses, and in tobacco and specialty shops. Sometimes, drug paraphernalia are labeled with misleading disclaimers to minimize the dangers associated with illicit drug use. Drug paraphernalia items are continually evolving along with illegal drug activity.

COMMON DRUG PARAPHERNALIA

Drug paraphernalia can be categorized as user or dealer specific. User paraphernalia consists of items that facilitate drug use, such as hypodermic needles and syringes, pipes (metal, wooden, acrylic, glass, stone, plastic, ceramic), pipe screens, bongs, roach clips, spoons, tubes, razor blades, mirrors, rolling papers, and drug kits. Dealer paraphernalia consists of items that facilitate the production, trafficking, and concealment of illicit drugs and include blenders, scales, bowls, baggies, capsules, balloons, vials, and diluents and adulterants for mixing illegal drugs.

Drug paraphernalia also encompasses drug storage or "stash cans" to conceal drugs. These items include bags, envelopes or flaps, purses, pen cases, small vials and containers, cigarette packs, pill bottles, film canisters, water bottles, gum and candy wrappers, pagers, soda cans, lipstick dispensers, and make-up kits. Stash cans may be specially constructed with hidden compartments to conceal drugs.

Drug paraphernalia can be difficult to identify because ordinary household products can be used to disguise illicit drug use. Sunglasses can be used to hide pupil dilation and red eyes. Breath sprays, mints, air fresheners, perfumes, and incense can be used to mask drug-related odors. Clothing may have hidden drug compartments.

DRUG-SPECIFIC PARAPHERNALIA

Different drug paraphernalia can be associated with different methods of drug transmission, such as inhaling, smoking, and injecting. Drug paraphernalia designed to aid in the inhalation and smoking of illicit drugs such as marijuana, crack, and cocaine includes pipes, smoking masks, roach clips, miniature spoons, bongs, hoses, tubes, and lighters. Hypodermic syringes, needles, and lighters are well-known drug paraphernalia for preparing and injecting drugs such as heroin and methamphetamine.

Drug paraphernalia can be associated with specific drugs such as ecstasy, cocaine, and marijuana and with methamphetamine production and inhalant use. Ecstasy paraphernalia includes pacifiers, lollipops, and mouth guards to aid in relieving jaw clenching, teeth grinding, and dry mouth. Glow sticks, flash lights, vapor rubs, and masks enhance stimulation while candy pieces and jewelry can be used to hide pills.

Cocaine paraphernalia includes pipes, glass tubes, small spoons, and lighters for smoking. Razor blades, cards, and mirrors are typically used to organize cocaine into lines for snorting through straws. Marijuana paraphernalia includes chillums or cone-shaped pipes, rolling papers to form cigarettes, stash cans, roach clips to hold the joint, and deodorizers or incense to disguise the odor.

Drug paraphernalia associated with methamphetamine production includes flasks, funnels, tubing, adaptors, joints, cooking equipment, and thermometers. Drug paraphernalia associated with inhalant use includes rags for sniffing, spray cans, glue, paint, plastic bags, balloons, nozzles, and bottles.

Rose Ciulla-Bohling PhD

Bongs are a type of drug paraphernalia, but can still be sold in shops for "tobacco use only." (C.P. Storm via Wikimedia Commons)

FOR FURTHER INFORMATION

Ginther, Catherine. *Drug Abuse Sourcebook*. 2nd ed. Detroit: Omnigraphics, 2004. Print.

Hagan, Holly, et al. "Sharing of Drug Preparation Equipment as a Risk Factor for Hepatitis C." *American Journal of Public Health* 91.1 (2001): 42–46. Print.

Inciardi, James A., ed. *Handbook of Drug Control in the United States*. Westport, CT: Greenwood, 1990. Print.

Korsmeyer, Pamela, and Henry R. Kranzler, eds. *Encyclopedia of Drugs, Alcohol, and Addictive Behavior*. 3rd ed. Detroit: Macmillan, 2009. Print.

Scheb, John M., and John M. Scheb II. *Criminal Law and Procedure*. 7th ed. Belmont, CA: Wadsworth, 2010. Print.

See also: Gateway drugs; Intravenous drug use and blood-borne diseases; Meth labs; Pipes and hookahs; Routes of administration

Drug testing

CATEGORY: Diagnosis and prevention

ALSO KNOWN AS: Drug screening; toxicology screening

DEFINITION: Drug testing is the screening of body fluids, breath and/or hair for the detection of various legal and illicit drugs including, but not limited to, alcohol, cocaine, amphetamine/methamphetamine, opiates, PCP, THC, benzodiazepines, barbiturates, methadone, propoxyphene and methaqualone.

DRUG SCREENING BASICS

Drug testing is the analysis of a sample for the presence of a variety of drugs. Usually, the sample tested is biological such as urine, blood, sweat, saliva, hair and breath, but the sample can be non-biological such as clothing, powder and/or a residue. A variety of legal, illegal and prescription drugs can be detected including alcohol, marijuana (THC), cocaine, amphetamines, methamphetamines, barbiturates, oxycodone, ecstasy, methadone, phencyclidine (PCP), propoxyphene and others. Blood alcohol is usually tested with a breathalyzer whereas most drugs are tested using urine. Drug testing is often used in the workplace, by law enforcement agencies and by athletic organizations. Some states prohibit drug testing in the workplace.

Government and private employers are the major users of drug testing methods. Although drug testing is not required except in certain occupations such as transportation, many private firms have created their own drug testing programs. The main reason for the implementation of drug testing was to deter workplace drug use. According to the US Substance Abuse and Mental Health Services Administration (SAMHSA), the number of positive drug tests at worksites around the United States declined steadily from 13.6 percent in 1998 to 3.5 percent in 2012, a 30-year low. However, according to Quest Diagnostics, the positivity rate for urine drug tests increased for the first time in 2013. In 2017, the positivity rate was 4.2 percent. The recent increase in positive tests is "led by a staggeringly fast rise in opiates". Quest also reports an increase in positivity for cocaine, methamphetamine and THC even though the overall positivity rate is relatively stable. As many as 80% of private employers used drug testing in 2017, but the number of employers testing for drugs, especially for marijuana, is declining since the employment market is shrinking and since nine states have legalized marijuana.

In the workplace, drug screens are used for several reasons: prescreening potential job candidates, randomly testing employees as a deterrent and to identify safety hazards, testing if there is a reasonable suspicion that an employee is abusing drugs, and testing following an accident.

Because it is quick and inexpensive, urine testing is most commonly used. Drug testing often uses a 5 drug (cocaine, amphetamine/methamphetamine, opiates, PCP, and THC) or a 10 drug (cocaine, amphetamine/methamphetamine, opiates, PCP, THC,

benzodiazepines, barbiturates, methadone, propoxyphene and methaqualone) panel that tests urine for multiple drugs. Drug tests can either detect the drug directly or metabolites of the drug. The window during which a drug and its metabolites can be detected varies from a few hours to several days and depends on a variety of factors including the person's age, weight, urine pH, metabolic rate and the amount and frequency of drug consumed. Tests using saliva and breath are similar to tests using urine although detection is more difficult. Saliva tests have not been approved for use in the workplace nor have they been approved by the Food and Drug Administration. Although a drug panel analyzes for several drugs simultaneously, specific drugs can be screened if requested. Drug testing can be done in a facility licensed for testing or can be done on site or at home by using one of a variety of available test panels. Although on site testing is less expensive, the tests used vary in their reliability and accuracy.

Urine drug tests usually employs the enzyme multiplied immunoassay technique (EMIT) which is an immunological method based on competitive binding. The test strip uses a drug-enzyme complex, an antibody for the specific drug, and a color reagent which will turn color if the enzyme acts on the reagent. A urine sample migrates up the test strip via capillary action. If no drug or metabolite is present or present below the cut-off level for detection, the drug-enzyme complex and antibody combine preventing the enzyme from acting on the color reagent so no color develops. If, on the other hand, the drug or metabolite is in the urine sample, it will compete with the drug-enzyme conjugate for the antibody and free the drug-enzyme from the antibody allowing the enzyme to act on the reagent resulting in color development. If a test is positive, the test will be repeated. If the test is again positive, it will be confirmed using gas chromatography—mass spectrometry (GC-MS) or liquid chromatography - mass spectrometry.

Color tests expose an unknown drug to a chemical or mixture of chemicals. What color the test substance turns can help determine the type of drug that's present. Here are a few examples of color tests:

Type of Test	Chemicals	What the Results Mean
Marquis Color	Formaldehyde and concentrated sulfuric acid	Heroin, morphine and most opium-based drugs will turn the solution purple. Amphetamines will turn it orange-brown.
Cobalt thiocyanate	Cobalt thiocyanate, distilled water, glycerin, hydrochloric acid, chloroform	Cocaine will turn the liquid blue.
Dillie-Koppanyi	Cobalt acetate and isopropylamine	Barbiturates will turn the solution violet-blue.
VanUrk	P-dimethylaminobenzaldehyde, hydrochloric acid, ethyl alcohol	LSD will turn the solution blue-purple.
Duquenois-Levine Test	Vanillin, acetaldehyde, ethyl alcohol, chloroform	Marijuana will turn the solution purple.

LAW ENFORCEMENT DRUG SCREENING

Law enforcement officials test for drug use by persons involved in automobile and other vehicle accidents to determine if alcohol and/or drugs may have been a factor in causing the accident. Law enforcement often uses drug screens to test persons who have been arrested to determine if that person was under the influence of drugs at the time the alleged crime was committed. Incarcerated persons, parolees and those on probation are often screened for drug use. A positive drug screen for a person on probation or parole often means he or she will be sent to prison because a positive drug screen is usually a violation of the terms of probation or parole.

Over 3000 courts throughout the United States have special drug court dockets that manage cases of persons convicted of drug offenses, and drug testing is an integral part of the program.

Drug testing may be ordered by law enforcement because some drugs are known to escalate the risk of violence. Thus, a person in custody for committing a violent act may be tested for recent use of a drug such as methamphetamine or cocaine which have been linked to violent behavior. According to research by SAMHSA, among adolescents age twelve to seventeen years, all of whom had engaged in violent behavior in the past year, 69.3 percent had used methamphetamine, 61.8 percent had used cocaine, and 61.4 percent had used hallucinogens in the past year.

Marijuana was found to be used by nearly half of the adolescents deemed violent.

ADDITIONAL REASONS FOR DRUG TESTING

The U. S. Anti-Doping Agency (USADA) manages the anti-doping program in the U. S. for those governing bodies involved with Olympic and other international athletic competitions to "Preserve the integrity of competition – Inspire true sport – Protect the rights of athletes". In addition to the USADA, various sports organizations such as major league sports and the National Collegiate Athletics Association (NCAA) have drug testing programs. These programs test for a variety of banned substances including, but not limited to, anabolic steroids and amphetamines.

In 2015, it was announced that the Electronic Sports League, one of the largest leagues in competitive video gaming, would be forming guidelines to institute a testing program for players involved in these e-sports. This decision came after it was revealed that some professional gamers had taken drugs such as Adderall to sharpen their focus during competitive gaming tournaments.

A 2002 ruling by the US Supreme Court (*Pottawatomie County v. Earls*) expanded the testing of student-athletes (Vernonia School District 47J v. Acton) to allow schools to randomly test non-athletes participating in competitive extracurricular activities. Schools that adopt such programs believe that random testing can deter students from abusing drugs and believe that testing allows for the identification of students with drug problems who would benefit from counseling. Many schools also use reasonable suspicion/cause testing if the school suspects or has evidence that a student is using drugs.

Pain management physicians may test their patients to ensure they are taking only the drugs that are prescribed and not taking any additional drugs of misuse. Some people who are prescribed drugs such as opiates, amphetamines, and benzodiazepines divert (mostly sell) their drugs to others. In this case, a negative test for the prescribed drug is problematic and indicates that the person is not taking the prescribed drug. Some pain management physicians require patients to sign a contract indicating that they are willing to be tested randomly for drugs. If the patient refuses to sign the contract, the physician will not provide treatment.

Persons admitted to emergency rooms with an altered mental state are often tested for drugs to help medical professionals determine whether the behavior is likely caused by drug misuse or by mental illness. One complicating factor is that some mentally ill persons also misuse drugs. It should be noted that few mentally ill persons are violent. However, research has indicated that the misuse of alcohol and drugs escalates the risk for violence among people with mental illness.

Substance use treatment facilities may require drug screening to ensure that patients in the facility are not using drugs that they have acquired illicitly, that is, drugs brought to the facility by visitors or others. Child protection workers may request drug screening to verify that former individuals who had misused or neglected their children in the past are no longer using drugs. Sometimes, young children are tested for drugs, particularly if it is known that a parent has used drugs. If drugs are found in a child, the child may be removed from his or her home. Additionally, small children often ingest drugs carelessly left in reach of children by those suffering with substance use disorders which leave these children at risk for cardiovascular or neurological symptoms, even death.

Pros and Cons of Testing Methods

Although urine is the most commonly screened body fluid, organizations do employ other means

for screening for drugs. Each screening method has advantages and disadvantages. For example, because hair grows about one-half inch per month, testing of the hair can determine the presence of drugs from several months prior to the test. With some exceptions, screens of blood or urine can detect drugs used within hours or days. As a result, if recent use of drugs is sought, then tests of the urine or blood are preferable, and if information on long-term drug use detection is sought, then hair testing may be preferable.

Another factor in determining what test to employ is the speed at which the test results are needed. Urine and blood test results usually can be obtained rapidly. In contrast, hair must be sent to a specialized laboratory for analysis. Oral fluid testing, often referred to as saliva testing, can be done on-site although this test is not as commonly used as urine and blood testing.

The reliability of a given test is another factor to consider. For example, hair testing can be affected by hair bleaches and dyes. Up to 60 percent of drugs may be removed through such processes. The drugs least affected by cosmetic substances for the hair include cannabis (marijuana and hashish) and opiates. Urine testing and blood testing are highly reliable although false positives can occur with urine testing. In addition, often there is no first-hand observation of the collection of urine for testing, as is with blood, hair, or oral fluids. As a result, some people deliberately attempt to alter urine test results by, for example, submitting the urine of another (likely drug-free) person.

The invasiveness of a given test is sometimes a consideration in choosing the type of test. Saliva testing is considered noninvasive because it requires that the person simply expectorate multiple times into a special container. Hair testing is noninvasive because it requires cutting only a few strands of hair close to the scalp. Urine testing is not considered invasive. Conversely, blood testing is the most invasive form of testing because it requires the penetration of the skin to collect the blood.

Drug Positives and False Positives

The accuracy of the tests, especially the rapid urine tests, varies depending on the specific test used and the manufacturer. From 5% to 10% of the tests give a false positive result whereas 10% to 15% of the tests give a false negative result. There are many factors including the consumption of some foods and legally prescribed and/or over-the-counter drugs that can

Drug testing and poppy seeds

Eating pastries and other food products with poppy seeds can cause positive test results for heroin. Opiates (such as heroin, morphine, and codeine) can be found in urine samples for as long as two days after eating poppy-seed-containing foods and for up to sixty hours if large quantities of the seeds are consumed.

Hair analysis is a more accurate, but less commonly used method of testing for recent heroin use. In a hair analysis, a false-positive test result would not occur after eating food containing poppy seeds.

One high-profile demonstration of the validity of poppy seed drug-test claims was conducted on the Discovery Channel's television program *MythBusters*. One participant ate a poppy seed cake and tested positive for opiates one-half hour later. The other participant ate three poppy seed bagels and tested positive two hours later. Both participants continued to test positive for sixteen hours.

lead to a false positive. Nonsteroidal anti-inflammatory drugs (NSAIDs) may give a false positive for the use of marijuana and/or barbiturates. The use of a Vicks inhaler and antidepressants such as bupropion, desipramine, and trazadone may give a false positive result for amphetamine use. The use of sertraline (Zoloft), a commonly used antidepressant, may give a false positive for benzodiazepine. Since a false positive can lead to a person not being hired for a position or a person facing disciplinary action, all false positives should be confirmed by an additional test.

Christine Adamec BA, MBA;
Updated by Charles L. Vigue, PhD

FOR FURTHER INFORMATION

American Management Association. "Medical Testing 2004 Survey." *American Management Association.* Amer. Management Assn., 3 Sept. 2003. Web. 11 Mar. 2011.

"Company Drug Testing: What Causes a False Positive Result?" DrugTestsInBulk.com. Jun 29, 2017. Web 30 July 2018.

"Frequently Asked Questions about Drug Testing in Schools". National Institute on Drug Abuse. NIH, May 2017 Web 30 July 2018.

Heller, Jacob. "Toxicology Screen." *MedlinePlus.* US Natl. Library of Medicine, 12 Feb. 2009. Web. 8 Mar. 2011.

Moller, Monique, Joey Gareri, and Gideon Koren. "A Review of Substance Abuse Monitoring in a Social Services Context: A Primer for Child Protection Workers." *Canadian Journal of Clinical Pharmacology* 17.1 (2010): 177–93. Web. 5 Mar. 2012.

Nasky, Kevin M., George L. Cowan, and Douglas R. Knittel. "False-Positive Urine Screening for Benzodiazepines: An Association with Sertraline? A Two-Year Retrospective Chart Analysis." *Psychiatry* 6.7 (2009): 36–39. Print.

Reynolds, Lawrence A. "Historical Aspects of Drugs-of-Abuse Testing in the United States." *Drugs of Abuse: Body Fluid Testing.* Eds. Raphael C. Wong and Harley Y. Tse. Totowa: Humana, 2010. Print.

US Department of Health and Human Services. "Mandatory Guidelines for Federal Workplace Drug Testing Programs." *Federal Register.* Federal Register, 25 Nov. 2008. Web. 11 Mar. 2011.

Vincent, E. Chris, Arthur Zebelman, and Cheryl Goodwin. "What Common Substances Can Cause False Positives on Urine Screens for Drugs of Abuse?" *Journal of Family Practice* 55.10 (2006). Web. 5 Mar. 2012.

Wingfield, Nick, and Conor Dougherty. "Drug Testing Is Coming to E-sports." *New York Times.* New York Times, 23 July 2015. Web. 29 Oct. 2015.

"Workforce Drug Positivity at Highest Rate in a Decade, Finds Analysis of More Than 10 Million Drug Test Results". Quest Diagnostics. 8 May 2018. Web. 30 July 2018.

See also: Diagnosis methods; Law enforcement and drugs; Legislation and substance misuse; Prevention methods and research; Screening for behavioral addictions

Drugged driving

Category: Social issues

Also known as: Driving under the influence; impaired driving

Definition: Drugged driving is the operation of a vehicle with a measurable quantity of an abusive or nonabusive substance in the body. Impaired driving results from any amount of illicit substance, such as heroin, cocaine, and marijuana, and impairing amounts of legal substances, such as sedatives or prescription painkillers. Driving under the influence of drugs can be particularly pronounced when the substance or substances are combined with alcohol.

Statistics

Drugged driving has become a growing problem in the United States and across the globe; twenty-first-century rates in the United States approach those of drunk driving, and the US Centers for Disease Control and Prevention estimates that 18 percent of vehicle accidents annually are related to drugs. Data collected by survey and reporting organizations, such as the Fatality Analysis Reporting System and the Monitoring the Future drug-use survey in teenagers, suggest that drugs are identified seven times more often than alcohol in youth drivers on weekend nights.

Nearly one-third of high school seniors admit to riding with an impaired driver or driving a car while impaired from drug use. Marijuana is the primary drug associated with drugged driving in youth and all other age groups; the second and third most frequently used are cocaine and methamphetamines, respectively.

A growing concern is the contribution of prescription painkillers and sedatives to drugged driving. In the United States, impaired driving rates from benzodiazepines or opiates approach those of drugged driving with cocaine.

Risk Groups

People age fifty-five years and older are at particular risk of impaired driving from the sedating effects of prescription drugs through normal use or misuse. Any person who uses a sedating prescription or nonprescription drug may experience impaired driving; people who obtain multiple prescriptions of painkillers, sedatives, or antidepressants are most likely to experience drug misuse and driving impairment.

The most common drugged-driving risk group, however, is youth, especially new drivers. Approximately 25 percent of vehicle-related fatalities that occur each year involve drivers younger than age twenty-five years. Prior offenders of drunk or drugged driving laws comprise another at-risk population.

Testing

Documenting drugged driving is complicated, in part because impairment thresholds are frequently unknown and evaluation methods are not standardized. For example, studies show that marijuana and stimulants increase the likelihood of poor decision-making and response times while driving. Connecting the use of these drugs with specific vehicle crashes is difficult, however, because of overlapping use, low testing rates, and poor understanding of the behaviors that cause reckless driving. Better and more frequent drug testing can support the connection between drug use and impaired driving.

Testing for drug impairment is more complex than testing for blood alcohol content (BAC). Choices about what drugs to test for and what methods to use remain unclear. Because drug levels in the body fluctuate nonlinearly, tested concentrations are not always predictive of effect. In addition, circulating drug metabolites can impair ability at least as much as the original drug but may not affect test results. Finally, drug testing must be conducted rapidly, because the primary drug can dissipate within hours despite lingering impairment.

Testing can be performed on urine, blood, or oral fluids. Blood tests report the most accurate drug concentrations but are invasive, costly, and time consuming. Urine is less indicative of drug effects and is difficult to test reliably in the field. Both blood and urine testing can require offsite laboratory evaluation, which adds to the cost and timeliness of results.

Oral fluid testing, conversely, is easy to administer and provides reasonable accuracy. However, these tests still do not evaluate metabolites, and they do not always have evidence-based cut points that reflect impairment. Oral kits have become preferred for field use because they are rapid-use tests that do not require a laboratory. Although rapid tests provide the best option for identifying drugged drivers quickly and are more accessible for law enforcement, they have lower sensitivity and more false positives than laboratory tests.

A barrier to frequent drugged-driving testing is appropriate drug identification. Law enforcement must identify behaviors representing drug use before ordering tests; the ability to distinguish the types of drugs by symptoms is crucial to minimize what drugs are tested for. Drug-recognition-expert programs are being developed to address this need and to educate law enforcement officers about the symptoms of specific drug use.

PREVENTION

Prevention is implemented through the education of three populations: new drivers, who are often unaware that drugged driving poses risks and consequences similar to those of drunk driving; law enforcement professionals, who need to identify and test persons who are suspected of drugged driving; and health professionals, who can identify risks associated with specific prescriptions or persons on multiple high-risk drugs.

A reduction in drugged driving rates and prevention of future offenses requires improved testing technology and application, greater professional education and outreach efforts, and broad public-health awareness campaigns. These efforts can be supplemented by clear legal restrictions, especially zero tolerance policies for illicit drug use while driving. Partnered efforts for public education, especially youth antidrug campaigns, are necessary deterrents, as are fines and arrests for drugged driving.

Over-the-counter and prescription drugs pose a greater challenge for prevention and legislation, as these drugs are legal and common. However, even therapeutic dosages can affect driving in some people. The efforts of health professionals to educate the public about the sedating effects of legal drugs and about the risks of misuse and drugged driving should be at the forefront.

Nicole M. Van Hoey PharmD

FOR FURTHER INFORMATION

"DrugFacts: Drugged Driving." *National Institute on Drug Abuse.* NIH, May 2015. Web.27 Oct. 2015.

Institute for Behavior and Health. "Drugged Driving Research: A White Paper." 31 Mar. 2011. Web. 2 Apr. 2012. http://www.whitehouse.gov/sites/default/files/ondcp/issues-content/drugged-driving/nida_dd_paper.pdf.

Maxwell, J. C. "Drunk Versus Drugged: How Different Are the Drivers?" *Drug and Alcohol Dependence* 121 (2012): 68–72. Print.

National Institute on Drug Abuse. "What Is Drugged Driving?" Dec. 2010. Web. 2 Apr. 2012. http://www.drugabuse.gov/publications/infofacts/drugged-driving.

Office of National Drug Control Policy. "Teen Drugged Driving Toolkit: Parent, Coalition, and Community Group Activity Guide." Web. http://whitehouse.gov/ondcp/drugged-driving.

See also: Designated drivers; Drunk driving; Law enforcement and drugs

---

Drunk driving

CATEGORY: Social issues

ALSO KNOWN AS: Alcohol-impaired driving; driving under the influence; driving while intoxicated

DEFINITION: By law, a driver of any motor vehicle is impaired by alcohol if his or her blood alcohol content is 0.08 percent [0.08 grams of alcohol per 100 milliliters (0.08 grams/deciliter, dl) of blood] or higher.

DRUNK DRIVING LAWS

Forty-nine US states have enacted a law making it illegal to drive with a blood alcohol content (BAC) of 0.08 percent [0.08 grams of alcohol per 100 milliliters (0.08 grams/deciliter, dl) of blood] or higher. In 2017, Utah enacted a law making it illegal to drive with a BAC of 0.05 percent or higher. Several states are considering following the Utah example. Most states make it illegal for drivers with a commercial license (buses and trucks for examples) to have a BAC over 0.04%. Also, each US state has set the minimum drinking age to twenty-one years and has established a zero-tolerance law that prohibits people younger than twenty-one years of age from driving after drinking. Most zero-tolerance laws set the drinking limit to a BAC of between 0.00 and 0.02 percent. Drivers convicted of alcohol-impaired driving (driving under the influence, DUI, driving while intoxicated, DWI) face suspension or revocation of their license.

Drivers who refuse to undergo BAC testing or who fail the test can have their license taken away immediately under a process called administrative license suspension, and the length of time a license is suspended ranges from seven days to one year, depending on the state. Many states will consider restoring limited driving privileges during a suspension if the person demonstrates a special hardship (such as needing to drive to work).

A mechanism that prevents suspended or probationary drivers from operating a vehicle while impaired by alcohol is the ignition interlock device or the breath alcohol ignition interlock device. This device is attached to the vehicle's ignition and forces the driver, before being able to start the vehicle, to blow into the device for an analysis of the driver's blood alcohol level. A device that registers a BAC of 0.08 or above will lock the vehicle's ignition and prevent the operator from starting the vehicle. Feasibility studies are also underway to examine alcohol ignition locks for motorcycles.

EFFECTS OF ALCOHOL.

Alcohol is quickly absorbed into the bloodstream and travels throughout the body and to the brain within thirty to seventy minutes of having an alcoholic drink. In the US, a standard alcoholic beverage (such as a twelve-ounce beer, a five-ounce glass of wine, or one shot of liquor) is defined as 6 fluid ounces (14 grams) of pure alcohol. How quickly a person's BAC rises will depend primarily on the amount of beverage consumed, the rate of consumption, and the amount of food in the person's stomach. Other factors that influence the rise in BAC are the person's weight, gender, age, excretory and metabolic rates. Some of these factors are, in part, determined by genetics and the environment. Having food in the stomach helps slow the absorption of alcohol through the stomach walls into the bloodstream. Moreover, heavier people

---

Sobriety checkpoints

The sobriety checkpoint, or roadblock, is a law enforcement tool used to arrest drunk drivers and to deter driving while intoxicated. Specifically, sobriety checkpoints occur when law enforcement officers set up a roadblock and stop cars to determine if their drivers have been drinking alcohol. According to the US Centers for Disease Control and Prevention, accidents involving drunk drivers were reduced by 20 percent in US states that have sobriety checkpoints. Thirteen states do not use sobriety checkpoints.

Sobriety checkpoints raise concerns, however. One is racial profiling and another is the targeting of unlicensed drivers. If a driver is unlicensed, his or her car can be impounded, making money for the state but penalizing drivers stopped at checkpoints who were not drunk. A third issue is the constitutionality of a sobriety checkpoint. Opponents say it violates the constitutional (Fourth Amendment) right against unreasonable searches.

---

have more water in their body, and this water dilutes their BAC. Women typically have less water and more body fat than men, and alcohol is not easily absorbed into fat cells, so more alcohol is absorbed into the bloodstream.

The effects brought on by alcohol start to appear with a BAC of 0.02 percent. These effects include a loss of judgment and a decline in the driver's ability to quickly track moving objects or perform two tasks at a time. Once a person's BAC reaches 0.05, the risk of a fatal crash substantially increases. At this level, the person is less alert and coordinated, has trouble focusing, has difficulty steering the vehicle, and is slower to respond to emergency driving situations. At a BAC of 0.08 percent, muscle coordination is affected, and the driver will have difficulty concentrating and controlling the vehicle, will have short-term memory loss, will have problems processing information (for example, signal detection), and will show impaired reasoning and depth perception. With a BAC of 0.10 the driver's reaction time and control deteriorates, cognitive ability slows further, and driving becomes even more difficult. By the time a driver's BAC reaches 0.15 percent, he or she shows a major loss of balance, impaired processing of information, inattention, and little control of the vehicle.

STATISTICS

The National Highway Traffic Safety Administration's National Center for Statistics and Analysis (NCSA) tracks statistics on alcohol-impaired driving and reports these results annually. The NCSA states that any fatal crash in which a driver has a BAC of 0.08 percent or higher is an alcohol-impaired-driving crash, and fatalities resulting from this crash are alcohol-impaired-driving fatalities. They further clarify that *alcohol-impaired* does not mean that the crash or the fatality was solely caused by alcohol impairment.

Another organization that monitors and reports statistics annually is the Insurance Institute for Highway Safety (IIHS). This organization uses data from the US Department of Transportation's Fatality Analysis Reporting System to analyze and report statistics.

FATALITIES

Some progress has been made to reduce alcohol-impaired driving and related injuries and deaths since about 1980. Reports from the NCSA and the IIHS show that from 1982 to 1994, the United States had a 32 percent decline in deaths among drivers with a BAC at or above 0.08. This decline has leveled off in fatalities per year, and alcohol-related traffic fatalities declined by 23 percent between 2004 and 2013. Between the early 1980s and early 2010s, alcohol-related traffic deaths per population have declined by 50 percent, with the greatest proportional declines among

individuals between the ages of sixteen and twenty. In the mid-1970s, alcohol was a factor in nearly two-thirds of all traffic fatalities. By 2013, alcohol was involved in roughly one-third of all traffic deaths. From 2012 to 2013, deaths in alcohol-related traffic accidents declined by 2.5 percent.

In 2016, alcohol impaired driving fatalities accounted for 28% of all motor vehicle traffic deaths. Of the 10,497 people who died in alcohol-impaired-driving crashes in 2016, there were 6,479 drivers (62%) who had BACs of 0.08 percent or higher. Of the children age fourteen years and younger who were killed in motor vehicle crashes in 2016, 54% were in a vehicle with a driver with a BAC of 0.08 percent or higher, 29% were occupants of other vehicles and 17% were either pedestrians or cyclists.

Time of day and day of the week are important indicators of an increased incidence of alcohol-impaired driving deaths. Midnight to 3 a.m. is the deadliest time for intoxicated drivers involved in crashes. The incidence of alcohol-impaired drivers involved in fatal crashes was nearly four times higher at night than at daytime and was two times higher on weekends than on weekdays.

DRIVER CHARACTERISTICS

Age is a significant predictor of a person driving drunk and being involved in a fatal crash. In 2016, 27% of drivers between the ages of 25 and 34 involved with a fatality had a BAC of 0.08 percent or higher. The percentages for other ages are 15% for ages 16 to 20, 26% for ages 21 to 24, 22% for ages 35 to 44, 19% for ages 45 to 54, 14% for ages 55 to 64, 9% for ages 65 to 74, and 5% for ages 75 and older.

Male drivers are consistently more likely to be involved in an alcohol related fatality in all age groups. In 2016, of those drivers involved in a traffic fatality, 21% of the males had a BAC of 0.08 percent or higher while 14 % of females had a BAC of 0.08 percent or higher.

Christine G. Holzmueller, BLA;
Updated by Charles L. Vigue, PhD

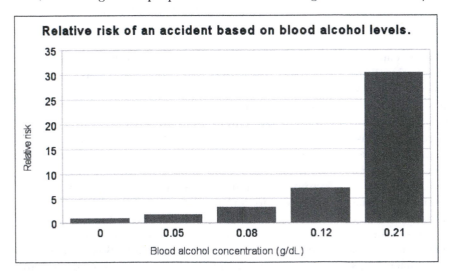

Relative risk of an accident based on blood alcohol levels.

Blood alcohol concentration (g/dL)

The relative risk of an accident increases exponentially with higher levers of BAC. (James Heilman, MD via Wikimedia Commons)

FOR FURTHER INFORMATION

"The ABCs of BAC: A Guide to Understanding Blood Alcohol Concentration and Alcohol Impairment." *National Highway Traffic Safety Administration.* Natl. Highway Traffic Safety Admin., n.d. Web. July 2016.

"Alcohol-Impaired Driving." *Insurance Institute for Highway Safety, 2015 Data.* Dec. 2016, https://crashstats.nhtsa.dot.gov/Api/Public/ViewPublication/812350. Accessed 1 Oct. 2017.

"Alcohol-Impaired Driving." Governors Highway Safety Association. 2017. Web. Accessed 27 July 2018.

Dasgupta, Amitava. *The Science of Drinking: How Alcohol Affects Your Body and Mind.* Lanham: Rowman, 2011. Print.

"Drunk Driving Laws." *Governors Highway Safety Association.* Governors Highway Safety Assn., Oct. 2015. Web. 27 Oct. 2015.

"Impaired Driving: Get the Facts." *Injury Prevention and Control: Motor Vehicle Safety.* Centers for Disease Control and Prevention, 16 June 2017. Web. Accessed 27 July 2018.

Natl. Highway Traffic Safety Admin. "Traffic Safety Facts, 2017 Data: Alcohol-Impaired Driving." *National Center for Statistics and Analysis.* Natl. Highway Traffic Safety Admin., Oct. 2017. Web. 27 July 2018.

See also: Designated drivers; Drugged driving; Mothers Against Drunk Driving (MADD); Students Against Destructive Decisions (SADD)

DSM-5: Diagnostic and Statistical Manual of Mental Disorders

CATEGORY: Treatment; research development

DEFINITION: Published in 2013 by the American Psychiatric Association, the *Diagnostic and Statistical Manual of Mental Disorder, 5th Edition,* is a widely used classification system for psychological disorders.

KEY TERMS:

Biopsychosocial history: an integrated approach that incorporates biological, psychological, and sociological data from a person's history.

Mental disorder: also referred to as a psychological disturbance, it is characterized by clinically significant symptoms that can adversely impact an individual's emotion, cognition, or behavior. It is usually associated with distress in one's life.

Nosology: this is the area of medicine that deals with the classification of diseases.

PURPOSE OF THE *DSM*

The *DSM-5* is the most current edition of a manual, published by the American Psychiatric Association (APA) that is widely used by mental and behavioral health professionals to increase the objectivity, precision, and accuracy of diagnosing mental disorders. The primary audience for the manual includes all types of mental health practitioners such as psychologists, psychiatrists, social workers, nurses, counselors and occupational therapists. In addition, the *DSM-5* can be a valuable resource to patients and their family members, support staff, legal specialists, and those who conduct research into mental health.

The *DSM-5* was published in 2013 as an updated version to the *DSM-IV-TR* (published in 2000). This latest version of the *DSM* was the product of a 12-year process that involved recruiting experienced mental health practitioners and academic researchers, of a wide range of multidisciplinary expertise, to participate on a taskforce that was divided into 13 different diagnostic work groups. The *DSM-5* includes descriptions of 19 categories of disorders (e.g., depressive disorders, anxiety disorders, substance-related and addictive disorders, etc.). In addition to these 19, a section on "other mental disorders" is used to capture mental disorders that do not fit the criteria for those previously discussed. An example of this "other" category would be an individual who experiences dissociative symptoms that includes forgetting large portions of his past, yet the condition was brought on by another medical condition such as complex partial seizures.

The *DSM-5* is accompanied with a web-based comprehensive assessment of clinical symptoms of mental health through the introduction of cross-cutting measures. More than 60 cross-cutting symptoms are organized into two levels. Level 1 measures include a brief screening of 13 domain areas for adults and 12 domain areas for children and adolescents. These areas include conditions such as depression, anxiety, suicidal ideation, anger, mania, psychosis, substance use, among others. After the assessment for Level 1 clinical symptoms are applied, Level 2 measures give a more in-depth assessment of elevated conditions along with measures that assess the severity of the disorder. The APA provides practitioners access to these assessment measures at no cost (the website is listed under additional resources). It is important to note that clinical training and experience is needed to use the *DSM-5* to properly diagnose a mental illness. The manual is not intended to be used by a non-trained layperson as a means to diagnose self or others.

A major objective of the *DSM-5* is to provide clinical utility to mental health professionals. This includes helping clinicians communicate clinical information to counselors, patients and their families. Another objective is to help clinicians implement effective treatment interventions to bring about better clinical outcomes. In order to accomplish this, practitioners need to be able to differentiate a mental health disorder from a non-disorder. Most significantly of all, the *DSM-5* provides a classification system that serves as a common language for mental health practitioners and researchers who come from a variety of theoretical orientations (psychodynamic, cognitive-behavioral, humanistic, client-centered, etc.) to be able to communicate with each other. If a group of counselors start a conversation on the topic of opioid use disorder, their common knowledge derived from the *DSM-5* enables them to better understand the clinically significant markers, regardless of their differing theoretical orientations.

CHARACTERISTICS OF *DSM-5* THAT FACILITATE ACCURATE DIAGNOSIS AND ASSESSMENT

The *DSM-5* is moving away from a categorical classification system that treats mental disorders as independent conditions and moving toward becoming a nosology that acknowledges most mental disorders are behaviorally heterogeneous with overlapping symptomology. This new emphasis reflects current research that demonstrates mental disorders are not usually seen as clearly delineated, narrowly defined categories. It is more common to see diagnostic criteria shared among several disorders. This could be due to the presence of multiple risk factors that are common to mental disorders and the possibility of comorbidity.

The *DSM-5* is not to be seen as a simple check off list for the number of primary symptoms associated with a particular disorder. When making a diagnosis, a mental health professional needs to consider a patient's clinical history and explore the psychological, social, and biological factors that might have contributed to the disorder. This includes taking into consideration cultural issues such as differences in cultural norms regarding specific behaviors. In addition, it is important to note that making a proper diagnosis is not the same as affirming that treatment is needed. The *DSM-5* does not attempt to provide practitioners with recommendations for treatment of any particular disorder.

Since ongoing clinical practice and research into mental illness continually broadens our understanding of the psychological, sociological, and medical aspects of these problems, it is expected and necessary to periodically revise diagnostic criteria. Just as has been the case with the *DSM-5* and its previous versions, future editions will delineate new disorders and subtypes. In some instances, this will require the deletion of current disorders. The *DSM* will always remain a work in progress.

Bryan C. Auday, PhD

FOR FURTHER INFORMATION

American Psychiatric Association. *Diagnostic and Statistical Manual of Mental disorders* (5th ed.). Arlington, VA: Author, (2013). This is the complete reference for the newest version of the *DSM*.

Buckley, Matthew R. "Back to Basics: Using the *DSM-5* to Benefit Clients." *The Professional Counselor*. Vol. 4, No. 3, (2014) 159-165. This lead article in a special issue of *The Professional Counselor* on the changes made in the *DSM-5* from its previous edition emphasizes how mental health professionals can apply these changes to assist them in making reliable diagnoses.

Cooper, Rachel. *Diagnosing the Diagnostic and Statistical Manual of Mental Disorders*. Philadelphia: Taylor & Francis, 2014. This book provides some of the background on how the *DSM-5* was developed. In addition, it offers a critique of some of the changes found in the new edition.

King, Jason H. "Clinical Application of the *DSM-5* in Private Counseling Practice." *The Professional Counselor*. Vol. 4, No. 3, (2014) 202-215. This article addresses some of the changes between *DSM*-IV-TR and *DSM-5*. In addition, a clinical scenario is presented to help counselors see how the new edition can be applied to clinical practice.

DSM-5: Criteria for substance use disorders

Category: Diagnosis and prevention

Definition: Substance use disorder describes the use or misuse of a substance that leads to impaired control, social impairment, risky behaviors, and/or pharmacological dependence.

Prevalence of Substance Use

The 2016 National Study on Drug Use and Health indicated that an estimated 28.6 million Americans over the age of 12 used at least one illicit substance during the month prior to when the study was conducted. The Substance Abuse and Mental Health Services Administration (SAMHSA) estimated that, during the year 2017, approximately 20.2 million adults (8.4% of the population) had a substance use disorder. Approximately 7.9 million adults had both a mental disorder and substance use disorder. Of note, in the year 2014, about 21.5 million adults in America (8.1% of the population) were diagnosed with a substance use disorder. The juxtaposition between these two years indicates an overall trend in increase of substance use within the United States. Marijuana is the most commonly used substance, followed by pain reduction medication.

Of particular note, the increase of use (both prescription and illegal) of controlled substances (e.g. pain medication) has surged substantially. For example, benzodiazepine prescription use (for adults) increased approximately 67 percent (from 8.1 million to 13.5 million) between the years of 1996 and 2013. Approximately 54 million adults have used prescription drugs for nonmedical reasons at some point in their life. With respect to gender use, men are more likely to die from opioid overdose, however the gap between overuse and death in men and women is shrinking. Perhaps most notably, between the years of 1996 and 2013, the rate of overdose and death from benzodiazepines more than quadrupled.

Although research methods have increased the accuracy of prevalence rates of substance use, the statistics are limited in several ways. Many users do not present for treatment or are unwilling to acknowledge their misuse of the substance. Additionally, users who do engage in some form of treatment may be inconsistent in their reporting of use or attendance in treatment.

DSM-5 Definition and Criteria

The chapter "Substance-Related and Addictive Disorders" is made up of 10 different (but not mutually exclusive) classes of substances: alcohol, caffeine, cannabis, hallucinogens, inhalants, opioids, sedatives (including hypnotics and anxiolytics), stimulants, tobacco, and other (or unknown) substances. The commonality amongst these substances includes stimulation of neurotransmitters in the brain, which lead to a reinforcement, and often increase, of use. The elevated level of reward from use often creates a scenario in which use may be accelerated to achieve an even greater degree of reward. In operant conditioning terms, the use becomes a positive reinforcement paradigm, as the substance consumption leads to the psychophysiological reaction that drives further (and often more frequent and intense) use.

Additionally, substance-related disorders are further separated into two groups: substance-induced and substance use disorders. Examples of substance-induced disorders include (but are not limited to): intoxication, withdrawal and other substance/medication-induced mental disorders (psychotic disorders, anxiety disorders, obsessive-compulsive and related disorders, sexual dysfunctions, and neurocognitive disorders).

In past versions of the DSM (e.g. the DSM-IV-TR, the edition of the DSM which immediately preceded the DSM 5), the delineation between substance use and substance dependence was modeled on the concept that chronic use would eventually lead to psychological, physiological (or both) dependence, which would lead ultimately to addiction. In the chapter (Substance-Related and Addictive Disorders) within the DSM 5, care is taken to note that a person may use a substance in a non-abusive manner; such as taking a prescribed opioid for pain as managed by a physician, and yet still develop a dependence on the substance. This example is all too common amongst community providers in the United States, as almost one-third (up to 29%) of patients prescribed opioids for pain management use them in a manner other than prescribed.

DIAGNOSTIC CRITERIA

For a diagnosis of substance use disorder to be made, a minimum of two of the eleven criteria must be met. As previously noted, many DSM 5 diagnoses are evaluated and qualified based on severity. For substance use disorders, an individual endorsing two to three criteria indicates a mild substance use disorder, endorsing four to five criteria indicates a moderate substance use disorder, and endorsing six or more of the eleven criteria indicates a severe substance use disorder. The eleven possible criteria for diagnosis are subdivided into four categories: impaired control, social impairment, risky use, and pharmacological dependence.

Although each substance use diagnosis has its own set of standards, the eleven criteria cover the general picture of the chapter. As the DSM 5 explains, a Substance Use Disorder is indicated when: A problematic pattern of substance use leading to clinically significant impairment or distress, as manifested by at least two of the following, occurring within a 12 month period: 1. The substance is often taken in larger amounts or over a longer period than was intended; 2. There is a persistent desire or unsuccessful efforts to cut down or control the substance use; 3. A great deal of time is spent in activities necessary to obtain the substance, use the substance, or recover from its effects; 4. Craving, or a strong desire or urge to use the substance; 5. Recurrent substance use resulting in a failure to fulfill major role obligations at work, school, or home; 6. Continued Substance use despite having persistent or recurrent social or interpersonal problems caused or exacerbated by the effects of the substance; 7. Important social, occupational, or recreational activities are given up or reduced because of substance use; 8. Recurrent substance use in situations in which it is physically hazardous; 9. Substance use is continued despite knowledge of having a persistent or recurrent physical or psychological problem that is likely to have been caused or exacerbated by the substance; 10. Tolerance, as defined by either of the following: A need for markedly increased amounts of the substance to achieve intoxication or desired effect, and/or a markedly diminished effect with continued use of the same amount of the substance; 11. Withdrawal, as manifested by either of the following: The characteristic withdrawal syndrome for the substance, and/or the substance (or closely related substance,

such as benzodiazepine with alcohol) is taken to relieve or avoid withdrawal symptoms.

Several specifiers are also noted for Substance-Related and Addictive Disorders in the DSM 5. The specifier of "In Early Remission" is indicated only after the diagnostic criteria for substance use disorder were previously met and none of the criteria for the substance use disorder have been met for at least three (but for less than 12) months. The specifier "In Sustained Remission" is indicated only after the diagnostic criteria for substance use disorder were previously met, and <u>none</u> of the criteria for a substance use disorder have been met at any time during a period of at least 12 months. The specifier "In a Controlled Environment" may be used if the person is in an environment where access to the substance is restricted (e.g. incarceration, rehabilitation program). Lastly, the specifier "On Maintenance Therapy" may be used if the person is taking a prescribed agonist medication (e.g. methadone, buprenorphine) and none of the criteria for opioid use disorder have been met for that class of medication (excluding tolerance to, or withdrawal from, the agonist).

An additional, non-substance related disorder is also described in this *DSM-5* chapter. Gambling Disorder is diagnosed by the presence of persistent and recurrent problematic gambling behavior leading to clinically significant impairment or distress. Nine criteria are listed for consideration, with a minimum of four criteria needed for a diagnosis of mild gambling disorder. In addition to the previously described specifiers of "In early remission" and "In sustained remission," two additional specifiers are available for this diagnosis. The specifier "Episodic" can be indicated when the person meets the diagnostic criteria at more than one instance, with the symptom abating between periods of clinically significant gambling behavior. The specifier "Persistent" may be indicated when the individual is experiencing the uninterrupted presence of symptoms, typically for multiple years.

SUBSTANCE USE DISORDERS INDICATED FOR FURTHER STUDY

Section III of the DSM 5 is reserved for disorders which require further evaluation and study before elevation to formal clinical disorder status. Two potential disorders are noteworthy for clinicians who study and treat substance use and addictive disorders. "Caffeine Use Disorder" refers to the potential addictive behavior that is caused by excessive and sustained consumption of caffeine. "Internet Gaming Disorder" describes a condition in which the compulsive preoccupation individuals may develop when participating in online gaming leads to the disregard, exclusion or abandonment of responsibilities or priorities. These potential disorders, in addition to several other (non-substance/addiction related) diagnoses are currently being evaluated for potential inclusion in the next edition of the DSM; which at the time of this publication has not yet been determined.

Robert S. Cavera, PsyD

FOR FURTHER INFORMATION

American Psychiatric Association. *Diagnostic and Statistical Manual of Mental Disorders.* 5th ed. Washington, DC: Author, 2013. Print.

Grant, B. F., Goldstein, R. B., Saha, T. D., Chou, S. P., Jung, J., Zhang, H., & Hasin, D. S. (2015). "Epidemiology of *DSM-5* alcohol use disorder: results from the National Epidemiologic Survey on Alcohol and Related Conditions III." *JAMA psychiatry,* 72(8), 757-766.

Hasin, D. S., Kerridge, B. T., Saha, T. D., Huang, B., Pickering, R., Smith, S. M., & Grant, B. F. (2016). "Prevalence and correlates of *DSM-5* cannabis use disorder, 2012-2013: findings from the National Epidemiologic Survey on Alcohol and Related Conditions–III." *American Journal of Psychiatry,* 173(6), 588-599.

King, D. L., & Delfabbro, P. H. (2013). "Issues for DSM-5: Video-gaming disorder?" *Australian & New Zealand Journal of Psychiatry,* 47(1), 20-22.

O'Brien, C. (2011). "Addiction and dependence in DSM V." *Addiction, 106*(5), 866-867.

Petry, N. M., Rehbein, F., Gentile, D. A., Lemmens, J. S., Rumpf, H. J., Mößle, T., & Auriacombe, M. (2014). "An international consensus for assessing internet gaming disorder using the new DSM 5 approach." *Addiction, 109*(9), 1399-1406.

Saha, T. D., Kerridge, B. T., Goldstein, R. B., Chou, S. P., Zhang, H., Jung, J., & Hasin, D. S. (2016). "Nonmedical prescription opioid use and DSM-5 nonmedical prescription opioid use disorder in the United States." *The Journal of clinical psychiatry,* 77(6), 772.

See also: Addiction; Alcohol misuse; Diagnosis methods; Drug misuse and addiction: Overview; Substance misuse

E

Economic impact of addiction

CATEGORY: Social issues

DEFINITION: The economic impact of drug and alcohol addiction includes the cost associated with drug and alcohol misuse as expressed in U.S. dollars, both in dollars spent (also called direct or resource costs) and in dollars not earned (also called indirect or productivity costs). The indirect costs are very difficult to measure.

ECONOMIC IMPACT OF THE DRUG OR ALCOHOL ADDICTED PERSON

The total costs of psychological changes due to addictions is difficult to calculate in dollars, since the costs of these changes vary with each person and where they live in the United States (U.S.) Many of these numbers need to be estimated and it is unrealistic to estimate the data by person. The types of addictions that are discussed are drug and alcohol misuse.

U.S. STATISTICS

Drug-addicted persons = 24.6 million

Alcohol-addicted persons = 17 million

Alcohol-addicted adolescents and young adults = 3 million

Alcohol-addicted adults = 14 million

Drug-addicted deaths in 2017 = 72,000

Alcohol-addicted deaths in a typical year = 79,000

Percentage of substance misusers with a family member who misuses substances = 53

Drug misuse-related emergency room visits in 2009 = 846,382

Alcohol misuse-related emergency room visits in 2009 = 658,263

Drug-related healthcare costs in a typical year = $11 billion

Costs of drug-addicted persons to society for the year 2007 = $193 billion

Costs of alcohol-addicted persons to society for the year 2010 = $249 billion

DRUG AND ALCOHOL MISUSE

Substance use disorders are a serious problem in the United States. The cost of drug and alcohol misuse consumes a great deal of money and resources. Misuse also takes a serious toll on the misusers themselves and their loved ones. Many drug- and alcohol-addicted persons give all they have to their addictions as addiction becomes the primary motivator in their lives. Frequently, they spend all of their money on drugs or alcohol, and miss large portions of their lives. There is a high mortality rate for those who misuse drug and alcohol. For those abusing drugs, the most common cause of death is overdose. For those with alcohol use disorder, liver disease is the most common cause of death.

HEALTHCARE COSTS

Those struggling with drug and alcohol addictions frequently need emergency room or inpatient medical care. The reasons for this are many: overdose, injection site infection, hepatitis C, other liver diseases, HIV/AIDS, behavioral and mental health problems, related medical problems including cardiovascular conditions, motor vehicle accident trauma, respiratory distress, injuries from falling, and attempted or successful suicide.

COSTS TO FAMILIES

The drug- or alcohol-addicted persons' home situation can play a large role in their cost of living. An adolescent or young adult may live with parents. Older adults can live alone, live with a spouse, or a friend. Where an addicted person lives determines the costs of their living situation.

If the misuser lives alone they could easily wipe out their bank accounts and "max-out" their credit cards in order to purchase drugs or alcohol. They will have to pay all of their bills by themselves. Addicted persons may have trouble paying their bills, their rent, their health insurance premiums, and not have enough to buy food. They will be unable to pay for drugs or alcohol if they use up all of their money. They could end up homeless. They may have to steal money to buy drugs or alcohol.

If the misuser lives with family they could still run out of money for drugs or alcohol. In this instance, they will have a home to go to. They won't have to pay the bills or rent. The drug or alcohol addicted could still run out of money for drugs or alcohol. Some parents may them money for drugs or alcohol, while some parents might ask them to leave as long as they are using drugs or alcohol.

If the misuser lives with a friend, a spouse, or children there could be other problems. Not all friends or spouses will allow actively addicted individuals to live with them. When parents are drug- and alcohol-addicted, they will need to find others to care for their children. If parents leave children unsupervised, they can have their child taken away by the Department of Children and Families (DCF), and lose custody. Many actively using parents leave their children with the children's grandparents.

LEGAL COSTS

The cost of government law enforcement in a typical year = $60 billion.

The costs of legal representation can become an issue if the substance use disorder individuals are arrested for illegal drug possession, or driving while drunk or otherwise impaired. They need legal representation in court. If they cannot pay, free legal aid may be available at no cost. Some states do not incarcerate addicted persons; some do.

JOBS AND SCHOOLS

The percentage of drug- and alcohol-addicted individuals in a typical year in the U.S. = 70%.

Cost of lost productivity due to drug or alcohol misuse in the typical year in the U.S. = $120 billion.

People misusing drugs or alcohol at work will not be able to do their job fully. Employers want motivated employees who can perform critical thinking and give the job their best. Frequent absences can lead to job loss with concomitant loss of health insurance when it is employer-sponsored.

Students struggling with addiction will not perform at their best either and the risk of failing out of school is significant. Scholarships are lost. Without treatment, students will find acceptance at another school difficult.

HEALTH DISPARITIES

Drug and alcohol addiction consume a much higher percentage of the income of those in the lower socio-economic group. To buy drugs or alcohol, addicted people often use their food money. This is particularly problematic if they have children. Children often emulate the behavior of their parents when they are adolescents. Multiple drug and alcohol misusers in a family are apt to encourage children to misuse as well. This has obvious consequences for their scholastic and social success. Living in a home with a limited and misspent income is frustrating and depressing.

DIRECT COSTS OF DRUGS AND ALCOHOL

Included in the following chart are both the cost of one dose of a drug and the annual cost, based on the cost of the single dose. The costs of alcohol are for a bottle of alcohol, and the total is for a single bottle every day. There is no way to accurately calculate the size of an actual dose of drugs or alcohol for a given day as use varies. Costs increase over the course of the addiction because the brain needs more drug or alcohol over time. There are scales on the internet that estimate costs for various kinds of alcohol and various kinds of drugs. Alcohol is typically purchased legally; drugs are typically purchased illegally.

ALCOHOL

One daily bottle of wine = $8 ($2,920 annually)

One daily 12 pack of beer = $9 ($3,285 annually)

One daily bottle of vodka = $15 ($5,475 annually)

Average legal and resulting costs of a charge of driving under the influence = $10,000

Average fines for public intoxication = $150 to $1,000

DRUGS*

Methamphetamine

One quarter daily gram = $25 ($9,125 annually)

One daily gram = $100 ($36,500 annually)

Federal penalty for first conviction for possession = one year in prison and $5,000 fine

Cocaine

One daily gram = $50 to $70 ($21,900 to $25,500 annually)

Three and half daily grams = $150 to $250 ($54,750 to $91,250 annually)

Federal penalty for first conviction for possession = one year in prison and $5,000 fine

Oxycontin
One daily pill = $10 to $80 ($3,650 to $29,200 annually)
Federal penalty for first conviction for possession of a controlled substance = one year in prison and $, 5,000 fine

Heroin
Single daily hit = $10 ($3,650 annually)
Average cost of a daily heroin habit= $150 ($54,750 annually)
Federal penalty for first conviction for possession of heroin = One year in prison and $5,000 fine

* These costs may vary in different cities and states.

DRUG-ADDICTED NEWBORNS

A newborn baby who is born to a mother who is drug-addicted, will be born addicted to the same substance the mother is. Often, addicted prenatal mothers are put on methadone in reduce the drug's harm to the baby. Because newborns are so much smaller than their mothers, the extent and degree of addiction is much greater than that of mothers. This condition is called neonatal abstinence syndrome (NAS). When they are born, they lose their source of opiates or the addicted substance, and they experience severe withdrawal symptoms. These newborns often have a low birth weight, and difficulty breathing. Also, they cry a lot, refuse to eat, shake, and vomit. The baby is not sent home until it is totally withdrawn from the opiates. This usually takes 17 days. The best treatments for these babies are cuddlers. Cuddlers are volunteer women who hold and comfort the baby continuously. The cuddlers also assist the new mother to feel comfortable in the neonatal intensive care unit. The number of addicted babies born in the U.S. is one every 25 minutes and this rate is increasing.

FETAL ALCOHOL SPECTRUM DISORDERS

Babies born to mothers who drink alcohol or are addicted to it can cause a condition called fetal alcohol spectrum disorders (FASD). Alcohol can cause a variety of symptoms in a newborn, depending on when during the pregnancy the mother drank alcohol and how much she drank. There is no amount of alcohol that is safe to consume during pregnancy. Of particular concern is drinking alcohol early in the pregnancy when many of the baby's organs are developing. Many of the symptoms of FASD are not apparent at birth, and may not be apparent until the baby is older. The child can have physical defects, brain and central nervous system disorders, and social and behavioral issues. The newborns often have a small head and a small brain. They may have small eyes and a turned up nose. They may have heart defects and problems with their kidneys and their lungs. Also, they may have visual or hearing problems. There is no data on the frequency of FASD.

DRUG AND ALCOHOL REHABILITATION

The only solution to the problems of drug or alcohol addiction is deciding to stop using the drugs or alcohol. The best place to do this is in a rehabilitation center that specializes in withdrawing from drugs or alcohol. The best way to find such a center is to look on the internet. There are day programs in many general hospitals called partial hospitalization programs. They help the addicted to detoxify, or "detox," or "dry out." The programs help them to change their feelings about drugs or alcohol, often putting them on methadone, Suboxone, or Naltrexone to ease withdrawal. It takes 90 days for the brain to return to normal, so it is a good idea to find a counselor for after the program. The costs of dropping drugs or alcohol addictions saves society between $4 and $7 per month in drug related crime, theft, and the criminal justice system.

Lisa M. Lines, MPH;
Updated by Christine M. Carroll, MBA

FOR FURTHER INFORMATION

Bosari, Jessica. (19 June 2012) The Cost of Addiction on Families. Retrieved on August 3, 2018 from https://www.forbes.com/sites/moneywisewoman/2012/06/19/the-cost-of-addiction-on-Families/#194cd7025097. This article describes what happens to a family when a member becomes addicted.

Maldonado, Lizmarie, MPH. (2018) Drug and Alcoholism Statistics and Data Sources. Retrieved on August 4, 2018, from https://www.projectknow.com/research/drug-addiction-Statistics-alcoholism-statistics/. This article has two parts. The first one discusses alcoholism statistics, and the second part explains drug abuse statistics.

Mayo Clinic Staff. (1998-2018) Fetal Alcohol Syndrome. Retrieved on August 4, 2018, from https://www.mayoclinic.org/diseases-conditions/fetal-alcohol-syndrome/symptoms-causes syc-20352901. This web site describes the fetal alcohol syndrome and what it does to the baby.

National Institute on Drug Abuse. (June, 2015) Nationwide Trends. Retrieved on August 4, 2018 from https://www.drugabuse.gov/publications/drugfacts/nationwide-trends. This is a report of a survey on addicting drugs. It explains drug abuse, alcoholism, and cigarette smoking.

See also: Addiction; Families and behavioral addictions; Families and substance misuse; Poverty and substance misuse; Socioeconomic status and addiction; Work issues and behavioral addictions; Work issues and substance misuse

Education about substance misuse

Category: Diagnosis and prevention

Definition: The methods for substance misuse education vary widely. Education can be as informal as a community-based health fair to practitioner-oriented education sessions and workshops at conferences. Colleges and universities offer highly formal and structured education and instruction. Media messages are often used to educate the public on the multiple issues related to substance misuse.

Overview

Throughout recent history, efforts have been developed to educate the public on the dangers of substance misuse. Much of this work has been targeted to youth populations, especially in school settings. Substance misuse prevention educators have assumed that educating people on the dangers and harmful nature of substance misuse alone will actually prevent drug use and addiction. However, many studies have questioned the effectiveness of this approach.

Traditionally, a common technique was to bring to the classroom a recovering addict to talk about drug use and how it negatively affected that person's life.

This approach was thought to be effective for preventing substance use. Another approach was for a teacher to show a film on substance misuse, a film that often included a number of scare tactics believed to deter youth from drug experimentation. Generally, the teacher would follow the film with a discussion of the dangers of drugs.

Another common method once believed to prevent substance misuse was for substance misuse educators to attend health fairs and simply hand out brochures to passersby. Health educators believed that if people knew about the negative effects of drug use, they would not use drugs. Much money and resources were spent in the hopes that educational brochures would deter people, primarily young people, from using tobacco, alcohol, or other drugs.

However, studies showed that these educational efforts were mostly ineffective. Substance misuse education is informative, but is not effective as a single, stand-alone approach to preventing substance use. Practitioners, who began to question their approach, also began to explore the nexus between substance misuse education and the prevention of drug misuse. In some cases, popular approaches to prevention education, such as the original Drug and Alcohol Resistance Education (D.A.R.E.) program and other singularly focused educational curricula, were shown to have adverse outcomes. For this reason, the National Institute on Drug Abuse (NIDA) substantially changed the D.A.R.E. curriculum.

Substance misuse education can be effective if the goal is to inform people of the facts of drug use and to train students of health care about the best practices associated with the substance misuse profession. Different disciplines offer their own perspectives on the issue of substance misuse. Some courses, in substance misuse counseling for example, teach student therapists how to work with clients who abuse substances.

Center for Substance Abuse Prevention

The Center for Substance Abuse Prevention (CSAP), part of the US Substance Abuse and Mental Health Services Administration (SAMHSA), created six strategies that many US states use to channel funding to their respective regions, counties, and community groups that conduct prevention programs. One of these areas is prevention education. This strategy includes two-way or multidirectional communication about substance misuse topics, including prevention programs that cover parenting techniques, social skills, and peer resistance skills.

Prevention education is one of six overall strategies that CSAP attaches to the Substance Abuse Prevention and Treatment block grant. The other five strategies include information dissemination, alternative activities, community-based processes, environmental approaches, and problem identification and referral.

The focus of prevention education is to provide substantive information. Simply passing out a brochure, for example, is considered information dissemination only. Adequate prevention education occurs in settings with interactive communication that leads, for example, to programs such as Life Skills Training (LST), which has been replicated nationally. This program has proven effective across multiple sites.

The LST program is a school-based program that prevents substance misuse and violence by targeting risky behaviors. The curriculum includes multiple sessions, over time, with interactive role-playing scenarios that engage the students in the program. A number of evidence-based educational programs in substance misuse exist on the National Registry of Evidence-based Programs and Practices (NREPP), which is sponsored by SAMHSA.

NATIONAL INSTITUTE ON DRUG ABUSE (NIDA)

NIDA, part of the National Institutes of Health, also provides some definitions and descriptions on substance misuse education and dissemination efforts. NIDA has two critical focuses. The first is the strategic support and conduct of research across a broad range of disciplines. The second is ensuring the rapid and effective dissemination and use of the results of that research to significantly improve prevention, treatment, and policy as it relates to drug misuse and addiction. Specifically, NIDA funds education and dissemination efforts that inform adults and youth about the neuroscience of addiction. Youth-focused curricula include Brain Power and NIDA Goes Back to School, programs with a substance-misuse educational component.

Many of the early programs identified by NREPP were programs that were funded in part by NIDA, which also published the book *Preventing Drug Use among Children and Adolescents* (1997). This work highlights a number of evidence-based, substance-misuse

prevention programs, many of which have an educational focus. A number of programs have since been created and are being studied for effectiveness. The contributions and research funding that NIDA provides is crucial. Research results are interpreted and then transferred to the field to influence educational practice.

NIDA's publication also highlights the risk-and-protective-factor approach to prevention. This approach, which has been adopted by most in the field of substance misuse prevention as the framework for programming, argues that there are multiple risk and protective factors in a person's life that can influence each stage of youth development. These factors operate across a number of domains, some of which include substance misuse. The implications for prevention specialists is that these factors must be assessed and understood before implementing a prevention program or a strategy designed to decrease risk factors and to increase protective factors. This is exciting research, and NIDA was one of the first federal agencies to disseminate information on this approach.

GUIDING PRINCIPLES AND BEST PRACTICES

As prevention knowledge continues to grow, new findings are being presented that have a role in guiding decision-making about funding and implementing prevention programs. Early findings on prevention education include the following:

- Providing information and educating people on the harms and risks associated with substance misuse is not an effective strategy when used in isolation from other approaches. Skill development in combination with education is preferred.
- Didactic approaches are not effective at preventing substance misuse. Interactive educational approaches are encouraged.
- When educating youth, peer approaches are preferred but require training and oversight.
- When implementing education programming in schools, lengthy curricula, including booster sessions, are preferred to short-term or one-time-only types of events.
- Social skills programs that include numerous risk-and-protective-factor approaches are preferred.
- Booster sessions are encouraged after the prevention education session has concluded.

- Role-playing components to substance misuse education programs are recommended.
- Educational programs that include parents and students are recommended.

This early work helped to guide the field of substance misuse prevention. Much of the early work of the Center for the Application of Prevention Technology, under CSAP contract, was to coordinate with states, jurisdictions, and tribal entities to transfer evidence-based information on substance misuse prevention programs and best practices to state leadership. It is within this context that education about substance misuse is often discussed. Communication covers what is effective and ineffective in this area.

COLLEGE AND UNIVERSITY EDUCATION

Substance misuse education is growing. Colleges and universities offer many educational courses in substance misuse prevention and treatment, and the content of these courses varies widely. Some focus on substance misuse prevention, others focus on pharmacology, and still others focus on substance misuse treatment. Courses cover the sociology of substance misuse, criminal justice solutions to substance misuse problems, the medical implications for patients with substance use disorders, and substance misuse counseling. Courses are being taught traditionally, in the classroom, but also online.

Substance misuse certification and licensure requirements have driven much of this increased activity in substance misuse education. Professional education in substance abuse prevention could not happen without careful pedagogical approaches and scientific findings to guide effective practice in the field.

NATIONAL YOUTH ANTI-DRUG MEDIA CAMPAIGN

The National Youth Anti-Drug Media Campaign is an educational vehicle for substance misuse messages in the United States. Millions of dollars are spent annually to create, distribute, and broadcast messages across the country. The campaign is part of the Office of National Drug Control Policy (ONDCP) in Washington.

A number of messages are offered as part of a comprehensive media campaign. Although the vast majority of these messages are one-way communication episodes, substance misuse organizations use the material too. Also, the ONDCP and state authorities discuss how media messages can support substance misuse services regionally.

Julie A. Hogan PhD

FOR FURTHER INFORMATION

Brounstein, P., Janet Zweig, and Steve Gardner. *Science-Based Practices in Substance Abuse Prevention: A Guide*. Rockville: Center for Substance Abuse Prevention, 1998. Print.

Fisher, Gary, and Nancy Roget. *Encyclopedia of Substance Abuse Prevention, Treatment, and Recovery*. Thousand Oaks: Sage, 2009. Print.

Goddard, Gillian, Viv Smith, and Carol Boycott. "Substance Abuse (Drugs) Education." *PSHE in the Primary School: Principles and Practice*. New York: Routledge, 2013. 213–24. Print.

Hogan, Julie, et al. *Substance Abuse Prevention: The Intersection of Science and Practice*. Boston: Allyn, 2003. Print.

Mignon, Sylvia I. "Substance Abuse Prevention." *Substance Abuse Treatment: Options, Challenges, and Effectiveness*. New York: Springer, 2015. 175–90. Print.

National Institute on Drug Abuse. *Preventing Drug Use among Children and Adolescents: A Research-Based Guide for Parents, Educators, and Community Leaders*. 2nd ed. Bethesda: DHHS, 2003. Print.

See also: Center for Substance Abuse Prevention (CSAP); Center for Substance Abuse Treatment (CSAT); Centre for Addiction and Mental Health (Canada); College and substance misuse; D.A.R.E. (Drug Abuse Resistance Education); Just Say No campaign; Media and substance misuse; National Institute on Alcohol Abuse and Alcoholism (NIAAA); National Institute on Drug Abuse (NIDA); Schools and substance misuse

Emergency treatment

CATEGORY: Treatment

ALSO KNOWN AS: critical care; urgent care

DEFINITION: Emergency treatment of drug and alcohol overdose requires urgent care for the particular drugs and other substances ingested, medical stabilization of patients, and subsequent follow-up care with substance use disorder treatment centers.

OVERVIEW

A person who has overdosed on a drug requires emergency treatment. Often, this treatment is initiated by friends, family, or coworkers. Emergency rooms (ERs) can be a challenging maze for persons not familiar with them, but some characteristics are common to most ERs.

Triage yields the first ER assessment, determining illness severity. *Triage* is a French word meaning "to pick or cull." Triage nurses record information related to the patient. Any family or friends accompanying the overdosed patient can be particularly helpful at this time by providing information they have about the overdosed patient. Medications, health history, allergies, and any drug paraphernalia found with the overdosed patient can help with diagnosis. The patient's vital signs are taken and recorded in triage, including his or her pulse, temperature, respiratory rate, and blood pressure.

Illness severity is usually broken into the following categories at triage: critical and immediately life threatening, such as a heart attack or a heroin overdose in which the patient is not breathing well; urgent but not immediately life threatening, such as most cases of abdominal pain or many cases of alcoholic intoxication; and less urgent, or the "walking wounded," including those with lacerations, coughs, and sore throats.

The emergency treatment of addictions and substance misuse is at first concerned with treating overdoses. After treatment of an overdosed patient and after medical stabilization, secondary care is initiated. Common substance misuse problems resulting in emergency treatment include alcohol intoxication, cocaine use, and heroin use. The following information outlines what can be expected if confronted with the care of an overdosed person.

A person overdosed on alcohol will often be obtunded (that is, will have a decreased mental status and will show lethargy and stupor). He or she may be vomiting, may lack muscle coordination, or may be passed out (unconscious). Severely intoxicated persons, who sometimes have a blood alcohol content (BAC) level above 0.35 percent and as high as 0.50 percent, should be transported to an ER as soon as possible. Alcohol levels in that high of a range often mean alcohol poisoning. (Legal limits of alcohol intoxication while driving in the United States is 80 milligrams of ethanol per 100 milliliters of blood, or a BAC of 0.08 percent.) Upon arrival at the ER, the alcohol-poisoned person is first assessed in triage.

An obtunded alcohol-intoxicated patient who is still conscious would most likely be assessed as a category two patient. A person overdosed on heroin, unconscious with the pinpoint pupils characteristic of narcotic overdoses, and with a severely depressed respiratory status, would be advanced to the category one or resuscitation section of the ER. Cocaine intoxication can lead to compromised cardiovascular dynamics. In such cases, pupils are dilated (large), breathing rates speed up, blood pressure elevates, and abnormal heart rates and rhythms occur with cocaine use. A person overdosed on cocaine and with a compromised cardiovascular function would be advanced to category one for emergency care and stabilization.

BASIC STABILIZATION

Overdose precautions taken "in the street" do not (and should not) typically include inserting a needle into the heart (as featured in films and on television). Street methods, which should not be used, sometimes include forced milk ingestion in an unconscious, narcotic-overdosed person, ice packing, or the injection of milk or saltwater (saline) solutions. Serious side effects can ensue, including aspiration pneumonia (milk vomited up from the stomach and into the lungs), hypothermia (dangerously low body temperature), blood infections, and cellulitis (skin infections).

Substance use overdose is a serious emergency requiring hospital treatment and evaluation. Someone trained in cardiopulmonary resuscitation (CPR) can check for a pulse in the unconscious person and initiate CPR after calling 911 for assistance; any home or street care should first be guided by accessing the emergency health care system. Recent programs have placed naloxone, a drug that treats narcotic overdoses, in the hands of nonmedical personnel so that they can treat life-threatening overdoses in the street. Training programs for this type of treatment exist in urban areas. A doctor-supervised training program organized through the Chicago Recovery Alliance, for example, has dispensed naloxone to drug users to provide lifesaving narcotic reversal on the streets. Narcan, previously only available as an injection, is now available as a nasal spray. Pilot studies considering the use of lockboxes on street corners containing Narcan nasal spray are taking place so that this potential life saver is more readily accessible.

EMERGENCY CARE

Initial ER treatment of a nonresponsive patient involves intravenous (IV) line insertion, oxygen administration, and heart monitoring. An IV provides direct access to blood vessels for medication injection and allows intravenous fluid replenishment if needed. Many obtunded overdose patients have depressed respirations, and oxygen applied through a mask or nasal cannula helps deliver oxygen to the brain and body. Cardiac or heart monitoring along with oxygen-saturation measuring devices offer valuable information related to blood transport in the body.

Emergency treatment of narcotic overdoses requires naloxone. Naloxone blocks the opiate receptors in the nervous system and reverses comas and breathing problems caused by opiates like heroin. Naloxone is rapidly effective, usually reversing the coma and respiratory depression within one or two minutes. A glucose solution is often administered intravenously to unresponsive patients to treat the possibility that low blood sugar is causing or contributing to the unconscious state.

Naloxone is helpful for narcotic overdoses, but it does not readily block alcohol poisoning. An alcoholic will be treated with IV fluids to replenish fluids and minerals and with the vitamin thiamine and multivitamins, and he or she will be observed for many hours until the excess alcohol is metabolized by the person's liver. Generally, a person's BAC level will drop from 0.20 to 0.10 in about five hours. This rate of metabolism will vary, and alcoholics often metabolize alcohol at a faster rate.

Tranquilizers, like Valium and Xanax, are benzodiazepines which can be a source of drug misuse. Flumazinil blocks the action of benzodiazepines and may be used intravenously in benzodiazepine overdose.

Cocaine overdose often leads to cardiac arrhythmias, requiring cardiac monitoring, analysis of abnormal rates and rhythms, and appropriate interventions to stabilize the heart. These interventions include IV medications or electrical defibrillation and cardioversion.

All of these treatments are subject to ongoing evaluation and reassessment. A category two alcohol-intoxicated patient could progress to a category one patient with no pulse or blood pressure, requiring advanced CPR and intervention. Narcotic overdosed patients may rapidly improve with naloxone treatments but could "crash" from secondary problems caused by the effects of multiple drug ingestions or by underlying heart, lung, kidney, or brain problems.

Emergency treatment is often followed by inpatient hospitalization, depending on the problems and recovery course. Follow-up care with substance use disorder treatment centers is necessary to prevent recurrence of these life-threatening overdoses.

Richard P. Capriccioso MD

FOR FURTHER INFORMATION

Capriccioso, Richard P. "Emergency Rooms." *Magill's Medical Guide.* Ed. Brandon P. Brown, et al. 8th ed. Pasadena: Salem, 2018. Print.

https://www.drugabuse.gov/about-nida/noras-blog/2015/11/narcan-nasal-spray-life-saving-science-nida

NARCAN Nasal Spray: Life-Saving Science at NIDA. November 18, 2015

Samet, J. A. "Drug Abuse and Dependence." *Goldman's Cecil Medicine.* Eds. Lee Goldman and Andrew I. Schafer. 25th ed. Philadelphia: Elsevier, 2015. Print.

Seelye, Katherine Q. "A Public Overdose. An Antidote at Hand. Would Passers-By Use It?" *New York Times.* 9 May 2017. https://www.nytimes.com/2017/05/09/us/opioids-narcan-drug-overdose-heroin-fentanyl.html

Walls, Ron M. Robert S Hockberger; Marianne Gausche-Hill. *Rosen's Emergency Medicine: Concepts and Clinical Practice.* 8th ed. Philadelphia: Elsevier, 2018. Print. ISBN 9780323390163 0323390161 9780323390170 032339017X

See also: Alcohol poisoning; Naloxone; Overdose

Emetic misuse

CATEGORY: Substance misuse

ALSO KNOWN AS: Ipecac misuse

DEFINITION: Emetic misuse is typically diagnosed in persons with psychological disorders such as bulimia nervosa, which affect eating behaviors. Emetics, which are poisonous irritants designed to induce intense vomiting by irritating the stomach, are regularly consumed to control weight through purging the body of consumables and their unwanted calories. Emetic misuse is a dangerous and damaging form of purging, but it is treatable.

CAUSES

Emetic misuse primarily affects adolescent girls and young women between the ages of twelve and twenty-five years who are exploring weight loss methods or who have an eating disorder such as bulimia nervosa. Childhood sexual abuse, food digestion problems, substance misuse, family history, and involvement in activities that value thinness, such as ballet, gymnastics, and modeling, also play a role in emetic misuse.

The best-known over-the-counter emetic is ipecac. Emetics are typically administered orally or by injection. These agents force vomiting by stimulating the gastric nerve endings responsible for muscle contraction and the brain chemoreceptor trigger zone. Emetics are officially prescribed in emergencies, for one-time-use only, to eliminate the absorption of poisonous toxins.

With repeated use, emetics can be lethal. They can accumulate in the body because of their long half-lives and can cause progressive weakening of the muscles. Misuse may lead to severe dehydration, electrolyte imbalances, and serious life-threatening cardiac complications, including heart muscle wastage. Some injuries can improve if the misuse stops.

RISK FACTORS

In addition to desired weight loss, as already discussed, other risk factors for emetic misuse include mental health issues such as depression, anxiety, low self-esteem, and obsessive-compulsive disorder.

SYMPTOMS

The short-term effects associated with emetic misuse and repeated vomiting include dental problems such as cavities, gum disease, bad breath, and staining and discoloration from stomach acids. Other health consequences include swollen glands, throat and esophageal irritation and inflammation, eye problems, muscle weakness, dizziness, fatigue, dry skin, blackouts, chest pain, and irregular heart beat.

Long-term effects associated with emetic misuse include electrolyte, mineral, and vitamin imbalances; alkalosis (loss of chloride); hypokalemia (low blood potassium); hypoglycemia (low blood sugar); dehydration; hypertension; menstrual abnormalities; gastric reflux; stomach ulcers; and esophageal tearing and bleeding (Mallory-Weiss syndrome).

Serious medical complications may result from repeated emetic use. These complications include seizures, stroke, paralysis, pancreatitis, kidney and liver damage, respiratory failure, heart arrhythmias, heart muscle wastage and poisoning (myocardial toxicity), cardiac arrest, and sudden death.

SCREENING AND DIAGNOSIS

Emetic misusers are usually secretive about their misuse and about the reasons for their misuse; health professionals should be familiar with behaviors and conditions associated with eating disorders. Primary care physicians should consult with a mental health professional and behavioral therapist for diagnosis and treatment.

Evaluation includes a medical history and physical examination to establish evidence of purging. Diagnostic screenings may include blood, urine, and electrolyte analysis to confirm emetic misuse and an electrocardiogram and echocardiogram to detect heart muscle damage.

TREATMENT AND THERAPY

Treatment for emetic misuse can be long and difficult and depends on the duration and severity of use. Emetic misuse tends to be chronic, so early intervention is critical for a successful recovery. Optimal care usually requires close patient monitoring and a combination of medical care, nutritional counseling, and psychotherapy. Withdrawal from emetics can be accomplished in an inpatient, outpatient, or residential setting specializing in eating disorders; most users can be managed as outpatients.

Antidepressant medications used to treat depression and reduce anxiety may be helpful in treating emetic abuse and in preventing relapse. Fluoxetine (Prozac) appears to reduce binge-purge behaviors and to improve eating perceptions. Other medications may be required to manage the physical complications associated with emetic misuse.

Cognitive-behavioral therapies are essential in eliminating binging-purging behaviors, restoring normal eating patterns, identifying and changing negative self images, and targeting the emotional issues that triggered the misuse. Therapy may be individual, family, or group based.

PREVENTION

The best preventive measure is to avoid using emetics and to better manage underlying illnesses associated with the misuse. Patients should be educated about possible health hazards related to emetic use, such as toxicity and potential for misuse.

Rose Ciulla-Bohling PhD

FOR FURTHER INFORMATION

Bulik, Cynthia M. "Abuse of Drugs Associated with Eating Disorders." *Journal of Substance Abuse* 4.1 (1992): 69–90. Print. Discusses the problem of drug use among women with bulimia nervosa.

Flomenbaum, Neal E., et al. *Goldfrank's Toxicologic Emergencies.* 8th ed. New York: McGraw-Hill, 2006. A comprehensive guide covering how toxins affect the body. Also covers clinical symptoms, emergency treatment guidelines, antidotes, and case studies.

Manoguerra, Anthony S., et al. "Guideline on the Use of Ipecac Syrup in the Out-of-Hospital Management of Ingested Poisons." *Clinical Toxicology* 43.1 (2005): 1–10. Print. Reviews the benefits and risks associated with ipecac use in the home.

Pritts, Sarah D., and Jeffrey Susman. "Diagnosis of Eating Disorders in Primary Care." *American Family Physician* 67.2 (2003): 297–304. Print. Examines the importance of the family physician in identifying, diagnosing, and treating patients with eating disorders.

Silber, Tomas J. "Ipecac Syrup Abuse, Morbidity, and Mortality: Isn't It Time to Repeal Its Over-the-Counter Status?" *Journal of Adolescent Health* 37.3 (2005): 256–60. Print. A literature overview of the clinical characteristics associated with ipecac abuse among young women and ways to eliminate it.

Steffen, Kristine J., et al. "The Eating Disorders Medicine Cabinet Revisited: A Clinician's Guide to Ipecac and Laxatives." *International Journal of Eating Disorders* 40.4 (2007): 360–68. Print. Reviews patterns of abuse and toxicities related to over-the-counter emetic and laxative use in persons with bulimia nervosa.

Yager, Joel, Harry E. Gwirtsman, and Carole K. Edelstein, eds. *Special Problems in Managing Eating Disorders.* Washington, DC: American Psychiatric, 1992. Describes the physical and psychological complications associated with diagnosing and treating eating disorders.

See also: Behavioral addictions: Overview; Laxative misuse

Emphysema

CATEGORY: Health issues

DEFINITION: Emphysema is a chronic obstructive disease of the lungs. The lungs contain millions of tiny air sacs called alveoli. In emphysema, these sacs lose their elasticity and air becomes trapped within. It becomes difficult to expel oxygen-depleted air from the lungs, which diminishes the normal exchange of air. Emphysema is classified as a chronic obstructive pulmonary disease (COPD).

CAUSES

Emphysema develops due to smoking; inhaling toxins or other irritants; and apha1-antitrypsin deficiency (A1AD), a genetic defect which can cause emphysema at an early age in nonsmokers.

RISK FACTORS

Factors such as smoking, exposure to long-term secondhand or passive smoke, and exposure to pollutants in the environment increase the chances of developing emphysema. Other risk factors include a family history of emphysema, a medical history of frequent childhood lung infections, HIV infection, and connective tissue disorders. Individuals at age fifty years or older also have a greater risk of developing emphysema.

SYMPTOMS

Early symptoms of emphysema include coughing in the morning, coughing up clear sputum (mucus from deep in the lungs), wheezing, and shortness of breath with physical activity. As the disease progresses, symptoms experienced may include increased shortness of breath, rapid breathing, fatigue, and a choking sensation when lying flat. Other symptoms include trouble concentrating, increase in chest size (barrel chest), enlargement of the right chamber of the heart, heart failure, swelling in the legs, weight loss, breathing through pursed lips, a desire to lean forward to improve breathing, and more frequent flare-ups (periods of more severe symptoms).

Screening and Diagnosis

A thorough review of the patient's medical history and a physical examination are performed. The examination may include testing, such as chest X-rays, a test that uses radiation to take pictures of structures inside the chest; CT scan, a type of X-ray that uses a computer to generate 3-D images of the internal organs; arterial blood gas test, a blood test used to assess the amount of oxygen and carbon dioxide in the blood; and lung function tests (spirometry).

Treatment and Therapy

There is no cure for emphysema. Instead, treatment aims to ease symptoms and improve one's quality of life. Treatments involve smoking cessation, which slows the progression of the disease; environmental management, or limiting the number of irritants in the air to make breathing easier; and medication, which helps to ease the symptoms and reduce complications.

Medications include bronchodilators to relax the airways and open breathing passages (may be given as pills or inhaled), corticosteroids to decrease inflammation and swelling in the breathing passages, antibiotics to fight bacterial infections, and expectorants to loosen mucus and make it easier to cough up.

Oxygen may also be given to supplement the air taken in by the body. Increasing the amount of available oxygen helps to increase energy levels and heart and brain function. In addition, because emphysema makes individuals prone to influenza and pneumonia, doctors recommend an annual flu shot and a pneumococcal vaccine.

Lastly, special exercises can strengthen chest muscles and make breathing easier. Physical activity builds endurance and improves quality of

Living with Emphysema: An Interview

Sandy, a fifty-year-old woman, is married with three grown children. She started smoking at age fourteen and continued until she was forty-eight years old. She quit for one full year, but has recently started smoking again. She says that one cigarette was all it took to return to smoking. She is struggling to quit again, and she is retired because of her emphysema. The following is a brief interview with Sandy:

Q. What was your first sign that something was wrong? What symptoms did you experience?

A. My first sign was being short of breath. I had been short of breath for years, but it became much worse over two years ago. I found it increasingly difficult to climb stairs or walk for any distance. I noticed that I could not even walk a whole city block without having to stop and rest. Surprisingly, it was after I had quit smoking for a month that I really noticed an increase in my shortness of breath. It was strange to me that I was more short of breath when my expectation was that I would be breathing easier.

Q. What was the diagnosis experience like?

A. I saw my primary care provider first. I wasn't referred to a specialist right away. My doctor felt that I probably was in the early stages of emphysema and decided to treat me first with medication and inhalers. He didn't feel that my condition was severe enough to require a specialist. I wasn't completely happy with that but felt that he must know what he was talking about. It wasn't until eight or nine months later, when I had a cold and possible lung infection, that I was referred to a specialist and given a pulmonary function test. When the test results came back, my primary care doctor admitted that he had not realized how bad my condition was.

Q. How do you manage your disease?

A. I am currently seeing a pulmonary specialist. This is my second pulmonary specialist; I was not happy with the attitude of the first specialist, so I switched. I am seen every three months and usually have a spirometry done in the office. I am on three different inhalers: Advair, Combivent, and Flovent. I also use Accolate twice a day and I keep prednisone on hand for flare-ups. I have had blood work, chest X-rays, and a dobutamine stress test. Next month, I will have a CAT scan on my lungs to see what kind of condition they are in.

Currently, I am operating at 30 percent lung function, and the doctor has told me that this is as good as it gets. I have been fortunate to not need supplemental oxygen yet. Recently, the doctor has mentioned the word *transplant*. He explained that at age fifty, I am young enough to endure a transplant. By the time I'm sixty, I may have only 15 percent lung function left.

I am also taking an antidepressant. So you can see that this illness has caused some stress and depression.

life, while special breathing exercises with and without an incentive spirometer can help to bring more air into the lungs and force trapped air out of the lungs. A small number of patients may benefit from surgery, including a bullectomy (removal of a bulla—a large, distended air space in the lung) or a lung transplant.

PREVENTION

Individuals can reduce the chances of developing emphysema by not smoking, avoiding exposure to secondhand smoke, avoiding exposure to air pollution or irritants, and wearing protective gear if exposed to irritants or toxins at work.

Debra Wood, RN

FURTHER READING

Chhabra, S. K., R. K. Gupta, and T. Singh. "Cutis Laxa and Pulmonary Emphysema." *Indian Journal of Chest Diseases & Allied Sciences* 43.4 (2001): 235–47. Discusses cutis laxa, a disorder of the skin due to a defective elastin synthesis, which can occur in those with pulmonary emphysema.

"COPD Resources." *AARC.org.* American Association for Respiratory Care. 2012. Web. 29 Mar. 2012. Information about chronic obstructive pulmonary disease (COPD), including basic facts, causes, diagnosis, comparison to asthma, treatments, patient information, and education about the lungs.

Petrache, I., et al. "HIV Associated Pulmonary Emphysema: A Review of the Literature and Inquiry into Its Mechanism." *Thorax* 63.5 (2008): 463–69. A review of the clinical studies that support a direct association between HIV infection and emphysema. Also reviews developments in the basic understanding of HIV and emphysema.

See also: Chronic obstructive pulmonary disease (COPD); Respiratory diseases and smoking; Smoking's effects on the body; Tobacco use disorder

Ephedrine

CATEGORY: Substances

ALSO KNOWN AS: Ma huang

DEFINITION: Ephedrine is an alkaloid drug derived from plants of the genus *Ephedra* (family Ephedraceae); it also is produced synthetically. Ephedrine is similar in chemical structure to amphetamine and methamphetamine drugs.

STATUS: Legal (certain formulations by prescription only in the United States and United Kingdom); illegal for use as a dietary supplement; sold over-the-counter in Canada as a nasal decongestant

CLASSIFICATION: Scheduled Listed Chemical Product (SLCP)

SOURCE: Primary natural source of ephedrine is as an extract from plants of the genus *Ephedra*, specifically *E. sinica* and *E. distachya*; most commercial supplies are grown in China. Because of the expense of extracting ephedrine from natural sources, most pharmaceutical sources of the drug are L-ephedrine, which is produced synthetically.

TRANSMISSION ROUTE: Ephedrine occurs as fine white crystals or powder; the drug is readily soluble in water. In capsule form it is administered orally, and when dissolved in water can be administered in a nasal spray. It also can be given subcutaneously or intravenously.

HISTORY OF USE

Ephedrine has been used as an herbal preparation (ma huang) for thousands of years in Chinese medicine as a treatment for asthma and bronchitis. A Japanese chemist, Nagayoshi Nagai, first isolated ephedrine from the plant *E. distachya* in 1885, and it has been used in Western medicine since that time.

Ephedrine acts to increase the activity of noradrenaline on adrenergic receptors in the brain. It indirectly stimulates the sympathetic nervous system and can cross the blood-brain barrier and affect the central nervous system directly by causing the release of noradrenaline and dopamine. Thus, its action is similar to that of the drugs amphetamine and methamphetamine. Ephedrine can also be used in the production of methamphetamine due to the drugs' similar chemical structures.

Ephedrine has been misused by athletes, particularly by weightlifters and bodybuilders, because it is thought to act as an appetite suppressant and may promote fat utilization. Many athletes need to maintain a certain weight and body fat percentage before competition, leading to ephedrine's use, often in combination with caffeine and aspirin. In 2004, the US Food and Drug Administration banned the use of ephedrine in dietary supplements aimed at weight loss.

EFFECTS AND POTENTIAL RISKS

Ephedrine has many legitimate medical uses, primarily in the treatment of respiratory problems but also to treat hypotension, narcolepsy, certain types of depression, and myasthenia gravis (an autoimmune neuromuscular disorder). However, ephedrine has many potentially serious side effects, and persons with heart disease, angina pectoris, hyperthyroidism, diabetes, and enlarged prostate must be closely supervised by their physicians during use of the substance.

Side effects of ephedrine include nervousness, panic disorder, insomnia, vertigo, difficult breathing, headache, tachycardia (rapid and erratic heartbeat), nausea, anorexia, and painful urination. Ephedrine should not be used during pregnancy except under extremely close medical supervision. Negative drug interactions occur between ephedrine and certain antidepressants, namely serotonin-norepinephrine reuptake inhibitors, and monoamine oxidase inhibitors. Ephedrine should not be used with medications for cough and congestion.

Lenela Glass-Godwin MS

FOR FURTHER INFORMATION

"Ephedra." *New York State Office of Alcoholism and Substance Abuse Services.* New York State, n.d. Web. 29 Oct. 2015.

Fontanarosa, Phil B., Drummond Rennie, and Catherine D. DeAngelis. "The Need for Regulation of Dietary Supplements: Lessons from Ephedra." *Journal of the American Medical Association* 289 (2003): 1568–70. Print.

Kuhar, Michael J., and Howard Liddle. Drugs of Abuse. New York: Marshall Cavendish Reference, 2012. Print.

Martin, Elizabeth. *An A to Z of Medicinal Drugs.* New York: Oxford UP, 2010. Print.

Maxwell, Jane Carlisle, and Beth A. Rutkowski. "The Prevalence of Amphetamine and Methamphetamine Abuse in North America: A Review of the Indicators, 1992–2007." *Drug and Alcohol Review* 27.3 (2008): 229–35. Print.

See also: Amphetamine misuse; Methamphetamine; Stimulant misuse

Esophageal cancer

CATEGORY: Health issues

DEFINITION: The esophagus is the muscular tube that transports food from the throat to the stomach. Esophageal cancer is the growth of cancer cells in the esophagus.

CAUSES

There are two main types of esophageal cancer: squamous cell cancer, which arises from the cells that line the upper part of the esophagus, and adenocarcinoma, which arises from glandular cells that are present at the junction of the esophagus and stomach. Cancer occurs when abnormal or mutated cells in the body divide out of control. If cells keep dividing, a mass of tissue forms. These are called growths, or tumors. If the tumor is malignant, it is cancer. Cancer can invade nearby tissue and spread to other parts of the body.

RISK FACTORS

Factors that may increase the chance of esophageal cancer include tobacco use, including cigarettes, chewing tobacco, or snuff; excessive alcohol consumption; and a history of gastroesophageal reflux, especially if this has caused Barrett's esophagus (a complication of chronic esophagitis, or inflammation of the esophagus). Other factors include achalasia, or chronic dilation of the esophagus; infection with *Helicobacter pylori*, which causes stomach ulcers; certain rare genetic conditions, such as Plummer Vinson syndrome and tylosis; a damaged esophagus from toxic substances, such as lye; a history of cancer of the head or neck; and the human papilloma virus (HPV) infection.

SYMPTOMS

Symptoms of esophageal cancer include trouble swallowing or painful swallowing; coughing, a hoarse voice; pain in the throat, back, and chest; nausea and vomiting; coughing up blood; and weight loss. The structure and location of the esophagus makes it easy for cancer to spread very early. This can make a cure more difficult. People who have related conditions, especially reflux, are encouraged to discuss regular screening tests with their doctors. This may include an endoscopy, in which a tube with a tiny camera is inserted into the body in order to see inside.

SCREENING AND DIAGNOSIS

After a thorough examination and a discussion of the patient's medical history, doctors perform tests to diagnose esophageal cancer. These tests may include a chest X-ray; an upper gastrointestinal series—a series of X-rays of the esophagus, stomach, and duodenum, or the first part of the small intestine; esophagoscopy, the examination of the esophagus using a lighted scope; biopsy, which is the removal of a small sample of esophageal tissue to test for cancer cells; CT scan, a type of X-ray that uses a computer to generate 3-D pictures of structures inside the body; and a bone scan to see if the cancer has spread to the bones.

TREATMENT AND THERAPY

Treatment for esophageal cancer may incorporate surgery to remove the tumor. The doctor may remove all or part of the esophagus, as well. A plastic tube might be used to replace the missing portion of the esophagus. Radiation therapy and chemotherapy are also options. Radiation therapy, or radiotherapy, is used to kill cancer cells and shrink tumors. Radiation may be external radiotherapy, which is radiation directed at the esophagus from a source outside the body, or internal radiotherapy, which is when radioactive materials are placed into the esophagus in or near the cancer cells.

Chemotherapy is the use of drugs to kill cancer cells. Chemotherapy may be given in many forms, including by pill, by injection, and via a catheter. The drugs enter the bloodstream and travel through the body. They will kill mostly cancer cells, but some healthy cells may also be killed. Chemotherapy alone will not cure this type of cancer. It is only used when the cancer has already spread and cannot be cured.

At this point, chemotherapy is used to help shrink the tumor and to ease pain or control nausea.

Chemotherapy and radiation therapy together are better than radiotherapy alone. They may also be as effective as surgery alone. Sometimes, chemotherapy and radiation therapy are followed by a surgery. This has been shown to be a most aggressive form of therapy and may be the best way to cure a patient of their disease.

Other treatment options are laser therapy, which is when high-intensity light is used to kill cancer cells, and photodynamic therapy, which is a combination of drugs and special lights used to try to kill cancer cells. This therapy is a promising treatment approach, but is only appropriate in a very small number of patients. There are limits to how far the infrared light source will travel into the cancer itself. The tumor must be very small (smaller than one-quarter-inch thick). It must not involve any lymph nodes or other structures.

PREVENTION

To prevent esophageal cancer, individuals should avoid or quit smoking or using other tobacco products, drink alcohol only in moderation, and seek medical treatment for gastroesophageal reflux disease.

Rosalyn Carson-DeWitt, MD

FURTHER READING

Abeloff, Martin D., et al. *Clinical Oncology.* 2nd ed. New York: Churchill Livingstone, 2000. A clinically focused reference of the latest oncology research. Includes information about esophageal cancer.

Far, A. E., et al. "Frequency of Human Papillomavirus Infection in Oesophageal Squamous Cell Carcinoma in Iranian Patients." *Scandinavian Journal of Infectious Diseases* 39.1 (2007): 58–62. A study of the role of human papilloma virus (HPV) in the development of oesophageal squamous cell carcinoma (ESCC).

Feldman, Mark, Lawrence S. Friedman, and Lawrence J. Brandt, eds. *Sleisenger & Fordtran's Gastrointestinal and Liver Disease.* 9th ed. Philadelphia: W.B. Saunders, 2010. A core, updated reference source on the techniques, technologies, and treatments in the fields of gastroenterology and hepatology.

See also: Alcohol's effects on the body; Cancer and substance misuse; Smoking's effects on the body; Tobacco use disorder

Ethanol addiction

CATEGORY: Substances

ALSO KNOWN AS: Alcohol; ethyl alcohol; EtOH; grain alcohol; neutral spirit

DEFINITION: Ethanol, a small molecule with the chemical formula CH3CH2OH, occurs as a natural result of the microbial fermentation of sugars. Humans control fermentation and distillation to produce ethanol for use in alcoholic beverages and for industrial purposes.

STATUS: Usually legal but highly regulated and taxed in the United States and many other countries

CLASSIFICATION: Controlled by various federal, state, and local laws

SOURCE: Produced for human consumption in alcoholic beverages; produced industrially to use as a solvent, a fuel additive, and for other applications; amateur winemakers and brewers may make small quantities legally in the United States; occurs naturally in foods such as fresh bread and some fruit juices

TRANSMISSION ROUTE: Ingestion, almost entirely of ethanol-containing liquids

HISTORY OF USE

Consumption of ethanol predates written human history. Even animals may behave as if inebriated when consuming overripe fruit containing ethanol naturally. Characteristic fermented grain and fruit beverages are part of many cultures. A current trend is mixing alcoholic beverages with so-called energy drinks containing caffeine and other pharmacologically active substances.

EFFECTS AND POTENTIAL RISKS

Ethanol metabolizes in a deceptively simple manner in animals, including humans. Ethanol oxidizes in two steps to acetate, which enters normal metabolism without pharmacologic effect. Acetate accounts for the high caloric content of ethanol (7.1 calories per gram). Reduced cofactors generated by oxidizing ethanol explain its fat-sparing ability and how it causes hypoglycemia (high blood sugar) and lactic acidosis when taken in excess.

Oxidative conversions are carried out by two enzymes widely distributed in nature: alcohol dehydrogenase and aldehyde dehydrogenase. The intermediate acetaldehyde is toxic and accounts for some of

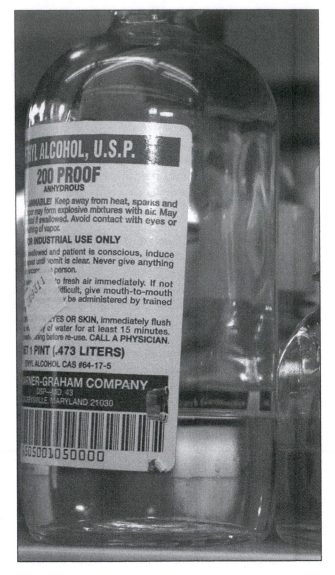

Ethanol, which is found in alcohol, is also used as a fuel. (National Cancer Institute, via Wikimedia Commons)

ethanol's toxic effects, such as hangover symptoms and cirrhosis (irreversible liver damage), and accounts for ethanol sensitivity in some people. Ethanol itself accounts for neurologic effects like inebriation (with loss of inhibition and coordination) and addiction (alcoholism).

After ingestion and absorption from the gut, ethanol in the bloodstream reaches liver, lungs, and other tissues and organs. Ethanol affects the brain directly, in a variety of complex and little-understood interactions. Excess imbibition leads to delayed oxidation in liver, inebriation and other brain effects, and release of acetaldehyde into the blood, which causes headache, nausea, and other delayed symptoms typical of hangovers.

Ethanol's neurologic effects on the brain result from the direct interaction of the ethanol molecule with protein receptors in the membranes of neurons. Several proteins and the genes that encode them have been implicated, including those responsible for neurotransmitters involved in addiction to other substances. Different gene frequencies probably account for ethnogeographic variation of ethanol metabolism and alcoholism among various human groups.

R. L. Bernstein PhD

FOR FURTHER INFORMATION

Berg, Jeremy M., John L. Tymoczko, and Lubert Stryer. *Biochemistry.* 8th ed. New York: Freeman, 2010.

Haseba, T., and Y. Ohno. "A New View of Alcohol Metabolism and Alcoholism: Role of the High-Km Class III Alcohol Dehydrogenase (ADH3)." *International Journal of Environmental Research and Public Health* 10 (2010): 1076–92. Print.

Manzo-Avalos, Salvador, and Alfredo Saavedra-Molina. "Cellular and Mitochondrial Effects of Alcohol Consumption." *International Journal of Environmental Research and Public Health* 12 (2010): 4281–4304. Print.

See also: Alcohol misuse; Caffeinated alcoholic drinks; Solvents

Exercise addiction

CATEGORY: Psychological issues and behaviors

ALSO KNOWN AS: Compulsive exercise; exercise bulimia; exercise dependence; overtraining

DEFINITION: Exercise addiction is an observable condition characterized by making physical activity central to one's life, often to the detriment of other responsibilities and obligations. Exercise addicts voluntarily and compulsively participate in excessive physical activity, typically of high intensity and duration. Exercise addicts may engage in multiple daily sessions of physical activity, avoid rest days, embrace compulsive thoughts about activity during work or social times, and experience symptoms of withdrawal when exercise patterns are interrupted. Exercise addiction may be a symptom of other emotional disorders or may be a phenomenon in itself.

CAUSES AND RISK FACTORS

Exercise addiction may be caused by emotional disorders, personality characteristics, and social influences. The desire to control one's weight and body image is typically a common rationale for exercise addiction, and the addiction often accompanies eating disorders such as bulimia. The pleasurable sensation associated with endorphin release (for example, the runner's high) can provide the exercise addict with a motivation for pursuing exercise beyond moderation. Oftentimes, regret about lapses in regular activity can give way to inappropriate guilt about missing any opportunity to exercise.

Persons with tendencies toward obsessive-compulsive behavior, persons with body- and self-image concerns, and endurance athletes are most vulnerable to engage in physical activity for its own sake. Participation in extreme exercise beyond that necessary for health benefits, pursuing increasingly greater exercise accomplishments, and comparing progress with others of similar behavior can place one at risk for developing an unhealthy addiction to exercise. Participants in other-than-team sports and those who self-coach are at highest risk.

SIGNS, SYMPTOMS, AND DIAGNOSIS

Exercise addicts may exhibit one or more of the following:

- activity sessions repeatedly lasting over one hour
- feeling remorseful about missing an activity opportunity
- substituting activity for social interaction
- exercising to and through pain
- adherence to a regular and rigid routine
- being overly concerned about exercise goals
- inability to maintain an overall sense of relaxation and acceptance when not active
- amenorrhea (in females), fatigue, and depression

Researchers have found that many people diagnosed with bulimia possess tendencies toward exercise addiction, and are therefore considered exercise bulimic. The anxiety felt when not exercising is lifted when one resumes the regimen.

Exercise addiction is not recognized as a primary disorder in the fifth edition of the *Diagnostic and Statistical Manual of Mental Disorders* (DSM-5, 2013) of the American Psychiatric Association, and diagnosis is challenging. The confirmation of exercise addiction ultimately rests with determining the importance and role of activity in a person's life while still exploring other conditions that may be present.

TREATMENT AND THERAPY

Exercise addiction is similar in concept to other addictions in that it shares a link with an underlying condition. Since regular physical activity is a desired behavior of health promotion and maintenance, efforts should be redirected to maintaining an active lifestyle while rebalancing the role that exercise plays in one's life. Because physical exercise is often recommended as a desirable substitute for many compulsive acts, it can become compulsive for those inclined to addictive behavior. Therefore, treating the exercise addict necessitates a multipronged approach, and it is unlikely that self-help or nonprofessional approaches to its cure will be effective.

Initially, a health care provider should determine the person's present state of health, including his or her physical and emotional well-being. Further analyses should focus on the patient's nutritional status and dietary habits, motivation for recovery and redirection of goals, capacity for implementation of coping strategies, and a health-focused activity prescription.

Treatment therapies would include the development of healthy eating habits; strategies for improving and maintaining a healthy self-esteem and body image; gradual incorporation of healthy, alternative recreational pursuits; and the monitoring of progress over time. It is likely that recovery from exercise addiction may take months and even years, and it must address underlying issues or other conditions. Even as the research into treatment efficacy progresses, individual counseling and monitoring will remain critical to achieving success.

P. Graham Hatcher PhD

FOR FURTHER INFORMATION

Cole, Cheryl L. "Addiction, Exercise, and Cyborgs: Technologies of Deviant Bodies." *Sport and Postmodern Times*, edited by Geneviève Rail, State U of New York P, 1998, pp. 261–76.

Friedman, Peach. *Diary of an Exercise Addict: A Memoir.* GPP Life, 2009.

Johnson, Marlys. *Understanding Exercise Addiction.* Rosen Publishing, 2000.

Kaminker, Laura. *Exercise Addiction: When Fitness Becomes an Obsession.* Rosen Publishing, 1998.

Powers, Pauline, and Ron Thompson. *The Exercise Balance: What's Too Much, What's Too Little, and What's Just Right for You!* Gürze Books, 2008.

Schreiber, Katherine, and Heather A. Hausenblas. *The Truth about Exercise Addiction: Understanding the Dark Side of Thinspiration.* Rowman & Littlefield, 2015.

Skupien, Scoop. *Wired to Run: The Runaholics Anonymous Guide to Living with Running Addiction.* Andrews McMeel Publishing, 2006. Print.

See also: Behavioral addictions: Overview; Compulsions; Work addiction

F

Families and behavioral addictions

CATEGORY: Social issues

DEFINITION: Behavioral addictions are those addictions that involve social, observable behaviors but not the misuse of or dependence upon chemical substances. The dynamics and features that characterize chemical addiction also occur in behavioral addiction, but without a person physically ingesting a substance that promotes the addictive response. Several findings report that chemical addiction and behavioral addiction share common processes regarding loss of control and repetitive compulsive actions. While a behaviorally addicted person may also have a simultaneous chemical addiction, these are understood as separate addictions even though treatment modalities overlap substantially. The most common behavioral addictions involve food, shopping, pornography, gambling, video gaming, online social networking, serial relationships, kleptomania, and exercise.

SCOPE OF THE ISSUE

While behavioral addictions are well accepted as serious mental and behavioral health problems, this historically was not the case. Mental health and even substance use specialists were slow to recognize the addictive properties in these behaviors for several reasons. First, the behaviors, such as shopping, were often engaged in routinely with no signs of addiction in most people. The activities themselves are usually ordinary, everyday, and common. There is nothing inherently addictive about them.

Second, some behavioral addictions that are not as ordinary (for example, pornography) occur privately, often hidden from public view. Performed in secret, people who are addicted are unseen and unchallenged. Others simply were unaware of the problem. Third, there was a general lack of awareness that such activities could become truly addicting in the same way that alcohol, cocaine, or prescription pain or anti-anxiety medications could become addicting. Among specialists, occasional disagreement still exists about whether behavioral addictions are true addictions.

With increased recognition of the underlying characteristics of behavioral addiction has come more accurate reporting and intervention. Physicians and other health care providers, educational and workplace personnel, friends, and families are now more likely to express concern and acknowledge a serious problem. While varying sources estimate the prevalence of behavioral addictions differently, most addiction specialists conservatively assume that one in ten families has a behaviorally addicted family member. Some specialists believe the prevalence is as high as one family in three.

FAMILIES AND CAUSES

It is established that chemical addictions run in families. That is, having one family member addicted to chemicals increases the likelihood, fourfold, that a first-order relative—a parent or sibling—will develop a chemical addiction at some time in his or her life. Behavioral addictions also run in families, though it is unclear just how much more likely it is that a second family member will develop a behavioral addiction when a first-order relation is addicted to a specific behavior.

The actual connections between one behaviorally addicted family member and a similar addiction in another family member are complex and far from fully delineated. Similarly, how particular family climates promote (or discourage) behavioral addiction is also far from being fully understood. Still, the existence of connections is indisputable.

The first, and most fundamental, connection is family-shared biology and genetics. The response in the brain's pleasure centers tends to be similar in genetically related persons. The enjoyment the video-gaming addicted person gets will be similar among his or her family members even if the particular source of enjoyment (such as addictive catalog shopping rather than video gaming) is different. The intensity of the reward and its recurrent allure will be similar. However, family genes do not cause addiction.

As many as three-quarters of families with a behaviorally addicted family member do not have a second addicted member. The genetic contribution lies in the degree of likelihood that each family member shares for developing addiction, not that they will develop the addiction. The strength of the tendency to become addicted is largely shared though the outcomes (being addicted to gambling as a primary force in one's life or merely enjoying gambling as a pastime) are not necessarily the same. One is not "doomed" to addiction if a sibling or parent has become addicted.

A second connection lies in what family members are exposed to and learn to imitate. A straightforward example would be how children learn to copy their parents. If a single mother has a relational addiction in which she serially and incessantly dates men regardless of the psychological health of these relationships, her children will gradually learn that their value and sense of safety, security, and meaning is dependent on being in a relationship. Though it could take years for the addictive properties of this behavior to develop in her children, the chances that they eventually will are multiplied.

The woman's children see and experience the emotional anxiety and panic that their mother feels when she lacks an active, current dating relationship. Even if they do not have the language to describe what their mother is doing, they notice their mother's pattern and learn how to ensure they are part of a relationship—any relationship. Even if the children come to understand the self-destructive pattern their mother is enduring (and putting her children through), they learn that having a relationship, even a bad one, prevents feelings of insecurity and insignificance that they believe are sure to come if they are not in a relationship. Their addictive pattern of incessant serial dating thus begins.

FAMILIES AND CONTINUATION

Though behavioral addictions are pathological, maladaptive, and harmful to the addicted persons and their families, the addictions persist because the families' way of functioning, how it achieves or fails to achieve what it sets out to do, has accommodated the addictive disease. As much as the family may want the addiction to stop and as much suffering as the addicted member causes, the family responds as a unit (or system, in the jargon of family therapy) in ways that end up supporting the addictive behaviors. Thus, the behaviors continue.

While this dynamic seems contrary to the well-being of the family and its members, it demonstrates the powerful emotional need within families to hold together for their survival—that no members can be lost. Families achieve this through maintaining a psychic balance, what social psychology describes as homeostasis: the drive within a family to keep itself going, regardless of the existence of harmful and hurtful family patterns (such as abuse, neglect, and addiction). Studies have shown that there is a low level of cohesion and adaptability in the families of those who exhibit behavioral additions.

As the family realizes there is a problematic behavior (for example, one member's addiction to food) it responds initially with efforts to correct the problem. Usually, however, families cannot control a member's addictive behaviors. As the family experiences repetitive failures, its emotional life becomes threatened, and though members do not consciously and explicitly coordinate their response, they react to the addicted person in ways that dysfunctionally balances the emotional energy within the family. Members become preoccupied with the addicted person's food consumption, where he or she is getting the food, where it is hidden, and how much is consumed, for example. This preoccupation involves everyone in the family with the well-intentioned, but unsuccessful, goal of getting the addicted person to eat normally.

Often, the addiction, known to all, is spoken openly by no one. It becomes this family's "public secret." As a secret, it cannot be effectively addressed. The addicted person reacts, in turn, to the heightened concern and scrutiny, and because the addiction must be fed, he or she reacts against the family's efforts to help.

These reactions take a variety of predictable forms: angry denial of the problem, in which family members are intimidated and told to mind their own business; avoidance of family encounters and generally being less visible, often in the guise of being too busy to participate in family activities, like meals, and spending large blocks of time at work, school, or in one's room; and helpless proclamations of guilt and shame while vowing to get help or promising to try harder.

This setting involves many negative emotions, including blame that surfaces and resurfaces. Questions are asked by the addicted person and by family members: Who really cares? Who is really selfish? Who really understands the addicted person? Who among us will take a stand? The emotional disconnection within the family grows.

FAMILIES AND TREATMENT

Just as families are typically central to the successful treatment of chemical and substance misuse, they are usually central to successful treatment of behavioral addiction. In some families, behavioral addiction arises due to an abnormal distance between family members with a corresponding low level of closeness and caregiving. So one of the most important tools in the road to recovery for the family would be to come together as a cohesive unit and openly acknowledge the problem, i.e. that it has reached the stage of addiction. This will allow the addiction to be treated.

In the early stages of treatment, or recovery, families are often confronted by the behaviorally addicted member's denial that there is a problem, that the problem is as bad as members say, that the addicted person can control it, or that the behavior is anyone else's business. Addicted video gamers, for example, will likely argue the benefits to their many hours of compulsive playing: It relieves stress for them. They enjoy it. They have friends online who play as much as they do and they enjoy their companionship. They are not bothering anyone else.

In such a case, family members must be supportive but honest in confronting both the addicted person and themselves, addressing how they have unintentionally enabled the addiction to continue. Family members need to recognize and openly declare what they used to do that allowed the addiction to continue and that they will no longer support the behavior. Members too should seek help, because it is inherently difficult to disengage from a loved one in trouble. Family members should assume a position of full support for helping the addicted person get help and of zero support for anything the addicted person does that does not promote recovery.

Paul Moglia, PhD and Eugenia Moglia, BA;
Updated by Eugenia Moglia, BA

FOR FURTHER INFORMATION

American Academy of Child and Adolescent Psychiatry. "Facts for Families." Washington, DC: AACAP, 2011. Print. An informational guide series for parents and families facing a variety of real-world issues, including behavioral addiction within families.

Bradshaw, John. *On the Family: A New Way of Creating Solid Self-Esteem.* Deerfield Beach, FL: Health Communications, 1996. Print. One of the best introductions for understanding families as systems with dynamic, reactive energies. Explains in clear, insightful language the family's role in supporting and maintaining ongoing problematic and addictive behaviors in an individual family member.

"Family Behavior Therapy." *National Institute on Drug Abuse.* NIH, Dec. 2012. Web. 29 Oct. 2015.

Hayes, Steven, and Michael Levin. *Mindfulness and Acceptance for Addictive Behaviors: Applying Contextual CBT to Substance Abuse and Behavioral Addictions.* Oakland, CA: New Harbinger, 2010. Print. Pioneers in the application of mindfulness in treating substance misuse and addictions in general. Focused on helping readers apply mindfulness to many types of behavioral addictions.

Sadock, B. J., and V. A. Sadock, eds. *Kaplan and Sadock's Comprehensive Textbook of Psychiatry. 10th Edition.* Philadelphia: Lippincott, 2017. Print. Written for professionals but intelligible for lay readers, contains detailed descriptions of various behavioral addictions.

See also: Behavioral addictions; Children and behavioral addictions; Domestic violence and addiction; Economic impact of addiction; Families and substance misuse; Marriage/partnership and behavioral addictions; Men and behavioral addictions; Women and behavioral addictions

Families and substance misuse

CATEGORY: Substance misuse

DEFINITION: A family with a substance-abusing member often experiences long-lasting, deleterious consequences from that misuse. An individual member's substance misuse or addiction is also the family's substance misuse or addiction. Addiction has been said to be a family disease. It is estimated that 1 in 5 children grows up in a home in which a parent or family member misuses drugs or alcohol. Self-pity, hatred, resentment, guilt, and anger disrupt family life that, while never perfect, should ideally be health-promoting, protective, supportive, and positive. Powerful and dangerous emotions intoxicate and ruin the functional life of the family. Treatment, however, is available for family members and for the addict.

CAUSES

Initial substance and chemical use is almost always voluntary, as the person decides to consume or not consume a substance; if they do consume, they decide how much. The person is in charge of the choices he or she makes.

Continued choices to use a drug produce chemical and structural changes in the brain that result in involuntary, compulsively driven needs to have the drug. This action compromises the functioning of the areas of the brain involved in the inhibition of drives. The urge is never more than temporarily satisfied, however. The substance, not the person, is in control.

What often starts as an experience of recreation, relaxation, excitement, experimentation, social bonding, or isolated escape from life's challenges becomes a need to satisfy and resupply. Users are now misusers, and misusers often become addicts of the substances they are using.

Substance misuse can involve any chemical, but more often it involves commonly used and legal substances such as tobacco (the nicotine in tobacco is addictive) and coffee or tea (the caffeine in coffee and tea is addictive) or illegal chemicals such as cocaine, heroin, and marijuana. Substances of misuse also include legal medications, such as anti-anxiety and pain medications, which require a physician prescription to obtain, and over-the-counter medications.

Although these substances are chemically quite varied, they all produce the same overt response in the misuser: an unrelenting need to achieve the next altered state of consciousness, be it a high, sleepiness or relaxation, or excitability. Satisfying the need becomes a priority over responsibilities with family, friends, or work. The addict becomes emotionally cut off from family, friends, and coworkers. Addiction and the quest to satiate the next urge control the addict's mental state.

Those struggling with addiction often have legal troubles and frequently use substances in dangerous situations (such as driving under the influence). The ability to resist the impulse to take the drug overtakes users' self-control, and they are left helpless and often beyond the help that their families and friends can typically provide.

RISK FACTORS

While vulnerability to substance addiction can come about for many reasons, the most common involve a prior history of substance misuse in one's family, which is dually suggestive of being exposed to and learning how to use substances (imitative, learned behavior) and a genetic predisposition to responding more strongly to drugs than might be true for the average person. The average person without an addiction is more likely to have been raised in a family free of substance and chemical misuse.

Geneticists are moving closer to identifying several genes and gene clusters that promote a much stronger pleasure response to certain substances than is typical in the average person. Neuroscientists, similarly, are increasing their focus on areas of the brain that become highly excitable in addicted persons exposed to drugs.

One in four families has one or more members who either misuses drugs or is addicted to drugs. This can be explained in part by research that shows that addiction and substance misuse occur more readily in persons with a family history in which a first-order relative is chemically addicted and in which there exists a genetic loading for an unusually pleasurable response to drugs and other substances. This extrapolates to one of every two families having to cope in a major way with a relation or close friend who misuses or is addicted to drugs.

Having a behavioral or mental problem or illness, even common ones like anxiety and depression, also increases the odds that one will develop an addiction.

Also more likely to become addicted are persons who were neglected or physically or emotionally abused as children. Children who were exposed to drugs and alcohol prenatally, besides experiencing a myriad of health problems, also have a higher risk of developing a substance use disorder. Research also shows that even the delivery system employed, that is, how the drugs are ingested, puts someone on a faster track to addiction. Snorting and intravenous injection are the most dangerous methods that can lead to drug addiction.

IMPACT ON THE FAMILY

Persons do not intend to become addicted or become substance misusers. People most often use substances to change an emotional state, to enhance a state of feeling good, or to combat a state of feeling bad.

The most vulnerable family members are children. (Andreas Bohnenstengel via Wikimedia Commons)

Use easily becomes frequent use, frequent use increases the odds of misuse; episodes of misuse, in turn, increase—and almost guarantee—the odds that addiction will overcome the person's state of mind and being. They live the life of addictive preoccupation; nothing else matters.

Having a substance-abusing member in a family has long-lasting, deleterious effects that take from the energy, bonds, and nurturance that characterize the traditional family group. The social dynamic in families is that each member reacts to all other members. Mothers react to spouses and their children. Fathers react to spouses and their children. Children react to each parent and their siblings. This mesh of reactions results in a long-term, developmentally progressive, complex social system that has its own lifecycle. Children and adolescents of parents with substance use disorders can experiencing a number of medical and psychobehavioral difficulties that will affect them throughout their lives. Any substance-abusing family member has an impact on this cycle, usually in one of three ways. Family members can respond to the substance misuse in a similar fashion.

The most prevalent of these three reactions is the desire to stay engaged with the substance misuser, and to advise, counsel, support, reason with, and show disappointment in the individual struggling with misuse while seeking the promise of abstinence and reform. This response by family members who love and are committed to each other is rarely effective, but nonetheless may last for decades. This relationship is referred to as codependency and denotes a pattern of unhealthy learned behaviors whereby the non-addicted family member focuses completely on the habits, behaviors, and day-to-day living of the substance misuser, often at the expense of the non-addicted family member's health, happiness, and general well-being. Engagement often produces depression and hopelessness in the family, which can then produce guilt and shame in the misuser. The pain of the guilt and shame is more than the misuser can withstand, and the negative emotions may drive him or her back to the substance of misuse.

The second most prevalent reaction, confrontation, usually arises some time after the addiction is accepted as a real problem, both for the family member and for the family. Although in some cases of parent substance misuse, the confrontation can arise from the child's pediatrician noticing the problem and confronting the parent about it. Confrontational responses generally have rapid onset with a short half-life. Most people cannot sustain high levels of intense anger and outrage. The addicted person often recoils in the face of such an emotional onslaught and will nervously try to avoid the drug or not get caught taking the drug. Inevitably, because the addiction or misuse is not being treated, its remission is brief; when it resurfaces, it will again be met by family outrage. The addicted person will then respond as before: recycling the pattern of misuse.

The third reaction, collaboration, can move family members from being contributors to and enablers of the problem to recognizing that, in the face of the disease, the family has become diseased itself; symptoms are often manifested in a long and varied series of unhelpful, maladaptive, dysfunctional responses that attempt the impossible: Remove the cause of the addiction, try to control the addiction, and find a cure for the addiction.

Engagement initially requires the emotional and psychological detachment from the addicted person and his or her disease. Genetic loading and family history notwithstanding, family members (often slowly) come to understand that they did not cause the disease, that they cannot (and have never been able to) control the disease, and that they cannot cure the disease.

TREATMENT FOR FAMILIES

Just as families have primary ways of reacting to their drug-abusing members, they also have fairly predictable developmental stages in reacting to these members. In the beginning, as an addicted person's behavior becomes harder to hide, family members begin to notice that something is wrong.

Family members will feel concerned and worried and will begin genuine attempts to look out for the troubled member's welfare. Families ask, remark, comment, suggest, and obtain promises of reduced or controlled use. Families will protect, make excuses, and try to carry on their normal lives. Slowly, as these efforts only prolong the addiction and delay treatment, families experience extreme emotional dissonance and self-doubt. Families become confused about whether they are tolerating addiction, enabling addiction, or just protecting themselves.

At this stage, families are immersed in the addiction, and treatment becomes necessary, even if the addicted person refuses. Often family members will employ a strategy of emotional or physical avoidance, a form of denial that parallels that of addicted persons.

For addicted persons and their families substance addictions are treatable diseases. As families accept the realities of the addiction, they can begin to make real changes. For many families, the treatment of choice will be a family-centered, twelve-step program such as Al-Anon or Nar-Anon. Individual family members may get their own treatment by meeting with a mental health specialist skilled at recognizing common dysfunctional family responses. As the family tends to its own health, it gets healthier. With the right kind of help comes healing, and the family can start to return to a normal way of life.

Family life involves intense emotions (good and bad), so it is almost impossible for families to have an engaged response without outside guidance, direction, and support. Help for families coping with addicted members is wide ranging. It comes in the form of twelve-step groups such as Al-Anon and Nar-Anon. Also available are licensed behavioral health care professionals who specialize in substance use treatment or specialized treatment centers or programs.

In addition to being an example of those invested in their own recovery, families can be huge catalysts for aiding the addicted persons' treatment and recovery processes. Ideally, the family should respond to the addiction with support and noninterference.

The role of the family is critical; its reactions will either promote health or enable disease. Though they may never have misused substances themselves, family members should accept that they are coping with more than the substance misuse habits of an individual member. They are facing a family disease, and they should seek help accordingly.

Paul Moglia, PhD and Eugenia Moglia, BA;
Updated by Eugenia Moglia, BA

FOR FURTHER INFORMATION

American Academy of Child and Adolescent Psychiatry. "Facts for Families." Washington: AACAP, 2011. Print. An informational guide series for parents and families facing a variety of real-world issues, including substance misuse.

Barnard, Marina. *Drug Addiction and Families.* Philadelphia: Jessica Kingsley, 2007. Print. The author, a senior research fellow at the Centre for Drug

Misuse Research at the University of Glasgow, Scotland, has written extensively on the contributory role family environments can plan in the development of substance misuse and how families can respond effectively.

Bradshaw, John. *On the Family: A New Way of Creating Solid Self-Esteem.* Deerfield Beach: Health Communications, 1996. Print. One of the best introductions for understanding families as systems with dynamic, reactive energies. Explains in clear, insightful language the family's role in supporting and maintaining ongoing problematic and addictive behaviors in an individual family member.

Congers, Beverly. *Addict in the Family: Stories of Loss, Hope, and Recovery.* Deerfield Beach: Health Communications, 2003. Print. Generally regarded as both realistic and inspirational, this work includes real-life perspectives from family members coping with a loved one's addiction. Discusses the need for self-care as well.

Foote, Jeffrey. *Beyond Addiction: How Science and Kindness Help People Change.* New York: Scribner, 2014. Print.

Friel, John C., and Linda D. Friel. *Adult Children Secrets of Dysfunctional Families: Secrets of Dysfunctional Families.* Deerfield Beach: Health Communications, 1988. Print. Based on their extensive experience working with families coping with members' substance misuse, the authors discuss how family dynamics promote conditions fostering substance misuse.

Hayes, Steven, and Michael Levin. *Mindfulness and Acceptance for Addictive Behaviors: Applying Contextual CBT to Substance Abuse and Behavioral Addictions.* Oakland, CA: New Harbinger, 2010. Print. Pioneers in the application of mindfulness in treating substance misuse and addictions in general. Focused on helping readers apply mindfulness to many types of behavioral addictions.

McCollum, Eric E., and Terry S. Trepper. *Family Solutions for Substance Abuse: Clinical and Counseling Approaches.* New York: Routledge, 2014. Print.

Rusnáková, Markéta. "Codependency of the Members of a Family of an Alcohol Addict." *Procedia-Social and Behavioral Sciences* 132 (2014): 647–53. Print.

Sadock, B. J., and V. A. Sadock, eds. *Kaplan and Sadock's Comprehensive Textbook of Psychiatry.* 10th Edition. Philadelphia: Lippincott, 2017. Print. Written for professionals but intelligible for lay readers, contains detailed descriptions of various behavioral addictions.

See also: Behavioral addictions; Children and behavioral addictions; Domestic violence and addiction; Economic impact of addiction; Families and substance misuse; Marriage/partnership and behavioral addictions; Men and behavioral addictions; Women and behavioral addictions

Fentanyl

CATEGORY: Substances

ALSO KNOWN AS: Apache; the bomb; China girl; China white; dance fever; friend; goodfella; jackpot; murder 8; perc-a-pop; poison; tango and cash; TNT

DEFINITION: Fentanyl is a highly potent opiate analgesic with biological effects indistinguishable from those of heroin.

STATUS: Legal in approved formulations as an anesthetic and analgesic; other formulations and uses are illegal

CLASSIFICATION: Schedule II controlled substance

SOURCE: Synthetic opiate analgesic with no natural sources. Similar to but more potent than morphine. Illegal formulations are either produced in underground laboratories or smuggled into the United States.

TRANSMISSION ROUTES: Legally administered by intravenous, transdermal (patch), and transmucosal (lozenge) routes; illegal formulations taken intravenously, snorted, or smoked

HISTORY OF USE

Fentanyl was first synthesized in a medical drug research laboratory in Belgium in the late 1950s. The original formulation had an analgesic potency of about eighty times that of morphine. Fentanyl was introduced into medical practice in the 1960s as an intravenous anesthetic. Subsequently, two other fentanyl analogs were developed for medical applications: alfentanil, an ultrashort-acting analgesic (of 5–10 minutes), and sufentanil, an exceptionally potent analgesic (5–10 times more potent than fentanyl) for use in heart surgery. Fentanyls are used now for anesthesia and analgesia. The most widely used formulation is a transdermal patch for relief of chronic pain.

Illicit use of fentanyl first occurred within the medical community in the mid-1970s. Among anesthesiologists, anesthetists, nurses, and other workers in anesthesiology settings, fentanyl and sufentanyl are the two agents most frequently misused. Potential misusers have ready access to these agents in liquid formulations for injection and can divert small quantities with relative ease. Transdermal patches cannot be readily adapted for misuse. The fentanyl lozenge has been diverted to illegal use. On the street, the lozenge is known as perc-a-pop.

More than one dozen analogs of fentanyl have been produced clandestinely for illegal use outside the medical setting. Since the mid-2000s, fentanyl misuse has emerged as a serious public health problem. Fentanyl-laced heroin or cocaine powders have become the drugs of choice for some addicts. In the 2010s, fentanyl played a major part in the drastic spike in overdose deaths due to opioid misuse, as the drug was often mixed with heroin or cocaine. Its potency means that users who are unaware of the mixture can easily overdose. Beginning around 2013 and accelerating in 2014 and 2015, the sharp rise of fentanyl-related overdose deaths contributed to the growing opioid crisis. In 2016 the National Institute on Drug Abuse (NIDA) estimated that over 20,000 deaths were caused by overdoses of fentanyl analogs.

EFFECTS AND POTENTIAL RISKS

The biological effects of fentanyl are indistinguishable from those of heroin, with the exception that illicit fentanyl analogs may be hundreds of times more potent. Short-term effects of fentanyl misuse include mood changes, euphoria, dysphoria, and hallucinations. Anxiety, confusion, and depression also may occur. High doses or long-term use may impair or interrupt breathing due to respiratory depression. Unconsciousness and even death can occur.

The 2000s and 2010s have seen a sharp increase in fentanyl use, as well as related overdoses and deaths.

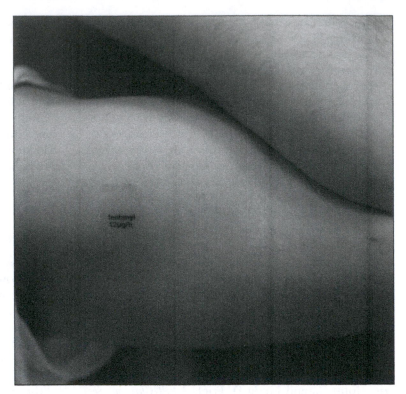

A fentanyl transdermal patch at release rate of 12 micrograms per hour, affixed to skin. (Daniel Tahar via Wikimedia Commons)

For example, in 2014 twenty-eight people died over a span of two months in Philadelphia due to the use of fentanyl-laced heroin. Police seizure of illegal drugs containing fentanyl tripled between 2013 and 2014; there were 942 fentanyl-related cases in 2013, compared with 3,344 in 2014. In 2015 the Drug Enforcement Administration (DEA) issued an alert about the spike in fentanyl-laced heroin. The problem was originally thought to be concentrated on the East Coast, but in April 2016 a spate of overdoses in the Sacramento area of California (thirty-six overdoses with nine deaths in a single week) showed that the problem was nationwide and growing. Notably, the drug used as a painkiller was responsible for the April 2016 death of the musician Prince.

With the rise of the opioid crisis, law enforcement and health care organizations began to press for wider availability of the overdose medication naloxone, also known as Narcan. The medication is effective in reversing the effects of overdose, though some critics claim it encourages drug users to use more recklessly, as they know they can be revived in case of overdose.

Ernest Kohlmetz MA

FOR FURTHER INFORMATION

Bryson, Ethan O., and Jeffrey H. Silverstein. "Addiction and Substance Abuse in Anesthesiology." *Anesthesiology* 109 (2008): 905–17. Print.

"Fentanyl" *Centers for Disease Control and Prevention,* 29 Aug. 2017, www.cdc.gov/drugoverdose/opioids/fentanyl.html. Accessed 4 Jan. 2018.

"Fentanyl." *National Institute on Drug Abuse.* Natl. Insts. of Health, Dec. 2012. Web. 28 Oct. 2015.

Kuhn, Cynthia, Scott Swartwelder, and Wilkie Wilson. *Buzzed: The Straight Facts about the Most Used and Abused Drugs from Alcohol to Ecstasy.* Rev. 4th ed. New York: Norton, 2014. Print.

McCoy, Krisha. "Opioid Addiction." Ed. Michael Woods. *Health Library.* EBSCO, Jan. 2014. Web. 27 Oct. 2015.

"Overdose Death Rates." *National Institute on Drug Abuse,* National Institutes of Health, Sept. 2017, www.drugabuse.gov/related-topics/trends-statistics/overdose-death-rates. Accessed 4 Jan. 2018.

Savelli, Lou. *Street Drugs: Pocketguide.* Flushing: Looseleaf Law, 2008. Print.

See also: Anesthesia misuse; Narcotics misuse; Opioid misuse

Fetal alcohol syndrome (FAS)

CATEGORY: Health issues, fetal alcohol syndrome

DEFINITION: Fetal alcohol syndrome (FAS) is part of a group of disorders called fetal alcohol spectrum disorder (FASD). FAS is caused when a woman drinks alcohol during pregnancy. Alcohol can cause birth and developmental defects in the baby leading to FAS.

CAUSES

Alcohol can cross from the mother's blood into the fetus's blood by passing through the placenta. Even a small amount of alcohol can damage the fetus and cause FAS. Doctors do not know how much alcohol it takes to cause defects. The risk increases with moderate to heavy drinking and with binge drinking. Even social drinking may pose a danger.

RISK FACTORS

Factors that increase a baby's chance of getting FAS include unplanned pregnancy (mother is not expecting to be pregnant and continues to drink alcohol), failure to recognize early pregnancy and continuing to drink, alcoholism, lack of knowledge about the risks of drinking while pregnant, advanced maternal age, and low socioeconomic status.

SYMPTOMS

Birth and developmental defects depend on when the fetus was exposed to alcohol. Babies with FAS may have a number of physical symptoms, including low birth weight, delayed growth, small head and eyes, flat cheeks and small jaw, vision and hearing difficulties, heart defects, minor joint defects, and ear infections.

As the infant grows and develops, other symptoms may also appear, including difficulty sleeping and eating, delayed speech, learning disabilities, poor coordination, behavioral problems, and a poor impulse control. Children do not outgrow these effects. Teenagers and adults with FAS often experience social and emotional problems. They may develop secondary conditions, such as mental health problems, the inability to hold a job, alcohol or drug dependence, and anger management issues.

SCREENING AND DIAGNOSIS

A doctor will ask patients about their alcohol intake while pregnant. The child's growth will be assessed and a physical examination will be done. The diagnosis is based on the mother's history of alcohol use and the child's characteristic facial appearance, slow growth, and problems with the nervous system.

Some children with this condition do not have the typical physical features. Their condition is described as fetal alcohol effect (FAE) or alcohol-related neurodevelopment disorder (ARND). An early diagnosis can help a child receive the proper services.

TREATMENT AND THERAPY

There is no specific medical treatment for this condition. Early intervention is helpful, as well as a supportive, nurturing home. The doctor may recommend hearing and vision testing, as well as testing for any other medical problems related to FAS. Professional support helps a family cope with caring for a child with birth defects. Services include respite care and parent training. Parents can learn ways to handle behavior problems and stress management techniques.

PREVENTION

Efforts to prevent FAS mainly include the avoidance of drinking alcohol if one is pregnant or trying to get pregnant. Women can also take folic acid to prevent other birth defects. Heavy drinking should be avoided when birth control is not being used, as damage can occur before a mother knows she is pregnant.

Debra Wood, RN;
Updated by Marianne Moss Madsen, MS, BCND

FOR FURTHER INFORMATION

"Alcohol During Pregnancy." *March of Dimes.* March of Dimes Foundation. Nov. 2008. Web. 29 Mar. 2012. Covers the risks of drinking while pregnant, fetal alcohol syndrome (FAS) and fetal alcohol spectrum disorder (FASD), and how to prevent alcohol-related birth defects. https://www.marchofdimes. org/pregnancy/alcohol-during-pregnancy.aspx.

Nykjaer C, Alwan NA, Greenwood DC, *et al.* "Maternal alcohol intake prior to and during pregnancy and risk of adverse birth outcomes: evidence from a British cohort." *J Epidemiol Community Health* 2014;**68**:542-549. Concludes that while the first trimester is the most dangerous one in which to consume alcohol, all women who are pregnant or may become pregnant should abstain from using alcohol.

Popova, Svetlana, Shannon Lange, Charlotte Probst, Gerrit Gmel, Jurgen Rehm. "Global prevalence of alcohol use and binge drinking during pregnancy, and fetal alcohol spectrum disorder." *Biochemistry and Cell Biology,* 2018, 96:237-240. Takes a worldwide view of drinking alcohol, particularly binge drinking, and how it leads to FAS.

See also: Alcohol's effects on the body; Birth defects and alcohol; Pregnancy and alcohol; Women and substance misuse

Flashbacks

CATEGORY: Health issues and physiology

ALSO KNOWN AS: Déjà vu; hallucinogen persisting perception disorder

DEFINITION: Flashbacks are spontaneous, vivid, sensory (usually visual) or emotional re-experiences, often associated with the past use of psychedelic drugs, such as LSD, or with a past severe trauma.

ACUTE FLASHBACKS

Acute flashbacks are sensory or emotional experiences in which a person relives a past event or experience. Most flashbacks are spontaneous and triggered by a particular sight, sound, or smell. The person undergoing a flashback recalls sounds, smells, images, and feelings often more vivid than they were during the original event or experience. Acute flashbacks are unexpected and short lasting. In most cases, they are benign, pleasant, even comforting. In some cases, however, they are disturbing and can lead to psychotic episodes, severe depression, or schizophrenia.

CHRONIC FLASHBACKS

Hallucinogen persisting perception disorder (HPPD) is a chronic condition in which recurring flashbacks interfere with a person's daily life. In mild cases, flashbacks occur infrequently. In extreme cases, flashbacks occur regularly and begin to distort a person's perception of reality. HPPD is associated with the use of hallucinogenic drugs. Flashbacks can occur any time, from a day to a year after taking a hallucinogen.

HPPD flashbacks cause visual disturbances. The person suffering HPPD may see flashes of intense color; auras around people's heads; dancing geometric shapes; images trailing moving objects; positive afterimages, in which objects remain in the brain after they have left the field of vision; or distortions in which objects appear larger or smaller than they are in actuality.

TRAUMA-RELATED FLASHBACKS

Trauma-related, or nondrug-related, flashbacks were first described medically by doctors treating World War I combat veterans. These types of flashbacks are seen not only in combat veterans but also in other people who have experienced severe trauma, such as witnessing violent death. Flashbacks affect many persons with post-traumatic stress disorder.

DRUG-RELATED FLASHBACKS

Hallucinogens are the drugs most associated with flashbacks. LSD (lysergic acid diethylamide, or acid); psilocybin in certain mushrooms; and PCP (phencyclidine, or angel dust), originally an anesthetic, are the main hallucinogenic, or psychedelic, drugs. By far, LSD is the most commonly used and studied psychedelic.

During LSD flashbacks, users experience an abbreviated version of an earlier drug trip, or experience, without taking the drug. Many users report that the flashbacks are even more intense than the original trips. The flashbacks can be isolated or recurring, brief or drawn-out, pleasant or disturbing, and benign or damaging. Because LSD flashbacks usually appear suddenly, without warning, they can disrupt a person's daily routine and lead to unpredictable behavior.

Chronic LSD users are more prone to flashbacks than occasional users. People with an underlying emotional problem and people highly susceptible to suggestion also are more prone to flashbacks than healthy users. Even emotionally healthy people who have used LSD only once or twice can experience flashbacks more than one year after taking the drug.

CAUSES

Scientists do not fully understand the biochemical processes through which hallucinogens affect the mind and body, and they do not know the causes of LSD flashbacks and HPPD. Research suggests several theories for flashbacks.

First, drugs can remain stored in body fat and in some organs—lungs, kidneys, liver, brain—long after they are taken. When the body burns fat during strenuous activity, the drugs might enter the bloodstream, causing the person to experience some of the drug's effects. Second, LSD might have damaged the brain, causing it to send incorrect signals. Third, LSD may have changed the way the brain functions and processes information, which may account for the accompanying visual disturbances. Another theory holds that flashbacks have nothing to do with psychedelic drugs, but that flashbacks are naturally occurring altered states of consciousness that are not understood and, consequently, mislabeled or misinterpreted by drug users.

TRIGGERS

Although scientists do not know the causes of flashbacks, they are reasonably sure of certain triggers. Common flashback triggers include physical or mental stress; physical or mental fatigue; lack of sleep; marijuana or alcohol binging; the use of certain prescription drugs, including antidepressants; and mild sensory deprivation. People sometimes deliberately induce mild sensory deprivation to alter their consciousness or to deeply relax. To induce mild sensory deprivation, a person might focus intensely on one particular sound, blocking out all other background sound, or might stare at a solid-colored surface without blinking for an extended period.

TREATMENT

No specific treatment exists for flashbacks. Doctors have prescribed certain medications, such as anti-seizure drugs, for people suffering HPPD. However, the effectiveness of these drugs remains debatable because of the unpredictability of flashbacks and because of the uncertainty of their cause. Treatment for trauma-related flashbacks generally follows the protocols for treating mild mental disorders: talk therapy or other forms of psychotherapy.

Wendell Anderson

FOR FURTHER INFORMATION

Baggott, Matthew, et al. "Abnormal Visual Experiences in Individuals with Histories of Hallucinogen Use: A Web-Based Questionnaire." *Drug and Alcohol Dependence* 114 (2011): 61–67. Print.

"Hallucinogens: LSD, Peyote, Psilocybin, and PCP." 18 Feb. 2012. Web. http://www.drugabuse.gov/infofacts/hallucinogens.html.

Heaton, Robert. "Subject Expectancy and Environmental Factors as Determinants of Psychedelic Flashback Experiences." *Journal of Nervous and Mental Disease* 161 (1975): 157–65. Print.

Lerner, Arturo, et al. "Flashback and Hallucinogen Persisting Perception Disorder: Clinical Aspects and Pharmacological Treatment Approach." *Israel Journal of Psychiatry and Related Sciences* 39 (2002): 92–99. Print.

Myers, Lin, Shelly Watkins, and Thomas Carter. "Flashbacks in Theory and Practice." *Heffter Review of Psychedelic Research* 1 (1998): 51–57. Print.

See also: Brain changes with addiction; Narcotics' effects on the body; Science of addiction

Food addiction

CATEGORY: Psychological issues and behaviors

ALSO KNOWN AS: Compulsive overeating

DEFINITION: Food addiction is characterized by the uncontrolled desire for and preoccupation with food. Food addicts are driven by obsessive-compulsive thoughts about food and eating despite knowing the negative effects of excess food intake, including obesity. Dependency on food, as with other dependent substances, occurs when destructive behavior persists despite the negative outcomes associated with repeated use.

CAUSES

Cited causes of food addiction include depression, loneliness, stress, hostility, boredom, childhood sexual or emotional trauma, and low self-esteem. Some scientists believe there is a biological explanation for food addiction that involves dopamine, a neurotransmitter in the brain. Neuroscientists and nutrition researchers continue to investigate the precise mechanisms by which food can trigger addiction-like eating behavior. Some hypotheses include attractiveness of certain foods, different reactions to sucrose and fructose than glucose, low satiation from energy-dense foods, and genetic variation in expressing the hormone leptin, which cues satiation.

Eating is typically a pleasurable experience, but food addiction is caused by a loss of control over the agent of abuse: food. Persons addicted to food may not recognize their addiction or may feel incapable of breaking the cycle of overeating. They have an undeniable preoccupation with food and are compelled to eat large amounts of food. For food addicts, this cycle eventually becomes the norm.

In an episode of binge eating it is not uncommon to consume in excess of 10,000 calories. These calories lead to obesity if not expended, yet it is not accurate to assume that all obese persons are food addicts. Food addicts continue to engage in compulsive overeating even when aware of its destructive effects. Those who eventually want to break the cycle often

feel incapable of doing so, while others feel they can stop but continue to postpone doing so.

Eating habits are established during childhood. The development of poor eating habits, including binge eating, may result from ineffective coping mechanisms. Food serves as a barrier or substitute to dealing with emotionally difficult situations and relationships. Poor eating habits continue into adulthood and become ingrained in behavior.

RISK FACTORS

Binge eating disorder is the most common eating disorder in the United States. This and other forms of food addiction most commonly affect girls and women age fourteen to thirty-five years, perhaps because of society's emphasis on appearance and thinness. Both women and men can be food addicts, but women more often seek treatment. Food addiction affects persons of all body types and body weights.

Although food addiction most often results in obesity, not all obese persons are food addicts. Persons with a family history of overeating and persons who lack adequate coping mechanisms for stress, disappointment, and anger may be more at risk for the disorder. Persons with a genetic predisposition for binge eating are enabled by family members, who often allow the cycle to continue through their own actions and expectations. Impulsivity may be another risk factor for food addiction (though not obesity), much as it increases vulnerability to other addictions.

SYMPTOMS

Binge eaters differ from individuals with bulimia in that they do not attempt to rid themselves of the consumed food after a binge. Binge eaters and food addicts spend overwhelming amounts of time planning and fulfilling food "frenzies," which occur publicly or privately. They may eat a reasonable portion in public yet overeat in private. They often eat when they are not hungry or when they are emotionally upset. Feelings of low self-worth and guilt often follow binges, yet these binges are followed by planning for the next episode of eating. Each encounter with food can perpetuate the cycle of destruction.

Though the majority of Americans eat more than what the US Department of Agriculture recommends, food addicts far exceed these same recommendations. Food addicts often feel full but may appear ravished,

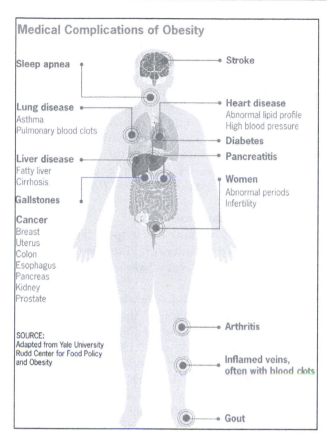

Medical Complications of Obesity

Sleep apnea

Lung disease
Asthma
Pulmonary blood clots

Liver disease
Fatty liver
Cirrhosis

Gallstones

Cancer
Breast
Uterus
Colon
Esophagus
Pancreas
Kidney
Prostate

SOURCE:
Adapted from Yale University
Rudd Center for Food Policy
and Obesity

Stroke

Heart disease
Abnormal lipid profile
High blood pressure

Diabetes

Pancreatitis

Women
Abnormal periods
Infertility

Arthritis

Inflamed veins,
often with blood clots

Gout

Morbid obesity is one possible result from food addiction and can cause further health issues. (CDC via Wikimedia Commons)

out of control, or on a high, or they may always claim to be hungry.

The insatiable appetite for food is a manifestation of other underlying problems. Food often becomes a substitute for other aspects of life that addicts do not perceive as fulfilled, including personal goals, finances, and personal and professional relationships. Food has filled these voids and temporarily provides the comfort, completeness, or pleasure that the addict so desperately seeks. Often, the addict makes food the object of obsession in attempts to delay or avoid dealing with uncomfortable situations or emotions.

Foods high in sugar and fat are thought to act as triggers for obsessive, compulsive eating. Therefore, withdrawal from these triggers is real and can cause cramps, tremors, and exaggerated feelings of depression and guilt.

SCREENING AND DIAGNOSIS

Screening tools in the form of questionnaires are available to determine if further evaluation may be necessary to aid in the diagnosis of a food addiction. However, these tools rely on self-reports. Food addicts are typically ashamed or in denial, or they feel they are too out of control to modify their behavior. These facts alter self-assessment tools.

Researchers have developed the Yale Food Addiction Scale (YFAS), based on an addiction scale for alcohol dependence, to screen takers for dependence on high-sugar and high-fat foods. Critics have pointed out that the scale does not clearly delineate the boundary between normal eating and problematic eating, however. This undermines the usefulness of the YFAS in determining whether an individual is overeating and whether food addiction can be said to exist as its own separate condition.

Health care providers are in a unique position to help those who may suffer from food addiction. Obesity is often attributed to other medical problems, such as thyroid disorders. However, appropriate laboratory tests can determine if a causal relationship exists. Among other complications, binge eating may lead to depression, suicidal thoughts and tendencies, obesity, heart disease, hypertension, type 2 diabetes, high cholesterol, and joint problems.

Notably, binge eating disorder, but not "food addiction," is a recognized diagnosis in the fifth edition of the American Psychiatric Association's *Diagnostic and Statistical Manual of Mental Disorders* (DSM-5). Binge eating is also a symptom of the well-known eating disorder bulimia, yet in bulimia, other dysfunctional behaviors such as vomiting or abusing laxatives are undertaken to mitigate negative feelings and to avoid weight gain. According to DSM-5 criteria, for a diagnosis of binge eating disorder to be made, the individual must have engaged in binge eating episodes a minimum of once a week for three months. The exclusion of food addiction as such from the DSM-5 reflects ongoing debate among scientists as to the nature of the problem—whether specific foods or behaviors are to blame, whether the label of addiction is helpful or harmful to individuals' treatment, and so forth. Nevertheless, problematic eating is a recognized health issue in need of treatment

TREATMENT AND THERAPY

Other substances of misuse (such as cocaine and heroin) are harmful to the addict regardless of dose. Treatment and therapy for substance addicts involves the elimination of the misused substance, which not only is detrimental to the body but also is completely unnecessary to sustain life.

Treatment and therapy for food addiction is unique because eating is required for human survival. The misused substance cannot be entirely removed from the person's environment. Also noteworthy is that eating is a social behavior. Eating's social aspects make it more challenging to control, given that humans are immersed in activities involving food and eating. Whether compulsive or not, overeating is more acceptable when others are also engaging in this behavior.

To sever their dependency on food, addicts must first realize and accept that they have a problem and must willingly receive treatment and support from trained professionals, such as physicians, dieticians, and mental health specialists. Food addicts must reclaim power and learn to control food instead of allowing it to control them.

Obesity that often accompanies binge eating and food addiction should also be addressed. Weight loss and psychological counseling may occur separately or simultaneously, but both are required to optimize the addict's future.

PREVENTION

Unhealthy foods tend to be more accessible and often are more affordable than sound, nutritious foods. Considering the predominance of hectic lifestyles in developed nations, this limited availability of healthy foods creates the perfect opportunity to make poor food choices. Obesity, the second leading cause of preventable death in the United States, can lead to premature death or disability. The United States spent an estimated $190 billion on obesity-related health care in 2012; obesity rates, and thus medical spending, have continued to rise.

Behavioral changes are required to prevent and correct binge eating and obesity. Apart from eating healthy and exercising regularly, several other strategies are suggested. Education is necessary to increase awareness of the problem, and educational efforts should be provided worldwide. Ideally, healthier food choices will be made equally available and healthy eating habits will be taught and reinforced. Also, researchers will continue to explore the underlying reasons behind unnecessary eating or overeating.

Virginia C. Muckler CRNA, MSN, DNP

FOR FURTHER INFORMATION

Blundell, J., S. Coe, and B. Hooper. "Food Addiction - What Is the Evidence?" *Nutrition Bulletin* 39.2 (2014): 218–22. *Academic Search Complete*. Web. 29 Oct. 2015.

Cawley, John, and Chad Meyerhoefer. "The Medical Care Costs of Obesity: An Instrumental Variables Approach." *Journal of Health Economics* , vol. 31, no. 1, Jan. 2012, pp. 219–30. *Science Direct*, www.sciencedirect.com/science/article/pii/S0167629611001366. Accessed 5 Oct. 2017.

Costin, Carolyn. *The Eating Disorder Sourcebook*. New York: McGraw-Hill, 2006. Print.

Kenny, Paul J. "The Food Addiction." *Scientific American* 309.3 (2013): 44–49. *Academic Search Complete*. Web. 29 Oct. 2015.

Kessler, David A. *The End of Overeating: Taking Control of the Insatiable American Appetite*. New York: Rodale, 2009. Print.

Power, Michael L., and Jay Schulkin. *The Evolution of Obesity*. Baltimore: Johns Hopkins UP, 2009. Print.

Wansink, Brian. *Mindless Eating: Why We Eat More Than We Think*. New York: Bantam, 2010. Print.

See also: Behavioral addictions: Overview; Binge drinking; Overeaters Anonymous; Sugar addiction

G

Gamblers Anonymous

CATEGORY: Treatment

DEFINITION: Gamblers Anonymous is a twelve-step recovery program based on Alcoholics Anonymous. There are no requirements for membership other than the desire to stop gambling. The purpose of Gamblers Anonymous is to support personal changes and daily behaviors that lead to a healthy way of living without gambling.

DATE: Established 1957

BACKGROUND

Gamblers Anonymous (GA) was founded in 1957 in Los Angeles by compulsive gamblers Jim and Sam (no last names are used in any of the anonymous programs). GA is a twelve-step program modeled after Alcoholics Anonymous (AA) and based on spiritual principles.

Following the medical model of addiction as an illness, compulsive gambling is seen as a progressive disease and an overactive behavior symptomatic of an emotional disorder related to low self-esteem and self-destruction. People who gamble compulsively want to be seen as generous (big spenders) and special (lucky), thus adding value to their lives. GA uses a list of twenty basic questions concerning gambling behavior; a person who answers "yes" to seven or more of these questions is considered a compulsive gambler.

Like other twelve-step-program meetings, GA meetings focus on the sharing of what it calls "experience, strength, and hope." Personal stories commonly include episodes of theft, deceit, lost relationships, and self-loathing. Members with some degree of abstinence from gambling describe where they are in working the steps of the program and how they have benefitted from the principles of the program, thus supporting and encouraging newer members.

Although GA is based on spiritual principles, interpretation is individual and independent of any religious dogma. Anonymity is paramount to creating a safe environment for revealing, learning, and growing, and members are reminded not to discuss what they have seen or heard in meetings.

In addition to focusing on emotional problems, GA provides resources to assist members with their financial and legal problems. Members are discouraged from filing for bankruptcy or borrowing money to repay debts. By abstaining from gambling, a person will usually have more earned income available to make restitution, leading to the resolution of financial pressures.

Membership in GA does not require dues payment; however, because GA declines funding from outside sources to remain self-supporting and self-governing, free-will contributions are accepted at meetings. Participants are encouraged to donate toward expenses that include meeting room rental and the cost of refreshments.

MISSION AND GOALS

The official literature of GA states that its members' "primary purpose is to stop gambling and to help other compulsive gamblers do the same." The nonprofit organization does not solicit members; persons must seek out the program. GA does not get involved with financial arrangements; members are responsible for paying off their own debts.

In the United States, one in sixty-two adults has a gambling problem. It has been estimated that six million compulsive gamblers in the United States lose $20 billion annually. However, less than 10 percent seek addiction treatment, and the rates of suicide and attempted suicide among gamblers remain high.

As of 2005, more than one thousand GA meetings were held in twenty-three cities in the United States; GA groups also meet in more than ten other countries. Many chapters are in cities where gambling is legal in some form, including cities in California, Nevada, and New Jersey.

Caesars Entertainment Corporation (formerly Harrah's Entertainment), one of the largest companies in the gaming industry, has been promoting responsible gaming since the late 1990s. While Caesars does not specifically endorse GA, it has been publicizing the signs and symptoms of compulsive gambling, thus helping to reduce the stigma.

An outcome study of GA conducted in 1988 found that less than 8 percent of people who begin attending GA meetings continue to work the program and stay away from gambling for more than one year. One reason may be that the stress of accepting responsibility for financial, legal, and employment problems in spite of abstinence from gambling is overwhelming. Another possible reason is that compulsive gambling also may be compounded by substance misuse: When the concomitant addiction is not addressed, relapse into gambling is easily triggered.

In addition, the recovery rate of GA members is still lower than that of AA members because the medical model of compulsive behavior as a progressive illness is less accepted by society for compulsive gamblers than for alcoholics. The medical community has labeled compulsive (pathological) gambling as an impulse control disorder similar to compulsive eating, kleptomania, and hypersexuality. The increasing incidence of compulsive gambling in persons with Parkinson's disease, for example, has prompted research that has discovered an associated dysfunction in the frontal lobe of the brain. Rat models of impulsivity are being developed to identify potential pharmacological targets and treatments for impulse control disorders.

Bethany Thivierge MPH

For Further Information

A Day at a Time: Gamblers Anonymous. Center City, MN: Hazelden, 1994. Daily affirmations and readings to inspire compulsive gamblers to pursue recovery.

Gamblers Anonymous. *GA Red Book: A New Beginning.* 3rd ed. Los Angeles: Author, 1998. Inspirational stories about persons who have successfully worked GA.

—. *Sharing Recovery through Gamblers Anonymous.* Los Angeles: Author, 1984. Handbook for compulsive gamblers following the twelve-step recovery program.

Sanders, Elizabeth. *Gambling Recovery: Working the Gamblers Anonymous Recovery Program.* Tucson, AZ: Wheatmark, 2010. A guidebook to working the twelve steps of the GA recovery program. Includes exercises at the end of each step.

See also: Behavioral addictions: Treatment; Gambling addiction; Group therapy for behavioral addictions; Support groups; Twelve-step programs for addicts

Gambling addiction

Category: Psychological issues and behaviors
Also known as: Compulsive gambling; disordered gambling; pathological gambling; problem gambling
Definition: Gambling is an activity that involves a degree of risk and an expenditure of money or goods with the hope of an increased return but with the possibility of a total loss. Some people gamble for pleasure, in a non-addictive fashion, and suffer no ill effects from gaming activities. Others have a problem with gambling, which is manifested by their increasing desire to gamble, even if doing so creates hardships. These hardships include money and debt problems, difficulties at work, relationship problems, and legal sanctions.

South Oaks Gambling Screen

The most common instrument used to screen for probable pathological-gambling behavior is the South Oaks Gambling Screen (SOGS), developed at South Oaks Hospital in New York. South Oaks Hospital is located on Long Island and is well known for work with psychiatric problems and addictions. SOGS has become one of the most-cited screening instruments in psychological research literature involving the measurement of pathological gambling.

Henry Lesieur, a psychiatrist and certified gambling counselor, and Shelia Blume, medical director at South Oaks Hospital, developed the twenty-item SOGS in the late 1980s to produce a scale that would be consistent and quantifiable. In use, responses to the twenty items are recorded, and agreement with five or more items is interpreted as evidence of the presence of pathological gambling. In the years since its development, SOGS has become the most commonly used scale to measure problem gambling in both clinical and nonclinical settings.

Causes

Problem gambling has a familial component because parents with a gambling addiction tend to socialize their children into the gambling world. Many of these young people, in turn, develop disordered gambling behavior. Research with twins suggests that there may be a genetic component underlying gambling addiction, which may be reinforced by cultural norms. Cultural components have also been associated with problem gambling, as have games that can be played without a gambling component, such as mahjongg and bingo.

RISK FACTORS

Greater numbers of men typically experience gambling addiction, although women are also at risk. People with gambling addictions often have other mental health issues (including personality disorders, mood disorders, and anxiety ailments) and other addictive disorders, which increase the challenge in determining what effects were caused by gambling and what were caused by other comorbidities. Problem gamblers often consume alcohol, nonprescription drugs, and tobacco in unhealthy ways, which also contributes to dysfunctional behavior.

Prevalence research in much of the developed world suggests that approximately 1 percent of the world's population may experience gambling problems. The disordered gambling figures for adolescents, in locations where such research has been completed, are much higher, with the implication that gambling-addiction numbers will rise as adolescents age and as increasing means to gamble become available. The growth of Internet gambling is particularly challenging for local authorities to license, control, or measure. Particular concerns with these web-based services are that young players are difficult to identify and, thus, cannot be prevented from accessing these sites, even when local laws do not permit children to gamble.

SYMPTOMS

According to the *Diagnostic and Statistical Manual of Mental Disorders* (DSM-IV), published in 1994 by the American Psychiatric Association (APA), pathological gambling is considered to be an impulse-control disorder. A text revision of this manual, called DSM-IV-TR, appeared in 2000, but this revision did not fundamentally change the definition of pathological gambling. The DSM volumes do not use the term *addiction* in connection with gambling, although other APA publications highlight the similarities to

South Oaks Gambling Screen

The most common instrument used to screen for probable pathological-gambling behavior is the South Oaks Gambling Screen (SOGS), developed at South Oaks Hospital in New York. South Oaks Hospital is located on Long Island and is well known for work with psychiatric problems and addictions. SOGS has become one of the most-cited screening instruments in psychological research literature involving the measurement of pathological gambling.

Henry Lesieur, a psychiatrist and certified gambling counselor, and Shelia Blume, medical director at South Oaks Hospital, developed the twenty-item SOGS in the late 1980s to produce a scale that would be consistent and quantifiable. In use, responses to the twenty items are recorded, and agreement with five or more items is interpreted as evidence of the presence of pathological gambling. In the years since its development, SOGS has become the most commonly used scale to measure problem gambling in both clinical and nonclinical settings.

substance addictions.

Pathological gambling is defined operationally by the presence of five of ten criteria. The measures focus on the negative effects of gambling for an individual (such as preoccupation, desire to gamble, and difficulty stopping) and the results for gambler's associates (such as lies, illegal actions, and loss of relationships). It is possible that some of the current criteria may be revised in updated editions of the DSM.

A person may manifest a gambling addiction for a period of time and then gain some control over his or her behavior, only to relapse and begin the cycle yet again. This is a common pattern for other addictive disorders, and this cyclical progression is challenging for persons in the gambler's family and social circles, and for the individual gambler.

SCREENING AND DIAGNOSIS

Several dozen screening and diagnostic devices have been used to measure problem gambling. Many of these are based on the DSM criteria for measuring pathological gambling. Two commonly used tools are the South Oaks gambling screen and the modified NORC DSM-IV screen for gambling problems.

Depending on the type of gambling screen used, a diagnosis typically places the person along a continuum of increasingly disordered behavior. At the lowest levels are people who have never gambled, although few people fit into this category at most locations, given the ubiquity of gaming activities in contemporary society. People who do not gamble excessively, or who cause no harm to themselves or others, may be described as recreational or social gamblers. Gamblers who display symptoms are termed *compulsive gamblers, disordered gamblers, excessive gamblers, intemperate gamblers, pathological gamblers,* or *problematic gamblers.* The term *gambling addiction* is not used typically in the social or the health sciences, although the general public uses it. Some treatment centers use this nomenclature as it is readily understood by clients.

TREATMENT AND THERAPY

Treatment traditionally involves talk therapy, although more recent approaches have focused on pharmacological interventions, especially antidepressants. A small number of studies have examined the effects of mood stabilizers and opioid antagonists (specifically naltrexone). Some of these medications had unpleasant side effects for the research volunteers, especially the participants in clinical studies using naltrexone.

Many people with gambling addictions have access to psychological and therapeutic treatments, including psychoanalytic approaches, psychodynamic-based treatments, behavioral therapy, cognitive approaches, addiction-based interventions, and self-help. Much of the research on these types of treatment relies on small sample sizes and no control groups, creating challenges in determining what treatments are most successful.

An additional problem for gamblers is that most treatments are offered at a cost, which can pose difficulties for this group given that, typically, gamblers have little money by the time they need treatment. Free Gamblers Anonymous groups are found in most urban centers, which is helpful for this client group.

In addition to methodological problems with studies that make it difficult to identify the most promising treatment options, there are conceptual issues. Generally, people with gambling addictions have been considered to be a fairly uniform subject group

by researchers; however, there are many differences within the group in terms of comorbidity and other factors, which might influence treatment outcomes. Also, there are many problem gamblers who manage to recover without treatment; it would be useful to learn more about this group and what factors account for their improvement.

Treatment efforts also have focused on spouses and other family members of problem gamblers. Because the addict also negatively affects others with his or her addiction, therapists have suggested that family members too could benefit from some intervention.

PREVENTION

It can be argued that the best prevention for gambling addiction is to avoid gambling, since most people do not realize their propensity for unhealthy and problematic gambling until they have a problem. Generally, government dollars have been spent on treatment rather than on prevention, but there are strong public health arguments that support greater efforts in prevention.

Susan J. Wurtzburg PhD

FOR FURTHER INFORMATION

Kaminer, Yifrah, and Oscar G. Bukstein, eds. *Adolescent Substance Abuse: Psychiatric Comorbidity and High-Risk Behaviors.* New York: Routledge, 2008. A broad consideration of substance abuse among adolescents.

Ladouceur, Robert, and Stella Lachance. *Overcoming Pathological Gambling: Therapist Guide.* New York: Oxford UP, 2006. Useful therapeutic information, from a cognitive-behavioral therapy approach, for the therapist, gambler, and affected family members.

Nathan, Peter E., and Jack M. Gorman, eds. *A Guide to Treatments That Work.* 3rd ed. New York: Oxford UP, 2007.

National Research Council. *Pathological Gambling: A Critical Review.* Washington, DC: National Academy, 1999. A clearly written overview of gambling technology, problem gambling, its effects on individuals and communities, and treatment.

Newman, Stephen C., and Angus H. Thompson. "The Association between Pathological Gambling and Attempted Suicide: Findings from a National Survey in Canada." *Canadian Journal of Psychiatry* 52.9 (2007): 605–12. Print. Identifies an association, although causality is unproven, between pathological gambling and attempted suicide.

Petry, Nancy M. *Pathological Gambling: Etiology, Comorbidity, and Treatment*. Washington, DC: American Psychological Association, 2005. Examines pathological gambling from a clinical perspective.

Wong, Irene Lai Kuen. "Internet Gambling: A School-Based Survey among Macau Students." *Social Behavior and Personality* 38.3 (2010): 365–72. Print. Discusses two growing gambling populations, each of which deserves more study: Internet gambling and adolescent participation in gambling.

See also: Behavioral addictions: Overview; Compulsions; Gamblers Anonymous; Gaming addiction; Impulse control disorders; Men and behavioral addictions

---

Gaming addiction

CATEGORY: Psychological issues and behaviors

Also known as: Pathological gaming; pathological video gaming; pathological video game use; problematic gaming; problematic video gaming; video game addiction

Definition: A behavioral addiction marked by excessive time spent playing games and, in particular, video games. The behavior displayed is a pattern of behavioral addiction in which self-care, health, familial, educational, and occupational obligations are unfulfilled or ignored. Those addicted invest inordinate time and focus to a degree it seriously impacting the other spheres which make up these individuals' worlds. The most prevalent form is being addicted to video games, alone or with others. Less common manifestations exist, such as board games and card games. When betting is involved, gaming addiction is referred to as compulsive gambling or gambling addiction. When excessive and problematic use of online sex video games occurs, this type of gaming addiction is referred to as pornography addiction.

KEY TERMS:

Avatar: Technically, refers to the physical manifestation of any one of the gods in Hinduism. Broadly, refers to the persona and physical appearance of a character in a game that represents the video game player.

Binge gaming: Gaming for more than six hours at a time with little or no interruption.

Carpel tunnel syndrome: When sustained or frequent pressure is maintained on the medial nerve running from the forearm to the wrist. The nerve physically passes through a canal or passageway, the carpel tunnel. Addicted gamers are at risk for developing the syndrome because of their frequent (how often) use of using game controllers and the duration (how long) while using them.

Dopamine: A neurochemically simple but potent neurotransmitter which significantly affects the brain's pleasure and reward centers and thus promotes these responses and the desire to continue to have them. It also facilitates physical movement and emotional responsivity.

Flow: An altered state of consciousness marked by a rewarding, focused sense of control with a simultaneous loss of a sense of time and place.

Gray matter: Covering most of the brain's surface and containing most of the brain's neuronal cells, it is a critically important part of the central nervous system. It is involved with speech, memory, self-control, production of emotions, seeing, hearing, and muscle control. Often compared and contrasted with the brain's "white matter."

Likert scale: Rensis Likert's invented method is the mostly widely used approach to scaling items or questions in survey research. Likert scales commonly appear like this statement: "On a scale of one to five, where one means strongly agree and five means strongly disagree, how would you rate the following."

MMORPGs Massively multiplayer online role-playing games. These are internet-based and involve large numbers of players from anywhere in the world. They often involve relationship play, military or combat themes.

CAUSES

Gaming addiction can have several underlying causes. In general, they addictions are triggered and cultivated when unmet or partially unmet social and psychological needs are fulfilled by playing games. One of the primary functions of playing games is to rehearse real-life situations and circumstances, allowing development of behavioral responses without risk. The reasons excessive gaming develops are many and can include releasing stress, relaxing, reducing anxiety, escaping from others, troubling events, avoiding responsibilities, escaping ennui, self-isolating, maintaining autonomy (or believing one is), avoiding social interaction or maintaining social interaction through the game itself..

Gaming addiction is similar to pathological gambling: both begin as rewarding entertainment. Video gaming, as does gambling, activates the brain's reward pathways, releasing dopamine.

Massively multiplayer online role-playing games (MMORPGs) have a significant mixture of social interaction and open-ended game play that has drawn many individuals in MMORPHs have considerable addictive potential. The interactive nature of video games and the increasing potential for realistic depictions of environments that allow for complex social interactions increase the potential that they become salient to the person playing the game.

RISK FACTORS

Adolescent and young adult males are predominant users of video games. Among this group there is also a greater incidence of dependency on others. Gaming can elicit a cognitive and affective state known as flow, which is characterized by a rewarding, focused sense of control and a loss of sense of time and place. Research data demonstrate that pathological gaming persists over time and is not a phase one matures out of. Impulsivity, absence of empathy, apathy, low social competence, and poorer emotional regulation correlate with pathological gaming. Experts, however, differ on the causal relationship of these factors in gaming development. These same factors also may be in response to problematic gaming.

Research increasingly shows that addictive or pathological gaming seems predictive of worse psychological health. Depression, moodiness, anxiety, reactivity, and social phobia are more present in individuals addicted to gaming than individuals who game in moderation. The role of these effects on psychosocial development, in the presence of continued gaming, is unclear. Youth gaming more than 30 hours per week are significantly more likely to develop gaming addiction than are those gaming less than 20 hours per week. While certainly not limited to them, games like

the MMORPGs, involve personally identifying with a gaming character or avatar, are much more prone toward gaming addiction. Open-ended games or those that regularly add content yet to be mastered, also pose addiction risk. Persons with a history of addiction, so those have, diagnosed or not, substance use disorder or a behavioral addiction, and who also have a lot of unstructured time are also at greater risk of become individuals with gaming addiction.

SYMPTOMS

Gaming addiction symptoms range from psychological and social to physiological and neurological, include game-binging, gaming late into the night, decreasing interest in school or occupational pursuits, becoming angry or frustrated when denied access to the game, say when a server is down, or being preoccupied with the next gaming session, downplaying the prevalence or effects of video gaming, having a distorted perception of time while gaming, difficulty abstaining from gaming, increased game-centered purchases on games and gaming platforms and equipment, and feeling distressed when unable to play. Relational symptoms include lying to others about how much time is spent gaming, decreased time spent with family and friends, increased preference for fellow gamers, and decreased interest in marital and romantic relationships.

Other issues, such as sleeping difficulties or a significant change in sleep habits, dry or red eyes, weight gain, lack of attention to personal hygiene and eating habits, and soreness to the back, neck, hands, or wrists (as carpal tunnel syndrome), can be symptomatic of pathological gaming. Using stimulants like coffee or highly caffeinated drinks or using medication prescribe for attention deficit disorder to promote attention, focus, and staying awake may also indicate a gaming addiction.

Research has identified and continues to identify through functional imaging, alterations of the brain's gray matter volume in those with gaming addiction.

SCREENING AND DIAGNOSIS

Several screening tools exist to diagnose pathological gaming, though none is the gold standard. They all use measures similar to those used to determine pathological gambling and substance use disorders. Two of these are the "Gaming Addiction Scale" (GAS) and the Problematic Videogame Playing (PVP). The

GAS for adolescents uses a Likert scale to measure the impact gaming addiction has on the individual. Core components of gaming addiction include salience, tolerance, mood modification, withdrawal, relapse, conflict, and consequences or problems. The PVP uses a nine-item, forced-choice questionnaire that focus on issues related to symptoms of excessive gaming.

Proponents of including gaming addiction in the *Diagnostic and Statistical Manual of Mental Disorders, Fifth Edition (DSM-5)* were concerned about the medical, educational, and social well-being of children who spend excessive time gaming. The *DSM-5* lists "Internet Gaming Disorder" as not a diagnosis, but as one of the many areas in psychiatric and psychological needing more research toward identifying this addiction as a formal behavioral disorder. In 2018, the World Health Organization named gaming addiction as a disease in its eleventh edition of the *International Classification of Diseases*. Given that gaming addiction is not in the *DSM*, it is not a clinical diagnosis. Gaming addiction can be considered a comorbidity with other clinical diagnoses like the mood, anxiety, and antisocial disorders. Diagnosis of gaming addiction should consider common addiction criteria, such as tolerance, psychological or physiological withdrawal with gaming abstinence, a progressive increase in time spent gaming, and a cycle of abstinence followed by relapse.

TREATMENT AND THERAPY

The most commonly used treatments are individual psychotherapy and psychoeducation about the effects of gaming consumption. Interpersonal therapy and cognitive-behavioral therapy are commonly employed to treat comorbid psychological issues. In addition, support groups (such as Online Gamers Anonymous) and group therapy can effectively treat gaming addiction, provided these groups consider matters of access, coping skills, relapse prevention, and recovery. Self-help and parenting books are also available for people who want to treat video game and other technology addictions.

Online communities for recovery also exist, although computer access and availability and the anonymous nature of this interface, which allows for viewing pornography, can be problematic. To address this, the use of filtering software to monitor use and prevent access to sexually explicit material is commonly regarded as a first-order behavioral or environmental intervention. Pharmacotherapy for gaming addiction or related diagnoses like anxiety disorder and mood disorder should also be considered for severe cases.

PREVENTION

Prevention of gaming addictions is best achieved by avoiding the regular use of video games. Refraining from extended play of video games, especially MMORPGs and those that are open-ended, also is recommended. The sooner treatment interventions are begun, generally the more successful. Established therapies used for most other behavioral addictions are also readily applied to gaming addiction.

William M. Struthers, PhD;
Updated by Paul Moglia, PhD

FOR FURTHER INFORMATION

Block, Jerald J. "Issues for *DSM-V*: Internet Addiction." *American Journal of Psychiatry* 165.3 (2008): 306–7. Print. Professional commentary on how behavioral addictions, like gaming, should be understood in developing diagnostic criteria in the *DSM-5*.

Clark, Neils, and Scott P. Shavaun. *Game Addiction: The Experience and the Effects*. London: McFarland, 2009. Print. Well-written. Addresses game addiction, symptoms, and developmental effects.

Driskell, Nathan, *30-Day Plan to Take Back Your Life*. Self-published: Cypress, TX. (2017). Print. https://nathandriskell.com. Highly readable, well received, and practical self-help work. Step-by-step guide to recovery.

Gentile, Douglas A., et al. "Pathological Videogame Use among Youths: A Two-Year Longitudinal Study." *Pediatrics* 127 (2011): 319–29. Print. Professional journal article presenting a longitudinal look at students' use of video games, measuring social competence, educational outcomes, and behavioral and mental health. While a study of students in Singapore, subsequent professional research supports the application of their findings much more universally.

Grüsser, S. M., R. Thalemann, and M. Griffiths. "Excessive Computer Game Playing: Evidence for Addiction and Aggression?" *Cyberpsychology and Behavior* 10 (2007): 290–92. Print. Academic investigation into the relationships among gaming addiction, aggression, and impulsivity.

Johnson, Nicola F. *The Multiplicities of Internet Addiction: The Misrecognition of Leisure and Learning*. Burlington: Ashgate, 2009. Print. Comprehensive text frames gaming addiction within the context of two of the elements which drives it, recreation and proficiency.

Roberts, Kevin, *Cyber Junkie: Escape the Gaming and Internet Trap*. Hazelton: Center City, MN (2017). Print. In recovery himself, the author presents an easy-to-read, easy-to-follow, step by step plan for recovering from gaming and internet addiction.

Robinson, Melia. "Korea's Internet Addiction Crisis Is Getting Worse, as Teens Spend up to 88 Hours a Week Gaming." *Business Insider*. Business Insider, 25 Mar. 2015. Web. 29 Oct. 2015.

Skoric, M. M., L. L. Teo, and R. L. Neo. "Children and Video Games: Addiction, Engagement, and Scholastic Achievement." *Cyberpsychology and Behavior* 12.5 (2009): 567–72. Print. Study of the effects of video gaming on educational and scholastic achievement.

Zahariades. Damon, *Digital Detox: The Ultimate Guide to Beating Technology Addiction, Cultivating Mindfulness, and Enjoying More Creativity, Inspiration, and Balance in Your Life!*. Self-published. No city given. Art of Productivity, https://artofproductitiy.com. Useful, well-written, well-received, practical, realistic guide to rebalance life in the wake of the omnipresence of technology and overuse of the internet. Readily applies to gaming addiction.

See also: Behavioral addictions; Computer addiction; Gambling addiction; Internet addiction; Pornography addiction; Social media addiction.

Gasoline (substance of misuse)

CATEGORY: Substances

DEFINITION: Gasoline is a volatile, flammable solvent that is inhaled by misusers of the substance. It is generally a mixture of hydrocarbons derived from petroleum and normally used as fuel in internal-combustion engines. Along with other aromatics, gasoline also contains various benzene compounds.

STATUS: Legal

TRANSMISSION ROUTE: Inhalants are readily absorbed through the lungs and then relatively rapidly metabolized in the liver, whereby different cellular mechanisms lead to pharmacologic and toxicologic effects. Gasoline is inhaled through the mouth and nose and into the trachea, often from a saturated cloth.

HISTORY OF USE

Prevalence of lifetime inhalant use among twelfth-graders has ranged between 10.3 percent in 1976 (when first measured) and 18.0 percent, at the 1990 peak. The 2006 rate of 11.1 percent has been stable since 2002. Misuse of gasoline is one of the most widespread inhalant abuses in the United States.

In the late 1990s it was considered that volatile solvent misuse was among the most difficult and refractory to treat. Inhalant misuse intervention has been characterized by the absence of even a rudimentary treatment model. There is no specific agent that can reverse or alleviate acute solvent intoxication, addiction, or the rare cases that present with withdrawal symptoms. Volatile substance misusers do not fit well within existing treatment regimens.

Reports of the misuse of leaded gasoline have been limited to northern Canada, the southwestern United States, and the Australian outback. To fight rampant gasoline sniffing in the outback, the Australian government introduced Opal, a fuel that has been in use since 2006 and has yielded a 70 percent reduction in the misuse of gasoline across outback communities.

EFFECTS AND POTENTIAL RISKS

Gasoline is a depressant that acts directly on the central nervous system. The vapors from gasoline trigger visual hallucinations, changes in consciousness, euphoria, and nystagmus. The user experiences a subconscious state, wherein he or she dreams while aware of his or her surroundings. This euphoric effect has a short duration and compels the user to inhale again. Adverse effects include dizziness, aggressiveness, impaired judgment, weakness, and tremors.

Long-term effects manifest as neurological and cognitive abnormalities in the absence of acute toxic brain diseases, and also include peripheral neuropathies and bone marrow damage. Chronic, heavy misuse of leaded gasoline results in an encephalopathy, cerebellar and corticospinal symptoms and signs, dementia, mental status alterations, and persistent organic psychosis. Chronic misuse also can lead to sudden death.

Stephanie Eckenrode BA, LLB

FOR FURTHER INFORMATION

Doweiko, Harold E. *Concepts of Chemical Dependency.* 8th ed. Belmont, CA: Brooks, 2012.

Fitzhugh, Karla. *Inhalants.* Chicago: Raintree, 2004.

Miller, Norman S., and Mark S. Gold. *Addictive Disorders in Medical Populations.* Hoboken, NJ: Wiley, 2010.

See also: Behavioral addictions: Overview; Computer addiction; Gambling addiction; Internet addiction; Social media addiction

---

Gateway drugs

CATEGORY: Substances

ALSO KNOWN AS: Gateway hypothesis; gateway theory

DEFINITION: Gateway drugs, especially marijuana but also tobacco and alcohol, are drugs thought to lead to the use of other (typically illegal) drugs. The drugs used initially are considered less harmful. The gateway is considered a "tunnel" that leads directly from simple drug use to hard drug use. Another view considers the gateway as a "funnel" that allows some people to move more easily to hard drugs. The term *gateway drugs* is thought to have been coined by Robert DuPont, the first director of the National Institute on Drug Abuse (NIDA). There is debate as to whether so-called gateway drugs actually lead to the use of more harmful drugs of misuse.

STATUS: Tobacco and alcohol are legal in the United States; marijuana is illegal under US federal law, though some states have legalized medical marijuana use and/or legalized or decriminalized recreational use. Gateway drugs are governed by certain regulations covering sales, conditions of use, and the minimum age for buying and using.

CLASSIFICATION: Marijuana is a schedule I narcotic; tobacco and alcohol are uncontrolled substances

SOURCE: Tobacco comes from leaves of seventy different species of the *Nicotiana* plant; consumable alcohol is known as ethanol; marijuana comes from the hemp plant *Cannabis sativa*

TRANSMISSION ROUTE: Tobacco is smoked, chewed, snuffed, and dipped; alcohol is ingested; marijuana is smoked and ingested

HISTORY OF USE

Chemicals derived from *Nicotiana* plants were used for medicinal purposes in the sixteenth century. Cigarettes were first made in the 1830s and were popular in the United States by the 1860s. By the 1950s studies showed that tobacco was hazardous to one's health and, in 1965, cigarette advertising in the United States had to include a warning of tobacco's health hazards.

Alcohol, specifically wine, was used as early as 5000 BCE. Alcohol use became rampant and problematic in the United States before 1920, leading to Prohibition. With Prohibition came moonshine, speakeasies, and even more problems, leading to the law's repeal in 1933. Alcohol sales and use were again legal in the United States.

Marijuana, which is often referred to as cannabis or THC (delta 9 tetrahydrocannabinol, its main chemical ingredient), was used for medicinal purposes as early as 3000 BCE and as an intoxicant by 1000 BCE. Marijuana use was illegal in the United States by 1920. It is now legal in certain US states for medicinal purposes and even recreational use, while other states have decriminalized marijuana possession.

One study (2001) found that the progression from alcohol and tobacco use to marijuana and harder drugs was first seen in the United States in people born after World War II, that it peaked in the baby boomers born in the 1960s, and that is has since shown a decline, indicating less of a gateway effect than in the past. Studies do indicate, however, that the younger a person begins smoking or drinking, the more likely he or she will progress to hard drugs. It is also commonly argued that as a user builds up a tolerance to the effects of tobacco, alcohol, or marijuana, they may become more likely to pursue other means of achieving the pleasurable effects associated with drug use, leading to an increased likelihood of experimenting with harder drugs. However, many researchers cite studies that suggest there is no proven evidence of a regular gateway effect, particularly with marijuana.

Another form of the gateway drug theory expresses concern that electronic cigarettes (e-cigarettes) could lead to use of regular tobacco products. Antismoking advocates particularly target e-cigarette marketing aimed at young audiences, such as candy-flavored formulas, that they argue could lead young people to become addicted to nicotine and eventually begin using cigarettes. Proponents of e-cigarettes counter that such products may by safer than traditional tobacco products and may even help regular tobacco smokers quit—essentially the opposite of the gateway effect.

EFFECTS AND POTENTIAL RISKS

Smoking causes dry mouth and thirst, after an initial increase in salivation. A sore throat and cough often follows dry mouth. Shortly after beginning the use of tobacco, the body will start to have problems with red-blood-cell production, which is often accompanied by cardiac arrhythmias. Long-term effects of smoking include cardiac problems, stroke, and lung problems, including cancer. According to most research, smoking, over time, affects almost every system in the body.

Alcohol is a sedative and a psychoactive drug, and it affects cells in the cerebral cortex, leading to disinhibition. As such, it tends to impair judgment. Driving under the influence of alcohol (above the legal limit) is illegal, and it is responsible for thousands of motor vehicle accidents and vehicle-related deaths in the United States each year. Long-term alcohol use can lead to liver and pancreatic problems, to cancer of the throat and esophagus, and to brain damage (such as Wernicke-Korsakoff syndrome).

Short-term effects of marijuana use can include disorders of perception, learning, memory, cognition, and coordination, and to symptoms of anxiety. While long-term effects of marijuana are unclear, it is thought that the drug may affect the immune system and the respiratory system, and that it can cause some forms of cancer.

Robin Kamienny Montvilo PhD

FOR FURTHER INFORMATION

Arkowitz, Hal, and Scott O. Lilienfeld. "Experts Tell the Truth About Pot." *Scientific American*. Scientific American, 1 Mar. 2012. Web 29 Oct. 2015.

DuPont, Robert L. *Getting Tough on Gateway Drugs: A Guide for the Family.* Washington, DC: American Psychiatric Association, 1984. Print.

Smokeless Tobacco

Smokeless tobacco, or snuff, is finely ground or cut tobacco that is sold in three formats: dry, moist, and sachet. Dry snuff is powdered and inhaled through the nose. Moist snuff, also called dipping tobacco, is sold in tins for oral use; sachet snuff is moist snuff packaged in small pouches similar to teabags. Swedish snuff, called snus, is pasteurized rather than fermented and induces less salivation in its users than does moist snuff.

Smokeless tobacco products regained popularity in the 1970s as people learned the dangers of smoking cigarettes and mistakenly thought that smokeless tobacco was a safe alternative to satisfy their nicotine addiction. In the United States in 2009, smokeless tobacco users were 3.5 percent of all adults (7 percent of adult men), 6.1 percent of all high school students (11 percent of males), and 2.6 percent of all middle school students (4.1 percent of males).

Golub, Andrew, and Bruce D. Johnson. "Variation in Youthful Risks of Progression from Alcohol and Tobacco to Marijuana and Hard Drugs across Generations." *American Journal of Public Health* 91 (2001): 225–32. Print.

"Is Marijuana a Gateway Drug?" *National Institute on Drug Abuse.* NIH, Sept. 2015. Web 29 Oct. 2015.

Kandel, Denise B. *Stages and Pathways of Drug Involvement: Examining the Gateway Hypothesis.* New York: Cambridge UP, 2002.

See also: Adolescents and alcohol misuse; Adolescents and drug misuse; Adolescents, young adults and smoking; Marijuana

---

Gender and addiction

CATEGORY: Social issues

DEFINITION: Though it is unclear whether men or women are more susceptible to alcohol or drug addiction based on gender-specific biological and environmental factors, data suggest that men and women often become addicted for different reasons. Diagnosis and successful addiction treatment are also gender-sensitive.

KEY TERMS:

Gender: Social and cultural identity differences between individuals.

Addiction: Condition of being dependent upon a certain substance, item, or activity.

PREVALENCE

Studies report that men are, overall, a larger group of individuals that use substances. However, studies evidenced some differences between genders. With respect to women with substance use histories, studies found that adolescent girls are more likely to be addicted to opioids or amphetamine-type stimulants. Age also appears to play a role in when a woman begins to use (e.g., methamphetamines are used at an earlier age). Women are more likely to attend the emergency room for overdosing and are, in general, more likely to die from overdosing on heroin. Women are less likely to inject heroin. When a woman is found to be an IV substance user, it is likely they began due to pressure from relationships, either romantic or otherwise.

CAUSES

More often than not, women use substances to cope with life stressors, such as a diagnosis of a mental health disorder or histories of trauma. Researchers described other reasons being related to hormones (e.g., fertility, pregnancy, breastfeeding, menopause, or menstrual cycle). Addiction is often due to a combination of environmental and genetic problems.

RISK FACTORS

Women report a variety of reasons as to why they use and each will be specific to the individual. Some of the common reasons for use include: weight loss/control; energy booster; maladaptive coping mechanism; or pain management. Trauma is a key element in why many women begin to use illicit substances. The women report this was their way of coping with life stressors, at a time when they did not have other means to cope.

ASSESSMENT

During a clinical interview/intake, it is imperative that the evaluation assesses for substance use, while focusing on coping skills the woman may utilize. For example, a woman may report they become stressed on Mondays because of the week ahead and instead of talking about this stressor, they use a Hydrocodone from a surgery they had last year. While this medication was prescribed to them, they are no longer in need of the medication from a medical standpoint. Thus, it is important to discuss this with the client to understand their use of the substance in order to best understand their cycle of misuse. Other important discussion points include a focus on if/how substance use has affected their family, if they have placed themselves/others at risk, if others have suggested they may have a problem, or if other important areas of functioning are impacted (e.g., school, work, or the community).

DIAGNOSIS

Women are more likely to be diagnosed with a mental health aliment and a substance use disorder. This is known as dual diagnosis. When programs and treatment focus on the specialized needs of women with dual diagnosis, researchers witnessed an increase in completion and success rates. More common diagnoses in women are anxiety, bipolar disorder, or major depressive disorder with suicide attempts.

GENDER-SPECIFIC TREATMENT

There are a number of gender-specific treatments. One of the more widely used programs is called *Seeking Safety*. In this program, women complete 24 structured sessions with a mental health professional. During this time, the participant begins to process their various lived experiences in order to come to understand their use, triggers, and they create new coping skills, along with a safety plan for after the completion of programming. In newer programs, agencies are incorporating *Seeking Safety* with Dialectical Behavioral Therapy, as a means to educate the individuals on new coping skills, while also addressing the concerns of addiction and mental health aliments. The programs are repetitive to ensure the participants understand the content and help them to remember the different components of the programs.

Another program, *Helping Women Recover: A Program for Treating Addiction*, utilizes a similar approach described above. The treatment includes women's psychological development, trauma, and addiction. The program is 17 sessions that address the following areas: self, relationships, sexuality, and spirituality. These areas are further broken down into self-esteem, sexism, family of origin, relationships, domestic violence, and trauma. The facilitator maintains a copy of the facilitator guide, while the women are provided a journal to complete different exercises throughout the program. This program has an additional specialized guide for working with those in the criminal justice system.

A third program is by Lisa M. Najavits called *A Woman's Addiction Workbook: Your Guide to In-depth Healing.* The program features certain problems associated with addiction such as body image, trauma, violence, relationships, stress, and thrill-seeking. The program is strength-based and provides healing exercises in feelings, beliefs, action, and relationships, in order to assist women with building self-respect. The final piece of the workbook is that it explains differences in gender and addiction.

BIOLOGICAL DIFFERENCES

The biological differences between genders suggest specific problems related to women who have addiction histories. Some of the concerns are related to hormones as previously identified. Women use smaller amounts of substances for less time, are quicker to become addicted to the substance, and some women report experiencing more cravings. Studies suggested women are more likely to relapse after treatment, which may be related to the woman's menstrual cycle. Research supported that adolescent girls who regularly use cannabis are at a higher risk of structural abnormalities in their brain.

Researchers found women may be more sensitive to the effects of a substance when compared to men. Women may also experience more physical effects on their heart and blood vessels. Recent trends suggested more women are drinking alcohol than previous decades. Over the last 40 years, it was estimated that women who consume alcohol increased from 45% to 66% and approximately 5% of that group of women consume a significant amount of alcohol. There are physiological differences between men and women as it relates to alcohol consumption. Women are generally smaller than men and have a larger percentage of fat. This allows for women to develop higher blood alcohol concentrations; thus, becoming intoxicated quicker. Further, the chemical that breaks down some alcohol (alcohol dehydrogenase) is found in lesser amounts in women under the age of 40, so more alcohol is being absorbed into their blood. Other concerns related to women and alcohol is the effects on the liver and pancreas, and the increased risk of breast cancer and high blood pressure. Furthermore, research supported that women who drink heavily are at a higher risk for domestic violence and sexual assault.

There are additional substances that appear to effect women differently than men. For example, it was found that women who used cannabis for longer periods of time experienced irregular menstrual cycles and impairment in spatial memory. This irregular menstrual cycle is also seen when women use opiates. While neither of these cases causes a woman to become infertile, it may make conception more challenging. Research provided that women who use opiates may also engage in unsafe sexual practices and may be at higher risk for sexually transmitted infections. An additional area of concern related to misuse of prescription medication is related to benzodiazepines. Women are more likely to obtain treatment for the misuse of sedatives (e.g., Xanax, Valium).

Lindsey L. Wilner, Psy.D.

FOR FURTHER INFORMATION

American Psychiatric Association. (2013). *Diagnostic and Statistical Manual of Mental Disorders – Fifth Edition (DSM-5)*. Arlington, VA: American Psychiatric Association.

Covington, S. (2008). *Helping women recover: A program for treating addiction* (2nd Ed.). Hoboken, NJ: John Wiley & Sons, Inc.

Kuhn, C., Swartzwelder, S., & Wilson, W. (2014). *Buzzed: The straight facts about the most used and abused drugs from alcohol to ecstasy* (4th Ed.). New York, NY: W. W. Norton & Company, Inc.

Najavits, L. (2002a). *A woman's addiction workbook: Your guide to in-depth healing*. Oakland, CA: New Harbinger Publications.

Najavits, L. (2002b). *Seeking safety: A treatment manual for PTSD and substance abuse*. New York, NY: Guilford Publications.

National Institute on Drug Abuse: Advancing Addiction Science. (2018, July). "Substance use in women." Retrieved from https://www.drugabuse.gov/publications/research-reports/substance-use-in-women/sex-gender-differences-in-substance-use

National Institute on Drug Abuse: Advancing Addiction Science. (2018, June). "Sex and gender differences in substance use." Retrieved from https://

www.drugabuse.gov/publications/drugfacts/substance-use-in-women

Springer, D. W., McNeece, C. A., & Arnold, E. M. (2003). *Substance abuse treatment for criminal offenders: An evidenced-based guide for practitioners.* Washington, DC: American Psychological Association.

See also: Age and addiction; Men and behavioral addictions; Men and smoking; Men and substance misuse; Socioeconomic status and addiction; Substance misuse and addiction in the elderly; Suicide and addiction; Women and behavioral addictions; Women and smoking; Women and substance misuse

Genetics and substance misuse

CATEGORY: Health issues and physiology

DEFINITION: Substance misuse is broadly defined as the over use and dependence (addiction) to substances such as drugs or alcohol. Evidence suggests some forms of misuse and addiction may have a genetic and/or an epigenetic basis.

GENETIC EVIDENCE

The functions of specific regions within the brain, including those that include pleasure centers and those that control other forms of reactions to specific drugs, are subject to hereditary control. The expression of cell receptors and the synthesis and activity of enzymes that control pathways in the brain, each regulating the response to drugs, have an underlying genetic control.

Studies indicate that the initial use of a drug is less affected by genetic factors than is the addiction that may develop from continued use.

Early attempts to estimate the relative contributions of genetics and the environment to the variance of drug and alcohol addiction involved twin and adoption studies. Identical (monozygotic) twins share 100% of their genes while fraternal (dizygotic) twins share only 50% of their genes. Comparing the concordance rate of addiction (or any other disease or behavior) in identical and fraternal twin pairs can give an estimate as to the relative contributions of genetic and the environmental factors. Comparing the incidence of addiction in monozygotic twin pairs raised together to those raised apart provides an even more powerful method to estimate the contributions of genetics and the environment. Adoption studies that compare adoptees to their adoptive and biological parents are also used to estimate the contributions of genetics and the environment to the variance of drug and alcohol addiction. These twin and adoption studies have determined that depending on the addictive drug studied between 40 and 70% of the variance of addiction is due to genetic factors.

Humans have about 20,500 genes, and the identification of those genes and the specific gene variants involved with addiction has not been easy since addiction and the development of drug dependence involves many genes (polygenic), and each gene involved probably has a very small effect. Completion of the Human Genome Project and the development of rapid DNA sequencing methods have facilitated the comparison of the genomes of addicted persons with those who are not addicted. These Genome Wide Association Studies as well as studies on lower primates and mice have indicated that the genetics of addiction is complex and polygenic, but some gene variants that may contribute to addiction have been identified. The identification of genes involved with addiction may lead to the development of treatments that target involved genes, enzymes and/or metabolic and signaling pathways.

Some of the genes which have been identified as being associated with drug addiction are the dopamine receptor gene (*DRD2*), the multiple PDZ domain crumbs cell polarity complex component (*Mpdz*), the cannabinoid receptor gene (*Cnr1*), the serotonin receptor gene (*Htr1b*), and the cyclic AMP responsive element binding protein gene (*CREB*). The molecular mechanisms and the specific roles these genes and their polypeptide products play in drug dependence are actively being investigated.

The dopamine receptor and its involvement with cocaine addiction is one example of the role genes play in drug dependence and addiction. Dopamine is a central nervous system neurotransmitter that is released by neurons (the presynaptic neurons), diffuses across the synapses, and binds to its receptors encoded by the *DRD2* gene on receiving neurons (the postsynaptic neurons) which are involved with motivation, emotion, thought, and movement. Once the dopamine has initiated a signal in receiving neurons, it is removed from its receptor and transported back in to presynaptic neurons by another molecule, the dopamine transporter. Cocaine binds to dopamine transporter molecules inhibiting their ability to remove and transport dopamine bound to the postsynaptic neuron. Dopamine accumulates causing the euphoria one experiences with cocaine use. The concentrations of two other neurotransmitters, norepinephrine and serotonin, are also affected by cocaine.

THE ROLE OF EPIGENETICS

Epigenetics refers to reversible and heritable molecular modifications in DNA that do not involve changes in DNA sequence and molecular modifications in histone proteins, those proteins that interact with DNA and form a DNA/protein complex known as chromatin. These epigenetic changes in DNA and histone modify gene expression. Although monozygotic twins have identical DNA sequences, their epigenetic chromatin modifications and the activity of several genes are not identical and diverge as they age. It is thought that epigenetic changes may be influenced by the environment where certain stimuli may interact directly or indirectly with chromatin and/or alter the enzymes that catalyze epigenetic changes resulting in a change in gene activity. The ingestion of drugs and/or alcohol could contribute to epigenetic modifications of chromatin and contribute to dependence and addiction. Evidence is accumulating that epigenetics may very well play a role in dependence and addiction. *In vitro* studies and studies with rodents indicate that cocaine, opioid and alcohol dependence involve epigenetic modifications to chromatin.

GENETICS, EPIGENETICS AND TREATMENT

The elucidation of drug and alcohol dependence physiology and the identification of genes and enzymes involved with dependence have led to the discovery of possible targets for treatment therapy. The enzyme histone deacetylase 5 (HDAC5) removes acetyl groups from certain amino acids in histones resulting in the remodeling of chromatin and changing the expression of specific genes. Studies in rodents has demonstrated that HDAC5 is found in high concentrations in the reward center of the brain which is influenced by serotonin and dopamine, neurotransmitters involved with drug and alcohol dependence. High concentrations of HDAC5 represses the activity of certain genes in the reward center and prevents the brain from forming a connection between cocaine

use and environmental cues. The loss of the cocaine use/environmental connection reduces the desire to ingest cocaine and removes the trigger for relapse. HDAC5 seems to be a potential target for cocaine (and possibly other drugs) dependence treatment.

Richard Adler, PhD; Updated by Charles L. Vigue, PhD

FOR FURTHER INFORMATION

"Cocaine Addiction Linked to Epigenetics." *Genetic Engineering and Biotechnology News*, September 28, 2017. Accessed June 27, 2018 https://www.genengnews.com/gen-news-highlights/cocaine-addiction-linked-to-epigenetics/81254983.

Family History and Genetics. *National Council on Alcoholism and Drug Dependence*. NCADD, 25 Apr. 2015. Web. 29 Oct. 2015.

Kendler, Kenneth, and Carol Prescott. *Genes, Environment, and Psychopathology: Understanding the Causes of Psychiatric and Substance Use Disorders*. New York: Guilford, 2007. Print.

National Institute of Drug Abuse. "How does cocaine produce its effects?" May 2016. Accessed June 28, 2018 https://www.drugabuse.gov/publications/research-reports/cocaine/how-does-cocaine-produce-its-effects.

Nielsen, David, A., Amol Utrankar, Jennifer A Reyes, Daniel D Simons, and Thomas R Kosten. "Epigenetics of drug abuse: predisposition or response." *Pharmacogenomics 13*: 1149–1160 (2012). Accessed June 27, 2018. https://www.ncbi.nlm.nih.gov/pmc/articles/PMC3463407/.

Palmer, Rohan H. C., Leslie Brick, Nicole R. Nugent, L. Cinnamon Bidwell, John E. McGeary, Valerie S. Knopik and Matthew C. Keller. "Examining the role of common genetic variants on alcohol, tobacco, cannabis and illicit drug dependence: genetics of vulnerability to drug dependence." *Addiction 110:* 530-537 (2014). Accessed June 26, 2018.

Taniguchi, Makoto *et al.*, "HDAC5 and Its Target Gene, *Npas4*, Function in the Nucleus Accumbens to Regulate Cocaine-Conditioned Behaviors." *Neuron* 96: 130-144 (2017). Accessed June 27, 2018 https://www.sciencedirect.com/science/article/pii/S0896627317308553.

Verhulst, B., M. C. Neale and K. S. Kendler. "The heritability of alcohol use disorders: a meta-analysis of twin and adoption studies." *Psychological Medicine* 45: 1061-1072 (2014). Accessed June 27, 2018 https://www.ncbi.nlm.nih.gov/pubmed/25171596.

See also: Adult children of alcoholics; Families and substance misuse; Science of addiction; Substance misuse; Suicide and addiction

GHB (Gamma-Hydroxybutyric acid)

CATEGORY: Substances

ALSO KNOWN AS: *Alcover*; Blue nitro; Cherry Meth; Easy Lay; Fantasy; Firewater; Fishies; G; Gamma-Oh; Georgia Home Boy; Gib; Gina; Great hormones at bedtime; Grievous Bodily Harm; G-Riffick; Goop; Heaven; 4-Hydroxybutanoic acid; Jib; Juice; K.-o.-Tropfen (German-speaking countries); Liquid E; Liquid Ecstasy; Liquid G; Liquid X; Mils; Organic Quaalude; Salty water; Scoop; Sleep; Sleep-500; Soap; Sodium oxybate; *Somsanit*; Vita-G; *Xyrem*.

DEFINITION: Gamma-Hydroxbutyric Acid (GHB) is a naturally occurring substance that resembles the neurotransmitter and energy metabolism regulator gamma-aminobutyric acid (GABA), and generally acts as a depressant of the central nervous system and intoxicant. Medically, GHB is used in general anesthesia, and to treat narcolepsy, insomnia, clinical depression, and alcoholism. GHB is used illicitly as an intoxicant, euphoriant, date-rape drug, aphrodisiac, and body-building supplement.

STATUS: Illegal in the United States, Australia, New Zealand, Canada, Chile, Hong Kong, and most of Europe.

CLASSIFICATION: Schedule 1 controlled substance, but *Xyrem*, the pharmacological preparation of GHB, is a Schedule 3 controlled substance.

SOURCE: GHB naturally occurs in the human central nervous system, and in animals, wine, beer, beef, and small citrus fruits. Drug suppliers can make GHB very easily and cheaply from sodium hydroxide, which is found in drain cleaner, and gamma-hydroxybutyrolactone, a readily available industrial solvent. GHB synthesis kits are available for purchase on the internet.

TRANSMISSION ROUTE: GHB appears either as a white powder or a colorless liquid. It is typically taken orally as a liquid. The dissolved powder can be injected, or solid GHB can be inserted rectally.

HISTORY OF USE

Russian chemist Alexander Mikhaylovich Zaytsev first reported the synthesis of GHB in 1874. The French physician Henri Laborit was one of the first to research the effects of GHB on human patients during the 1960s. Laborit and others evaluated the potential therapeutic uses of GHB in obstetrics, anesthesia, alcohol and opiate withdrawal, and treatment of narcolepsy and cataplexy. As an anesthetic, GHB showed poor analgesic effects and tended to cause seizures and delirium, but it was still registered in Germany for use as an intravenous anesthetic that was marketed under the sobriquet *Somsanit*. Likewise, despite poor evidence of efficacy, GHB was approved in Italy and Austria, under the trade name *Alcover*, to treat alcohol dependence and withdrawal. In July 2002, the United States Food and Drug Administration (USFDA) approved a form of GHB called *Xyrem* that is marketed worldwide for the treatment for narcolepsy and attacks of cataplexy. On the 17th of January 2017, the USFDA approved a generic form of GHB to treat cataplexy and excessive daytime sleepiness in patients with narcolepsy.

In the late 1980s and 90s, GHB was sold over-the-counter in the United States as a sleep aid, and as a body-building supplement that purportedly enhanced growth hormone secretion. In 1990, there were approximately 100 reported cases of GHB poisoning, which persuaded the USFDA to ban the sale of GHB, and the Centers of Disease Control and Prevention (CDC) to issue warnings regarding its potential dangers. However, GHB availability and incidents of GHB poisonings continued to increase.

In the late 1990s, GHB was used in several highly-publicized drug-facilitated cases of sexual assault. Because of this, people labeled GHB as a "date-rape drug." Because illicit formulations of GHB are commonly colorless, odorless liquids, surreptitious addition of GHB to drinks in bars and clubs is difficult to detect. Also, several GHB side effects (sedation, euphoria, decreased inhibitions, enhanced sex drive, and mild amnesia) enhance its effectiveness in drug-facilitated sexual assaults. In March 2000, the FDA placed *Xyrem* on Schedule III, and listed non-medical GHB as a Schedule I controlled substance.

Also during the 1990s, GHB became widely used as a "club drug." Club or party drugs are used by people who attend nightclubs, raves, and circuit parties. These drugs include cocaine ("Blow"),

GHB is also known as:		
Bedtime Scoop	G-Juice	Liquid Ecstasy
Cherry Meth	Gook	Liquid X
Easy Lay	Goop	PM
Energy Drink	Great Hormones	Salt Water
G	Grievous Bodily Harm (GBH)	Soap
Gamma 10		Somatomax
Georgia Home Boy	Liquid E	Vita-G

methamphetamine ("Speed"), 3,4-methylenedioxy-N-methylamphetamine or MDMA ("Ecstasy"), lysergic acid diethylamide ("Acid"), and ketamine ("Special K"). GHB, MDMA, and ketamine are frequently used together, also in combination with alcohol, marijuana, and other types of amphetamines. Surveys have shown that an estimated 3 of 1,000 young adults, aged 18-25, in the United States have ever knowingly taken GHB, but in the nightclub scene, the rate of GHB use increases to about 10%. GHB use surges among gay men and men who have sex with men (MSM) in party scenes. Studies have shown that more than half of MSM nightclub attenders in South London have reported GHB use in the past year. GHB is one of the leading "ChemSex" drugs (drugs used to intensify sex).

The popularity of GHB as a club drug resulted from the ease of its synthesis and low cost. At bars or "rave" parties, GHB is sold in liquid form for $5 to $25 per "swig," or capful. GHB was once popular in "under 21" dance clubs where alcohol is not sold, but teenagers sip water spiked with GHB. Club drugs related to GHB include gamma-butyrolactone (GBL) and 1,4-butanediol, both of which are liquids and found in paint strippers and varnish thinners. These chemicals are GHB "prodrugs" since they are converted to GHB by the body after ingestion. GBL is inexpensive and while it is not illegal to possess, its distribution is highly regulated. GBL has twice the potency of GHB per unit volume, and is usually mixed with other liquids to mask its strong solvent-like taste.

In September 2002, a 42-year-old mother of three named Dianne Brimble from Brisbane, Australia, died on board a *P & O* cruise ship after consuming GHB and alcohol. The Brimble death, combined with the surfeit of GHB overdoses, caused a gradual decline in the recreational use of GHB. However, around 2013, GHB use as a club drug and as a ChemSex drug among MSM began to increase, as did cases of GHB overdoses, GHB-caused deaths, and arrests for GHB possession. GHB use has also increased among fitness-conscious professionals who use the drug as a growth hormone and workout booster. On June 10, 2015, celebrity John Stamos was arrested in Beverly Hills, California for driving under the influence of GHB. Stamos admitted to using GHB as a fitness booster to lose weight for an upcoming television show.

EFFECTS AND POTENTIAL RISKS

In the brain, cells called neurons generate and propagate nerve impulses. GHB exerts its effects by binding to specific receptors on the surfaces of neurons. GHB weakly binds to the $GABA_B$ receptor and strongly binds to the GHB receptor. By binding and activating $GABA_B$ receptors in the "thalamo-cortical loop," which regulates sleep and arousal, GHB induces sedation. Conversely, when GHB binds and activates the GHB receptor, it increases the release of the neurotransmitter glutamate. Glutamate is the principal excitatory neurotransmitter in the brain. This explains GHB's contradictory combination of sedative and stimulatory properties.

At low concentrations, GHB induces the release of the neurotransmitter dopamine in the ventral tegmental area (VTA). The VTA is one of the key reward regions of the brain, and dopamine release in the VTA produces a feeling of pleasure or satisfaction, and is the reason for the addictive nature of GHB. At higher concentrations, GHB predominately activates the $GABA_B$ receptor, which inhibits dopamine release and induces sedation. However, once GHB concentrations fall below the threshold for $GABA_B$ receptor activation, GHB receptor activation predominates, which stimulates wakefulness and alertness. This causes people who have taken GHB to awaken abruptly after several hours.

The effects of GHB are dose related. At 10 milligrams per kilogram body weight (mg / kg), GHB depresses the central nervous system and causes a general sense of calm and relaxation. GHB doses of 20-30 mg / kg induce sleep for 2-3 hours. A dose of 40-50 mg / kg induces even longer periods of sleep, but also causes amnesia, nausea and vomiting, dizziness, weakness, loss of peripheral vision, confusion, hallucinations, agitation, and low heart rate (bradycardia). Doses above 50 mg / kg cause seizures, unconsciousness, respiratory depression, and coma. GHB effects appear within 15 minutes of oral ingestion, but the acute symptoms cease after 7 hours.

Combining GHB with alcohol increases depression of breathing and can cause death, as can combining GHB with other drugs, such as benzodiazepines, barbiturates, opiates, gabapentinoids, and thienodiazepines. GHB is rather addictive and long-term use can cause depression and suicidal tendencies. A 2016 study published in the journal *Neuropsychobiology* showed that taking GHB repeatedly, three to six times per day, can lead to tolerance or dependence. GHB withdrawal can also cause excruciating symptoms that include sweating, anxiety, tremors, insomnia, increased heart rate, and increased blood pressure. High-profile deaths as a result of GHB withdrawal include former Mr. America, Mike Scarcella, who died from GHB withdrawal in 2003, and Mike Fox, the close friend and personal trainer of professional baseball star Mike Piazza, who shot himself in the Fall of 2000 while trying to give up GHB.

From 1995-2005 in the UK, US, and Canada there were 226 GHB-related deaths. According to research published in the journal *Forensic Science International*, of the 61 GHB-related deaths in the UK from 2011 to 2015, all but one were men and most occurred in the inner London areas. However, the actual number of GHB-induced deaths are probably significantly higher, since GHB is rapidly eliminated from the body (half-life of 30-50 minutes) and difficult to detect after death.

Michael A. Buratovich Ph.D.

FOR FURTHER INFORMATION

Abadinsky, Howard. (2013). *Drug Use and Abuse: A Comprehensive Introduction.* 8th ed. Florence, KY: Wadsworth Publishing. A readable, interdisciplinary introduction to drug misuse by a criminal justice academic who spent many years as a parole officer and inspector for the Cook County Sheriff's Office.

Gahlinger, Paul. (2003). *Illegal Drugs: A Complete Guide to their History, Chemistry, Use and Abuse.* New York: Plume. An extremely informed compendium on the chemical, medical, and historical aspects of illegal drugs by a physician who is also a certified substance use disorder review officer.

Grim, Ryan. (2010). *This is Your Country on Drugs: The Secret History of Getting High in America.* Hoboken, NJ: Wiley. A journalist's foray into the seedy world of illegal drugs that examines drug supply lines, the culture of drug misuse and those with substance use disorders, the political and economic ramifications of American drug misuse, and the problems facing drug enforcement in the United States.

Kamal, Rama M., van Noorden, Martijn S., Franzek, Ernst, Dijkstra, Boukje A. G., Loonen, Anton J. M., & De Jong, Cornelius A. J. (2016). "The neurobiological mechanisms of gamma-hydroxybutyrate dependence and withdrawal and their clinical relevance: A review." *Neuropsychobiology, 73,* 65-80. A definitive review of our present understanding of the multiple mechanisms by which GHB causes addiction and withdrawals and the clinical significance of GHB activity in the brain.

Kuhn, Cynthia, Swartzwelder, Scott, & Wilson, Wilkie. (2014). *Buzzed: The Straight Facts about the Most Used and Abused Drugs from Alcohol to Ecstasy.* 4th ed. New York: W. W. Norton & Company. A popular, highly useful information guide to illegal drugs by three professors from Duke University Medical Center.

Palamar, Joseph. (2018, January 25). "The comeback and dangers of the drug GHB." *The Conversation.* Retrieved from https://theconversation.com/the-comeback-and-dangers-of-the-drug-ghb-90736. A public health researcher who investigates the use of party drugs provides a troubling picture of the deleterious consequences of GHB from inside the nightclub scene.

Strudwick, Patrick. (2017, January 13). "Deaths from the drug GHB more than double in one year." *BuzzFeed*. Retrieved from https://www.buzzfeed.com/patrickstrudwick/deaths-linked-to-chemsex-drug-ghb-have-risen-by-119-in-one-y?utm_term=.xoojZ5Y5r#.lvpAXRjRM. A well-regarded British reporter's investigation of the precipitous rise of GHB-caused death among MSM in the UK.

Townsend, Catherine. (2015, October 19). "The scary reason GHB is making a comeback." *The Daily Beast*. Retrieved from https://www.thedailybeast.com/the-scary-reason-ghb-is-making-a-comeback. An investigative reporter describes her own experience with GHB and several high-prolife arrests and deaths because of GHB use.

See also: Anesthesia misuse; Club drugs; Date rape drugs; Depressants misuse

Government warnings for addictive substances

CATEGORY: Diagnosis and prevention

ALSO KNOWN AS: Health warning labels; US surgeon general warnings; warning labels

DEFINITION: Health warning labels issued by the US government are evidence-based statements of risk associated with the general use of legal substances such as alcohol and tobacco and with the misuse of prescription drugs or other substances of misuse. Warnings are required on products themselves and on related advertisements as a part of public health campaigns. Government warnings are frequently issued through the Office of the Surgeon General as part of the US Department of Health and Human Services.

PURPOSE AND FUNCTIONS

The primary function of a government warning is to increase public knowledge about unsafe use of substances, particularly tobacco and alcohol products that can be purchased without a prescription by adults who have proper identification. These health warnings attempt to minimize dangerous substance activity by discouraging drug misuse and overuse. Warning label goals include the complete cessation of tobacco use and total abstinence from alcohol during any stage of pregnancy.

The first alcohol and tobacco warning labels developed as a result of acts by the US Congress. The Alcoholic Beverage Labeling Act of 1988 was passed in response to birth defects connected with alcohol use during pregnancy. Similarly, tobacco use has been tracked by the Office of the Surgeon General (OSG) since the 1920s. In the 1960s, tobacco use became a public health issue that resulted in government warnings because of early reports about the health damage to nonsmokers from exposure to secondhand smoke.

Government warning labels on alcohol and tobacco are intended to call separate attention to multiple risks. Label text may be decided by the OSG but enforcement is often implemented by affiliate agencies, such as the Alcohol and Tobacco Tax and Trade Bureau (TTB). One goal of the TTB is to protect public safety through oversight of federal laws about alcohol and tobacco product-labeling.

LABEL FORMATS

Product health warnings require text introductions of "Warning" or "Government Warning" in bold type on every package. To ensure visibility, all statements must be placed prominently on high-contrast sections of the package label, separate from other information.

Warning texts expand as evidence builds on the dangers of alcohol and tobacco use. Since 1989, the US government has mandated two warnings on alcoholic products. These warnings are "According to the Surgeon General, women should not drink alcoholic beverages during pregnancy because of the risk of birth defects" and "Consumption of alcoholic beverages impairs your ability to drive a car or operate machinery, and may cause health problems."

In 2001, horizontal boxed text and conspicuous statements with surrounding white space were encouraged on beverage labels to increase attention to the warnings. In 2005, the OSG supplemented alcohol label warnings with an online news advisory to recommend total avoidance of any amount of alcohol during all stages of pregnancy, as evidenced by expanded research on fetal alcohol syndrome disorders.

Like alcohol warnings, tobacco warnings were initiated in Congress and adapted in time. Government warnings about tobacco changed little since the 1960s, until the statements were strengthened by the

US Food and Drug Administration in response to the Family Smoking Prevention and Tobacco Control Act of 2009. The new warnings, effective September 2012, comprise nine separate statements, a resource site (1-800-QUIT-NOW), and images of harmful tobacco effects on the body. Each warning contains one statement, one image, and the toll-free quit hotline.

The plain-language warnings, identified through literature review and public commentary, are as follows: cigarettes are addictive, tobacco smoke can harm your children, cigarettes cause fatal lung disease, cigarettes cause cancer, cigarettes cause strokes and heart disease, smoking during pregnancy can harm your baby, smoking can kill you, tobacco smoke causes fatal lung disease in nonsmokers, and quitting smoking now greatly reduces serious risks to your health. These changes, especially the new graphics, are negative reminders to heighten risk awareness, increase quit rates, and empower youth to avoid smoking.

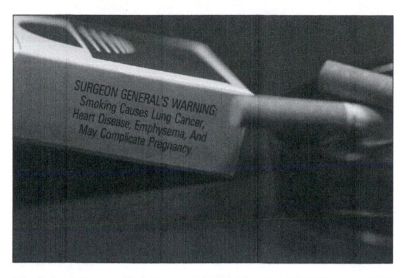

The Federal Cigarette Labeling and Advertising Act of 1965 required this Surgeon General's message on all cigarette packs. (CDC via Wikimedia Commons)

LABEL EFFICACY

Government warnings are updated infrequently, and public awareness of the standard labeling may introduce complacency. Government warnings on alcohol and tobacco are acknowledged by consumers, but effects on behavior are variable. For example, in the Alcoholic Beverage Label Evaluation survey from 1989 to 1995 (which surveyed persons in the Midwest), alcohol risks were noted by participants, but no significant changes in alcohol use resulted. Positive changes, such as lower rates of alcohol use while driving, appeared to level off after approximately three years. Thus, although awareness appears commonplace, the warnings do not appear to affect any long-term behavioral change.

Strategies for calling greater attention to the health risks include point-of-purchase notices, graphic images to supplement text labels, and even more prominent placement of warnings on the products. For example, cigarette products now require warning label placement on the top half of the front and back of each package or advertisement to pointedly display potential consequences of use. The use of graphics to transmit any health information is known to increase knowledge of risks, increase quit rates, and prevent new smokers.

Even greater distribution of warnings is available through state-regulated point-of-purchase programs, which require establishments that sell alcohol and tobacco to display warning signs at checkouts. For example, businesses that sell liquor must post the government warning about pregnancy and birth defect risks, and tobacco warning signs must be present where the tobacco products are sold.

Nicole M. Van Hoey PharmD

FOR FURTHER INFORMATION

Alemanno, Alberto, and Amandine Garde, eds. *Regulating Lifestyle Risks: The EU, Alcohol, Tobacco and Unhealthy Diets.* New York: Cambridge UP, 2015. Print.

Centers for Disease Control and Prevention. *How Tobacco Smoke Causes Disease: The Biology and Behavioral Basis for Smoking-Attributable Disease.* Rep. Washington, DC: DHHS, 2010. Print.

Hammond, David, et al. "Text and Graphic Warnings on Cigarette Packages: Findings from the International Tobacco Control Four Country Survey." *American Journal of Preventive Medicine* 32.3 (2007): 202–9. Print.

MacKinnon, David P., and Liva Nohre. "Alcohol and Tobacco Warnings." *Handbook of Warnings.* Ed. M. Wogalter. Mahwah: Erlbaum, 2006. Print.

Thomas, Gerald, Ginny Gonneau, Nancy Poole, and Jocelynn Cook. "The Effectiveness of Alcohol Warning Labels in the Prevention of Fetal Alcohol Spectrum Disorder: A Brief Review." *International Journal of Alcohol and Drug Research* 3.1 (2014): 91–103. Print.

Voon, Tania, Andrew D. Mitchell, and Jonathan Liberman, eds. *Regulating Tobacco, Alcohol, and Unhealthy Foods: The Legal Issues.* New York: Routledge, 2014. Print.

See also: Education about substance misuse; Legislation and substance misuse; Prevention methods and research; War on Drugs

---

Group therapy for behavioral addictions

CATEGORY: Treatment

DEFINITION: As the medical community debates whether behavioral addictions are true addictions, research has proven that support groups (group therapy) that are similar to those for substance misusers can help people to overcome the compulsion for certain unhealthy behaviors. Many of these groups are twelve-step programs. Other behavioral addiction groups focus on cognitive-behavioral therapies, which stress that thoughts precede actions.

OVERCOMING BEHAVIORAL ADDICTIONS

All support groups help a person addicted to a harmful behavior to become aware of the problem, find solace in the company of other people with similar issues, and develop new ways of coping with stress. Behavioral addictions are destructive patterns of behavior that mimic substance misuse. They begin when a person experiences pleasure in association with a behavior and then later engages in that behavior to reduce stress.

Eventually, through frequent and ritualized indulgence, the behavior becomes part of the person's daily routine. A person addicted to behaviors such as gambling, eating, sex, video games, exercise, shopping, or work or affection from another person (codependency) has a strong urge to engage in the behavior to experience relief and euphoria, despite persistent negative consequences.

Whether caused by substances or undesirable behaviors, all addictions have three things in common: physical and mental cravings, a habit, and denial of both craving and habit. Denial is a key factor with behavioral addictions, and it must be overcome if the person is to recover. Group therapy is successful in such cases because sitting in a room and listening to others describe situations and feelings that one has experienced in painful isolation tends to turn denial into identification. People who have recovered from the same affliction can also offer compassion, which is needed to offset feelings of self-loathing in the addict.

Evidence suggests that behavioral addictions involve the same brain mechanisms as substance addictions, although more research is needed to clarify and confirm this. For now, it is clear that behavioral addictions present problems with relationships similar to substance misuse by undermining trust and by putting pressure on family members to compensate for difficulties caused by the addiction.

Unlike treatment for most types of substance misuse, behavioral addiction treatment does not require a detoxification period. A person with a behavioral addiction can stop doing it suddenly without experiencing physical withdrawal symptoms. Psychological withdrawal symptoms are common, however, and include feeling restless or anxious and having a strong desire to engage in the harmful behavior.

PATHOLOGICAL GAMBLING AND GAMBLERS ANONYMOUS

Pathological gambling (PG) is the only behavioral addiction included in the *Diagnostic and Statistical Manual of Mental Disorders* (DSM). PG is classified as an impulse control disorder, in which the "essential feature is the failure to resist an impulse, drive or temptation to perform an act that is harmful to the person or to others." It has been proposed that PG be renamed gambling disorder and moved to a new category, addiction and related disorders.

PG is a serious problem not only for the addict but also for the addict's family and for society at large. The disorder produces financial insecurity, family dysfunction, domestic abuse, legal problems, employment difficulties, psychological distress, and higher rates of suicide. The problem is likely to become more prevalent, as state governments derive significant revenue from and thus promote gambling-related activities, such as lotteries. Also, Internet gambling increases access and anonymity.

Gamblers Anonymous (GA) was founded in Los Angeles in 1957 by two men who focused on fostering a character change within themselves in order to stop gambling. This fellowship of men and women has since grown to thousands of groups in the United States, Australia, Brazil, Israel, Japan, Kenya, Korea, the United Kingdom, and Spain. GA's website offers a questionnaire to help people determine if they need the program.

Family members of compulsive gamblers can attend Gam-Anon, another twelve-step program, founded in 1958. Through Gam-Anon, members come to understand their problem and learn how to give emotional support to the troubled person without enabling him or her in the illness. Children can attend Gam-A-Teen, part of the Gam-Anon program.

OVEREATERS, CODEPENDENTS, AND SEX ADDICTS

The idea for Overeaters Anonymous (OA) came to a woman who attended a GA meeting in 1958 and "heard her story," though she related the speaker's turmoil to her eating compulsion instead of a gambling problem. Not until 1960, though, did she find another person willing to recover from the addiction. As of 2015, OA offers recovery from compulsive eating through a worldwide fellowship of sixty-five hundred groups in seventy-five countries.

The organization's website includes a fifteen-item questionnaire to help people determine if they have an eating problem. Compulsive eating is a threefold illness, affecting physical condition, mental state, and the spirit. In the mental dimension, a compulsive eater is not "eating down" feelings but is expressing an inner hunger that leads to a loss of spiritual values.

Co-Dependents Anonymous, which celebrated its twenty-fifth anniversary in 2011, is a fellowship of men and women whose common purpose is to develop healthy relationships. Rather than a questionnaire, its website offers a list of patterns and characteristics of codependence, in five categories.

Under the category of denial, for example, co-dependent behaviors include minimizing one's feelings or expressing negativity in passive-aggressive ways. Low-self-esteem behavior patterns include difficulty making decisions and constantly seeking recognition. Compliance patterns emerge in compromising one's integrity to avoid rejection or anger and being hypervigilant of other people's feelings. Control patterns include freely offering advice and direction to others without being asked and needing to be needed. Avoidance patterns show up in pulling people close and then pushing them away.

Sex and Love Addicts Anonymous, or SLAA, offers help to anyone who has a sex addiction, love addiction, or both, and who wants to recover from that addiction. The fellowship was founded in 1976 by an Alcoholics Anonymous member who was serially unfaithful to his wife. SLAA recognizes that an obsessive-compulsive pattern exists when relationships or sexual activities become destructive to one's career, family, and self-esteem. Advances in computer technology have made it easier for people to access sex-related websites with great anonymity, leading to a problem called Internet-enabled sexual behavior, which affects family relationships, work productivity, and academic success.

INTERNET ADDICTION

Internet addiction is a behavioral problem affecting a growing number of people who use the web, according to the American Psychiatric Association. People who lose track of time while using the Internet become more socially isolated, depressed, and challenged by family discord, divorce, academic failure, financial failure, and job loss.

In the United States, one-on-one cognitive-behavioral therapy (CBT) has been shown to reduce the amount of time a person spends online. A study in Shanghai found that group therapy using CBT techniques, which emphasize that thoughts precede actions, was successful in treating teenagers addicted to the Internet.

Laura B. Smith

FOR FURTHER INFORMATION

Hecht Orzack, Maressa, et al. "An Ongoing Study of Group Treatment for Men Involved in Problematic Internet-Enabled Sexual Behavior." *Cyberpsychology and Behavior* 9.3 (2006). Print.

Jiménez-Murcia, Susana, et al. "Cognitive-Behavioral Group Treatment for Pathological Gambling: Analysis of Effectiveness and Predictors of Therapy Outcome." *Psychotherapy Research* 17.5 (2007). Print.

Ladouceur, R., et al. "Group Therapy for Pathological Gamblers: A Cognitive Approach." *Behavior Research and Therapy* 41.5 (2003): 587–96. Print.

See also: Behavioral addictions: Treatment; Gamblers Anonymous; Group therapy for substance misuse; Overeaters Anonymous; Support groups; Treatment methods and research

Group therapy for substance misuse

CATEGORY: Treatment

DEFINITION: Group therapy, a critical component of the substance-misuse recovery process, is promoted by the US Substance Abuse and Mental Health Services Administration as a cost-effective treatment for substance misuse. Although group therapy is important to a comprehensive treatment plan, it does not replace core mental health and physician services that focus on substance misuse treatment.

RATIONALE

By the time a person reaches the point of seeking treatment for substance misuse, he or she most likely has become alienated from friends and family because of poor behavior resulting from long-term substance misuse. Therefore, as the recovering user steps into a community of persons facing similar concerns, the most important benefit of group therapy is a reduction in the feeling of social isolation.

This sense of community experienced in group therapy rewards participants with peer support and the feeling that they are not alone in the recovery process. Participants benefit by learning how others in recovery are coping with the process, gaining feedback, encouragement, and insight. Group therapy participants also develop or relearn social skills, namely, how to interact with others while sober.

On a practical level, group therapy is cost-effective, as a single psychotherapy professional helps several persons at a time, keeping costs down. By participating in a low-cost group therapy program, substance misusers in recovery may gain a substantial return in treatment for their financial investment.

MODELS

The Substance Abuse and Mental Health Services Administration (SAMHSA), part of the US Department of Health and Human Services, endorses five group-therapy models as effective approaches to substance misuse treatment. These models involve psychoeducational groups, skills development groups, cognitive-behavioral/problem-solving groups, support groups, and interpersonal process groups. The appropriate model for a substance misuser depends on his or her life experience and psychological background.

Psychoeducational groups inform participants about substance misuse and provide them with information about the behaviors, risks, and effects of substance misuse. Psychoeducational groups raise awareness of the science behind the problems of substance misuse, enabling participants to understand why they need medical and psychological help. These groups also help participants understand their own behaviors, the stages of the recovery process, and what resources are available to help them cope during recovery.

Skills development groups help participants develop special skills for recovery. Chiefly, these groups help the user learn how to abstain from drug or alcohol use. According to SAMHSA, these development groups should teach social skills and skills that address substance refusal, communications, anger management, parenting, and money management.

Cognitive-behavioral groups are especially important during early recovery, as they help participants identify the psychological factors leading to substance misuse. Participants are guided in exploring their thoughts, beliefs, and feelings as they relate to their substance misuse behavior. Negative thoughts and beliefs, such as feelings of failure and inadequacy, are uncovered and addressed. The goal is for participants to resolve destructive, errant beliefs about their potential and worth so that they can move forward in the recovery process.

Support groups are valuable for treating substance misuse in that they offer a nonjudgmental forum where participants may openly discuss their experiences and struggles with substance misuse. Ground rules for discussion are important for facilitating an environment where recovering substance misusers may freely express feelings and events related to recovery. The psychotherapist leading the support group models active listening, positive feedback, and appropriate, nonjudgmental discussion. Types of group therapy include relapse prevention groups, communal and culturally specific groups, and expressive groups.

Interpersonal process groups apply psychological process-oriented methods to promote substance misuse recovery. Interpersonal groups focus on individual members, interpersonal interaction among members, and the group dynamic as a whole.

STRUCTURE

Because the appropriate placement of a person into a particular model of group therapy is important, a care provider first evaluates the substance misuser's background, needs, and stage of recovery. Depending on the substance misuser's circumstances and preferences, the care provider matches him or her with a group type and group leader equipped to treat any adjunct issues the person has, such as psychological disorders or traumatic experiences. The caregiver also considers the substance misuser's gender, age, race, ability to cope, stage of recovery, and interpersonal skills.

At the first meeting, the group therapy leader establishes participant expectations and ground rules through a presentation of a "group agreement." Issues addressed in the agreement usually include confidentiality, physical contact, use of substances, contact outside the group, financial obligations, and actions that would lead to expulsion from the group. Though the leader will require that participants accept the agreement, it is unlikely that he or she will discipline or dismiss members for violating the agreement. Rather, if a participant defies the rules of the agreement, the leader will use the situation as a discussion point and a part of the group-therapy process.

There are three phases of group therapy: beginning, middle, and end. The beginning phase includes explanation of the group agreement and ground rules, and an explanation of the rationale and goals for the therapy. The middle phase centers on two things: the leader providing group members with information, including facts about substance misuse or feelings expressed by participants in the group, and on moving participants forward in the process of recovery. The middle phase is the time for participants to connect their experiences and struggles to knowledge about substance misuse and the

recovery process. During the end phase, the group leader provides closure by acknowledging what was shared and learned by participants. The leader then summarizes the process and suggests how participants can continue to move forward in the process outside the group therapy environment.

ALTERNATIVE APPROACHES

In 2010, one care provider introduced an online group-therapy community. The interactive twelve-step substance misuse group therapy program, accredited by the Commission on Accreditation of Rehabilitation Facilities, is designed to help misusers who are seeking initial help for the recovery process.

In 2009, the journal *Anthrozoos* published the results of a study of applying animal-assisted therapy (AAT) to group therapy for substance misuse. Researchers concluded that, among clients who had no fear of or abusive tendencies toward dogs, the therapeutic process was significantly improved by adding a therapy dog to sessions. Connection to the recovery process through therapy is critical for clients in overcoming addiction and substance misuse. Toward that end, therapy dogs assist in attaching clients emotionally to the recovery process by reducing their anxiety so that they may disclose feelings and thoughts about their experience of substance misuse.

A group of men meet to discuss their issues with substance dependence. (Rehab Center Parus via Wikimedia Commons)

Researchers, however, urged counselors and psychotherapists to apply AAT not as an isolated or replacement method for group therapy. Rather, AAT should be used as a complementary technique within the group therapy setting and process. A therapy dog becomes valuable as a healing presence in group therapy as he or she performs therapeutic "tricks" during sessions, such as bringing a tissue to a client who is crying and moving to the client who is speaking so that he or she may touch the dog while sharing feelings. "The dog was available when called, was nonjudgmental, and predictable in her responses," the researchers wrote in their study. The dogs provided for an enhanced substance-misuse recovery process, they concluded.

Melissa Walsh

FOR FURTHER INFORMATION

Brook, David W., and Henry I. Spitz. *The Group Therapy of Substance Abuse.* New York: Haworth Medical, 2002. Print.

Cleland, Charles, et al. "Moderators of Effects of Motivational Enhancements to Cognitive Behavioral Therapy." *American Journal of Drug and Alcohol Abuse* 31.1 (2005): 35. Print.

Minatrea, Neresa B., Joshua C. Watson, and Martin C. Wesley. "Animal-Assisted Therapy in the Treatment of Substance Dependence." *Anthrozoos* 22.2 (2009): 137. Print.

"SAMHSA Guide Supports Benefits of Group Therapy." *Addiction Professional* 3.3 (2005): 60. Print.

Substance Abuse and Mental Health Services Administration. "Substance Abuse Treatment: Group Therapy, Quick Guide for Clinicians Based on TIP 41." Washington, DC: Dept. of Health and Human Services, 2005. Print.

See also: Alcoholics Anonymous: The Twelve Steps; Cocaine Anonymous; Group therapy for behavioral addictions; Narcotics Anonymous; Support groups; Treatment methods and research

H

Halfway houses

CATEGORY: Treatment

ALSO KNOWN AS: Sober houses; sober-living houses; transitional housing

DEFINITION: Halfway houses are drug- and alcohol-free transitional living environments for people in recovery from drug or alcohol misuse. These houses provide a safe place for addicts and alcoholics to transition back into mainstream society.

BACKGROUND

Recognizing the need for a safe environment for alcoholics in recovery, Alcoholics Anonymous (AA) established the first halfway houses in the 1940s in the United States. These group living facilities were called twelve-step houses and provided safety and support for alcoholics who were not ready or able to return to their lives before addiction.

In 1975, Oxford House, established by and for persons in recovery, was established in Silver Spring, Maryland. Sixteen Oxford houses were established between 1975 and 1988. The Oxford House manual for running a group home was first published in 1978.

Several factors led to an expansion in the halfway house movement in the 1990s. One factor was the loss of residential treatment centers because of decreases in government and private insurance funding for these centers. A second factor was the 1988 amendments to the federal Fair Housing Law. These amendments allowed recovering addicts and alcoholics to be considered persons with disabilities, giving those in recovery the right to live together as a "family" of unrelated persons. As part of the 1988 Anti-Drug Abuse Act, all states were required to maintain funds for establishing sober houses based on the Oxford model, and halfway houses are now found throughout the United States.

Halfway houses are not licensed or accredited by the federal government, however, and they are restricted from offering drug and alcohol treatment. Instead, they are permitted to offer a drug- and alcohol-free environment. Also, halfway houses are limited to groups of unrelated adults, disabled through addiction and working toward recovery. To receive government aid, halfway houses can accept only those persons who have completed or who are involved in some type of formal treatment program.

MISSION AND GOALS

Although halfway houses are not licensed to treat alcohol or drug misuse, they do provide support for the recovering addict or alcoholic. Other goals include providing an environment that is safe, structured, and affordable. Most addicts and alcoholics come to a halfway house directly from detoxification and treatment programs. Some continue aftercare and outpatient care at a treatment center while living in the halfway house.

Government-funded halfway houses offer affordable rates, and payment is usually on a month-to-month basis. Although the average stay in a halfway house is three to six months, each house may have different arrangements. Most houses are run by a house manager, who is not required to have a special credential for the position. House manager selection varies greatly, as does the establishment of house rules and regulations.

A person seeking residence at a halfway house often gets a referral from a treatment facility. Houses may cater to men, women, women with children, and to special populations. House rules for residences generally include remaining drug and alcohol free, completing or attending a drug or alcohol treatment program, continuing to make payments for care, and avoiding negative or disruptive behavior. Other house rules may cover check-in times, visitors, attendance at house meetings and twelve-step meetings, and completion of assigned chores and other responsibilities.

Sober living houses are similar to halfway houses but may have less stringent rules. A resident may be admitted without having completed or without involvement in formal treatment. These houses are less likely to be government funded, may be more expensive, and may allow residents to remain indefinitely. Sober living houses provide an alcohol and drug free environment and usually encourage attendance at self-help programs, such as AA.

Numerous studies have documented that the lack of a stable, alcohol- and drug-free environment is a significant barrier to any sustained recovery from addiction. Involvement in twelve-step groups and strong social support remain strong predictors of successful recovery. A variety of studies have shown that halfway houses improve treatment outcomes for both drug and alcohol addiction.

Christopher Iliades MD

FOR FURTHER INFORMATION

Hoffman, John. *Addiction: Why Can't They Just Stop?* New York: Rodale, 2007. Print.

Jason, L. A., et al. "An Examination of Main and Interactive Effects of Substance Abuse Recovery Housing on Multiple Indicators of Adjustment." *Addiction* 102.7 (2007): 1114–21. Print.

Polcin, D., et al. "A Model for Sober Housing During Outpatient Treatment." *Journal of Psychoactive Drugs* 41.2 (2009): 153–61. Print.

Polcin, D., et al. "What Did We Learn from Our Study on Sober Living Houses and Where Do We Go from Here?" *Journal of Psychoactive Drugs* 42.4 (2010): 425–33. Print.

See also: Alcoholics Anonymous: The Twelve Steps; Residential treatment; Sober living environments; Treatment methods and research

Hallucinogen misuse

CATEGORY: Substance misuse

ALSO KNOWN AS: Illusionogenic misuse; psychedelic drug misuse

DEFINITION: Hallucinogen misuse is the repeated use of hallucinogens, which are drugs that distort a person's perception of reality, after they have caused impairment that undermines the user's ability to fulfill obligations at home, school, and work.

CAUSES

The mechanism by which hallucinogens exert their effects is not fully understood. However, it is recognized that hallucinogens bind with 5-HT serotonin receptors in the brain. Serotonin facilitates transmission of nerve impulses. When a hallucinogen binds with serotonin receptors, it blocks serotonin from these receptor sites, thus altering nerve transmission. Unbound serotonin increases in the brain, contributing to the distortions in vision, hearing, and the perception of time and space, as well as in the alterations in mood and thought processes that occur under the influence of hallucinogens. Misusers regard this as a consciousness-raising experience that can lead to increased creativity and self-awareness.

RISK FACTORS

Hallucinogens are easily and cheaply obtained, making them attractive to adolescents who want to experiment with mind-altering drugs. Older adolescents and young adults use them in the party scene to heighten their experiences. The National Institute on Drug Abuse reports that about 6 percent of high school seniors have tried lysergic acid diethylamide (LSD, or acid) or other hallucinogens at least once. Persons who misuse hallucinogens are also likely to abuse alcohol and marijuana.

SYMPTOMS

Physical symptoms of hallucinogen misuse include increased blood pressure and heart rate; nausea, vomiting, and diarrhea (especially with psilocybin and mescaline); dilated pupils; blurred vision; paraesthesia (burning, tingling, or itching skin); and sweating. With ecstasy (3,4-methylenedioxymethamphetamine, or MDMA), symptoms include muscle cramping, dehydration, and severe elevations in body temperature.

Psychological symptoms of hallucinogen misuse include distortion of sight, sound, and touch; synesthesia, which is confusion of the senses, such as "seeing" sounds; depersonalization, or "out-of-person" experiences; delusions of physical invulnerability (especially with LSD); elation or euphoria; blissful calm or mellowness; reduced inhibitions; poor judgment and increased risk taking; impaired concentration and motivation; anxiety attacks; and paranoia.

Misusers can experience recurring flashbacks of their drug-induced psychological symptoms long after the immediate experience. These flashbacks are referred to as persisting psychosis and perception disorder and posthallucinogenic perceptual disorder. Flashbacks occur in 30 to 50 percent of frequent misusers and far less often in occasional misusers. Use of alcohol or marijuana, or extreme fatigue, can trigger flashbacks. Chronic misuse can affect long-term memory and cause personality changes. Frequent misuse can trigger latent psychiatric disorders, such as depression, anxiety, and psychosis. Frequent misusers can develop psychological dependence on hallucinogens.

SCREENING AND DIAGNOSIS

Most persons who are treated for hallucinogenic misuse are experiencing an acute "bad trip." Key to diagnosis is that their distress will be evident. Routine blood or urine sampling does not detect the use of hallucinogens. Hallucinogen misusers do not develop a tolerance to the drug that would require more frequent and higher dosing. Frequent or high-dose use indicates a psychological rather than a physiological need. Detectable withdrawal symptoms do not occur when a misuser stops using hallucinogens.

TREATMENT AND THERAPY

A bad trip can be a frightening and anxiety-provoking experience, as can flashbacks. The immediate goal of treatment in these situations is to prevent the person from harming the self or others. The user needs to be assured that the experience will pass as the drug wears off.

The effects of LSD, the longest-acting hallucinogen, can last up to twelve hours. The user should be kept in a quiet, comfortable, and lighted environment and allowed to move around under supervision. An anti-anxiety drug such as lorazepam or another benzodiazepine may be helpful. A user of ecstasy may develop a dangerously high body temperature, which needs to be brought under control.

Persons who have recurrent flashbacks or who were long-term frequent misusers of hallucinogens may require long-term psychotherapy after stopping the misuse. Any underlying psychiatric disorders will have to be addressed. Many people find group support or a twelve-step program to be helpful in the recovery process. Hallucinogen intoxication delirium is a rare syndrome that can occur when a hallucinogen is contaminated with another drug or chemical, such as strychnine.

PREVENTION

Education regarding hallucinogen misuse should begin with children or early adolescents, before they experiment with the drugs. Educators should stress that the effects of hallucinogens cannot be predicted or controlled. Any user, even a first-time user, is at risk of a bad, even life-threatening, trip and of recurrent, disturbing flashbacks.

As all hallucinogen products are prepared in illegal, unregulated laboratories, there is no guarantee of their potency or purity, furthering the user's risk of serious consequences. Parents should be alert to the availability and use of hallucinogens in their communities and should keep children from these sources.

Ernest Kohlmetz MA

FOR FURTHER INFORMATION

Abadinsky, Howard. *Drug Use and Abuse: A Comprehensive Introduction.* 7th ed. Belmont, CA: Wadsworth, 2011. Print.

Julien, Robert M. *A Primer of Drug Actions.* 11th ed. New York: Worth, 2008. Print.

Kuhn, Cynthia, Scott Swartwelder, and Wilkie Wilson. *Buzzed: The Straight Facts about the Most Used and Abused Drugs from Alcohol to Ecstasy.* 3rd ed. New York: W. W. Norton, 2008. Print.

Laing, Richard R., ed. *Hallucinogens: A Forensic Drug Handbook.* San Francisco: Elsevier, 2003. Print.

Lowinson, Joyce W., et al., eds. *Substance Abuse: A Comprehensive Textbook.* 4th ed. Philadelphia: Lippincott, 2005. Print.

National Institute on Drug Abuse. "NIDA InfoFacts: Hallucinogens: LSD, Peyote, Psilocybin, and PCP." 2009. Web. 10 Mar. 2012. http://www.nida.nih.gov/infofacts/hallucinogens.html.

See also: Flashbacks; Hallucinogen's effects on the body; LSD; MDMA; Mescaline; Mushrooms/psilocybin; PCP; Psychosis and substance misuse

Hallucinogen's effects on the body

CATEGORY: Health issues and physiology

ALSO KNOWN AS: Dissociatives; psychoactives; psychomimetics

DEFINITION: Hallucinogens, hallucinogens are members of a variable drug class stemming from plant and synthetic sources that induce experiences of fantasy as altered reality and distortions of self and senses.

HALLUCINOGEN SOURCES

Plant sources. LSD, or lysergic acid diethylamide, lysergic acid diethylamide, the prototypical and most potent natural hallucinogen, is extracted from fungal rye. Related hallucinogens are mescaline, mescaline from peyote cacti, psilocybin, psilocybin and psilocin, psilocin from mushrooms, and ibogaine, ibogaine from the shrub Tabernanthe. All plant hallucinogens have serotonin-like chemical structures.

Synthetic sources. Of the synthesized hallucinogens, PCP (phencyclidine, phencyclidine) and ketamine, ketamine are key examples. PCP was developed in the 1950s and used through 1965 as an anesthetic, and ketamine was designed as a less potent veterinary anesthetic. Both of these drugs and dextromethorphan induce glutamate-related hallucinations.

Newer designer drugs, including the tryptamines, tryptamine, methylenedioxymethamphetamine (MDMA, or ecstasy, ecstasy), the herbal *Salvia divinorum*, Salvia divinorum, and numerous amphetamine-like drugs, are not specifically members of the hallucinogen drug class. However, they can exert hallucinogenic effects through non-serotonin or non-glutamate pathways.

IMMEDIATE EFFECTS

Hallucinogens distort perceptions of self, emotion, sensations, and moods; they also impair judgment and cause dissociation. Depersonalization, or a disconnection from the physical body and surroundings, and dissociation, or a separation of the mind from the physical self and environment, can lead users to lose control of their body and actions. Each drug experience, or trip, causes unpredictable hallucinations according to the user's environment, the user's emotional state of mind, and the timing, type, and amount of drug used.

LSD, mescaline, psilocybin, and ibogaine affect serotonin (5HT) actions at the 5HT-2 receptors in the cerebral cortex and locus cerebellum to impair control of mood, senses, hunger, and body temperature. The onset of effect is thirty to ninety minutes; LSD and mescaline trips can last up to twelve hours, but psilocybin trips are often only four to six hours. Serotonin blockade results in rapid psychologic fluctuations of fear to euphoria; bizarre but peaceful delusions of enhanced abilities are as likely as time alterations and loss of control that cause panic and terror. Sensory experiences of plant hallucinogens become uniquely confused and overlap. This crossover, called synesthesia, is common and causes an intense and unusual ability to see sounds, to hear or feel colors, and to taste sights.

Unlike these sensory delusions, PCP and ketamine induce primarily dissociative effects by N-methyl-D-aspartic acid antagonism at glutamate brain receptors to cause bizarre distortions of reality. Glutamate blockade results in feelings of power, impaired memory, numbness to pain, detachment from the body and bodily responses, and altered senses. As with plant hallucinogens, out-of-body sensations may be pleasantly empowering or terrifying. Ketamine and PCP both cause an immediate dopamine-related rush of euphoria, followed by anxiety and emotional lability after the dopamine peak. Although PCP is more potent and longer-lasting than ketamine, both drugs are delivered straight to the brain when smoked or snorted, so they take effect within minutes.

PCP-like hallucinogens are known for their quicker onset, shorter duration, and reduced potency compared with plant hallucinogens. For example, dimethyltryptamine, dimethyltryptamine (DMT), a designer drug with hallucinatory properties, takes action within two to five minutes, but the effects last only twenty to sixty minutes. Of the PCP-like hallucinogens, dextromethorphan, dextromethorphan (DXM) alone has specific dose-effect plateaus. Two ounces of 3 milligrams (mg) per milliliter of DXM cough medicine causes mild sensory changes, and complete dissociation occurs at 10 ounces or greater. DXM effects can last for six hours after use and are particularly dangerous because of overdose risk with combination products.

Hallucinogens cause physiologic changes in part through sympathetic nervous system activation. Immediate effects include increased heart rate and blood pressure, sweating and flushing, increased body temperature, nausea and dizziness, pupil dilation, and loss of appetite. Motor changes include tremor, muscle weakness, and ataxia. Mushroom poisoning from psilocybin use can begin within twenty minutes and last for six hours, causing nausea, vomiting, and excessive sleepiness. Increased respiratory rate and shallowness of breathing are particular to PCP and ketamine, and PCP doses greater than 5 mg can induce a dangerous reduction of blood pressure, heart rate, and respiratory rate.

Risk of death from overdose is twofold, through suicidal psychologic impairment of judgment and body dysregulation. At extremely high doses, hallucinogens cause deadly hyperthermia and seizure. Anesthetic nervous system sedation causes coma and dangerously low heart and respiratory rates. Spontaneous muscle contractions lead to muscle breakdown and kidney overload.

DELAYED AND PROLONGED EFFECTS
After the initial trip, adverse psychological, psychological effects, hallucinogens and physical effects, physical effects, hallucinogens of drug use last from hours to days. The sense of detachment and the prolonged psychological changes after a trip ends can lead to panic and increased risk of suicide with any drug in the class. Depression, memory loss, visual changes, and long-term psychoses are not uncommon after even a single trip, particularly with LSD or psilocybin. Users with a history of psychiatric disorders more often experience depression and psychoses that can become more pronounced following hallucinogen use.

After use of anesthetic hallucinogens, paranoia and schizophrenic episodes may develop, regardless of the prior state of mind or drug experience. Up to 50 percent of PCP users experience anxiety within forty-eight hours of drug use, and PCP can alter thought, speech, and memory for up to one year after a trip.

Perhaps the most characteristic delayed hallucinogenic response is the psychologic flashback experience. Flashbacks occur primarily after LSD, peyote, or psilocybin use and can occur spontaneously or can be triggered by fatigue, stress, or the use of certain drugs (such as alcohol, barbiturates, and marijuana). These sudden episodes can develop after just a single trip, can occur once or multiple times, and can develop within days or years. A hallucinogenic flashback may repeat the initial trip or may manifest as a visual hallucinatory experience, although any distortion is possible.

Although hallucinogens are considered non-addictive, serotonin-related tolerance among the plant hallucinogens develops, and dissipates, quickly. Conversely, chronic PCP use leads to addictive cravings and drug-seeking compulsions. Physical dependence on PCP is rare, but PCP may induce reduced heart and respiratory rates as withdrawal.

LONG-TERM IMPAIRMENT
Semi-permanent psychological and physical impairments occur as extensions of the drug assault. LSD in particular is associated with psychotic episodes years after drug use has ended; plant hallucinogens induce long-lasting visual changes, disorganized and irrational thought patterns, and fluctuating depression and mania. Conversely, PCP mediates continued depressive symptoms and long-term memory loss.

The flashbacks from natural hallucinogens can recur for up to five years in chronic users and may impact psychological health for much longer. Hallucinogenic persisting perception disorder, hallucinogenic persisting perception disorder, or HPPD, is a psychiatric diagnosis of hallucinatory flashbacks that persist for five or more years after a single trip. HPPD flashbacks occur most frequently in persons with a history of LSD use and are typically experienced as repeated false visual sensations and alterations; the effects can be confused with symptoms of neurologic stroke or brain tumor in otherwise healthy persons.

Nicole M. Van Hoey PharmD

FOR FURTHER INFORMATION
Cunningham, Nicola. "Hallucinogenic Plants of Abuse." *Emergency Medicine Australasia* 20 (2008): 167–74. Print. A review of natural hallucinogens that focuses on the drug sources, intoxication effects, and presentation in an emergency medicine setting.

Laing, Richard R., ed. *Hallucinogens: A Forensic Drug Handbook.* San Francisco: Elsevier, 2003. Comprehensive textbook detailing structures, identification techniques, and pharmacologic and pharmacokinetic actions of both common and more unusual hallucinogenic substances of abuse.

Substance Abuse and Mental Health Services Administration. "NSDUH Report: Use of Specific Hallucinogens, 2006." Rockville, MD: Author, 2008. Periodically released government report that discusses hallucinogenic drugs of abuse, in particular the effects of use, drug types used, rates of use, types of users, and results of use. Also includes usage descriptions of new hallucinogenic substances, including herbals and ecstasy.

Wu Li-Tzy, et al. "Recent National Trends in *Salvia divinorum* Use and Substance-Use Disorders among Recent and Former *Salvia divinorum* Users Compared with Nonusers." *Substance Abuse Rehabilitation* 2 (2011): 53–68. Print. Introduces *Salvia divinorum* as a new herbal hallucinogenic substance, identifies the most common users, and discusses adverse health effects.

See also: Brain changes with addiction; Flashbacks; Hallucinogen misuse; LSD; Narcotic's effects on the body; Psychosis and substance misuse

Harm reduction

CATEGORY: Treatment

DEFINITION: Harm reduction in the context of addiction and substance use disorder includes policies and practices that aim to reduce the level of physical and emotional damage as well as the mortality rate that are consequences of chronic drug and alcohol use.

BACKGROUND

Harm reduction focuses on behavior and practices that jeopardize a person's health and well-being. Such behaviors and practices include risky sexual practices, over-use of drugs and alcohol to the point of becoming unconscious or overdosing, using drugs alone and in seclusion, and sharing needles during intravenous drug use that can result in spreading diseases such Hepatitis C and HIV and drug misuse. Harm reduction is based in pragmatism, or realism, rather than in the idealism reflected in abstinence-only drug policies. Harm reduction methodology does not aim to stop a person from misusing drugs and alcohol but rather to reduce the individual's level of harm and risk often associated with such behavior.

Harm reduction practices are often controversial in that opponents view them as promoting an unhealthy, immoral, and sometimes illegal behavior. Advocates of harm reduction policies believe that prohibitionist drug policies can increase the risk and danger to users beyond those risks already associated with a drug. Focusing on reducing the levels of potential harm that results from drug and alcohol use while still maintaining a compassionate and nonjudgmental stance when working with individuals suffering from substance use disorder has been shown to have a greater impact on whether or not the afflicted choose to enter treatment and rehabilitation for their disease. Advocates believe that state and federal drug policies that are based on the prohibition of drugs will not eradicate drug use; people will still break laws and use drugs regardless of the laws in place. Drug policies, they argue, should seek to reduce the harm caused by drug use. Harm reduction policies regarding illegal substances are the most contentious in terms of public support.

TYPES OF PROGRAMS

In the United States, harm reduction policies surrounding the use of heroin are among the most controversial yet the most prevalent as well. Canada, Australia, and many European nations have embraced harm reduction policies. Needle exchange programs (also referred to as syringe services programs, or SSPs), in which addicted person exchange a used needle for a clean one, are among the most disputed harm reduction programs. Controversy exists even though research consistently shows needle exchange programs minimize the risk of contracting blood-borne diseases such as those caused by the human immunodeficiency and hepatitis viruses.

The US Congress banned federal funding for needle exchange programs in the late 1980s but lifted the ban in 2009. Two years later, however, Congress re-imposed the ban. In 2016, the Federal government once again lifted the ban resulting in an increase in states offering SSPs. In 2013, there were around 200 SSPs in thirty-four states, the District of Columbia, and the Commonwealth of Puerto Rico. In 2018, this had increased to over three hundred SSPs operating throughout forty-one states, the District of Columbia, the Virgin Islands, and the Commonwealth of Puerto Rico. The federal funding allows state, tribal, and territorial health departments to apply for funding upon demonstrating that they are experiencing, or at risk of experiencing, an increase in hepatitis or HV due to injection drug use.

Since the early 2000s, the US has been in a heroin/opioid epidemic. The alarming increase in prescription opioid analgesics use over the past few years has resulted in more attention being given to harm reduction strategies. This has been particularly true for those involved in the criminal justice system where drug arrests constitute a large number of incarcerated offenders, many of whom are opioid users. Currently in the US, Medical Assisted Treatment (MAT) is a successful method of treating opioid users and while the majority of prisons do not use MAT, it remains a viable treatment option. MAT includes methadone, naltrexone, and buprenorphine. These drugs act as opioid agonists, antagonists, and partial agonists respectively. An additional HIV prevention strategy includes pre-exposure prophylaxis (PrEP). PrEP is an effective medication in preventing HIV. In addition to MATS, harm reduction advocates emphasize the effectiveness of safe injecting facilities in other countries, as well as syringe exchange programs for reducing opioid harm resulting from the recent epidemic.

Tobacco use in the United States has been steadily declining since the 1960s and currently about 16% of adults are current smokers. Despite the decline in use, tobacco harm reduction remains among the more controversial harm reduction strategies in recent years. Tobacco harm reduction focuses on reducing the harm of smoking as opposed to smoking cessation. It includes nicotine replacement products such as gums, lozenges, and patches, as well as alternative or electronic cigarettes that may reduce exposure to carcinogens, and oral tobacco. Collectively, these products have been labeled as potentially reduced-exposure products (PREPs). Public health officials continue to emphasize smoking cessation over PREP use. They emphasize concerns that nonsmokers may initiate use of PREPs believing that they are safe and that current smokers may choose to use PREPs as an alternative to eventually quitting. Electronic cigarettes have often been the center of this harm reduction debate as the use of electronic cigarettes, also known as vaping, has grown tremendously over the past decade. The Food and Drug Administration (FDA) does not currently regulate electronic cigarettes and recently announced that regulation would not be considered

until the year 2022. Instead, the FDA, and their subsidiary department the Center for Tobacco Products, are focusing on reducing the nicotine level of tobacco cigarettes. While the FDA will continue to focus on a regulatory path for less harmful products, it has expressed concerns over the use and sale of electronic cigarettes to minors. The FDA has issued warnings, however, to some online retailers believed to be using marketing tactics to attract minors to their products. Critics of electronic cigarette use assert that there is not enough long term research conducted to assess the potential dangers of these products.

Additional harm reduction strategies include distributing condoms to prevent the spread of sexually transmitted diseases, promoting moderate and thoughtful drinking practices over abstinence for recovering alcoholics, and conducting responsible drinking campaigns on college campuses. Safe injection rooms, also known as supervised injection facilities, exist in many European nations providing onsite medical personnel, sterile equipment and referrals to treatment programs. Canada is currently the only North American country to provide supervised injection facilities although a few US states and cities are considering, or have attempted to adopt, legislation to allow safe injection sites. Drug zones have also been implemented in some European cities to contain the spread of drug use into other areas.

US DRUG POLICY

Despite a slight shift in thought and perception surrounding illicit drug use, substance use disorder, and opiate addiction in particular, the US drug policy continues to be shaped around punitive actions that promote zero-tolerance for drug use and heavy prison sentences for possession and distribution of drugs. The federal government continues to wage a war on drugs that seeks to eradicate drug use. US drug policy has created significant barriers to implementing harm reduction strategies.

Michelle Petrie PhD

FOR FURTHER INFORMATION

Brinkley-Rubinstein, Lauren, David Cloud, Ernest Drucker, and Nickolas Zaller "Opioid Use Among Those Who Have Criminal Justice Experience: Harm Reduction Strategies to Lessen HIV Risk.". *Current HIV/AIDS Reports*. 11 May 2018.Web. 15 June 2018.

Directory of Syringe Exchange Programs. North American Syringe Exchange. https://nasen.org/directory/ Web.10 June 2018.

"Federal Funding for Syringe Services Programs: Saving Money, Promoting Public Safety, and Improving Public Health." *AMFAR: The Foundation for AIDS Research.* amfAR, Mar. 2013. Web. 29 Oct. 2015. PDF file.

Hulse, Carl. "Surge in Cases of HIV Tests US Policy on Needle Exchanges.: *New York Times.* New York Times, 16 May 2015. Web. 29 Oct. 2015.

Inciardi, James, and Lana D. Harrison, eds. *Harm Reduction: National and International Perspectives.* Thousand Oaks, CA: Sage, 2000.

Marlatt, G. Alan, ed. *Harm Reduction: Pragmatic Strategies for Managing High Risk Behavior.* New York: Guilford, 1998.

McCann, Eugene, and Cristina Temenos. "Mobilizing Drug Consumption Rooms: Inter-place Networks and Harm Reduction Drug Policy." *Health and Place* 31 (2015): 216–23. Print.

Nadelmann, Ethan A. "Common Sense Drug Policy." *Foreign Affairs* 77.1 (1998): 111–26. Print.

Stark, Emily, Eugene Borgida, Anita Kim, and Brandy Pickens. "Understanding Public Attitudes Toward Tobacco Harm Reduction: The Role of Attitude Structure." *Journal of Applied Social Psychology* 38.10 (2008): 2615-2635. Print.

Syringe Services Program. Center for Disease Control and Prevention. 10 June 2018. Web. https://www.cdc.gov/hiv/risk/ssps.html

Wheeler, Lydia. "FDA Lets Vaping Flourish as it Eyes Crackdown on Cigarettes." *The Hill,* 03 May 2018. Web. 15 June 2018. http://thehill.com/regulation/healthcare/385930-fda-lets-vaping-flourish-as-it-eyes-crackdown-on-cigarettes

See also: Abstinence-based treatment; Alternative therapies for addiction; Treatment methods and research

Hashish

CATEGORY: Substances

ALSO KNOWN AS: Charas; hash; kif

DEFINITION: Hashish is a drug made from the resin, plant oils, or flowers of *Cannabis sativa,* also the source of marijuana.

STATUS: Illegal in the United States and other countries

CLASSIFICATION: Schedule I controlled substance in the United States; schedule II in Canada

SOURCE: Historically, hashish was prepared in the Indo-Iranian regions of Asia, although it now is manufactured in many parts of the world; it is either smuggled into the United States or made in homes or laboratories.

TRANSMISSION ROUTE: Inhaled and ingested

HISTORY OF USE

According to some studies, people have been using cannabis for thousands of years. It now is the most commonly used illicit drug worldwide. Hashish, a potent substance derived from cannabis, has a long history of its own. The word *hashish* is of Arabic origin and refers to preparations made from strong resins, plant oils, and sometimes flowers, which are dried and shaped into various forms; these can then be smoked or, after being dissolved in a liquid, baked into foods.

Hashish originally was used for religious purposes in what is now Pakistan, but its use had spread throughout India and the Middle East by the Middle Ages. Marco Polo and other medieval writers thought that the drug was used to motivate a particularly fierce group of warriors in northern Syria. Somewhat later, hashish was experimented with in Europe, most famously by French writers and doctors in the mid-nineteenth century. Several of these persons believed the hallucinations associated with the drug could be of use in psychotherapy.

EFFECTS AND POTENTIAL RISKS

Like other forms of cannabis, hashish contains dozens of substances called "cannabinoids," the general functions of which are not well understood. The

Hashish is derived from the Cannabis sativa plant. (via Wikimedia Commons)

most psychoactive substance is delta-9-tetrahydrocannabinol (THC), which binds to specific receptors in the human forebrain and cerebellar cortex. The flowering top and the resins and oils of cannabis are comparably richer in THC than are the other parts of the plant. Once bound to receptors, THC affects motor activity, reward and reinforcement, memory, and the sensation of nausea.

In practical terms, the person consuming small amounts of hashish may experience hallucinations and euphoria. Larger doses may produce increased anxiety and paranoia. With chronic and heavy use, users can experience disorganized or scattered thinking, cognitive deficits, decreased motivation, social withdrawal, and decreased range of affect.

Like other psychoactive substances, THC use can induce dependence. Dependent users tend to experience anxiety, insomnia, and loss of appetite without the drug.

Michael R. Meyers PhD

FOR FURTHER INFORMATION

Benjamin, Walter. *On Hashish.* Ed. Howard Eiland. Cambridge: Harvard UP, 2006. Print.

Breivogel, Chris, and Laura Sim-Selley. "Basic Neuroanatomy and Neuropharmacology of Cannabinoids." *International Review of Psychiatry* 21.2 (2009): 113–21. Print.

"DrugFacts: Marijuana." *National Institute on Drug Abuse.* Natl. Insts. of Health, Sept. 2015. Web. 27 Oct. 2015.

"Effects of Hashish Use." *Narconon.* Narconon International, n.d. Web. 27 Oct. 2015.

Sewell, R. Andrew, Mohini Ranganathan, and Deepak Cyril D'Souza. "Cannabinoids and Psychosis." *International Review of Psychiatry* 21.2 (2009): 152–62. Print.

See also: Marijuana; Opium; Pipes and hookahs; Psychosis and substance misuse; *Salvia divinorum*

Hazelden Foundation

CATEGORY: Treatment

DEFINITION: The Hazelden Foundation is a nonprofit organization that provides a wide range of programs for alcoholics, drug abusers, and their families. Hazelden has multiple sites in the United States.

DATE: Incorporated on January 10, 1949

BACKGROUND

The Hazelden Foundation was established in an old farm house in Center City, Minnesota, in 1947. It began as a treatment program for men who were alcoholics and was based on the twelve-step program of Alcoholics Anonymous. Initially, Hazelden's founder, Austin Ripley, himself a recovered alcoholic, intended to treat alcoholic Catholic priests, but this plan was quickly dropped.

Hazelden struggled to survive, until several of its key supporters took over the program. The Hazelden

Foundation was incorporated in 1949, but it did not begin to grow until 1952, when the Butler family took over. Hazelden soon began to flourish by providing inpatient care for recovering alcoholics, particularly those who needed extended care.

In 1955, Hazelden opened a facility for women called Dia Linn, which was in Dellwood, Minnesota. During the 1960s, Hazelden began providing a comprehensive approach to the treatment of alcoholics, adding psychologists, chaplains, social workers, and family services personnel to its staff. Also during this time, the Hazelden Foundation more than quadrupled the number of beds for its treatment programs. In 1966, Hazelden began treating men and women together and, in 1968, it opened an extended care treatment center for patients who needed a longer period of residential care.

In 1953, Hazelden purchased the rights to *Twenty-Four Hours a Day*, a book of inspirational messages for alcoholics. The publication of this book led the way for Hazelden's own publications business, which started off slowly and did not become successful until the 1970s. Hazelden has published books related to substance misuse, alcoholism, and codependency.

In the 1970s and 1980s, Hazelden expanded further and opened treatment centers in Plymouth, Minnesota; West Palm Beach, Florida; New York City; Chicago; and Newberg, Oregon. The treatment center in Plymouth serves young people (age fourteen to twenty-five years), whose needs may vary from those of adults. In 1984, the foundation opened a retreat center in Center City. In September of 1999 the foundation began a graduate degree program in addiction studies (accredited in 2007). In December of 2003, Hazelden opened a halfway house in St. Paul, Minnesota, and in 2010 it opened a treatment center in Naples, Florida.

The Hazelden treatment programs use the Minnesota model of treatment, which follows the ideas of Alcoholics Anonymous. The Minnesota model is based on the premise that alcoholism is a physical, spiritual, and mental disease, and not a moral failure on the part of the substance misuser. Accordingly, substance misusers are to be treated with dignity and respect. Primarily, the model includes group therapy because it is thought that substance misusers can be helped by discussing their experiences with other addicts. This is a central concept of the model. The goals of treatment include withdrawal from all mood-altering substances, improving the quality of life of the client, helping the client to achieve feelings of self-worth, increasing spiritual awareness in the client, assisting clients in developing relationships with other clients and with therapists, and educating clients in personal choice and responsibility.

The Minnesota model is based on existential philosophy. Existentialism is a philosophy that professes that the individual person determines the meaning of his or her life through the choices he or she makes. The presence of free will is essential to this philosophy. The role of therapists is to provide a comfortable, nurturing, caring, and client-centered environment for therapy.

The Minnesota model is considered the gold standard of treatment for substance misusers, although it does have limitations. One limitation is that its concept of the client having a disease contradicts the assumption of personal responsibility for one's own behavior.

Mission and Goals

The mission of the Hazelden Foundation is to assist persons addicted to alcohol and other drugs in achieving recovery and to assist in maintaining their recovery throughout their lives. The mission includes the goal of helping as many people as possible.

Hazelden intends to achieve this mission through its addiction treatment programs and by publishing books about addiction and codependency, speaking out for persons with addictions, researching addictions and their treatments, providing education for addiction treatment professionals, and sharing research and results with other addiction treatment organizations.

The Hazelden Foundation remains committed to the twelve-step recovery program; to treating clients and their families with dignity and respect; to treating each client as an individual, and not treating their addiction only; and to keeping an open mind to new information and research about addictions. Hazelden continues to maintain a vital presence in the treatment and recovery of addicted persons.

Christine M. Carroll RN, BSN MBA

FOR FURTHER INFORMATION

McElrath, Damian. *Hazelden: A Spiritual Odyssey.* Center City, MN: Hazelden, 1987. Written by a former administrator at Hazelden, this book provides a history of the Hazelden Foundation and the development of its treatment method for substance abuse, known as the Minnesota model.

National Institute on Drug Abuse. "Minnesota Model: Description of Counseling Approach." Web. 12 Mar. 2012. http://archives.drugabuse.gov/ADAC/ADAC11.html. Provides an outline of the Minnesota model of substance abuse treatment.

Spicer, Jerry. *The Minnesota Model: The Evolution of the Multidisciplinary Approach to Addiction Recovery.* Center City, MN: Hazelden, 1993. A comprehensive overview of the challenges, changes, history, and tenets of the Minnesota model.

Substance Abuse and Mental Health Services Administration. *National Survey of Substance Abuse Treatment Services, 2007: Data on Substance Abuse Treatment Facilities.* 2008. Web. 12 Mar. 2012. http://www.oas.samhsa.gov/nssats2k7/nssats2k7toc.cfm. A US-government survey of treatment facilities in the United States.

The Way Home: A Collective Memoir of the Hazelden Experience. Center City, MN: Hazelden, 1997. Four former Hazelden patients describe their recovery from substance abuse.

See also: Alcoholics Anonymous: The Twelve Steps; Minnesota Model; Rehabilitation programs; Treatment methods and research; Twelve-step programs for addicts; Twelve-step programs for family and friends

Health disparities and substance misuse

CATEGORY: Health issues and physiology

Definition: The Department of Health and Human Services (DHHS) describes health disparities as "differences in health outcomes that are closely linked with social, economic, and environmental disadvantage." The National Institute of Health (NIH) defines a health disparity as a "difference in the incidence, prevalence, mortality, and burden of disease and other adverse health conditions that exist among specific population groups in the United States." The National Institute of Allergy and Infectious Diseases states: "Health disparities are gaps in the quality of health and health care that mirror differences in socioeconomic status, racial and ethnic background, and education level. These disparities may stem from many factors, including accessibility of health care, increased risk of disease from occupational exposure, and increased risk of disease from underlying genetic, ethnic, or familial factors."

Health disparities are those differences in health-related treatment or outcomes that disproportionately affect ethnic and racial minorities, women, the working class and the poor, lesbian and gay persons, and the undereducated.

BACKGROUND

Since 1946, the Center for Disease Control and Prevention (CDC) has monitored and responded to challenges in the nation's health, with particular focus on reducing gaps between the least and most vulnerable U.S. residents in illness, injury, risky behaviors, use of preventive health services, exposure to environmental hazards, and premature death. The CDC defines health disparities as differences in health outcomes between groups that reflect social inequalities. Since the 1980s, according the *CDC Health Disparities and Inequalities in the United States – 2011,* the federal government has made substantial progress in improving residents' health and reducing health disparities.

In 1999, Dr. Kevin Schulman and colleagues published "The effect of race and sex on physicians' recommendations for cardiac catheterization" in the *New England Journal of Medicine,* which explored how doctors treated patients of different races. Their study found significant differences in doctors' responses to identical symptoms and presented a stark picture of pure racial bias. The study lead to congressional mandate and resulted in the Institute of Medicine's (IOM) *Unequal Treatment: Understanding Racial and Ethnic Disparities in Health Care* in 2001.

The IOM report demonstrated that minorities receive lower quality of health care even when insurance status, income, age, and severity of conditions are comparable. In order to address the problem, the IOM recommends:

- The use of evidence-based guidelines ("best practices").
- Culturally competent care, more interpreters; cross-cultural education to train providers on racial bias in medicine.
- Community-based health care workers who can act as a liaison between patients and health care providers and offer patient education.
- Medicaid should help beneficiaries access high quality health care.
- All health care agencies receiving federal funds should collect data on race and ethnicity.

HEALTH DISPARITIES AND SUBSTANCE MISUSE

Some groups of people may be more vulnerable to alcohol problems than other groups. For example, although Native Americans are less likely to drink than white Americans, those who do drink are more likely to binge drink, have a higher rate of past-year alcohol use disorder (AUD) compared with other racial and ethnic groups, and are approximately twice as likely to die from alcohol-related causes than the general American public. In addition, Hispanics and blacks who drink are more likely to binge drink than whites who drink, but Hispanics with AUD are less likely than whites to receive alcohol treatment at a specialty facility. The lesbian, gay, bisexual, and transgender (LGBT) communities are also important subpopulations to consider. Lesbian and bisexual women are about seven times more likely than heterosexual women to meet criteria for AUD. Although rates of alcohol use and AUD among men who have sex with men (MSM) are comparable to rates in the general population, alcohol misuse among MSM is an important public health problem. Alcohol misuse is a known risk factor for HIV, and MSM account for more than half of all new HIV infections each year in the United States.

The *CDC Health Disparities and Inequalities in the United States – 2011* reports on key findings across health care and highlights a couple regarding substance misuse:

- Rates of drug-induced deaths increased between 2003 and 2007 among men and women of all race/ethnicities, with the exception of Hispanics, and rates are highest among non-Hispanic whites. Prescription drug misuse kills more persons than illicit drugs, a reversal of the situation 15-20 years ago.

- More than half of alcohol consumption by adults in the United States is in the form of binge drinking (consuming four or more alcoholic drinks in one or more occasion for women and five or more for men). Younger people and men are more likely to binge drink and consume more alcohol than older adults and women. The prevalence of binge drinking is higher in groups with higher incomes and higher educational levels, although people who binge drink and have lower incomes and less educational attainment levels binge drink more frequently and, when they do binge drink, drink more heavily. American Indian/Native Americans report more binge drinking episodes per month and higher alcohol consumption per episode than other groups.

Several studies indicate that health disparity is a problem in the primary care and behavioral healthcare system. Health disparities differentially affect ethnic and racial minorities, women, and other groups who, historically, have lacked access to adequate health care.

DIFFERENCES IN HEALTH AND HEALTH CARE

The disparities differ depending on the indicator or outcome examined; however, there are some underlying trends. Minorities tend to have poorer outcomes when compared with whites; women have poorer outcomes when compared with men; and gay and lesbian individuals have poorer outcomes when compared with heterosexual individuals. These disparities are noted even when researchers control for other variables, such as socioeconomic status and availability of health care.

Health disparities are especially disconcerting when it comes to substance misuse. Although racial and ethnic minorities use drugs and alcohol at roughly the same rate as whites, racial and ethnic minorities suffer more adverse effects from substance misuse. Researchers note health disparities related to substance misuse in several areas, including human immunodeficiency virus (HIV) infection rates, transmission of sexually transmitted diseases (STDs), and cardiovascular health as it relates to substance use, hepatitis and tuberculosis infection, and drug-related deaths. These diseases are more prominent in individuals with addictions due to sharing needles, engaging in risky behaviors, having unprotected sex, and having impaired immune systems from poor overall health. Drug and alcohol misuse can impair judgement leading a person to engage in risky sexual behavior and alcohol misuse may make it difficult for those infected with HIV/AIDs or tuberculosis to follow treatment regimes.

- Hispanics and African Americans have higher rates in general of complete abstinence from alcohol while at the same time have a higher risk for developing alcohol-related liver disease than whites if they do drink.

- According to the Centers for Disease Control and Prevention (CDC), all racial minorities, with the exception of Hispanics, had increases in drug-related deaths between 2002 and 2007.

- The CDC reports that in 2014 the diagnosis rate for HIV in the United States was 13.8 per 100,000 persons and 49.4 among African Americans.

- African Americans make up approximately 11 percent of the US population but account for 44 percent of people living with AIDS; they also represent almost one-half of new AIDS diagnoses.

- According to 2015 data, 6.5 percent of the world's prison population are women and, overall, incarcerated females have higher HIV prevalence than men. Drug use, as well as sexual abuse, are linked in the disproportionately high prevalence of HIV infection.

- The prevalence of smoking among whites and African Americans is almost identical, though a 2015 study suggests that African Americans who are heavy smokers have an increased risk of diabetes. American Indians are twice as likely to smoke as Hispanics and almost three times as likely to smoke as Asian Americans, according to the 2015 National Health Interview Survey

- When examining the disparities for lesbian, gay, bisexual, and transgender (LGBT) people, similar results are noted. LGBT persons have higher rates of alcohol and substance use disorders when compared with the rates noted among heterosexuals, are less likely to abstain from alcohol and drug use, and are more likely to continue with heavy drinking into later life. All of these behaviors also may contribute to an increased risk for HIV and other STDs.

DIFFERENCES IN TREATMENT

In addition to the disparities noted in health care among minority populations, disparities also found in access to and participation in treatment. For example, those of lower socioeconomic status access substance use disorder treatment at levels significantly lower than persons in higher socioeconomic brackets.

Asian Americans access substance use disorder treatment at lower levels than other racial and ethnic groups, even when controlling for prevalence of substance use disorders. Lesbians are less likely to access treatment services for substance use disorders. African American men are less likely to access residential treatment when compared with men of other racial and ethnic groups, and African Americans overall are less likely to complete substance use disorder treatment when compared with whites.

Health disparities also affect persons who have both a mental illness and a substance use disorder (co-occurring or comorbid disorders, or COD). Persons with COD have a more difficult time accessing treatment, perhaps because of a lack of adequate training for the professionals who treat substance use and those who treat psychiatric disorders. This is particularly true of persons whose psychiatric illness (such as schizophrenia or bipolar disorder) is more complex and requires medication management.

CONCLUSION

The effect of the disparities goes beyond limited access to treatment or increased risk of infection with an STD. Disparities significantly affect the individual and their community, which may lead to increased morbidity and mortality.

To address the wide-ranging scope of the problem, the National Institutes of Health (NIH), the American Psychological Association (APA), the Office of Minority Health, and other state and federal organizations have made reducing health disparities a priority for the last several years. Healthy People 2020, an ongoing program of the Office of Disease Prevention and Health Promotion, which focuses on American health disparities, has expanded their goal to eliminate, not just reduce, health disparities by the target date of 2020. Some of the actions taken include developing special task forces, funding for research to examine and address disparities, and encouraging minority and other scholars to engage in research in this area by offering grants and opportunities for training.

Desiree A. Creuecoeur-MacPhail. PhD;
Updated by Duane R. Neff, PhD, MSW

FOR FURTHER INFORMATION

Brown, L. S., et al. "Disparities in Health Services for HIV/AIDS, Hepatitis C virus, and Sexually Transmitted Infections: Role of Substance Abuse Treatment Programs." *Journal of Addiction Medicine* 3.2 (2009): 95–102. Concludes that services do exist that are tailored for special populations, despite barriers.

Burlew, A. K., et al. "Measurement and Data Analysis in Research Addressing Health Disparities in Substance Abuse." *Journal of Substance Abuse Treatment* 36.1 (2009): 25–43. Print. Discusses some of the issues with conducting substance abuse research with ethnic minorities and provides some strategies to increase the validity of such research.

Carter-Pokras, O & Baquet, C. "What is a Health Disparity." *Public Health Reports 117* (Sep.-Oct. 2002):426-434.

Centers for Disease Control and Prevention (CDC). "Alcohol-attributable deaths and years of potential life lost among American Indians and Alaska Natives—United States, 2001–2005." *MMWR Morb Mortal Wkly Rep.* 2008 Aug 29; 57(34):938–941.

Center for Disease Control and Prevention. "CDC Health Disparities and Inequalities Report – United States, 2011." *Morbidity and Mortality Weekly Report 60* (Jan. 2011): 55-114.

Jacobson, J. O., P. Robinson, and R. N. Bluthenthal. "A Multilevel Decomposition Approach to Estimate the Role of Program Location and Neighborhood Disadvantage in Racial Disparities in Alcohol Treatment Completion." *Social Science and Medicine* 64.2 (2007): 462–76. Print. Attempts to explain the treatment disparities with regards to treatment completion.

Lowman, C., and C. E. Le Fauve. "Health Disparities and the Relationship between Race, Ethnicity, and Substance Abuse Treatment Outcomes." *Alcoholism: Clinical and Experimental Research* 27.8 (2003): 1324–26. Print. Describes some counter-intuitive findings concerning disparities research that compared treatment outcomes between whites and African Americans.

National Institute on Alcohol Abuse and Alcoholism. "HIV/AIDS." www.niaaa.nih.gov/alcohol-health/special-populations-co-occurring-disorders/hivaids. Accessed 23 Oct. 2017.

Schulman, et al. "The effect of race and sex on physicians' recommendations for cardiac catheterization." *New England Journal of Medicine.* 1999

United States Department of Health and Human Services, *HHS Action Plan to Reduce Racial and Ethnic Health Disparities.* Washington, DC: Department of Health and Human Services, April 2011.

Wray TB, et al. "Systematic review of interventions to reduce problematic alcohol use in men who have sex with men." *Drug Alcohol Rev.* 2016 Mar; 35(2):148–157.

See also: Gender and addiction; Insurance for addiction treatment; Poverty and substance misuse; Socioeconomic status and addiction

Heart attacks and substance misuse

CATEGORY: Health issues and physiology
ALSO KNOWN AS: Myocardial infarction
DEFINITION: A heart attack is an abrupt interruption of the flow of blood to the heart that results in damage to the heart or death because of a lack of oxygen to the heart muscle. The foods and substances one takes in are major contributors to coronary heart disease. Misuse of four addictive substances in particular—tobacco, alcohol, cocaine, and methamphetamine—increases the risks of a person developing coronary heart disease.

HEART ATTACK

A heart attack occurs when one of the coronary arteries (the vessels that supply blood to the heart) becomes blocked, thus preventing oxygen-rich, or oxygenated, blood from reaching the heart. A lack of oxygenated blood damages heart muscle and kills cells. The severity of a heart attack depends on how much heart muscle dies. For the patient, this could mean a long recovery period, permanent disability, or death. Coronary heart disease, the precursor of heart attack, is the leading cause of death for both women and men in the United States.

Coronary heart disease, also called coronary artery disease, atherosclerosis, or hardening of the arteries, is caused by deposits called plaques that form on the inside walls of coronary arteries. Plaques are a mixture of fat, calcium, cholesterol, and certain white blood cells. Plaques develop gradually over time. All adults have some plaques in their coronary arteries. When plaques are dense enough to restrict the normal healthy flow of oxygenated blood to the heart, coronary heart disease develops. When a section of a plaque deposit suddenly ruptures, blood clots form naturally to seal the crack. When a clot is large enough to block most of or the entire artery, a heart attack follows.

HEART ATTACK AND TOBACCO

Cigarette smoking increases the amount of artery-clogging plaque. An international study in 2007 found that chewing tobacco more than doubles the risk of heart attack, and that smoking and chewing quadruples the risk. The study also found that cigarette smoking triples the risk of heart attack and that the risk increases with every cigarette smoked. Even after quitting, heavy smokers continue to be at risk of heart attack up to twenty years later.

When combined with other risk factors for heart attack, smoking and chewing become even more lethal. Smoking raises blood pressure, increases the likelihood of blood clot formation, lowers the body's ability to benefit from exercise, and decreases high-density lipoprotein (HDL), the good cholesterol. HDL helps to remove bad cholesterol from arteries.

HEART ATTACK AND ALCOHOL

A number of studies have suggested that moderate alcohol consumption, especially of red wine, actually benefits the heart by reducing plaques in the coronary arteries and by increasing HDL cholesterol. How this happens in unclear. Moderate consumption is one drink per day for women and two for men. One drink is generally established as 12 ounces of beer, 5 ounces of wine, or 1.5 ounces of spirits.

However, consuming more than three drinks per day or binge-drinking has a toxic effect on the heart. In addition, heavy drinking over time adds fat to the blood, which increases cholesterol that can settle in the coronary arteries. Heavy drinking also leads to alcoholic cardiomyopathy, a condition in which the heart muscles are weakened and the heart becomes less efficient in pumping oxygenated blood throughout the body and back to the heart. Furthermore, heavy drinking causes high blood pressure, one of the major risks for coronary heart disease.

HEART ATTACK AND COCAINE

Cocaine misuse, whether long-term use or binging, also can lead to a heart attack. One study found that about 66 percent of heart attacks associated with cocaine misuse occurred within three hours of taking the drug, whether by inhaling it or taking it intravenously. A heart attack can occur anywhere from one minute to four days after consuming cocaine.

Cocaine triggers a heart attack in several ways. First, cocaine constricts the coronary arteries, thus reducing the amount of oxygenated blood flowing to the heart. There is no way to measure the amount of cocaine in the system or the duration of use before the constriction becomes so severe that it completely impedes the blood flow. Second, cocaine increases the heart's need for oxygen by speeding up the heart rate and raising blood pressure. Third, cocaine adds to the deposits of plaques in the coronary arteries, and fourth, cocaine produces changes in the blood that make the blood more likely to clot and block arteries.

HEART ATTACK AND METHAMPHETAMINE

Methamphetamine (meth) is dangerous to the heart. Prolonged use or binging leads to rapid heartbeat, irregular heartbeat, inflammation of the heart muscle, inflammation of the lining of the heart, and inflammation of blood vessels within the heart. Meth increases blood pressure and damages blood vessels throughout the body. It also constricts coronary arteries, the major cause of heart attack.

Furthermore, meth's damage to the heart and to the entire cardiovascular system is often irreversible. Even after years of abstaining from the drug, meth users still run a higher risk of suffering a heart attack than does the general population. Furthermore, because meth is so detrimental to every major organ in the body, meth misusers go through a much more difficult and longer recovery period from heart attack than do nonusers.

Wendell Anderson BA

FOR FURTHER INFORMATION

Aslibekyan, Stella, Emily Levitan, and Murray Mittleman. "Prevalent Cocaine Use and Myocardial Infarction." *American Journal of Cardiology* 102.8 (2008): 966–69. Print. Reports on a study of the association between cocaine use and heart attack.

Institute of Medicine. *Secondhand Smoke Exposure and Cardiovascular Effects: Making Sense of the Evidence.* 15 Oct. 2009. Web. 13 Mar. 2012. http://www.nap.edu/catalog.php?record_id=12649. Results of a study showing the link between secondhand smoke and coronary heart disease.

Westover, Arthur, Paul Nakonezny, and Robert Haley. "Acute Myocardial Infarction in Young Adults Who Abuse Amphetamines." *Drug and Alcohol Dependence* 96 (2008): 49–56. Print. Reports on a study of the association between amphetamine abuse and heart attack.

See also: Alcohol's effects on the body; Cocaine use disorder; Methamphetamine; Smoking's effects on the body

Heroin

CATEGORY: Substances

ALSO KNOWN AS: Big H; black; black tar heroin; boy; brown sugar; diacetylmorphine; diamorphine; dope; dragon; horse; junk; mud; skag; smack; snow; snowball; tar; white

DEFINITION: Heroin is a highly addictive opioid drug derived from the poppy plant. As an opiate, it functions as a central nervous system depressant similar to morphine, opium, methadone, and hydromorphone (Dilaudid).

STATUS: Illegal in the United States and worldwide

CLASSIFICATION: Schedule I controlled substance

SOURCE: A synthetic derivative of morphine, the most potent constituent of the opium poppy; formed by adding two acetyl groups to the morphine molecule; most of the illicit supply is smuggled into the United States from opium refinement sources in Southeast Asia, Afghanistan, and Mexico or is produced in illegal laboratories

TRANSMISSION ROUTE: Primarily exists in three forms: as a pure white bitter-tasting powder, an impure brown powder, and a black sticky substance called black tar heroin. Most street heroin is mixed or cut with other drugs, additives, and impurities, causing variations in color and potency. Heroin can be smoked, snorted, sniffed, or injected intravenously.

HISTORY OF USE

Diacetylmorphine, later named heroin, was originally synthesized in 1874 in London by the English chemist C. R. Alder Wright. However, it was not until 1898 that Bayer Pharmaceutical Company of Germany commercially introduced heroin as a new pain remedy and nonaddictive substitute for morphine. During the next several decades, heroin was sold legally worldwide and aggressively marketed as a cough medicine and as a safer, more potent form of morphine.

By the early twentieth century, heroin's intense euphoric effects were fully recognized, leading to widespread misuse. Numerous restrictions on the production, use, sale, and distribution of heroin were established to help prevent further misuse. These restrictions included the Harrison Narcotics Act of 1914, the Dangerous Drug Act of 1920, and the Heroin Act of 1924. As a result, heroin consumption briefly declined, but illicit production and trafficking grew. Heroin became one of the most sought after drugs in the world and, by 1970, the US Drug Enforcement Administration (DEA) classified heroin as a schedule I controlled narcotic. Class I drugs are those with a high misuse potential and no legitimate medical use.

Various methods have been used to gain heroin highs over the years, depending on user preference and drug purity. The most common and economical method of heroin use is injection, or "shooting up." Popular forms of shooting up include "mainlining" (injecting directly into a vein) and "skin-popping" (injecting directly into a muscle or under the skin).

Snorting and smoking heroin became popular as a result of the availability of higher quality heroin, the fear of contracting blood-borne illnesses, such HIV/AIDS and Hepatitis C, through needle sharing, and the erroneous belief that inhaling heroin would not lead to addiction. The best-known method of smoking heroin is "chasing the dragon." Originating in the 1950s in Hong Kong, this method involves heating and liquefying the drug on tin foil and inhaling the vapors. Heroin is such a potent and addicting drug, however, that most users soon are forced to begin using the drug intravenously as their tolerance increases and greater amounts are needed to achieve a high and forestall the horrendous physical symptoms of withdrawal.

Some users crave an even greater high and engage in "speedballing" or "crisscrossing," which involves simultaneously injecting or snorting alternate lines of heroin and cocaine, respectively. Heroin is considered one of the most dangerous and psychologically and physically addictive drugs available. It remains a serious health issue throughout the world.

EFFECTS AND POTENTIAL RISKS

Heroin is the fastest acting of the opiates; it is three times more potent than morphine. It acts by depressing the central nervous system through an endorphin-like mechanism. Heroin rapidly crosses the blood-brain barrier because of its high lipid solubility. It is quickly metabolized into morphine and binds to the opioid receptors responsible not only for suppressing pain sensation and relieving anxiety but also for critical life processes.

The short-term effects of heroin are attributed to its properties as an opiate. These effects have made heroin one of the most desirable drugs in the world. Heroin produces a warm surge of pleasure and euphoria referred to as a rush. This rush is followed by feelings of peacefulness, well-being, contentment, and physical relaxation. Users alternate between wakeful and drowsy states, a condition commonly referred to as "nodding" since the user will be awake one moment then will fall asleep the next. At this point the user's neck relaxes and the chin drops down toward the chest, which in turn wakes the user enough to lift the head back up. This action of nodding the head up and down continues, with the user seemingly unaware it is occurring. While high on heroin, the user will also experience little sensitivity to pain. Minor, negative, short-term effects of heroin use include nausea, vomiting, constipation, severe itching, dry mouth, difficulty urinating, heavy extremities, impaired mental functioning, and constricted, pin-point pupils. Non-pleasurable sensations, such as severe irritability, irrational anger, and depression, can occur as the high dissipates.

The most serious and most common side effect of heroin use is overdose, which is a result of respiratory depression and is fatal unless an opioid antagonist such as Narcan (naloxone) is administered. Narcan, which is dispensed nasally as a spray or

Buprenorphine

Buprenorphine is an opioid analgesic approved for use in the treatment of moderate to severe pain and for treatment of opioid dependence. Buprenorphine has been investigated for treating symptoms associated with opioid and heroin withdrawal. It is available as a sublingual tablet for treating dependence, and it is classified as a schedule III controlled substance.

Buprenorphine therapy is divided into three phases: the induction phase, when treatment is initiated after a patient has abstained from opioid products for twelve to twenty-four hours; the stabilization phase, during which time a patient gradually reduces or discontinues the use of opioid products; and the maintenance phase, in which a patient continues a steady buprenorphine dose for an indefinite time to control cravings and withdrawal symptoms associated with opioid abstinence.

injected intramuscularly, reverses the overdose by removing the opioids from the opiate receptors in the brain. This will then send the user into immediate withdrawal, which is painful but not life-threatening. Because the half-life of Narcan is much shorter than that of heroin, it is critical that the revived, overdosing user be medically monitored after administering Narcan since the potential for a recurrence of respiratory depression is possible.

The most immediate and intense heroin rush is achieved by intravenous injection. However, this transmission route also has the most dangerous potential side-effects. The risk of contracting infectious diseases such as human immunodeficiency virus (HIV) and hepatitis viruses is substantial. Furthermore, illegal street heroin is contaminated with unknown additives and impurities such as sugar, starch, and poisons, which can cause blood vessel inflammation, blockage, and permanent damage. Beginning in the 2010s, cities and towns along the eastern coast of the United States began seeing heroin laced (or "cut") with the synthetic opioid fentanyl. Fentanyl, which was first developed in the 1960s, is eighty to one hundred times more potent than morphine and is an effective palliative care medication for cancer treatment. Once mixed with heroin, it is often fatal since the user is sent into immediate respiratory distress, and unless

Narcan is administered within minutes, irreversible brain damage and/or death occurs.

Long-term heroin use can lead to adverse physical effects, including collapsed veins, heart and skin infections, liver and kidney disease, and pulmonary complications. Continuous heroin use may affect brain functioning as a result of repeated respiratory suppression and lack of oxygen. However, the most detrimental long-term effect of heroin use is physical and psychological dependence and addiction, which can occur as quickly as after using heroin for the first time; users soon crave larger and larger doses of the drug to achieve the original high and to keep from experiencing the painful physical effects of withdrawal.

Black tar heroin. (DEA via Vikimedia Commons)

Heroin misuse is a problem that affects people across the world at every socioeconomic and education level. Afghanistan is the world leading producer of the opium poppies used to make heroin. Opiate use is most prevalent in the Middle East, as a result, but is also a significant problem in the United States. In 2012 the National Survey on Drug Use and Health (NSDUH) found that there were 669,000 heroin users in the United States; 156,000 of those people were new users. Heroin use saw a steady increase between 2006 and 2012; however, use among adolescents decreased during that period.

Heroin Epidemic

The US Food and Drug Administration (FDA) approved the opioid pain medication Oxycontin in December 1995. Its manufacturer, Connecticut-based Purdue Pharma, assured prescribers and the public and managed to dupe the FDA into believing that the drug was "misuse resistant." Purdue then specifically targeted and marketed the drug to physicians nationwide who, based on a database the company had compiled, were known for prescribing large amounts of pain medication in their practice. From 1999 to 2010, the sale of prescription painkillers quadrupled in the United States.

Because Oxycontin is so chemically similar to heroin and because heroin is a fraction of the cost of illegal pain medication, individuals who first become addicted to prescribed opiate medication will often turn to heroin. According to the American Society of Addiction Medicine, four in five heroin users were first addicted to prescribed painkillers. The rate of deaths from heroin overdose quadrupled in the United States from 2000 to 2013, with a 67 percent increase in heroin-related overdoses during the 2010–13 time period. The Substance Abuse and Mental Health Services Administration (SAMHSA) noted a 51 percent increase in the number of heroin users in the Untied States between 2013 and 2014, despite double the seizure amounts of heroin by law enforcement between 2010 and 2014.

Recognized public ally as an epidemic by US President Barrack Obama and such agencies as the DEA, the US Department of Health and Human Services (HHS) announced in a 2015 report that 2014 was a peak year for drug overdoses, with 60 percent of those deaths attributed to opioids. A report released by the DEA noted that in 2015, drug overdose deaths in the United States outnumbered deaths from firearms and from motor vehicle accidents combined for that year.

Rose Ciulla-Bohling PhD

FOR FURTHER INFORMATION

Brezina, Corona. *Heroin: The Deadly Addiction.* New York: Rosen, 2009. Print.

Cobb, Allan B., and Ronald J. Brogan. *Heroin: Junior Drug Awareness.* New York: Chelsea, 2009. Print.

Elliot-Wright, Susan. *Heroin.* Chicago: Raintree, 2005. Print.

Libby, Therissa A. *Heroin: The Basics.* Center City: Hazelden, 2007. Print.

Morales, Francis. *The Little Book of Heroin.* Berkeley: Ronin, 2000. Print.

"National Drug Threat Assessment Summary." *DEA.* US Dept. of Justice/Drug Enforcement Administration, Oct. 2015. Web. 24 June 2016.

"Opioid Addiction: 2016 Facts and Figures." *ASAM.* Amer. Soc. of Addiction Medicine, 2016. Web. 25 June 2016.

"The Truth about Heroin." *Foundation for a Drug-Free World.* Foundation for a Drug-Free World, 2016. Web. 15 Jan. 2016.

Van Zee, Art. "The Promotion and Marketing of OxyContin: Commercial Triumph, Public Health Tragedy." *Amer. Jour. of Public Health* 99.2 (2009): 221–27. Print.

"What Is the Scope of Heroin Use in the United States?" *National Institute on Drug Abuse.* NIH, Nov. 2014. Web. 15 Jan. 2016.

"World Drug Report 2014." *United Nations Office on Drugs and Crime.* United Nations, June 2014. Web. 15 Jan. 2016.

See also: Intravenous drug use and blood-borne diseases; Morphine; Narcotics misuse; Recreational drugs

History of addiction

CATEGORY: Social issues

DEFINITION: Drugs and alcohol have been part of human history for centuries but the nature of addiction and dependence has changed considerably. There were so-called drug cults, historically located in traditional cultures. Drugs and alcohol were sometimes associated with religious ceremonies. They have changed in some modern societies into alarming mass tendencies leading to addictions. The nature of addictive drugs also has evolved, particularly since the mid- to late twentieth century.

EARLY HISTORY OF DRUG ADDICTION

The history of drug addiction can be traced to prehistoric times. Certain areas of the world, most notably pre-Columbian America, may be said to have developed a culture of drugs as part of religious (or ceremonial) belief systems. The use of plants with narcotic effects by ruling elites and priests was noted by Spanish conquistadors who came in contact with the Incas of Peru. Drugs such as peyote (derived from a spineless cactus growing in Mexico and parts of Texas) have been used by indigenous populations around the world for their transcendental effects and as meditation.

Probably the most widely known historical example of addiction is the case of opium dens in China. Although popular views may have distorted the image of opium addiction in China, the problem of opium consumption definitely increased during the eighteenth and into the nineteenth century. The Chinese imperial administration, acting in response to a push by India-based British merchants to flood the Chinese market with opium imports, attempted several times to outlaw opium use. Historians also note the use, and the production, of opium in eighteenth century colonial America, in which local militias seem to have used the drug before entering battle. They did so with the knowledge and even encouragement of commanders. An example is the American Civil War where injured soldiers were given opium as an analgesic and then became addicted to the opium.

MODERN RISE OF DRUG ADDICTION

Drug addiction in some form was probably present in all societies from ancient times into modern times. A general consensus exists, however, that the socially damaging spread of addiction has become the hallmark of modern mass cultures, particularly in the Western world, beginning in the twentieth century. Certain addictive drugs have played a significant role in the modern world. They include: marijuana (cannabis and hashish), cocaine (a product of the coca plant), opium (a product of the poppy plant), morphine (derived from opium), and heroin (derived from morphine). Drugs that have spread throughout the world have disastrous addictive effects. They also are the cause of thousands of deaths each year. Among these drugs are methamphetamine and crack cocaine. In the United States several addictive drugs became particularly popular in certain periods and among certain population groups. While the dangers of smoking marijuana (or any of the common drugs associated with marijuana) continue to be debated, there is general agreement that, compared with hard drugs, marijuana is not necessarily an addictive drug. This is not the case with other drugs that became popular in recent history.

The prohibition of alcohol was passed as the 18th Amendment to the United States Constitution, in 1919. The law was passed due to pressure from the Temperance Movement. The law made the manufacture, distribution, and sale of alcoholic beverages illegal in the U.S. The American people did not care for this law, so they made their own alcohol, or bought wine from criminals who had a black market for alcohol.

The 18th Amendment was repealed by the 21st Amendment in 1933. Each state was to have a convention to approve the 21st Amendment. Most states approved it, but not all states. One side effect of the Prohibition era (1919–1933) in the United States was near glorification of illicit consumption not only of alcohol but also of cocaine and other drugs for partygoers. Some people became prostitutes in order to earn money for alcohol or drugs.

Statistical studies were limited in the first half of the twentieth century. The studies that were performed indicate that the number of people struggling with addiction in the United States declined between 1940 and 1945. This was probably due to wartime effects on international supply lines. Drug addiction became an increasing problem, however, in the second half of the century. By the 1950s news of rising drug addiction was spread rapidly through the media. Starting in 1953 in the United States, the Federal Bureau of Narcotics began collecting detailed statistics on drug and alcohol addiction. A growing body of data covering the next five decades of the century revealed the different levels of susceptibility to the dangers of addiction. What was considered alarming in the first years after 1950 was that the use of "soft" drugs (such as marijuana) was becoming almost commonplace... Debate about the presumed non-addictive nature of marijuana and its potential medical benefits continued, and so did debate about the dangers of hard drugs. Addiction was soon an unavoidable subject for government agencies, educational institutions,

churches and synagogues, medical treatment centers, and, inevitably, the penal system.

Perhaps foremost on the list of hard drugs associated with addiction before the 1960s is heroin. Near the end of World War I, chemists discovered a process to derive heroin from morphine. Private users of illegal drugs may have welcomed heroin for its illusory and temporary euphoric effects (later referred to as a heroin rush). Attraction to such sensations had its costs, as heroin users began to enter alternate periods of wakefulness and drowsiness (a state known as the nod). Mental faculties declined, and other bodily functions such as speech, vision, digestion, and bowel elimination were affected. Withdrawal symptoms were experienced by those addicted. They included muscle and bone pain, muscle spasms, insomnia, and severe upset stomach. These symptoms would reach their height after about forty-eight hours without the drug.

1960s DRUG CULTURE

Probably more than any other decade, the 1960s stood out as the era both of increasing hard drug addiction and of a rising level of popular experimentation with drugs. Public consumption of marijuana became synonymous with anti-establishment youthful rebellion. The use of dangerous psychedelic drugs, particularly acid, or LSD (lysergic acid diethylamide), was more limited. Acid was part of a counter-culture wave not only among youth but also among the adult population. By the end of the 1960s, however, the term "drug culture" began to be associated with widespread social, economic, and political problems. There were rising levels of addiction in the economically depressed environments of large cities in the United States. This phenomenon became increasingly alarming. U.S. military authorities announced a significant number of cases of service members using drugs in Vietnam. For an entire generation of Americans, the decade of the 1960s will be remembered for the presumed attraction of "tripping" and for the growing signs of the psychological, economic, social, and politically destructive effects of addiction. Commonly used drugs were heroin, LSD, methamphetamine, crack, marijuana, cocaine, and hallucinogenic mushrooms. A treatment for drug misuse became available. Methadone was the treatment and although it is a narcotic it has milder symptoms of withdrawal than heroin. It was developed in Germany at the end of World War ll. Methadone needed to be prescribed by a physician. The individual was required to visit a methadone clinic, every day or two. Initially, it was a liquid, but soon it was converted to a powder or a pill. Methadone had some dangerous side effects, most notable was a heart arrhythmia. There was also an antidote for opioid drugs. It was Narcan (naloxone). There were two versions of Narcan. It could be inhaled or injected into the person's thigh.

CRACK COCAINE AND METHAMPHETAMINE

Crack cocaine's lower cost appealed to economically depressed inner-city users in the United States. In the mid-1980s, there began the use of a new and dangerous drug. This drug appealed to confirmed those already with a substance use disorder and new drug misusers. Crack is a highly addictive rock-like substance that is a by-product of a chemical process that converts normal powder-form cocaine. Sometimes, illicit manufacturers of crack cocaine omitted certain steps in the production process and they would then use cheap sodium bicarbonate as a substitute additive. This product could be marketed at lower prices, thus attracting the poorer drug users.

Methamphetamine (meth), a stimulant, became a significant addictive substance in the 1990s.It was produced from synthetic ephedrine (the basic component of amphetamine). It was originally produced by chemists in Germany and Japan in the last decades of the nineteenth century. As early as the 1930s the derivative amphetamine became a major prescription drug used to treat a number of illnesses. They included epilepsy, schizophrenia, and various forms of depression. Methamphetamine itself became an important new arrival on the drug scene. Some individuals used the relatively simple but dangerous chemical methods to produce their own meth. The chemical process is quite dangerous, because of risks of fire and explosions. An explosion can lead to potentially deadly contamination of so-called cooking sites and surrounding buildings, some of which must be permanently condemned. To discourage methamphetamine production by users, pseudoephedrine, the main ingredient, can only be purchased in small amounts and the customer must present a picture identification card to purchase it.

CRIMINAL INVOLVEMENT IN DRUG ADDICTION

The history of drug addiction includes not only the consideration of specific drugs and their effects but also the effects of addiction on society. Such effects inevitably involve illegal acts and legal sanctions to control the effect of drug violations on society as a whole. Large-scale international drug dealings are considered among the most dangerous and harmful arenas of criminal activity, affecting certain areas of the world, in particular, Latin America, Southeast Asia, and Afghanistan. However, street-level criminality involving those drug addicted and drug dealers in many cities of the United States and Europe has at times reached near-epidemic rates.

Addiction forces many with addiction to spend money that they don't have. To remedy that problem, the temptation is great to earn money by selling drugs to others. In economically depressed neighborhoods, selling drugs is a cash trade. Over time there are groups of drug sellers, like gangs that develop, Some gangs or drug sellers will develop a "turf" that is where they sell their drugs. Many of these people get upset if someone else invades their turf. Another problem can develop if a person tried to obtain drugs without money. Gang members frequently possess guns to use to protect their "rights." Sometimes guns are traded for drugs. Violence can happen and people may be killed because they haven't paid their debts. Drug purchasing can be risky for all involved.

Although drug addiction is almost always associated with the use of hard drugs such as crack cocaine and heroin, sometimes young people are given drugs to try for their first experience. Young people may use a household chemical to sniff. New ways to get high with common, legal substances are found regularly. In mid-July 2011, for example, the *New York Times* reported rising evidence that young people were using certain bath salts containing the dangerous chemicals mephedrone and methylenedioxypyrovalerone as recreational drugs. In this case, harmful effects may be immediate and drastic. Efforts to stop over-the-counter sales of such products have been unevenly successful, and vary from state to state.

DRUGS IN THE 2000S

Early in the new millennium, drug culture was similar to the1990s. In the last 6 months of 2007 and all of 2008, the U.S. experienced a major recession. It was particularly hard on people in their 50s and 60s. Many had worked for the same employer for most of their career, and were unable to find a comparable job. This caused feelings of hopelessness. Many of them self-medicated with alcohol or drugs. There were new opioids available for post-surgery analgesia and physical injuries. They were Dilaudid, Oxycodone, oxycontin (MS Contin), fentanyl, and carfentanil. Dilaudid and oxycodone were opioids. Oxycontin was an opioid but the pharmaceutical company marketed it as non-addicting because it was slowly released over 12 hours. This was false. There were also additional drugs for treating alcohol and drug addiction. For alcohol there was Antabuse, Campral, and Naltrexone. For drug misuse, there was Suboxone (nuprenorphine), and Naltrexone. These drugs are similar to methadone, in that they had decreased symptoms of withdrawal.

It was common for drug sellers to cut the drugs and replace it with an inert substance. Opioids began to be cut and replaced with fentanyl or carfenanil. Fentanyl was used as an anesthetic and when it was added to opioids, the risk of overdose was increased. Carfentanil was even more potent than fentanyl. Both of these drugs were lethal if they were inhaled or if they got on the skin. First responders had to wear hazmat suits to care for someone who had used an opioid cut with fentanyl or carfentanil.

The U. S. had a new drug crisis with older victims, as well as, adolescents or young adults. The older people were not expected to be doing drugs, and often they were found unconscious while babysitting a grandchild. While there were more treatments, there was an increased demand for them. Narcan was given to police and first responders, who were frequently faced with a person who had overdosed. Both the old and new opioids were illegal to possess or to use. So, drug users and sellers often ended up in Prison. In 2016 to 2018, many U.S. state governments decided not to prosecute these people. Prison costs were increasing and they were overloaded. The current thinking is that addiction is a disease, and not a human flaw. There is no easy solution for these problems, unfortunately.

Byron D. Cannon, PhD;
Updated by Christine M. Carroll, BSN, MBA

For Further Information

A Forever Recovery. (2018) The History of Drug Abuse in the United States. Retrieved on August 2, 2018 from Http://aforeverrecovery.com/blog/drug-abuse/the-history-of-drug-abuse-in-the-united-states/

Narconon. (2018) Alcohol History. Retrieved on August 2, 2018 from https://www.narconon.org/drug-information/alcohol-history.html.

See also: Addiction; Just Say No campaign; Trends and statistics: Alcohol misuse; Trends and statistics: Behavioral addictions; Trends and statistics: Illegal drug use; Trends and statistics: Prescription drug misuse; Trends and statistics: Smoking

HIV/AIDS and substance misuse

Category: Health issues and physiology
Key terms:

CD4 T-Lymphocyte (CD4 cells): a type of lymphocyte that organizes other immune cells when fighting off pathogens

Human Immunodeficiency Virus (HIV): a pathogen that enters CD4 T-helper immune cells and destroys them during its replicative stage

Acquired Immune Deficiency Syndrome (AIDS): the most severe form of HIV, which is defined by a CD4 cell count of below 200 cells/mm or if there is the presence of AIDS-defining illnesses, regardless of the CD4 cell count

Opportunistic Infections: an infection that is found within those with a weakened immune system, such as those with advanced HIV

Substance Misuse: when a substance user consumes enough of the substance on a regular basis to cause harm to themselves or others whether it be physical, mental, or financial harm

Pre-Exposure Prophylaxis (PrEP): a combination drug of tenofovir/emtricitabine taken daily that can prevent a person without HIV from getting it

Syringe Services Programs (SSPs): community-based programs that allow intravenous drug users to receive access to sterile needles and provide users to safely dispose of used needles; also referred to as *needle-syringe programs (NSPs), syringe exchange programs (SEPs),* and *needle exchange programs (NEPs)*

How Does HIV Work?

When a person becomes infected with HIV, the virus enters the bloodstream and begins replicating itself inside the CD4 cells. The immune system recognizes both the virus and these infected CD4 cells as pathogens and becomes activated. Immune cells such as CD8 T-Lymphocytes begin to kill off infected CD4 cells and B lymphocytes create antibodies against the virus. At the beginning of infection, CD4 count goes down but then starts to come back up as the immune system creates new CD4 cells. However, if left untreated, the virus will continue to replicate and destroy CD4 cells and the immune system is unable to keep up. Once the CD4 cell count gets to be below 200, the patient now has what is called AIDS. This low CD4 count leaves the patient susceptible to developing opportunistic infections. However, opportunistic infections such as *P. jirovecii* pneumonia (PCP), cryptococcal meningitis, and CMV retinitis can all occur in those assumed to be HIV negative because these patients have not been properly checked in the past for the virus. Therefore, if a person has one of these opportunistic infections, regardless of the CD4 cell count, then the person is said to have AIDS.

There are two strains of HIV, HIV-1 and HIV-2. HIV-1 is by far the more common strain, accounting for 95% of infections worldwide. Within HIV-1, there are four groups and within each group, there are different subtypes. HIV-2 is concentrated in West Africa and has a slower progression than HIV-1. Also, the treatments are different. More about treatment of HIV-1 has been studied than what is efficacious for HIV-2.

Causes and Prevention

HIV is a blood-borne pathogen, meaning that it can be transmitted through unprotected sex or intravenous drug use. HIV cannot be transmitted through saliva, so kissing or sharing utensils/drinks cannot transmit the virus. The virus also can be transmitted through sharing cocaine straws among users with damaged nasal mucosa.

As of July 2018, there is no efficacious vaccine for HIV. However, one of the most recent studies is promising. At the time of publication, there is a clinical trial that is in Stage 2b that shows promise in a vaccine that can be made available to the public.

In addition to avoiding IV drug use and cocaine straws, one can use condoms while participating in sexual activity. However, there are many IV drug users who resort to prostitution to pay for drugs and in those scenarios, it's very difficult for these people to use condoms. Recently, a new medication called Truvada by Gilead Sciences was released as is a form of *pre-exposure prophylaxis* (PrEP). It is a combination drug of tenofovir and emtricitabine, two of the three common drugs used to treat HIV. Note that it is not intended to treat HIV, as it will not completely combat the virus, nor is everyone eligible for PrEP. There are weight limitations and medical conditions that can prevent someone from being able to take it, and this is something that should be discussed with a physician. What should also be of note is that Truvada does not replace condom use; it only prevents against HIV-1 infection and not HIV-2 or other sexually transmitted infections.

Symptoms

The symptoms of HIV can vary depending on the stage of the infection. In the early stages, the patient can develop with is known as *Acute Retroviral Syndrome* (ARS). ARS is defined as a collection of symptoms such as fever, lethargy, muscle pain, headache, and sore throat. It is commonly misdiagnosed as a flu or other viral type illness. Unfortunately, less than half of people infected with HIV do not present with these symptoms upon infection and those who are symptomatic do not attribute this to an acute HIV infection. Because of this, patients do not go and get tested for their status and could potentially continue to spread the virus to others.

After this stage, a person ends up in an asymptomatic stage and even if a patient gets tested, there is a time frame called the "window period". During the window period, a person who is infected with HIV can show up as HIV negative. This is because the immune system is still healthy enough to create antibodies to the virus and the HIV antibodies are attached to the virus, creating complexes. As there are no free antibodies to be detected, the person comes up as being a false seronegative.

As stated earlier, AIDS is the latter stage of HIV infection and is defined by either the presence of an AIDS-defining illness (opportunistic infections) or a CD4 count below 200. By the time a person reaches this stage, which can take up to 10 to 15 years, the immune system is unable to keep with the replication of the virus and the virus ends up destroying CD4 cells faster than they could be replaced. The opportunistic infections are now present, as well as more frequent non-opportunistic infections.

SCREENING AND DIAGNOSIS

Four rapid HIV tests are available. Each has received marketing approval by the US Food and Drug Administration. These tests are OraQuick Advance Rapid HIV-1/2 Antibody Test, manufactured by OraSure Technologies; Reveal G2 Rapid HIV-1 Antibody Test by MedMira; Uni-Gold Recombigen HIV Test, made by Trinity BioTech; and Multispot HIV-1/HIV-2 Rapid Test by Bio-Rad Laboratories. Each of these tests is an HIV enzyme immunoassay (EIA), and each is considered a screening test. Also, each test mandates additional confirmatory tests if the results are positive.

The basis of these tests is the ability to detect anti-HIV antibodies in body fluids. Antibodies are products of the immune system that are produced in response to exposure to a virus and its component proteins. Antigens, or proteins, from the virus are embedded in or affixed to a filter. Because antibodies generated after exposure to HIV bind specifically to the viral proteins, antibodies in a person's body fluids will bind to the filter exactly where the protein in the test kit was placed. To determine if antibodies from the sample are present on the filter, a second antibody from the test kit is added.

The secondary antibody specifically binds to the person's antibodies. When an exposed person takes the test, the secondary antibody binds and creates a complex. The complex is created only when the person has anti-HIV antibodies in his or her fluids.

Detection of the complex on the filter paper is possible because the secondary antibodies in the test kit come with an enzyme linked to them. This enzyme catalyzes a reaction that results in a color change. The color is detected by visual inspection of the filter paper. Because these kits detect the presence of antibody in the person's fluids and not the virus, a positive result requires additional testing.

The polymerase chain reaction works by detecting the genetic material unique to the HIV virus. This assay works by adding the necessary components for the replication of genetic material to the sample. If HIV genetic material is present, it will be multiplied to generate quantities that can be detected by a color-forming reaction not unlike the EIA tests.

Needle Sharing

Intravenous (IV) drug users often share needles (syringes), cookers, and other injection paraphernalia. This practice is associated with the injection of illicit substances, most commonly heroin or other opiates. Users also inject a combination of heroin and cocaine (speedball), cocaine by itself, or any other drug. Needle sharing can lead to blood-borne diseases such as hepatitis and human immunodeficiency virus (HIV) infection.

Needles are shared among users mainly because of a scarcity of clean needles. Needle exchange programs have been implemented in some US states and in some countries outside the United States, but they are controversial. Some persons believe the programs simply enable drug misuse; program advocates disagree, arguing that the availability of clean needles reduces potential harm among users and helps to connect users with treatment programs. Needle exchange programs also distribute needle-cleaning kits among IV-drug users. These kits include materials that help to kill any viruses the needles might contain.

TREATMENT AND THERAPY

Highly active antiretroviral therapy (HAART) is the recommended treatment for HIV, where the goal is to bring the viral load to an undetectable level and consequently increase the CD4 cell count. HAART is administered as a combination of three or more anti-HIV medications from a minimum of two different classes. Nucleoside reverse transcriptase inhibitors comprise one class of anti-HIV drug. These drugs inhibit the HIV enzyme reverse transcriptase by means of blockage with a nucleoside. Non-nucleoside reverse transcriptase inhibitors inhibit the same viral enzyme through means other than the addition of nucleosides. Protease inhibitors block another key enzyme from the virus.

Three additional classes of anti-HIV drugs block functions critical to the infection process. They are entry inhibitors, fusion inhibitors, and integrase inhibitors. Because each class of medications blocks the virus in a different way, the combination of several medications increases the chances of preventing viral replication and decreases the chance that the virus will survive long enough to mutate into a resistant form. Some of the drugs are available as a combination pill of two or more different anti-HIV medications from one or more classes.

There are two preferred regimens of medications at the time of publication: bictegravir-emtricitabine-tenofovir alafenamide (brand name Biktarvy) and do-lutegravir plus tenofovir alafenamide/emtricitabine. The first drug combination mentioned is a single pill and is preferred in terms of compliance. The second drug combination mentioned are two pills, but it has a more studied side effect profile.

SYRINGE SERVICES PROGRAMS

Intravenous (IV) drug users often share needles (syringes), cookers, and other injection paraphernalia. This practice is associated with the injection of illicit substances, most commonly heroin or other opiates. Users also inject a combination of heroin and cocaine (speedball), cocaine by itself, or any other drug. Needle sharing can lead to blood-borne diseases such as hepatitis and human immunodeficiency virus (HIV) infection.

Needles are shared among users mainly because of a scarcity of clean needles. *Syringe Services Programs (SSPs)* have been implemented in some US states and in some countries outside the United States, but they are controversial. Some persons believe the programs simply enable drug misuse; program advocates disagree, arguing that the availability of clean needles reduces potential harm among users and helps to connect users with treatment programs. SSPs are programs that provide sterile needles and syringes for free and allow an IV drug user to dispose of used needles and syringes in a safe manner. These kits include materials that help to kill any viruses the needles might contain. They also provide information on HIV and Hepatitis C (another common virus caused through IV drug use and sex), along with access to treatment, counseling, and other social services.

Kimberly A. Napoli, MS;
Updated by Steven Shanab, MD, MBA
and Vijay Rajput, MD, FACP, SFHM

FOR FURTHER INFORMATION

Avert. (23, January 2018). *HIV Strains and Types.* Retrieved from Avert Global Information and Education on HIV and AIDS: https://www.avert.org/professionals/hiv-science/types-strains

Barouch, D. H. (2018, July 6). *Evaluation of a mosaic HIV-1 vaccine in a multicentre, randomised, double-blind, placebo-controlled, phase 1/2a clinical trial (APPROACH) and in rhesus monkeys (NHP 13-19).* Retrieved from The Lancet: https://www.thelancet.com/journals/lancet/article/PIIS0140-6736(18)31364-3/fulltext

CDC. (2017, May 30). *Centers for Disease Control and Prevention.* Retrieved from Opportunistic Infection: https://www.cdc.gov/hiv/basics/livingwithhiv/opportunisticinfections.html

CDC. (2018, April 19). *Centers for Diseae Control and Prevention.* Retrieved from Syringe Services Programs: https://www.cdc.gov/hiv/risk/ssps.html

CDC. (2018, March 16). *Centers for Disease Control and Prevention.* Retrieved from About HIV/AIDS: https://www.cdc.gov/hiv/basics/whatishiv.html

CDC. (2018, May 15). *Centers for Disease Control and Prevention.* Retrieved from Pre-Exposure Prophylaxis: https://www.cdc.gov/hiv/risk/prep/index.html

NIH. (2018, June 20). *AIDS Info.* Retrieved from CD4 T Lymphocyte: https://aidsinfo.nih.gov/understanding-hiv-aids/glossary/113/cd4-t-lymphocyte

NIH. (2018, March 27). *AIDSInfo.* Retrieved from Department of Health and Human Services Adults and Adolescents Antiretroviral Guidelines Panel* Classifies a Fixed-Dose Combination Product of Bictegravir/Tenofovir Alafenamide/Emtricitabine as One of the Recommended Initial Regimens for Most People with : https://aidsinfo.nih.gov/news/2044/adult-arv-panel-classifies-bic-taf-ftc-as-recommended-initial-regimen-for-hiv

Peter A. Leone, M. (2010). *NC Department of Health and Human Services.* Retrieved from Acute HIV Syndrome: http://epi.publichealth.nc.gov/cd/lhds/manuals/std/training/2010/PeterLeone3.pdf

Ruiz, Pedro, Eric C. Strain, and John G. Langrod. "HIV Infections and AIDS." *The Substance Abuse Handbook.* Philadelphia: Wolters, 2007. Print.

Tortora, Gerard J., Berdell R. Funke, and Christine L. Case. *Microbiology: An Introduction.* 11th ed. New York: Pearson, 2012. Print.

See also: Heroin; Intravenous drug use and blood-borne diseases; Substance misuse

Hoarding

CATEGORY: Psychological issues and behaviors

DEFINITION: Hoarding involves the compulsive acquisition and accumulation of objects, animals, and trash and other debris. The hoarder, who often has another mental illness such as depression, is unable or unwilling to discard items, frequently resulting in health and safety hazards to those who reside in or visit the dwelling.

CAUSES AND SYMPTOMS

The precise cause of hoarding is not known and doubtless varies, although common denominators among hoarders do exist. Stressful life events and social isolation both appear to contribute. Most have problems with decision-making, perfectionism, categorical organization, and risk assessment. Many people with hoarding disorder buy compulsively. They may collect items purchased years earlier that remain unused in the original wrapping. Hoarders may vaguely anticipate future need for the item or keep items for remembrance. When the hoarder must discard items she tends to feel a terrible loss, regardless of the items' objective worth or value.

Between two and five percent of the US population is estimated to have hoarding disorder, which affects both sexes equally. For diagnosis to be confirmed, hoarding behavior must either cause distress to the individual or impair his ability to function. Symptoms of the disorder include persistent difficulty discarding or giving away that which is hoarded; these problems arise because the person feels a need to retain the items and anticipates anguish at their loss. Eventually, accumulations interfere with normal use of the living space. Hoarding may be comorbid with OCD, clinical depression, attention-deficit disorder, psychosis, or other disorders.

Animal hoarding may be a symptom of larger issues. Over 70% of animal hoarders in one study were women, with about half of participants hoarding both animals and objects. The hoarder may feel she has a special ability to care for and empathize with her animals despite overcrowding and lack of care. People who hoard animals may also have combative attitudes toward authorities, and violence is a potential hazard of enforcement.

RISK FACTORS

Many begin exhibiting signs of hoarding disorder during adolescence. Although symptoms may begin early, they tend become more entrenched with age. Three times as many over the age of 55 hoard than people aged 34 to 44. People with hoarding disorder often share the trait with other family members. Stressful events such as divorce or death can cause or worsen hoarding symptoms. Symptoms of hoarding disorder have occurred in people after brain injuries. It was once thought that hoarding might be a subset of obsessive-compulsive disorder (OCD). However, hoarding disorder is linked to certain discrete anomalies of brain function not seen in people with OCD or, for that matter, other disorders.

EFFECTS OF HOARDING

Severe hoarding is bound to cause problems in relationships at home and work. Assorted items such as newspapers, magazines, and articles of clothing may line walls in stacks reaching the ceiling, limiting access to whole sections of the residence and threatening collapse. Years of accumulation lead to fire, health, and safety concerns.

Family members who don't share the disorder are often embarrassed by the chaos created by hoarding and may even cut off communication with the hoarder. A person with hoarding disorder who is isolated from friends and family may hoard even more obsessively until intervention occurs.

People who hoard animals may tolerate vermin, animal waste, decayed food, and inadequate or absent sanitation procedures that threaten their own health as well as that of their animals. All who live under such conditions face high ammonia levels, insect and rodent infestations, parasitic diseases, and food-related illnesses. The effects on overcrowded, underfed, medically neglected animals legally constitute animal cruelty. Animals that survive such conditions may require extensive rehabilitation, and some will not recover.

TREATMENT

The main goal of treating people who hoard is to change behaviors, particularly the compulsion to hoard but also behaviors that contribute. Oftentimes, this involves changing the relationship a person has with his possessions, which is a long, slow process that can involve discarding items one by one.

Cognitive-behavioral therapy can help hoarders become aware of factors that can foster hoarding. Therapists can help people fully consider the need for and consequence of acquiring an item before purchase. With help from a therapist or a professional organizer, a hoarder can consciously make the choice, for example, to recycle used magazines and newspapers, to sort mail regularly, and to organize important paperwork. A therapist and perhaps medication can also help address the anxiety that the prospect of unloading the hoarded can induce. In cases of comorbid anxiety or depression, medication may reduce negative feelings incurred by the prospect of loss. Although tendencies to hoard will probably never be eliminated, those tendencies can, with help if needed, be controlled.

Difficult to treat successfully, animal hoarding requires extended follow-up care long after the animals have been removed. Although not everyone concurs, some believe that animal hoarding differs sufficiently from 'inanimate' hoarding that it should be classified separately. Animal hoarders may have different motivations, and unlike most object hoarders they tend not to respond to medications effective for people with OCD. In 2013 the DSM's governing body reclassified hoarding in a new chapter titled Obsessive-Compulsive and Related Disorders, with animal hoarding a subtype of hoarding disorder.

Mary Hurd; Updated by Jackie Dial, PhD

FOR FURTHER INFORMATION

Adee, Sally. "Possessed by Possessions." *New Scientist* 221.2962 (2014): 44. *Academic Search Complete.* Web. 28 Oct. 2015.

Arluke, Arnold, and Celeste Killeen. *Inside Animal Hoarding: The Case of Barbara Erickson and Her 552 Dogs.* Lafayette: Purdue UP, 2009. Print.

Bratiotis, Christiana, Cristina Sorrentino Schmalisch, and Gail Steketee. *The Hoarding Handbook: A Guide for Human Service Professionals.* New York: Oxford UP, 2011. Print.

Frost, R. O., G. Patronek, and E. Rosenfield. "Comparison of Object and Animal Hoarding." *Depression and Anxiety* 28.10 (2011): 885–91. Print.

Jabr, Ferris. "Step inside the Real World of Compulsive Hoarders." *Scientific American.* Nature America, 25 Feb. 2013. Web. 29 Oct. 2015.

Neziroglu, Fugen, Jerome Bubrick, and Jose A. Yaryara-Tobias. *Overcoming Compulsive Hoarding: Why You Save and How You Can Stop.* Oakland: New Harbinger, 2004. Print.

Parekh, Ranna, MD (reviewer). "What is Hoarding Disorder?" American Psychiatric Association, July 2017. Web 2018: https://www.psychiatry.org/patients-families/hoarding-disorder/what-is-hoarding-disorder

Price, Michael. "Animal hoarding is its own mental disorder, study argues." *Science* 10.1126 (2017). doi: 10.1126/science.aap9750; web: https://www.sciencemag.org/news/2017/09/animal-hoarding-its-own-mental-disorder-study-argues

Steketee, Gail, and Randy Frost. *Stuff: Compulsive Hoarding and the Meaning of Things.* New York: Mariner, 2011. Print.

See also: Behavioral addictions: Overview; Compulsions; Families and behavioral addictions

The living room of a compulsive hoarder. (Shadwwulf via Wikimedia Commons)

Homelessness and addiction

CATEGORY: Social issues

DEFINITION: Homelessness is the state of not having a stable, adequate place of residence. Homeless persons include those sleeping outdoors and in buildings not intended as housing and persons temporarily dwelling in shelters or other institutions meant to lodge people without permanent housing. Substance use disorder can precipitate and develop from homelessness. Conversely, homelessness is often a consequence of substance use disorder. Those experiencing homelessness have significantly higher rates of substance use disorders and higher mortality rates by drug overdose than national averages.

OVERVIEW

Homelessness is the state of not having a stable, adequate place of residence. Homeless persons include those sleeping outdoors and in buildings not intended as housing and persons temporarily dwelling in shelters or other institutions meant to lodge people without permanent housing. Though homelessness is difficult to measure, the Department of Housing and Urban Development's Annual Homeless Assessment Report estimates that in 2017, about 554,000 people were without a permanent place to sleep on a given night in the United States. About 193,000 of those people were unsheltered, which means that they were living on the streets, with no access to emergency shelters or transitional housing. The total homeless population in the US increased in 2017 for the first time since 2010. From 2016 to 2017, the total number of homeless people in the US increased by 0.7%, but the number of unsheltered homeless grew by 9.4%. The majority of people who experience homelessness are located in urban areas, particularly in places with high cost of living such as California, Oregon and Washington. For example, in Seattle, the unsheltered population grew by 44% over the past few years. In fact, eight of the ten states with the highest rate of homelessness are also among the ten most expensive states by median price of housing.

Substance use disorder can develop from homelessness; conversely, homelessness is often a consequence of substance use disorder. According to the National Healthcare for the Homeless Council, those experiencing homelessness have higher rates of substance use disorders and higher mortality rates by drug overdose than national averages. Additionally, drug overdose is one of the major causes of death among people experiencing homelessness. For example, a study in Boston showed that those experiencing homelessness were nine times more likely to die from an overdose than those who were stably housed.

PREVALENCE AND PATTERNS OF HOMELESSNESS

Though homelessness is difficult to accurately measure, the Department of Housing and Urban Development's Annual Homeless Assessment Report estimates that in 2017, about 554,000 people were without a permanent place to sleep on a given night in the United States. The number of people who face homelessness rose dramatically toward the end of the twentieth century, as the economy deteriorated and budget cuts were made in the areas of housing and social services. Homelessness rose again following the Great Recession from 2007 to 2009. It is now increasing yet again as rents in many cities skyrocket and as drug addiction rates across the nation rise.

In 2017, most people experiencing homelessness were adults without children (67%). 40% of people experiencing homelessness were women. 21% of the yearly homeless population were children. The racial and ethnic makeup of the homeless population reveals a striking disparity, with African Americans being grossly overrepresented. Though African Americans represented only about 12.5 percent of the total US population, they accounted for 41 percent of homeless persons in 2017. Homelessness among Blacks increased 6 percent or 7,299 people in 2017, compared with a 2 percent increase or 2,856 people among Whites. Hispanics are also overrepresented—while they make up about 17.8 percent of the nation's total population, they make up about 22 percent of the homeless. White and Asian Americans are underrepresented among the homeless. Whites make up about 77% of the US population, yet only constitute 47% of the homeless; Asian Americans make up about 6% of the US population, and only constitute about 1% of the homeless. A UCLA study found that about 20 to 40% of homeless youth in the US are LGBTQ, compared to 5 to 10 percent LGBTQ among the overall youth population in the US.

CAUSES OF HOMELESSNESS

Poverty and lack of affordable housing are leading causes of homelessness. Persons who are unemployed or underemployed often cannot afford housing, food, healthcare or education. Low wages and insufficient social welfare benefits often cannot match the rising costs of living, leaving many in debt and unable to pay their bills. Furthermore, any unexpected event such as an illness or an accident may also lead these individuals to homelessness. The decreases in the availability of affordable housing and lack of housing assistance programs, along with the increased number of foreclosures, have led an increasing number of families to homelessness.

Health care, domestic violence, mental illness, and substance use also are related to homelessness. An unexpected illness can lead to job loss, and medical bills can leave individuals and families with an insurmountable debt leading to homelessness. Many women and children are affected by domestic violence, and are often left with the choice of living in an abusive environment or homelessness. Domestic violence shelters often limit the amount of time a woman and her children can stay. In the midst of housing shortage and lack of affordable housing, more and more women lack the resources to secure housing when they leave.

Individuals who suffer from mental illness are at increased risk of homelessness, as they often have difficulty living independently and do not have adequate access to programs and supportive housing options. In addition, substance use disorder can also contribute to and prolong homelessness. In fact, approximately 30 percent of chronically homeless persons suffer from substance use disorder, with alcohol being the commonly used substance.

SUBSTANCE MISUSE AND ADDICTION

Substance use disorder can both precipitate and develop from homelessness. Substance use disorder often causes problems in both an individual's family life as well as work life, which can lead to homelessness, particularly for those with a limited income. Use of alcohol and other drugs can also lead to physical ailments such as seizure disorders and liver diseases, which can precipitate homelessness. For others, homelessness serves as an introduction to substances of misuse, which are often used to cope with the difficulties of being homeless. Rates of misuse and addiction are substantially higher among the homeless than among the general population, and substance misuse often co-occurs with mental illness. In fact, a study in Boston showed that individuals experiencing homelessness were nine times more likely to die from an opioid overdose that those who were stably housed. Reports also show that a high percentage of homeless people are infected with viruses such as HIV (human immunodeficiency virus) due to high risk behaviors such as injection drug use, resulting in high rates of morbidity and mortality compared to the general population.

Being homeless often makes it difficult to engage in proper substance use treatment, as many community health centers and social service agencies do not have the capacity to treat alcohol or drug problems, particularly among mentally ill or homeless clients. Treatment options are severely limited, and these individuals often return to the streets or shelters after short substance use or substance use interventions. A lack of long-term comprehensive care has prompted researchers and advocates to recommend nationwide implementation of integrative housing, treatment, and support programs that address substance misuse and

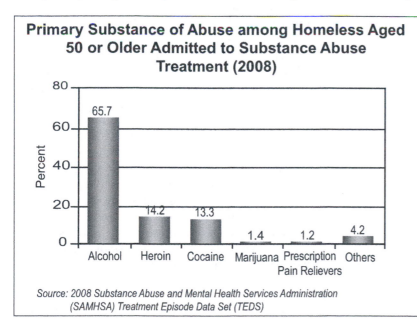

Primary Substance of Abuse among Homeless Aged 50 or Older Admitted to Substance Abuse Treatment (2008)

Source: 2008 Substance Abuse and Mental Health Services Administration (SAMHSA) Treatment Episode Data Set (TEDS)

addiction, as well as, other problems that result from homelessness and mental illness.

Tammy Arford, MA; Updated by Shiliang Alice Cao, BA

FOR FURTHER INFORMATION

Benedict, Kizley. "Estimating the Number of Homeless in America." *The DataFace*, 20 July 2018, thedataface.com/2018/01/public-health/americanhomelessness.

Bourgois, Philippe, and Jeff Schonberg. *Righteous Dopefiend.* Berkeley: U California P, 2010. Print.

"Current Statistics on the Prevalence and Characteristics of People Experiencing Homelessness in the United States." *SAMHSA.* Substance Abuse and Mental Health Services Administration, July 2011. Web. 5 Nov. 2015. PDF file.

Durso, L.E., & Gates, G.J. (2012). Serving Our Youth: Findings from a National Survey of Service Providers Working with Lesbian, Gay, Bisexual, and Transgender Youth who are Homeless or At Risk of Becoming Homeless. Los Angeles: The Williams Institute with True Colors Fund and The Palette Fund.

Hopper, Kim. *Reckoning with Homelessness.* Ithaca: Cornell UP, 2009. Print.

Kusmer, Kenneth L. *Down and Out, On the Road: The Homeless in American History.* New York: Oxford UP, 2002. Print.

Levinson, David, ed. *Encyclopedia of Homelessness.* Thousand Oaks: Sage, 2007. Print.

Office of Community Planning and Development. *The 2016 Annual Homeless Assessment Report (AHAR) to Congress.* US Dept. of Housing and Urban Development, Nov. 2016, /www.hudexchange.info/resources/documents/2016-AHAR-Part-1.pdf. Accessed 6 Oct. 2017.

Pauly, Bernadette Bernie, et al. "Housing and Harm Reduction: What Is the Role of Harm Reduction in Addressing Homelessness?" *International Journal of Drug Policy* 24.4 (2013): 284–90. Print.

Rayburn, Rachel L. "Understanding Homelessness, Mental Health and Substance Abuse through a Mixed-Methods Longitudinal Approach." *Health Sociology Review* 22.4 (2013): 389–99. Print.

Schutt, Russell K., and Stephen M. Goldfinger. *Homelessness, Housing, and Mental Illness.* Cambridge: Harvard UP, 2011. Print.

Tsemberis, Sam J. *Housing First: The Pathways Model to End Homelessness for People with Mental Illness and Addiction.* Center City: Hazelden, 2010. Print.

"Substance Abuse." *USICH.* United States Interagency Council on Homelessness, 2013. Web. 4 Nov. 2015.

"Substance Abuse and Homelessness." *National Coalition for the Homeless,* July 2009, www.nationalhomeless.org/factsheets/addiction.pdf.

Yıldırım, Neşide, and Kazım Yıldırım. "Homelessness with Social Change." *Mediterranean Journal of Social Sciences* 5.22 (2014): 418. Print.

See also: Domestic violence and addiction; Mental illness; Poverty and substance misuse; Socio-economic status and addiction

---

Household chemicals of misuse

CATEGORY: Substance misuse

DEFINITION: Household chemicals of misuse are commonly found in homes as cleansers, aerosols, beauty products, and adhesives. These substances are inhaled to reach an altered state of consciousness, or high. When used in this manner, household chemicals can produce a number of permanent, negative side effects, including death.

STATUS: Legal to obtain in the United States, some sales to minors are restricted

CLASSIFICATION: Uncontrolled substances

SOURCES: Household chemicals of misuse include more than one thousand products: hairspray, fabric and room deodorant sprays, nail polish, cough syrup, tub and tile cleaner, correction fluid, felt-tip marker fluid, compressed-air computer dusters, drain cleaner, video-machine-head cleaner, air freshener, furniture polish, carpet cleaner, canned whipped cream, cooking spray, static cling spray, glass cleaner, all-purpose cleaner, oven cleaner, ant and roach bait, lighter fluid, spray paint, butane, insect spray, paint thinner, gasoline, adhesive, wood stain, motor oil, windshield washer fluid, house paint, antifreeze, freon, pesticide, weed killer, and pool chemicals.

TRANSMISSION ROUTE: Inhalation

History of Misuse

The main users of common household products are adolescents because these products are mostly inexpensive and readily accessible. Misuse of these chemicals by teens and preteens has steadily increased since the 1980s. Misuse of these chemicals by teens and preteens has steadily increased since the 1980s. In the USA in 2016, the National Survey on Drug Use and Health found 600,000 people over the age of 12 admitting to the current use of inhalants of some type.

A National Household Survey on Drug Abuse found that one in five persons reported having misused common household goods one or more times in their lives. Different products tend to be misused at different ages. Among children age twelve to fifteen years, the most commonly misused inhalants are glue, shoe polish, spray paint, gasoline, and lighter fluid. Among children age sixteen or seventeen years, the most commonly misused product is nitrous oxide, which is found in whipped cream cans.

Effects and Potential Risks

Inhalants (except nitrites) act by producing short-term effects similar to barbiturates or anesthetics, which inhibit nervous system functioning. Breathable household chemicals are inhaled by dousing a cloth or bag with the substance and holding it up to the nose and mouth, or by directly spraying the chemicals into the nose or inhaling the vapors to produce a short-term high. This method is known as sniffing, huffing, bagging, or dusting. Because this type of high lasts a few minutes only, users may inhale the chemical again and again to maintain the high.

Inhalants are classified into four categories: solvents (fluids that vaporize at room temperature), gases (butane, propane, whipped cream cans, refrigerants), and aerosols (spray paint, hairspray. Initial inhalation introduces the substance into the brain and nervous system and produces a stimulating effect, whereas ongoing inhalation may produce a loss of inhibition and control. Because the high of inhalants resembles alcohol intoxication, users may exhibit such symptoms as trouble speaking or walking, dizziness, agitation, increased heart rate, hallucinations, delusions, vomiting, muscle weakness, depression, lightheadedness, confusion, and even loss of consciousness.

Chronic inhalant users tend to exhibit such external signs as loss of appetite, facial rashes and blisters, runny nose, coughing, dilated pupils, extremely bad breath, glassy or glazed eyes, chemical smells, signs of paint or other products on face or fingers, headaches, slurred speech, nosebleeds, and reddened eyes. The chemicals in inhalants cause intoxication by inducing hypoxia (decreased oxygen to the brain), which may lead to brain damage and damage to the heart, liver, lungs, and kidneys. The effects of hypoxia vary according to which regions of the brain are damaged.

There are many permanent effects that may be caused by the misuse of inhalants. Some of these include hearing loss, limb spasms, bone marrow damage, brain damage (problem-solving, planning, memory loss, inability to learn new things), loss of sense of smell or hearing. White matter degeneration has been demonstrated in chronic use and may be permanent, leading to long-term cognitive dysfunction. Equally serious but potentially reversible effects include heart arrhythmia, liver and kidney damage, and reduced muscle tone and strength.

Inhalant use can lead to fatal cardiac arrhythmia. This effect is known as sudden sniffing death syndrome and can occur in otherwise healthy persons. This syndrome is mainly associated with aerosols and gases. Inhalants also may cause death by suffocation by displacing oxygen in the lungs. Bagging, or using an inhalant in an enclosed area, increases the chances of suffocation, which is why proper ventilation for the legitimate uses of the products is essential. In addition, death may be caused by the aspiration of vomit. Emergency care includes rapid activation of the emergency response system and contacting local poison control centers.

Eugenia M. Valentine PhD;
Updated by Denis Folan, DO

For Further Information

Del Bigio, Marc R. "Toluene Abuse and White Matter Degeneration." *Neuropathology of Drug Addictions and Substance Misuse.* 2016. 1004-1011.

Foden, Charles R., Jack L. Weddell. *Household Chemicals and Emergency First Aid.* Boca Raton, FL: Lewis, 1993. This manual covers 386 household chemicals, discusses the effects of mixing with other chemicals, and details emergency first aid treatment.

Guo, Ting-Jang. "A rare but serious case of toluene-induced sudden sniffing death." *Journal of Acute Medicine* 5.4 (2015): 109-111.

Butane

Butane is a flammable aliphatic hydrocarbon that is a colorless gas at room temperature and at atmospheric pressure. Butane occurs in natural gas and in the atmosphere. It is sold as a bottled fuel for cooking and camping, and it is used as a fuel in cigarette lighters, as a propellant in hair sprays and deodorants, and as a refrigerant in refrigerators and freezers. It was classified as an inhalant drug in 1987.

When used as an inhalant, butane's chemical vapors can produce mind-altering effects. Sniffing, huffing, or spraying of butane allows the gas to enter through the pulmonary system, where it immediately enters the bloodstream. Rapidly absorbed by the body, and being lipid soluble, butane can be trapped in the body's fat cells and continue to be released to the bloodstream in time. If a person sniffs highly concentrated amounts of butane, he or she can die. Sudden sniffing death, as it is called, can result from heart failure within a few minutes.

In 1999, a US law banned the sale of butane lighter-fuel to anyone under the age of eighteen years. By 2000, butane was the most commonly misused volatile substance in the United Kingdom, where it accounted for 52 percent of all solvent-related deaths. Since 2005, butane use has decreased worldwide.

Perron, Brian E., and Matthew O. Howard. "Adolescent Inhalant Use, Abuse, and Dependence." *Addiction* 104 (2009): 1185–92. Print. Provides the demographics and psychological profiles of inhalant users. Personal histories include high levels of trauma, suicidal ideation, distress, antisocial behavior, and other substance-related problems.

Marsolek, Melinda R., Nicole C. White, Toby L. Litovitz. "Inhalant Abuse: Monitoring Trends by Using Poison Control Data, 1993–2008" *Pediatrics* (2010), peds.2009-2080; DOI: 10.1542/peds.2009-2080

Substance Abuse and Mental Health Services Administration. (2017). "Key substance use and mental health indicators in the United States: Results from the 2016 National Survey on Drug Use and Health (HHS Publication No. SMA 17-5044, NSDUH Series H-52)." Rockville, MD: Center for Behavioral Health Statistics and Quality, Substance Abuse, and Mental Health Services Administration. Retrieved from https://www.samhsa.gov/data/

Tormoehlen, L. M., K. J. Tekulve, and K. A. Nanagas. "Hydrocarbon toxicity: a review." *Clinical Toxicology* 52.5 (2014): 479-489.

Winter, Ruth. *A Consumer's Dictionary of Household, Yard, and Office Chemicals: Complete Information about Harmful and Desirable Chemicals Found in Everyday Home Products, Yard Poisons, and Office Polluters.* Lincoln, NE: iUniverse, 2007. A layperson's guide to the ingredients printed on the labels of certain common products. Listings are cross-indexed by subject and synonym. A directory lists poison control centers and regional offices of the US Environmental Protection Agency.

See also: Cough and cold medications; Dextromethorphan; Gasoline; Inhalants misuse; Solvents

Hydrocodone

CATEGORY: Substances
ALSO KNOWN AS: Dihydrocodeinone; Lortab; Vicodin
DEFINITION: Hydrocodone is the most frequently prescribed opiate (narcotic) in the United States. It is an antitussive (cough suppressant) and analgesic (pain relief) agent.
STATUS: Legal
CLASSIFICATION: Schedule II controlled substances
SOURCE: Semisynthetic with either of two naturally occurring opiates: codeine and thebaine
TRANSMISSION ROUTE: Hydrocodone comes as a tablet, a capsule, a syrup, a solution (clear liquid), an extended-release (long-acting) capsule, and an extended-release (long-acting) suspension (liquid) to take by mouth. Generally misused orally, often in combination with alcohol, but hydrocodone tablets can also be crushed and inhaled.

HISTORY OF USE

Hydrocodone was first synthesized in Germany in 1920 by Carl Mannich and Helene Löwenheim. The first report of euphoria and habituation was published in 1923, and the first report of dependence and addiction was published in 1961. Hydrocodone was approved by the US Food and Drug Administration in 1943 for sale in the United States.

Hydrocodone relieves pain by changing the way the brain and nervous system respond to pain, that

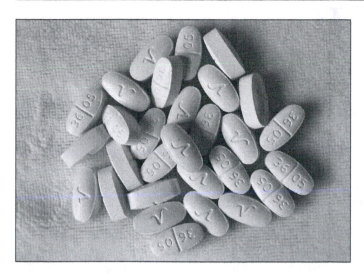

Hydrocodone tablets. (via Wikimedia Commons)

is, by binding to the opioid receptor sites in the brain and spinal cord. It is not usually produced illegally; diverted pharmaceuticals are the primary source for misuse. Misuse comes in the form of fraudulent call-in prescriptions, altered prescriptions, theft, and illicit purchases online. Diversion and misuse have been increasing. In 2008, hydrocodone was the most frequently encountered opioid in drug evidence submitted to state and local forensics laboratories, as reported by the National Forensic Laboratory Information System.

EFFECTS AND POTENTIAL RISKS

Short-term effects are improvement of mood, reduction of pain, euphoria, sedation, light-headedness, and changes in focus and attention. Side effects include nausea, vomiting, constipation, anxiety, dry throat, rash, difficulty urinating, irregular breathing, and chest tightness. When inhaled, burning in nose and sinuses usually occurs. A newborn of a woman who was taking the medication during pregnancy may exhibit breathing problems or withdrawal symptoms.

Symptoms of overdose include cold and clammy skin, circulatory collapse, stupor, coma, depression, respiratory depression, cardiac arrest, and death. Mixing hydrocodone with other substances, including alcohol, can cause severe physical problems or death.

Misuse of hydrocodone is associated with tolerance, dependence, and addiction. There is no ceiling dose for hydrocodone in users tolerant to its effects. Acetaminophen carries the risk of liver toxicity with high, acute doses (of around 4,000 mg per day).

Stephanie Eckenrode BA, LLB;
Updated by Marianne Moss Madsen, MS, BCND

FOR FURTHER INFORMATION

Amer. Soc. of Health-System Pharmacists. "Hydrocodone." *MedlinePlus.* US Natl. Lib. of Medicine, 15 March 2018.

Amer. Soc. of Addiction Medicine. "Opioid Addiction, 2016 Facts and Figures." https://www.asam.org/docs/default-source/advocacy/opioid-addiction-disease-facts-figures.pdf

McCoy, Krisha. "Opioid Addiction." Ed. Michael Woods. *Health Library.* EBSCO, Jan. 2014. Web. 27 Oct. 2015.

See also: Narcotics misuse; Opioid misuse; Painkiller misuse; Vicodin and Norco

I

Impulse control disorders

CATEGORY: Psychological issues and behaviors

DEFINITION: Impulse control disorders (ICDs) comprise a specific group of diagnoses categorized in the fifth edition of the American Psychiatric Association's *Diagnostic and Statistical Manual of Mental Disorders* (*DSM-5*) under the broader chapter on disruptive, impulse control, and conduct disorders. These disorders include pyromania, kleptomania, and intermittent explosive disorder. The *DSM* category "not elsewhere classified" allows the inclusion of rare disorders that share ICD criteria but that do not fit easily into one of the main diagnoses.

CHARACTERIZATION OF IMPULSE CONTROL DISORDERS

Impulse control disorders (ICDs) are grouped based on the concept of impulsivity. In this context, impulsivity is an urge to engage in a specific behavior that overwhelms normal inhibitions. The behavior is unplanned and is prompted by a stimulus that induces internal tension; the behavior relieves the tension and may bestow a sensation of pleasure. Affected persons are unable to resist the impulse because the usual inhibitions that limit harmful behavior are insufficient or absent.

A key component of an ICD is the disregard for consequences of the behavior, whether by the person with the disorder or by others. For some ICDs, the behavior is by definition a criminal act. The extent of research into individual ICDs varies, and new research has led to significant changes in classification. For example, both compulsive gambling and trichotillomania were considered ICDs under DSM-4 before being reclassified in DSM-5. Some also consider disorders such as sexual compulsion, compulsive shopping, and various forms of Internet addiction to be ICDs.

Pyromania. The media and public often misuse the term *pyromania* to apply to any unlawful fire setting. For a behavior to qualify for a diagnosis of pyromania, several DSM criteria must be met. Early and excessive interest or fascination with fire is one prerequisite. The act of fire setting must be deliberate, repetitive, and without seeming motivation. The fire itself is the reward.

In several studies of arsonists, one-half or more are under the influence of alcohol when they start fires, which precludes the pyromania diagnosis. The disorder as strictly defined, therefore, is extremely rare.

Kleptomania. Kleptomania is the uncontrollable impulse to steal objects that have no personal use. The person with kleptomania disregards the likelihood of incurring legal consequences. Kleptomania should not be confused with shoplifting, in which items are stolen for personal use or monetary gain.

The onset of kleptomania occurs late in adolescence or in early adulthood; more women than men are affected. Impairment in social and occupational functioning is usually significant, and kleptomania appears to have a familial element. First-degree relatives of those affected are more likely than comparison groups to have an alcohol-use problem or other psychiatric disorder.

Intermittent Explosive Disorder. Recently reported and least known of the ICDs, intermittent explosive disorder is thought to be more common than has been recognized; one estimate of prevalence in the adult population is 7 to 11 percent. Features of this disorder are unpredictable, recurrent outbursts of extreme anger, frequently accompanied by unprovoked physical violence. Seemingly normal behavior follows. These episodes commonly result in injuries and property damage. Those affected average forty-three lifetime attacks.

The average onset of intermittent explosive disorder is about fourteen years of age, although most cases may occur in late adolescence to the late twenties. The frequency is higher among men than women.

318

QUESTIONS ABOUT THE ICD DIAGNOSIS

Impulsivity is a complex trait that is not limited to ICDs; rather, it cuts across a spectrum of psychiatric disorders. Many authors have noted the similarity between ICDs and substance use disorders. The occurrence of one or another ICD together with alcohol misuse or drug dependence is common, and much genetic and neurobiologic evidence links ICDs to disorders of substance misuse. According to estimates, ICDs as a group account for as much as 10 percent of psychiatric diagnoses.

For persons who investigate or treat ICDs, the category as listed in the DSM may become confining and questionable. Several heterogeneous behaviors with impulsivity as a hallmark have been proposed for inclusion. These behaviors include compulsive purchasing (items are paid for, as distinguished from kleptomania and shoplifting), compulsive Internet use, compulsive sexual behavior, and compulsive skin-picking and nail-biting. DSM-5 attempted to take such distinctions into account by creating more specific classifications

Compulsions that characterize some ICDs have a strong resemblance to other disorders marked by compulsive behavior, notably obsessive-compulsive disorder (OCD) and related disorders. Although compulsive and impulsive disorders have been considered distinctive traits, the behaviors overlap and the theoretical differences are blurring. Behavioral disinhibition marks both impulsive and compulsive disorders.

Shared neurologic and genetic mechanisms are suggested by the occurrence of impulsive and compulsive behaviors in the same person and by their clustering in first-degree family members. Research into the neurobiology of the brain is increasingly finding links among all these disorders.

DRUG-INDUCED ICDS

Dopamine is a neurotransmitter that takes part in regulating behavior linked to pleasure and rewards. When dopaminergic systems fail to work normally, they contribute to ICDs and addiction.

The importance of dopamine to impulse-related disorders is well illustrated by Parkinson's disease, which primarily results from a massive loss of dopaminergic nerve cells in a midbrain structure that is a major player in reward-seeking and addiction. The relevance of Parkinson's disease to ICDs lies in a standard therapy for the disease, which is to replace the lost neurons with dopamine agonists—drugs that mimic the action of dopamine.

Several disorders related to impulsivity and pleasure-seeking have been reported in a significant proportion of persons with Parkinson's disease who have been treated with dopamine agonists. Pathologic gambling, hypersexuality, compulsive shopping, and binge eating are the most frequent behaviors in this subgroup of otherwise low-risk adults. Restless leg syndrome (RLS) is another neurologic disorder that has been treated with dopamine agonists. In one group of one hundred persons undergoing treatment for RLS, 17 percent had one or another ICD.

Overstimulation of the dopaminergic system has been proposed to explain the development of ICDs in these persons; enhanced dopamine release in the brain has been shown with neuroimaging. An addiction to dopamine replacement therapy develops in some persons with Parkinson's disease, who self-administer excessive doses of their prescribed dopamine agonists.

TREATMENT

The treatment for many impulse control disorders is often composed of seven steps:

1. Conduct an assessment and provide education
2. Develop stress reduction skills
3. Challenge distressing thoughts
4. Prevent damaging behaviors
5. Develop emotion regulation and distress tolerance skills
6. Develop problem-specific coping skills
7. Prevent relapse

Medications can play an important role in both treating and preventing the development of an impulse control disorder. A variety of pharmacologic agents are being applied to ICDs, but research has been limited and general guidelines are not established. Reports of treatment in the medical and psychiatric literature are often based on a single case or a small patient group.

Studies testing pharmacologic treatments are generally directed to a single disorder, and more than one author has suggested that strategies should focus on targeting underlying mechanisms common to several ICDs. An important consideration that will influence treatment choice is the frequent presence of comorbid psychiatric disorders—mood, substance misuse, and personality disorders—in many persons with an ICD.

In general, treatment has moved away from psychodynamic approaches (talk therapy). Most frequently prescribed are cognitive-behavioral therapy and selective serotonin reuptake inhibitors (SSRIs), which are antidepressants. Treatment with other drug classes is being explored, and mixed success has been reported with opioid antagonists, anticonvulsants, mood stabilizers, atypical antipsychotics, and antidepressants other than SSRIs. Gold-standard, randomized, double-blind, placebo-controlled trials are rare for ICDs, although a few have been reported for pathologic gambling. Some individuals benefit from a type of therapy known as "habit reversal." Habit reversal was developed in the 1970s to treat stammering, tics and skin picking. The theory is based on helping the person identify the action when it is occurring and then learn to replace that action with something less harmful. Habit reversal provides an individual with something they can do when feeling compelled to engage in the destructive impulse. If the person pulls their hair, they might be asked to clench their fists instead. If one were to pick at their skin, they might learn to close their eyes until the feeling passes. Sometimes breathing exercises can help relax the body, soothe tense muscles and control the impulsive urges.

Twelve-step, self-help groups and various therapies usually aimed at substance-use disorders have been applied to ICDs, also with varying results. High dropout rates limit the effectiveness of the twelve-step programs.

Judith Weinblatt, MA, MS; Updated by Jeffrey Larson

FOR FURTHER INFORMATION

American Psychiatric Association. *Highlights of Changes from DSM-IV-TR to DSM-5.* American Psychiatric Assn., 2013. *dsm5.org.* Web. 30 Oct. 2015'

Chattopadhyay, K.). "The genetic factors influencing the development of trichotillomania." *J Genet,* 91(2), 263. (2012).

Cooper-Kahn, Joyce. *Late, Lost, and Unprepared: A Parents' Guide to Helping Children with Executive Functioning.* Bethesda, MD: Woodbine House, 2008. Print.

Davis, Diane Rae. *Taking Back Your Life: Women and Problem Gambling.* Center City, MN: Hazelden, 2009. Print.

Grant, Jon E., and Suck Won Kim. *Stop Me Because I Can't Stop Myself: Taking Control of Impulsive Behavior.* New York: McGraw-Hill 2003. Print.

Grant, J. E., Odlaug, B. L., Kim, S. W. "Impulse control disorders: clinical characteristics and pharmacological management." *Psychiatric Times,* 24(10), 64-9. (2007).

Kalisiki, Sean Z. "Impulse Control, Impulsivity, and Violence: Clinical Implications." *Psychiatric Times.* UBM Media, 31 Aug. 2015. Web. 30 Oct. 2015.

Karakus, G., Tamam, L. "Impulse control disorder comorbidity among patients with bipolar I disorder." *Compr Psychiatry,* 52(4), 378-85. (2011).

Linden, David J. *The Compass of Pleasure: How Our Brains Make Fatty Foods, Orgasm, Exercise, Marijuana, Generosity, Vodka, Learning, and Gambling Feel So Good.* New York: Viking, 2011. Print.

See also: Behavioral addictions: Overview; Compulsions; Crime and behavioral addictions; Gambling addiction; Kleptomania; Pyromania

Inhalants misuse

CATEGORY: Substance misuse

ALSO KNOWN AS: Bagging; chroming; dusting; glading; huffing; sniffing; snorting

DEFINITION: Inhalants misuse is the repeated inhalation of fumes, vapors, or gases from common household and commercial products despite evident negative effects.

CAUSES

Inhalation of fumes, vapors, or gases leads to the rapid onset of a high that resembles alcohol intoxication. The chemicals in the inhalants are quickly absorbed from the lungs into the bloodstream and from there to the brain and other organs. The initial high lasts for only a few minutes, so most misusers inhale repeatedly over time to maintain a sustained high. Repeated use builds up tolerance, leading to the need for higher and more frequent dosing.

RISK FACTORS

Inhalant products, such as glues, nail polish removers, hairsprays, felt-tip markers, lighter fluids, and spray paints, are readily available in the home and the community. Over one thousand inhalant products can be purchased for relatively low cost and, for the most part, without legal restrictions on purchase or use. State laws within the United States prohibiting the sale of products containing certain inhalants to minors are difficult to enforce. Legal consequences for abusing the few restricted inhalants are minimal.

Most first-time users are preteens or young adolescents who begin by experimenting with friends. Among the youngest users, girls are about as likely as boys to try inhalers. In contrast, among young adults, misuse is twice as common among men as among women. The National Institute on Drug Abuse estimated in 2016 that about 8 percent of all eighth graders had some experience with abusing inhalants and that 10 percent of misusers were younger than age eighteen years when their inhalants misuse began.

SYMPTOMS

The initial, brief high experienced with inhalants misuse is followed by drowsiness, lightheadedness, and agitation. Short-term adverse effects that can develop include headache, numbness and muscle weakness, nausea, and abdominal pain. Hearing loss and visual disturbances, even hallucinations, may occur.

Long-term use may result in weight loss, disorientation, incoordination, irritability, depression, and irreversible damage to the brain, heart, kidneys, liver, and other organs. Even a first-time user is at risk of death. The misuser can develop a rapid and erratic heartbeat, which can lead to cardiac arrest and death. Misuse also can reduce the body's oxygen level, leading to suffocation.

SCREENING AND DIAGNOSIS

Changes in a misuser's appearance and behavior are the primary indicators of misuse. A misuser may have red or runny eyes and nose, spots or sores around the mouth, paint or other products on the face, lips, nose, or fingers, or unusual breath odor or the odor of chemicals on clothing. The misuser may have slurred speech and appear to be dazed or drunk.

Behavioral changes include increased anxiety, excitability, and irritability. The misuser may become belligerent, even violent, with swings between extreme agitation and lethargy. Speech may be slurred. Disciplinary problems or truancy may develop. Extracurricular activities may be dropped in favor of

---

Glue

Like other misused inhalants, including cleaning compounds and petroleum products, many adhesives, including glue, contain a potent blend of chemicals, many of which can be intoxicating when inhaled in sufficient quantity. A common way of misusing adhesives is to squeeze an amount into a plastic bag, hold the bag against the nose and mouth, and then inhale the substance, which is made up of various chemicals; inhaling from a bag also limits oxygen intake and increases the effects of the inhalant.

Although their effects pass quickly, several of these chemicals, including toluene and hexane, affect gait and balance, movement, the brain's speech centers, and higher executive functions. In turn, these effects can lead to increased aggression or euphoria.

Many of these effects are augmented by low oxygen levels in the brain, leading to increased loss of balance and coordination and poor decision making. US government studies conducted in the early twenty-first century have shown an increase in inhalant misuse among older adolescents and young adults.

---

socializing with friends or staying home. The misuser may develop a new set of friends or become a loner. Conflict with siblings and parents may increase.

No test, such as urinalysis, will detect inhalants misuse. The user has to be confronted and admit to the problem.

TREATMENT AND THERAPY

For most misusers, treatment is community-based and focuses on behavioral changes. One should listen to what a misuser has to say and remain calm and nonjudgmental. This may provide clues to underlying problems, such as peer pressure or problems at home, which can be resolved or redirected. One should focus on the serious health risks of inhalants misuse, not on such behavior being "bad," and should redirect a misuser to constructive, safe, and healthy activities.

A frequent or relapsing misuser will require professional help to identify and address underlying causes for the abuse and any concomitant physical or psychological problems. An initial step is a medical examination to determine if inhalants misuse has caused

Brittany Roberts, sophomore, reads another teenager's tragic huffing experience to fellow high school students. The Consolidated Substance Abuse Counsel Center held a brief on misuse of inhalants. (US Department of Defense via Wikimedia Commons)

organ damage. Neurologic, psychological, and cognitive assessments should be part of the initial examination. Family stability, structure, and dynamics may contribute to the misuser's behavior. An effort should be made to obtain constructive participation in treatment by the misuser's family.

Few treatment centers address inhalants misuse. Detoxification may take up to thirty or forty days because inhaled chemicals stored in fatty tissue take a long time to break down and be flushed from the body.

During withdrawal, the misuser may experience headaches, nausea, excessive sweating and chills, tremors, muscle cramps, hallucinations, and even delirium. Relapse is common among heavy misusers, especially if underlying behavioral problems are not addressed.

PREVENTION

Children should be informed about the dangers of experimenting with inhalants, preferably before they try them. Inhalants misuse can be the gateway to further substance abuse. Parents, teachers, and other adults involved with children and young adolescents should know and be on guard for warning signs, including behavior changes, and should be prepared to discuss the dangers of inhalants misuse with the young person.

Parents should be aware of what inhalant products are in the home and how they can be used and stored so the risk of misuse is minimized. Similarly, school personnel should assess the use and storage of inhalant products in schools. Programs such as the Alliance for Consumer Education Inhalant Abuse Prevention Program can help parents, teachers, school administrators, and community leaders.

Ernest Kohlmetz MA

FOR FURTHER INFORMATION

Abadinsky, Howard. *Drug Use and Abuse: A Comprehensive Introduction.* 7th ed. Belmont, CA: Wadsworth, 2011.

Donovan, Dennis M., and G. Alan Marlatt, eds. *Assessment of Addictive Behaviors.* Guilford Publications, 2013.

Julien, Robert M. *A Primer of Drug Actions.* 11th ed. New York: Worth, 2008.

Kuhn, Cynthia, Scott Swartwelder, and Wilkie Wilson. *Buzzed: The Straight Facts about the Most Used and Abused Drugs from Alcohol to Ecstasy.* 3rd ed. New York: W. W. Norton, 2008.

Lowinson, Joyce W., et al., eds. *Substance Abuse: A Comprehensive Textbook.* 4th ed. Philadelphia: Lippincott, 2005.

Nguyen, Jacqueline, Casey O'Brien, and Salena Schapp. "Adolescent Inhalant Use Prevention, Assessment, and Treatment: A Literature Synthesis." *International Journal of Drug Policy*, vol. 31, 2016, pp. 15–24.

See also: Gasoline; Household chemicals of misuse; Solvents

Insurance for addiction treatment

CATEGORY: Treatment

DEFINITION: Insurance is payment for health care services by a third party payer. Health insurance includes private insurance provided by an employer and Medicare, Medicaid, military health insurance, and individual health insurance. Some health insurance also covers inpatient, outpatient, physician, and counselor care for persons with addictions.

HISTORY

Although experts have known for some time that rehabilitation treatment is important for sustained addiction recovery, not until 2008 did health insurers, on a wider scale, begin to cover addiction treatment. Typically, health insurers contract with health care facilities and providers to obtain a discounted reimbursement rate.

Mental health and addiction treatment facilities and providers have been reluctant to contract with health care insurers because they did not want to accept the reduced reimbursement and because many of their patients did not have health insurance covering mental health and addiction treatment. Less than 70 percent of addiction treatment facilities were contracted with public and private insurers. Health insurers, when they did cover addiction services, only covered detoxification. They provided little or nothing for rehabilitation services for the misuser.

A few US states had mandated that health insurers cover addiction treatment. Other states required that health insurers include options for addiction treatment but did not mandate this form of coverage; still other states did not require coverage at all for addiction services. There were exceptions, however. Self-insured employers opted not to cover addiction services, and employers covered by the Employment Retirement Income Security Act of 1974 (ERISA) were exempt from these state requirements.

ERISA is a federal law that sets minimum standards for pensions and health care insurance in private industry, but it does not require pension plans or health care insurance. Many substance misusers were not employed and had no health insurance. This left addiction treatment facilities and providers without any assurance of payment. As a result, addiction treatment facilities and providers frequently required that persons pay in advance for their treatment.

MENTAL HEALTH AND ADDICTION COVERAGE

In 2008, after years of lobbying by mental health advocates, the Mental Health Parity and Addiction Equity Act (MHPAE) was signed into law in the United States. This federal legislation requires that health insurance policies with coverage for mental health and substance misuse treatment include coverage at the same level as that for physical treatment. This means that co-payments, co-insurance, out-of-pocket expenses, office visit and days-of-service limitations, and in-network and out-of-network benefits, must be comparable to those for care for physical ailments.

In addition, this law requires equal mental health and substance misuse treatment coverage for self-funded health plans and for ERISA employers' health plans; exclusions were no longer permitted. However, MHPAE has a large loophole: Health insurers and employers are not required to offer any mental health and addiction coverage.

Upon enactment of MHPAE, the greatest concern among businesses was that the act would increase the cost of health insurance. Few studies have been performed to determine whether this concern is valid. One study utilizing data from federal employees' health plans has been performed to evaluate this change. Federal employees were granted mental health parity in 2001. The study used claims data from 1999 through 2002. The mental health costs before parity were compared with those after parity. The study found little increase in the utilization and costs of mental health and addiction treatment. However, out-of-pocket costs for members were lowered significantly.

Another flaw in the mental health parity law is the way that health insurers validate and pay for coverage. Often, they have special criteria for claims' reimbursement that interfere with payments. For example, a health insurer might require that the mental health or substance misuse patient receive outpatient care before inpatient care. Only if the outpatient treatment fails can the person be admitted for care. Also, visits to a psychiatrist or a counselor are often limited in number by calendar year.

ISSUES

Even with parity for mental health and addiction treatment, additional reimbursement issues arise. First, a majority of addicted persons have no health insurance. Often they have no job or they have a job that does not provide any health insurance. Second, addicted persons often have relapses. Costs for addiction treatment are controlled through limited admissions for treatment, resulting in limited treatment for relapses.

Third, addiction treatment programs, both outpatient and inpatient, have patient rules. For example, patients cannot take any drugs while they are in the program. They are tested weekly for the presence of drugs in their urine. If they violate this rule, they can be discharged from the addiction treatment program, even if they have health insurance.

Fourth, insurers may require that substance misusers use in-network (contracted) providers. Often, only a few such facilities and providers exist in a given network, and there may be a waiting period for treatment. Programs using cognitive-behavioral therapy are more likely to accept health insurance for payment. If a patient does not respond well to this type of therapy, their health insurance is of little use to them. Fifth, denial is a common symptom of substance misuse. It can be difficult to get the patient to accept their problem and to go for treatment, even if he or she has health insurance.

Christine M. Carroll RN, BSN MBA

FOR FURTHER INFORMATION

"Acceptance of Private Health Insurance in Substance Abuse Treatment Facilities." 6 Jan. 2011. Web. 21 Feb. 2012. http://www.oas.samhsa.gov/2k11/305/305privateins2k11.htm. Examines data on the extent to which treatment facilities are ready to accept private health insurance for substance abuse treatment services.

"Health Insurance and Substance Use Treatment Need." Substance Abuse and Mental Health Services Administration. 2007. Web. 21 Feb. 2012. http://www.oas.samhsa.gov/2k7/insurance/insurance.htm. Describes health insurance coverage for mental health and addiction services prior to the passing of the mental health parity legislation.

Johnson, Teddi Dineley. "Mental Health Advocates Laud New Federal Parity Law: Equal Coverage for Mental Health Care." *Nation's Health* 38.10 (2008).

Print. This article discusses the features of the Federal Mental Health and Substance Abuse parity legislation.

"Understanding the Federal Parity Law." Substance Abuse and Mental Health Services Administration. Web. 21 Feb. 2012. http://www.samhsa.gov/healthreform/docs/ConsumerTipSheetParity508.pdf. A brief overview of the Mental Health Parity and Addiction Equity Act of 2008.

See also: Health disparities and substance misuse; Legislation and substance misuse; Mental illness; Socioeconomic status and addiction; Substance Abuse and Mental Health Services Administration (SAMHSA)

Internet addiction

CATEGORY: Psychological issues and behavior

ALSO KNOWN AS: Compulsive behavior; compulsive internet use; excessive internet use; internet addiction disorder; internet-enabled internet gaming disorder; internet gaming disorder; pathological internet use; virtual addiction; web addiction

DEFINITION: Internet addiction (IA) is a compulsive-impulsive disorder consisting of three main subtypes: gaming, sexual preoccupation, and social media. Excessive lack of control in the use of various internet applications leads to a host of physiological, psychological and social problems. Researchers and scholars provide empirical evidence and theoretical support for the disorder even though is it not yet formally recognized in the American Psychiatric Association's *Diagnostic and Statistical Manual of Mental Disorders* (*DSM-5*). However, the American Psychological Association (APA) and the World Health Organization (WHO) recognize the disorder, as do many scholars in diverse disciplines.

CAUSES

Researchers have identified diverse factors that contribute to IA. Lack of parental control and peer pressure increase the likelihood of the disorder developing. The anonymous character of the internet appeals to persons with low self-esteem, negative thinking, and psychological traits ranging from narcissism to hostility. Chinese researchers maintain that the internet serves a compensatory function and represents an avenue for forming social networks in an increasingly demanding and threatening society. Some research indicates that situational factors, including the loss of a loved one, social rejection, unemployment, and relocation, might prompt a person to seek solace on the internet, thereby precipitating the development of IA. Psychological variables such as feelings of helplessness, difficulty communicating with others, a strong need for reward, and a desire for attention, also play a role in problematic internet use. Neurological studies show that changes in the activity and structure of the brain engender and reinforce IA. These changes effect diverse phenomena, such as reinforcement (in mitigating loneliness or social awkwardness), repeated use, tolerance, and withdrawal, all of which are symptomatic of addiction.

An internet café. (via Wikimedia Commons)

RISK FACTORS

A large body of research confirms the existence of problematic internet use across cultures and age groups. Surveys by the Pew Research Institute in 2018 show that 90% of people in developed nations frequently use the internet compared to a little less than two-thirds in less developed countries. Nearly 70% of Americans whose income is less than $30,000 are likely to use Facebook; however, only 36% of those whose incomes are above $75,000 use it frequently. Females are more likely to demonstrate excessive use of social media; males with video games. Teens report the greatest use of excessive internet use and the prevalence is increasing. Twenty-four percent of American teens reported that they were "almost constantly" online in 2015 but that percentage rose to 45% in 2018.

The status of the internet in modern culture ensures that all susceptible persons (that is, persons with a genetic predisposition to addiction or those with psychological disturbances) spend time on the internet and can develop IA. Persons undergoing life-changing events (such as bereavement, divorce, or job loss) are more vulnerable to developing problematic internet use. In some young individuals, studies show that the pressure to succeed can lead to internet overuse as a means to relieve stress.

Socially isolated persons and persons with attention deficit hyperactivity disorder (ADHD), depression, and other psychological disorders are at an increased risk for developing IA. Depression, ADHD, social phobia, and hostility predicted the occurrence of IA in follow-up studies. Hostility and ADHD were the most important predictors of IA in male and female adolescents, respectively. Persons with multiple addictions have a high risk of becoming addicted to the internet and to subsequently relapsing.

SYMPTOMS

Although IA lacks formal diagnosis criteria, significant progress has been made, however, in diagnosing IA since it was first described in the mid-1990s. The *DSM-5* includes internet gaming disorder in Section III as a disorder that warrants further clinical research; however, the *DSM-5* does not include problematic use of the internet in general. Overall, the fundamental components of the addictive process applicable to IA are as follows: preoccupation with internet use, greater usage than desired, numerous unsuccessful attempts to reduce usage, withdrawal (with anger and tension when not online), tolerance (including the need for more hours and better equipment), and lying about internet usage. The *DSM-5* criteria for internet gaming disorder include playing internet games compulsively, to the exclusion of other interests; causing clinically significant impairment or distress due to internet gaming; experiencing withdrawal; and incurring negative consequences at school or work. Affected persons also may overuse digital devices such as smartphones and tablets. Some of these behaviors likely indicate underlying psychological disorders (such as gambling and compulsive shopping), while others represent internet-specific behaviors (such as gaming, texting, and browsing). Ultimately, the computer or other digital device becomes the person's primary relationship.

Research has demonstrated that IA results in diverse problematic changes in one's well-being. Psychologically, excessive internet use decreases empathy, life satisfaction, sense of identity, and feelings of security. It increases the likelihood of depression, anxiety, hostility, peer aggression, victimization, procrastination, and a sedentary lifestyle. A 2018 study found that decreased digital engagement and happiness were inversely related and that increased use contributed to attention deficit disorders. Overuse of the internet results in less sleep, poorer school performance, maladaptive thinking, and narcissism.

Socially, preoccupation with cellphones and tablets is associated with the rise of pedestrian deaths in the United States (27% increase, 2007-2018) and other countries. Research has found that texting while driving quadruples the times a driver's eyes leave the road and increases accidents 23-fold. In Seoul, Korea, traffic accidents tripled from 2011 to 2016, primarily attributable to drivers and pedestrians being fixated on their internet devices.

Of great concern are the physical consequences of IA. Using a computer for extended periods leads to weight gain, sleep deprivation, back pain, carpal tunnel syndrome, and vision impairment. Numerous international studies have documented that excessive internet use increases gray matter volume in neural areas involved in pleasure and reward (e.g., ventral striatum, nucleus accumbens). In contrast, gray matter volume is decreased in areas of the brain associated with planning, impulse control, problem solving, and emotional regulation (e.g., medial prefrontal cortex), memory (e.g., hippocampus), and decision making based on experience (e.g., anterior cingulate cortex). While digitally engaged, brains show decreased empathic responsiveness, distorted perception of faces, and less activity in areas critical to a sense of self (e.g., precuneus).

SCREENING AND DIAGNOSIS

Unlike illegal drugs or gambling, the internet has widespread legitimate uses in fields such as education, research, business, industry, and communications. In this context, IA is easily masked, and therapists may have difficulty detecting the disorder. Obtaining a history of symptoms and previous treatment attempts, and gathering information about other potential addictions are essential in making a correct diagnosis.

Screening tests available include internet addiction expert Kimberly Young's Internet Addiction Test (IAT) and the Diagnostic Classification Test for Internet Addiction (DCT-IA). Even so, diagnosing IA can prove difficult because of the lack of rigorous diagnostic criteria. Experts agree, however, that internet activities become problematic when the person loses her or his ability to control the use and when time spent online impairs daily functions and jeopardizes relationships, employment, education, and personal health. Studies generally indicate significant distress if internet usage exceeds twenty to twenty-five hours per week.

The first validated instrument to assess the disorder is the IAT. This questionnaire addresses the duration and frequency of online activities, job productivity, ability to form new offline and online relationships, fear of life offline, attempts to reduce internet use, and many other behaviors. The person answers each IAT question using a scale of 0 to 5. The higher the final score, the greater the level of addiction. In addition to the severity of the addiction, the therapist identifies the applications (such as gaming, pornography, and chat rooms) that are most problematic for a particular person. The assessment is completed by obtaining a history of earlier treatment attempts, identifying the most detrimental types of usage, analyzing the family environment, and conducting a motivational interview.

TREATMENT AND THERAPY

While China was one of the first countries to label IA as a clinical disorder, hospitals and clinics all over the world have established treatment centers and "detox" facilities for internet addiction. These programs aim to reconnect internet-dependent youth and adults to the offline world by temporarily eliminating all avenues for electronic communication or by gradually reducing online time. In the United States, Young founded and opened the country's first inpatient treatment program for IA in a hospital in 2013 at Bradford Regional Medical Center in Pennsylvania. A ten-day program, the treatment includes evaluation, therapy sessions, and seminars.

A 2014 documentary titled *Web Junkie*, screened at the Sundance Film Festival, examined problematic internet use in Chinese culture and offered a glimpse into one of the treatment centers for IA. In the United States, a 2016 documentary titled *Screenagers*, chronicled the dilemma that parents face with their children and their overuse of technological devices.

Given society's increasingly online nature, many therapists argue that traditional abstinence treatment models may not yield good outcomes, at least for some types of IA. Reorganization of time usually spent online, using timers and reminder cards, and setting goals may help to limit the extent of online activities. Cognitive-behavioral therapy is often recommended as a first therapeutic approach, in addition to couples' therapy (especially for networking and "internet infidelity" addictions), cultivating hobbies, home maintenance skill building, and socializing opportunities.

Two factors make IA treatment difficult. First, many of individuals with internet addiction have an additional psychiatric diagnosis, making IA highly resistant to treatment and, in turn, rendering the coexisting psychiatric disorder more difficult to treat. Consequently, any therapeutic attempt should consider the person struggling with addiction's comorbid conditions and address them promptly. Second, structural changes to the brain that lead to enhanced sensitivity to pleasure and reward but diminished executive cognitive control, militate against attempts to change behavior and thought patterns. Biological treatments, such as transcranial magnetic stimulation of the brain may help to overcome IA.

PREVENTION

Despite providing undeniable benefits, the internet can be detrimental when used inappropriately or obsessively. An expanding body of research aims to clarify the causes, evaluation methods, and treatment outcomes for this phenomenon, which threatens to reach epidemic proportions. Meanwhile, persons at risk of IA, especially youth, can benefit from safeguards that ensure appropriate internet usage in schools and colleges. Setting limits for usage time is necessary for children and adolescents at home. Guardians and teachers should monitor and limit online time, especially among at-risk children with pre-existing psychosocial difficulties.

South Korea is a country in which hundreds of thousands of South Korean young children and teens experince IA and require treatment for the disorder. That country has identified IA as a prominent public health issue and started training counselors to address the problem. Other countries have enacted laws ranging from the banning cell phone use while driving to limiting internet access in certain situations that may help prevent individual maladjustment and societal problems. Competent, aware, technology-savvy professionals now help to identify populations at risk and provide correct diagnoses and therapeutic strategies. Perhaps the best approach is to educate the youngest members of society on the dangers of IA, thus inoculating children to the intense societal pressures to "turn on" … online, that is.

Mihaela Avramut MD, PhD;
Updated by Paul John Chara Jr, PhD

FOR FURTHER INFORMATION

Aiken, Mary. *The Cyber Effect*. New York: Spiegel & Grau, 2017. Presents research on how the cyber culture is affecting the development of children, increasing addictive behavior, and shaping societal values. Print.

Alter, Adam. *Irresistible: The Rise of Addictive Technology and the Business of Keeping Us Hooked...* New York: Penguin Press, 2017. Alter asserts that half of the American population has at least one addictive behavior and businesses are reinforcing those addictions. Print.

Braunstein, Danya. "Internet Use Disorder: What Do Parents Need to Know?" *Huffington Post*. TheHuffingtonPost.com, 12 Mar. 2013. Web. 30 Oct. 2015.

Davidow, Bill. "Exploiting the Neuroscience of Internet Addiction." *Atlantic*. Atlantic Monthly, 18 July 2012. Web. 1 Dec. 2014.

Konnikova, Maria. "Is Internet Addiction a Real Thing?" *New Yorker*. Condé Nast, 26 Nov. 2014. Web. 1 Dec. 2014.

Lachmann, B., C. Sindermann, R. Y. Sariyska, R. Luo, M.C. Melchers, B. Becker, A.J. Cooper, and C. Montag. "The Role of Empathy and Life Satisfaction and Smartphone Use Disorder." *Front. Psychol.*, 27 March 2018. Web. 25, Jul. 2018. doi. org/10.3389/fpsyg.2018.00398.

Lanier, Jaron. *Ten Arguments for Deleting Your Social Media Accounts Right Now.* New York: Henry Holt and Company, 2018. Lanier offers ten reasons why social media platforms are dangerous.

Palaus M., E.M. Marron, R. Viejo-Sobera, and D. Redolar-Ripoll. "Neural Basis of Video Gaming: A Systematic Review." *Front Hum Neurosci.* 2017. May 22, 11:248. doi: 10.3389/fnhum.2017.00248. eCollection 2017. Web. 25 Jul. 2018.

Radesky J. "Digital Media and Symptoms of Attention-Deficit/Hyperactivity Disorder in Adolescents." *JAMA.* 2018, 320(3):237–239. Web. 25 Jul. 2018. doi:10.1001/jama.2018.8932.

Sax, Leonard. *Boys Adrift: The Five Factors Driving the Growing Epidemic of Unmotivated Boys and Underachieving Young Men.* New York: Basic Books, 2016. Sax identifies factors leading to underperforming males in school and society, including problematic video gaming.

Tu, D., X. Gao, D. Wang, and Y. Cai. "A New Measurement of Internet Addiction Using Diagnostic Classification Models." *Frontiers in Psychology,* 10 October 2018. Web. 25 Jul. 2018. Doi: 10.3389/fpsyg.2017.01768. Web. 25 Jul. 2018.

Young, Kimberly S., and Cristiano Nabuco de Abreu, eds. *Internet Addiction: A Handbook and Guide to Evaluation and Treatment.* Hoboken: Wiley, 2011. Print.

See also: Behavioral addictions: Overview; Computer addiction; Gaming addiction; Social media addiction

Intervention

CATEGORY: Treatment

ALSO KNOWN AS: Brief intervention; Johnson model; structured intervention

DEFINITION: In general medicine, intervention can refer to any action intended to produce an effect (such as surgery or administering a medication) or to interrupt or stop the progression of a disease. In the field of addiction and treatment, intervention refers more specifically to an attempt to break the cycle of addiction by persuading the addict to seek professional help. The intervention may be brief and relatively informal or highly structured and led by a professional interventionist.

BRIEF INTERVENTION

There is no universally accepted classification of addiction and substance misuse intervention. However, it is useful to begin with a distinction between brief (sometimes called simple) intervention and formal or structured intervention. This second category can be subdivided into direct and indirect interventions. Although structured interventions were introduced in the 1960s as a method of moving alcoholics into treatment, these intervention models have been increasingly used in treating such behavioral problems as sexual addiction, gambling or shopping addiction, and video gaming addiction.

The term *brief intervention* is sometimes used to include informal attempts by family members or friends to confront the addict or to coax him or her into getting help, but it is more often applied to short, one-on-one counseling sessions between the addict and his or her physician, psychotherapist, social worker, or religious leader in a setting familiar to the addict. Brief interventions in primary care settings are considered to be most appropriate for persons who are not dealing with an immediate legal or social crisis caused by the addiction, are not intoxicated or high at the time of the office visit, and do not have a coexisting major psychiatric disorder. Brief interventions in emergency departments or trauma centers may be helpful, but only with patients who are open to counseling after an alcohol- or drug-related accident or injury.

The National Institute on Alcohol Abuse and Alcoholism (NIAAA) and the National Institute on Drug Abuse (NIDA) have published pamphlets for physicians, psychotherapists, and other helping professionals on conducting brief interventions. Possible settings for such interventions include prenatal care, primary care, emergency care, and college health centers.

The first step in a brief intervention is screening the patient for alcohol or drug use. NIDA has drawn up a "screener" called ASSIST that can be filled out by the patient in the doctor's office on paper or on a computer. After the screener is scored, the doctor then discusses the results with the patient, giving personalized advice according to the patient's likelihood of developing a substance use disorder. NIDA recommends referring high-risk patients to an addiction specialist for further evaluation and treatment, counseling moderate-risk patients to lower their drug or alcohol intake, and advising low-risk patients to continue to be responsible and moderate in their use of alcohol.

After the initial brief intervention, the primary care physician then schedules follow-up visits with ongoing support. Office handouts and other printed educational materials are often given to a patient as part of a brief intervention.

STRUCTURED INTERVENTION

Structured interventions have become increasingly familiar to the general public through such media as reality television shows, popular magazines, social media, and personal memoirs. In a structured intervention, the addicted person is confronted in one of two ways: directly by concerned family members, friends, and possibly employers or religious leaders or indirectly through a professional interventionist's work with the addict's family.

The first type of structured intervention is known as the Johnson model; the second type is variously known as the invitational or family systems model. In actual practice, however, a structured intervention may incorporate features of both the Johnson and the family systems models. The reason for the overlap is that structured interventions are highly individualized; that is, they are tailored to the addict's age, gender, occupation, drug or addictive behavior of choice, living situation, and extended family structure or friendship network.

The goal of a structured intervention is to persuade the addict to enter treatment at once. Plans include transportation to the treatment center and caring for the addict's children, pets, and residence to lower his or her resistance to accepting treatment.

JOHNSON MODEL

The Johnson model is named for Vernon Johnson (1920–1999), an Episcopal priest and recovering alcoholic who pioneered the use of structured interventions in alcohol rehabilitation in the 1960s. In the Johnson model, also known as the confrontational or direct model of intervention, those closest

to the addict form a team that will confront him or her under the guidance of a trained interventionist. Johnson believed that a confrontational approach is necessary to break through the addict's denial and other psychological defenses.

Members of the team have a pre-intervention meeting in which they learn about the disease model of addiction, decide on treatment options for the addict, and prepare letters or statements in which they describe the effect of the addict's substance misuse (or behavioral addiction) on their lives. They also may prepare a list of the addict's behaviors that they will no longer tolerate, along with specific consequences if the behaviors continue. The statements are written in a straightforward but caring tone that avoids judgmental expressions or accusations.

The actual intervention is usually a surprise to the addict, who may be told that he or she is being taken to lunch or to some other get-together but is instead confronted by the interventionist, family members, and other concerned persons. Following an introductory explanation by the interventionist, the members of the team take turns reading their prepared statements. At the end, the addict is offered the option of immediate treatment.

FAMILY SYSTEMS MODEL

The family systems model of intervention, also known as the indirect or invitational model, focuses on the addict's family rather than the addict alone. The theory underlying this model is that changes in the family system—the behavior patterns and interactions of family members—will affect the addict also and will reduce the severity of his or her self-destructive behaviors. A common form of this type of structured intervention is to hold an educational workshop for family members, to which the addict is invited; however, the workshop takes place as scheduled even if the addict refuses to attend.

The workshop, which typically lasts for two days, is led by a professional interventionist and includes discussion of intergenerational patterns of addiction and enabling as well as the biological and medical dimensions of addiction. Each family member is helped to understand his or her role within the family system and how his or her behavior may have enabled the addict. The participants may be asked to read some educational materials before the workshop. During the workshop, the various treatment options—including codependency treatment for family members—are explained. If the addict has chosen to attend, treatment is offered to him or her at the end of the workshop.

The general atmosphere of a family systems intervention differs from that of the direct model in that it is non-confrontational. Interventionists who use this model usually maintain contact and follow-up with the family for as long as one year after the intervention.

PROFESSIONAL INTERVENTIONISTS

While structured interventions can be led by an addict's friend or family member, the chances of success are low because the addict has already had considerable practice in manipulating those close to him or her. Most treatment centers recommend consulting a professional interventionist when brief interventions have failed and when a structured intervention is necessary.

A professional interventionist—who may be a physician, psychotherapist, social worker, nurse, psychologist, or member of the clergy—is a person who has completed training programs and field supervision approved by the Association of Interventionist Specialist Certification Board. After two years of experience in the field, the interventionist may be licensed as a board-certified interventionist, level one. Level-two interventionists have had an additional three years of field experience and have completed an oral or written examination. Lists of certified interventionists can be obtained from treatment centers, community mental health centers, or the Association of Intervention Specialists.

Rebecca J. Frey PhD

FOR FURTHER INFORMATION

Johnson, Vernon. *Intervention: How to Help Someone Who Doesn't Want Help: A Step-by-step Guide for Families and Friends of Chemically Dependent Persons.* Minneapolis: Johnson Inst., 1986. Print.

Morgan, Oliver J., and Cheryl H. Litzke, eds. *Family Intervention in Substance Abuse.* New York: Haworth, 2008. Print.

Recovery Connection. *Intervention: A Free Resource for Addicts, Friends, and Family.* Pompano Beach: Recovery Connection, 2010. PDF file.

Substance Abuse and Mental Health Services Administration. *Brief Interventions and Brief Therapies for Substance Abuse.* Washington, DC: SAMHSA, 2012. PDF file.

See also: Drug misuse and addiction: Treatment; Treatment methods and research

Intoxication

CATEGORY: Health issues, intoxication
ALSO KNOWN AS: Inebriation
DEFINITION: Intoxication is a temporary physical and mental state resulting from having consumed a psychoactive substance. Intoxication is characterized by disruptions to a person's physiological, psychological, and cognitive processes.

CAUSES, SYMPTOMS, AND DIAGNOSIS

Intoxication results from the consumption of substances such as alcohol, caffeine, marijuana and other illicit drugs, some mushrooms and plants, or even over-the-counter and prescription drugs.

Intoxication is diagnosed via identification of the substance in the body system and the observation of characteristic symptoms in the person affected. Specific substances have certain effects on the body and therefore create certain symptoms. Breath tests and urine samples often are used to detect intoxication. Additionally, simply watching the individual for psychological and behavioral signs of intoxication, or asking the individual to perform certain tasks can help with detection. For instance, police officers suspecting alcohol intoxication may request individuals to try to walk a straight line or to close their eyes and try to stand up straight. Such tests allow the officers to observe the person's balance and body sway. Loss of balance or significant body sway can indicate alcohol intoxication.

Each substance has specific symptoms associated with its intoxication state. Therefore, when testing someone for intoxication, different tests may be needed to determine whether any individual substance has been used.

Alcohol intoxication is marked by symptoms such as slurred speech, coordination problems, unsteady gait, nystagmus (an involuntary condition affecting the eyes in which they do not track the movement of objects smoothly), impairments in memory or attention, and stupor. Stupor is a condition in which the person is in a daze and has numbed senses. With alcohol intoxication, stupor can escalate to a coma. In addition to these symptoms, problematic behaviors may also manifest themselves, such as aggression, impaired judgment, mood problems, or problems interacting socially or at work.

The level of intoxication is directly related to dose and individual characteristics, such as body weight. A substance may produce different symptoms at various doses. For example, whereas small amounts of alcohol have a stimulant effect on behavior, high levels of alcohol cause sedation.

TREATMENT AND THERAPY

Intoxication is short-lived; once a substance has been processed out of the body, the effects dissipate. The intensity of intoxication lessens over several hours after ingestion. Treatment of chronic intoxication usually consists of a process called detoxification, or detox. This is usually done in inpatient units in hospitals or in treatment centers. Sometimes, however, detoxification may be done in community settings where nonmedical models of intervention are practiced. In all of these settings, symptoms are monitored closely as the person withdraws from the substance, as withdrawal can be dangerous. Withdrawal varies from drug to drug. It also varies depending on how long the person has used the substance and how much has been used. Severe withdrawal from certain substances, such as alcohol, can be fatal without appropriate medical supervision.

PREVENTION

Intoxication for some substances is easier to identify than for others. Increasingly, methods are being developed to identify intoxication with greater ease via objective measures. For instance, technology to assess the iris of the eye to detect marijuana intoxication and the use of patches to detect substance use, such as with drugs that may be excreted in sweat, are two recent developments.

Nancy A. Piotrowski, PhD;
Updated by Marianne Moss Madsen, MS

FOR FURTHER INFORMATION

American Psychiatric Association. *Diagnostic and Statistical Manual of Mental Disorders: DSM-5.* 5th ed. Arlington, VA.: American Psychiatric, 2013. An updated, comprehensive review of research about mental disorders. Covers the associated character-

istics of mental disorders and information on their prevalence, course, and familial patterns.

Julien, Robert M., Claire D. Advokat, and Joseph Comaty. *A Primer of Drug Action: A Comprehensive Guide to the Actions, Uses, and Side Effects of Psychoactive Drugs.* 12th Ed. New York: Worth, 2011. A nontechnical guide to drugs, written by a medical professional. Describes the different classes of drugs, their actions in the body, their uses, and their side effects. Basic pharmacologic principles, classifications, and terms are defined and discussed.

Weil, Andrew, and Winifred Rosen. *From Chocolate to Morphine: Everything You Need to Know About Mind-Altering Drugs.* Rev. and updated ed. Boston: Houghton Mifflin, 2004. Identifies and defines psychoactive substances. Also outlines the relationships between different types of drugs, the motivations to use drugs, and associated problems.

See Also: Alcohol poisoning; Alcohol's effects on the body; Blood alcohol content (BAC); Brain changes with addiction; Drug interactions

---

Intravenous drug use & blood-borne diseases

CATEGORY: Health issues and physiology

DEFINITION: Intravenous drug use is the administration of drugs, usually proscribed substances, by injection directly into the bloodstream. Numerous pathogenic microorganisms are transmitted in this way, which can lead to infectious diseases in the drug misuser.

CAUSES

Blood-borne pathogens such as parasites, viruses, and bacteria can be transmitted by injection drug misuse. Some of these pathogens, and associated diseases, are described here.

Malaria. Plasmodium outbreaks among injection drug addicts have been reported since the early twentieth century, when the first cases were reported in Africa. Needle sharing was suspected, but analysis of blood found in syringes did not show the *Plasmodium falciparum* parasite. Malaria eventually became common in injection drug addicts in New York City, with fatal cases numbering about 135 in the ten-year period preceding US involvement in World War II. Nonfatal cases of *P. vivax* malaria also were reported. The outbreak was limited to intravenous heroin addicts. Cases were typically attributed to sailors who traveled to the tropics. The sharing of needles was the mode of transmission during these outbreaks. The addition of quinine, an antimalarial drug, to cut, or dilute, heroin dramatically reduced cases.

Hepatitis. Sharing of needles by addicts was noted as the cause of hepatitis B virus (HBV) transmission in the mid-nineteenth century. HBV outbreaks associated with injection drug use are still noted today. Research into the prevalence of HBV among injection drug users shows that 50 to 60 percent of all addicts have been exposed to the virus. Combined HBV, hepatitis delta, or hepatitis C virus (HCV) infection causes hepatitis outbreaks among injection drug misusers that are sometimes fatal. HCV is now the most common blood-borne infection in the United States. Each of the hepatides is most common among those exposed to blood, including addicts.

Human immunodeficiency virus (HIV). Intravenous drug users are the second largest risk group for acquired immunodeficiency syndrome (AIDS) in the United States, comprising one-fourth of all cases. Needle sharing is the greatest risk for exposure and transmission. Forty-three percent of injection drug addicts test positive for the virus. Other human retroviruses, such as human T-cell lymphotropic virus, types I and II, also are transmitted among addicts.

Clostridial disease. Tetanus among addicts is not uncommon in female misusers, though the reason for elevated susceptibility in women is unclear. The *Clostridium tetani* bacterium and spores likely originate in the environment. However, contamination of heroin is possible too. Also, botulism caused by *C. botulinum* infection originating at the injection wound site has been reported among parenteral drug misusers.

Candida. Candida parapsilosis is the most common etiologic agent of fungal endocarditis among injection drug addicts. Viable cells have been recovered from both heroin and injection paraphernalia. Because this fungus is a member of the oral flora, addicts may be the reservoirs. *C. albicans* infection of the skin, eyes, bones, and joints has also been noted.

Pseudomonas aeruginosa. Serogroup 0-11 *P. aeruginosa* endocarditis is noted almost exclusively in intravenous drug misusers. Tablets of pentazocine, an

analgesic, and tripelennamine, an antihistamine, are crushed, diluted in tap or toilet water without boiling, then injected. The bacterium grows readily in these preparations.

Polymicrobial bacteremia. Seventy percent of blood cultures from injection drug addicts with polymicrobial bacteremia grow *Staphylococcus aureus* along with other bacteria. Therefore, skin contamination and poor hygiene are risk factors. As with *P. aeruginosa* bacteremia, pentazocine and tripelennamine misuse is a risk factor for polymicrobial bacteremia.

Staphylococcus aureus. A common cause of bacterial endocarditis, skin and soft tissue infections, and bacteremia in addicts is *S. aureus*. The source of the bacteria is likely the addict's own skin. Outbreaks of methicillin-resistant *S. aureus* (MRSA) have been reported. Antibiotic misuse, long periods of injection drug misuse, and frequent hospitalizations are associated with MRSA bacteremia.

Mycobacterium tuberculosis. The incidence of active tuberculosis is higher among hospitalized or methadone treatment patients than in the general population. Suppression of the immune system from drug misuse likely leads to an elevated number of infections among those exposed.

RISK FACTORS

The lifestyle of injection drug misusers makes addicts vulnerable to infection. Addicts repeatedly inject substances with immunosuppressive effects that are frequently in contaminated diluents. Immunologic defenses also are compromised by the simultaneous misuse of alcohol and tobacco and by personal neglect.

Several factors may influence the susceptibility in addicts exposed to bacteria, viruses, or parasites. The most important factor in reduced tolerance to infection is the damaged skin of the injection drug misuser. Needle wounds lead to abscesses and result in higher *S. aureus* skin colonization. Destruction of nasal mucosa, depression of cough and gag reflex, and dental carries lead to increased susceptibility. The addict also may have impaired functioning of phagocytosis, reduced superoxide production, and reduced T-cell function.

SYMPTOMS

The symptoms of blood-borne disease vary with the specific diagnosis. General symptoms of infection include fever and inflammation. Also common are body ache, headache, nausea, and vomiting. Hepatides cases can result in jaundice.

SCREENING AND DIAGNOSIS

Diagnosis of infectious diseases among addicts is performed in a manner identical to nonaddicted patients. Fluid or tissue samples must be obtained aseptically and delivered to the microbiology lab. Growth of the specimen is limited to about two hours so that the composition of the flora represents that in the original sample.

A fixed smear is Gram-stained for preliminary identification of Gram-positive or Gram-negative bacteria. Multiple test kits are available for more specific identification of bacterial pathogens. The presence of antibodies directed against a pathogen is used in presumptive diagnosis of hepatitis viruses and HIV. In rare cases, genetic analysis is performed to identify an infectious agent.

A urinalysis and a complete blood count checking white blood cell differential, serum electrolytes, urea, nitrogen, creatinine, glucose, and transaminases should be obtained. A chest X-ray and films of any involved soft tissues and bone should be taken. While bone scans are a valuable diagnostic tool, they are usually not available in emergency rooms, where addicts with infections frequently are treated. A computerized tomography scan of the brain should be ordered if there are neurologic symptoms or signs.

TREATMENT AND THERAPY

The treatment of blood-borne disease in injection drug misusers varies by diagnosis. Chloroquine is frequently used in the treatment of malaria, but quinidine or quinine plus doxycycline, tetracycline, or clindamycin, or atovaquone plus proguanil, are used in the treatment of chloroquine-resistant infections. The hepatitis viruses are treated with antivirals, and HIV is treated with antiretroviral drugs.

Mifepristone and misoprostol are used in the treatment of clostridial disease. Amphotericin B has been the most frequently used antifungal in the treatment of candida infections. Fluconazole is frequently administrated as an alternative to amphotericin B. *P. aeruginosa* is naturally resistant to a host of antibiotics. However, several injectable drugs can be effective. Ceftaroline is a broad-spectrum cephalosporin used in the treatment of MRSA infections. With any

---

Hepatitis C

Hepatitis C is an infectious disease with a viral etiology that usually leads to chronic infection with persistent liver inflammation (hepatitis). The disease is caused by a ribonucleic acid virus that infects liver cells and has six known genotypes (genetic makeup). Infection is transmitted primarily through exposure to contaminated blood.

Drug users commonly share needles and other drug injection paraphernalia, so a history of current or past use of injectable drugs carries a high risk for hepatitis C. Infection with the human immunodeficiency virus increases vulnerability to the disease, as does alcohol consumption, which accelerates liver damage. Other risk factors include unprotected sexual contact, especially with multiple partners, and nonsterile tattooing techniques.

Most people remain asymptomatic in the early stages of infection, although some may experience mild flu-like symptoms such as fatigue and fever. In time, the infection becomes chronic, and persistent liver inflammation may lead to cirrhosis (scarring of the liver) or liver cancer.

---

infectious disease, treatment of the addiction is essential to the long-term health of the addict.

PREVENTION

It remains difficult to control and prevent infectious diseases among addicts. Most addicts are elusive and seek care in the mainstream health-care system only when very ill or when facing withdrawal. Such socioeconomic factors as poverty, illiteracy, and language and cultural barriers are often further impediments to effective care.

With the fear that HIV-infected addicts may be a significant reservoir for the general public, health departments have become innovative. For example, they often employ former addicts to educate current intravenous drug users about blood-borne diseases and risk reduction. If such programs are successful, health experts can anticipate a concomitant reduction in the incidence of other infections associated with needle sharing and patronage of injection-drug "shooting galleries." Hepatitis B and tetanus immunization are effective in the prevention of these diseases.

Kimberly A. Napoli MS

FOR FURTHER INFORMATION

Centers for Disease Control and Prevention. "HIV/AIDS." http://www.cdc.gov/hiv. Comprehensive consumer-based information on HIV and infectious diseases.

Levine, Donald P., and Jack D. Sobel, eds. *Infections in Intravenous Drug Abusers.* New York: Oxford UP, 1999. A comprehensive text written for advanced readers and specialists.

Tortora, Gerard J., Berdell R. Funke, and Christine L. Case. *Microbiology: An Introduction.* 9th ed. New York: Pearson, 2007. A microbiology textbook focusing on infectious diseases.

See also: Heroin; HIV/AIDS and substance misuse; Substance misuse

J

Jail diversion programs

CATEGORY: Treatment

DEFINITION: Jail diversion programs are alternatives to sentencing and allow for rehabilitation within the community for nonviolent offenders who have a history of mental illness, substance use, or co-occurring disorders.

OVERVIEW

In order to rectify the high number of arrested individuals with an SMI, jail diversion programs were created. A jail diversion program is one that is an alternative means to sentencing and allows for rehabilitation in the community, under strict supervision, and for those with nonviolent substance use or mental health problems. The goal of these programs is to assist with a (1) decrease of incarcerated persons, (2) provide community-based treatment, and (3) provide supportive services for nonviolent offenses.

Diversion programs were created due to the high number of incarcerated individuals. The U.S. contains not only the most prisons throughout the world, but also the highest number of incarcerated persons. As of 2017, the U.S. contains 325.7 million people, 2.3 million of which are incarcerated. This number includes those in local jails, state and federal prisons, military prisons, immigration detention facilities, civil commitment center, state psychiatric hospitals, prisons in U.S. territories, and juvenile detention centers. The U.S. contains 5% of the world's population and 25% of the world's incarcerated persons. According to researchers, 1 in 5 persons are held on a substance use offense; while at least half of all incarcerated persons have some type of history of SMI. Those with a dual diagnosis of mental health and substance use are often incarcerated as well.

In the 1950s, deinstitutionalization began, which is also when the U.S. began to witness an increase in correctional facilities that housed SMI. Currently, the larger city jails are the largest mental health facilities in the U.S. (e.g., Cook County Jail, Los Angeles County Jail, or Riker's Island Complex in New York). It was the hope that with deinstitutionalization, there would be increased community-based treatment; however, the funds from each state were not applied to community facilities. Mental health clinicians began to see a rise in the number of individuals diagnosed with a SMI in nursing homes, homeless, or in correctional facilities.

As a response to the increased number of incarcerated individuals with an SMI, the Court Systems began to create specific diversion programs for substance use or mental health. Not all states have specific court systems for such programming; however, over the last decade the U.S. Court Systems increased their use of such programming. The goal of these programs is to help decrease the number of incarcerated individuals who engaged in a nonviolent offense. The purpose of the programs is also to help the individual obtain treatment in the community. This type of programming is not only effective for treatment of the SMI or substance use problem, but also aids in the individual maintaining employment, connection with family or friends, and a sense of connectedness to their community, all of which has been shown to decrease recidivism.

In addition to helping the individual, jail diversion programs are advantageous for the community. Depending on the State, the cost of housing an inmate is quite costly (e.g., for someone with an SMI the cost per day is about $130 versus $80 for someone without a SMI). This reduced cost to the County is an effective means to apply the funds elsewhere in the community. Further, research evidenced the advantages of jail diversion programs for those with SMI and the community, outweigh the advantages of incarceration.

TYPES OF JAIL DIVERSION PROGRAMS

There are two types of jail division programs; namely, prebooking and postbooking. The prebooking occurs prior to the individuals arrest and prior to formal changes being filed. In prebooking, the arresting officer(s) must have some type of training in order to determine if the individual has a SMI or substance use disorder, in order to determine how the situation should be handled on the scene. This type of jail division programming often is completed with both trained mental health officers and mental health professionals from the community. In certain cases, the officer may not have the training and/or mental health professional available, so the arresting officer may choose to take the individual to the hospital prior to filing any formal charges.

Postbooking programs occur after the individual was arrested and formal charges filed. This type of jail diversion program is often utilized in comparison to prebooking. There are five elements to postbooking programs: (1) screening for the presence of a SMI or substance use disorder; (2) treatment eligibility in lieu of incarceration by a qualified mental health professional; (3) negotiation with prosecutors, defense attorneys, other court officials, and community-based treatment providers; (4) development of a treatment plan for the community-based facility and the individual; and (5) clinical monitoring and supervision.

The Court Systems may, or may not, have specialized courts for mental health and substance use. The number of specialized courts continues to grow within the U.S., as research supports the efficacy of such programming. There are no specific guidelines or laws set to assist states or the Federal Government with how a specialty court should be outlined and/or executed. What researchers found was that most programs have the following components: (1) mental health aliments are outlined in a report; (2) the defendants must enter a plea of guilty prior to enrolling the program; (3) there is an option of alterative sentencing; and (4) a plea agreement that includes conditions, such as medication compliance, psychotherapy compliance, and case manager/status hearing compliance. Some of the sanctions imposed for those who are noncompliant with the voluntary participation of a jail diversion program includes: (1) increased treatment or supervision, or (2) re-incarceration.

EFFECTIVENESS

Longitudinal studies evidenced jail diversion programs are effective with positive outcomes, such as decreased recidivism and substance use, with an increase in the individuals overall functioning and quality of life. One of the drawbacks to utilizing longitudinal studies is that this type of research design is costly with high attrition rates, as many of the clients do not complete 6- and 12-month follow-up interviews. Researchers found though that the problem related to follow-up with clients was not just related to research attrition rates, case managers also had challenges in following-up with their clients. Crisanti, Case, Isakson, & Steadman (2014) determined there are specific characteristics that appear to be implicated in those who will not follow-up (e.g., men, individuals with a Hispanic background, those diagnosed with a bipolar disorder, longer periods of incarceration, and those living in suburban areas). These results suggest that while the effectiveness of jail diversion programs is effective, there is still a need to assess for certain groups. This indicates that case managers, researchers, and courts must increase creative and/or intensive procedures in order to obtain data for the effectiveness of the aforementioned groups.

While there are some drawbacks to the research on this topic, it appears that the evidence from most of the research is promising. One study assessed completers and non-completers over a 5-year period. The researchers found that those who completed the jail diversion program were less likely to spend time incarcerated, less re-incarceration rates, increased community integration, increased overall functioning, and overall increased management of symptoms. Furthermore, there was less termination from mental health services, and increased compliance with those services (Gill & Murphy, 2017). Overall, it is apparent that the literature supports the cause for jail diversion programs, as it not only helps the individual, but also assists the community.

Jack A. Lasky;
Updated by Lindsey L. Wilner, PsyD

FOR FURTHER INFORMATION

Barber-Rioja, V., Rotter, M., & Schombs, F. (2016). Conducting mental health diversion evaluations. In T. Masson (Ed.), *Inside forensic psychology* (pp. 80-105). Santa Barbara, CA: Praeger.

Collier, L. (2014). Incarceration nation. *Monitor on Psychology, 45*(9), 56. Retrieved from http://www.apa.org/monitor/2014/10/incarceration.aspx

Crisanti, A. S., Case, B. F., Isakson, B. L., & Steadman, H. J. (2014). Understanding study attrition in the evaluation of jail diversion programs for persons with serious mental illness or co-occurring substance use disorder. *Criminal Justice and Behavior, 41*(6), 772-790.

Gill, K. J., & Murphy, A. A. (2017). Jail diversion for persons with serious mental illness coordinated by a prosecutor's office. *Biomedical Research International, 2017*.

Wagner, P., & Sawyer, W. (2018, March 14). Mass incarceration: The whole pie 2018. *Prison Policy*. Retrieved from https://www.prisonpolicy.org/reports/pie2018.html

See also: Co-occurring disorders; Crime and behavioral addictions; Crime and substance misuse; Mental Illness; Rehabilitation programs; Treatment methods and research

Just Say No campaign

CATEGORY: Diagnosis and prevention

DEFINITION: The Just Say No campaign was a substance misuse awareness and prevention program for youth promoted by US First Lady Nancy Reagan.

DATE: Established 1982

BACKGROUND

In 1982, Nancy Reagan, then-US First Lady, had been working on the problem of drug misuse through speeches and visits to various national organizations. That same year she was approached by a school girl in Oakland, California, who asked the First Lady what she should say if she were asked to use drugs. Reagan responded with "just say no," which became the name of Reagan's nationwide awareness and prevention program.

Reagan continued her crusade against substance misuse among children. She spoke nationally to parent groups, community groups, schools, and other audiences about drug misuse and its effects on children. In 1986, US president Ronald Reagan signed a proclamation creating the first official Just Say No to Drugs Week. By 1988, more than twelve thousand Just Say No clubs had formed across the nation and around the world.

Early research supported the focus of the Just Say No program. This research, especially the work of Richard Evans on the social inoculation model, supported the claim that these programs "inoculated" students with peer-pressure-resistance skills that included refusing drugs if approached by peers.

In 1989, Reagan established the Nancy Reagan Foundation to continue the campaign against drug misuse. The foundation merged with the BEST Foundation for a Drug-Free Tomorrow in 1994, which developed the Nancy Reagan Afterschool Program, promoting drug prevention and life skills for youth.

MISSION AND GOALS

The Just Say No campaign became a national effort on substance misuse. The mission of the campaign was to teach children to resist drug use by simply teaching them to say "no" to anyone who approached them with the idea of using drugs. The slogan was simple and catchy, and it helped to initiate a national dialogue about the problems of drug misuse in the 1980s.

The program was widely disseminated across the county, but no evidence exists to demonstrate that the program was effective. Also, it is not entirely clear what specific program elements the Just Say No campaign actually contained.

By reviewing numerous sites and old publications, one can see that the Just Say No campaign was linked to a number of early drug prevention efforts. A series of Just Say No media messages was created, and Just Say No clubs were implemented in elementary and secondary schools. A Youth Power program existed, and numerous schools implemented Just Say No afterschool programs. The Just Say No campaign became, in some respects, more of a slogan interwoven with early drug prevention work.

This drug prevention work included the Red Ribbon Campaign of the National Federation of Parents, school-based drug-prevention assemblies, and drug-free weeks that were politically highlighted to bring national attention to the problem of drug use for young people. Although some of these components attempted to teach children positive resistance skills, it is not clear if rigorous evaluations were conducted or if any positive findings exist on the program. Documents link research roots to the development of various programs, but it is not clear what specific components or curricula were created and later evaluated for effectiveness. It appears that the Just Say No campaign evolved into a movement that involved concerned parents and community members.

Dated studies conducted in 1984 concluded the following: One, most substance misuse prevention programs have not contained adequate evaluation components. Two, increased knowledge has virtually

First Lady Nancy Reagan founded the Just Say No campaign. (US National Archives and Records Administration via Wikimedia Commons)

no impact on substance misuse or on intentions to smoke, drink, or use drugs. Three, effective education approaches appear to be experiential in their orientation and place too little emphasis on the acquisition of skills necessary to increase personal and social competence, particularly those skills needed to enable students to resist interpersonal pressures to begin using drugs. Four, few studies have demonstrated any success in preventing substance misuse. In the late 1980s and early 1990s drug prevention programs were created based on research ideas but were not commonly evaluated to determine their effectiveness in preventing substance misuse.

A group called Just Say No International, formerly Just Say No Foundation, was formed in Oakland, California, in 1986. This organization was led by Ivy Cohen, who brought attention and focus to the problem of drug misuse internationally. One publication by Far West Laboratory for Educational Research and Development published in 1993 contains an introduction by Cohen unveiling a new Just Say No program entitled Youth Power. Youth Power was developed with the premise that a "whole child" approach to substance misuse prevention was needed. The program is described in this 1993 publication as treating children as individuals with the ability and desire to help provide solutions to drug problems through empowerment models. Again, no evaluation findings were presented in this report.

Information on the Just Say No campaign is difficult to find and locate, and questions remain whether the program actually prevented substance misuse behaviors as measured through rigorous program evaluations. The Substance Abuse and Mental Health Services Administration's National Registry of Evidence-based Programs and Practices does not list the Just Say No campaign as an evidenced-based substance-misuse prevention intervention. The campaign did, however, bring national attention to the problems of drug misuse and American youth in the 1980s and early 1990s.

Julie A. Hogan PhD

FOR FURTHER INFORMATION

Evans, R. I. "A Historical Perspective on Effective Prevention." *Cost-Benefit/Cost-Effectiveness Research on Drug Abuse Prevention: Implications for Programming and Policy.* Eds. W. J. Bukoski and R. I. Evans. Washington, DC: GPO, 1998. Print.

Hart, Carl L., and Charles Ksir. *Drugs, Society, and Human Behavior.* 14th ed. New York: McGraw, 2011. Print.

National Institute on Drug Abuse. *Preventing Drug Use among Children and Adolescents: A Research-Based Guide for Parents, Educators, and Community Leaders.* 2nd ed. Bethesda: NIDA, 2003. Print.

Stricherz, Mark. "What Ever Happened to 'Just Say No?'" *Atlantic.* Atlantic Monthly Group, 29 Apr. 2014. Web. 27 Oct. 2015.

See also: D.A.R.E. (Drug Abuse Resistance Education); Education about substance misuse; Government warnings; History of addiction; Prevention methods and research

K

Ketamine

CATEGORY: Substances

ALSO KNOWN AS: K; special K; vitamin K

DEFINITION: Ketamine hydrochloride is a short-acting anesthetic. It has pain-killing and hallucinogenic properties.

STATUS: Legal in the United States for use as an anesthetic in medical settings; nonmedical use is illegal

CLASSIFICATION: Schedule III controlled substance

SOURCE: Synthetic drug with no natural sources; supplies are diverted from legal sources for illegal use

TRANSMISSION ROUTE: Intravenous, intramuscular, ingestion, inhalation

HISTORY OF USE

Ketamine was first synthesized in 1962 in the laboratories of the Parke-Davis pharmaceutical company. It was developed as an alternative to phencyclidine (PCP) for use as an anesthetic. Clinical use in short-term surgery in humans was initiated in 1975. Many patients began reporting hallucinations while under the drug's influence. Its use is now limited in humans, but it has more widespread applications in veterinary medicine. The drug was soon diverted from hospitals, medical offices, and medical supply houses.

Ketamine became a popular drug for recreational use among teenagers and young adults in the club scene. The US Drug Enforcement Administration added ketamine to its list of emerging drugs of misuse in the mid-1990s. It was classified as a schedule III controlled substance in 1999.

Since the early 2000s, various institutions have been conducting studies to determine whether ketamine can safely be used as an antidepressant and mood stabilizer. With one of the first small studies conducted at the National Institutes of Health, other larger studies have been performed by scientists at Yale University and Mount Sinai Hospital. It is believed that ketamine could relieve depression within hours, and researchers have continued to test the drug's effect on depression on patients for whom other medications have not worked; however, as of 2015, the US Food and Drug Administration had not approved ketamine for the treatment of depression.

EFFECTS AND POTENTIAL RISKS

Primary side effects of ketamine observed in medical settings include increased heart rate and blood pressure, impaired motor function and memory, numbness, nausea, and vomiting. While sedated, patients are unable to move or feel pain. Once the drug wears off, patients have no memory of what occurred while they were sedated.

In unmonitored situations, ketamine produces a dose-related progression of serious adverse effects from a state of dreamy intoxication to hallucinations and delirium. A "trip" on ketamine has been

Ketamine is also known as:		
Black Hole	Jet	Psychedelic Heroin
Bump	K	Purple
Cat Valium	K-Hole	Special K
Green	Kit Kat	Super Acid

described as being cut-off from reality—"going down into a K hole"—and as an out-of-body or near-death experience. Users may be unable to interact with others around them or even see or hear them. Ketamine has been used as a date rape agent because the victim has no memory of what occurred.

Because misusers feel no pain, they may injure themselves without realizing they are doing so. Chronic use can lead to panic attacks, rage, and paranoia. High doses or prolonged dosing can lead to respiratory depression or arrest and even death. Ketamine is often mixed with heroin, cocaine, or ecstasy. Any of these combinations can be lethal.

Ernest Kohlmetz MA

For Further Information

Dillon, Paul, Jan Copeland, and Karl L. R. Jansen. "Patterns of Use and Harms Associated with Non-Medical Ketamine Use." *Alcohol and Drug Dependence* 69 (2003): 23–28. Print.

Kuhn, Cynthia, Scott Swartwelder, and Wilkie Wilson. *Buzzed: The Straight Facts about the Most Used and Abused Drugs from Alcohol to Ecstasy.* 3rd ed. New York: Norton, 2008. Print.

Savelli, Lou. *Street Drugs: Pocketguide.* Flushing: Looseleaf Law, 2008. Print.

Winter, Caroline. "Is Ketamine the Best Hope for Curing Major Depression?" *Bloomberg Businessweek.* Bloomberg, 19 Aug. 2015. Web. 30 Nov. 2015.

See also: Anesthesia misuse; Club drugs; Date rape drugs; Recreational drugs

Kleptomania

Category: Psychological issues and behaviors, psychological issues and behaviors, kleptomania

Definition: Kleptomania is the uncontrollable impulse to steal. Oftentimes it is marked by an inability to stop stealing despite attempts to stop. Kleptomania may be accompanied by other conditions, such as anxiety, mood disorders, eating disorders, and chemical dependency. Other psychological or psychiatric conditions may exacerbate urges to steal and stealing behaviors. Obsessive-compulsive disorder and major depression have been documented to coexist with kleptomania in some cases.

Causes and Risk Factors

The causes of kleptomania are not known, although it may have roots in neurobiology, neurochemistry, psychology, and psychiatry. In addition to intrapersonal factors in kleptomania, environmental or situational factors can affect urges to steal. For example, stressful home or work situations may influence urges. More general factors, such as neighborhood violence or environmental overcrowding, also may be involved.

Some researchers have shown that functional-neuroimaging, biochemical, and genetic data implicate multiple neurotransmitter systems in the pathophysiology of impulse control disorders. The existence of multiple systems may elucidate the failure of traditional pharmacotherapy approaches to yield consistently efficacious results. Some researchers propose the development and implementation of targeted therapies to address impulse control disorders. Genetic influences in kleptomania may be present and are being considered, in part, by examinations of stealing behaviors among first-order relatives.

From a psychosocial perspective, stressful childhood experiences, sibling difficulties, and parenting issues may play roles. Failures in impulse control can be addressed through behavioral interventions. Such interventions focus on teaching coping strategies for resisting urges. Cognitive antecedents involve maladaptive thoughts and beliefs. Such interventions involve cognitive-behavioral modification, identifying triggers, avoiding such triggers, and countering maladaptive thoughts and beliefs. Cognitive-behavior therapy is being used in the treatment of kleptomania.

Kleptomania may be a manifestation of underlying conditions such as mood disorders, eating disorders, and anxiety. It is important to note that different factors may be involved for different people. Also, kleptomania may result from more than one factor. Additional causes may underlie the course of kleptomania over time. For example, difficulties with impulse control may underlie kleptomania in its earlier manifestations, while compulsions may develop later in the course of the disorder. Addictive influences may impact people even later in the course of the disorder, with corresponding feelings of anger.

Course of Symptoms

The course of kleptomania reflects sporadic, brief episodes accompanied by long abstinent periods; longer periods of stealing accompanied by periods of abstinence; and chronic stealing with some degree of variability. Prevalence in the general population is believed to be rare, with fewer than 5 percent of individuals who shoplift meeting the criteria for kleptomania. More than 65 percent of affected individuals are female. The age of onset of symptoms and beginning of treatment is younger for women than it is for men.

DIAGNOSIS

According to the DSM-IV-TR, the following five diagnostic criteria must be present for a diagnosis of kleptomania:

- recurrent failure to resist impulses to steal objects that are not needed for personal use or their monetary value
- increasing arousal immediately before committing the act
- pleasure, relief, or gratification at the time the act is committed
- the person is not committed to express anger or vengeance and not committed in response to a delusion or a hallucination
- the act is not better accounted for by a conduct disorder, a manic episode, or by antisocial personality disorder

TREATMENT PROGRAMS

Treatments for kleptomania can be linked to the antecedents of the condition. Treatment methods for kleptomania specifically include the following:

- *Pharmacologic.* While pharmacologic research is ongoing, and drug regimes are administered for some persons, this research has met with complex, sometimes mixed, results. Several classes of drugs are being used.
- *Antidepressants.* Selective serotonin reuptake inhibitors (SSRIs) are the antidepressants most commonly used to treat kleptomania.
- *Mood stabilizers.* Mood stabilizers are intended to reduce rapid or uneven mood changes that may trigger urges.
- *Benzodiazepines.* Such drugs are central nervous system depressants.
- *Antiseizure medications.* Some studies have reported data with respect to possible benefits in addressing kleptomania.

- *Addiction medications.* Opioid antagonists are intended to block the part of the brain that experiences pleasure during certain addictive behaviors.
- *Covert sensitization.* When an urge to steal arises, patients are instructed to imagine negative consequences until the urge subsides.
- *Aversion therapy.* Patients are taught to hold their breath when they experience the urge to steal until physical discomfort is felt. An association can develop between the urge and the discomfort.
- *Systematic desensitization.* Patients are taught to substitute relaxing feelings for urges to steal.

Ronna F. Dillon PhD and Laurel D. Dillon-Sumner BA

FOR FURTHER INFORMATION

Grant, Jon E. *Impulse Control Disorders: A Clinician's Guide to Understanding and Treating Behavioral Addictions.* New York: W. W. Norton, 2008. Provides information on impulse control disorders, including extended coverage in treatment.

Halgin, Richard, and Susan Krauss Whitbourne. *Abnormal Psychology: Clinical Perspectives on Psychological Disorders.* 6th ed. Columbus, OH: McGraw-Hill, 2010. Contains material on psychological disorders and how they affect functioning. Includes portrayals and case studies of persons living with the various psychological conditions.

Hollander, Eric, Heather Berlin, and Dan Stein. "Impulse Control Disorders Not Elsewhere Classified." *The American Psychiatric Publishing Textbook of Psychiatry.* Eds. Robert Hales, Stuart Yudofsky, and Glen Gabbard. 5th ed. Arlington, VA: APA, 2008. The range of conditions discussed includes kleptomania, pathological gambling, trichotillomania, and pyromania.

Moore, David. P., and James Jefferson. *Handbook of Medical Psychiatry.* 2nd ed. Philadelphia: Mosby, 2004. Covers psychiatric and neurological conditions and numerous general medical conditions that affect mental functioning.

See also: Behavioral addictions: Overview; Compulsions; Crime and behavioral addictions; Gambling addiction; Impulse control disorders; Pyromania

L

Laryngeal cancer

CATEGORY: Health issues and physiology

ALSO KNOWN AS: Cancer of the larynx, cancer of the vocal chords

DEFINITION: Laryngeal cancer is a disease in which cancer cells grow in the larynx. The larynx is a tube-shaped organ inside the neck that lies between the throat and the windpipe. Its main function is to produce sound for speaking.

CAUSES

Cancer occurs when cells in the body, in this case laryngeal cells, divide without control or order. Normally, cells divide in a regulated manner. If cells keep dividing uncontrollably when new cells are not needed, a mass of tissue forms, called a growth or tumor. The term cancer refers to malignant tumors, which can invade nearby tissues and can spread to other parts of the body. A benign tumor does not invade or spread.

RISK FACTORS

Smoking, cigarettes, and laryngeal cancer is by far the most common high-risk behavior associated with laryngeal cancer. Other risk factors include the excessive use of alcohol and occupational exposure to certain air pollutants, such as wood dust, chemicals, and asbestos. Race and age also play a factor: African Americans and people who are age fifty-five years and older have a greater chance of developing laryngeal cancer. Gastroesophageal reflux (stomach acid that backs up into the esophagus and throat where it may come in contact with the larynx) and a weakened immune system are also associated with an increased risk of laryngeal cancer.

SYMPTOMS

The following are symptoms of laryngeal cancer: a persistent cough, hoarseness, or sore throat; an abnormal lump in the throat or neck; difficulty swallowing or pain when swallowing; frequent choking on food; difficulty breathing or noisy breathing; persistent ear pain or an unusual ear fullness, or sensation in and around the skin of the ear; unplanned, significant weight loss; and persistent bad breath.

SCREENING AND DIAGNOSIS

A thorough review of the patient's medical history and a physical examination are performed. Tests may include laryngoscopy, a thin, lighted tube inserted down the throat to examine the larynx; biopsy, the removal of a sample of laryngeal tissue to test for cancer cells; chest X-ray, a test that uses radiation to take a picture of the larynx and nearby structures; CT scan, a type of X-ray that uses a computer to make pictures of the inside of the larynx; or MRI scan, a test that uses magnetic waves to make pictures of the inside of the larynx.

TREATMENT AND THERAPY

Once laryngeal cancer is found, staging tests are performed to find out if the cancer has spread and, if so, to what extent. Treatment depends on the stage of the cancer. For early stage laryngeal cancer, either surgery or radiation alone are the most common and appropriate therapies offered. For more advanced stages of the disease, either radiation with chemotherapy or surgery followed by radiation are the most common treatments given.

Surgery requires the removal of a cancerous tumor and nearby tissue, and possibly nearby lymph nodes. The surgeries for laryngeal cancer are total laryngectomy, which involves the removal of the larynx, including the vocal cords; partial laryngectomy, in which the surgeon removes the cancerous tissue while leaving as much of the vocal cords as possible; tracheotomy, in which a hole is made in the neck below the larynx to assist with breathing; and neck dissection, which involves the removal of the lymph nodes and part of the neck muscles to determine the spread of cancer.

Radiation therapy is the use of radiation to kill cancer cells and shrink tumors. This may mean external radiation therapy, in which the beam is directed at the tumor from a source outside the body. Chemotherapy is the use of drugs to kill cancer cells. This form of treatment may be given in many forms, including pill, injection, or catheter. The drugs enter the bloodstream and travel through the body, killing cancer cells but also some healthy cells. Chemotherapy may be used to reduce the size of a particularly large tumor.

PREVENTION

Since laryngeal cancer is extremely rare in non-smokers, the best way to prevent this type of cancer is by not smoking. A person can also reduce the risk of laryngeal cancer by avoiding excessive alcohol consumption and by protecting against toxic exposures.

Rick Alan

FOR FURTHER INFORMATION

Beers, Mark H., ed. *The Merck Manual of Medical Information.* New York: Gallery Books, 2004. Updated information from medical experts covering numerous medical issues, such as cancer, heart disease, mental illness, pediatric care, eating disorders, and AIDS.

"Laryngeal and Hypopharyngeal Cancer." *American Cancer Society.* American Cancer Society. 2012. Web. 30 Mar. 2012. An overview and detailed guide about laryngeal and hypopharyngeal cancer. Includes information about clinical trials and resources for talking about cancer.

"Laryngeal Cancer Treatment." *National Cancer Institute.* National Institutes of Health. 2012. Web. 30 Mar. 2012. General information about laryngeal cancer as well as its stages, recurrence, treatment options, and resources for more information.

See also: Cancer and substance misuse; Esophageal cancer; Lung cancer; Smoking's effects on the body; Tobacco use disorder

Law enforcement and drugs

CATEGORY: Social issues

DEFINITION: In the United States, the passage of drug laws that define substances as illegal or under the regulatory control of the government necessitated a mechanism for ensuring that these laws are obeyed. Law enforcement agencies at the federal, state, and local levels provide that mechanism. These agencies have been entrusted with the responsibility of enforcing drug laws by interrupting the production, importation, distribution, and sales of drugs in a collective effort known as supply reduction.

HISTORY OF DRUG LAWS

With the passage of the landmark Harrison Narcotics Tax Act in 1914, introduced by US Representative Francis Burton Harrison of New York, the US federal government began its continuous oversight of psychoactive substances. The new law made illegal and began regulating such drugs as narcotics, cocaine, and marijuana and numerous prescription and non-prescription drugs, including amphetamines.

The act taxed physicians only $1.00 annually for the right to legally prescribe opium, morphine, and coca leaves and their various derivatives, mislabeling the latter as a narcotic instead of a stimulant. However, nonphysicians were charged $1,000 for each exchange of any of these drugs, essentially prohibiting exchange under the strict penalty of law for tax evasion. Also, physicians were prohibited from prescribing opiates to treat addicts for maintenance purposes because addiction was not considered a disease, and physicians had to register with the federal government each prescription written and the name of each user.

From its enactment until 1970, the act was the prototypic antidrug law, spawning a succession of legislation drafted to limit the production, distribution, sale, and possession of unlawful substances. Following the legislative model of the 1914 act, the 1937 Marijuana

Tax Act was introduced by Robert Doughton of North Carolina and passed over the objections of the American Medical Association. The law prohibited the sale of hemp, cannabis, or marijuana by anyone other than registered and licensed commercial establishments. Each transaction of these products required a transfer tax. The Marijuana Tax Act was repealed by the Comprehensive Drug Prevention and Control Act of 1970, known as the Controlled Substances Act (CSA), which incorporated under one statute many of the extant federal drug laws (for example, the Opium Poppy Control Act of 1942, the Boggs Act of 1951, and the Narcotic Control Act of 1956).

The CSA created a schedule of drugs (I–V) that classified substances, in a hierarchy, according to their widely accepted medical use (ascending order) and potential for misuse and dependence (descending order). According to this hierarchy, drugs in schedule I have no accepted medical use and the highest potential for misuse and dependence, whereas drugs in schedule V have an accepted medical use and the lowest potential for misuse and dependence. Many schedule V drugs (such as codeine) were available as over-the-counter medications (in small amounts in cough syrup). The CSA also transferred the authority for drug regulation from the US Department of Commerce to the Department of Justice, thereby criminalizing all aspects of the drug trade—from production to trafficking, sales, and possession.

A crew member aboard the Coast Guard Cutter Legare *stacks a bale of cocaine during a contraband offload at Coast Guard Base Miami Beach, FL.* (Mark Barney via Wikimedia Commons)

FEDERAL ANTI-DRUG AGENCIES

The US Drug Enforcement Administration (DEA) was established in 1973 as the federal government's lead agency for ensuring that domestic drug laws are obeyed and that drug offenders are arrested and punished. With an annual budget of more than $2 billion as of 2014, the DEA also directs many drug investigations abroad. The forerunner to the DEA was the Federal Bureau of Narcotics (FBN), housed under the Department of Treasury and led by Harry Anslinger. The FBN undertook numerous domestic and international operations in an effort to halt narcotics smuggling.

Reflecting the federal government's abiding and serious interest in eradicating illegal drugs, it created, through the passage of the Anti-Drug Abuse Act of 1986, the White House Office of National Drug Control Policy (ONDCP), which remains under the auspices of the executive branch of the federal government. The ONDCP sets policy, allocates resources, and engages in public information campaigns to prevent and control drug sales and use throughout the country and to prohibit illegal drugs from entering the United States. The director of the ONDCP, the so-called drug czar, is appointed by the US president to serve as the leading authority on drug enforcement initiatives. The directorship, once a cabinet-level post, has been held by William Bennett (former secretary of education), Barry McCaffrey (a retired US Army general), and John Walters (former assistant to the secretary of education). Michael Botticelli, a longtime recovering alcoholic and former deputy director, was sworn into the position in February 2015.

ENFORCEMENT ACTIVITIES

The enforcement of drug laws in general occurs at four levels: international, national, state, and local. The international and national levels are under the aegis of the federal government. State and local police departments have specialized units for drug enforcement activities.

In certain instances, resources at each level are combined and coordinated through special task forces that concentrate on a particular drug (such as methamphetamine) or on a particular drug-trafficking enterprise (for example, outlaw motorcycle gangs). To prevent drugs from being smuggled across country or state borders in conveyances (for example, airplanes, boats, cars, trucks, and trains), the government employs agents from the FBI, DEA, Department of Homeland Security (US Customs and Border Patrol), and Transportation Security Administration to perform searches for illegal substances in a multistage interdiction process that involves intelligence gathering, surveillance, pursuit, and capture of smugglers.

To identify smugglers, trained officers implement drug-courier profiling techniques, watching vehicles and persons for telltale signs of drug trafficking. Drugs can be hidden in legitimate cargo or in false compartments in suitcases and in vehicle trunks and door panels. To uncover illegal substances, agents use advanced imaging technologies, trained dogs, pat-downs, body scans, and searches of persons. Drug smugglers have attempted to thwart officials by swallowing drug-filled balloons or by hiding drugs in bodily orifices—a dangerous practice that can result in death if the balloons burst and their contents are absorbed through the stomach or mucosa.

In cooperation with foreign governments, the DEA has engaged in crop eradication efforts that destroy the plants that are later processed into drugs for street sales. Such efforts to destroy crops involve the use of deracination (uprooting) techniques and chemical (for example, paraquat) and incendiary agents. US and foreign governments have subsidized the growers of illegal crops (for example, poppies for opium) to encourage them to cultivate legal crops and to discourage them from participating in the drug trade.

Drug enforcement efforts also focus on interrupting the processing of crops into saleable substances. For example, the milky juice from poppies, which is turned into a brownish gummy matter and then to a powder, becomes heroin for sale and consumption. Other drug factories produce cocaine from coca leaves. More sophisticated factories produce the main ingredient for methamphetamine (pseudoephedrine). The makeshift drug laboratories that produce methamphetamine are usually located in rural areas to hide the noxious odors and toxic, environmentally hazardous chemicals that are by-products of the production process. Drug enforcement agents seize, close, and destroy drug-producing factories of every type.

At the street level, police officers in specialized drug enforcement units gather intelligence from hotlines, local residents, and low-level criminals and informants to uncover drug-selling entities, such as street gangs in urban areas or freelance drug sellers. Officers disrupt operations by raiding houses in which drugs are packaged and stored for sale. Large amounts of drugs and money are seized from these premises as evidence.

In poor communities, drugs are often sold on the street. The public nature of these transactions makes it easier for police to engage in undercover enforcement activities known as buy-and-bust operations. In sting operations, officers pose as drug customers. In reverse-sting operations, officers pose as drug sellers. In both types of activities, an arrest is made after money and drugs are exchanged.

Closed markets are more difficult to police because drug sellers engage in transactions only with known drug customers or those vouched for by trusted friends or criminal associates. Local police can enforce drug laws by implementing other strategies as well, including the use of visible area patrols, crackdowns or sweeps in drug-infested neighborhoods, and partnerships with community-based antidrug programs. Police also can enforce nuisance abatement laws, which close down or seize properties where drugs are stashed or sold, and ordinances that allow them to seal vacant buildings, which are havens for drug sellers and users.

Arthur J. Lurigio PhD

FOR FURTHER INFORMATION

Levinthal, Charles F. *Drugs, Society, and Criminal Justice.* Boston: Prentice Hall, 2012. Print.

Rowe, Thomas C. *Federal Narcotics Laws and the War on Drugs.* New York: Haworth, 2006. Print.

Zilney, Lisa Anne. *Drugs: Policy, Social Costs, and Justice.* Boston: Prentice Hall, 2011. Print.

See also: Crime and substance misuse; Drug Enforcement Administration (DEA); Legislation and substance misuse; War on Drugs

Laxative misuse

CATEGORY: Substance misuse

DEFINITION: Laxative misuse is the repeated and routine use of laxatives to lose weight, shed unwanted calories, feel thin, feel empty, manage bowel movements, or treat constipation. There are different types of laxatives, but stimulant and bulk agents are the most common. Stimulant laxatives and osmotic laxatives physically alter the bowel's ability to function, and with excessive use can cause permanent damage. Bulk agents do not have the same physical effects as stimulant laxatives if taken as directed, but the user may become psychologically dependent on these laxatives.

CAUSES

There are several causative factors associated with the misuse of laxatives. One is the mistaken belief that laxatives will prevent the absorption of calories and help with weight reduction. Another factor is the mistaken belief that daily bowel movements are a necessary part of good health and that laxative use is a harmless remedy to ensure this occurs. A third factor is the repeated use of laxatives to relieve constipation.

RISK FACTORS

There are four groups of people at risk for laxative misuse. The largest group to misuse laxatives includes persons who have an eating disorder, such as anorexia nervosa and bulimia nervosa. Adolescents and young adults with low self-esteem and poor body image are particularly prone to disordered eating and laxative misuse. Anorexia nervosa is the severe restriction of food intake to bring about drastic weight loss, which in turn causes dehydration and subsequent constipation. Bulimia nervosa is characterized by a cycle of binge eating followed by behaviors such as vomiting or laxative misuse to compensate or reverse the effects of binge eating.

A second group to misuse laxatives includes athletes who need to stay within a specific weight range; these athletes include wrestlers, boxers, and jockeys. A third group is made up of middle-aged and older people with frequent bouts of constipation. In this group, excessive use often comes with the misperception that daily bowel movements are part of good health. The fourth group includes persons with a factitious disorder, wherein they misuse laxatives to intentionally cause diarrhea.

SYMPTOMS

Several physical warning signs and personality traits indicate laxative misuse. The physical signs include a history of alternating diarrhea and constipation or chronic diarrhea of an unknown origin; physical signs also include gastrointestinal complaints such as cramping or pain, dehydration, and retention of fluids that cause severe bloating and the feeling of being fat.

Certain personality traits are characteristic of those who misuse laxatives. These traits include an obsession with weight and body shape, low self-esteem, impulsiveness, and anxiousness. Exhibiting one of these traits does not mean a person is a laxative misuser, but having a combination of traits may increase the risk of laxative misuse. For example, if a person is obsessed with weight and has low self-esteem, they may binge eat. When this behavior does not make that person feel better, he or she may turn to laxatives to get rid of the calories just consumed.

SCREENING AND DIAGNOSIS

Screening and diagnosis of laxative misuse is tricky and oftentimes difficult because many misusers want to hide the behavior. The best screening tool is a clinician's suspicion. Once a clinician suspects laxative misuse, he or she can order blood tests to check for an electrolyte (potassium, magnesium, sodium, and chloride) imbalance, as chronic diarrhea will remove electrolytes through the stool and will prevent them from being absorbed into the body.

Persons with an eating disorder typically have low potassium levels in their blood (a condition called hypokalemia). Clinicians can check urine for the presence of a laxative. Another screening method is to perform a personality assessment by having the person complete surveys related to body dissatisfaction, low self-esteem, and level of drive to stay or be thin.

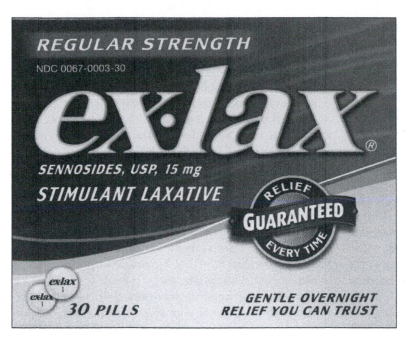

Box of Ex Lax laxatives. (iStock)

because intense exercise can worsen constipation. Physicians may start their patients on fiber and osmotic supplements to help the bowel function properly and to establish normal bowel movements.

PREVENTION

No guaranteed mechanism prevents laxative misuse. However, education can be a powerful tool in helping people understand that laxatives will not prevent the body from absorbing food or losing weight. Moreover, routine laxative use will have a reverse effect on the body, causing dehydration and constipation. Also, social support from friends and family and being aware of the signs and symptoms of misuse are crucial; intervention could prevent long-term laxative misuse and irreversible physical and psychological consequences.

Christine G. Holzmueller BLA

TREATMENT AND THERAPY

To overcome laxative misuse, users will need the medical expertise of a general physician, will need therapy with a psychologist or psychiatrist, and will need consultation with a registered dietician. The most immediate treatment is to stop taking laxatives and to seek a physician's care.

Many people will experience withdrawal symptoms that usually last from one to three weeks; in rare cases symptoms have lasted two days to two or three months. Side effects of withdrawal include constipation, fluid retention, feeling bloated, and temporary weight gain. To treat these side effects one should drink six to ten cups of water per day and decaffeinated beverages to hydrate one's body. (Caffeine is a diuretic and promotes fluid loss, and dehydration causes constipation.) One should eat regular meals and foods that promote normal bowel functioning, such as whole-grain or wheat bran foods with plenty of fluids, vegetables, and fruits.

Routine physical activity also helps regulate the bowel, but a physician should be consulted first

FOR FURTHER INFORMATION

Daniels, Glenda, and Marilee Schmelzer. "Giving Laxatives Safely and Effectively." *MEDSurg Nursing* 22.5 (2013): 290–302. *Consumer Health Complete.* Web. 29 Oct. 2015.

Heller, Jacob L. "Laxative Overdose. *MedlinePlus.* US Natl. Lib. of Medicine, 13 Oct. 2013. Web. 29 Oct. 2015.

Le Grange, Daniel, and James Lock. *Eating Disorders in Children and Adolescents: A Clinical Handbook.* New York: Guilford, 2011. Print.

Pomeranz, Jennifer L., Lisa M. Taylor, and S. Bryn Austin. "Over-the-Counter and Out-of-Control: Legal Strategies to Protect Youths from Abusing Products for Weight Control." *Amer. Jour. of Public Health* 103.2 (2013): 220–25. *CINAHL Complete.* Web. 29 Oct. 2015.

Roerig, James L., et al. "Laxative Abuse: Epidemiology, Diagnosis, and Management." *Drugs* 70.12 (2010): 1487–1503. Print.

See also: Emetic misuse

Legislation and substance misuse

CATEGORY: Social issues

DEFINITION: Substance misuse, also known as drug misuse, is characterized by overuse of and dependence on addictive substances, most often narcotic drugs or alcohol. Legislative issues affecting and addressing substance misuse and substance misusers are addressed at the federal, state, and local levels.

SCOPE OF THE ISSUE

In 2015, according to the Federal Bureau of Prisons, nearly one-half of persons in prisons in the United States were imprisoned for drug-related crimes. According to the National Substance Abuse Index, the United States is the largest single market in the world for illegal drugs. States generally are left to legislate substance misuse issues.

Federal law, however, may require states to take certain actions, such as tracking specific instances or reporting some types of infractions. Laws also generally distinguish between legal substances, such as alcohol, and illegal substances, including the unlawful use of prescription medication.

Each state chooses what federal laws to enact. Though there are thirty-nine federal laws pertaining to alcohol, for example, states are not bound by them. States also are required to follow the parameters of federal sentencing guidelines.

HISTORY OF SUBSTANCE MISUSE LEGISLATION

The criminalization of drugs in the United States began in 1914 with the Harrison Tax Act. Under this law, a tax of $1,000 was imposed for the nonmedical exchange of certain drugs; the law, however, pertained to tax evasion, not drug use or transfer.

In the early and middle decades of the twentieth century several federal agencies had varying responsibilities and power in drug law enforcement. By the 1960s most of this enforcement was in the hands of the federal Bureau of Narcotics and the Bureau of Drug Abuse Control. Changing attitudes toward drug use during the 1960s and into the 1970s gradually led to increases in crime. Federal law enforcement agencies continued to evolve, as did legislation.

The US Congress passed the Controlled Substances Act, part of the 1970 Comprehensive Drug Abuse Prevention and Control Act, launching national substance control campaigns. The law consolidated legislation that regulates the manufacture and distribution of illicit substances—anabolic steroids, depressants, hallucinogens, narcotics, and stimulants—and some chemicals used to produce controlled substances. As public health threats from other substances became known, the act was amended. In its infancy, the Controlled Substances Act was enforced by the Bureau of Narcotics and Dangerous Drugs under the Department of Justice (DOJ).

In 1973, US president Richard M. Nixon created the Drug Enforcement Administration (DEA) within the DOJ to centralize efforts to combat substance misuse. Interagency rivalry and the necessity of coordinating investigation and prosecution efforts were among the reasons cited for the creation of the DEA. In announcing the DEA, Nixon declared the United States' global war on drugs.

As the war on drugs continued, investigators developed intelligence units and technology to aid agents. Laboratories were built and staffed to support the DEA's efforts. The DEA has continued to monitor substance misuse developments and to respond to emerging trends. In 2011, for example, the DEA took action against three synthetic cathinones, widely called bath salts, following alarming and increasing reports of misuse of the substances.

CLASSIFICATION AND PENALTIES

There are five classifications of controlled substances. Laws mandate the penalties for crimes of trafficking based in part on the classification, or schedule, of the drugs, and in some cases, as with trafficking marijuana, on the amount of drug confiscated. Penalties may include incarceration and fines. Each state sets its own penalties for sale and possession of these substances within the federal guidelines.

Schedule I drugs are classified as substances with high potential for misuse and no accepted medical use in the United States. The law requires that these drugs be tightly controlled, including mandating security for manufacturing and storing them, and establishing quotas and licensing guidelines. Schedule I drugs include heroin, LSD, marijuana, peyote, and ecstasy.

Schedule II substances may have accepted medical use and high potential for misuse; they also are likely to lead to severe physical or psychological dependence. Methadone, oxycodone, amphetamine, methamphetamine, and cocaine are examples of schedule II drugs.

Schedule III drugs include anabolic steroids, codeine with aspirin, and some barbiturates; these substances have less potential for misuse than schedule I and II drugs, have accepted medical uses, and have some potential for dependence.

Schedule IV and V substances have low potential for misuse or dependence and also have accepted medical uses. Valium and Xanax are among the schedule IV drugs. Over-the-counter medicines, such as cough medicines with less than 200 milligrams of codeine per 100 milliliters, are examples of schedule V drugs.

Much of the federal legislation regarding illegal substances pertains to alcohol, marijuana, cocaine, heroin, and methamphetamine. Persons who have been convicted of drug offenses may lose some federal benefits, such as grants and loans, and assistance including food stamps and Social Security benefits. A college or university student receiving federal financial aid, for example, could lose the aid if convicted of a drug offense; the penalty could be temporary for a first offense of possession, but permanent following multiple offenses.

The Controlled Substances Act also includes prohibitions and penalties for selling drugs to minors or near schools and other locations. Federal penalties are often more severe than those for crimes prosecuted at the state level. Local jurisdictions also may pass laws pertaining to drug possession and trafficking.

CURRENT LEGISLATIVE ISSUES

Substance misuse issues continue to arise as chemists develop new synthetic drugs and as others experiment with substances. Such issues often develop in other countries and eventually arrive in the United States. Drug enforcement authorities are continually monitoring and responding to developments.

Designer Drugs

One example of a developing issue is the collection of designer drugs commonly called bath salts, which were first seen in Europe. Hospitals and health care workers reported sharp increases in the number of patients being seen for the effects of bath salts beginning in 2009 and escalating in 2011. These designer drugs were being used for their psychoactive properties.

Under the Comprehensive Crime Control Act of 1984 the US attorney general has the authority to temporarily place substances into schedule I for up to one year. The DEA took action on bath salts in 2011; an order in October temporarily scheduled the bath salt substances into schedule I because the drugs were deemed threats to public safety. The following year, President Barack Obama signed a bill into law that banned the active ingredients of many types of synthetic drugs, including bath salts. However, by 2015, concerns had risen over the increased use of flakka, a synthetic drug similar to bath salts but deemed even more dangerous.

Misuse of Prescription Medicine

Many people who misuse prescription medicine believe that these substances are safe because they are prescribed by doctors. Some people take a larger dose than was recommended because they believe more is better, while others take the medication to induce euphoria. The latter is an example of drug misuse.

Misuse of prescription medication can cause harm or death. According to the Substance Abuse and Mental Health Services Administration (SAMHSA), approximately 15 million people in the United States age twelve years and older used prescription drugs for nonmedical purposes in 2014. Among the most common prescription drugs misused are oxycodone, Valium, amphetamine, methamphetamine, and barbiturates.

Penalties for prescription drug misuse vary by state. North Carolina, for instance, mandates prison sentences of seventy to eighty-four months for anyone with more than 4 grams of opium, opium derivatives, or heroin. A person illegally in possession of six Vicodin pills, for example, would be in prison for up to seven years. Penalties increase with the amount of the drug a person has. In contrast, someone caught in North Carolina with more than 10 pounds of marijuana could be sentenced to twenty-five to thirty months in prison.

Prenatal Exposure

According to data from the SAMHSA, for the years 2012 and 2013, 5.4 percent of pregnant girls and women age fifteen to forty-four years, including 8.6 percent of women age eighteen to twenty-five years, admitted to some kind of current illicit drug use. A number of states require health care professionals to screen infants for prenatal drug exposure, and many states go further, requiring that women suspected of prenatal substance misuse be reported to child protective services. Federal laws such as the Child Abuse Prevention and Treatment Act, however, regard such actions as referrals for treatment and investigation of child safety issues, not grounds for criminal prosecution.

Eighteen US states classify substance misuse during pregnancy as child abuse as of 2015. Some states also require actions including reporting parents to authorities. Responses to substance misuse also vary widely from state to state; some make treatment for pregnant women a priority, others make furnishing drugs to pregnant women crimes. Women who have been charged criminally for prenatal actions often face charges of child endangerment or abuse, fetal murder or manslaughter, or illegal drug delivery to a minor (via umbilical cord), depending on the state.

Federal Alcohol Laws, State Discretion

All fifty states have adopted some federal alcohol laws, such as the law making it illegal to operate motor vehicles with a blood alcohol concentration (BAC) at or above 0.08. Most states have adopted the administrative license revocation law, which suspends licenses of those who fail the BAC test.

Several states have adopted the federal law making driving under the influence with a minor child in the vehicle a separate offense or increasing the penalty for doing so. Another federal law mandating jail for a second offense of driving under the influence has been adopted by forty-six states. By 1987, all fifty states had laws making age twenty-one years the legal drinking age; national statistics indicated that per capital consumption of alcohol dropped considerably.

Josephine Campbell

FOR FURTHER INFORMATION

Campo-Flores, Arian. "Potent New Stimulant Flakka Ravages Florida." *Wall Street Journal.* Dow Jones, 12 Aug. 2015. Web. 30 Oct .2015.

Gray, James. *Why Our Drug Laws Have Failed and What We Can Do about It.* Philadelphia: Temple UP, 2011. Print.

Haggin, Patience. "Obama Signs Federal Ban on 'Bath Salt' Drugs." *Time.* Time, 10 July 2012. Web. 30 Oct. 2015.

Lyon, Joshua. *Pill Head: The Secret Life of a Painkiller Addict.* New York: Hyperion, 2009. Print.

Valverde, Mariana. *Diseases of the Will: Alcohol and the Dilemmas of Freedom.* New York: Cambridge UP, 1998. Print.

See also: Drunk driving; Opioid misuse; Prescription drug addiction: In depth; Prescription drug addiction: Overview

Leukoplakia

CATEGORY: Health issues and physiology
ALSO KNOWN AS: Smoker's keratosis
DEFINITION: Caused by chronic irritation, leukoplakia is a disorder of the mouth's mucous membranes. White patches form on the tongue or inside of the mouth over weeks or months. This can also occur on the vulva in females, but for unknown reasons.

CAUSES

Leukoplakia is caused by chronic irritation. Irritants can come from cigarettes and pipe or cigarette smoking, chewing tobacco or snuff, rough teeth, and rough places on dentures, fillings, or crowns. One type, known as hairy leukoplakia, results from a virus that becomes active in the body when the immune system is weak. This is found primarily in people with the human immunodeficiency virus (HIV) or other types of severe immune deficiency. Infection may play a role in other cases, as well. Most cases of leukoplakia get better once the source of the irritation is removed.

RISK FACTORS

Risk factors that increase the chance of developing leukoplakia are old age (sixty-five years or older); lifestyle, such as tobacco use or long-time alcohol use; and a weakened immune system. More men than women are at risk of developing leukoplakia. In women, the condition more often develops into cancer.

SYMPTOMS

Leukoplakia is usually harmless, but it can lead to cancer. In some cases, leukoplakia resembles oral thrush, an infection also associated with HIV/AIDS and lowered immune function. Symptoms can include a lesion on the tongue or gums, inside of the cheeks, or on the vulva. The lesion can be white, gray, or red in color, and is typically thick and slightly raised, or it may have a hardened surface. Other symptoms include sensitivity to touch, heat, or spicy foods, as well as pain or other signs of infection. With hairy leukoplakia, painless and fuzzy white patches appear on the tongue.

SCREENING AND DIAGNOSIS

In most cases, a dentist can diagnose leukoplakia with a mouth exam. To confirm a diagnosis or to check for cancer, an oral brush biopsy may be needed. This involves removing some cells with a small brush. A pathologist then checks these cells for signs of cancer. Sometimes the dentist uses a scalpel to remove cells after numbing the area.

TREATMENT AND THERAPY

Leukoplakia can be treated by removing the irritant, which may involve quitting smoking or correcting dental problems; removing patches, particularly if signs of cancer are present; and taking medicine. Medicines include valacyclovir and famciclovir or a topical solution, such as podophyllum resin. For hairy leukoplakia, the doctor may prescribe antiviral medicines.

PREVENTION

Smoking cessation, limiting or avoiding alcohol use, good oral hygiene, regular visits to the dentist, and consuming plenty of fruits and vegetables (full of antioxidants) are all effective methods of reducing the chance of developing leukoplakia.

Annie Stuart

FOR FURTHER INFORMATION

"Leukoplakia." *American Osteopathic College of Dermatology*, www.aocd.org/?page=Leukoplakia. Accessed 17 Feb. 2017.

"Leukoplakia." *Mayo Clinic*, Mayo Foundation for Medical Education and Research, 26 July 2013, www.mayoclinic.org/diseases-conditions/leukoplakia/basics/definition/con-20023802. Accessed 17 Feb. 2017.

"Leukoplakia." *MedlinePlus*, US National Library of Medicine, 10 Sept. 2015, medlineplus.gov/ency/article/001046.htm. Accessed 17 Feb. 2017.

"Leukoplakia." *UMMC*, University of Maryland Medical Center, 2011, umm.edu/health/medical/ency/articles/leukoplakia. Accessed 30 Mar. 2012.

"Oral Hairy Leukoplakia." *AETC National Resource Center*, AIDS Education & Training Centers National Resource Center, 2012, aidsetc.org/guide/oral-hairy-leukoplakia. Accessed 30 Mar. 2012.

See also: Smoking; Smoking's effects on the body; Substance misuse and addiction in the elderly; Tobacco use disorder

---

Librium

CATEGORY: Substances

DEFINITION: Librium, trade name for chlordiazepoxide, is a psychoactive drug used to treat anxiety and insomnia. It is also used for agitation, seizures, muscle spasms, alcohol withdrawal, and as a premedication for certain medical and dental procedures. Librium was the first in the class of benzodiazepines, the minor tranquilizers.

STATUS: Available by prescription only

CLASSIFICATION: Schedule IV controlled substance

SOURCE: A chemical structure formed by the fusion of a benzene ring and a diazepine ring; other trade names include Libritabs, Novapam, Risolid, Silibrin, Tropium, and Zetran

TRANSMISSION ROUTE: Ingestion, intravenous, intramuscular, rectal

HISTORY OF USE

Librium works by acting on gamma-aminobutyric acid (GABA), a chemical that occurs naturally in the brain. Brain cells affected by GABA slow down and stop firing, calming the muscles and heart rate and alleviating anxiety and insomnia. When first prescribed, Librium and other benzodiazepines were considered safe and effective. By the 1970s, there were reports of adverse physical and psychological effects. Some persons developed a tolerance to and even a physical dependence on the drug. The US Congress investigated benzodiazepines three times, unusual for a drug legally prescribed. The majority of people taking the drug were middle-class women.

The women's health movement of the 1970s argued that Librium was an agent of social control, a drug that tranquilized women into submission. Addiction specialists considered Librium to be prone to misuse. Emergency rooms often found Librium and other benzodiazepines in persons who overdosed. From a peak of more than 120 million prescriptions per year in the mid-1970s, Librium fell to 60 million prescriptions by 1979. The US Food and Drug Administration now limits Librium to short-term use.

EFFECTS AND POTENTIAL RISKS

Persons taking Librium sometimes experience paradoxical reactions such as seizures, aggression, impulsivity, irritability, or suicidal behavior. Long-term Librium use risks deterioration of physical and mental health. Sudden withdrawal from Librium can cause severe pain in the muscles and joints, insomnia, or suicidal thoughts. A person may experience extrapyramidal symptoms, such as restlessness, involuntary movements, or uncontrollable speech.

Librium may cross the placenta with other substances, putting a fetus at risk for withdrawal, extrapyramidal symptoms, or perinatal complications. Benzodiazepines affect the metabolism of estrogen and may have an association with ovarian cancer.

Benzodiazepines pose the greatest risk to the elderly, causing memory problems, daytime sleepiness, impaired motor coordination, and increased risks of car accidents and falls. Long-term effects may include depression, dementia, and acute anxiety.

Merrill Evans MA

FOR FURTHER INFORMATION

"Drug Abuse and Addiction: Benzodiazepines." *Cleveland Clinic: Current Clinical Medicine.* 2nd ed. Cleveland, OH: Elsevier, 2010.

Harlow, Bernard L., and Daniel W. Cramer. "Self-Reported Use of Antidepressants or Benzodiazepine Tranquilizers and Risk of Epithelial Ovarian Cancer." *Cancer Causes and Control* 6 (1995): 130–34. Print.

Herzberg, David. "The Pill You Love Can Turn on You," *American Quarterly* 58 (2006): 79–103. Print.

Sinclair, Leslie. "Antipsychotic Labels to Cite Risks to Newborns." *Psychiatric News* 46 (2011): 12. Print.

Tallman, John F., et al. "Receptors for the Age of Anxiety: Pharmacology of the Benzodiazepines." *Science*, n.s. 207 (1980): 274–81. Print.

See also: Addiction medications; Anxiety; Anxiety medication misuse; Benzodiazepine misuse; Controlled substances and precursor chemicals

Liver disease and alcohol use

CATEGORY: Health issues and physiology

ALSO KNOWN AS: Alcoholic hepatitis; alcoholic liver disease; cirrhosis; Laennec's cirrhosis; steatohepatitis

DEFINITION: Alcohol (ethanol) is a toxin metabolized in the liver; hence, the organ is the site of major injury from repeated alcohol use. According to the National Institute of Diabetes and Digestive Kidney Diseases, cirrhosis ranked as the twelfth leading cause of death in the United States in 2014. The course of alcoholic liver disease (ALD) is a continuum of damage in which multiple areas of liver function become impaired, as fatty liver develops into inflammation and necrosis (hepatitis), then fibrosis, and then cirrhosis and liver failure.

THE LIVER

The liver is the largest organ in the body and the only organ able to regenerate itself. Performing more than five hundred vital functions, it is the conduit where blood from the stomach and intestines passes and where toxic substances and waste products are removed from the blood. The liver is responsible for protein, carbohydrate, and lipid metabolism and for detoxification and metabolism of ethanol and its toxic by-products.

The liver consists of two main lobes containing small units called lobules. These hexagonal plate-like structures are made up of hepatocytes (liver cells) and are attached to interconnecting ducts that end in the hepatic duct. Hepatocytes constitute the functional component of the liver, making up 70 to 80 percent of its cytoplasmic mass, and the cells are damaged by prolonged alcohol ingestion. A connective tissue capsule covering the liver acts as scaffolding; its branching extends throughout the liver as septae, enabling vessels and bile ducts to traverse the liver.

DISEASE MANIFESTATION

ALD is a spectrum of evolving liver injuries, progressing from mild steatosis and fatty infiltration to hepatitis and fibrosis, and finally to cirrhosis, which

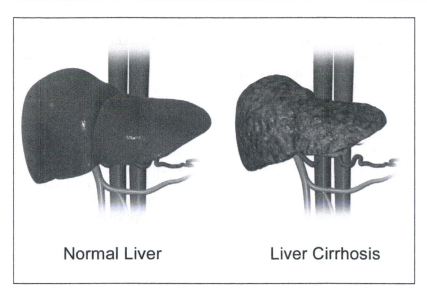

Normal Liver   Liver Cirrhosis

A diseased liver versus a normal liver. (Bruce Blaus via Wikimedia Commons)

evolves to complications of portal hypertension, hepatic encephalopathy, or hepatocellular carcinoma. Although ALD is often devoid of clinical symptoms and best observed histopathologically, the course of the disease can be insidious.

Steatosis, the abnormal retention of lipid (fat) within a cell, is the earliest manifestation of ALD and is seen in 90 percent of heavy drinkers. The lipid droplets are mostly triglycerides, and as they accumulate in hepatocytes, the liver becomes infiltrated with fatty deposits—hence, the term *fatty liver.* Injury is most evident in the perivenular area (zone three), a diamond-shaped area of the hepatic lobule located around central veins. Fatty liver is a relatively benign condition that reverses itself quickly with abstinence.

Continued drinking causes necroinflammation and the onset of alcoholic hepatitis (AH), an acute form of alcohol-induced liver injury, marked by intralobular inflammation and necrosis. AH is characterized by a group of morphological changes in cell integrity, ranging in severity from detection of distinct necroinflammatory components (steatohepatitis) to evidence of biochemical damage and lesions to fulminant liver failure, triggering sudden and rapid deterioration of liver function.

The pattern of fatty liver development is macrovesicular, such that swelling of the cytoplasm occurs; this process is called ballooning degeneration and it reflects widespread disturbances in lipoprotein transport in and out of hepatocytes. With ballooning, fat accumulation inside hepatocytes is so large it distorts the cell's nucleus and displaces the cytoplasm. In staining it appears as single-shaped white spaces or vacuoles. Ballooning leads to lytic necrosis, causing cell contents to decompose, with subsequent condensation of reticulin fibers (fibrosis). Common lesions in AH are neutrophilic infiltrates, Mallory hyaline inclusions or bodies, megamitochondria, and lipogranulomas that form from ruptured hepatocellular fat.

Clinical diagnosis of AH remains rather nebulous, as there are no positive markers or reliable tests that differentiate simple fatty liver from steatohepatitis or more advanced stages of ALD. The short-term mortality rate for patients with severe AH is high, and the disease is a precursor to cirrhosis, with an associated long-term risk nine times higher in AH than in fatty liver alone.

FIBROSIS

Fibrosis is an exaggerated response to the wound-healing process elicited by liver damage involving the production of excessive type 1 collagen and other extracellular matrix (ECM) proteins and their deposition as scar tissue. Collagen deposition occurs primarily in an area of the liver known as the space of Disse. The fibrosis common to ALD is called sclerosing hyalin necrosis and involves wide pericentral areas of fibrosis extending to portal fields.

With overspreading necrosis, the ECM becomes overwhelmed and loses its ability to express enzymes that degrade lesions. This results in unbalanced synthesis and decomposition of collagen, causing proliferation of connective tissue and, over time, increases to wider bands of collagen that form bridging fibrosis. Lesions then span between septae and cause disturbances in lobular structure, loss of hepatocytes, and deterioration in liver function.

Hepatic stellate cells (HSCs) are known to generate fibrosis. Normally dormant, HSCs become activated in response to liver injury. Activated HSCs are differentiated myofibroblast-like cells with a changed phenotype, characterized by proliferative, fibrogenic, and contractile properties. The process affects a cascade of histologic events in which HSCs elicit inflammatory signaling, cytokine release, and matrix metalloproteinase dysregulation, resulting in increased accumulation of ECM and further fibrosis.

Liver fibrosis is reversible and liver transplantation improves survival. However, most transplant centers do not recommend transplants unless a patient demonstrates a minimum of six months of abstinence from alcohol.

CIRRHOSIS

Cirrhosis is a diffuse pathologic process of architectural disorganization involving the entire liver, whereby normal liver architecture is replaced by abnormal structures called regenerative nodules. These nodules are completely surrounded by fibrous-band bridging between portal tracts. Cirrhosis usually develops over many years and produces a nodular, firm liver. In ALD, cirrhosis is usually micronodular and most prominent in the central vein area. Often called Laennec's cirrhosis, it is characterized by a fine mesh-like pattern of small uniform yellow nodules and narrow, regular fibrous septa.

Decompensated cirrhosis occurs when liver function is overridden by architectural remodeling and is accompanied by complications of portal hypertension or hepatic encephalopathy. Portal hypertension causes phlebosclerosis (hardening of venous walls), resulting from abnormal blood flow patterns of cirrhotic liver, and its effects extend to other organs. Encephalopathy is a clinical state of disordered cerebral function caused by impaired hepatic metabolic function. Decompensated cirrhosis is often further complicated by hepatocellular carcinoma, is irreversible, and has high mortality.

By eliminating alcohol before cirrhosis develops, it is possible for the liver to heal—a sobering fact, considering ALD claimed 18,146 lives in the United States in 2013, according to mortality data from the US Centers for Disease Control and Prevention.

Barbara Woldin BS

FOR FURTHER INFORMATION

"Alcoholic Liver Disease." *Cleveland Clinic: Current Clinical Medicine*. Ed. William Carey. 2nd ed. Philadelphia: Saunders, 2010. Print.

"Cirrhosis." *National Institute of Diabetes and Digestive and Kidney Diseases*. Natl. Inst. of Diabetes and Digestive and Kidney Diseases, 23 Apr. 2014. Web. 27 Oct. 2015.

"FastStats: Alcohol Use." *Centers for Disease Control and Prevention*. CDC, 20 July 2015. Web. 27 Oct. 2015.

Feldman, Mark, Lawrence Friedman, and Lawrence Brandt. *Sleisenger and Fordtran's Gastrointestinal and Liver Disease*. 9th ed. Philadelphia: Saunders, 2010. Print.

Schiff, Eugene, Michael Sorrell, and Willis Maddrey, eds. *Schiff's Diseases of the Liver*. 10th ed. Philadelphia: Lippincott, 2006. Print.

See also: Alcohol's effects on the body; Ethanol

Love and relationship addiction

CATEGORY: Psychological issues and behaviors

ALSO KNOWN AS: Codependency; obsessive relationship; pathological relationship; relational dependency; relationship pursuit

DEFINITION: A love or relationship addiction is a behavioral addiction involving an unhealthy preoccupation with a person or an obsession with the idea of romance or love. It can be a one-sided romantic relationship or can involve partners who are codependent, or it can define a nonromantic, pathological relationship, such as that between a child and parent.

CAUSES

A relationship addiction can be caused by many different factors. Common contributors include depression, low self-esteem, loneliness, and a sense of helplessness. Some behavior can be traced to childhood abuse or inadequate bonding experiences with caregivers early in life, which can result in a high level of neediness.

Some people remain in an addicted relationship or fall into a pattern of addicted relationships due to lack of education or social skills, or because of impaired judgment. Pursuers often enjoy exploiting or controlling others, or they seek revenge for being rejected.

Couples who are codependent feed off each other's most vulnerable or negative qualities. In those situations in which a person is obsessed with the idea of romance or love, he or she becomes addicted to the mood-enhancing qualities of "falling in love" and is unable to move forward into a more mature relationship.

RISK FACTORS

People most at risk for relationship addictions are those who have failed to develop a sense of worth and self. Other people at high risk are victims of child abuse or child abandonment or persons who grew up with codependent parents and failed to learn about healthier relationships. Persons with a substance addiction, sexual addiction, or another mental disorder are also at risk, as are those brought up in a fundamentalist religion or a culture that advocates strict passive and dominant gender roles and a sense of martyrdom between spouses.

SYMPTOMS

When a person falls in love, a sense of being "swept away" or losing oneself is common and normal. In a healthy relationship, this state of being is temporary and eventually blossoms into a deeper sense of love and responsibility, qualities of a successful long-term relationship. Also normal is the need to establish multiple relationships before the "right" person comes along.

Those who are addicted to love, however, establish a pattern of leaving partners just when the initial romantic high begins to fall away, never taking a relationship to the next level. Love addicts also can exhibit a pattern of extramarital affairs, tend to spend abnormal amounts of time fantasizing, and may miss work or destroy friendships and family relationships because they are too busy looking for their next attraction.

Signs that one is invested in an unhealthy relationship include situations in which values are being compromised, in which positive rewards are lacking, and in which one's health and safety are at risk. The inability to leave a pathological relationship can cause anxiety, high blood pressure, moodiness, digestive problems, eating disorders, depression, and substance misuse. In some cases, the shame or guilt associated with codependent relationships causes people to withdraw from society. A partner who is manipulative, controlling, and abnormally jealous may stalk the other, invade his or her privacy, and resort to violence or even murder when rejected.

Although it is normal for those who have been rejected in a love relationship to feel sad, worthless, and "lost" for a temporary period of time, the pathological love addict finds the pain so unbearable that he or she has thoughts of suicide and may carry out the act. The dependency upon another can be so overwhelming that it prohibits the person from imagining a life without the partner.

SCREENING AND DIAGNOSIS

There is no official diagnosis of a relationship addiction as determined by the American Psychological Association or any other major professional group. Mental health professionals rely on questionnaires or surveys to measure jealousy, anger, and other emotions, and to uncover related psychological motives.

Examples of surveys that can be administered by professionals or used for self-diagnosis are available from Sex and Love Addicts Anonymous, Co-Dependents Anonymous, and other organizations. As these tests rely upon personal reflection and honest answers, they work best when the client has admitted to a problem. In other situations, family members and current or former partners might be interviewed for additional insight.

When a person has been accused of stalking, the victim may be asked to complete the stalking behavior checklist or similar surveys, which commonly are used in domestic violence cases. Clients will also be screened for mental disorders, including substance misuse, depression, sexual addictions, and borderline personality disorder, which are often present with relationship addicts. A physical examination and medical history also may be conducted.

TREATMENT AND THERAPY

Treatment for a relationship addiction usually involves a twelve-step program similar to the model devised by Alcoholics Anonymous in addition to individual or couples therapy. Twelve-step programs rely on peer support, fellowship, and a belief in a higher power to help the client abstain from the unhealthy behavior or to end an addictive relationship. Individual psychotherapy can help to uncover underlying problems, attitudes, or disorders and to focus on treatment.

An important part of treatment for those who have been involved in an addictive relationship is finding activities that offer a distraction; getting rid of the reminders of a relationship, such as gifts, cards, and music; and participating in a healthy lifestyle. Education is also essential, as clients may need to learn certain coping or interpersonal skills to build healthy relationships. When depression, borderline personality disorder, or another mental disorder is present, treatment also will consist of additional psychotherapy and medication.

PREVENTION

The best way to prevent a relationship addiction is to develop a healthy and happy self-identity. Persons should pursue a career and leisure activities that are fulfilling, should develop a spiritual or humanistic side of life, and should participate in social activities that build healthy relationships. A person who likes and respects him- or herself conveys that and other healthy attitudes to others.

Learning about normal human development and the qualities of healthy relationships, and developing critical thinking skills that can be used to judge relationships, also are important. A person should seek professional help at the first signs of a problem relationship, before a partner becomes abusive or violent, and should be aware that stalking, abuse, and sexual harassment are not only unacceptable, but are also crimes.

Sally Driscoll MLS

FOR FURTHER INFORMATION

Beattie, Melody. *The New Codependency: Help and Guidance for Today's Generation.* New York: Simon, 2009. Print.

Cupach, William R., and Brian H. Spitzberg. *The Dark Side of Relationship Pursuit: From Attraction to Obsession and Stalking.* Mahwah: Erlbaum, 2004. Print.

Fisher, Helen. *Why We Love: The Nature and Chemistry of Romantic Love.* New York: Holt, 2004. Print.

Fjelstad, Margalis. "Getting Out of an Addictive Relationship." *Psychology Today.* Sussex, 30Dec. 2013. Web. 30 Oct. 2015.

Katz, Dian. "Checking the Health of Your Relationship." *Lesbian News* 29.7 (2004): 51. Print.

Moore, John D. *Confusing Love with Obsession: When Being in Love Means Being in Control.* 3rd ed. Center City: Hazelden, 2006. Print.

Peabody, Susan. *Addiction to Love: Overcoming Obsession and Dependency in Relationships.* 3rd ed. New York: Celestial Arts, 2005. Print.

Schaeffer, Brenda. *Is It Love or Is It Addiction: The Book That Changed the Way We Think about Romance and Intimacy.* Center City: Hazelden, 2009. Print.

Tallis, Frank. *Love Sick: Love as a Mental Illness.* New York: Thunder's Mouth, 2004. Print.

See also: Behavioral addictions: Treatment; Compulsions; Men and behavioral addictions; Self-destructive behavior and addiction; Sex addiction; Women and behavioral addictions

LSD

CATEGORY: Substances

ALSO KNOWN AS: Acid; lysergic acid diethylamide

DEFINITION: LSD, a synthetic amide of lysergic acid found in ergot, a fungus on grains, is a psychoactive intoxicant, similar to but stronger than psilocybin or mescaline. LSD has powerful mind-altering effects, usually called hallucinogenic or psychedelic.

STATUS: Illegal in the United States and other countries

CLASSIFICATION: Schedule I controlled substance in the United States

SOURCE: A synthetic chemical with no natural sources; produced illegally in laboratories

TRANSMISSION ROUTE: Crystals are diluted into liquid form and ingested orally; also injected intramuscularly

HISTORY OF USE

LSD was synthesized in 1938 by Albert Hoffman, of Sandoz Laboratories in Basel, Switzerland, as part of a research program seeking new medicines. LSD did not seem to offer such promise, but in 1943 Hoffman accidentally ingested a dose, experienced its psychoactive effects, and described these effects as being surprisingly transformational.

Albert Hofmann, discoverer of the mind-altering drug LSD and former head of the research department of Swiss chemical company Sandoz in Solothurn, Switzerland. (Phillip H. Bailey via Wikimedia Commons)

For the next twenty years, Sandoz Laboratories marketed LSD for research purposes. Among early research was that by the US Central Intelligence Agency from the 1950s through the 1970s, in an attempt to discover whether LSD could be used for mind-control purposes. Mostly, however, psychiatry and psychology became involved, initially because LSD seemed to simulate a "model psychosis."

The perceptual distortions induced by LSD, however, are not experienced as hallucinations in the sense of something that is not there; rather, they transform what is given in the perceptual field. This distinction led Canadian psychiatrists Humphry Osmond, Abram Hoffer, and Duncan Blewett to use LSD as a treatment for psychosis. LSD was also studied as an adjunct in psychotherapy, especially by Stanislav Grof in Czechoslovakia. Before its criminalization, more than forty thousand patients were treated with LSD psychotherapy. Notable results occurred in alcoholics, felons, and the terminally ill, persons who normally are resistant to successful therapeutic outcomes.

In the United States, research was conducted at Harvard University by Timothy Leary, Ralph Metzner, and Richard Alpert (who later became Ram Dass). The trio's 1964 book *The Psychedelic Experience* popularized the view that LSD could be useful in enhancing human potential. Leary, in particular, became a public advocate for LSD with his slogan to "turn on, tune in, drop out."

Soon writers such as Aldous Huxley and Ken Kesey and musicians, most famously the Beatles, also reflected a view of LSD's possibilities. Cary Grant, a major film star, attributed a "new assessment of life" to his experience on LSD. By the 1960s, LSD had become a common drug for American youth, especially in California, where it spread among the burgeoning counterculture. Owsley Stanley, who made and distributed a large amount of LSD in San Francisco in the mid-1960s, is known for fueling the upsurge of interest there. Largely because of this sense that LSD contributed to a rejection of mainstream values, the drug became intensely controversial and the subject of much negative publicity. The manufacture and sale of LSD was made a crime in 1965 and possession was criminalized in 1966.

According to the US Substance Abuse and Mental Health Services Administration, LSD use peaked in the early 1970s, fell slowly to a low in 2003, and has been increasing since. The National Household Survey on Drug Abuse indicated that 20.2 million Americans age twelve years and older used LSD at least once in their lifetime. The most common age of first-time users is eighteen years.

EFFECTS AND POTENTIAL RISKS

The effects of LSD become noticeable within thirty to sixty minutes and last six to eight hours or more. The threshold dose is 25 micrograms (mcg), and 100 to 250 mcg is typical; beyond 400 mcg no further change seems to occur. A feature of LSD is how widely its effects vary. Researchers quickly realized the keys to this variability are the mental set (or state) of the user and the setting in which the drug is used.

The physiological effects of LSD include changes to the pulse rate, muscular tension, blood pressure, constriction of arteries in the periphery, and pupil dilation. These effects tend to be mild and do not last beyond the psychoactive period. Longer term physiological effects have been reported, but these claims have not survived rigorous research.

Negative experiential effects of LSD are cognitive and emotional. Judgment is impaired such that the user is not as concerned with safety. Emotionally, a user can become so disoriented as to feel anxiety or panic, a reaction augmented if the setting were conducive to disorientation. A rare longer-term negative effect is the unwelcome vivid memory of an emotionally charged moment from the LSD event, known as a flashback.

The experiential effects of LSD include positive aesthetic, psychological, and spiritual transformations. Aesthetically, the effects center on perceptual changes, especially to the visual field, which is intensely enhanced with greater mobility, colorfulness, transiency, luminosity, energy, swelling, vividness, and synesthesia. Psychologically, the effects of LSD include mood changes, particularly feelings of well-being and euphoria; a new and greater awareness of the world and of self; a deeper understanding of human relationships; a transcendence of time and space; and a sense of ineffability. Spiritually, the effects of LSD include a sense of rebirth; a sense of encounters with divinity; a sense of the world as sacred; and a sense of communion, unity, and nonduality.

These effects tend to be experienced as an inward journey; they are remembered and are felt by the user to be of lasting benefit. The effects are so unmistakable that blinded research studies are impossible. For this reason too, substances other than LSD are rarely sold as LSD.

LSD is not addictive. A tolerance is built up after a few days if used daily, but the tolerance is diminished quickly following cessation of use and uncontrolled drug-seeking behaviors are not caused by LSD. Studies of lethal overdose levels in animals indicate it would require an extremely huge amount for humans, and no lethal overdoses have been shown in humans.

Christopher M. Aanstoos PhD

FOR FURTHER INFORMATION

Dobkin de Rios, Marlene, and Oscar Janiger. *LSD, Spirituality, and the Creative Process.* Rochester: Park Street, 2003. Print.

Grof, Stanislav. *LSD: Doorway to the Numinous.* Rochester: Park Street, 2009. Print.

Hoffman, Albert. *LSD: My Problem Child.* San Francisco: MAPS, 2005. Print.

Shroder, Tom. *Acid Test: LSD, Ecstasy, and the Power to Heal.* New York: Penguin, 2014. Print.

See also: Flashbacks; Hallucinogen misuse; Hallucinogen's effects on the body; MDMA; Mescaline; Mushrooms/psilocybin; PCP; Psychosis and substance misuse

Lung cancer

CATEGORY: Health issues and physiology

ALSO KNOWN AS: NSCLC; non-small cell lung cancer; non-small cell bronchogenic carcinoma; small cell lung cancer

DEFINITION: Lung cancer is a disease in which cancer cells grow in the lungs. Cancer occurs when cells in the body divide without control or order. If cells keep dividing uncontrollably, a mass of tissue forms. This is called a growth or tumor. The term cancer refers to malignant tumors. They can invade nearby tissue and spread to other parts of the body.

CAUSES

Cancer is caused by cell division that occurs within the body without control or order. Any damage to the cells in the lungs can lead to the development of lung cancer, including damage caused by first- or secondhand smoke from cigarettes, cigars, or pipes; and exposure to asbestos (a type of mineral), radon (radioactive gas), or other toxins. There are two types of lung cancer: non-small cell lung cancer, which is more common and generally grows and spreads more slowly; and small cell lung cancer, which generally grows more quickly and is more likely to spread to other parts of the body.

RISK FACTORS

There are numerous risk factors that can increase the likelihood of developing lung cancer. They include cigarette, cigar, or pipe smoking; using chewing tobacco; exposure to secondhand smoke; exposure to asbestos or radon; having a lung disease such as tuberculosis; having a family or personal history of lung cancer; exposure to certain air pollutants; exposure to coal dust; radiation therapy (used to treat other cancers); and infection with the human immunodeficiency virus (HIV).

SYMPTOMS

The symptoms of lung cancer are many, and may include a persistent cough, especially one that worsens over time; constant chest pain; coughing up blood; shortness of breath, wheezing, or hoarseness; repeated problems with pneumonia or bronchitis; swelling of the neck and face; loss of appetite or unexpected weight loss; and fatigue. It should be noted that these symptoms might be caused by other conditions.

SCREENING AND DIAGNOSIS

A discussion of symptoms and medical history followed by a medical examination is usually the first step toward a diagnosis. A doctor will also typically inquire about a possible family history of cancer as well as any exposure to environmental and occupational substances. The following tests will help to diagnose lung cancer: chest X-ray, which uses radiation to take a picture of structures inside the body, especially bones; sputum cytology, a test that examines a sample of mucus from the lungs; spiral CT, a special type of X-ray of the internal organs; PET scan, an image created using a tiny amount of radiation that is put into the body; PET/CT scan, a type of imaging test that combines PET and CT scan techniques; bone scintigraphy, a test that detects areas of increased or decreased bone activity; and biopsy, which is the removal of a sample of lung tissue to be tested for cancer cells.

Methods of biopsy include bronchoscopy, in which a thin, lighted tube is inserted into the mouth or nose and through the windpipe to look into the breathing passage and to collect cells or tissue samples; needle aspiration, in which a needle is inserted through the chest into the tumor to remove a sample of tissue; thoracentesis, which involves the use of a needle to remove a sample of the fluid in the lungs to check for cancer cells; and thoracotomy, which is surgery to open the chest and examine the lung tissue.

TREATMENT AND THERAPY

Once lung cancer is found, staging tests are done to find out if the cancer has spread. The goal of treatment is to eliminate the cancer or to control symptoms. Surgery involves removing the tumor and nearby tissue. Lymph nodes may also need to be removed. The type of surgery depends on the location of the tumor. Segmental or wedge resection requires the removal of only a small part of the lung, lobectomy surgery is the removal of an entire lobe of the lung, and pneumonectomy requires the removal of an entire lung.

Radiation therapy and chemotherapy are other possible treatments. Radiation therapy is the use of radiation to kill cancer cells and shrink tumors. This may also be used to relieve symptoms, such as shortness of breath. Radiation may be external, or directed at the tumor from a source outside the body, or internal, using radioactive materials placed into the body in or near the cancer cells. External radiation therapy is more common for treating lung cancer. Chemotherapy is the use of drugs to kill cancer cells. This may be given in many forms, including pill, injection, and via a catheter. Chemotherapy is often used to kill lung cancer cells that have spread to other parts of the body.

There are two newer therapies as well, which are not yet widely used: photodynamic therapy (PDT), for lung cancerphotodynamic therapy and, cryosurgery, for lung cancer cryosurgery. Photodynamic therapy is a type of laser therapy. A chemical is injected into the bloodstream and is then absorbed by the cells of the body. The chemical rapidly leaves normal cells, but it will remain in cancer cells for a longer time. A laser is aimed at the cancer, activating the chemical. This chemical then kills the cancer cells that have absorbed it. This treatment may also be used to reduce symptoms. Cryosurgery is a treatment that freezes and destroys cancer tissue.

PREVENTION

To help prevent lung cancer, one should cease smoking, avoid places where people are smoking, test for radon gases and asbestos in the home, and avoid workplaces with asbestos. A US Task Force recently updated its recommendation for annual screening to advise adults aged 55 to 80 years who have a 30 pack-year smoking history and currently smoke or have quit in the past 15 years to undergo a low-dose computed tomography (LDCT) screening for lung cancer.

Laurie LaRusso, MS, ELS;
Updated by Marianne Moss Madsen, MS

FOR FURTHER INFORMATION

Munden, R. F., S. S. Swisher, C. W. Stevens, and D. J. Stewart. "Imaging of the Patient with Non-Small Cell Lung Cancer." *Radiology* 237.3 (2005): 803–18. Reviews the role of radiologic imaging in patients with NSCLC, which is important for assessing the extent of the disease.

Pantanowitz L., and B. J. Dezube. "Evolving Spectrum and Incidence of Non-AIDS-Defining Malignancies." *Current Opinion in HIV and AIDS* 4.1 (2009): 27–34. Reviews literature about non-AIDS defining cancer (NADC), an increasing cause of morbidity and mortality in HIV patients.

US Preventive Services Task Force. "Published Final Recommendations: Lung Cancer Screening." March 2014. https://www.uspreventiveservices-taskforce.org/Page/Document/UpdateSummary-Final/lung-cancer-screening.

See also: Cancer and substance misuse; Esophageal cancer; Laryngeal cancer; Respiratory diseases and smoking; Smoking; Smoking's effects on the body